ARTISTS UNDER HITLER

ARTISTS UNDER HITLER

COLLABORATION AND SURVIVAL IN NAZI GERMANY

JONATHAN PETROPOULOS

Yale UNIVERSITY PRESS/NEW HAVEN & LONDON

Published with assistance from the foundation established in memory of Amasa
Stone Mather of the Class of 1907, Yale College.

Yale University Press books may be purchased in quantity for educational, business, or promotional use. For information, please e-mail sales.press@yale.edu
(U.S. office) or sales@yaleup.co.uk (U.K. office).

Designed by Mary Valencia.
Set in Minion and ITC Franklin Gothic type by Integrated Publishing Solutions, Inc.
Printed in the United States of America.

Library of Congress Cataloging-in-Publication Data
Petropoulos, Jonathan.
Artists under Hitler : collaboration and survival in Nazi Germany / Jonathan
Petropoulos.
        pages   cm
Includes bibliographical references and index.
ISBN 978-0-300-19747-1 (hardback)
1. National socialism and art.   2. Arts, German—20th century.   3. Artists—
Germany—Social conditions—20th century.   4. Germany—Social conditions—
20th century.   I. Title.
NX180.N37P48 2014
701'.03094309033—dc23
2014021451

A catalogue record for this book is available from the British Library.

This paper meets the requirements of ANSI/NISO Z39.48–1992 (Permanence of
Paper).

10 9 8 7 6 5 4 3 2 1

To Dennis, Christopher, and David

WHEN I VISITED France and Italy right after the war, I was full of that righteous antifascist feeling that we all had in the safety of America. I didn't want to meet the people who had, if not exactly collaborated, certainly had not fought the Nazis. I was too prissy. And then, as I began to learn more about Europe under the occupation, and what it was like, and to compare it to us, I became less prissy about it. Because the people who were defending their children and their lives were in a different situation from the people who were defending their swimming pools and their contracts at Metro. They weren't brave enough to be partisans, but they hadn't sent any Jews to Auschwitz, either. I wasn't gonna be the one from America to tell them they were wrong. Of course, I never forgave the people who sent Jews to the camps. But I did get so I could forgive the people who entertained the German troops. What else were they gonna do—not entertain them? Not entertain, and go where? If you had no group, if you were a group of one, what could you do? I can make a case for all the points of view.

ORSON WELLES

CONTENTS

Gallery follows page 176
The bibliography for the book can be accessed at http://www
.claremontmckenna.edu/hist/Artists-Under-Hitler/bibliography.php

PREFACE

IS THE NOTION of Nazi culture an oxymoron? Was any "good" culture produced during the Third Reich? There are, of course, the well-known accomplishments of Albert Speer and Leni Riefenstahl, Carl Orff, and Ernst Jünger. But conventional wisdom insists that any genuinely interesting art was rooted in the modernism of the Weimar Republic, while Nazi culture, with its rigidity and monumentality, was bad. This view is both coarse and wrong.

The cultural life of Nazi Germany was complex. Fascism did not defeat modernism. It persisted as an unresolved issue throughout Hitler's reign. Simply put, what are we to make of those cultural figures, many already with significant international reputations, who tried to find accommodation with the Nazi regime? And what effect, if any, did doing so have on their work? This book offers a more comprehensive and complicated understanding of culture during the Third Reich. While no single volume will ever be exhaustive, the history of these modernist (and modernist-influenced) artists goes a long way to capturing the rich and contentious cultural life of this period.

"Modernism" and "modernist" are terms that I use to refer to cultural figures—and their ideas and works—that were in sympathy with avant-garde movements that rose and flourished in the last decades of the nineteenth and the first half of the twentieth century. Some historians have employed the phrase "classic modernism," while others prefer "modernisms" to denote the plurality of styles and projects.[1] Yet these modernists were united in questioning the social realism of the period and in arguing that the world as it appears to our senses constitutes an inadequate representation of reality. Instead, they argued for a deeper interiority, a greater appreciation of our instincts, and a heightened awareness of the subjectivity of our perceptions. In rejecting verisimilitude and traditional historicist idioms, they developed new aesthetic strategies, including the use of abstraction and alternative color schemes. In the visual arts the key modernist movements include Post-Impressionism, Cubism, Expressionism, Dada, and New Objectivity. In music, atonality and dissonance were its hallmarks, with Arnold Schoenberg playing a particularly important role. Literature, for its part, featured an expressionist style of its own, although modernism in this discipline might also extend to nonlinear narrative structures and the efforts to give a voice to the poor and marginalized (for example, the works of Émile Zola). There were parallel stylistic trends across the disciplines, as well as common intellectual projects: among them, Sigmund Freud's quest to understand the unconscious; a fascination with irrational impulses; an exploration of social alienation, and a desire to challenge the stale and oppressive conventions of the regnant order. That said, modernism can be an elusive concept, and for some it has more to do with a visceral impression. It is akin to U.S. Supreme Court Justice Potter Stewart's famous definition of pornography—that he knew it when he saw it.

My approach in this book rests upon a fairly expansive conception of modernism. I recognize that certain figures do not qualify as ideal types— that their work and aesthetic philosophies contain contradictory elements. But all the figures treated at length here engaged modernist ideas in a meaningful manner at some stage of their careers. Rather than advancing a narrow conception of modernism—and trying to force figures as varied as Barlach and Riefenstahl into a procrustean bed—I argue for a broader and more flexible conception of the term: one that allows for more fruitful analytical comparisons and a more holistic examination of the multifaceted cultural history of the Third Reich.

I am also aware of the sensitivities that arise when one explores the engagement with National Socialism on the part of individuals who have long been viewed as anti-Nazi or, for that matter, those who were pro-Nazi. This finds expression in the word *collaboration,* which has myriad associations. While some scholars have used the word to denote complicity in the crimes of the Nazi regime, I take a more expansive definition that includes accommodation and the pursuit of accommodation.

The sensitivities attendant with the study of Nazi Germany demand certain responsibilities from the historian. Chief among them is scholarly and moral precision, and I take care to ensure that my sources are clearly identifiable. Researching this book compelled me to visit numerous archives and examine original documents, as well as to synthesize a vast secondary literature. In terms of the former, some figures presented particular challenges: for example, the painter Emil Nolde. I was denied access to his papers in Seebüll in northern Germany and was advised simply to consult the existing scholarly literature. But this does not prevent a deeper understanding of the subjects. Even with figures as elusive and as private as Nolde in North Schleswig or Ernst Ludwig Kirchner in the Swiss Alps, there are rich sources to consult. Understanding the past is inherently fraught. I undertake it with humility in the hope that my efforts will shed light on what remains a dark and haunting time.

ARTISTS UNDER HITLER

Introduction

IN **MARCH 1945,** with the Soviet Red Army pursuing its brutal Vistula-Oder offensive and the Western Allies advancing from the opposite direction, battling to cross the Rhine at Remagen, all of Germany's major cities lay in ruin. Basic services were disrupted, and transport proved a difficult if not impossible proposition (many German soldiers had recently fled the Netherlands on stolen bicycles). Yet amid this chaos and destruction something remarkable occurred—or, more precisely, continued. Art dealers carried on with transactions involving the paintings of Emil Nolde and other Expressionist artists. Renowned dealer Ferdinand Möller had long based his operations in Berlin, where he provided one of the havens for lovers of modern art, but he had recently relocated to his home in eastern Pomerania, where he persevered with his trade in modern works. Möller negotiated with his counterpart Ludwig Gutbier, who had left Munich for the more secure environs of rural Bavaria. On 26 February 1945, Möller had written to Gutbier to request the transport of several modern paintings to him in the East: "I would ask you to please send the crates to me here."[1] Gutbier responded on 9 March 1945—their correspondence having been delayed—"Yesterday I received your lines from 26 February. . . . [but] there is no possibility of sending objects to Berlin, or to the locations of both of my [Karl Schmidt-] Rottluff and [Erich] Heckel customers." He added, "I have marked as unsellable the two other paintings by Nolde and [Swiss modernist Lothar] Bechstein that are kept in my study. We follow the events in Berlin with great excitement and communicate to you our hopes that there will soon be a turn of events." In other words, Gutbier had finally accepted that the current situation precluded the transport of these Expressionist works in his possession, but he continued to hope for a change of fortune. Möller and Gutbier had sustained their enterprises until that point, and other colleagues of theirs actually continued to sell modern works until late April 1945—some two weeks before the final defeat. Their establishments had become rubble-strewn and lacked heat, but they carried on. They even used the official Reichspost to transact their business. The dealers also did not appear unduly concerned about the Gestapo or other intelligence agencies pursuing them for trading in officially proscribed art.

A second revealing episode involves Max Beckmann, the legendary artist who had left Germany in July 1937 when the Nazi regime had opened the twin shows in Munich, *The Great German Art Exhibition,* which featured officially accepted works, and the *Degenerate Art Exhibition,* which mocked and vilified modernist works. Beckmann had relocated to Amsterdam, where he enjoyed one of his most productive periods. He completed over seven hundred paintings during his time in the Netherlands, many of them during the war. Despite being a modernist and a figure associated with the Weimar Republic—which the Nazis reviled—Beckmann continued his work unimpeded after the Nazi occupation commenced in May 1940. He also overcame the logistical challenges when canvas and paints proved difficult to come by. How did he manage this? The answer lies in his close friend, Erhard Göpel, an art historian and dealer. Göpel also served as an agent for Adolf Hitler and scoured the Netherlands and France for artworks that would go to the Führermuseum planned for Linz. Göpel trafficked in looted art, playing a central role, for example, in the liquidation of the famed Schloss collection in France, consisting of some 330 paintings. Yet even while working as a plunderer and navigating networks of nefarious characters, Göpel remained friends with Beckmann. He carried letters back and forth between the artist and various contacts in Germany and, on occasion, transported paintings. Beckmann painted Göpel's portrait during the war, including a well-known picture created in the midst of the infamous Dutch "Hunger Winter" of 1944 in which he portrayed Hitler's agent in seemingly full health, seated in a comfortable interior and holding an art book. The two men continued their close relationship into the postwar period. Later, after the artist had succumbed to a heart attack in 1950, Göpel edited Beckmann's diaries for the war years, and also published a series of well-regarded books on the artist, including a catalogue raisonné of Beckmann's paintings. Erhard Göpel, along with his wife, art historian Barbara Göpel, became authorities on Beckmann in the postwar period.

Max Beckmann would not be the only modernist cultural figure to consort with plunderers and perpetrators in Nazi Germany.

A third vignette took place even earlier—in February of 1933—and concerns a competition to design a new Reichsbank in Berlin. Hitler had been appointed chancellor on 30 January and had immediately set out to define his regime by way of architecture and other cultural initiatives. He ordered bank president Hans Luther, a former Reich chancellor, to organize a competition, which Luther in turn entrusted to Heinrich Wolff, the head of the Reichsbank's building department. Rather than commence a time-consuming open competition, Wolff and his committee selected thirty architects to submit designs. Among them were Bauhaus founder Walter Gropius and the current Bauhaus director, Ludwig Mies van der Rohe. The Bauhaus, which counted as the most famous art school in Germany—if not the world—stood as a vivid symbol of the Weimar Republic. The locus of controversy since its founding in 1919—the Bauhaus had been forced to move from Weimar to Dessau in 1925 due to local opposition, and then to Berlin in 1932 for similar reasons—the school had been a favorite target of the Nazis. Yet here were two of its leaders asked to undertake a design for Hitler's first public building. Gropius and Mies complied, submitting elaborate plans and models. Indeed, Gropius provided a great deal more material than was called for, including blueprints, cost estimates, a philosophical statement, and photographs of a mock-up.[2] The image of Walter Gropius working feverishly on the new Reichsbank headquarters in early 1933 and hoping that he would become an official architect in the Third Reich needs to be integrated into the cultural history of Nazi Germany.

Examining the experiences of those modernist cultural figures who sought to find a place in the Third Reich prompts a central question: why did they seek accommodation with the Nazi regime? The answer is multifaceted. People are complex and rarely, if ever, act due to a single motivation. Rather, several factors entered into the thinking of the figures in this book: first, a misunderstanding of the Nazi leaders and their goals; second, an unchecked ego and sense of self-importance, whereby they thought their work to be indispensable to their field; third, a highly developed survival instinct—in part a legacy of an earlier time when modernism provoked veritable culture wars—combined with a more garden-variety opportunism; fourth, the mixed signals from the Nazi leaders themselves, some of whom embraced modernism and buoyed the cultural figures' optimism; and finally, a belief that the intellectual goals of modernism and fascism were compatible—that a new and meaningful synthesis between the two was possible. It is helpful, before considering specific figures and their experiences, to elaborate briefly on these factors.

A key to understanding the history of Nazi Germany is the realization that the regime gradually grew more radical. The dark, totalitarian society of 1943, with the ongoing murder of European Jews, the violent response to dissent, and the near complete mobilization of the population as part of the "total war" measures, was quite different from Germany in 1933— or even 1937. Of course, intimidation and violence also characterized the earlier years, and anti-Semitism proved an enduring facet of National Socialism, but many initially held out hope for a "kinder and gentler" Nazi regime. Hitler had checks on his power—for example, in President Paul von Hindenburg until August 1934, and in the armed forces and the Foreign Office. Correspondingly, there was also considerable cultural heterogeneity. The Nazis' efforts at coordination (the virtually untranslatable word they coined was *Gleichschaltung*) had not yet run their course. Furthermore, most artists did not endorse a racial war of conquest or mass murder. Their efforts at accommodation were born out of fundamental misapprehensions about the Nazi regime. This does not mean that they were not anti-Semitic, or fervently anti-Communist, or chauvinistically nationalistic. Some were all of the above. But when they sought out a place in the Reich, they scarcely imagined what would transpire during the war. The modernists were not the only ones to underestimate Hitler. Kurt Hahn, the Jewish educator who had overseen an elite school at Salem on Lake Constance before emigrating to the United Kingdom (where he founded the Gordonstoun School, among other institutions), initially believed that the responsibilities of office would moderate the behavior of the Nazi leader; but this, according to historian Golo Mann, "was not the real Hitler but an imaginary one that had a place in Hahn's political thought."[3]

Their own egos often blinded them to the realities of the time. Some saw themselves as gods in a kind of modernist pantheon and were often celebrated as such on an international level. For example, the Museum of Modern Art in New York organized a grand retrospective on the Bauhaus in 1938, and Gropius was the star of this show—just as he had been in the 1930 exhibition on the Bauhaus organized in Cambridge, Massachusetts, by a coterie of Harvard students.[4] Many cultural figures believed their work was so central to their fields that excluding them would be virtually impossible. They had altered the courses of their disciplines and remained confident that they would continue to play a pivotal role, even if this meant making concessions to the new regime. The triumphs they had enjoyed in the 1920s—professorships, directorships, commercial success, and fame—had only added to their sense of self-importance. The last director of the Bauhaus before it was closed in 1933, Ludwig Mies van der Rohe, to take another example, was a gruff man, a "difficult genius" type. He preferred the word "Baukunst" (literally, building art) to "Architektur." Years after he had immigrated to the United States, Mies remained brusquely demanding. With regard to the Seagram Building in New York that he designed with Philip Johnson, his biographer Elaine Hochman noted that between 1954 and 1958 "the Seagram employees were not allowed to close the Venetian blinds in their offices in his skyscraper in New York, lest the resulting disorder mar the appearance of the façade from the street. Only Mies's death released them from this constraint."[5] Comprehending his colleague's belief that art came first and that he possessed the extraordinary talent that enabled him to design for anyone, Philip Johnson quipped, "If the devil himself offered Mies a job he would take it."[6]

Of course, these modernist icons expected certain difficulties in Nazi Germany, but they had weathered storms throughout their careers. Before World War I, audiences rioted at Stravinsky concerts and few bought Expressionist paintings. Even during the Weimar Republic, when, to play upon historian Peter Gay's famous phrase, "The outsider became an insider," they faced strong opposition in many quarters, especially in the countryside and in provincial cities.[7] But just as they had endured attacks and insults before, they expected to find a way to move forward after 1933. The figures in question were not Jewish. Most Jewish modernists recognized that it would be impossible to make a career in Nazi Germany and therefore emigrated. Those non-Jews who sought accommodation with the Nazi regime did not want to lose their positions, or to part with family and friends. Reality eventually set in for many—especially those who were iconic figures in their fields prior to the Nazi seizure of power—who gradually came to the realization that they would never be accepted. Despite their egos and predilection for opportunism, many departed Germany in the mid-to-late-1930s, finally giving up in the face of the regime's unrelenting radicalization.

Another key component that induced many modernists to seek accommodation was the perceived sympathy for their cause exhibited by certain Nazi leaders. The central figure in the early years of the Third Reich was Joseph Goebbels, the intensely energetic Propaganda Minister who styled himself as the "czar of Nazi culture." With his Reich Ministry for People's Enlightenment and Propaganda, which came into existence in March 1933, and the establishment of his Reich Chamber of Culture the following September (every practicing artist was obliged to join the latter group) he was well on his way to realizing his ambitions. His appointment as Reich Minister included the provision that Goebbels was "competent for tasks concerning the cultural molding of the nation," and this augured well for the pro-modernist camp. In the spring of 1933, Goebbels engaged a young and then unknown architect-designer named Albert Speer to remodel his home on Lake Wannsee in Berlin. The Reich Propaganda Minister expressed his approval of Speer's choice of landscapes by Emil Nolde as part of the decoration. Indeed, Goebbels's wife, Magda, had accompanied Speer to the Berlin Nationalgalerie and helped select the pictures by Nolde, an act that suggested even greater solidarity in support of the artist.[8] Back in 1924, after visiting the Wallraf-Richartz Museum in Cologne, Goebbels noted in his journal that he had discovered "a Spanish dancer by Nolde. Wonderful colors. An exquisite, deep red."[9] Goebbels also kept a small figure on his desk (*Man in a Storm*) by Expressionist artist Ernst Barlach. In a January 1936 letter to his son, Barlach wrote that he believed that Goebbels actually owned two of his sculptures (the other was apparently *Begging Woman*). In 1924, Goebbels had written about another Barlach sculpture, *The Berserker* (1910), that was also exhibited in the Wallraf-Richartz Museum, exclaiming that he was "gripped by the sculpture. . . . The true spirit of Expressionism! Brevity raised to the level of grandiose interpretation."[10] In mid-1935, Goebbels commissioned a portrait by Berlin Secessionist Leo von König, an aristocratic painter who worked in a distinctly modern style (his paintings were purged two years later as part of the "degenerate art" action). Goebbels admired the painting and ordered a second rendition (paid for with ministerial funds). Baron von König signed his letters to the Propaganda Ministry "Heil Hitler!"—indicating that he also hoped for official acceptance.[11]

Modernists continued to have sympathizers in the upper reaches of the Nazi state and carved out room to create and exhibit their work. For example, in the late 1930s Nazi Foreign Minister Joachim von Ribbentrop and his wife, Annelies, commissioned painter Otto Dix to paint a portrait of their children, despite the fact that Dix had been a prominent modernist in both the Expressionist and the *Neue Sachlichkeit* (New Objectivity) movements and had always been associated with the political left. The Ribbentrops hung works in their homes by Franz Radziwill (a former member of the left-wing Novembergruppe), André Derain (a French Fauve), and Gustave Courbet (a leader of the Paris Commune and radical in his day).[12] The art of the former Communist and Neue Sachlichkeit painter Georg Schrimpf, whose works were included in the *Degenerate Art Exhibition,* hung in the homes of Deputy Führer Rudolf Hess, Reich Peasant Leader Richard Walter Darré, and Bernhard Rust, Reich Minister for Science, Education, and People's Culture.[13] Modernist works were also exhibited in public spaces during the Third Reich. In Vienna, for example, an exhibition of young artists, many of whom worked in abstracted styles, opened in February 1943, the same time the regime was moving to a "total war" footing and growing more malignant. That the Viennese governor and former Hitler Youth Leader Baldur von Schirach had sponsored the show made it all the more remarkable. The exhibition *Junge Kunst im Deutschen Reich* (*Youthful Art in the German Reich*) elicited controversy and was shut down on Hitler's orders. But Vienna's cultural life continued to include modernist elements until 1945. Exhibitions of the art of Gustav Klimt and the regular sale of works by Egon Schiele at the Dorotheum, the state-owned auction house, were but two indications of the persistence of modernism in the former Habsburg capital.

Fascist Italy, where Mussolini had embraced Futurism and other cultural modes associated with the avant-garde, provided yet another reason for the modernists' hopefulness. The acceptance of modernism prevented the alienation of key constituencies and helped legitimate the political leaders —validating them as sophisticated elites, which was especially important after years of "thuggery and vulgarity."[14] Fascism and modernism also shared many core principles, starting with the "myth of national regeneration." As historian Emilio Gentile has noted, exponents of "the modernist avant-garde . . . proposed a spiritual revolution that, starting from a philosophy or art, should affect all areas of life, including the world of politics."[15] Gentile mapped much of the common terrain shared by the Italian modernists and the Fascists, including the notion of a spiritual revolution, the belief in youth as a regenerative force, and the glorification of violence. The Futurists also celebrated speed and technology, detested Bolshevism, and styled themselves as nationalists, and did so publicly (and in the German press) well into the late 1930s.[16] All of these ideas could easily be reconciled with the German brand of fascism. It also did not hurt that Mussolini had been influenced by his mistress, Margherita Sarfatti, and had come to appreciate German Expressionism, with a special regard for the artists in Die Brücke (The Bridge). Young Fascisti also often evinced enthusiasm about other German modernists. The Neue Sachlichkeit works of Otto Dix, for example, were exhibited in Milan in 1933.[17] Mussolini himself believed that his German counterparts should embrace modernism, albeit with distinctive national characteristics. Because the Nazis had borrowed heavily from the original Fascists—the Roman salute ("Heil Hitler!") and the black shirts of the Squadristi as uniforms for the SS, to take two examples—many observers believed that the Fascists and the Nazis would share a common cultural policy. Even the contemporaneous Austro-fascist leaders in Vienna promoted modernism, despite their nationalistic, anti-Bolshevist, and staunchly Catholic orientation. Certain Nazi officials appreciated the potential for a common, or at least coordinated, cultural policy among fascist countries, and invited Mussolini's government to send exemplars of its modernist art to Berlin in the spring of 1934.

The reconciliation of fascism and modernism emerged as an international trend and constitutes the fifth key factor frequently underlying the search for accommodation. French author Louis-Ferdinand Céline, American poet Ezra Pound, American architect and designer Philip Johnson, and Finnish composer Jean Sibelius count among the modernists who exhibited sympathies for fascism. In many respects, this quest for a synthesis between modernism and, in the German case, National Socialism brings to mind literary critic George Steiner's question that he posed in his 1971 essay "A Season in Hell":

> Art, intellectual pursuits, the development of the natural sciences, many branches of scholarship flourished in close spatial, temporal proximity to massacre and the death camps. It is this structure and meaning of that proximity which must be looked at. Why did humanistic traditions and models of conduct prove so fragile a barrier against political bestiality? In fact, were they a barrier, or is it more realistic to perceive in humanistic culture express solicitations of authoritarian rule and cruelty?[18]

As Steiner suggests, certain aspects of modernism dovetailed with the National Socialist ideology. While this synergistic relationship took many forms, three elements stood out: a desire to explore and exploit the irrational side of humans; a belief that modernist cultural forms corresponded to specifically German national characteristics; and an appreciation of technology and machines.

Many modernists and National Socialists shared a belief in the power of irrational instincts. An earlier generation of modernists had tried to tap into the Dionysian forces—the wild, instinctive, and animalistic aspects of humanity that played a role in sublime art (at least according to Friedrich Nietzsche). This energy was part of the appeal of the "neo-Primitivism" of Picasso and others—what George Steiner called "the charismatic appeal of 'barbaric forms.'" Hitler and his cohort also proved adept at uti-lizing irrational appeals to followers. Standing among hundreds of thou-sands of spectators in Nuremberg, surrounded by vibrant red and black swastika banners and otherworldly lighting effects, the viewer lost himself (or, less often, herself) in an amorphous crowd. The religious qualities of the event—the "longing for transcendence"—and the hypnotic appeal of the dictator affirmed these irrational impulses. With the chorus of "Heil Hitler" chants shouted in unison, among other theatrical effects, the Nazis organized a kind of *Gesamtkunstwerk* that touched people on a deep, vis-ceral level. Thomas Mann realized this when he opined in the 1930s that National Socialism and Expressionism stemmed from the same "root."[19] A number of modernist cultural figures who tried to find accommodation with the Nazis—Martin Heidegger, Gottfried Benn, even Albert Speer—identified commonalities based on emotions, instincts, and profound life forces. Historian Richard Wolin coined the phrase "the seduction of unrea-son" to describe certain intellectuals' gravitation to fascism.[20]

Another argument advanced in this effort to reconcile modernism with National Socialism concerned national character. In the realm of visual arts (along with architecture, the focal point of the debate about modernism in the Third Reich), many believed that Expressionism captured essentially Germanic qualities. The landscapes of Emil Nolde, with their rural settings and spiritual overtones, seemed a perfect representation of the "Blut und Boden" (Blood and Soil) motif favored by the Nazis—or, certainly, the con-servative, *völkisch* faction. It did not hurt that Nolde was an avid supporter of the Nazis and begged to play a meaningful role in the "new" Germany. Ernst Ludwig Kirchner painted mountain scenes that glowed incandescently in vibrant hues—suggesting a deeper spiritual resonance—and he populated many of his canvases with isolated peasant herders and their animals. The focus on the power of nature and the soul-killing effects of modern society provided additional linkages between German Expressionism and National Socialism. The black and white wood-block print, a favored medium for German Expressionists, harkened back to the German medieval tradition, and the historic Gothic style resonated in the work of sculptors like Ernst Barlach. These affinities between the medieval, Romantic, and modernist cultural forms offered an intellectual underpinning for those who hoped for a more tolerant *Kunstpolitik* (arts policy). The phrase "Nordic Expres-sionism," which occurred with greater frequency in the early 1930s, also reflected a belief that Expressionism and National Socialism could be rec-onciled (Plates 4–7).[21]

On a more practical level, Germans had often taken the lead with modernist projects in the twentieth century, and this provided Goebbels and his cohorts with plenty of German talent to exploit. Goebbels believed with good reason that having gifted people in Germany would reflect positively on his ministry and the regime more generally. He therefore sought to enlist the most prestigious cultural figures he could. The Reich Chamber of Culture offered the best opportunity. The seven arts-specific chambers (literature, journalism, radio, theater, music, film, and visual arts) each needed a president and a vice president, and there would be a Reich Cultural Senate to which he could appoint those luminaries whom he favored. Goebbels, for example, explored the idea of luring director Fritz Lang back from Hollywood to head up the Reich Chamber of Film. Both Goebbels and Hitler greatly admired Lang's 1926 epic, *Metropolis,* which explored the theme of a leader's psychological power over the masses. In particular, they praised the manner in which the director coordinated the movement of people. Although an iconic figure in the Weimar modernist renaissance, Fritz Lang came into consideration for the post, just as Goebbels turned to Richard Strauss, who served as the first president of the Reich Chamber of Music. According to Lang, he met with Goebbels in March 1933 and, rather than being castigated for putting "Nazi slogans into the mouth of a pathological criminal," which he had done in *The Last Will of Dr. Mabeuse,* Lang was offered "a leading post in the German film industry." The director, of course, did not accept the offer from Goebbels. He later engaged in some self-mythologizing about his departure from Germany—he did not, as he claimed, flee to Paris that very night "practically penniless"—yet the discussions about his assuming the presidency of the film Chamber are in themselves illuminating.[22]

The Reich Propaganda Minister was also prepared to mend fences with Thomas Mann, who had so forcefully defended the Weimar Republic and denounced National Socialism. Because Mann had been a patriot in World War I, was loyal to the imperial monarchy, and was not Jewish, Goebbels believed it might be possible to bring him into the fold.[23] Mann's books, such as his modernist novella *Death in Venice,* were not thrown into the pyres during the protests "against the un-German spirit" on 10 May 1933. Thomas Mann as head of the Reich Chamber for Literature would have been a sensation. There were other appointments to make, and other cultural luminaries to co-opt. Goebbels would compel Wilhelm Furtwängler, arguably the most famous conductor in the world at the time, to continue on at the Berlin Philharmonic, which Goebbels effectively controlled. He also made Furtwängler the vice president (under Strauss) of the Reich Chamber of Music. Perhaps he could even lure Marlene Dietrich back from Hollywood?

An enthusiasm for technology offered another affinity shared by modernists and Nazis. Granted, one must avoid the simplification that an embrace of technology equals modernity, which in turn equals modernism. The relationships are far more complicated and provisional. Yet machine aesthetics intrigued many modernists, especially those with a more rationalistic approach (as compared to the Expressionists). Machines offered a highly favored metaphor, with Le Corbusier, for example, articulating his well-known credo, "A house is a machine for living in." Kurt Weill and Paul Hindemith engaged modern technology in another way in their opera *Der Lindberghflug* (*The Lindbergh Flight*) (1929), which also allowed them to explore myths about the United States (a country that itself constituted one of the "quintessential symbols of modernity").[24] Modernist architects typically engaged technology, with most favoring austere, streamlined design and embracing new machine-made materials such as glass, concrete, and steel. This kind of architecture persisted throughout the Third Reich. Modernists during the Weimar period also worked in the diverse fields of industrial design—what Pierre Bourdieu would later call (with an element of sarcasm) "the illegitimate arts": that is, the less established fields such as graphic design, advertising, and photography, among others.[25] Because these newer arts did not attract the same publicity as more traditional genres, with practitioners working out of the limelight and often as members of larger teams, it was often possible to continue this work during the Third Reich. The graphic artists for the magazine *Die neue Linie* (*The New Line*), for example, which was published in Leipzig, continued with progressive design techniques until the magazine ceased production in 1943.[26] Bauhaus "Werkmeister" Christian Dell, who created sleek modernist lamps, also continued his industrial design work during the Third Reich. And Herbert Bayer, who conceived so many of the iconic images associated with the Bauhaus and was later known for the ski posters he did in Aspen, produced images for a propagandistic exhibition staged by the Nazi regime in 1934. Bayer also contributed to a brochure in the mid-1930s "meant to lure people from all over the world to see the Führer's achievements."[27] Despite the relatively low visibility of most of these designers with modernist ties, they were important to the culture of the Third Reich.

Modernists, therefore, often sought accommodation with the National Socialist regime, and did so for both ideological and personal reasons. This is not to deny that some modernists were truly against Hitler and chose to emigrate. The German émigré community during the Third Reich represented the greatest assemblage of cultural talent ever to leave a country. Yet the image of virtuous émigrés has long overshadowed the fact that a wide array of cultural figures who were trained or who worked in a modernist tradition attempted to find a place in Hitler's Reich. This includes Walter Gropius, Paul Hindemith, Gottfried Benn, Ernst Barlach, Emil Nolde, Richard Strauss, Gustaf Gründgens, Leni Riefenstahl, Arno Breker, and Albert Speer, as well as Ludwig Mies van der Rohe, Wilhelm Furtwängler, Carl Orff, Werner Egk, Herbert von Karajan, Martin Heidegger, Gerhart Hauptmann, and Ernst Jünger. The list goes on. Although it is important to preserve distinctions and recognize significant differences between these figures, including their different relationships to modernism, they all shared a belief that their work would be an asset to the new Germany.

Some of the modernists successfully acted on this belief and, by altering the styles of their work, reached the apogees of their careers. Speer and Riefenstahl, who were trained in modernist traditions, offer vivid examples. Others went even further in terms of adapting to the regime and meeting its "needs." Fritz Ertl, for example, who was one of about 1,300 students to pass through the Bauhaus, studying at the Dessau facility between 1928 and 1931, became a Waffen-SS officer, and an urban planner at the Auschwitz site.[28] Ertl obviously represented an extreme example, while most other modernists sought accommodation in a less injurious manner. These efforts, as indicated earlier, were more common in the early years of the Third Reich. For example, an August 1934 petition in support of Hitler succeeding Paul von Hindenburg as head of state bore the signatures of many leading cultural figures, including Ludwig Mies van der Rohe, Wilhelm Furtwängler, Richard Strauss, Emil Nolde, Erich Heckel, and Ernst Barlach. Granted, as detailed later, these signatures were obtained in certain instances by subjecting the artists to a measure of duress, but their compliance nonetheless attested to a yearning for a peaceful coexistence with the Nazi regime.

Other documents penned by modernist heroes prove more troubling. Ernst Ludwig Kirchner, a founding member of Die Brücke and a pioneer of German Expressionism, responded to pressure to resign from the Prussian Academy of the Arts (Preussische Akademie der Künste) on 17 May 1933 by sending the executive secretary the following response:

> I have never derived any personal advantages from the membership.
> I have instead tried to honor the institution and have always sent my

best work for your exhibitions. For more than thirty years now, I have struggled through my work for a new, strong, and authentic German art and will continue to do this as long as I live. I am neither a Jew nor a Social Democrat, nor otherwise been politically active; and in general, have a clean conscience. I am therefore waiting patiently to see what the new government will do with regard to the question of the Academy and leave with confidence the question of my membership in your hands.[29]

The Prussian Academy held off making a decision about Kirchner, as it did with architect Mies van der Rohe and sculptor Rudolf Belling. All three tried to find accommodation with the Nazi regime. As artist Max Pechstein said about Belling, "he is performing the most fantastic leaps, like a salmon he is trying again and again to overcome the weir to climb the heights, but until now in vain."[30] Yet all three were later forced out of the Academy in 1937. Of course, they were not alone in expressing regret about being unable to play a role in the new Reich. In July 1937, architect Bruno Paul wrote, "I would still like to emphasize how much I have regretted, and still regret, that I was not able to use my extensive experience and knowledge in the area . . . of art . . . in the service of National Socialistic principles."[31]

This book in no way seeks to minimize the sacrifices or suffering of the many modernist cultural figures who opposed the regime, especially during the war. Painter Max Pechstein went fishing in order to feed himself, and former Bauhaus Master Oskar Schlemmer painted camouflage for the Luftwaffe and then worked in a lacquer factory in Wuppertal.[32] At a different level of hardship, Bauhaus-trained artist Franz Ehrlich, who had studied with Wassily Kandinsky, Paul Klee, and Lázló Moholy-Nagy, designed the gates of the Buchenwald concentration camp, where he had been a prisoner since 1935. Ehrlich rendered the inscription, "Jedem das Seine" (To each his own), in such a way that the Bauhaus influence was readily apparent.[33] A number of cultural figures opposed to the regime paid with their lives, including writer Erich Mühsam (1878–1934), journalist Carl von Ossietzky (1889–1938), film director Herbert Selpin (1904–1942), and pianist Karlrobert Kreiten (1916–1943). And Jews always faced grave dangers, as evidenced by the tragic fates of modernist painters Felix Nussbaum (1904–1944), Ignaz Kaufmann (1885–1941), and Charlotte Salomon (1917–1943), as well as sculptor Otto Freundlich (1878–1943). Yet this clearly was not the entire story.

The figures in this book have been selected for a variety of reasons, but

Bauhaus-trained artist Franz Ehrlich, who studied at the Dessau school from 1927 to 1930, designed the gates of Buchenwald in 1938 while incarcerated in the camp. It features the famous slogan "Jedem das Seine" (To each his own). (Peter Hansen/Sammlung Gedenkstätte Buchenwald)

largely because of their important artistic work and high-profile careers, and because they were representative of the most important fields in the cultural life of the Third Reich. In both Chapter 2 (about failed attempts to find accommodation) and Chapter 3 (accommodation realized), I have selected five figures that broadly cover the cultural life of Nazi Germany. Chapter 3 does not include a painter (only a sculptor, Arno Breker), which in part speaks to the more stridently anti-modernist policies that eventually prevailed with regard to pictures. Of course, there were painters with modernist roots that found official acceptance—Paul Mathias Padua, Albin Egger-Lienz, and even Adolf Ziegler, among others—but none rivaled Breker in terms of importance of their work to the field of the visual arts. These ten figures, when considered collectively, cannot reflect every facet of culture in Nazi Germany, but they go a long way toward capturing this complex history.

Part I

"The Summer of Art" and Beyond

MODERNISTS CAME CLOSEST to realizing their vision of reconciliation with the National Socialists in 1933—more specifically,
during "the summer of art," as some have called it. At least, this
proved true in terms of the coalescence of support for modernism among certain Nazi leaders. The summer of 1933 marked the
apogee regarding the debate over Expressionism. Hitler remained
indecisive with respect to cultural policy, and this created an environment rife with impassioned debate. In order to understand
the modernists' quest for accommodation, one must appreciate
the uncertainty, the aspirations, and the alliances that provided the
basis for this hopefulness. This "summer of art" saw the misap-
prehension of the true nature of National Socialism and the belief
in the importance and compatibility of the modernists' own work
in a revived Germany. These views would persist until 1937, when
Hitler induced Goebbels to organize the *Degenerate Art Exhibition*.
Even then, support for Expressionism and other forms of modernism continued, but not with the transparency and optimism of the
earlier years. A cohort of former Bauhaus architects, for example,
constructing the massive Hermann Göring Works in Linz in the
late 1930s in a modern, functional idiom, might offer a different
high point in terms of practice. Hitler himself cared most about
architecture among all the arts (although painting, his former profession, and opera, especially Richard Wagner's work, also occupied important parts of his mental life). Yet in the early years of the
Third Reich, the visual arts offered the most dramatic contest over
aesthetic policy.

In late July 1933, the exhibition *Thirty German Artists* opened.

The show featured works by established Expressionists, such as Emil Nolde, Ernst Barlach, and Christian Rohlfs, but also by a younger generation, including Otto Andreas Schreiber and Hans Weidemann. The latter two were Nazis who, in addition to painting modernist canvases, were storm troopers (members of the Sturm Abteilung, or SA). Schreiber and Weidemann, along with Fritz Hippler, also headed the Berlin chapter of the National Socialist German Students' League—the NSD-Studentenbund. The leaders of the Students' League, along with modernist art dealer Ferdinand Möller, organized *Thirty German Artists*. Prior to the opening of the exhibition, the students staged a pro-modernist rally. They advertised the event by making posters themselves. Many were titled "Youth Fights for German Art" and "Witness of Youth for Art." These were bright red in color and covered the walls of the university in the days prior to the rally. The students also extended special invitations to a number of luminaries, including Mies van der Rohe, Karl Hofer, and Berlin Nationalgalerie director Ludwig Justi. On the evening of 29 June, the students and their special guests convened in the main auditorium at the Humboldt University on Unter den Linden. Observers reported that the atmosphere was electric, with the auditorium bursting with an overflow crowd. Fritz Hippler—later a key aide to Goebbels —delivered a speech in which he railed against the "restoration of Wilhelmian academicism and all regulation of art."[1] He was followed by other speakers who defended Expressionism. The last speaker was Otto Andreas Schreiber, who announced that the art exhibition was formally under the protection of the student group. The participants at the rally approved a resolution that declared, "The principal threat to the birth of a new art lies in the narrow-minded exclusion of valuable German artists from this collaborative effort [to regenerate the nation and its culture]—this, for reasons not related to their personalities or work."[2]

During this pro-modernist rally at the Humboldt University, Hippler and Schreiber whipped the crowd into a frenzy. But they had more in mind than an emotional catharsis. The carefully phrased resolution that they had drafted (with the aforementioned line about "the principal threat to the birth of a new art lies in the narrow-minded exclusion of valuable German artists from this collaborative effort"), and that they proceeded to pass by acclamation, had unambiguous political undertones. Historian Peter Paret noted, "The meeting attracted attention in the public and the press, not only because of the speakers' challenging words but also because one of the organizers [Weidemann] worked in the Propaganda Ministry, which suggested that the meeting represented Goebbels's views, or at least was being

Ferdinand Möller, a modernist artwork dealer and co-organizer of the
important but controversial 1933
exhibition *Thirty German Artists*.
(Berlinische Galerie)

used by Goebbels to test how far disagreements on cultural issues were still permissible."[3] If there were any doubts about the implications of the rally, Schreiber also "proclaimed the dissolution" of the anti-modernist pressure group, the Fighting League for German Culture, at the Berlin art schools and academies. Schreiber's speech was published on 10 July 1933 in the *Deutsche Allgemeine Zeitung,* and then again a second time on 14 July. The paper also published declarations of support from student groups at other universities. There was widespread optimism in the bourgeois press, which had not yet been taken over by the Nazis. For example, the *Deutsche Allge-meine Zeitung* reported that Hitler "regretted the breach with Barlach."[4] Word then leaked that Goebbels had borrowed several Nolde paintings from the Berlin Nationalgalerie. Rumors also circulated that Goebbels had expressed regrets about the 10 May 1933 book burnings, which had pro-voked negative reactions abroad.[5]

Three weeks later, the *Thirty German Artists* exhibition opened at the Fer-dinand Möller Galerie on the Lützow-Ufer in central Berlin—just down the street from Jewish modernist Alfred Flechtheim's famous gallery. Throngs

of students, artists, and other culturally aware observers packed the premises so that one could hardly move, let alone see the Expressionist works.
But the opening was less about viewing the art than it was a demonstration
of support for a more "liberal" arts policy. If Hitler and the other Nazi leaders were serious about empowering German youth, if they were to act on
their promises for change and renewal, and if they were dedicated to finding a truly Germanic form of art, then they would respect this bold student-
led initiative. But in a foreshadowing of events to come—such as the Röhm
Purge of June 1934, when the more socialistic branch of the Nazi Party came
under attack, including its figurehead, the storm trooper chief—Hitler and
key subleaders moved against the overly "progressive" students. Three days
after the exhibition's opening, Reich Minister of the Interior Wilhelm Frick,
who controlled the police, set his forces on the Möller Galerie. Utilizing the
powers derived in the wake of the Reichstag fire from the Emergency Decree
of 28 February 1933, Frick closed the exhibition and stationed uniformed
officers at the entrance. This was by no means the end of the battle, and the
show's organizers managed to arrange for its reopening a week later; it was,
however, a clear signal that the fight would be arduous.

1

The Fight over Modernism

Leo von König, *Portrait of Dr. Goebbels* (1935)—a work that
featured modernist stylistic influences and so pleased the Reich
Propaganda Minister that he commissioned von König to execute
a replica. (Reprinted from Bruno Kroll, *Leo von König,* Berlin:
Rembrandt Verlag, 1941)

THE DEBATE OVER Expressionism, which stood out as the most visible fault line in the battle over modernism, actually represented a struggle for overall control of Nazi cultural policy. The two chief combatants, the figureheads of their respective camps in the early years of the Third Reich, were Alfred Rosenberg, a rabidly anti-modernist philosopher, and Joseph Goebbels, the recently appointed Reich Minister for People's Enlightenment and Propaganda and the Gauleiter (Nazi Party district leader) of Berlin. Goebbels and the pro-modernists had a distinct advantage in terms of bureaucratic standing. Rosenberg headed up the Fighting League for German Culture (Kampfbund für Deutsche Kultur)—a kind of cultural nongovernmental organization—but had no state or Party position with regard to culture in 1933. On the other hand, the slippery Goebbels was wavering in his support of modernism—at least publicly—and reluctant to expend political capital on a cause that he knew Hitler opposed on a personal level. Having grown up in provincial Linz, Austria, Hitler never developed an appreciation for modernist culture and instead developed affinities for more traditional historicist styles. One of the pro-modernists' problems grew out of the less than firm support shown by the Reich Propaganda Minister. For example, curator Ernst Holzinger wrote Berlin Nationalgalerie director Eberhard Hanfstaengl in 1937 that Goebbels was reported to have said back in 1934 that "[Franz] Marc would probably have been the leading German artist if he had not fallen in war."[1] The two museum officials were uncertain whether Goebbels actually uttered these words, but the fact that the rumor circulated among museum officials captures the sense among those engaged in this debate that he supported modernism, but not in an unwavering or open manner. Rosenberg and his allies, on the other hand, were never lacking in resolve or self-assuredness.

Rosenberg had been the first among the Nazi leaders to build an organization for cultural affairs. The editor of the Nazi newspa-

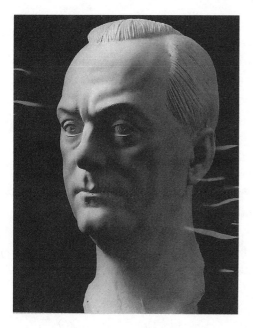

Arno Breker, *Portrait Bust of Alfred Rosenberg* (1940), the Nazi ideologue and unofficial leader of the *völkisch* movement. (Zentralinstitut für Kunstgeschichte, Munich)

per, *Der Völkische Beobachter,* Rosenberg had founded the Fighting League for German Culture in Munich in 1927, and by 1933 the pressure group had branches stretching across Germany. He oversaw an ambitious initiative to lobby politicians, publish periodicals, and organize various kinds of lectures and exhibitions. Yet Rosenberg and the Munich leadership of the Fighting League felt somewhat marginalized by their colleagues in Thuringia, who had entered into a coalition government in 1930. This situation came about in the September 1930 elections, when the Nazis fared so well in the provincial elections that they earned a place in the state's government. On a national level, the Nazis saw their percentage of the vote jump from 2.6 percent in 1928 to 18.3 percent, netting an additional 103 seats in the Reichstag. In the Thuringian provincial government, negotiations for cabinet posts resulted in the Nazis gaining hold of the Ministry of Interior, which gave them considerable influence over cultural matters.

In both Thuringia in 1930 and the Reich government in 1933, Wilhelm Frick served as the Minister of the Interior. Although he seemed a rather dull and forgettable lawyer on the surface, Frick was a radical National Socialist. In Thuringia, he immediately transferred control of the state art academy in Weimar to Paul Schultze-Naumburg, a capable traditional architect and radical *völkisch* (or culturally conservative) activist. The Weimar art academy had formerly housed the Bauhaus before Walter Gropius moved the school to Dessau in the neighboring province of Saxony-Anhalt in 1925. Frick and his cohorts sought to draw attention to their new cultural policies in Thuringia. Most notoriously, they focused on the iconic mural that Oskar Schlemmer had executed in 1923 at the Weimar facility. The now-famous wall painting climbed the central stairs in the workshop that Henry van de Velde had designed. Rendered in a kind of three-dimensional style and featuring man-machine imagery, Schlemmer's Bauhaus murals captured the spirit of Weimar modernism. Paul Schultze-Naumburg and his Nazi associates arrived at the Bauhaus one day in October 1930 and destroyed the murals, pulling some parts down and plastering over other sections. Alfred Barr Jr., the founding director of the Museum of Modern Art (MoMA) in New York, subsequently acquired a related work—a 1932 painting that served as an "homage" to the Bauhaus. Schlemmer's painting of the Bauhaus staircase was purchased by architect Philip Johnson during the Third Reich and later donated to MoMA in 1942.[2]

The Nazis' cultural policies in Thuringia in 1930 foreshadowed what transpired after 1937. Just as with the sensational *Degenerate Art Exhibition,* the Nazis tried their best to be incendiary, using provocative language in the 5 April 1930 decree "Against Negro Culture—For Our German Heritage."[3] Frick and his aides also purged the Schlossmuseum in Weimar of some seventy works by Otto Dix, Wassily Kandinsky, and Emil Nolde, among other modernists. The rationale was that these works had "nothing in common with Nordic-German essence, but rather limited themselves to depicting Jewish, Slavic, or otherwise inferior sub-humanity."[4] "'The battle for art' was," as art historian Berthold Hinz has noted, "by no means a National Socialist invention. The slogan and the issue [of a "German" art] had been of central concern in German cultural life for decades."[5] Modernism had elicited strong opposition prior to World War I, with nationalistic and even racist arguments wielded as weapons. Yet starting in Thuringia, the Nazis took this battle to a new level, purging museums, closing schools, and censoring books, among other initiatives. The Thuringian Nazis and their Fighting League allies would also disrupt concerts of atonal and other modern music. This training ground produced many of the key spokesmen for the National Socialists in the cultural sphere: joining Schultze-Naumburg were Adolf Bartels, Hans F. K. Günther, Richard Walther Darré, and Hans Severus Ziegler, among others. They became standouts in the völkisch faction, waging a relentless campaign against the pro-modernists.

The Thuringian Nazis enjoyed a generally positive popular response to their anti-modernist agitation, and intensified their harassment of opponents. Yet they also faced resistance. For example, the purging of modernist art from the Schlossmuseum in Weimar resulted in challenges that they had exceeded their legal authority. The Thuringian parliament issued a vote of no-confidence, citing Frick's action in the Schlossmuseum as part of his excesses. Frick was subsequently forced to resign his position as minister in April 1931.[6] But again, despite such setbacks, the Nazis' policies in Thuringia met with widespread public support. In the July 1932 elections, the National Socialist German Workers Party (Nationalsozialistische Deutsche Arbeiter Partei [NSDAP]) received 42.5 percent of the vote in Thuringia (as compared to 37 percent nationwide). This resulted in Nazi Gauleiter Fritz Sauckel leading a coalition government—meaning that Thuringia fell under Nazi rule even before Hitler's appointment as chancellor in January 1933. The stridently anti-modernist policies in Thuringia appeared to have considerable popular support.

The völkisch faction, of course, extended far beyond the Fighting League. One umbrella organization for smaller societies, the Führer's Council for German Art and Cultural Organizations, had 250,000 members in 1933. The völkisch camp had genuine grassroots support, and many of those in these pressure groups were not hesitant to assert themselves as activists. Historian Hildegard Brenner suggests that many members were "motivated largely by resentment."[7] One such example would be Bettina Feistel-Rohmeder, an unsuccessful Dresden-based artist who published several journals, including *Deutsche Bildkunst* and *Deutscher Kunstbericht*. Feistel-Rohmeder was an activist who devoted most of her energy to attacking art and artists whom she did not like. While she had no standing in the Nazi Party—even the Nazi leaders found her unpleasant—Feistel-Rohmeder's periodicals had relatively large circulations and served as a platform for her allies, especially before 1933 (*Deutsche Bildkunst* had some three thousand subscribers).[8] With the advent of the Third Reich, Feistel-Rohmeder and her supporters allied themselves with Alfred Rosenberg and tried to induce Hitler to appoint him the Minister of Culture.

Although mocked by rivals as "almost Rosenberg" because he was almost a philosopher, almost an artist, and almost a foreign policy expert, Rosenberg remained a force with which to reckon. Serving as editor of *Der Völkische Beobachter* in itself would serve as a solid power base until Nazi Party and state positions came his way during the Third Reich. Rosenberg had his own foreign policy office within the Party and would later oversee the largest Nazi looting operations in World War II (a Party post called the Einsatzstab Reichsleiter Rosenberg, or ERR); he also served during the war as Reich Minister for the Occupied Eastern Territories (a state post). But his first official appointment in the cultural sphere did not come until January 1934, when Hitler appointed him to a Party office for ideological supervision (the title was so prolix that it was known by the acronym DBFU).[9] Rosenberg's unofficial status in 1933 was one reason for the modernists' optimism.

While Rosenberg was left out of Hitler's initial cabinet, at least his old friend and ideological ally Wilhelm Frick held a post—and a key one at that, as Reich Minister of the Interior. Of course, this gave the Nazis control over the police, but the Ministry of the Interior also had jurisdiction in the cultural sphere. As Frick had shown when he was the Minister of the Interior in Thuringia, the post afforded almost limitless possibilities. After his appointment as Reich Minister, Frick returned to the Thuringian model by engaging Paul Schultze-Naumburg as his adviser on artistic issues. The architect, who had been made a Nazi Reichstag deputy in 1932, appeared to be a rising star. Schultze-Naumburg met with Hitler and briefed him on a range of issues, including the presence of modern art in museums. Therefore, through mid-1933, most members of the völkisch groups, although cognizant of their organizational disunity, believed that they were destined to prevail, especially with Frick in office in the Reich Interior Ministry.

Because the völkisch faction had gained so much momentum in early 1933, many in this camp were shocked and mystified by Goebbels's appointment as Reich Minister for People's Enlightenment and Propaganda on 13 March 1933. Of course, no one knew what this newly fabricated and curiously titled ministry meant at that point (that it came into existence due to a decree from President Hindenburg further confused matters). Perhaps Goebbels and Rosenberg had a better understanding of the appointment: that it entailed a major victory for Goebbels. But Rosenberg did not succumb and, true to form, redoubled his efforts to challenge his rival. Both the principals believed that the debate over modernism was the key to resolving the competition. Hildegard Brenner noted, "Art policy became a factor in the struggle for power. . . . In this conflict the political interest groups were mobilized above all by one question, which led to a bitter confrontation. This was the question of modernism, particularly in the fine arts."[10] Hitler therefore kept his subordinates Goebbels and Rosenberg balanced in a state of tense opposition, as was common in the Third Reich, believing in the "divide and rule" philosophy, and also the Social Darwinian notion of struggle determining who was most fit.

With the subleader rivalry as a backdrop, and the Reichstag turned into a rubber-stamp body by way of the 23 March 1933 Enabling Act, the Nazi government took another aggressive step against many modernists with the landmark 7 April 1933 Law for the Protection of a Professional Civil Service. This statute gave the government the power to cashier any employee of the state, and was meant to target those who were left-wing or Jewish. Yet it also led to the firing of many modernists. Among the notable figures who lost their teaching posts in the initial round of purges in the spring of 1933 were Max Beckmann (Frankfurt), Willi Baumeister (Frankfurt), Otto Dix (Dresden), Karl Hofer (Berlin), Paul Klee (Düsseldorf), Käthe Kollwitz (Berlin), and Oskar Schlemmer (Stuttgart); as well as a number of professors of architecture, including Hans Poelzig (Berlin) and Bruno Taut (Berlin). One could add some thirty museum directors, including Gustav Hartlaub from Mannheim, who coined the term *Neue Sachlichkeit* in 1925; Max Sauerlandt, the influential director of the Museum for Arts and Crafts in Hamburg who then died shortly thereafter; Ernst Gosebruch, who had taken over the Folkwang Museum from its founder, Karl Ernst Osthaus, and helped turn it into a world-class public institution in Essen; and Ludwig Justi, who co-founded the Berlin Nationalgalerie in the Kronprinzenpalais after World War I when the Hohenzollern palace was turned into a museum. The purge also resulted in the dismissal of the Reichskunstwart Edwin Redslob, who was in charge of design throughout most of the Weimar Republic. From the state theater, those dismissed included Jewish impresario Max Reinhardt. These were the people who had been most responsible for institutionalizing modernism during the Weimar Republic, transforming the "outsiders" to "insiders."

Similar events occurred in the musical sphere, with a purge of Jewish and also modernist artists from their posts. By late 1934, "49 out of 85 opera houses had experienced a change of intendant, a considerable turnover of personnel."[11] The transformation of the musical sphere included the departure of Jewish conductors Otto Klemperer and Bruno Walter, as well as Jewish composers Arnold Schoenberg and Hanns Eisler. Schoenberg was forced to resign his professorship at the Prussian Academy in Berlin—"the Nazis viewed his expulsion as a precondition for musical reconstruction along *völkisch* lines."[12] All of these figures, and many others, emigrated, an avenue that appeared distinctly more open for musicians than those in any other field due to the nature of the profession (including less of a reliance on a native language). Of course, a number of non-Jewish musicians joined the exodus from Nazi Germany, including conductors Hermann Scherchen, Fritz Busch, and the latter's brother, violinist-composer Adolf Busch. That said, most serious musicians remained in Germany, even if they more often ended up playing the compositions of officially approved composers such as Werner Egk, Hans Pfitzner, and Gottfried Müller, rather than Alban Berg, Ernst Krenek, or Kurt Weill.

Being sacked from a state position did not preclude joining the Reich Chamber of Culture. Many modernists availed themselves of this possibility of joining one of the seven arts-specific chambers, knowing that it was necessary in order to work. Thus, one finds today in various archives the Reich Chamber of Culture identity cards for a range of figures, from Otto Dix to Walter Gropius.[13] Even certain Jews were admitted to the Chamber—at least from the autumn of 1933 until it was purged in 1935–36. In 1935, there were 1,328 Jews expelled from the Reich Chamber for the Visual Arts alone, which gives a good indication of the numbers.[14] The Nazi authorities made exceptions beyond this point, such as the *Devisenjude,* or Jews who brought in foreign currency. Famed art dealer Curt Valentin, for example, received authorization to sell art abroad from the Reich Chamber for the Visual Arts in November 1936, but this was unusual. German Jews were then expected to join the Jüdischer Kulturbund, where, in principle, they could practice their art.[15] This distinct Jewish cultural sphere also offered a space for modernism—for a limited time—that yielded some surprising results: for example, the memorial exhibition of the work of painter Max Liebermann that took place in 1936—a year after his death—in the Berlin Jewish Museum.[16] A number of his works rendered in Impressionist and Post-Impressionist styles were included in the show.

The forces of aesthetic open-mindedness, or the pro-modernists, were certainly aware of the consequences of the 7 April 1933 law, yet many found ways to rally. Musician Wilhelm Furtwängler led the way, writing Reich Propaganda Minister Goebbels about the regime's future cultural policies. Goebbels responded and allowed the exchange to be published in the national press on 11 April 1933. Furtwängler, the conductor of the Berlin Philharmonic (among other posts) and one of the most revered artists in Germany at the time, maintained that he recognized only good and bad art—and contended that the dismissal of Jewish artists was justifiable only if they were bad artists. Goebbels offered vague assurances that "artists of real ability, whose work outside the field of art does not offend the elementary norms of state, politics, and society, will continue to find the future, as they have always in the past, the warmest encouragement and support."[17]

Granted, the Bauhaus Berlin was raided and the school closed that very day (11 April). Yet this was the initiative of Reich Interior Minister Wilhelm Frick, with the backing of Prussian Minister President Göring. The fiefdom created by Goebbels in the cultural realm remained in its protean state, but his initial signals about freedom and his willingness to engage in dialogue emboldened the pro-modernists. The director of the Bauhaus in Berlin, Ludwig Mies van der Rohe, responded to the institution's closure by seeking out Alfred Rosenberg. On 12 April 1933—the day after the raid—they met at Rosenberg's office in Berlin at 11 p.m. Rosenberg had also trained as an architect, and Mies hoped to have a serious discussion with him. Mies reportedly initiated the exchange by asking, "Where do you, as the cultural leader of the new Germany, stand on the aesthetic problems which have emerged as the result of technical and industrial development?" Rosenberg, who appeared unprepared for this kind of discussion, deflected the question, "Why do you ask?" He added, "Why do you want the backing of political power? We are not thinking of stifling individual initiative. . . . If you are so sure of what you are doing, your ideas will succeed anyway."[18] The two men talked past one another, but it seemed there was an element of mutual respect. Rosenberg terminated the meeting abruptly but reportedly said, "I will see what I can do for you." Mies responded, "Don't wait too long."[19]

2

Otto Andreas Schreiber and the Pro-Expressionist Students

A factory exhibition organized by Otto Andreas Schreiber, Hans Weidemann, and associates. Because one needed security clearance to visit most factories, they provided spaces for the pro-modernists to show controversial works. (*Der Arbeiter und die bildenden Kunst* [Berlin: NS-Gemeinschaft KdF, 1938])

IT WAS IN this unsettled environment that a group of Berlin university students, who led the local branch of the NSD-Studentenbund, made the decision to offer a more public defense of modernism. Theirs was a remarkable and important undertaking. The students, of course, were Nazis. Just because they were agitating for a more pluralistic cultural policy (which makes them sympathetic in certain ways), they remained anti-Semitic, hypernationalistic, and misogynist, among other less-than-attractive qualities. The NSD-Studentenbund was formed in 1926 and initially had little to do with cultural policy.[1] Although it served as an umbrella organization for Nazi student groups at the various universities in Berlin, the leaders eventually found a natural linkage between university affairs and cultural policy. Significantly, art students moved into leadership positions. Like their cohort in cities like Hamburg and Munich, the Berlin students gravitated to the debate about modernism. In a very real sense, they responded to the destructive policies of the Nazis in Thuringia after 1930. The Berlin students had no desire to have Paul Schultze-Naumburg or some other *völkisch* leader impose restrictions on them. They were open-minded in the sense that they saw multiple aesthetic styles as fitting into the new Reich, as compared with the more restrictive and monolithic aesthetic vision that characterized the völkisch camp.

The leaders of the Berlin students' group viewed the Fighting League members as provincial and regarded the völkisch art favored by Alfred Rosenberg and his allies as dull and reactionary. The students looked down on the anti-modernists, and many in the völkisch faction accused them (with good reason) of arrogance. As Elaine Hochman has noted, the members of the NSD-Studentenbund in Berlin "tended to be younger, better educated, and more accustomed to artistic experimentation than their [Fighting League] counterparts. German Expressionism had been part of their own formative aesthetic experiences, and many were unfamiliar with the longstanding Nazi antipathy for modernism, which had occurred mostly outside Berlin."[2] The German capital, of course, acted as a magnet for the more culturally "progressive" types, even during the Third Reich. It is no accident that former Bauhaus instructor Lyonel Feininger moved to Berlin in 1933. Even though his wife was part-Jewish (and he American-born), Feininger remained in Berlin until mid-1937, when he returned to the land of his birth to teach at Mills College in Oakland. But up until his emigration, Feininger, like so many others who hoped that modernism might find acceptance in Nazi Germany, believed that the metropolis would offer the greatest freedom for him to continue with his work.

The pro-modernist campaign of the NSD-Studentenbund captivated the imagination of many Berlin students and faculty—especially those studying or teaching studio art and art history. The students knew that they were entering the fray, what with the pressure-cooker atmosphere of the first months of the Third Reich. All the dismissals from the universities and academies, not to mention the state of emergency that followed the Reichstag fire of 28 February, had created a highly charged atmosphere. Fritz Hippler, the leader of the Brandenburg section of the NSD-Studentenbund, hailed from the "left-wing" element of the Nazi Party: those with a more anti-bourgeois, anti-capitalist, and anti-establishment animus to their thinking. He had joined the NSDAP in 1925 at age seventeen.[3] In 1932, Hippler had been dismissed from the University of Berlin as a result of his involvement in violent protests, but after the Nazi seizure of power he was reinstated by order of Reich Minister Bernhard Rust, who granted amnesties to all students sanctioned due to "national" demonstrations. Hippler continued to pursue violent methods, for example helping organize an aggressive rally outside the Berlin stock exchange in opposition to Hitler's alliance with "reactionary" Alfred Hugenberg. The event turned disorderly and a number of windows were broken in the surrounding neighborhood.[4] Historian Peter Paret has characterized Hippler as fairly unsophisticated and opportunistic, but he had been awarded a doctorate in philosophy at Heidelberg with a dissertation on Karl Marx, John Stuart Mill, and Paul Lagarde.[5] Hippler was also a capable organizer. He is now best known as the producer of the 1940 pseudodocumentary *The Eternal Jew,* which counts among the most anti-Semitic works of the Third Reich, with the visual metaphor of Jews and rats and actual footage from ghettos in the newly formed General Government. One scholar described it as "a preview of coming atrocities, preparing the German populace for the 'final solution.'"[6] *The Eternal Jew* also featured modernist techniques, such the dissolves where "'the

Eastern Jew, with his caftan, beard, and sideburns' [is transformed in-]to the camouflaged and grinning 'clean-shaven, Western European Jew.'"[7] Hippler became a powerful cultural bureaucrat, serving as the head of the film department in the Reich Propaganda Ministry until a falling out with Goebbels in March 1943. That year also marked the discovery that he had a Jewish great-grandmother, which resulted in his expulsion from the SS (Schutzstaffel—Himmler's elite corps that began as a protection staff).[8]

Hippler's deputy, painter Otto Andreas Schreiber, had joined the NSDAP at age twenty-four in November 1931. He had been born in West Prussia, but his family was driven out in 1919 when the League of Nations determined that this territory would be the "Polish Corridor."[9] Schreiber was trained by Jesuits and had been a member of their New Germany Society, a Catholic youth group. Later, between 1927 and 1931, he studied philosophy at the University of Berlin, and painting at the State Art Academies in Breslau, Königsberg, and, again, in Berlin. Among his teachers were leading Expressionist painters Otto Mueller (who exhibited with both Die Brücke and Der Blaue Reiter) and Oskar Moll, with whom Schreiber studied in Breslau. Both encouraged the young artist to become part of the next generation of Expressionists. Schreiber gradually grew more committed to National Socialism in the early 1930s. He joined the storm troopers (SA) and assumed a leadership role in the NSD-Studentenbund—even though he had been appointed an *Assistent* (and was therefore a kind of faculty member) at the State Art School in Berlin-Schöneberg after passing his examinations in 1931. By 1933, he represented four Berlin art schools within the organization. Schreiber was a self-assured, aggressive Nazi who added to this reputation on 17 February 1933 when he led an uprising of Nazi students at one of the Berlin art schools. He compelled some of his Brown Shirt friends (members of the SA) to storm the school and evict several professors. They then proceeded to beat up those students who attempted to defend the targeted faculty. The assault occurred during the state exams, when nerves were already on edge; the disruption of the important tests only amplified the impact of the rampage. Peter Paret noted, "Schreiber represented a familiar type in the regime's early stages: the university-educated humanist, whose ready use of intimidation and even violence was motivated by intense ideological conviction but coexisted with a cultural idealism beyond the mental horizon of the Party's rank and file bullies."[10] This incongruity found expression in a letter that Schreiber wrote in March 1933 to artist Otto Pankok. After describing the attack that he and other storm troopers had carried out at the Berlin Kunstschule, Schreiber concluded

Otto Andreas Schreiber, a painter and leader of the pro-Expressionist National Socialist German Students' League (NSD-Studentenbund) in Berlin. Schreiber later organized factory exhibitions of modernist artworks. (Bundesarchiv-Berlin)

the letter by talking about his career as an artist, relaying news about three upcoming exhibitions and noting, "My painting, I think, goes forward."[11]

The Berlin students were in contact with officials at the Propaganda Ministry, and several eventually found positions in Goebbels's ministry. These pro-modernist student leaders were relatively capable individuals who went on to considerable success in both Nazi and postwar Germany. In short, they were not inept or without influence, and they had a reasonable chance of realizing their vision of more tolerant cultural policy. Another key figure in this younger cohort was Hans Weidemann, who although not a matriculated student in 1933 served as the main representative of Goebbels in the minister's dealings with the Berlin students. Weidemann had joined the Nazi Party in 1927. His low Party membership number—below one hundred thousand—would be a significant asset in his career.[12] He first served as the deputy to the Gauleiter of Essen, Josef Terboven, before moving on to work for the Berlin Gauleiter Goebbels in 1930. Both Gauleiters situated themselves in the left wing of the Nazi Party, although the latter was clearly more important as a mentor. Weidemann was a painter as well as a musician. He had spent four years studying at the Düsseldorf Art Academy and a year at the State Music School in Cologne. He had then worked as an "independent painter" until 1930. Weidemann had been trained in an

Hans Weidemann, another leader of the NSD-Studentenbund. He went on to work for Goebbels's Reich Propaganda Ministry, where he promoted modernist art. Weidemann also became a member of the SS and is shown here in uniform. (Bundesarchiv-Berlin)

Expressionist style and was described as "a young protégé of Nolde."[13] He was not without artistic talent. The Folkwang Museum in Essen acquired one of his works, and only his personal appeal to the director of the museum, Count Klaus von Baudissin, prevented its inclusion in the *Degenerate Art Exhibition.* Weidemann noted after the war that "Baudissin regarded it as a special favor to me."[14]

Regardless, Hans Weidemann was far more important as a cultural bureaucrat. In March 1933, Goebbels made him a section chief in the newly minted Reich Propaganda Ministry, where he headed up Section II (simply titled "Propaganda"). Goebbels then selected him to be the liaison with Robert Ley, the head of the mammoth Nazi trade union known as the German Labor Front, which featured the Strength Through Joy leisure time organization. Weidemann in turn headed up the Culture Office of the Strength Through Joy initiative, although this proved short-lived due to conflict at the ministerial level. Yet Goebbels held Weidemann in high regard, and subsequently appointed him a vice president of the Reich Chamber for the Visual Arts, among other posts. While this also proved a short-lived assignment—Weidemann was sacked when he pushed for Nolde to become president of the Chamber—he retained his position on the Chamber's Presidential Advisory Board until 1937, when the new President, Adolf Ziegler, appointed a new group of more stridently anti-modernist advisers.[15] Weidemann henceforth ceased to be a force in the administration of the visual arts, although his career took an interesting turn and he remained active in the cultural sphere more broadly. Weidemann, like his friend Hippler, turned to film and oversaw the newsreel division in the Reich Propaganda Ministry. Shortly after this appointment, in May 1938, Weidemann joined the SS.[16] During the war, he personally went to the Eastern Front, where he filed reports for the Waffen-SS unit Kurt Eggers and for the SS-Totenkopf (Death's Head) Division. This was a kind of exile for the once prominent and well-connected cultural bureaucrat, yet he received positive reviews as an "exemplary SS-Man" and was promoted to the rank of SS-Second Lieutenant in early 1943.[17] Weidemann experienced brutal frontline conditions in the Soviet Union, but he managed to survive. In a letter to former museum director Alois Schardt in 1949, he expressed remorse for his "political error" and blamed it on "a great measure of idealism and youthful inexperience." But this was before he faced a denazification trial, and he was looking for witnesses who were not Nazis to vouch for him. In his appeal to Schardt, he claimed that "Barlach is dead [but], Nolde, Heckel and others have remained true to me." Schardt, who had headed up the modern section of the Berlin Nationalgalerie in 1933, replied with a helpful letter and Weidemann went on to rehabilitate his career as a journalist, even working for the prominent magazine *Stern* from 1964 to 1970.[18]

In the spring and summer of 1933, Hippler, Schreiber, and Weidemann realized that they needed a wider range of allies in order to advance their pro-modernist agenda. More specifically, they sought to enlist members of the art world. To do so, they created an organization they called "The Ring of German Artists" and invited both high profile and relatively unknown artists to join. The motto of the "Ring" was "Against French Aesthetics— For a Nativist German Art." More specifically, they built upon the ideas of prominent art historians Heinrich Wölfflin and Wilhelm Worringer, who posited a distinction between Germanic and Mediterranean cultures, and opposed Impressionism, which they viewed as French/Latin and hence superficial and insubstantial. Instead, they rallied on behalf of the spiritually deeper "Nordic Expressionism," which in their minds communicated fundamentally German attributes. As Nazis, they phrased their ideas in terms of "the mythic powers of German blood" and talked of "the essential bond between the German people and the German artist, who served the race, and whose work expressed in spirit . . . Nordic Aryan values."[19] Anti-Semitism also permeated their thinking: Impressionism, for example, had been foisted upon the Germans by Jewish dealers. The leaders of the Weimar Republic ("the Jewish Republic," in Schreiber's words) had entered into this conspiracy on behalf of the Impressionists, and in the process "betrayed" Expressionist artists such as "Barlach, Nolde, Heckel, Schmidt-Rottluff, Marc, and Rohlfs." Toward the end of one of his most important speeches Schreiber asserted, "Our blood instinctively rejects the Jewish people and its art."[20]

Several art dealers emerged as key allies for the pro-modernist students. One was Ferdinand Möller, who had founded his first gallery in Breslau in 1917 and made it a point of pride—especially during the Third Reich—to stress that he focused on German artists. Möller wrote to one Nazi museum director, Count Baudissin, in mid-1936,

> In the years of the Weimar regime, not one of these artists gained advantages from the state or received a state position. Their work was only valued by a few museum directors and private collectors domestically and abroad, and was collected by a few patrons, but the Jewish art trade ignored them. When Flechtheim declared to me that he could not understand how I could make a living with this "German garbage," well then you have an approximate idea of how the majority of the Jewish dealers opposed this art.[21]

Möller went on to say that one could criticize modernist artists on a variety of grounds—as part of the avant-garde they were accustomed to attacks—but "the accusation that they were Jewish, or that Jewish art dealers had intervened on their behalf, was not true."[22] While Möller was by no means a Nazi, he could find common cause with certain Nazi officials: he became a dealer of the purged "degenerate" art in part due to his relationship with Joachim and Annelies von Ribbentrop.[23] It is therefore understandable that Schreiber and his allies turned to Möller once they had decided to organize an exhibition of German Expressionism.

Alfred Rosenberg, as was his nature, did not sit by passively but rather mounted a counterattack in the summer and fall of 1933. He made a series of speeches and penned articles dated 6 July and 14 July 1933 that ran in his paper, the *Völkischer Beobachter,* where he criticized the pro-modernist element in the Party.[24] He accused Schreiber of being "a cultural Otto Strasser" (a former Nazi leader in the left wing of the Party who was out of favor in 1933—and had fled the country, while his brother, Gregor Strasser, was later murdered in the Röhm purge of 1934). Rosenberg vilified these leaders of the "Black Front." But he was onto something: the left wing of the NSDAP featured a disproportionate number of those in the Party who evinced a sympathy for modernism, as Schreiber, Weidemann, and Hippler demonstrated. Perhaps it was the interest in socialism that translated into an internationalism with regard to art; more likely, it correlated to education level. There were myriad factors that made the left-wing Nazis gravitate to the pro-modernist camp. Because they constituted formidable opponents for Rosenberg, he did not completely dismiss their views. He also still hoped to occupy an official post in the Nazi cultural administration, and took pains to appear reasonable and judicious. It is in this light that we should understand his review of 7 July 1933 in the *Völkischer Beobachter,* in which Rosenberg praised Nolde's seascapes as "strong and powerful," yet lamented other works, which he "declared to be negroid, raw, without piety and inner strength of form."[25]

Rosenberg could leave much of the dirty work to others. For example, he turned to an anti-modernist drawing teacher and journalist from Hamburg, Walter Hansen, to pen articles for the *Völkischer Beobachter.* Hansen labeled the 29 June rally "an effective blow against the art policy of the Führer and Rosenberg"; "a maneuver of falsification directed against national art and the racial principle"; and "an act of sabotage."[26] Hansen would later help instigate the *Degenerate Art Exhibition,* as he and Nazi artist/ideologue Wolfgang Willrich prepared a study of the "degenerate" works in the Berlin Nationalgalerie. Another article, authored by Hans Schemm, the Bavarian Minister of Education, and featured in the Nationalsozialistische *Lehrzeitung (National Socialist Teachers' Magazine)*, labeled the *Thirty German Artists* exhibition an "open attack on the sovereignty of the Party."[27]

Otto Andreas Schreiber replied to Rosenberg's first piece in the *Völkischer Beobachter* by sending a letter to the *Deutsche Allgemeine Zeitung* that was published on 12 July 1933. While Schreiber affirmed his support for modernism and a more tolerant cultural policy, he also tried to reduce the escalating tensions by giving "his word of honor . . . that student youth . . . are not attacking his [Rosenberg's] personal view of art."[28] Schreiber acknowledged that he had written the piece as an individual, not as a representative of the NSD-Studentenbund, an attempt to defuse the explosive situation. However, both sides were caught up in a pitched battle, and these minor concessions did little to help matters. The exchanges became so acrimonious that Bernhard Rust, the Reich Minister for Education, issued an order on 15 July prohibiting further discussion of these issues—especially in the press. Hans Hinkel, a State Commissioner who also worked for Goebbels, repeated this edict in an article published in the *Völkischer Beobachter* on 16–17 July 1933. Hinkel threatened that disciplinary actions would be taken against "all those who twist the words of sincere National

Socialists and so attempt to bring division into the front of the true new German art."[29] Many observers had recognized that the debate over modernism threatened the unity of the Party, giving rise to divisions that could undermine the fledgling Nazi regime.

Thirty German Artists opened the following week, on 22 July 1933. It actually featured the work of thirty-three artists. As noted above, both the elder and the younger generation of Expressionists were represented. Among the elders were August Macke, a member of Der Blaue Reiter who had fallen in World War I, and Karl Schmidt-Rottluff, who had designed the symbol of the German eagle for the fledgling Weimar Republic.[30] The show received a number of positive critical responses in the local press, including strong praise for the younger artists, such as Schreiber and Weidemann, as critics found their work "refreshing" and "vividly filled with the desire for the new and contemporary."[31] Certain artists whose work was featured in the exhibition subsequently found official acceptance in Nazi Germany, including Georg Kolbe. But it was a provocative and risky undertaking for the organizers. Their decision to borrow two carvings by Ernst Barlach from his Jewish dealer, Alfred Flechtheim, for example, would have opened them up to even harsher attacks had this fact become public.

Despite efforts on the part of Rust and others to minimize conflict over the show, the völkisch faction would not back off. They had been encouraged by the firing of Ludwig Justi from his post as director of the Berlin Nationalgalerie right after the 29 June rally. They now pressured Reich Interior Minister Frick to close the *Thirty German Artists* exhibition, and he complied. Three days after the opening, on 25 July, Frick sent uniformed police to enforce the decision; two SS men were subsequently placed at the entrance to the Möller Gallerie. The presence of SS men appeared to send a message of support from SS leader Heinrich Himmler and signaled this was a Nazi Party measure (as compared to a Reich or a state action). Members of the völkisch faction therefore believed they had the upper hand, and they were able to induce Party leaders to expel both Hippler and Schreiber from NSD-Studentenbund. Both students, however, were permitted to go on with their studies at the university.

Yet this was not the end of the saga surrounding *Thirty German Artists*. A week later, on 2 August 1933, Reich Minister Frick and the National Socialist authorities allowed the show to reopen, but this time without the sponsorship of the NSD-Studentenbund. The modification was an attempt to render it an "ordinary" exhibition, although its previous history made this effort impossible. Institutional support mattered a great deal in the debate over modernism, and the separation from the powerful Berlin student association greatly undermined the pro-modernists' initiative. This brought the matter of the *Thirty German Artists* show to a gradual close. Each side believed that it had advanced its cause, but neither could conclude it had prevailed. Members of both camps continued to agitate as best they could. In a 7 January 1934 article he wrote for the magazine *Deutsche Zukunft*, for example, museum director Max Sauerlandt referred back to the students' support of modernism the previous summer: "To have made the first attempt to clear the way for these most authentic among artists of the recent past and to have set them apart from the mass of incompetents and charlatans will redound to the eternal credit of the National Socialist Students' League and its leaders."[32] And so the debates and battles persisted.

Otto Andreas Schreiber's most significant accomplishments in his fight for modernism in the Third Reich were still to come. In November 1933 he launched a journal, called *Kunst der Nation* (*Art of the Nation*), that would become the most important venue for the pro-modernists. It had approximately 3,500 subscribers and could be purchased at newsstands for thirty Pfennigs. Goebbels not only sponsored *Kunst der Nation* but even contributed articles under his own name. Schreiber, who was the lead editor, took responsibility for its contents, and he was bold in his vision. For example, in a special *Winterhilfswerk* (Winter Relief) issue in 1934, he put a sculpture by Ernst Barlach on the cover.[33] The article, written by Alfred Hentzen, a curator at the Berlin Nationalgalerie, praised Barlach as a German master (Hentzen would go on to be director of the Hamburger Kunsthalle from 1955 to 1969). Historian Hildegard Brenner noted, "This excellently written magazine was able to appear for almost two years. Although the butt of much hostility, the editors managed to come out openly and militantly for Expressionism without being prosecuted for opposition to the Party."[34] This would be the case until 1935, when Alfred Rosenberg and other völkisch Nazis took more careful aim at the magazine.

To state that it was "excellently written" arguably heaps too much praise on this Nazi organ, which was, after all, a product of the Reich Propaganda Ministry. Some dubious premises surfaced within its pages, such as "Van Gogh als Deutscher," whereby the Dutch artist, who lived in France during his most productive period, was claimed by the Nazis as one of their own (or closely related as a *Niederdeutsch*).[35] Yet a series of distinguished figures penned pieces for *Kunst der Nation,* including art historian Werner Haftmann, a passionate champion of modern art who later directed the Berlin Nationalgalerie from 1967 to 1974, and Wilhelm Pinder, the es-

Otto Andreas Schreiber, *Double Portrait* (1936): a work with pronounced Expressionist elements. (*Kunst für Alle,* 1936)

teemed academic who held endowed chairs in Munich and then, as of 1936, in Berlin, and who was among the foremost art historians in Germany (if also a supporter of Hitler and a convinced anti-Semite). Dealer Ferdinand Möller also offered his support to the enterprise. Indeed, Schreiber had to deflect criticism that the periodical was "not published by true National Socialists, but the Galerie Ferdinand Möller."[36] This charge had been leveled by a drawing teacher named Jansen at a museum opening in Jena and provoked a passionate response from Schreiber. *Kunst der Nation* proved sufficiently important that Alfred Rosenberg contacted the Gestapo and demanded that the police agency close down the operation and confiscate all existing issues. The request was denied, but the periodical nonetheless folded in mid-February 1935 with the appearance of the last of its thirty-two editions.

For sixteen months, however, *Kunst der Nation* provided Schreiber and his allies with an important platform. Besides serving as editor, Schreiber authored seven articles in which he articulated his vision reconciling modernism and National Socialism. His most important programmatic statement was a piece published in the first edition of *Kunst der Nation,* titled "Do We Young Artists Have a New Art Ideal?"[37] Here he emphasized the national and racial components of art, rejecting, for example, an "international artistic impulse [*Kunstwille*]," which he saw as a "betrayal of our foundational principles." That said, he also believed many different styles and genres could bring out the "heroic spirit" of a people. He would later follow up on this theme in his other articles, for example quoting Goebbels's speech to open the Reich Chamber of Culture on 15 November 1933, where the Propaganda Minister talked about a National Socialist *Kunstpolitik* that was "free and unlimited," as long as the artists respected the laws of the state.[38]

Impressionism was one kind of art that Schreiber rejected, and he continued to view it as a "French art cult" that was "ushered in by the Jewish people." Here he was in sync with more mainstream National Socialist art critics, such as the *Völkischer Beobachter*'s Wilhelm Rüdiger, who argued that Impressionism stood as an "empty form of art"—one that involved "merely registering on the canvas impressions from the retina in a 'very routine process' that was 'utterly lacking in content.'"[39] In one of his articles, Schreiber talked about how Expressionists such as "Barlach, Nolde, Heckel, Schmidt-Rottluff, Marc und Rohlfs . . . [had led] the war of destruction against Impressionism." He added that the artists he listed had rejected the "Jewish Republic" and "recognized [in the democrats] their opponents." Schreiber also noted, "In the same way, our blood instinctively rejects the Jewish people, just as we reject [the Impressionist] forms." Here one gains a sense of the pro-modernists' strategy: they aimed to separate Expressionism from the Weimar Republic, to place it in opposition to Impressionism and French culture, and to use racial concepts (above all anti-Semitism) to appeal to the National Socialist base. Schreiber argued that what was needed was not a rehabilitation of Expressionism, but its "further development," and he maintained that it was Expressionists, in fact, who counted as the "exponents of a true völkisch culture."[40]

Schreiber developed this populist line of argumentation and, following Goebbels, lashed out against "Kitsch"—especially the "unmodern" variety—which he saw as a threat to the masses, who often succumbed to the easy and sentimental fare.[41] This concern for the masses and the art to which they were exposed served as the rationale for another initiative of Goebbels and the pro-modernist camp: appointing Weidemann and Schreiber to head the Cultural Office (Kulturamt) of the Strength Through Joy (Kraft durch Freude, or KdF) organization. The Strength Through Joy program would later be taken over by Robert Ley and featured as the showpiece of the German Labor Front (Deutsche Arbeitsfront). But until then, it was a model program in Goebbels's Propaganda Ministry. With Weidemann as

40

the main art adviser for the organization, and Schreiber as his deputy, the two pro-modernists gained a base from which to operate, although they would experience difficulties when the Goebbels-Ley relationship turned from alliance to rivalry. In 1934, Ley forced Weidemann to resign and replaced him with his own man. Weidemann went back to work for Goebbels in the Reich Propaganda Ministry, but Schreiber continued on as head of the office for the visual arts and organized a remarkable series of exhibitions that were held in German factories. These shows almost invariably included modernist works. As Hildegard Brenner later noted, with some exaggeration, "These exhibitions were to be the last refuge of the National Socialist avant-garde."[42]

While the exhibitions were justified by the anodyne formulation that workers and artists needed to develop greater respect for one another, the reality was that pro-modernists planned a series of truly extraordinary events. Schreiber explained shortly after the war in a letter to Paul Ortwin Rave of the Berlin Nationalgalerie that by the end of 1933 he and Weidemann had organized "small degenerate art shows" in factories that had been sealed due to the security measures related to rearmament. He recalled, "It occurred to me that before long almost every factory was an armaments operation for which entry was forbidden to outsiders; almost never did the eyes of someone not employed there see the exhibitions."[43] Schreiber and Weidemann organized a series of art competitions with jurors such as Emil Nolde, Erich Heckel, Ernst Barlach, Ludwig Mies van der Rohe, and Richard Strauss. The first was scheduled for December 1933. These shows would travel from factory to factory, often with individual works available for purchase. Design products, such as housewares promoted by the Strength Through Joy subagency Office for the Beauty of Labor (Amt Schönheit der Arbeit), were sometimes also included—many in a modernist style in the tradition of the Deutscher Werkbund (often translated as the German Association of Craftsmen). Graphic works predominated, but they were often by major artists, including Karl Schmidt-Rottluff, Gerhard Marcks, Max Pechstein, and Renée Sintenis. By moving these exhibitions to different factories, a remarkable number of people were exposed to Schreiber's vision. Schreiber organized eighty factory exhibitions in his first six months on the job, and by 1939 counted three thousand different "Fabrikausstellungen," with more than five million viewers. Ultimately, some four thousand exhibitions were organized, although Schreiber departed in 1939, whereupon he entered the military while continuing his own work as a painter.[44]

Precisely what percentage of the works in the factory exhibitions could be counted as modernist remains unclear, but long after the war—in a 1977 essay—Schreiber suggested that many of the pieces were Expressionist in style, and that he had been rather successful in sustaining this kind of art in the Reich. He also noted in a 1949 letter to Paul Ortwin Rave that "at the beginning of the undertaking we put at the disposal of twenty-five modern artists a wood-block press, an etching table, or a stone press; we took thirty prints from each work, signed by the artist. In this way, we had thirty sheets by Schmidt-Rottluff, Gerhard Marcks . . . , Edwin Scharff, etc. These graphic works formed the basis for the twenty-five exhibition collections."[45] The shows were supplemented by works loaned by sympathetic dealers, such as Eduard van der Heyde and Ferdinand Möller—the latter, for example, providing works by Nolde for one show at the A.E.G. factory in Berlin in the spring of 1936. Schreiber also noted, "Additional works were provided from private collectors and by the artists, whereby a great deal of idealism was demanded from all involved . . . there was nothing to be earned; never would an exhibition be seen by a critic, never would it be discussed in the press, and for all of that, the works often suffered through the frequent transport on the trucks to the factories."[46] This idealism included showing modern art in an industrial setting—a gesture consistent with the mechanistic tendencies associated with modernism—and the commercial availability of many of the exhibited items, which would result in many pieces finding their ways into workers' homes.

Considering that Hitler and others opposed modernism on the grounds that it was unintelligible to the masses and hence elitist (among other reasons), Schreiber's program to exhibit works in places like turbine halls seems exceedingly audacious. Schreiber claimed, "In the years up until the start of the war in 1939, we had only about five denunciations from workers that were directed to the leadership of the German Work Front; but the matter got stuck in the sand because the German Work Front leadership wasn't particularly interested in art problems."[47] Thus, these pro-modernist Nazi cultural bureaucrats had been given a free space in which to operate by a relatively negligent minister, Robert Ley, and his senior staffers. Schreiber recalled,

> The whole thing was for us—and often the factory directors—great fun; we were delighted by the associated excitement, all of the skirmishes, etc. There is no reason to regard it as an "act of heroism," but the reality is interesting: that one really could do this throughout almost the entire year and unnoticed by the public. [This was also

due] thanks to the cluelessness of the German Work Front people, and thanks to the cluelessness of the millions of workers, who saw these 4,000 exhibitions and must after all have sometimes wondered what "the Party" had come up with for them.[48]

The factory exhibition undertaking eventually encountered difficulties in mid-1939 when Hans Schweitzer, a graphic artist and notorious anti-modernist who worked for Goebbels, caught wind of the program. Schweitzer sent a long memorandum to the leadership of the German Work Front, demanding access to the exhibitions. Schreiber rightly construed Schweitzer's inquiry to be a "massive attack" and the start of bigger problems. As this drama unfolded, the war broke out and the factory exhibitions were put on hold, declared "non-essential during the war."

Their campaign to promote Expressionism was helped greatly by the fact that Schreiber and Weidemann were artists. Back in the autumn of 1933, both had joined an exhibition group called Der Norden (The North), which comprised modernist artists. They exhibited at the Ferdinand Möller Galerie and, later, at the Galerie van der Heyde, both in Berlin. That Weidemann and Schreiber were painters gave them additional legitimacy in these culture wars. They were not mere bureaucrats or dilettantes, but actual artists who appeared to evince a deep concern for the *Volk*. Their own work also gave them cover in times of difficulty or defeat. In the August 1934 issue of *Kunst der Nation,* when Schreiber announced that he would step down as editor, he justified the measure by asserting that his work in the Strength Through Joy Culture Office left no time for painting. Schreiber continued to edit *Die Kunstkammer* (the official journal of the Reich Chamber for the Visual Arts), in which he also wrote anti-völkisch pieces well into 1935. Among those contributing to *Die Kunstkammer* were two former Bauhaus members, Lothar Schreyer and Margaret Leischner. Although this magazine also went under amid continued attacks from Rosenberg's faction—in this case in 1936—Schreiber had his art (and, at this point, the factory exhibitions).[49] His identity as an artist would sustain him psychologically and, to a lesser extent, financially throughout the war.

The battles surrounding *Thirty German Artists, Kunst der Nation, Die Kunstkammer,* and the Strength Through Joy factory exhibitions were by no means the only fronts in the fight over modernism. Another important skirmish occurred in February–March 1934 on the occasion of the exhibition *Aeropittura* (or *Flugmalerei,* in German), a traveling show that had opened in Hamburg at the end of February and then moved to Berlin, before going to Vienna in 1935. Many observers concluded that this show, which featured Italian depictions of airplanes—and, more generally, Futurist works that glorified speed, modernity, and violence—was a means of bolstering the cause of German modernism. The argument that the Italian Fascists had reconciled modernism with their ideology rested upon a rationale that differed from that advanced by Schreiber and his partners (that Expressionism was quintessentially German), but both groups shared a view that modernism would help rejuvenate their respective countries. This was the theme of the lecture that Italian Futurist poet Ruggero Vasari delivered at the Hamburg opening in February 1934 and that was translated into German and published in 1935.[50]

The *Aeropittura* exhibition came at a crucial time in the debate over modernism in the Third Reich. Even the slippery Goebbels was forced to disclose his support for modernism in a more explicit way than ever before. He belonged to the Committee of Honor sponsoring the show. Others on the committee included Hermann Göring, Reich Education Minister Bernhard Rust, Eugen Hönig (president of the Reich Chamber for the Visual Arts), and Eberhard Hanfstaengl, the director of the Berlin Nationalgalerie. The Italian members included Filippo Marinetti and Ambassador Vittorio Cerrutti. The Berlin exhibition was held in the space formerly occupied by the Galerie Flechtheim on the Lützow-Ufer—arguably the most famous gallery of modern art during the Weimar Republic. It had been taken over by a Nazi trustee, with Alfred Flechtheim relocating to Paris and then London. Was the selection of this venue purely utilitarian? The record is silent on this point. The opening of the *Aeropittura* show on the evening of 28 March 1934 was another highly charged event, akin to the June 1933 rally prior to the *Thirty German Artists* exhibition. Dada-Constructivist Kurt Schwitters journeyed from Hannover just to attend the event and reacted with tremendous enthusiasm when he met Marinetti. Gottfried Benn, then vice president of the Union of National Authors, defended modernism and argued that "'discipline and form as symbols of domination' must mold 'the cold style of the future.'"[51] It is not clear whether Goebbels, Göring, Rust, and all of the other members of the Committee of Honor were present. If so, it would have added yet another element of excitement.

The pro-modernist forces in Germany used the occasion to advance their cause in the reviews that followed. The critic for *Die Weltkunst* argued that the exhibition was of "inestimable importance as an indication of the tie between the political forces and artistic endeavors of an allied nation."[52]

The most enthusiastic response to the exhibition, not surprisingly, came from Gert Theunissen in *Kunst der Nation,* who wrote,

> Marinetti and his disciples of the Manifesto are the artistic incarna-
> tions of an idea, born about 1909 from the Vesuvius of Marinetti's
> mind and the inferno of his heart. This idea was to capture time,
> time as such, to seize it by the hair as it speeds over Europe's asphalt
> roads, polished smooth by balloon tires . . . the new continent is in-
> habited by airplanes, automobiles, and Marinettis. . . . We hail the
> Futurist exhibition on the Lützow-Ufer . . . as welcome testimony
> to the many-sidedness of artistic endeavors and to the justification
> of many-sidedness.[53]

Otto Andreas Schreiber added his own endorsement of Futurism, noting how it had a "historic parallel" with Expressionism. Schreiber was less than gushing about the works in the show, but he was clear about the implica-tions for German art: "The young painters of today . . . continue to build on the artistic experience of color and form which they found present. On the strength of this organic continuity a higher development of German paint-ing is to be hoped for."[54] Lest this seem too opaque, Schreiber also called for "a continuation of Expressionism." He and his allies would not go down without a fight.

The völkisch faction, of course, responded immediately to what they perceived as a provocation. Robert Scholz, Alfred Rosenberg's chief art critic, penned a series of attacks in the *Völkischer Beobachter.* The first ap-peared on the morning of the opening, 28 March 1934, labeling the show "an attempt at propaganda" and arguing that Futurism was "a movement without significance in Italy itself."[55] Scholz was wrong in this respect, but he was correct in noting that Mussolini had recently been pushing for a new style that would supplant Futurism. The "imperial style" that emerged in the 1930s would be the result. Scholz also helped elucidate what would become the dominant view among the Nazis with regard to their Fascist co-hort to the south: the Italians were lazy and self-indulgent people and there-fore permitted a lax cultural policy. This view would find resonance with regard to the Austrians as well, who were viewed as "schlampig" (sloppy) and lacking the discipline of the "Prussians." Scholz had actually showed considerable sympathy for modernism up through 1933, praising Barlach and Kokoschka in one article that ran in the more centrist *Steglitzer Anzei-ger* in 1933; he could also point to both artists as veterans of the Great War, with Kokoschka having joined the Austro-Hungarian cavalry and fighting on the Eastern Front, barely surviving a bayonet stab to the lung.[56] Scholz therefore at times evinced sympathy for certain modernist artists, Edvard Munch included, whose work he did not consider "degenerate."

Despite these views, Scholz quickly learned how to do his boss's bidding and proved very effective as a cultural bureaucrat. While not the most radical of the anti-modernists—he was outdone by, among others, the aforementioned Walter Hansen, Wolfgang Willrich, and Franz Hofmann—Scholz counted as one of the most influential.[57] He wrote dozens of articles for the *Völkischer Beobachter,* especially between 1933 and 1938, and as of 1934 held a high ranking post in Rosenberg's organization, the DBFU—a Nazi Party office for cultural and ideological initiatives—where he organized art exhibitions. Beginning in 1937 Scholz also edited the glossy official art journal *Kunst im Deutschen Reich* (one of the most important publications of the era). As of 1938, he directed the Moritzburg Galerie in Halle, a fairly prominent museum not far from Berlin. During the war, Scholz served as the Leader of the Special Staff Visual Arts within the ERR, the Special Task Force of Reichsleiter Rosenberg. He received an initial appointment to work on the Sonderstab at the end of 1940, where he oversaw the creation of inventories, but he gradually grew more hands-on. By 1943, Scholz and his colleague Hermann von Ingram effectively managed the ERR—supplanting Kurt von Behr and art dealer Bruno Lohse in this regard. This put Scholz in the stratosphere of the art looting bureaucracy, where he corresponded frequently with Martin Bormann and other top Nazis. The most intense engagement with the Führer's secretary came at war's end, when the stolen and safeguarded art stored at *Schloss* Neuschwanstein and in salt mines at Altaussee came under threat by radical SS elements that threatened to destroy the objects rather than relinquish them to the enemy. Scholz helped preserve the treasured cultural objects, once again showing that he was a formidable administrator.

Rosenberg also pressed the attack in his own right, but largely from behind the scenes. An indefatigable bureaucrat who generated an almost unimaginable quantity of documents from his various agencies, Rosenberg inundated Goebbels with complaints about cultural policies he viewed as too tolerant. In one August 1934 letter, Rosenberg charged:

> The high point was unquestionably the successful attempt to put on a Futurist exhibition of Berlin art Bolshevists by the detour of Italy, sponsored by you among others, evidently in ignorance of the trends

represented. Perhaps indeed it was unknown to you that the organizer of this exhibition was for many years active in Berlin as an art Bolshevist and spokesman of the Sturm group. I can assure you that this fact was appropriately deplored among National Socialist artists.[58]

Goebbels mostly ignored these rants, but they wore on him and made him less inclined to expend political capital to protect modernists.

Goebbels's more cautious approach became evident as early as February 1934, when the Reich Minister ordered Hans Weidemann to remove Expressionist paintings that he had just installed in the ministry's premises on the Wilhelm-Strasse. Weidemann, who viewed himself as a principled and courageous person, refused to disavow German Expressionism and withdraw the offending works. After all, just six weeks earlier, in December 1933, Goebbels—in a statement with flowery language drafted by Weidemann —had sent a congratulatory telegram to Norwegian modernist artist Edvard Munch on his seventieth birthday. It did not hurt that Munch had spent his formative *Wanderjahren* in Germany between 1892 and 1908, self-identified as a Nietzsche enthusiast, and was widely thought to have fascist sympathies.[59] Weidemann apparently believed he knew his chief's sincere views, and he decided to take a stand with regard to the works that he had placed in the ministry. Goebbels interpreted this as an act of insubordination and demoted him (albeit temporarily) to a less important position in the Propaganda Ministry. The two men met on 8 February 1934, and Goebbels put his aide in his place, noting in his diaries that Weidemann's reaction had been "reserved."[60] The contretemps had negative repercussions for the pro-modernists. For example, they scrapped an exhibition that Weidemann and Schreiber were planning, where Emil Nolde and Mies van der Rohe were to serve on the jury. At the time, few had little idea what Weidemann's demotion meant for modernism in Germany. Elaine Hochman concluded, "In fact, contrary to what was perceived at the time, the disgrace of Hans Weidemann, Nazi idealist and outspoken Party advocate for modernism (and Mies), meant that modernism would never be the 'official' art of the Third Reich."[61]

By September 1934, then, Goebbels appeared to retreat from his support for modernism. He wrote to Rosenberg at the end of the month, "It is not true that gentlemen employed in the Reich Chamber for the Visual Arts have the closest relationships to those in the Barlach-Nolde circle."[62] Was this a bald-faced but expedient lie that concealed his enduring support for Expressionism, or a sign that he had decided to betray his old allies? It is difficult to know for certain, but likely a combination of the two. Hitler had criticized modernism at the Nuremberg Party Rally a few weeks earlier, and this swayed the sycophantic Propaganda Minister, who, to use a phrase now favored by historians, was "working toward the Führer." Hitler had expressed disapproval of the Nolde watercolor in Goebbels's Schwanenwerder home, and this had resulted in its removal.[63] But at the same time, Goebbels kept certain modern works, such as the statues by Barlach, in his private collection. He also did not move against certain public collections of modernist art, including the Abstract Cabinet in the Hannover Museum, which featured a dazzling array of works by Mondrian, Picasso, Moholy-Nagy, and Malevich, among others. This modern section of the Hannover Museum remained open well into late 1935. Goebbels, on the other hand, sent signals in 1935 that he would be less laissez-faire: this included new requirements for organizing exhibitions, whereby the Reich Chamber for the Visual Arts received greater supervisory authority and he mandated, among other requirements, a list documenting the names of all participating artists. Modernist cultural figures still had spaces in which to operate, and yet they also perceived the escalating threats that characterized the mid-1930s.

3

The Continuation of Modernism
in Nazi Germany

The cover of the Nazi magazine *Die neue Linie* (September 1939),
which illustrates the continuation of modernist design principles
during the Third Reich.

WHILE MANY MODERNIST cultural figures remained uncertain whether Goebbels could be counted on to champion their cause, certain individuals remained cautiously optimistic up through 1937 for the reasons noted earlier. The Reich Chamber of Culture, for example, continued to include many modernist figures. Most of the luminaries from the pathbreaking Expressionist group Die Brücke, for example, were members of the Chamber, including Erich Heckel, Max Pechstein, Karl Schmidt-Rottluff, and Emil Nolde. Goebbels had not completely reneged on his earlier promises of artistic freedom, or reversed his public stance regarding Expressionism. His most encouraging early statement had been a May 1933 speech to leaders in the world of theater, where he spoke of the "healthy view of Expressionism" and also praised *Neue Sachlichkeit* as "the German art of the next decade," and he had yet to repudiate these stances publicly.[1] Goebbels in all likelihood preserved considerable sympathy for various kinds of modernist culture, including Expressionist art. A landscape that did not have colors true to nature or a work with abstraction—as long as there was a strong figurative component—might well please him. His purchases of artwork after 1937 reflect this sympathy. For example, Goebbels in May 1938 bought a painting by Franz von Stuck.[2] Stuck was a fin-de-siècle painter, a Munich professor often placed in the Symbolist category, who created works with modernist features. For Goebbels, buying a work by Stuck was akin to his supporting Fritz Klimsch, Georg Kolbe, and the other artists who had modernist elements, but who, in his eyes, did not cross over the line into decadence.[3]

There were other Nazi leaders who indicated their support for modernist culture in the years up through 1937. In June 1936, for example, word circulated that Reich Minister Bernhard Rust had commented that he considered Emil Nolde to be "the greatest living German painter." Berlin dealer Ferdinand Möller wrote to Nolde in breathless prose a few days after the event and asked if he had "heard about the very positive remarks about your work made by Reich Minister Rust on the occasion of an assembly of art teachers convened by the Reich Education Ministry."[4] Nazi officials in the Foreign Ministry also appreciated a more tolerant arts policy because it could facilitate better foreign relations. In the autumn of 1937, they signed off on an exhibition of Italian art that included Futurist paintings by Umberto Boccioni and Enrico Prampolini that took place at the Berlin Academy of the Fine Arts in the Pariser Platz. Italian diplomats, such as counselor Massimo Magistrati, lobbied a number of Nazi officials, including Goebbels's personal aide in the Reich Propaganda Ministry, Karl Hanke, and implored the Germans to adopt a more open-minded policy toward certain kinds of modernism. According to counselor Magistrati, Hitler visited the exhibition, but scarcely looked at the controversial works.[5] The dictator would not budge on this issue, and this proved decisive. Put another way, Goebbels and others would have not have caved in their support for modernism if Hitler had not intervened and attempted to settle the debate.

It is important to gain some sense of how Hitler was brought around to repudiate Goebbels and act against the pro-modernists. Bear in mind that this was a process, and not a bolt out of the blue. Hitler, of course, had expressed anti-modernist views going back to his early writings, including *Mein Kampf,* where he lashed out against the proponents of modernism, whom he viewed as "spiritual degenerates or slimy swindlers." He continued to disparage them in his statements on art. In his September 1933 speech at Nuremberg on the "Führer's Day of Culture," he said, "We will not allow these charlatans and untalented artists to enter our arts scene even if they change their opinion. Under no circumstances must the representatives of decadence become the voices of the future. This is our state, not theirs, we will not be soiled."[6] But this speech was also viewed by many as "a dazzling display of equivocation." Oskar Schlemmer wrote to artist Willi Baumeister on 9 October 1933, "The Nazi policy on art remains undefined." Schlemmer had earlier written to Baumeister on 22 March 1933, reporting that some of his works were being taken down in Stuttgart, but, he added, "[Karl] Hofer tells me that there are apparently some decent people among the Nazis."[7] The notion of "decent people" among the Nazis helped sustain hope for some observers. Accordingly, Schlemmer joined the Reich Chamber for the Visual Arts and remained a member into the war years. He hoped that Hitler's speech on 15 October 1933 at the groundbreaking ceremonies for the Haus der Deutschen Kunst would provide clarification. But Hitler did not answer the key questions and offered only platitudes about the building rising from the ashes of the previous structure (the Glaspalast museum had burned down in 1929).

Hitler's reluctance to take a stand gave the pro-modernists continued hope that Expressionism would find a place in the Third Reich. Additionally, Hitler traveled to Italy in June 1934 and visited the German pavilion at the Venice Biennale. The German exhibition contained works by New Objectivity painter Franz Radziwill and Expressionist sculptor Ernst Barlach, among others with a modernist orientation. Yet Hitler did not offer any objections or negative comments—at least none that were recorded. At the September 1934 Nuremberg Party Rally, he criticized modern art but also rebuked the *völkisch* faction, bemoaning "the sudden emergence of those backward-lookers who imagine that they can impose on the National Socialist revolution, as a binding heritage for the future, a 'Teutonic art' sprung from the fuzzy world of their own romantic conceptions."[8] By attacking both camps, Hitler delayed a resolution of the modernism debate.

Up until 1937, Hitler refrained from making his personal views state policy. Years later Hans Weidemann reflected, "I must repeat it. In 1933 we all held Hitler's artistic view to be his own personal opinion. Quite certainly. Mies thought so too."[9] There were multiple factors that most likely induced Hitler to delay the official campaign against modernism. One was that Hitler tended to be more flexible with artists. He could, for example, be slightly more understanding with regard to Jewish heritage and associations: opera singer Margarete Slezak performed at the German opera despite Jewish grandparents; art dealer Maria Almas Dietrich had a Jewish father, a Jewish husband, and a child by another Jewish man, yet she sold more works to Hitler than any other of her cohort; composer Arthur Piechler was reinstated to his post at the Augsburg conservatory despite being Jewish (architect-designer Gerdy Troost intervened on his behalf); and composer Franz Lehár had Jewish relatives yet found protection. While these figures represented exceptions, there was nevertheless more latitude in the cultural sphere than elsewhere. Hitler was certainly more understanding about artists' politics and their sexual orientation. He gave passes to sculptor Josef Thorak and others for earlier left-wing views, and he was generally too formal or prudish to inquire about homosexuality among artists. Actor Gustaf Gründgens and certain others widely thought to be gay were permitted to work (see Chapter 10). Granted, it did not take much to incite Hitler to rage against Jews, socialists, homosexuals, and modernists as well. This is what had happened in June 1933, when Hitler received a delegation that included

Paul Schultze-Naumburg. The architect proceeded to show him illustrations of modernist works being exhibited in the Kronprinzenpalais (which had over five hundred modernist paintings, making it the "world's premier museum of the avant-garde"). This tactic worked; Hitler was outraged and ordered the paintings removed to storerooms. The director, Ludwig Justi, was then demoted to curator. But to a considerable extent Hitler refrained during the early years of the Third Reich from personal involvement in the determination of cultural policy.

Until 1937, numerous pockets of tolerance remained in Nazi Germany, at least when it came to modern art. As Elaine Hochman has observed, "The absence of any apparent logic in the Nazi actions kept many people off their guard. Some cities were left free to pursue their normal cultural activities, while others were subjected to extensive police harassment. An artist respected and praised in one city often found his works banned and politically suspect in another."[10] Eberhard Hanfstaengl, the director of the Nationalgalerie in Berlin who succeeded Alois Schardt (a figure who had himself tried to reconcile Expressionism and National Socialism by way of the concept of "Nordic art"), continued to acquire modernist art for the museum, including purchasing works by Barlach, Kokoschka, and Otto Dix in 1935. In early 1936 the Nationalgalerie acquired sixty-four pictures and graphic works of a *kulturbolschewistischer Tendenz*: the objects had been pulled from an auction organized by the Gestapo and the Reich Interior Ministry held at the auction house Max Perl.[11] Hanfstaengl was told to make a selection, which he did—commandeering works by Dix, Hofer, Pechstein, and others. Hanfstaengl also acquired modernist works seized from the estate of Ismar Littmann, a Jewish lawyer from Breslau who had committed suicide in 1934.[12] In April 1937, Hanfstaengl bought a color sketch of *Ecce Homo* done by Lovis Corinth: the artist's widow had agreed to part with it for RM 1,000 (about $400) and was honored to have the work in the collection of the Nationalgalerie.[13] This was a work Corinth made in an Expressionist style after he had recovered from a debilitating stroke; some of his earlier pictures were so "tame" that even Hitler had one in the collection for the Führermuseum. Otto Andreas Schreiber had one of his own Expressionistic watercolors purchased by the Berlin Nationalgalerie from the Galerie van der Heyde in 1936 (it was later purged by Ziegler's committee and sold off). Art historian Dieter Scholz wrote of Schreiber, "The year 1936 appeared to mark the artistic pinnacle of his artistic career."[14] Dresden art historian/critic Will Grohmann included him in that year's edition of the *Thieme-Becker-Künstlerlexikon,* attesting to his status as an artist.

Architect Fritz Höger, one of the leading exponents of "Brick Expressionism" (*Klinker-Expressionismus*) because of the elaborate masonry of his soaring structures, offers another important case of a modernist hoping to find accommodation in Nazi Germany. Höger had shown sympathy for National Socialism for some time—he would speak at events organized by the Nordische Gesellschaft (Nordic Society), a Nazi-affiliated organization— and he joined the Party in 1932. After the war, he claimed to have joined the Party in order to limit the attacks from the anti-modernists. Although he claimed to be horrified by the violence of the Nazi regime, Höger maintained that Party membership was the only way to pursue his "ideal" and create a "true, honest German architecture."[15] Höger was an important and visible modernist—perhaps not of the stature of Gropius or Barlach, but not too far behind. He designed many structures for sites across Germany in the 1920s, but especially in Hamburg, where he conceived a number of iconic structures, most notably the sleek and curvaceous Chilehaus (1924). It is therefore striking that Höger had supporters in such key positions. Fritz Mackensen, a painter and utopian who founded the Worpswede Artists' Colony and befriended many artists, including Expressionist painter Paula Modersohn-Becker and poet Rainer Maria Rilke, counted as a committed ally of Höger. Mackensen also joined the NSDAP, although not until 1937. Prior to that, he founded the only art school created by the Nazis: the Nordische Kunsthochschule (NKH) in Bremen. Opened in April 1934 as a kind of counter to the Bauhaus, the Nazi art academy integrated Nazi racial ideology into a wide-ranging curriculum, including painting, applied arts, and architecture. Höger held a chair in architecture at the NKH from 1934 to 1935, a signal that the Expressionism debate was far from resolved. At this time he had the support of Alfred Rosenberg and his chief art critic, Robert Scholz, who both believed that Höger had talent that could be shaped in an appropriate way.[16] Rosenberg even commissioned Höger to design an exhibition organized by one of his agencies, the Office for the Nurturing of Art (Amt für Kunstpflege) in Berlin. Even with this support, Höger could not hold on. The sharper anti-modernist turn in the mid-1930s translated into acute pressure for Höger to give up his chair at the Nazified institution. Höger explained after the war that he was one of the few architects in Germany who were financially comfortable and did not need to earn a living by teaching. Yet he continued to search for acceptance, and had some success. In 1937, for example, he received an invitation to enter the competition for a Nazi Party building (a *Gauforum*) in Hamburg. Höger, like many others, held out hope that he could combine Expressionism and National Socialism.

Even Max Pechstein, formerly a member of Die Brücke, had works included in an exhibition of one of Rosenberg's organizations, the NS-Kulturgemeinde, in July 1936. The show was held in the town of Stolp in Pomerania, and reports of the presence of pictures by this "convinced cultural Bolshevist" immediately made their way to Rosenberg.[17] It was not clear whether the pictures remained in place, but a representative of the president of the Reich Chamber for the Visual Arts, an art historian named Benno Griebert, wrote to the local Nazi official in Pomerania that Pechstein was a member of the Chamber in good standing, and that his artwork could be shown so long as it was approved by the exhibition leader. Previously, in 1934 Pechstein had executed a design of four blacksmiths grouped around an anvil, with a large swastika in the center; the design was evidently for a Strength Through Joy competition and, in the words of his biographers, constituted "more troubling evidence of Pechstein's conformity."[18] The artist also had his pictures collected by the Berlin Nationalgalerie into 1935, including a still life and a work called *Man in Repose,* which the museum acquired in August 1935. Pechstein claimed in his memoirs, which were published in 1960, that he had suffered a ban on exhibiting his work (*Ausstellungsverbot*) in 1935, but clearly if such a prohibition existed it was not enforced throughout the Reich.[19]

Pechstein played up to the Nazis in an attempt to find acceptance, often in ways that proved rather unbecoming. After he was asked to resign, he wrote to the Prussian Academy on 12 July 1937: "I am not aware of any dishonorable wrong-doing on my part which would justify the withdrawal of my membership—neither personally nor politically. I and my wife are proven Full-Aryans, my eldest son is in the SA [storm troopers], my youngest son already in his second year of the Hitler Youth, and apart from that I am myself since 1934 a member of the N[ational] S[ocialist] Welfare Organization and the NS Air Sports Association."[20] Ten days later, Pechstein wrote Professor Arthur Kampf about his possible exclusion from the Prussian Academy, which he saw as the "finishing off of him as a person." Pechstein added, "I read the names of the newly appointed members and I would mention only one: [Josef] Thorak, who among other things, was married to a full Jew, with whom he had a child. After the upheaval [Nazi seizure of power] he disavowed them!"[21] Desperation did not always bring out the best in persecuted modernists. Despite his protestations, Pechstein lost his position at the Prussian Academy on 6 September 1937. He subsequently managed a few victories, such as an exhibition of his recently painted landscapes at the Galerie van der Heyde in Berlin in 1939. Pechstein continued to hope for acceptance throughout the Third Reich and remained a member of the Reich Chamber of Culture until 1945.

There was much wishful thinking on the part of the pro-modernists. When Hitler approved a functionalist design for industrial production, or when he incorporated modernist elements in *Autobahn* design, this was interpreted as a sign of a more tolerant cultural policy. And indeed, Hitler saw the merits of modernism when it came to certain kinds of industrial or mechanical projects. He said to architect Hermann Giesler, for example, "I will have nothing to do with Romantic eccentricity or anachronistic buildings—as, for example, a service station on a contemporary autobahn of all places that tries to give the impression, through half-timber and gables, of being part of the landscape. Instead, they should be declaring, 'Here autos are fuelled, not horses given water.'"[22] At the 1935 Nuremberg Party Rally, Hitler made yet another address on culture and, more specifically, identified eight key principles with regard to architecture. Several of them were decidedly pro-modernist, such as "modern construction might require modern means; architects should therefore not shun modern building materials."[23]

Hitler opted for modernist design in a number of projects. Many of the bridges designed during the Third Reich offer a case in point: at Rüdersdorf, just east of Berlin, and over the Mangfal Valley in Bavaria, among others. The sleek bridges often soared over deep gorges, a striking advertisement for German engineering and design. Hitler came around to appreciate steel and glass, as well as reinforced concrete. Speer tells of a visit to the Hermann Göring Works in Linz in 1943, where the dictator praised the design: "When we left the big steel plant, Hitler expressed appreciation of modern steel and glass architecture. 'Do you see this façade more than three hundred meters long? How fine the proportions are.'"[24] Hitler also changed his views on skyscrapers: although he once viewed them as inhuman, he came to understand them as "symbols of technological advance and a nation's scientific prowess." He therefore planned for a future Germany with skyscrapers "sensibly integrated"—with the caveat that it applied only to certain kinds of projects.[25] The socialist strains of the Nazi ideology also generated support for large-scale public housing programs, and these visions were often modernist. Even critics for the *Völkischer Beobachter* evinced admiration for the technological modernity of the new architecture, believing it could be harmonious with Hitler's grand visions of urban planning.[26] This is why Fritz Höger could serve as a consultant to the *Völkischer Beobachter* as of 1927. Hitler openly admired Henry Ford (whom he awarded the Great Cross of the Order of the Eagle), ostentatiously rode around in high-powered Mercedes, and even allowed himself to be photographed in 1938 "sitting contentedly" in a sleek, curved Bauhaus chair.[27]

The Nazis struggled to reconcile modernism and anti-modernism. "Reactionary modernism," as historian Jeffrey Herf put it, proved an alluring if elusive concept.[28] Could the Germans be rooted in the soil and tied to tradition (a.k.a. "ruralist romanticism") while at the same time develop their modern industrial power? Could they have a folk culture and still fashion themselves as the progenitors of the West? Hitler and his subleaders clearly could not realize their ambition of imperial conquest without modern means. As such, they praised and patronized those who advanced technological development throughout the Third Reich.

With great fanfare, the Nazis glorified the accomplishments of technocrats, or "techno-princes," during the Third Reich. The list is extensive but includes Professor Dr. Ferdinand Porsche, who along with his son Ferry Porsche took the lead in developing the Volkswagen, as well as the family's own eponymous automobile. While not many people received an actual People's Car, there were many military vehicles, tanks, airplane engines, and other tools of war designed and built by the Porsches (and Ferdinand Porsche joined the SS in 1937, rising to the rank of SS-Oberführer, or colonel, in 1942). Hitler and the Nazis enthusiastically pursued the "motorization" of German society in the 1930s. Another example would be the aircraft designer Wilhelm Messerschmitt, who along with Walter Rethel in 1934 designed the Messerschmitt Bf 109, which subsequently became the most produced fighter in history. Willy Messerschmitt enjoyed the patronage of Hermann Göring and Rudolf Hess and grew increasingly famous in the Third Reich. In 1938, the Bayerische Flugzeugwerke underwent a change of name and became Messerschmitt AG, and the aircraft designer received the German National Prize for Art and Science, the highest honor of its kind in the Third Reich. The German National Prize had been created by Hitler in 1937 as a substitute for the Nobel Prize and came with an RM 100,000 (or $40,000) stipend. The award lasted only until 1939, with just nine recipients in total. These technocrats were exalted by the Nazi publicity machine in a manner that affirmed a pro-modern agenda. The aviator Hanna Reitsch, known for both her bold feats and her dedication to National Socialism, became the first woman to fly a helicopter and a jet fighter; she later became the only woman to win the Iron Cross in World War II, among other high honors.

And so the pro-modernists persisted into the mid-1930s, looking for clues about official policy, seizing upon the small victories. American Monuments, Fine Arts, and Archives officer Hellmut Lehmann-Haupt noted in 1947 that "it would be a great mistake to assume that there was no cultural resistance, that there were no men or women who defended their intellectual and artistic integrity with courage and skill. . . . They lived on isolated islands, inhabitants so to speak of a small oasis surviving here and there in the Nazi desert."[29] These "inhabitants" knew they had their detractors, and that Hitler might shut them down at any moment. But members of the avant-garde had suffered attacks since the concept came into existence in the early nineteenth century. It was, after all, a military term. Many believed that Hitler and Nazi Germany needed them. Their own egos usually came into play: Hitler needed cultural leaders—individuals to advance the specific disciplines—and they saw themselves as the leaders of their fields. Especially in the early years of the Third Reich they hoped for, and often expected, a leadership role. Of course, the rationales for staying and trying to find a place in Nazi Germany proved complex and variable. For this reason, it is important to look at specific case studies.

Part II

The Pursuit of Accommodation

WHY DID SO many modernists seek a place in Nazi Germany? How did their work change as a result of the evolving and conflicted aesthetic policies of the new leaders? What did they aspire to do and what role did they see themselves playing in the Third Reich? The fate of five exemplary figures helps tell the tale. These figures hoped for accommodation with the Nazi regime but ultimately failed to find a meaningful modus vivendi. They were compelled either to emigrate or to retreat from public life. Their struggles for acceptance reveal a great deal about the Third Reich, and their diverse responses to the Nazi cultural administration show that the resolution of the modernist debate was not prede-termined. With artistic figures accustomed to success, there was an even heightened element of human agency. These figures had risen to leading positions in their respective fields, often overcom-ing enormous hardship, and most had strong instincts for survival.

Walter Gropius, for one, after augmenting his fame as the founder and first director of the Bauhaus, enjoyed a successful private practice. The other architect who could rival Gropius in terms of reputation, Ludwig Mies van der Rohe, was the last director of the Bauhaus, and he too enjoyed the patronage of an array of important clients (although his practice languished during the Depression and Third Reich). Mies viewed himself as an artist—a visionary whose "less is more" became a guiding principle for many modernists. Within certain German circles, their reputations remained undiminished after 1933. Both Gropius and Mies immigrated to the United States, with the former taking a position at Harvard University and the latter at the Armour Institute in Chicago. But before their departures in late 1934 and in 1937, respectively, they sought official acceptance and support. Architectural historian Richard Pommer quipped, "Politically, Mies was the Talleyrand of modern architecture," designing within the span of ten years for the Communist Party in Germany and the Nazis.[1]

Because writers are so tied to language, which they usually convey in their native tongue, emigration presented special challenges for Germany's distinguished cohort of modernists. About two thousand writers are estimated to have left Nazi Germany, which still represented a minority of the discipline. Although certain figures departed—especially those who had been translated into English and could head to the West, such as Thomas and Heinrich Mann, Bertolt Brecht, Erich Maria Remarque, Ernst Toller, Carl Zuckmayer, Lion Feuchtwanger, Franz Werfel, and Alfred Döblin— many others stayed and endured Nazi rule. Expressionist writer Gottfried Benn offers an instructive example. With his interest in the irrational and in violence, and his strong sense of nationalism, Benn believed that his work would find a place in Nazi Germany. In this way, he was much like fellow writer and World War I veteran Ernst Jünger, who also eschewed emigration and found a place in the Reich.[2]

The cases of Ernst Barlach and Emil Nolde are likewise enlightening. Born in 1867, Nolde was seven years older than Barlach, who also experienced the travails and consequences of World War I. Nolde genuinely admired Hitler and embraced many tenets of National Socialism, while Barlach, who was anti-Nazi, believed that his art was essentially German, and that he belonged in his homeland. The aging and increasingly frail Barlach could scarcely imagine living in another country, and instead retreated to the Mecklenburg hinterland, where he hoped to avoid politicized attacks. Of course, each artist responded with unique hopes and concerns. There were even German artists living outside the Reich, such as Ernst Ludwig Kirchner in Switzerland, who also harbored fantasies of success in his native country during the 1930s. His painting *Three Peasants*, dated 1936–37, featured two women (one holding what appears to be a milk jug) who are joined by a man, with the three figures surrounded by cows (Plate 6).[3] The picture bears a distinct resemblance to many National Socialist works—and seemed to echo the "Blood and Soil" theme that informed so many works in the *Great German Art Exhibitions*.

These artists were exceptional in many respects, but also representative. Their motivations, fears, and decisions echoed those of others. They were tremendously influential during their own time. Other cultural figures were watching how Gropius, Hindemith, Benn, Barlach, and Nolde responded to the Nazi regime. With the exception of Nolde, none of the figures discussed here were members of the Nazi Party. They were seeking accommodation with a regime that they understood to be dangerous. But they believed this could be accomplished, just as many had contended with hostile critics in the years before 1933. They also shared certain personality traits. Mies van der Rohe's biographer Elaine Hochman wrote about "his authoritarian instincts, single mindedness, and refusal to acknowledge the validity and diversity of human claims."[4] He was not alone.

There was one characteristic above all others that compelled these figures to collaborate: careerism. They all desperately wanted to work, and saw an unprecedented opportunity with Hitler and the Nazi regime, especially with so much of the rest of the world mired in an economic depression. Never before in modern history had a regime invested so much in cultural projects, and there were even greater prospects for the future (assuming one could find favor with the regime). Hitler had big plans. He conceived "Germania": the remodeling of Berlin into a capital befitting the Nazi empire. With structures such as the Great Hall, which would hold 180,000, and the Führer Palace, a fortress that would tower over one end of the North–South Axis and replace part of the Tiergarten, the madly ambitious project could be accomplished only by conquest—the cost and requirements for raw materials were so enormous. Even Albert Speer later conceded that Hitler "was planning buildings expressive of an imperial glory which could be won only by war."[5]

There was also Special Project (*Sonderauftrag*) Linz, with the Führermuseum at its core, but also a library, a symphony hall, and an entire cultural complex. The art collection alone, for which Hitler acquired over eight thousand works prior to 1945 (even if only about a thousand were specifically designated for the museum), represented the most manic acquisition program in history. Hitler and his subleaders outpaced Napoleon, Baron Denon, and the Grande Armée by a considerable margin. The efforts by Hitler and other Nazi leaders to amass collections offered tremendous opportunities for many in the art world. It did not hurt that the first director of the Führermuseum, Hans Posse, admired modern artists like Oskar Kokoschka and Otto Dix and protected their works in his other capacity as head of the Dresden Gemäldegalerie.[6] Of course, he did not acquire such art for Hitler's museum. But some dealers who sold to Hitler and Posse also continued their trade in modern works: Erhard Göpel, yet also Hildebrand Gurlitt, Karl Haberstock, Ludwig Gutbier, and Eduard Plietzsch, to name a few. Hitler's agents, as well as those representing other Nazi leaders, also helped sustain the auction houses, such as Hans Lange in Berlin, Adolf Weinmüller in Munich, and the Dorotheum in Vienna.[7]

Artists had ample opportunity to benefit from the many other official projects initiated by Hitler. There were the "Führer cities"—Hamburg, Nuremberg, Munich, Berlin, and Linz—that would be graced with massive building projects, ranging from the world's longest suspension bridge in Hamburg to Speer's coliseum in Nuremberg. There would be the elite Nazi schools—the Adolf Hitler Schule and the castle-like *Ordensburgen*— and there would be the *Autobahnen,* with their attendant sculptures and buildings. Artists in all fields benefited from the Nazis' ambitious cultural plans. The Reich Chamber of Music as of 1939 had "more than 170,000 professional members who benefited from generous state and party subsidies, an expanding market for music at all levels of German society, and the increasing availability of specialist positions in the many Party offices and ensembles, such as the National Socialist Reich Symphony Orchestra [NSRO] under the batons of Franz Adam and Eric Kloss, which performed at home and abroad in their brown tuxedos designed by Hitler himself."[8] The Nazi leaders, at least for a time, appeared to improve the circumstances of a wide range of people in the cultural sector.

There were many cultural figures who viewed, with good reason, the Nazi leaders as generous patrons. The kleptocratic leaders who enriched themselves during the Third Reich subscribed to a trickle-down philosophy with regard to wealth, especially because so much of it involved state funds, not to mention plundered assets.[9] The Nazis provided support that ranged from scholarships for promising artists to the renovation of the Munich Künstlerhaus (Hitler authorized RM 2 million [or $800,000] for the project).[10] Hitler also awarded favored cultural figures tax-free cash gifts, called *Dotationen.* These were usually in the hundreds of thousands of Reichsmarks when the average worker earned RM 2,000 (or about $800) per year. Sculptors Arno Breker and Josef Thorak were among the recipients of a "*Führer-Dotation.*"

Clearly there was more to the drive to collaborate than profit and the opportunity to work on compelling projects. There were also artistic principles at play. Most believed that their art would represent a positive contribution to the Third Reich and would also help determine the direction of their discipline. Max Beckmann observed, "After the simplification practiced by van Gogh and Gauguin, it's time to go back to multiplicity. There is no way past those two: You have to take what they have achieved, turn back, and look for a new path from some earlier point on the route."[11] The ambition for many was to find that path—but one that would be accepted in Nazi Germany.

4

Walter Gropius

(1883 Berlin–1969 Boston)

Walter Gropius in 1928 in front of his entry for the Chicago Tribune
Tower from 1922. (Associated Press)

I **F ONE ATTEMPTED** to identify Germany's greatest architects in the twentieth century, the list would certainly include Walter Gropius. The founder of the Bauhaus, as historian Peter Gay has rightly noted, helped pioneer modernist design in the years before World War I: the Fagus Shoe Factory of 1911 and the factory building for the Deutscher Werkbund exhibition in Cologne in 1914 immediately emerged as modernist landmarks.[1] The influence of Gropius's work, which involved designing with rectilinear lines, avoiding unnecessary ornamentation, and exploring the possibilities of prefabrication, among other features, can scarcely be overestimated. Married to Gustav Mahler's widow, Alma Mahler, from 1915 to 1920, Gropius occupied a place among modernist royalty. His transformation of the Weimar art school into an iconic institution, and the epic battles he waged with the forces of reaction, eventually made Gropius an international celebrity. His relocation to Great Britain and then to the United States before becoming too complicit in the programs of the Third Reich, and his acceptance of a distinguished position at Harvard University's Graduate School of Design in 1937, helped to obscure the period he spent in Germany trying to find accommodation with the Nazi regime.

Like many who have enjoyed success and renown, Gropius possessed tremendous self-confidence. When he resigned his post as director of the Bauhaus in 1928 in order to focus on his private architectural practice, he believed not only that he had established an institution of world-historical importance, but also that he had conceived a pathbreaking movement in architecture—"the New Architecture," as he would call it.[2] Gropius also maintained that he personally played a leading role in rehabilitating the reputation of modern technology, which had been so badly damaged during the slaughter of World War I. The machine gun stood as the most potent symbol of technology run amok: an industrial product that operated in an automated way, spewing out bullets at a steady rate as it mowed down scores of victims. If Gropius could rehabilitate technology during the 1920s, he reasoned in 1933, then he could resolve the modernist/anti-modernist dilemma that roiled the new Reich.

Of course, rehabilitating technology's negative reputation during the Weimar Republic and reconciling the "reactionary modernism" that preoccupied so many National Socialists were two different projects. During his tenure as director of the Bauhaus, it had helped that Gropius had served as an army officer and could speak with authority about how technology had been utilized in the Great War. He and his Bauhaus colleagues showed how machines could improve living standards: how automation, mass production, prefabrication, and multiusage strategies could serve as a basis of social reform. A key, for Gropius, was green architecture: both in the sense of the conservation of resources and with regard to nature. The homes and housing complexes he designed always featured garden spaces, and the buildings stood in proportion to nature (never exceeding four stories). The idea was to have people surrounded by trees and grass, and to make it easy to access these resources (no long elevator rides as in a skyscraper). This, in concert with the technology, would provide a life-enhancing balance. Gropius's efforts to reclaim technology, to use it for benign purposes, proved a viable project. His success in this regard led him to be overconfident about his ability to find common cause with the Nazi regime, which had its own "green" agenda, albeit as part of a broader racist worldview. Hitler marketed the *Autobahnen,* for example, as providing the means for urban residents to escape the unhealthy city and connect with the supposedly pristine and restorative German countryside.[3]

An appreciation for the potential of technology and the desire to counterbalance modernity with a regard for the environment—these were to be the points of common cause between Gropius and the National Socialists. He would design rational, efficient, cutting edge buildings and cities that would arise in the reinvigorated Reich. Gropius's design would serve the *Volksgemeinschaft.* His planned communities, what with their populist and communitarian notions of social engineering, would fit in well with Nazi values. Even *Der Völkische Beobachter* exhibited support for certain modernist housing projects in the 1920s, regarding the undertakings as consistent with the National Socialist worldview.[4]

Most people who moved into the housing projects that Gropius and his colleagues designed in Berlin, Karlsruhe, and Dessau from 1926 to 1932 were leaving squalid tenements, often without indoor plumbing and always overcrowded, among other limitations. Gropius's housing projects represented a signal improvement in the quality of the environment, and were considerably healthier than the inner-city complexes. Viewed from a certain perspective, his desire to ameliorate the urban experience responded to the assertion made by many Nazis that cities caused widespread alienation and degeneration, as compared to the life-affirming qualities of an organic rural community. One might think of sociologist Ferdinand Tönnies's value-laden distinction between *Gemeinschaft* (community) and *Gesellschaft* (society), but with a racial twist: the former being the healthy organic community found in small towns, and the latter designating the commodification of labor and alienation so common in cities. In short, Gropius's communities had certain points of convergence with the "Blood and Soil" ideology embraced by most Nazis.[5] This is not to say that Gropius was a Nazi. He was not. He detested their intolerance and, in the course of battling for acceptance, came to view the Nazis as "them" (and not "us"). But there was enough common ground for the two sides to undertake exploratory forays.

Gropius not only viewed his vision of a community shaped by architecture as consistent with the aspirations of the Nazis, but also saw himself as possessing the qualities that would enable him to flourish in the Third Reich. He thought of himself as an artist above politics. True, Gropius himself had initially professed enthusiasm for left-wing views in the early years of the Weimar Republic. He had been a member of the November-Gruppe and in 1922 had designed a memorial for the victims of the right-wing Kapp Putsch in Weimar, and one of his first moves as director of the Bauhaus was to hire Wassily Kandinsky, who had just helped set up the Moscow Institute of Art and Culture for Vladimir Lenin.[6] In 1923, Gropius engaged Lázló Moholy-Nagy, who had supported Béla Kun's Hungarian soviet regime. Kandinsky and Moholy-Nagy were lightning rods for the extreme right. It did not help matters that, at the inception of the school, the faculty shared a building and lived in an almost communal way. This and the rowdiness of the students exacerbated the "town-gown" rift. That the Bauhaus was a state institution with state funding made it all the more political.

Gropius, however, was a diplomat and a pragmatist at heart and he recognized the need for political neutrality. Early in his tenure as director of the Bauhaus, he (like Mies later on) took steps in that direction by telling students not to attend certain events: for example, the funeral of striking workers who had been killed by government authorities in 1920. He was to exhibit his penchant for avoiding confrontation at an early stage. Already in December 1919, when the Bauhaus was just months old, charges arose that it was an "un-German" institution. This was code for too many Jews.

Gropius responded that there were "only 17 students . . . of Jewish extrac-
tion, of whom none has a grant and most have been baptized. All others are
Aryans."[7] He was to adopt similar tactics and play to the Nazis in an explicit
way after 1933. But, in fairness to Gropius, he also found opportunities to
express more critical opinions in his dialogues with the Nazi authorities.

In many ways, the Nazis could have utilized such a charismatic figure
as Gropius to oversee the national architecture and design programs. Gropius seemed to know everyone in the cultural sphere. Wherever he turned,
he had significant ties to other cultural luminaries—with a preponderance
on the modernist side. For example, in 1934, when his eighteen-year-old
daughter Manon (born to him and Alma in 1916) contracted polio and
then passed away, famed modernist composer Alban Berg wrote his violin
concerto in memory of her. Of course, Gropius had recruited for the Bauhaus the greatest assemblage of modernist talent ever brought together at
one institution: not only Kandinsky and Moholy-Nagy, but also Paul Klee,
Oskar Schlemmer, Marcel Breuer, Josef Albers, Johannes Itten, and Lyonel
Feininger, among many others. Gropius was their boss—and at the center
of their lives while at the Bauhaus—and he would forever remain a figure
of authority for them. Gropius had impressive skills as an administrator,
having kept the Bauhaus afloat in treacherous waters.

Gropius resigned from the Bauhaus in 1928, with the institution firmly
established and the political situation relatively stable. This all changed after
1929 once the Depression set in and the Nazis grew in numbers and influence. He would always be associated with the institution. Having done so
much to promote the school, this was unavoidable. Similarly, the Bauhaus
could never escape its left-wing reputation and its perceived connection to
the Weimar Republic, the government having provided the core funding
and then the commissions for the housing projects. Gropius had always
been high on the conservative Nazis' "most wanted" list. He was sometimes
referred to, with a certain wry humor, as "Mister Bauhaus"—a moniker that
would cut the other way and help him when he moved to the United States
and assumed a leading role within the Bauhaus diaspora.[8]

Despite looming large in the imagination of many Nazis, Gropius be-
lieved that he could find a place in the Third Reich. Partly this had to do
with his social background. Gropius hailed from an old and distinguished
Berlin family. His father was a city building councilor and his great uncle,
Martin Gropius, was a famous architect and follower of Karl Friedrich
Schinkel, who designed the School of the Berlin Arts and Crafts Museum.
Walter Gropius attended excellent schools—four Gymnasia and the pres-

tigious Technische Hochschule in Berlin, among others. Due to his social status and connections, Gropius found a place in a distinguished cavalry regiment in World War I. In short, Gropius counted as a *salonfähig* (socially acceptable)—and not Jewish—gentleman, and he believed that, as such, he would be acceptable to the Nazis. Gropius's privileged background meant that he did not need an income from his work in the 1930s. He had family money. When he and Mies worked for Peter Behrens before the Great War, Gropius, according to Mies, "did not need a salary."[9] He had become only wealthier in the intervening years, what with his patents (many from his time at the Bauhaus) and his architectural commissions. Gropius worked because he believed in his design philosophy and because he coveted the recognition.

When the Nazis came to power, however, Gropius did not stand squarely upon his principles. While he never joined the Nazi Party, he did become a member of the Reich Chamber of Culture and, more specifically, of the Reich Chamber for the Visual Arts. On 12 December 1933, Gropius became architect-engineer member number 706 of the Reich Chamber of Culture. His biographer Reginald Isaacs observed of Gropius's membership card, "His signature is dramatic, but his photo shows him stern, tight-lipped, appearing less sad than resentful, and older than his fifty years."[10] Gropius knew he needed the card in order to practice his profession as an architect and designer. Becoming a member of a Chamber entailed submitting proof of one's "Aryan" ancestry, although some Jews were in fact initially admitted. Gropius submitted his *Ahnentafel* (family tree) and remained a member in good standing with the Reich Chamber of Culture until the war years.[11] He never suffered restrictions on his work, or the dreaded *Berufsverbot* —banned from practicing one's profession. But Gropius went further than just maintaining his position within the Nazis' corporatist organization.

For starters, he developed a convivial relationship with the first president of the Reich Chamber for the Visual Arts, fellow architect Eugen Hönig. A professor of architecture at the University of Munich, Hönig exhibited a certain intellectual sophistication. He had also been a practicing architect, designing a number of buildings in central Munich, including the famed Dallmayr food emporium. Although Hönig had been the head of the Munich chapter of the Fighting League for German Culture, he was not beholden to Fighting League leader Alfred Rosenberg, whom he opposed with considerable frequency, and he counted as a moderate in most respects. Besides initially allowing Jews to join the Chamber, he supported the right of modernists like Max Pechstein to exhibit their work—so long as they were

REICHS-
KULTURKAMMER
Reichskammer der bildenden Künste
Fachverband:
Bund Deutscher Architekten e. V. (BDA)

Mitglieds-Nr.: **AI 706**
Herr/Frau/Fräulein
Prof. Dr. ing. e.h. Walter Gropius
Landesstelle:
Berlin

Der Präsident
der Reichskammer der bildenden Künste

Unterschrift:

Ausgefertigt
Berlin, den

Walter Gropius's membership card for the Reich Chamber for the Visual Arts from December 1933. (Landesarchiv, Berlin)

members of the Chamber in good standing.[12] Hönig was a key reason the modernists held out hope in the early years of the Third Reich, and his departure at the end of 1936 would signal a sharper and more anti-modernist shift in policy. Gropius and Hönig corresponded about a number of topics, including the exhibition of Italian Futurist art in Berlin in 1934 and Filippo Marinetti's speech at the opening of the show. Gropius also wrote to Hönig in March 1934, "Shall this strong new architectural movement [modernism] which began in Germany, be lost to Germany? Can Germany afford to throw overboard the new architecture and its spiritual leaders, when there is nothing to replace them?"[13] Gropius complained about defamatory comments (*Verleumdungen*) in the Nazi press, and Hönig proved supportive. For example, in a 4 October 1934 letter in the Bauhaus-Archive, Hönig praised Gropius as a "deutschempfindenen" (literally, a "German-feeling") person, advising that he should "calmly defend himself"; Hönig added, "You can always give proof of your value that you were admitted into the Reich Chamber for the Visual Arts."[14] Hönig even came to visit Gropius when the latter was living in the United Kingdom in 1936. The president of the Reich Chamber for the Visual Arts arrived with Carl Christoph

Lörcher, the president of the Confederation of German Architects (and also a storm trooper), and, according to Gropius's wife, Ise, who wrote to former *Bauhäusler* Xanti Schawinski in Fascist Italy, they all got on well. Hönig was a moderate Nazi, but he was a Nazi in a high office, and Gropius's friendship with him suggests that the Bauhaus founder was not an opponent of the regime at this point.

Gropius often fell back on his self-image as an unpolitical artist. In 1936, he wrote in regard to the criminal trial of Dessau Lord Mayor Fritz Hesse and the latter's involvement with the Bauhaus,

> At the inauguration of a Bauhaus exhibition in 1923, in my absence while on vacation, a text by Professor Oskar Schlemmer was drafted and published. Because I believed there was a misunderstanding of the text with the sentence about the "Cathedral of Socialism"—which was meant in a completely non-party political way—I ordered that this page of the program be cut out and destroyed. . . . Subsequently, I did all that I could throughout the entire tenure of my leadership of the Bauhaus to avoid that which was party-political—to shield the institution from the considerable danger that existed at the time and to prevent it from becoming a ball batted around by political parties in Parliament.[15]

Gropius claimed that the history of the Bauhaus had been compressed (*verquickt*) so as to blur the distinction between him and his successor, the politically engaged Communist Hannes Meyer, and that Gropius had always been against the politicization of the school. While Meyer had moderated his Communist politics during his tenure as director from 1928 to 1930, Gropius nonetheless distanced himself from him.

Gropius was a German nationalist, perhaps not surprising considering that he hailed from a prominent family and had been an officer in World War I. Even after he left Germany in late 1934, he would sign important letters with the phrase "mit deutschen Gruss" (with German greetings), and while living in England and the United States in the 1930s he invariably took pains to emphasize that he was a German citizen. On 27 March 1934, Gropius wrote to Hönig, "It goes thoroughly against my nature, dear Professor Hönig, to have to be negative in what I say, but it is a natural consequence of the fact that my own country forcefully represses the positive in me. You demand the German man. I feel very German—and who can make himself a judge over what is German and what is not—in my ideas and the ideas of my spiritual brothers of German origin."[16] Later, in 1938, after Gropius became chair of the architecture department at Harvard's Graduate School of Design, the German authorities demanded that he pay the Reich Flight Tax. Gropius wrote an angry letter: "I find it shameful and without foundation to be treated as someone who has jumped ship [*Überläufer*]," and added that he was "a loyal German citizen."[17]

This nationalism played into Gropius's efforts to find ideological common ground with the Nazis. Gropius wrote, "Above all, I myself see this new style as the way in which we in our country can finally achieve a valid union of the two great spiritual heritages of the classical and the Gothic tradition. Schinkel sought this union, but in vain. Shall Germany deny itself this great opportunity?"[18] Gropius wrote on several occasions that he simply wanted the opportunity to express his views, and to defend himself against attacks—and that, given this opportunity, his views would prevail. He wrote fellow architect Paul Schmitthenner in June 1934 that it was an "old German code of martial honor" to give one's opponents not only the same weapons, but the same space to fight (*Kampfraum*).[19]

An early test in the Third Reich regarding this synthesis of modernism and National Socialism concerned the Deutscher Werkbund (often translated as the German Association of Craftsmen). Gropius, like many others, thought that the movement (which came to include Peter Behrens, Heinrich Tessenow, and Henry van de Velde) could be adapted to serve the goals of the new Reich. The Deutscher Werkbund had featured a joint effort of designers and manufacturers who tried to integrate arts and crafts into the modern industrial mass-production system. For certain observers, the ideas of the Werkbund could be apolitical, or even "a surrogate for political involvement."[20] For others, they had a nationalistic thrust: making German industry more competitive. The reform program of the Deutscher Werkbund certainly lent itself to co-optation. Speer's Office for the Beautification of Work (Amt Schönheit der Arbeit) took over the remnants of the Werkbund in 1934. Speer believed in its potential because "the underlying philosophy of this modern movement was the fusion of architecture and the machine into the 'machine aesthetic.'"[21] Gropius deserves credit for being one of the few members of the Deutscher Werkbund to vote in a June 1933 meeting against handing the organization over to new leaders who were aligned with the Nazi regime, and he opposed the expulsion of Jewish members. Gropius quit the Werkbund once it became Nazified, but it was difficult to deny that the Werkbund fit into National Socialist Germany in many respects.

Gropius also looked to Mussolini's Italy as a model for reconciling modernism with Fascism. Other Bauhäusler had found acceptance in Italy, including ex-Bauhaus-Master Xanti Schawinski, who used Bauhaus typography in his designs of fascist posters.[22] Many Italians embraced Gropius and the New Architecture, and he had a formidable reputation in Italy. Gropius had helped design the German pavilion in the Triennale in Milan in 1934, and he also spoke at a theater conference in Rome in October 1934. He followed the Italian Fascist *Kulturpolitik* closely. His letter to Hönig in spring 1934 about Marinetti's visit to Germany and the exhibition of Futurist art showed how he hoped to use Mussolini's more pluralistic cultural policy as a model. Gropius took it as an encouraging sign that the Italian Futurist exhibition in Berlin earlier that spring had featured Göring, Goebbels, and Reich Education Minister Bernhard Rust as patrons. Fascist politician Dino Alfieri, who later became Minister of People's Culture in 1937 (and then ambassador to Germany), proved especially enthusiastic about Gropius's work and helped arrange for the architect to come to the 1934 Rome conference, sponsored by the Fondazione Allessandro Volta. This solicitation came at a time when Italian Fascists sought to attract high-profile foreigners to witness their national transformation, and they invited luminaries like Gropius in the belief that it would both showcase and legitimize the regime. With the approval of President Hönig, Gropius delivered a speech where he talked about the "purification and renewal of theater . . . in a materialistic age of the machine."[23] While Gropius's remarks in Rome did not meet with universal approval among those in attendance, he seemed to make an effort to reach out to the Fascists. Even Ise Gropius, the architect's second wife (they married in the early 1920s after his divorce from Alma Mahler), did her part. She accompanied him to the conference, and, in a highly visible gesture, entered the lavish dining room at the Palazzo Farnese for the celebratory dinner arm in arm with Fascist Party Secretary Achille Starace—a moment captured and then exploited by the state propaganda machine.[24]

When the Nazis closed the Bauhaus on 11 April 1933, a number of younger Bauhäusler tried to re-found the school under the name "Deutsches Bauhaus." They, like Gropius, believed that the institution could be reconciled with the Nazi regime. Some even applied for membership in the Fighting League for German Culture. This pro-Nazi cohort could never overcome the fact that the Bauhaus had been one of the "best known enemies" targeted in the Nazis' Kulturpolitik of the 1920s. That said, a number of former Bauhäusler joined the Nazi Party. Architectural historian Winfried Nerdinger noted, "It is, to say the least, astonishing how many leading colleagues from Gropius's office went over to the Nazis" and offers numerous examples, including Ernst Neufert, who became Speer's expert for standardization (Beauftragter für Normungsfragen); and Hanns Dustmann, who served as the Reich Architect of the Hitler Youth, which he followed with a stint with Speer in Berlin and finally, to cap off his Nazi career, a post as Schirach's architect-in-chief in Vienna. Nerdinger observed succinctly, "The direct origins in the office of the Bauhaus-founder caused no professional problems during the National Socialist period."[25]

The battle for the Bauhaus raged most fiercely in the 1920s and early 1930s. By 1936–37, there were some legal reverberations stemming from the property of the Bauhaus, but mostly the famed art school remained a nonissue in the ongoing culture wars. This made it all the easier for the Bauhäusler to work in Nazi Germany. They were most active in what Nerdinger has labeled "neutral fields of activity," which would include industrial design, the graphic arts, and photography. Wilhelm Wagenfeld, for example, headed the Vereinigten Lausitzer Glaswerke after 1935, and Carl Bauer served as an architect in the German Labor Front. Many alumni subsequently found employment at the Hermann Göring Works, a massive industrial firm founded in July 1937 that by 1940 employed over six hundred thousand people and represented one of the "great concentrations of industrial power" in the world.[26] Some former Bauhäusler went further than the "neutral fields" and created propaganda. Hinnerk Scheper completed many commissions for murals, including one for Göring's Karinhall residence, and Kurt Kranz became a combat artist.

Another extraordinary instance of a former Bauhäusler seeking accommodation was Oskar Schlemmer, who tried to hold on to his professorship in Stuttgart. In April 1933, having heard rumors that he was accused of being Jewish, he wrote to Reich Minister Bernhard Rust and informed him of his "Christian-Protestant origins dating back to the Thirty Years' War that is impeccably documented."[27] This did not save him from losing his post. Having just been released from his professorship, Schlemmer wrote a friend in June 1933, "At this time, everything is being investigated: ancestry, political party, Jew, Marx, Bauhaus. . . . I myself feel pure and that my art corresponds to National Socialist principles—namely, heroic, steel-hard-romantic, unsentimental, hard, sharp, clear, a productive working type, etc. But who sees it?"[28] In these remarks, Schlemmer referenced a speech by Goebbels inaugurating the Reich Chamber of Culture. Later, in 1934, Schlemmer entered the mural competition for the Congress Hall in the Deutsches Museum in Munich. His figures were posed in marching positions, standing in clean rows and making the "Hitler-greeting" (Plate 3). Art historian Magdalena Droste noted of the design for the 130-meter-long wall, "From left to right in a rising movement the figures should reach out to the central god-like figure [*Sonnenjüngling*] at the high point of the wall."[29] The repetition of the figures, making the highly politicized gesture, brought to mind the Nuremberg Party rallies, what with the coordinated movement of the thousands of Nazi faithful. Schlemmer himself commented, "My designs are not bad . . . I am the only one who tried to portray the *Volksgemeinschaft* [people's or racial community]."[30]

Oskar Schlemmer also engaged in a spirited and lengthy correspondence with Count Klaus von Baudissin, the Nazi director of the Folkwang Museum in Essen between 1934 and 1938 and the brother-in-law of SS General Karl Wolff. Baudissin had taken over what Harvard art historian Paul Sachs called "the most beautiful museum in the world"—this after his 1932 visit to the collection, which impressed him greatly; the museum had major works by Gauguin, Nolde, and Franz Marc, among others.[31] Baudissin and Schlemmer exchanged a series of letters in which they discussed aesthetic policy in very frank terms. Baudissin explained in one letter from May 1934 that Schlemmer's murals (*Wandbilder*) had already been moved to the storeroom when he assumed leadership of the museum, and he promised, "A destruction or painting-over of the panels will, as long as I am in office, not occur."[32] Such promises would eventually prove hollow, but up until 1937 Schlemmer believed that he was attacked due to an error or a misunderstanding. And indeed, he had his supporters, as reflected in a commission from Stuttgart collector Hugo Borst to paint the door to his dining room (Borst organized private shows of modern art for those whom he trusted), and in the positive review Schlemmer received from critic Will Grohmann in January 1937 that appeared in the *Deutsche Allgemeine Zeitung* (Grohmann commented on his energy-filled canvases).[33] Schlemmer was not alone in this cautious optimism during the 1930s, although he grew more pessimistic and depressed during the war years, even as he kept working. Just prior to his death in 1943, he queried, "My actions in recent years were all mistakes and entanglements, growing out of causes relating to one's existence. How will I come out of this honorably?"[34] For his part, Will Grohmann found a way forward, writing throughout the war for Goebbels's periodical *Das Reich,* among other Nazi publications.

One source of hopefulness for Gropius and other modernists was the competition for the new Reichsbank, which was among the first of the Nazis' representational buildings undertaken in 1933. With its expanding

Gropius's design for the Reichsbank competition of 1933. Note its monumental scale, symmetry, and neoclassical elements, all of which became hallmarks of fascist architecture. (Bauhaus-Archiv, Berlin)

responsibilities in an ever more complicated economic environment and its growing staff, the Reichsbank was in urgent need of a new headquarters. The competition was announced in February, and thirty of Germany's leading architects were invited to submit proposals. Six finalists were then chosen and paid an RM 5,000 ($2,000) participation fee—about twice the annual income of a worker. Making this short list helped induce Gropius to think he could find a place in Nazi Germany. To what extent Gropius actually believed that he could win is not known, but he expended a colossal effort on the submission—including twenty-three different architectural drawings and an array of artfully rendered photographs of the model—as noted earlier, far more than was needed.[35] Gropius clearly tried to address the issues raised by the selection committee. For example, he made herculean efforts to limit costs—then very important amid the Depression—and he spent seven pages in his explanation of the design describing the "measures to protect against an aerial attack," detailing how it would fare when threatened by incendiary bombs, poison gas, and bacterial agents.[36] More significantly, his entry for the new Reichsbank suggested accommodation in terms of style.

Gropius's Reichsbank was monumental, and from street level it dominated the viewer much like the structures one sees from Paul Ludwig Troost, Albert Speer, and Hermann Giesler, among others. The structure had four parallel sections, each separated by an open space that would bring in light; in other words, it was not an undifferentiated pile of stone. But the façade, with its regularized and rectilinear windows and the absence of ornamentation, when combined with its size, can be seen as having qualities associated with National Socialism. The building material, or at least the stone cladding, also proved suggestive of the architecture that would prevail after 1933. Gropius's model represented a fusion of Weimar modernist design (he also proposed the project on a modular basis with standard materials) with that which emerged during the Third Reich. The model of the building submitted by Gropius, when viewed from above, showed that it was more daring in certain respects, but it also represented an effort at compromise and bore much in common with the historicist structures that would surround it.[37]

In contrast, Mies van der Rohe's submission had utilized a glass façade, and while the building was monumental, it was more geometric and sleek. His was a monumental civic architecture in modernist style, but it was historically informed. One critic called it "a brilliant reinterpretation of the neoclassical tradition of Schinkel and Behrens."[38] Mies later acknowledged that he had been reading *völkisch*-Nationalist cultural historian Arthur Moeller van den Bruck on the Prussian style.[39] Around the same time, on 15 November 1933, Mies appears to have attended the first meeting of the Reich Chamber of Culture and apparently came away impressed with Goebbels, who made assurances of artistic freedom that had decidedly pro-modernist undertones.[40] In short, Mies also believed that he could synthesize modernism with the new ideas advocated by members of the Nazi regime.

Yet in September 1933, Hitler had rejected all the entries coming from the six finalists and chose a design by Reichsbank Building Director Heinrich Wolff, despite the fact that Wolff served on the jury for the competition. Wolff's design, which was completed in 1938, was a massive affair, housing over four thousand employees. His structure on the Kurstrasse has been described as a "typical Nazi building: sleek, cold, unadorned, and disturbing," but also as featuring "a stripped-down classicizing style."[41] It rested upon a steel frame, and the structure more generally contained rectilinear shapes, as well as windows organized in a geometric pattern, among other modernist touches. It later served as Communist Party headquarters in the German Democratic Republic and is part of the Foreign Ministry today.

While Gropius did not prevail in the Reichsbank competition, he derived some benefit from having been a finalist. The press coverage in Germany did not conceal that the founder of the Bauhaus was one of the six whose designs received careful consideration from Hitler.[42] Gropius himself used the press at this time to signal his eagerness to come to terms with the Nazi regime. In an interview that appeared in a Spanish newspaper in late April 1933—around the time of the Reichsbank competition—he stressed his close connections to industry, and how he had served as an artistic adviser for the Adler Automobile Works in Frankfurt.[43] Because Gropius continually faced the perception that he was a Communist or a Socialist, this statement contained undertones that he was prepared to make certain accommodations—in this case, with capitalists. Such statements were similar to Mies's underscoring his designs for villas and houses for the wealthy.

Gropius could hope to make inroads in other places, and like many modernists seeking accommodation he turned to Hans Weidemann in the Reich Propaganda Ministry. Weidemann asked Gropius, as well as Mies, Herbert Bayer, and about ten other former Bauhäusler to participate in the German People—German Work (Deutsches Volk—Deutsche Arbeit) exhibition that opened in the spring of 1934. The Gropius-Weidemann correspondence from this period shows that the two men got on well. For example, writing on stationery of the German Labor Front, Weidemann told Gropius in January 1934, "Of course, I would be very happy to discuss the fundamental questions of German architecture and your personal matters. . . . Heil Hitler!"[44] Despite this relationship, Gropius was rather skeptical about his participation in the German People—German Work exhibition—certainly more so than Mies, who initially thought he might become the show's "architectural director" (but ended up designing only the sections concerning the mining of potash and coal, as well as the glass and ceramics industries).[45] Gropius, along with his former Bauhaus colleague Joost Schmidt, received the commission in April 1934 to design the part of the exhibition for the nonferrous metal industries.

What is striking is that this exhibition was so ideological and propagandistic: it emphasized Nazi racial ideas and conceptions of the "people's community." The opening line of the exhibition catalogue read, "For the entire world, the Germans are the people [Volk] of work and nothing can generate more courage than to look back upon these successes." The text continued, "The exhibition brings together under the title Deutsches Volk a knowledge of race [Rassenkunde] and racial hygiene. . . . Only when the Volk as a living organism is returned to its original strength, to blood and soil, is a recovery, a resurrection as a nation, possible."[46] These propaganda exhibitions were to become a hallmark of the National Socialist cultural program—"a useful tool in leading the people," in the words of Nazi bureaucrat Leopold Gutterer, who was one of the overseers of the undertaking.[47] The *German People—German Work* show also featured a monumental yet modernist mural with a swastika and other Nazi insignia painted by Cesar Klein, who happened to be a founding member of the left-wing Novembergruppe fifteen years earlier. The mural offered a fitting symbol of the hopes that existed at that time for reconciling modernism and Nazism. The same could be said for the cover of the exhibition catalogue, which featured a tire that appeared to be made from leaves, giving it the appearance of a laurel wreath. This modernist-inflected image was designed by Herbert Bayer, who had been director of printing and advertising at the Bauhaus under Walter Gropius (Plate 2).

The participation of Gropius, Mies, Bayer, and others who were not Nazis in the *German People—German Work* exhibition raises a number of questions. Did they know beforehand that the show would be so ideological and propagandistic? To what extent should it be viewed in the international context of racism and eugenics? Did they understand that muscle-bound, steel-jawed figures would adorn the panels just feet from their own streamlined designs? Could they have influenced the other designers participating in the exhibition in some way so as to lessen the effect of this exercise in fascist propaganda? This last question most likely can be answered in the negative, but they presumably had the opportunity to withdraw from the project. In a sense, the exhibition stood as a microcosm of their experiences in the Third Reich. Gropius (like Mies and Bayer) was not a Nazi, and he viewed the Nazis as opponents who needed to be treated with caution. But in seeking to find accommodation with the new regime, he made decisions that could give an entirely different impression. And undaunted by his experiences with this show, Mies van der Rohe agreed to design the *Reich Exhibition of German Textiles and Clothing,* which opened at the Berlin convention center in March 1937—although again, Mies experienced difficulties with the appointment and Göring replaced him with architect Ernst Sagebiel prior to the completion of the project.[48]

Around the same time that the *German People—German Work* exhibition entered the planning stages, Gropius, along with his partner, Rudolf Hillebrecht, entered a design for a Nazi project to construct *Häuser der deutschen Arbeit* (Houses of German Work). The project was overseen by the German Labor Front—or, in other words, by the pro-modernist cul-

The Nazi Propaganda exhibition *German People–German Work* in Berlin, which Gropius helped design in 1934. This panel, which Gropius created with Joost Schmidt and Heinz Loew, concerns the transformation of metal into a final product, highlighting the muscular might of men in the German industrial process. (Bauhaus-Archiv Berlin)

tural bureaucrat Hans Weidemann. Gropius wrote to Weidemann about his designs for the project in January 1934, "The Houses of German Work should be a temple to the German spirit of work [*Kultstätte deutschen Arbeitsgeistes*]. They should be a permanent and impressive embodiment of the newly recognizable conception of community—one without class distinctions. The form of the Houses of German Work will be an expression of the National Socialist worldview."[49] This project concerned a relatively

Walter Gropius and Rudolf Hillebrecht, a detail of an image in their proposal for the House of Work competition in 1934. This undertaking was overseen by the German Work Front's Strength Through Joy Movement. This design, which was intended for the Berlin Tiergarten, was never constructed. (Bauhaus-Archiv, Berlin)

benign leisure-time facility—one that Gropius envisioned would be suitable for hosting sporting events, theater, and concerts. For him, it differed in nature from a school for political leaders that Ley was also building; Gropius wanted no part of that project.[50] But with the Houses of German Work, Gropius was clearly pandering to the Nazi regime. That he permitted the above-quoted statement to be published in the *Deutsche Bauzeitung* in January 1934 indicates that he was making a public declaration in support of the regime. That same month Gropius wrote the President of the Reich Chamber for the Visual Arts, Eugen Hönig, and remonstrated, "I have never been politically active in my entire life and also never belonged to a political party, but only attended to my business. . . . I could not and cannot do better for myself and for my homeland [*Heimat*] than work responsibly and conscientiously."[51] Additionally, in the drawings submitted by Gropius and Hillebrecht as part of their submission, the proposed structures were amplified by swastika banners—long, rather narrow flowing flags similar to those used by Albert Speer in his designs for various Party rallies. One of their drawings had four long swastika banners placed in a row, seemingly blowing in the wind.[52]

The jury for the Houses of German Work competition included Hans Weidemann, Heinrich Tessenow, Albert Speer, and Paul Bonatz, among others who evinced some sympathy for modernism. Weidemann served as chair, which again raised Gropius's hopes. The sites of the project were in the Berlin Tiergarten—right in the heart of the capital—and in Berlin-Treptow further east. It would have been a coup for Gropius to secure a commission: a public declaration that the regime embraced his work and welcomed his political support. But the odds were still long that he would be chosen for such a representative building. Indeed, Hitler intervened and quashed the competition.[53] Robert Ley persisted in his efforts to build a House of German Work and commissioned his "house architect" Clemens Klotz to design a structure for Cologne, although it was never completed. Klotz's work often featured modernist elements: streamlined design, rectilinear forms, and prefabricated materials. His massive Strength Through Joy resort Seebad Prora on the island of Rügen offers a striking example.[54]

Gropius's submission for the House of German Work project is in many respects reminiscent of Mies van der Rohe's entry for the German Pavilion at the Brussels World Fair of 1935. In June 1934, Mies was invited by the Propaganda Ministry to submit a design. This was not a public competition, but a more private discussion between Mies and Goebbels's representatives. The Nazi authorities moved cautiously as they explored a rapprochement with a modernist like Mies. The layout and themes of the pavilion were drawn up by the Propaganda Ministry in May 1934: a "hall of honor" would be surrounded by four major exhibits, as well as an additional section for industrial objects. It was another highly ideological undertaking, with sections titled "Peasant and Soil" and "People and Nation" (which would focus on the Nazi Party, the storm troopers, and the German Labor Front). Mies grasped the essence of the project and in his design made a concerted effort to appeal to the Nazis. He wrote in the text accompanying his proposal, "The exhibition building must express the will of National Socialist Germany through an imposing form; it must act as the symbol of . . . National Socialist fighting strength and heroic will."[55] His sketches included flags with hand-drawn, but slightly abstracted, swastikas. A huge German eagle also featured prominently. Mies wrote in his submission that the Hall of Honor "serves to accommodate the national emblems and the representations of the Reich."[56]

Hitler judged the competition personally, with the models and plans brought to the Prussian Academy on the Pariser Platz near the Brandenburg Gate. According to eyewitness reports, when Hitler saw Mies's submis-

Ludwig Mies van der Rohe, design for the German Pavilion planned for the Brussels World Exposition in 1935. Note the hand-drawn swastika banners—evidently part of his effort to find accommodation with the Nazi regime. A German pavilion was never constructed. (Digital Image © The Museum of Modern Art/Licensed by SCALA/Art Resource, New York)

sion he reacted violently; he smashed the model, knocking it off his desk. The remnants were found by Mies's assistant, who was sent to retrieve it ("lying in a heap behind his desk"). Hitler, it turns out, did not like any of the entries. He subsequently ordered that Germany withdraw from the Brussels exhibition of 1935.[57] This made the Speer-designed pavilion at the Paris World Exposition in 1937 all the more significant. Hitler later also rejected Mies's service station, although not as violently. A former associate of Mies's, Sergius Ruegenberg, heard that Hitler was impressed by the plans and returned to them as he contemplated the future design aesthetic on the *Autobahnen.*[58]

Gropius also expressed interest in contributing to industrial and urban planning projects. For example, he helped develop a housing plan for East Prussia in 1934. Critical of an existing proposal to develop the region—one that entailed industrial development along new transport routes, rather than building upon existing towns and cities—Gropius and famed city planner Martin Wagner elaborated a vision which stressed that new settlements were a matter of "humanity and civilization," and not mere economic development.[59] They sent their reflections to Hans Weidemann and requested that he forward the letter to the governor (Oberpräsident) of

East Prussia as a kind of open letter. Gropius and Wagner, in the words of Reginald Isaacs, "called for a city-region, to be planned and constructed as a prototype for Germany."[60] Gropius had worked in Pomerania as a young architect before World War I and always professed a fondness for the region.

Gropius's decision to relocate to England in the fall of 1934 should not be considered a form of political opposition to the Nazi regime. A number of architectural historians have noted that Gropius's choice was based above all on the lack of work in Germany. Walter Scheiffele wrote, "We know that Gropius had little success securing the commissions for which he applied [in these early years of the Third Reich]."[61] In 1933 his tenure as part of the Board of Trustees for the Design of Motor Cars at the Adlerwerke came to an end. His failure to win the competitions for the Reichsbank or the House of German Work also came as blows. Gropius designed only two private homes in 1933–34, an exceedingly lean period for him. The lack of work in Germany left Gropius feeling underappreciated, an alien sentiment for someone who had previously enjoyed considerable success.

The reason for his fateful trip to London in December 1934 was an exhibition of his work at the Royal Institutes of British Architects. Gropius traveled to Great Britain to address a conference of the Congrès internationaux d'architecture moderne, an indication of his undiminished international reputation at the time of his resettlement. When British modernist architect Maxwell Fry approached him about forming a partnership, and made a compelling argument about the potential of their collaboration in the United Kingdom, Gropius accepted the offer. Their partnership lasted two years and bore fruit, including the main building of the Impington Village College in Cambridgeshire. Gropius also made money by overseeing design for Isokon Furniture Company, including teapots, lamps, and wastepaper baskets—with the latter being the most popular. His relative success in Great Britain helped open his eyes to the possibilities of living outside his homeland.

Yet Gropius traveled back to Germany on several occasions in 1935 and 1936 and openly expressed the possibility of returning up until 1939. He therefore worked assiduously to keep a distance from all political complications. Historian Kathleen James observed, "Anxious to protect family members and property he had left behind and motivated by a respect for Germany that transcended the character of its government, he vacillated between private denunciations and public accommodation, refusing to allow his critical comments about the new regime to be quoted in the press."[62] To avoid closing the door to his return to Germany, Gropius dutifully reported his annual income to the Reich Finance Ministry and paid the appropriate taxes. And in his correspondence with Nazi authorities, he made it clear that he had not emigrated for good—hence, his objection to the Reich Flight Tax in 1938.

Up until the entry of the United States into World War II, Gropius stayed clear of almost all political involvement. Gropius wrote in a 9 September 1936 letter to journalist Gerald Berry, "You will understand that I as a German citizen must protect against having my name associated with an attack on my native country. To my believe [sic], the development of modern architecture has nothing whatever to do with any political system. I should be very grateful therefore if you would bear this in mind and prevent my name from getting involved in a political argument."[63] He declined to write for the BBC periodical *The Listener,* on "modern art and architecture in relation to the social crisis"—fearing that his remarks would be construed as political. In his letter to the editors Gropius explained, "I feel unable to make any comments to whatever opinion a German official may express, because I am still a German subject and am working here with the legal permission of the present government. As there is in Germany—as well as in Russia and Italy—no art which is not approved of by the government, any criticizing remark about the present policy made by me would easily be taken as a hostile act. I cannot have my name put up against an official report from Germany without risking very unpleasant consequences."[64] He retained this outlook for a time in America. For example, in 1938, Gropius refused to lend his name to the American Guild for German Cultural Freedom. Gropius's biographer Reginald Isaacs noted, "Until late 1940, he expressed only his concern for the setback in social and cultural development resulting from the political tension in Europe."[65] Defenders have argued that Gropius feared that speaking out would cause harm to friends back in Germany, including former Bauhäusler in especially vulnerable circumstances. Once the United States entered the war, Gropius was classified as an "Enemy Alien," whereby he had to secure permission to travel outside the Boston area. While the American authorities always acceded to his requests, such circumstances were hardly conducive to political activism.

Up until the start of the war, Gropius toed the line between loyal submissiveness to the Nazi regime, on the one hand, and a position of leadership in his adopted land on the other. In terms of the former, Gropius checked in regularly with Nazi authorities once he had left Germany for Great Britain in late 1934, giving the impression that he was cooperative.[66] Gropius even took care to secure the approval of the Nazi authorities after he received the offer from Harvard University in December 1936. He used an old friend from the Deutscher Werkbund, Ernst Jäckh, and President Eugen Hönig from the Reich Chamber for the Visual Arts to facilitate approaches to the authorities. Gropius did his utmost to explain that the appointment at Harvard constituted a high honor, and that he would be replacing a French architect, Jean-Jacques Haffner, a proponent of the Beaux Arts style. Gropius wrote to Eugen Hönig, "It is now of the greatest importance to me that the responsible authorities in Berlin [be apprised of] the appointment to this cultural chair [*kulturelle Lehrstuhl*] [and recognize] that it is now held by a German. . . . It would be of inestimable value to me if you, with your connections in the Propaganda Ministry, could help me in this regard. . . . Just as up until now, I will conduct myself in the future in a loyal manner and see my mission at Harvard as one that serves German culture."[67] The words in German—"loyal verhalten," "meine Mission," and "dienen deutschen Kultur"—served to create a sense of deference and subservience. Gropius's request made its way to Goebbels, who approved the appointment, "granted on the rationale suggested by Gropius that for the first time a German would replace a Frenchman."[68] It was indeed Nazi policy in the mid-1930s to encourage German professors to travel abroad to promote "German types and German ways."

Gropius knew full well of the risks attendant with emigration and wrote to his friend Ernst Jäckh in February 1937 "that it went well is like a stone has been lifted from my heart."[69] The Nazi regime had implemented measures to confiscate the property of those deemed *staatsfeindlich* (hostile to the state), and this is what had happened to Thomas Mann. Despite penning a letter to the Nazi authorities, the Nobel Prize–winning author was stripped of his German citizenship in 1936 and lost his villa in Munich, as well as its entire contents.[70] Emigration also made one subject to the Reich Flight Tax, which had been increased to 81 percent in October 1936 (it rose to 96 percent in September 1939). Gropius therefore pondered how he could avoid or obtain a reduction of the Reich Flight Tax.[71] He also made sure that the landmark exhibition *The Bauhaus, 1919–1928*, which opened in December 1938 at the Museum of Modern Art in New York, did not appear as an anti-Nazi initiative. Gropius, along with the other co-organizers, Herbert Bayer and Alfred Barr Jr., offered what architectural historian Karen Koehler has described as a "depoliticized and incomplete history of the Bauhaus."[72] But it was common for émigrés to tread gently, at least initially, with regard to the Nazi authorities—in part because many imagined that they might return.

But lest these efforts to avoid a break with the German state obscure the full picture, Gropius also endeavored to support other modernists. For example, among his first acts after arriving at Harvard was to help Marcel Breuer, a friend from the Bauhaus, obtain an appointment there. He later did the same for Martin Wagner, formerly the city architect for Berlin and planner for Ankara, Turkey, who arrived at Harvard in 1938.[73] At times, Walter and Ise Gropius opened their house to emigrants and used their own money to help get these émigrés established in the United States. Gropius remained at Harvard for fifteen years, and, like the august university that benefited from the talents of so many European scholars, he would be identified with the remarkable émigré community in the United States—the "apples" from the tree that Hitler had shaken, to borrow the famous phrase of Walter Cook, the director of the Institute for Fine Arts of New York. Gropius was immediately celebrated as the embodiment of German creativity in the face of Nazi persecution. He admitted in a June 1937 letter to Maxwell Fry that he and Ise had gone on holiday "to recover from the 63 parties they had attended since arriving on American soil in March."[74] His broader fame among the American public, however, was still to come.

Gropius later transformed himself and his work into symbols of America. He obtained American citizenship in the summer of 1944 and became part of the postwar movement to utilize modernist designs as a symbol of liberal, progressive society. He instructed his Harvard students to "work on solutions to the university's problem of space and design," and incorporated their input as he had his colleagues from The Architects Collaborative— a private firm that he helped found in Cambridge, Massachusetts—plan seven dormitories and a student center that now form Harkness Commons, a part of the Harvard Law School.[75] Between 1958 and 1966, Gropius helped design the Pan American World Airways (now the MetLife) building on Park Avenue in New York, the U.S. embassy in Athens, and the John F. Kennedy Federal Building in Boston. These structures, which were designed and realized during the Cold War, served as symbols of American power. Winfried Nerdinger noted that the cult of Gropius and the Bauhaus reached its peak in the United States in the post-1945 period: "The international luster of the postwar period finally closed this phase [concerning the Third Reich] of his life for 'Mister Bauhaus.'"[76]

Gropius remained chair of the architecture department within the Harvard Graduate School of Design until 1952, although by 1945 he devoted much of his time to The Architects Collaborative (known as TAC). Gropius worked mostly with younger architects, reprising in a certain way his days at the Bauhaus but with far less Sturm und Drang. Returning to the collaborative work he so liked, and continuing his focus on the social responsibilities of architecture, Gropius helped make TAC a legendary modernist firm. The founder of the Bauhaus lived out his years in a house he designed in Lincoln, Massachusetts, and died at age eighty-six in 1969, long before TAC went under in the mid-1990s. But his reputation endured. Peter Gay's thoughtful treatment of the architect in a 1976 book had a significant impact on scholars, while the creation of the Bauhaus-Archive/Museum of Design in Berlin in 1979, housed in a structure based on Gropius's own designs and containing a museum, archive, and library, helped institutionalize his legacy.[77] Thanks to Gropius's biographers Reginald Isaacs and Winfried Nerdinger, as well as others who have followed their lead, a more critical and nuanced understanding of Gropius has subsequently emerged.[78] The brilliant but complicated visionary was never a Nazi—or even sympathetic to them—but he did seek to find accommodation with the regime in the prewar period.

5

Paul Hindemith

(1895 Hanau near Frankfurt–1963 Frankfurt)

Paul Hindemith with his viola in January 1935. (Getty Images-
Hulton Archives)

ALTHOUGH REGARDED AS a leading modernist composer of his generation—often mentioned in the same breath as the older Arnold Schoenberg and his famous students Alban Berg, Anton Webern, and Hanns Eisler—Paul Hindemith believed that he and his work fit into the new German Reich.[1] By 1933, his most radical work was behind him. The compositions of the early Weimar Republic, including the score for Oskar Kokoschka's Expressionist play *Mörder, Hoffnung der Frauen* (*Murder: The Hope of Women*) from 1919 (about ritualized sexual murder), *Das Nusch-Nuschi* from 1920 (a "mildly erotic" piece performed by Burmese marionettes), and *Sancta Susanna* of 1921 (which features nuns experiencing sexual ecstasy) had gradually given way to a more tonal and accessible idiom. True, Hindemith had reverted back to his earlier, more daring style in 1929, when he wrote the *Badener Lehrstück vom Einverständnis* (a work of musical theater utilizing a text by Bertolt Brecht) and *Neues vom Tage* (a wild satiric opera that incorporated jazz, blues, and cabaret), but these works signaled the culmination of his most pronouncedly avant-garde work. Even prior to this shift in the late Weimar Republic, Hindemith had written in a "neo-Baroque" style that he later imagined would meet with acceptance in Nazi Germany.[2]

Hindemith occupied an important place in the modernist movements of the Weimar Republic. Early on, he had incorporated Expressionist elements into his music: certain of his works borrowed heavily from Arnold Schoenberg, while others have been compared to the Futurist and Dada movements (the blaring siren at the end of Chamber Music Nr. I with Finale, op. 24, of 1921).[3] He developed new strategies about harmony and utilized both popular and avant-garde idioms in his compositions. Besides working with the texts from Kokoschka and Brecht noted above, he composed music for Bauhaus master Oskar Schlemmer's *Triadic Ballet* in the mid-1920s, a piece written for a small mechanical organ. Hindemith had a strong interest in mechanical music, and wrote in this style for films like the cartoon *Felix the Cat at the Circus* (shown at the renowned modernist Baden-Baden festival in 1927) and the surrealistic *Ghosts at Breakfast* (*Vormittagsspuk*), by Hans Richter.[4] Hindemith also joined the administrative committee for the Donaueschingen Festival in 1923 (which later moved to Baden-Baden) and promoted modern music through this famous festival. In his earlier years, he often composed for smaller instrumental groups, a conscious rejection of the massive post-Romantic orchestras. This penchant for chamber ensembles would facilitate the shift in his music toward the neoclassical idiom in his more mature work, although he would also later pursue larger productions, composing five symphonies after the landmark *Mathis der Maler,* which he completed in the first years of the Third Reich.

As David Stanley Smith, then dean of the Yale School of Music, noted in 1940, "At one time, [Hindemith] was an extreme modernist but lately has softened his style so that it is accessible to the average listener."[5] His compositions became more melodic, harmonic, and lyrical. They retained the tremendous energy but sounded more akin to the work of Gustav Mahler or Sergei Prokofiev; that is, still modern, but not stridently so. Musicologist James Paulding argued that Hindemith expanded the "Austro-German symphonic tradition" by pursuing "a balance between strong, linear writing and a new expansion of the traditional tonal system."[6] The composer continued to incorporate jazz-inspired rhythms and found other ways to remain modern, even while decreasing the atonality and dissonance in his music. His use of motifs from folksongs and his fondness for chorale arrangements would also provide a firmer basis for establishing a foothold in the Third Reich.[7]

Paul Hindemith's upbringing in Hanau, near Frankfurt, also provided a basis for finding accommodation with the Nazi regime. His father was a house painter and a decorator, while his mother hailed from a farming family. Hindemith himself would later enjoy woodworking and other crafts (as well as drawing), suggesting a continuity with his family roots.[8] Indeed, he sometimes claimed that composers and musicians were more craftsmen (*Handwerker*) than artists (*Künstler*). Despite modest financial means, his father encouraged music among the three children (indeed, he enforced disciplined practice in a domineering way), and the elder Hindemith himself was a passionate player of the zither, providing a further linkage to folk culture. The town of Hanau, as well as the city of Frankfurt, to which the family moved in 1905 when Paul was ten, lay in the Hessen region.

Known for its half-timbered (*Fachwerkhäuser*) building style, the quintes-sentially Germanic province had been the home of the brothers Grimm, who had collected folktales about a century earlier. Hindemith studied at the Hoch Conservatory in Frankfurt, where he had earned a scholarship (and won every significant prize in performance and composition offered there), and after graduation went on to serve in the army during World War I.[9] He entered the army in August 1917 and moved with his regiment to the front lines in Flanders in the summer of 1918. Although Hindemith himself avoided combat, having joined the musical corps of his regiment (his commanding officer also asked him to form a string quartet and play private concerts), he witnessed the carnage and suffering, which affected him deeply. His upbringing and tenure as a soldier nonetheless suggested a nationalistic orientation: he had written to the family doctor back in Sep-tember 1914 that "the *Volk* is hugely enthusiastic" about the war, putting him in the mainstream of patriotic Germans.[10] His father also saw action and fell in Flanders. Hindemith's status as a veteran would be advantageous during the Third Reich. More generally, his background and upbringing augured well for finding a modus vivendi with the Nazi regime.

Another reason for Hindemith's hopefulness grew out of his sterling and increasingly global reputation. Because Goebbels sought to utilize cul-ture to enhance Germany's international prestige, Hindemith would prove extraordinarily useful. Michael Kater noted how "Hindemith had been the most prominent composer of the younger generation in Germany at the beginning of Nazi rule."[11] The composer had been appointed a profes-sor at the Hochschule für Musik in Berlin in 1927—this at age thirty-two. He was also an exceptionally skilled performer—among the greatest of his generation—playing the viola and the viola d'amore, although he also had a facility with the piano, clarinet, and violin. In the 1920s, he starred in the celebrated ensemble the Amar-Hindemith String Quartet. They per-formed both traditional chamber music (J. S. Bach and Handel) as well as modern compositions (Stravinsky, Webern, Bartók, and Schoenberg). Hindemith therefore enjoyed a reputation both within traditional classical music circles and amid the modernist avant-garde. He left the string quar-tet in 1929 due to his other commitments, but his reputation continued to spread. He became increasingly well known in the United States beginning in the second half of the 1920s, and in 1930 received a commission from Serge Koussevitzky to compose a piece for the fiftieth anniversary of the Boston Symphony Orchestra.[12] Further success on foreign stages ensued, and he himself gladly accepted the role as a kind of cultural ambassador. He also generated a sizable income both at home and abroad, with American patron Elizabeth Sprague Coolidge, for example, paying him RM 10,000 ($4,000) in 1930 for one piece she commissioned.[13] Yet in September 1933 he wrote to friends that he had no plans to emigrate, that he "had been asked to cooperate and had not declined," and that he thought it his task to "export German culture, beginning with music."[14]

Another reason for optimism concerned the lack of a coherent policy on the part of Nazi officials with regard to music. Most scholars now question whether a specific Nazi aesthetic for music ever existed.[15] While Nazi music policy had the appearance of orderliness, it often proved haphazard and contradictory—this, in the words of music scholar Pamela Potter, "despite relentless propaganda, to devise clear guidelines for distinguishing between 'good' and 'bad' music; and, in the case of jazz, a pragmatic policy of balancing suppression with toleration, bending ideological principles in order to appease popular tastes."[16] To take a more specific example, German musicologist Michael Walter studied opera in the Third Reich and found "stark inconsistencies between the pronouncements against 'degeneracy' and the new operatic works that thrived—and even won Hitler's praise—in the Third Reich, despite their atonal and jazz-inspired scores that were directly reminiscent of works by Schoenberg, Krenek, and Weill."[17] Music was so decentralized—with public performances and private activities (known in German as *Hausmusik*)—that it proved exceedingly difficult to control.[18] Additionally, as Pamela Potter argues "Nazi leaders, like their predecessors, valued the centrality of music in Germany's culture so much that they were willing to grant composers and musicians a considerable degree of personal and political leeway."[19]

With the shift away from his most aggressively modernist music behind him, and with a sense that Nazi music policy was inchoate and inconsistent, Paul Hindemith set out to find a place in the Reich. He understood that his best hopes rested on developing personal relationships with those in positions of influence and took steps to cultivate allies. An important if surprising cohort of supporters came from within Alfred Rosenberg's Fighting League for German Culture.[20] More specifically, a well-regarded musician in the Berlin chapter by the name of Gustav Havemann embraced Hindemith's cause. A violinist and conductor who had his own ensemble, the Havemann Quartet, the Fighting League subleader had been a proponent of modernist music going back to the 1920s. In the summer of 1932, he and a group of colleagues proposed the creation of a kind of corporatist music chamber—one that anticipated the Goebbels-led body—under the aegis of the Fighting League.[21] Havemann invited Hindemith to help, and the composer submitted "a detailed programme for the teaching of music theory."[22] While the envisioned reforms did not come about, the two men became allies, and Havemann could at least perform Hindemith's music in the Fighting League Orchestra, which he conducted (another Fighting League orchestra, conducted by Heinz Dressel, also performed Hindemith's work in early 1934).[23] Havemann subsequently worked for the Reich Chamber of Music, providing the composer with a supporter in a strategic post. Like Otto Andreas Schreiber, Havemann strove to integrate an intense anti-Semitism with pro-modernist views. His proposals for "reform" invariably entailed a purge of Jewish musicians from orchestras and organizations. Another figure in Rosenberg's cultural bureaucracy, his music expert Herbert Gerigk, also became a proponent of Hindemith's music (not to mention, during the war, a plunderer of Jewish-owned music instruments and manuscripts). Back in the early 1930s, Gerigk "conceded that in the 'right hands' (read: Aryan hands), atonal music could be highly expressive."[24] While intensely anti-Semitic—Gerigk later contributed to the slanderous *Lexikon der Juden in der Musik* that appeared in multiple editions during the war—he opined in a 1934 article on Arnold Schoenberg that "even from the so-called atonality, a worthwhile art can spring up if the composer remains true to his race and irreproachably creative. [Hans] Pfitzner's C-Sharp Minor Symphony leaves behind the realms of tonality in places without one feeling somewhat negative about it."[25] Although Pfitzner more accurately conformed to a late-Romantic style, Gerigk's formulation offered a glimmer of hope, especially because it came from one of Rosenberg's staffers. Around the same time, another critic, writing for the pro-Nazi *Zeitschrift für Musik*—a journal that had previously published pieces critical of modern music—opined that Hindemith was truly German, stating, "After the searching and roving restlessness of the years of development, new instrumental works have been composed with an allegiance to classicism and a sense of clarity and firmness which expresses the essence of German music in masterly economy of sound and form."[26]

The composer also saw himself as a pedagogue who would help usher in a new era of music in Germany. Throughout the early years of the regime, he retained his professorship in Berlin, and this gave him standing with regard to educational initiatives. He also had a strong interest in music for amateurs (*Gebrauchsmusik,* or utility music), which could be presented in a way consistent with the Nazis' populist policies. Hindemith reported in April 1933 to his friend and publisher Willy Strecker:

> Recently, just after my return from England, I had a long talk with some of the higher-ups in the Kampfbund [Fighting League]. It was only about educational matters, but I got the impression (after satisfying them that I was neither a half- nor any other fractional Jew) that they have a good opinion of me there. Since then they have commissioned me (though not quite officially) to work out plans for a new system of teaching composition and musical theory. Since I know how mistrustful people are, and have also seen how several who have tried to curry favor have sunk without trace, I, who have absolutely no desire to curry favor, am none too eager to carry out this tidying-up operation just now. If you will leave it to me here to watch out for the most favorable time to start something like this, you can rest assured that I shall do whatever is possible. One of these days I shall of course have to get the Kampfbund to support my things officially, but it is a bit too early yet for that.[27]

The remonstration here that he had "no desire to curry favor" with Nazi officials indicates that Hindemith understood how fraught, how ethically precarious, accommodation would be. But he also held that composers had a social responsibility—that they worked not for themselves alone, but for a larger public. He sincerely believed he could effect positive developments in terms of music education.

The passage above sheds some light on his interactions with new leaders, although there is much that we do not know. These discussions about youth education most certainly would have involved ideological rhetoric on both sides. After all, they were discussing educating the *Volk* about German music. Hindemith exhibited a willingness to use an ideologically charged vocabulary in his dealings with Nazi officials and in certain of his public statements, although these formulations were absent from his private correspondence.[28] Yet merely the fact that Hindemith entered into conversations with representatives of Nazi agencies controlled by Alfred Rosenberg, Hitler Youth Leader Baldur von Schirach, Reich Science and Education Minister Bernhard Rust, and German Labor Front chief Robert Ley shows that the composer took an active role in trying to reconcile with the Nazi leaders. The following year, in February 1934, he wrote Willy Strecker again, reporting, "Quite a lot is going on in Berlin. I am still 'conferring' with all sorts of higher-ups in the Arbeitsfront, the Dopolovoro, and the Arbeitsdienstlager.

The outcome will be that I shall make suggestions for a very far-reaching musical education system for the German people and, if things continue as they have now begun and these people continue to show goodwill to me, I hope to provide the impetus for vast plans to cooperate in putting them into effect."[29] Hindemith reportedly went so far as to invite Hitler to attend one of his composition classes.[30]

In consultation with his publisher, Hindemith promoted his work by contrasting it with the "sonic orgies" of émigrés Kurt Weill, Ernst Krenek, and Arnold Schoenberg.[31] Hindemith's caustic remarks predated the Nazi seizure of power. He told his students that he did not embrace "twelve-note composition"—comments directed at Schoenberg. He had also been critical of Kurt Weill back in 1929, and this led to Weill's revamping of *Der Lindberghflug,* replacing the Hindemith-written sections with his own. During the Third Reich, Hindemith continued with critical statements about other modernist composers in a way that suggests opportunism. For example, in March 1935, at a time when he hoped to revive his career, he sanctioned a letter from his publisher, Willy Strecker, to Gustav Havemann in the Reich Chamber of Music, where Hindemith was quoted as rejecting "the decadent intellectual efforts of a Schoenberg."[32] Michael Kater also noted, "Nor was there much love lost between Hindemith and Carl Orff, with whom he was associated at the Munich contemporary-music festival."[33]

Hindemith saw his work as Germanic in spirit and his larger task to be the reform of German music. For example, he promoted his opera *Mathis der Maler* as "a decidedly German work."[34] Hindemith had begun the opera in 1932 and focused on it in 1933. He proceeded to fashion parts of the unfinished work into three movements, known as the *Mathis-Symphony,* which premiered in Berlin March 1934. This piece told the story of sixteenth-century German painter Matthias Grünewald, a figure best known for the *Isenheimer Altar* and who was revered by Nazi art historians like Wilhelm Pinder and pro-Nazi artists like Emil Nolde.[35] Certain themes in the libretto resonated with prevailing ideas. Kater noted how "Hindemith's Mathis exhibited typically German attitudes, not the least of which turned out to be acquiescence to the powers that be, as repeatedly, [Archbishop Albrecht] extended to him favors and understanding, ultimately causing the introspective Mathis to resign himself to temporal authority."[36] The libretto was also extremely personal: Albrecht had been Archbishop of Mainz, which is close to the Frankfurt-Hanau area where Hindemith grew up. Albrecht's final order is to "go out and create."[37] Hindemith hoped this composition would enable him to do just that.

The music was largely accessible and very much in the German Romantic and post-Romantic tradition. James Paulding described how it revealed a "great richness of orchestral sound . . . based on tonal and often triadic harmony. The underlying forms are constructed on classical models and, in contrast with much of his earlier music, true development occurs here."[38] *Mathis* also incorporated motifs from German folk songs, a technique Hindemith had developed earlier, such as in his Concert Music for Piano, Brass, and Two Harps, op. 49, in which he quoted a *Volkslied* (folk song).[39] In *Mathis,* he quotes *Three Angels Sang a Sweet Song,* which appears several times and "exerts an uncanny spell over the whole work."[40] Early in the Third Reich, Hindemith composed *Lieder* (art songs for voice and piano) based on texts by Wilhelm Busch (a populist humorist of the late nineteenth century), as well as German Romantic authors, including Novalis and Hölderlin. Utilizing this German literary tradition would have appealed to the National Socialists, although Hindemith had mined this vein prior to 1933.[41] Accordingly, the *Mathis-Symphony* elicited many positive reviews, even among a number of Nazi critics. Historian Claudia Maurer Zenck argued that *Mathis* "conformed very precisely to the official expectations for modern music in the Third Reich."[42]

Hindemith's initial efforts seemed to have succeeded, and he enjoyed a momentary ascendance to prominence. His compositions were played across Germany in the early years of the Third Reich—in Lübeck, Wiesbaden, Munich, Leipzig, Cologne, and Berlin, among other cities—as well as, at times, on the radio (such as the Königsberg station). He received numerous offers for what he called "smaller commissions," yet rejected them "because the time doesn't seem to be right for them."[43] He also wished to focus on the *Mathis* opera project. He had situated himself in a place where a triumphant opera would secure his future in Germany. Munich critic Claus Neumann wrote in June 1933 that he was "the leader of the younger, contemporary generation of modernist," and many contemporaries shared this view.[44] Hindemith hoped to show Hitler that this was indeed the case and offered personally to perform a cantata he had written back in 1932. Discussions about a private concert ensued, but they proved fruitless in the end.[45]

Hindemith also secured an appointment in the Reich Chamber of Music in February 1934. The post came as a result of his relationships with Chamber President Richard Strauss and Vice President Wilhelm Furtwängler. Strauss had approached Hindemith back in November 1933 and inquired whether he would join the executive council of the composers' section in the Chamber. The appointment was subsequently widely reported. It also certainly entailed Goebbels's assent as president of the Reich Chamber of Culture. The appointment within the Reich Chamber of Music helped in other ways. It facilitated the above-noted discussions about music pedagogy with Ley, Schirach, and Rust. It was much safer to interact with him now that Hindemith was a high-ranking official in the Chamber. The appointment also enhanced his reputation as a composer. At the 18 February 1934 concert to celebrate the inauguration of the Chamber, his 1930 piece Concert Music for Strings and Wind Instruments was performed by the Berlin Philharmonic, along with works by Richard Strauss, Hans Pfitzner, and others on the executive council. The event was billed as the "First German Composers' Day," and Hindemith himself climbed the podium to conduct his piece. As he noted in one letter, "One really could not ask for more in the way of an official introduction."[46] Many of the ensuing reviews of his piece were also glowing.

But the performance of his work at this high profile *Festkonzert* also elicited "outrage" from certain Nazi stalwarts, and Hindemith continued to endure a rash of attacks. According to Pamela Potter, these arose out of the political rivalries beyond his control, rather than out of any heroic acts of resistance on his part. She stated, "Rosenberg and Goebbels, for their part, displayed relatively little knowledge of music and showed far less interest in engaging in the aesthetic debates surrounding it, and even Goebbels's keynote speech for the opening of the Reich Music Days in 1938, where he outlined the 'ten commandments' for German music, was strikingly vague."[47] Goebbels, as Gauleiter of Berlin, controlled the former city opera in Charlottenburg, as well as the Berlin Philharmonic, which he transformed into the Reich Orchestra, and he exhibited more interest in administrative issues than in aesthetic policy. When he did engage in the latter, he proved inconsistent with regard to modernism—just as with the visual arts. Rosenberg also relied on aides when music policy was involved. While some, like Herbert Gerigk, exhibited sympathy for Hindemith, others reverted to a more predictable anti-modernist policy. These two elements in the Rosenberg camp neutralized one another until the early summer of 1934, but the anti-Hindemith forces gained the upper hand. They used the journal *Die Musik,* among other outlets, to launch attacks on the composer and his work and lobbied for a broadcast ban, which made it difficult, but not impossible, to play his music on the radio. The anti-Hindemith faction proved unrelenting; in late 1934, Berlin critic and music teacher Eberhard Preussner noted, "Again, people are talking about a new wave against

Hindemith."[48] Rosenberg's minions even monitored his foreign concert tours lest he use Jewish musicians—which he did, including violinist Szymon Goldberg and conductor Paul Breisach, who performed with him in Holland and Austria respectively. Hindemith's enemies also took heart in rumors that Hitler himself appeared unsympathetic to the musician and his work. Reports circulated that certain figures in Hitler's inner circle, such as pianist Ernst ("Putzi") Hanfstaengl, lobbied against Hindemith. Even the composer heard an account from Furtwängler that Hitler "had once walked in horror out of a concert hall in Munich when something of mine was played"—although, he added, Furtwängler "hadn't the slightest doubt that everything would be all right."[49]

The composer had advocates, of course, and they continued their campaign on his behalf. Heinz Tietjen, the General Intendant of the Prussian State Theater, lobbied Göring on his behalf and met with some success. Yet it was conductor/composer Wilhelm Furtwängler who counted as his most notable advocate. Although Furtwängler did not embrace Hindemith's most radically atonal works, which he believed suffered from "intellectualism," he respected the younger musician and offered assistance both publicly and privately. Efforts regarding the former included conducting the symphonic version of *Mathis der Maler* on 12 March 1934—an especially important gesture because it was performed by the Berlin Philharmonic (arguably the most prestigious orchestra in the world); as to the latter, this included personal interventions with Hitler, with a notable meeting occurring in the autumn of 1934. Furtwängler sought to convince Hitler of Hindemith's importance both inside and outside Germany, and to overcome the dictator's "deep-seated resentment."[50] The director of the Berlin Philharmonic, among other posts, tried to induce Hitler to permit a staging of the opera *Mathis der Maler,* which Hindemith had recently completed. Furtwängler asked Hitler to read the libretto—believing that there was nothing the Nazi leader would find objectionable—and also suggested a staging in early 1935 in a city less visible than Berlin, such as Leipzig. Hindemith was accustomed to tactics of this nature: the premiere of the *Mathis-Symphony,* for example, took place not at the "politically sensitive" Staatsoper—a so-called hallowed hall—but rather at the Prussian Staatskapelle.[51]

Furtwängler ardently desired to stage the opera version of *Mathis,* believing a performance would both help rehabilitate Hindemith and also set the tone for music in the Reich going forward. His push to stage the opera in August 1934 evidently provided part of the motivation for his signing the petition by artists supporting Hitler's move to become "Führer and

Reich Chancellor." By exhibiting loyalty and offering this gesture of support, he hoped for reciprocal understanding from the Nazi leaders. In the fall of 1934, as the debate over the opera raged, with Rosenberg's forces leading the attack, Furtwängler arranged a meeting with Hitler to discuss the matter. With an appointment scheduled for 30 November, Furtwängler decided that the best tactic would be for him to elaborate his views before the meeting, and he chose as a venue the relatively liberal *Deutsche Allgemeine Zeitung*. He consulted Hindemith prior to publication, and he confirmed with the editor of the paper "that he knew the risk that he was taking." But he argued that what was at stake—"the freedom of the artistic personality"—merited the step. The article that he published, titled "The Hindemith Case" ("Der Fall Hindemith") indeed proved controversial.[52] But Furtwängler made a series of compelling arguments: for example, he compared Hindemith to Richard Strauss, whose *Salome* had caused a furor when it premiered in 1909. He also noted that Hindemith had moved to composing in a tonal style and that he incorporated elements of folk music in his work, providing a viable way forward for modern music in the new Reich. Furtwängler also strategically called Hindemith "purely Germanic" and noted the composer had "never been politically active." He clearly believed that this talented colleague should have an opportunity to evolve and adapt, that the public should have the right to judge, and that Hindemith would serve as an effective cultural ambassador for Germany abroad. In short, Furtwängler employed arguments he hoped would resonate with the Nazi elite.

This turned out not to be the case, and certain key Nazi leaders—Goebbels, Göring, and even Hitler—interpreted Furtwängler's defense of Hindemith as an act of insubordination. Furtwängler had gone so far as to offer "a warning against the dangers of political denunciation being 'applied in the fullest measures in the matter of art,'" and this angered the Nazi leaders.[53] Even Goebbels and Rosenberg found common cause on this issue, and Reich Education Minister Bernhard Rust joined in, writing, "Hindemith showed signs of an un-German attitude that disqualifies him from taking part in the movement's reclamation work."[54] The Nazi leaders' aggressive reaction to Furtwängler's article grew stronger after the audience responded with thunderous applause when Furtwängler conducted the Berlin Staatsoper a few days later. With Goebbels and Göring attending the performance and sitting in their quasi-royal boxes, the audience began with a rousing twenty-minute ovation even before the start of Wagner's *Tristan und Isolde,* and then applauded again after every act. This gesture, which violated opera etiquette, clearly transcended the performance itself and signaled a show of support for Furtwängler. After witnessing the demonstration, Göring reportedly muttered, "Such things cannot be tolerated," and after the performance phoned Hitler to report that Furtwängler was "endangering the authority of the government."[55]

It was not only the issue of Paul Hindemith—and modernist music more generally—that generated friction between Furtwängler and the Nazi leaders. A second area where Furtwängler and members of the regime clashed concerned Jews in the German music world. Furtwängler cared, above all else, about music. He wanted the best musicians, regardless of ethnicity or religion. Although hardly a philo-Semite, he refused to let the music suffer. The world of classical music in Germany, as in many countries, had a pronounced Jewish presence. In Germany, Otto Klemperer and Bruno Walter were Jewish, not to mention Arnold Schoenberg, Erich Korngold, and Kurt Weill. In June 1933, a professional census recorded that 1,915 of the 93,857 musicians in Germany were Jewish, which came to just over 2 percent (2.04). This was higher than the percentage of Jews in the general population (just under 1 percent). Music historian Fred Prieberg estimated that this figure was about double during the Weimar Republic, prior to the diaspora. Up until 1938, there were more expulsions on racial grounds from the Reich Chamber of Music (2,310) than from any other (next was the Chamber for the Visual Arts, with 1,657). This would also attest to the large number of Jewish musicians who stayed for a time.[56] Back on 11 April 1933 Furtwängler had written an open letter to Goebbels, published in the *Vossische Zeitung,* in which he argued that "men like Walter, Klemperer, and [Max] Reinhardt, and the like, must be able to have a voice in Germany in the future."[57] Several months later, in June 1933, he spoke out against the firing of Jewish musicians in the Berlin Philharmonic. In other words, his call for cultural policy based solely on the quality of the artist, and his defense of Jewish musicians in the Berlin Philharmonic, had already placed him at odds with the Nazi leaders.[58] One administrator in the Reich Chamber of Culture had written to Hans Hinkel, a vice president of the Chamber, "Can you name one Jew for whom Furtwängler has not intervened?"[59]

Furtwängler's defense of artistic autonomy led to an open conflict between the conductor and the Nazis, albeit only a temporary one. Three days after Furtwängler's 25 November 1934 article about Hindemith, a critic for Goebbels's newspaper, *Der Angriff,* ran a piece titled "Why Honor Hindemith the Opportunistic Musician?"[60] Below this heading, which was plastered in large type at the top and center of the first page, the critic, Erich

Roeder, alleged that Hindemith had used his post in the Reich Chamber of Music to advance his own career—and to the detriment of others. The following week, on 6 December 1934, Goebbels spoke at an event celebrating the one-year anniversary of the Reich Chamber of Culture. Although he did not mention Hindemith by name, his remarks were clearly directed at the composer and his advocates. Goebbels railed that "technical craftsmanship never excuses, but is rather an obligation. To misuse it in writing purely motoric empty mechanical music [*Bewegungsmusik*] is a mockery of the generation that stands above every true art."[61] In other words, Goebbels took Furtwängler's words as a personal affront and, true to form, reacted with vitriol. Göring met privately with Furtwängler and "censured him for having taken the matter [about Hindemith] to the public," while Hitler canceled their planned meeting.[62] That Furtwängler persisted in a kind of brinksmanship, reiterating his wish to conduct the opera version of *Mathis,* exacerbated matters. That same week, in early December 1934, he was told to submit letters of resignation from his posts, which he did, writing to Goebbels with regard to the Berlin Philharmonic and the vice presidency at the Reich Chamber of Music, and to Göring to relinquish his post at the Berlin State Opera.[63] Furtwängler also tried to renounce his appointment as state counselor, but Göring informed him that the Prussian state awarded the post, and therefore only the Prussian state could take it away (and that was not happening). Furtwängler moved to the countryside, and the Propaganda Ministry issued instructions to reduce the mention of his name in the media.

The contretemps over Hindemith therefore led to a major crisis in Furtwängler's career. He recovered in due time—in part because subscribers by the hundreds demanded refunds from the Berlin Philharmonic for their season tickets.[64] In late February 1935, he met with Goebbels and then published a statement saying that they had reconciled. A Propaganda Ministry press release explained that when Furtwängler wrote about Hindemith in November 1934, the intention was to raise musical issues, not to engage in remarks of a political nature. Hindemith was reportedly disappointed by the way the conflict was resolved—and he knew the reconciliation diminished the chances that the opera version of *Mathis* would be performed in Germany (but he remained grateful to Furtwängler and wrote a moving obituary of the conductor in 1954).[65] Furtwängler then resumed his posts at the Berlin Philharmonic and the Berlin State Opera, among others that he held in the Reich. By 1937, he was considered for the German National Prize for Arts and Sciences, as Goebbels himself placed his name on the list of potential recipients.[66] Although Furtwängler did not win this award that was meant to replace the Nobel Prize—which Hitler forbade Germans to accept—the nomination confirmed his rehabilitation.

The same cannot be said for Paul Hindemith, who increasingly suffered from the polarized reaction to his work. He wrote to Johannes Schüler, a conductor in Essen who had performed the *Mathis-Symphony* on 20 November 1934, about "the unearthly amount of muck that has been emptied out over my head in recent days," as he thanked Schüler for his support.[67] In the wake of "The Hindemith Case" article, he sought to turn down the temperature. Along these lines, he requested and received a temporary leave from his teaching duties at the Berlin Hochschule für Musik. Yet despite the deteriorating situation, Hindemith remained in Nazi Germany in the mid-1930s and continued to hope for official acceptance. While certain earlier biographers have claimed that he went into a kind of "inner emigration," music historian Claudia Maurer Zenck, among others, has argued convincingly that this did not occur.[68] Hindemith, for example, kept working to have his productions performed. At one point in early 1935, it looked like *Mathis* might be staged in Frankfurt, and he pursued this possibility. He firmly believed that *Mathis* was the key to his career fortunes in the Third Reich. Richard Strauss allowed Hindemith to remain part of the executive council of the Reich Chamber of Music, and this also offered some encouragement. He then traveled to Turkey in 1935 in order to consult on a reform of the music higher educational system there, including the creation of a conservatory for advanced students. Hindemith hoped that a successful mission to Ankara would reflect positively on him and help him find acceptance. The trip was sanctioned by the Reich Ministry of Education and the Reich Foreign Ministry and had an official character. At no time, Kater pointed out, did he contemplate emigration, even though President Mustafa Kemal Atatürk welcomed German emigrants. Hindemith wrote to his friend Willy Strecker in February 1935, "I do not wish to go for good . . . but wish to stay living in Germany."[69]

Paul Hindemith and his wife, Gertrud, arrived in Turkey on 6 April 1935 and stayed until the end of May. Hindemith made every effort to elicit positive reviews from the German authorities, both in Turkey and back in the Reich. Even before his departure, he wrote to the rector of the Berlin Hochschule für Musik, Fritz Stein, "still his nominal superior, a convinced Nazi, but also a staunch Hindemith supporter, that his upcoming journey should not be interpreted as 'an action against the Hochschule or even against Germany.' Turkey, which Hindemith said, was in the potential sphere of influence of nations other than the Reich, should be secured for a 'cultural influence' by the Germans."[70] Hindemith pointed to other experts from the Soviet Union and France, whom he viewed as rivals. Instead, as he wrote in his June 1935 report on the mission, he had aimed to secure for "the German musical culture a future field of influence of the greatest possible extent, and hence work for German prestige abroad."[71] He therefore promoted German teaching methodologies, as well as German music. It is unclear whether this rhetoric was meant for effect or whether he actually believed what he wrote (or both). Regardless, with his mission to Turkey, Kater noted, "Hindemith obviously wanted to buy the Nazi regime's benevolence."[72] His report on the mission to Turkey was circulated among various Nazi leaders—and he penned a special separate report for Goebbels. Hindemith appeared optimistic about the reports' reception ("I think it should have a good effect"), and indeed, they seemed to elicit the desired reactions.[73] Goebbels, for example, initially appeared to have lifted his objections to a Frankfurt premiere of the *Mathis* opera, and there were reports that Hitler "seemed more favorably disposed" to the composer.[74] A performance of the *Mathis-Symphony* in Paris on 29 May 1935, which Hindemith had attended together with Furtwängler, seemed to bolster the case that his work brought positive publicity abroad.

But the situation again quickly deteriorated. Richard Strauss's subversive correspondence with his librettist Stefan Zweig was discovered, and the aging composer was forced to resign as president of the Reich Chamber of Music, thereby depriving Hindemith of a key ally. To make matters worse, Gustav Havemann, another avid supporter in the Chamber, was also forced out. In his 5 July 1935 diary entry, Goebbels linked the dismissal of both Strauss and Havemann and lamented, "These artists are all so politically characterless."[75] The atmosphere with regard to controversial modern figures appeared to change, as reflected in a memorandum sent by Goebbels's state secretary, Walther Funk, to Hans Hinkel, another important figure in the cultural bureaucracy at the Reich Chamber of Culture, in which Funk criticized the notion of Hindemith's rehabilitation. With a faction within Rosenberg's organization still agitating against Hindemith, there were few individuals prepared to take the risk of advocating for the composer. Even several opera directors who had earlier expressed an interest in staging *Mathis* backed away at this point, although the prospect of a production was not yet completely dead.[76] It finally premiered—with Goebbels's tacit acceptance—in Zurich in May 1938, but there was veritable press silence about it in the Reich. At least it was performed in a nearby land that permitted certain German musical luminaries, such as Carl Orff, to attend.[77]

Hindemith continued to fight for acceptance. On 17 January 1936, he "willingly" signed an oath of allegiance to Hitler—this, in part, an attempt to retain his professorship at the Hochschule für Musik.[78] Shortly thereafter, he sought to use another opportunity to his advantage in Nazi Germany: just after Britain's King George V died on 20 January, the BBC commissioned him to write an elegy. Hindemith finished the piece quickly—building on the *Mathis* work he had recently completed and adding a Bach chorale at the end—and it was very well received in Great Britain. He noted that the Bach chorale was "very suitable for kings" and, as it turned out without his prior knowledge, "a tune every child in England knows."[79] Hindemith wrote to a friend, "Should we not make use of this story? Would you like to circulate it to the German press? It is after all no everyday occurrence when the BBC gets a foreigner to write a piece on the death of their king and sends it out over the complete network." He added, "My various pupils are now busy writing articles about the affair, they are very proud that the old man can still do things so well and so quickly."[80] A German periodical, *Deutsche Zukunft,* reflected the positive press coverage at home, with the reporter boasting that writing funeral music for a king "within the space of an evening" constituted a feat "that could only have been achieved by a German."[81] Hindemith therefore again hoped that he could play the role of cultural ambassador, and in light of Hitler's well-known desire for accommodation with England, he believed he could prove useful in this specific situation. Hindemith enjoyed a short spell of other positive developments in early 1936: he performed a viola concerto in Berlin on 14 February, his recently composed Sonata in E Major was played at the Baden-Baden new-music festival in April, and later that month one of his viola sonatas was played in a Hamburg concert organized by a Nazi student organization. In June, Göring's Luftwaffe commissioned a work from him—in Hindemith's words, "a highly official orchestral concert"—and he threw himself into the project. As he wrote to Willy Strecker on 8 July 1936, "I want to give them something really good—I am certain that this piece, if reasonably successful, will mean 'Mathis' in the State Opera. The prospects are not quite so gloomy as they looked at first sight."[82] He never fulfilled the commission, but it is remarkable that he received it in the first place. Hindemith was also charged with making a second trip to Turkey to advise on musical education, which he did in 1936—again spending six weeks in Ankara.

But the pendulum quickly swung the other way, and the mirage of acceptance disappeared. Walther Funk and other officials in the Reich Propaganda Ministry had been offended by the enthusiastic applause violinist Georg Kulenkampff had received in a Berlin performance of Hindemith's recently composed violin sonata (plans for the performance of a piano sonata were then scrapped). Hitler's cultural address at the September 1936 Nuremberg Party Rally featured a strident attack on "Bolshevism in politics and culture, art, and politics," sending a message that pro-modernists were in dire straits. Goebbels took this as a cue and, using the Reich Chamber of Music that he controlled, issued a ban on the public performance of Hindemith's work. From October 1936 until the end of the Third Reich, Hindemith's compositions were rarely played in public. On 22 March 1937, Hindemith resigned his professorship in Berlin (effective the following October) and set sail three days later for a concert tour of the United States.[83]

With his fortunes rapidly deteriorating, the composer induced Furtwängler to intervene with Hitler yet again, with this meeting taking place in August 1937. The discussion did not go well. Furtwängler reported, "It is the Führer's opinion that H. is backed by merely a small circle of followers, about the size and significance of which we are all dead wrong, and that it would not make any sense to alter the general direction of his cultural policy because of such a small clique."[84] Again, in this specific case, the fate of a modernist cultural figure was effectively settled by Hitler personally. The inclusion of the composer and his work in the *Degenerate Music Exhibition* that opened in Düsseldorf in May 1938 underscored his status as a proscribed artist. The show featured blown-up photographs of the vilified contemporary composers, as well as a series of listening booths where visitors could sample the music of Hindemith, Kurt Weill, Ernst Krenek, and others. Hindemith was accused of having "deteriorated into a Jewish sensibility" ("Gesinnung verjudet"), among other insults.[85]

Hindemith and his wife, Gertrud, reluctantly undertook plans to emigrate. That she was half-Jewish made their lives increasingly untenable as the Nazi regime grew more radical. The Hindemiths remained in Berlin until late summer 1938. In September, they relocated over the border in Switzerland to an Alpine village called Bluche. Michael Kater has suggested that "Hindemith chose Switzerland because it was close enough to Germany to facilitate an easy and quick return should the occasion present itself."[86] Indeed, the historian labels Hindemith "the reluctant émigré," and there is ample evidence to support this assertion. For one, he passed up numerous earlier opportunities to emigrate—most notably to Turkey, Switzerland, and the United States. Back in March 1937, as Hindemith submitted his resignation from the Berlin Hochschule für Musik, he turned down a permanent position in Basel because, as his wife wrote, he feared being "definitively blacklisted in the Reich."[87]

Certain attitudes he exhibited in 1939 also suggest an effort to identify with the prevailing spirit in Nazi Germany. In October, he wrote his friend Willy Strecker regarding American Jewish musician Louis Krasner that "his was not a very enlightening presence, 'in consideration of which it would be understandable if one were to be caught up in anti-Semitism.'"[88] While it would be inaccurate to label him an anti-Semite—he collaborated with the Jewish Kulturbund in staging a children's opera, and he defended Jewish colleagues in various instances—he did not appear to evince great sympathy for them or their plight.[89] His biographer Ian Kemp, for example, noted that Hindemith "seemed oddly unmoved by the dismissal of Jewish musicians from the Hochschule."[90] That the Hindemiths remained in Switzerland until after the outbreak of war, relocating to the United States only in February 1940, also speaks to their hopes for a return to Germany. This move away from Europe, motivated by the need for an income, by the threat of being overrun by the Wehrmacht, and by the urging of concerned friends, elicited mixed feelings. Paul Hindemith wrote his wife while on board the S.S. *Rex* from Genoa to New York, "If I could return with good grace and with the prospect of a somewhat secure existence I would have the ship turned around right away."[91]

So why did Paul Hindemith fail to find accommodation with the Nazi regime? The main reason for his failure in this respect stemmed from his identification with the modernism of the Weimar Republic. He was simply too closely associated with the atonal modern music that flourished in the 1920s, with Nazi critics pointing, for example, to his collaboration with Bertolt Brecht in the late 1920s (the *Badener Lehrstück*), his appearances at new-music festivals such as Donaueschingen and Baden-Baden, and his "close collaboration with modernist and politically left-wing conductor Hermann Scherchen," among other elements contributing to these optics.[92] Hindemith's association with Weimar modernism in part grew out of the musical renaissance that took place after World War I, especially in Berlin. Furtwängler biographer Sam Shirakawa noted that the conductor's "appointment was among the numerous phenomena that contributed to making Berlin even greater as the center of Europe's cultural universe from 1922 to 1933. Paris may have had its writers and painters, and London many have had its novelists and poets, but for sheer variety, energy, and importance of the work being produced in that period, there was nothing quite like Berlin during Weimar."[93] The German capital featured four opera houses and twenty orchestras and constituted the center of the Weimar modernist renaissance—musical and otherwise.

Of course, the perceptions linking Hindemith to Weimar modernism predated the Nazis' seizure of power: Wilhelm Frick and the Ministry of Education in Thuringia, for example, had banned all performances of Hindemith's music in the province back in 1930.[94] Even though modernist music persisted in various ways throughout the Third Reich—ranging from performances of Richard Strauss's *Elektra* in state theaters to Carl Orff's progressive compositions, to more private performances within the *Hausmusik* genre—there was a deeply ingrained antipathy among many Nazis toward atonality and dissonance. As Erik Levi noted, "The ideological objection against atonal music was that it was subversive, a mode of musical expression cultivated by composers with Left-wing sympathies and a manifestation of anti-German sentiments."[95] While modernism in music was more than atonality, the two concepts were fundamentally linked.

The cultural figures who had modernist roots or qualities and who found a place in Nazi Germany generally did not have reputations as modernists in the same highly visible way as the figures treated in this chapter—that is, those who tried to find accommodation but failed. Many lesser-known modernist musicians, although experiencing some difficulties in Nazi Germany, established a modus vivendi with the regime (composer Hermann Reutter, for example).[96] Granted, pre-1933 visibility could cut both ways. Pamela Potter has argued, "Closer examinations of the varying degrees of conformity will likely show that the greater the reputation of the artist (or organization), the lesser the need to profess the party line." She adds, "For the most part the prestige they lent to the cultural reputation of the Third Reich earned them a surprising degree of freedom in pushing the boundaries of tolerance." The musical figures who toed the Nazi line—anti-Semitism, an opposition to "degeneracy," a belief in German music—"tended to be less well-known or, in the case of Hans Pfitzner, trying to revive fading celebrity."[97] She noted that the same applied to organizations: the Berlin Philharmonic and the Prussian State Opera held on to Jewish members longer than second-tier ones, such as the Mannheim Orchestra.

A second reason for Hindemith's difficulties with many Nazi officials grew out of both his marriage to a half-Jewish woman and his friendships with Jewish musicians. His wife, née Gertrud Rottenberg, had a Christian mother, but her father was the highly visible Jewish director of the Frankfurt opera. "Frankfurt," according to music historian Erik Levi, had "attained a

Paul Hindemith (center), with Emanuel Feuermann (left) and Szymon Goldberg (right) in the early 1930s. (Bundesarchv-Koblenz, Bild Nr. 183-1984-0104-524)

special reputation for promoting audacious repertoire," including the first performance of Hindemith's *Sancta Susanna* in 1922.[98] According to the Nuremberg Laws of 1935, Gertrud Hindemith qualified as Jewish, and this presented significant (but not insurmountable) problems. In certain instances cultural figures with Jewish spouses found a measure of tolerance in the Third Reich: composer Rudolf Wagner-Régeny, for example, who enjoyed the support of Baldur von Schirach.[99] Yet Hindemith's difficulties in this regard were exacerbated by his friendships with Jewish musicians, such as violinist Simon Goldberg and cellist Emmanuel Feuermann. Hindemith also had Jewish students, such as Franz Reizenstein, who were perceived as linked to him, and this situation exacerbated the attacks. In March 1934, at a critical time in the debate about whether Hindemith and his music should be tolerated in the Third Reich, critic Friedrich Welter wrote in the journal *Die Musik*, "How was it possible . . . for Hindemith to be accepted as a genuine representative of German art, when he had continually associated with Jews?"[100]

Why did Hindemith hope for acceptance? While the reasons are myriad, one related to his ego or, to be more precise, his arrogance. In the spring of 1941, he signed a three-year contract to teach at Yale University, which he renewed in 1944. He negotiated these temporary appointments because, in his words, he "still prefer[red] not to commit himself to a longer term."[101] Besides believing himself so gifted as not to require binding commitments—some other prestigious institution would surely snap him up—Hindemith behaved in an autocratic manner with regard to both his teaching and his administrative work. Michael Kater described him as "stern to the point of being callous" and added that while "at Yale, he treated even the most gifted and advanced of his students as if they were mere beginners."[102] In the thirteen years he taught at Yale, the composer awarded only twelve master's degrees in composition. Hindemith also taught during the summers at the Tanglewood music venue in western Massachusetts, where he clashed with his colleague Aaron Copland, who encouraged his students to stage public performances. Hindemith, in his own words, would "forbid any pieces by my students to be performed publicly."[103] He initially even refused to look at the scores they had submitted and remanded them to remedial work on counterpoint. One young Jewish student from Egypt evidently drowned himself in a local river after Hindemith subjected him to harsh criticism. With regard to the reform of the Yale music program, Hindemith elaborated a series of measures that would have made the institution far more hierarchical (not unlike the German system). His Yale colleagues resisted, and a hard-fought compromise ensued. Hindemith reported to Willy Strecker, "The school has been totally reformed, essentially according to my plans."[104] Many émigrés behaved in an arrogant fashion, finding America less culturally advanced than their homeland, but his new milieu accentuated a trait already present in the composer.

A second factor grew out of Hindemith's political naïveté. A left-wing democrat during the Weimar Republic, Hindemith reportedly expressed anti-fascist views in his classes at the Berlin Hochschule für Musik, even after January 1933.[105] On Christmas eve in December 1933, he went to the Moabit prison in Berlin and played viola music by Bach: his brother-in-law Hans Flesch was incarcerated there while being investigated, and Hindemith hoped this demonstration, this sign of solidarity, would help. While capable of a noble gesture, he clearly failed to comprehend the malignant intentions of Hitler and his cohort. As Hindemith endeavored at a compromise with the new leaders by growing more nationalistic and less modernist in his music, he expected the Nazi leaders to moderate their behavior in turn. He also did not believe that they would remain in power.[106] But of course the opposite occurred, certainly in terms of foreign policy and Jewish policy, but also in terms of cultural policy. The *Degenerate Art Exhibition* of 1937 and *Degenerate Music Exhibition* of 1938 signaled the sharper key, and musical censorship also increased in the latter years of the Third Reich. Hindemith miscalculated in predicting the course the Nazi regime would take.

A third reason for his belief that he and his work should find a place in the Third Reich stemmed from his German identity. While he did not go as far as his friend and supporter Wilhelm Furtwängler, who "felt able to declare that . . . 'a genuine symphony has never been written by a non-German,'" it is significant that Hindemith relocated back to a German-speaking land in the early 1950s, taking a permanent post at the University of Zurich in 1953.[107] This left "his American colleagues to wonder whether Hindemith had ever liked being in the United States in the first place" (although the main reason for the relocation was his wish to reduce his teaching load so that he could focus on composing and conducting).[108] Certain passages from his letters in the 1930s, when he visited North America, are suggestive: "These people, incidentally, are a fantastic hotchpotch. Their jaws, including the feminine ones, move continuously from left to right like cows chewing the cud; the gum consumption must be enormous."[109] While he found many positive elements in the United States (he became a citizen in 1946) and also developed ambivalent views about Germany, his self-conception and his understanding of his work was founded on an essential German identity.[110] His decision not to return to Germany rested upon the physical destruction of the country, "Hindemith's own hurt pride, after what Germans had done to him from 1933 to 1938; and not least, uncertainty over how he and his music would be treated."[111] Resettling in Zurich afforded him a manageable distance from his troubled homeland, while also allowing the many benefits.

A point related to his German identity, but also somewhat separate, concerned his belief that leaving his native country "would sap his creative energy."[112] During the three tours of the United States from 1937 to 1939, Hindemith began to contemplate the idea of emigration. He had certain positive experiences on these tours—he was feted wherever he went, including a reception at the Washington, DC, home of Secretary of the Treasury Henry Morgenthau—such that he wrote his patron Elizabeth Sprague Coolidge at the end of the 1937 tour, "I left the country where I was so warmly received with a feeling of artistic satisfaction."[113] Yet many of his other reactions to America conveyed his fear that emigration would spell creative disaster. At a Carnegie Hall performance of his piece *Der Schwanen-dreher* on the 1937 tour, the New York Philharmonic played poorly. He noted in his journal that "the harpist played a lot of wrong notes and the trombonist never played his important solo part," among other errors.[114] In early 1939, when visiting Los Angeles, he toured several Hollywood studios, including the Walt Disney film studio, where he met Leopold Stokowski, who was scoring the film *Fantasia*. Hindemith wrote his wife about the visit, commenting about the visual artists, "The place is so tightly regulated that it makes you ill. They have a special school where talented young artists are taught to draw only Mickey Mouse or Donald Duck and are not allowed to try anything on their own." He was even more critical of the musicians, including Stokowski: "When I saw what kind of trash he was making and that he was wearing an ultramarine blue silk shirt and a lemon-yellow cravat with his albino-like face I really could not muster up the proper feeling of awe."[115] Even though he once entertained the possibility of joining other German émigrés in Hollywood, he clearly viewed the culture there as inferior, derivative, and, ultimately, soul-draining. He wrote in 1939, "I think I am pretty well cured of the urge to do anything with the films here (I once had the completely mad thought I could create something of artistic value). This idea simply cannot be pursued seriously."[116]

Any portrait of Paul Hindemith must also include the many positive qualities he possessed. The discussion above shows clearly that he cared deeply about the quality of art. Even with his often caustic demeanor, others understood this and often responded well. He noted in one letter after teaching at Tanglewood how the students had responded to his demanding regimen and, at the end, were "complaining that the course lasts only six weeks."[117] He enjoyed rigorous intellectual exchange and thrived at Yale University and in other academic settings. Stretching back to the 1920s, Hindemith embraced a wide range of art forms, both "high" and "low." His account of visiting the Cotton Club in Harlem and hearing Duke Ellington's orchestra is illustrative: "The orchestra played continuously for about three hours, the wildest I have ever heard. Trumpets screamed all the way up to high B, trombones and saxophones did elaborate 'hot flourishes.' The whole thing was really a rhythmic and tonal orgy, done with remarkable virtuosity."[118] After visiting several other clubs, he finished off the evening "back downtown" with "a final glass of beer." Even though the Cotton Club was a problematic institution of its times, with a "Whites only" clientele, his account showed that he was not always the tightly wound mandarin. Similarly, upon arrival in the Swiss town of Bluche in the summer of 1939, he and Gertrud expressed their fondness of gardening and canning vegetables, for making wine, and for joining in local theatrical productions. In short, Hindemith was a complex person, with both positive and negative attributes.

Pamela Potter has described a prevailing assumption among musicologists, albeit one that she and other scholars have challenged in recent years: "An image has emerged of a dystopia in which all musical activity was strictly controlled by a core of ruthless dictators and a few willing collaborators, and in which all music produced was artistically impoverished."[119] She added, "The canon of German music history—by tacitly honoring the admonitions to assume the worst about any music produced within Nazi Germany and to privilege the music of all who can be regarded as victims—has virtually erased the Nazi years, sketching a narrative that jumps from Weimar-era experimentation to the exile activities of those who fled the Third Reich."[120] In other words, it is important not to overlook the important music that was produced in Germany from 1933 to 1945 and to recognize its linkages to the periods preceding and following Hitler's rule, as well as the way it connects to the creations of contemporaries in foreign lands.

Researchers began to gain access to the archives and publish their findings in the 1980s, leading to a reassessment of this conception. They began to question "the extent to which 'forbidden' music was actually suppressed, and the extent to which the government had terrorized practicing musicians."[121] Clearly, Hindemith remained productive up until his departure in September 1938—his *Symphonic Dances* of 1937 and ballet suite *Nobilissima Visione* (based on the life of Saint Francis) of 1938 deserve mention. And within Germany, despite the proscriptions imposed on him and his music, his work percolated with force from a kind of pro-modernist underground spring. It helped that his publisher, the preeminent music publishing house in Germany, Schott's Söhne, continued to offer his music in its catalogue throughout the war. The publisher released the first part of his textbook *Unterweisung im Tonsatz* (usually translated as *The Craft of Musical Composition*) in 1937, and it sold exceedingly well—more than two thousand copies in a short period of time.[122] *Unterweisung im Tonsatz* represented a plea for chromatic music, his thoughts about the rules by which one writes such music, and a critical brief against serialism. By this point, Hindemith viewed tonality as an inescapable part of human existence or, as he put it, "a natural force, like gravity."[123] Many of his recordings were also still available, including a rendition of the *Mathis der Maler* symphony produced by the Telefunken label in 1934, for which Hindemith himself had conducted the Berlin Philharmonic. This recording remained available well after Hindemith's works ceased to be performed publicly in Nazi Germany.[124] Michael Kater also noted, "Music educators continued to concern themselves and their students with Hindemith's compositions, with the students sometimes taking the initiative, for Hindemith's legacy as a composer and pedagogue persisted tenaciously underground. Throughout the war, a number of party, government, and cultural agencies in Germany were interested, despite the official ban, in performing or holding instructive lectures about Hindemith's music—and a few actually got away with it."[125] Going back to the early years of the Third Reich, Hindemith, like modernist cultural figures in a range of disciplines, attracted especially strong support from the younger generation of National Socialists. In hoping for a "new" Germany, they envisioned correspondingly innovative forms of culture.

Just as many key Nazi leaders could not be shaken from their early anti-modernist views, Hindemith's supporters continued to advocate for him after his emigration. In 1940, music historian Otto Schumann wrote, "Hindemith's last works reflect a change . . . the former adversary is aware, above all (in the music drama *Mathis der Maler*), of an art truly responsible to the life-giving forces of the nation. Should Hindemith continue along this path, he may perhaps be reclaimed for Germany."[126] The composer, of course, was not given that opportunity, but it was not for lack of trying on the part of his supporters—or of Hindemith himself. Even though he disliked the Nazis and their policies, he went to great lengths artistically and professionally to find accommodation with the regime.

6

Gottfried Benn

(1886 Mansfeld [Brandenburg]–1956 West Berlin)

Dr. Gottfried Benn at his medical practice in Berlin circa 1928.
(Deutsches Literaturarchiv, Marbarch)

AN EXPRESSIONIST POET and essayist, Gottfried Benn initially evinced considerable sympathy for National Socialism. Some have even called him "an avid Nazi"—at least, at the beginning of the regime.[1] Benn was unusual in many respects: he was a physician who spent part of World War I serving as a doctor in an army brothel and later, during the Third Reich, returned to the armed forces as a physician in what he termed "an aristocratic form of emigration." His view of the world was dark, but he advocated an escape from the harsh realities by way of dreams, myths, and even drugs (see his 1917 poem "Cocaine," where he wrote about the "Sweet deep desired disintegration of what was me").[2] Benn developed into a German nationalist yet repeatedly pointed to "the South"—and more specifically, "the classical world and the warm blue sea"—as humanity's salvation.[3] In spite of these complexities, Benn was representative of many well-educated Germans in that he initially believed in the ideals of National Socialism and thought that Hitler would help revive the flagging country. Benn took an extreme course as a response to the country's profound problems. Certain critics would say that Benn ultimately chose modernism over National Socialism—he was an "unreconstructed Expressionist," they argued. Yet as with many modernist figures, it was the dominant forces within the regime turning against him, and the stylistic idiom in which he worked, that proved decisive in his relationship to National Socialism.

Benn was among the most distinguished modernist writers in the Weimar Republic: a member of the (metaphoric) twentieth-century German-language pantheon that ranged from Thomas Mann to Günter Grass and Elfriede Jelinek, among many others. His work has also been compared to Anglo-American authors, such as T. S. Eliot ("in scrupulousness of style"), Ezra Pound ("in scope"), W. H. Auden ("in formal invention and use of the vernacular"), and Wallace Stevens ("in content . . . ideas on the value of poetry and expression").[4] Benn had been elected a member of the Prussian Academy in 1932 and was singled out for his poetry, even though he wrote in various genres. He helped pioneer a radical sense of language and used the German language to plumb the depths of the human condition, including the powerful irrational forces that he, like many Nazis, saw as so important. Later, in 1952, Theodor Heuss, president of the German Federal Republic, awarded Benn the Cross of Merit (*Verdienstkreuz*), as the West German regime attempted to harness modernism as part of the cultural Cold War. Yet Heuss was correct in regarding the writer as a titan of German literature. That the Stuttgart publishing house Klett-Cotta has issued a dozen volumes of Benn's letters from 1914 to 1956, featuring his exchanges with Ernst Jünger and Paul Hindemith, among others, says a great deal about his importance.[5]

Gottfried Benn hailed from eastern Germany, having been born in the town of Mansfeld in Saxony-Anhalt, not too far from the city of Halle. The son of a Lutheran pastor, he would go on to study theology and philology at the University in Marburg, the distinguished historic university in the western province of Hesse. His upbringing in the conservative, pietistic, and largely rural environment shaped the writer. Benn took enormous pride that he was born in the same house and, in fact, in the same room, as his father. In 1934, when securing documents about his "Aryan" ancestry, he pointed to church records showing his family residing in the town back to 1704, and indicated that they were farmers and "complete peasants" (*Vollbauern*).[6] Previously, in an August 1933 article titled "The German Man: Genotype and Leadership" ("Der deutsche Mensch. Erbmasse und Führertum"), Benn recalled that the family house had been built in the seventeenth century, taking pride that it was "indistinguishable from a sheep's stall."[7] His charismatic preacher-father influenced him profoundly—Benn compared him to a prophet of the Old Testament—as did his mother, who had been born in the French part of Switzerland. Benn would later point to the "Latin" influence on his worldview, and how his mother hailed from the same landscape as Jean-Jacques Rousseau's father. This evidently deepened his spiritual proclivities and love of nature. The Benn family moved to the Neumark when he was only two, to the village of Sellin (today Zielen in Poland), not far from Küstrin, near the Baltic Sea. The scenic Pomeranian landscape would become his *Heimat,* and he evinced a love for the region that fed into certain "Blood and Soil" tropes.[8] There were many ironic elements in Benn's career: one was that he styled himself as connected to the rural east while at the same time presenting himself as a poet of the metropolis, with all its decadence, cosmopolitanism, and cynicism.[9]

Benn grew even more complex as he matured. His experiences studying military medicine in Berlin at the Kaiser Wilhelm Akademie (also known as the Pépinière, because of its French Huguenot roots) shaped him profoundly. As J. M. Ritchie noted, "This magnificent establishment for training medical officers offered not only first class and up-to-date scientific facilities, but also general lectures on philosophy and art as well as training in the social graces required of an officer."[10] Yet his time at the Akademie also made him more aware of the darker side of human existence, a realization that would inform his work and provide a linkage to National Socialism. He spent five years at the Pépinière (1905–10) and, for part of that time, was also a soldier in the Prussian Guard. That he entered into duels, and received several scars from the sabers—one *Mensur* from 1909 resulted in a cut to the bone below his left eye and left a deep scar—speaks to his conservative proclivities.[11] Benn continued to study philosophy and art as a medical student, and he began writing poetry on his own. His literary interests developed further even as he took a position as a junior physician for the Infantry Regiment 64 in Prenzlau in October 1910, as well as the following year as he began his residency at the Berliner Charité hospital.

Benn crafted Expressionist prose even before World War I, publishing a collection of poems in 1912 that he titled *Morgue and Other Poems*. Here he explored themes such as the decay of the flesh and the transitory nature of life. For example, in the poem "Man and Woman Go Through the Cancer Ward [*Krebsbaracke*]," he described how "one bed stinks next to the next" and how this sapped the life forces of those present. His own mother was suffering from a terrible cancer at the time and would die in April 1912—"the most difficult death [he] had ever seen," as he wrote a friend.[12] One critic noted, "His poetry offers an introverted nihilism: an existential philosophy which sees artistic expression as the only purposeful action. In his early poems, Benn used his medical experiences and terminology to portray a morbid conception of humanity as another species of disease-ridden animal."[13] His concern with the irrational forces in life—the passions, emotions, and instincts that drove human beings—and the way he expressed a longing for regression, placed him in the mainstream of many fin-de-siècle modernists, including painters such as German Expressionist Franz Marc (who also favored animals as subjects) and Viennese Secessionists Gustav Klimt and Oskar Kokoschka, whose visions were similarly dark. It is not surprising that Benn was invited to read his poems at modernist art dealer Paul Cassirer's *Kunstsalon* and that his work was featured in the Expressionist periodical *Die Aktion*.[14] Benn grew increasingly discontented with his work at the pathological institute in the Berlin hospital and quit his post in March 1914. He signed on as the physician for a steamship called the *Graf Waldersee* and in April 1914 made his only trip to the United States. While in New York he had the opportunity to attend the Metropolitan Opera and hear Enrico Caruso, but the poet left unimpressed by the tenor and, evidently, by the country as a whole.

As one would expect for someone with his background, Benn volunteered for military service in 1914, joining the Brandenburg Pioneer Battalion. He served as a military physician and accompanied his unit into Flanders, where they took part in the attack on Antwerp. Despite serving as a medic, he entered into harm's way and was awarded the Iron Cross, Second Class. Benn spent most of the war at a hospital in Brussels, which proved relatively comfortable and afforded him the opportunity to write. Yet his experiences in Belgium were far from uneventful. For example, he was on hand for the trial and execution in 1915 of British nurse Edith Cavell, who had helped secure the freedom of some two hundred Entente troops. She was convicted of treason and shot by a firing squad; Benn was present at the execution (he later wrote a journalistic account in 1928). Benn's tenure as a doctor in an army brothel also proved colorful, if in a rather bizarre manner. He described his time as "a completely isolated post where I lived in a confiscated eleven-room house with my boys. I had little to do and could wear civilian clothes."[15] Benn continued to pen verses about a variety of topics, including, in his words, "the victims of the slaughter."[16] He lost a number of family members and friends during the war; most notably his younger brother Siegfried (1892–1916) as well as two step-brothers who fell in action. Benn himself was able to leave the front before war's end, returning to Berlin in November 1917, when he set up a practice in Kreuzberg treating venereal diseases.

While this specialty might contribute to a pessimistic worldview in any person, Benn was a cerebral type who thought in grand ideological and cosmological terms. In the 1920s, he developed a strong antipathy to Marxism, which he saw as stifling individual will and creativity. His letters most often referenced figures like Friedrich Nietzsche and Rainer Maria Rilke, who affirmed the potential of the individual and the cosmic importance of nature. Benn would later reference Swiss historian Jacob Burckhardt in discussing the individual in world history, noting how "great" men would appear, especially in terrible times, and this buttressed his defense of Hitler.[17] Benn also had a pronounced anti-American streak, seeing the rising power as a threat to German values. In particular, he railed against the effects of capitalism: the materialism, the exploitation of workers, and the emergence of unhealthy cities, among other aspects. For these and other reasons, Benn developed a friendship with artist George Grosz (who, ironically, would find sanctuary in the United States in 1932). The two men met in places like the Café des Westens and often inspired one another. Grosz, for example, executed drawings inspired by Benn's collection of poems titled *Fleisch* (*Meat*)—works that showed naked prostitutes and corrupt war profiteers—and Benn dedicated poems (such as "Café") to the artist.[18] They shared a dark, cynical worldview but also incorporated the liberated and modern Berlin atmosphere into their work, representing the jazz cadences, mercurial financial swings (Benn would reference casinos), and perceptible eroticism so prevalent in the German metropolis. Benn flourished in the modernist subculture of 1920s Berlin, publishing works in periodicals such as Alfred Flechtheim's *Der Querschnitt* and enjoying widespread critical acclaim. His circle at this time also included Bertolt Brecht, Alfred Döblin, and Paul Hindemith—collaborating with the latter by writing the text for *Das Unaufhörliche* (*The Incessant*) in 1931.[19] Early the next year, Benn was elected to the Prussian Academy of the Arts. The success Benn enjoyed in Weimar would not prevent him from detesting the republic and celebrating its demise.

Although he never joined the Nazi Party, Benn initially believed that Hitler would usher in a revolution that would transform the country into a vibrant and positive force. Naturally, he believed that Expressionism should be part of that transformation. He never embraced a *völkisch* conception of culture but instead believed that the spiritual depth of Expressionism was consonant with Hitler's ideals. A vast and contentious literature has resulted from Benn's decision to support the National Socialists. Augustinus Dierick provides a sense of the debates, writing, "Whether Benn's reactions were purely emotional, or whether Benn really built his hope for social and cultural stability on the Nazi regime, whether he finally thought he had the 'high life' within his grasp, or whether we must speak of opportunism or political blindness, all this depends to a great extent not only on what sources are used to back up the arguments, of course, but also on the political convictions of the critics themselves."[20] In that individuals rarely, if ever, act for a single reason, all of the aforementioned explanations possess some merit. Benn himself did not articulate one sole reason for his support for Hitler. A strong proponent of the power of irrational forces and an avid German nationalist, he had a general sense that his art belonged in the new Reich. He articulated this almost religious conviction in the compatibility of Nazism and Expressionism in "Confession of Faith in Expressionism," his 1933 essay that invoked a tradition that included Kleist, Nietzsche, and Rilke.[21]

Benn's optimistic feelings appeared to find confirmation in mid-February 1933, when he was appointed the provisional head of the poetry section of the Prussian Academy. He held this position only until 7 June 1933, but this was a crucial three-month period when many venerable writers were forced out and replaced by a pro-Nazi cohort. The Academy was wracked with controversy in these early months of the Third Reich, as Bernhard Rust, then provisional Prussian Minister of Education, applied pressure on left-wing and Jewish members, calling for the resignations of Heinrich Mann, Käthe Kollwitz, Max Liebermann, and Arnold Schoenberg, among others. Rust singled out Kollwitz and Heinrich Mann, who had signed a petition endorsing cooperation between the Social Democrats and the Communists in the upcoming elections scheduled for 5 March. Rust threatened that he would hold the entire Academy responsible unless they expelled Kollwitz and Mann. Kollwitz resigned just prior to the 15 February 1933 meeting of the Academy, but events that day proved particularly dramatic. The members of the Academy debated the expulsion of Heinrich Mann, and Benn asked whether Mann had been informed. It appeared that he had not been told that this item was on the agenda, but he was contacted by telephone and arrived shortly thereafter. Mann was ordered to resign as head of the poetry section, and from the Academy altogether. After an impassioned debate—with Alfred Döblin speaking on Mann's behalf on several occasions—Mann stepped down. Shortly thereafter, Benn took over as the new (but provisional) head of the Poetry Section.[22] In other words, Benn helped facilitate the Nazis' *Gleichschaltung* of culture. Benn could rationalize the purge on the grounds that Mann and Kollwitz espoused left-wing political views and actively opposed the Nazis. He could also point to the modernists that remained in the Academy, including Ernst Barlach, Max Pechstein, Ernst Ludwig Kirchner, and Karl Hofer—although all would fall victim to the second round of purges in 1937–38. Some literary scholars have seen opportunism as a key factor in Benn's support of the Nazis. J. M. Ritchie noted, "As far as external symbols of acceptance were concerned, the outsider seems to have been so delighted with his election to the Prussian Academy that he was prepared to throw his colleagues to the wolves."[23]

Benn oversaw other measures associated with the coordination of the Academy. The first round of expulsions provoked heated debates among Academy members. Alfred Döblin took the lead drafting a resolution protesting the forced resignations, which constituted a bold move against the

Nazi leadership. As the poetry section chief, Benn had considerable influence, and he worked to moderate the tone of the communication. But he did more than this. Elaine Hochman observed, "Gottfried Benn altered the version that appeared in the press release, to a mere expression of regret at [Heinrich] Mann's resignation and praise for his artistic merits."[24] A fair characterization would be to say that Benn tried to decrease friction between the Prussian Academy and the Nazi government. At the 13 March 1933 meeting of the literature section, members were asked to sign a loyalty oath stating that they would "forgo public political activity against the Reich government, dedicating themselves instead to 'loyal cooperation.'"[25] Benn led the pro-accommodation contingent, which also included Nobel Prize winner Gerhart Hauptmann. With his dramas focused on workers and naturalistic prose style, Hauptmann also occupied a place in the history of modernism, and yet he also went on to find a place in the Reich (he counted Baldur von Schirach as a patron and Arno Breker as a friend). Hauptmann remained a suspect figure in the eyes of many Nazis because he had once championed social engagement, but it helped that he signed a loyalty oath to Hitler in March 1933 and applied to join the Nazi Party later that summer.[26]

The pro-accommodationists manipulated the rules governing the proceedings of the crucial meeting at the Academy to get their way, although some found these tactics unsavory. Notably, the accommodationists successfully lobbied for the ruling that "only a written yeah or nay reply would be permitted." This prompted the resignation of four members, including Thomas Mann, then living abroad after having fled to Paris via Switzerland in the wake of the burning of the Reichstag on 28 February, and Alfred Döblin. An arrest warrant for the Jewish and politically left-wing Döblin followed the next day. The remaining members signed the loyalty oath and made Benn the official chief of the poetry section. By May 1933, a new German Academy of Poetry had been founded within the Prussian Academy, and Rust proposed a list of writers more sympathetic to the Nazis, including Hanns Johst, Hans Grimm, and Erwin Guido Kolbenheyer.[27] Perhaps more interesting is that Ernst Jünger, best known for his works that portrayed the combat experience of World War I in a positive light, turned down an offer to join the Academy. Citing the "uniqueness of his work," he did not wish to have any institutional ties. Jünger noted in a subsequent letter to the Academy that he hoped for "positive cooperation with the new state," yet offered another model for artistic survival within the Third Reich.[28]

Gottfried Benn also provided the intellectual justification for the purges.

A crucial moment for Benn and his relationship to the Nazi regime came on 24 April 1933, when he delivered a radio address titled, "The New State and the Intellectuals." Literary scholar Egbert Krispyn summarized his remarks: "He derided all liberalism and proclaimed that intellectual freedom had to be subordinated and sacrificed to the totalitarian state. At the same time he hailed the National Socialists as representing the new heroic biological type to which the future belonged."[29] Two days after delivering this radio address, Benn spoke in his capacity as section chief of the Prussian Academy at a graveside ceremony to commemorate writer Arno Holz, who had died in 1929. In a widely reported address, he intoned "that he would take the opportunity to show publicly that an intellectual at this time in his life, who had always adhered to a specific social class, could nevertheless stand in positive relation to the new state—indeed, must adopt such a stance!" Benn continued, "Naturally it is painful to renounce and distance oneself from old 'liberal' works and people. But the law of history is so completely clear that in my opinion, no delay is possible."[30]

By the spring of 1933, a distinguished cohort of writers and intellectuals had already emigrated—many of them initially residing in neighboring European countries. One of the most prominent anti-Nazi exiles, Klaus Mann, responded to Benn's address with an open letter of 9 May 1933, in which he first professed great admiration for Benn's writing, and then expressed his disillusionment. Mann "respectfully raised the question how someone whose name had been synonymous with the highest moral level and with an almost fanatical purity of spirit could in this critical hour lend his support to the Nazis." Klaus Mann wrote that he wished Benn had resigned from the Academy (like Klaus's father, Thomas), and criticized Benn's obsession with the irrational. In Benn, Klaus Mann saw a "repudiation of civilization" that could feed into "the worship of brute power."[31] Gottfried Benn responded in turn. In yet another radio address, this one on 24 May 1933, he offered his "Answer to the Literary Emigrants." Benn defended the new regime once again, claiming that "German workers are better off now than ever before.... They get better treatment in their shops; their supervisors are more cautious, the personnel chiefs more courteous; the workers have more power, are more respected, work in a better mood."[32] It was a remarkable assertion in light of the loss of civil liberties that resulted from the emergency decrees that followed the 28 February Reichstag fire, the 23 March Enabling Act that had turned the Reichstag into a rubber-stamp body, and the 7 April law that had resulted in the dismissal of thousands of civil servants. Benn, in a thinly veiled reference to Thomas Mann and other émigrés, also criticized those authors who "are writing to me from the neighborhood of Marseilles, in the little resorts along the Gulf of Lyons, in the hotels of Zurich, Prague, and Paris." They had not lived through the historic events in Germany and this invalidated their arguments. Benn defended the regime against charges of violence and "barbarism" as the polemics of the Left. He wrote, "You put it as if what happens in Germany now were threatening culture, threatening civilization, as if a horde of savages were menacing the ideals of mankind as such. But let me ask you in turn: how do you visualize the movement of history? Do you regard it as particularly active at French bathing resorts?"[33] With barbed comments such as these (he also labeled them "superficial, irresponsible and hedonistic"), Benn took the fight to the émigrés, many of whom had formerly been colleagues and supporters.

While his taunts about being out of touch on the French Riviera angered certain émigrés, Benn's racist formulations in the early years of the Third Reich provoked even more enmity. At times, he combined the two themes, writing, for example, "Will you not finally realize, on your Latin shore, that the events in Germany are not political tricks, to be twisted and talked to death in the well-known dialectical manner, but are the emergence of a new biological type, a mutation of history and a people's wish to breed itself?" He also remarked, "Will you amateurs of civilization, you troubadours of Western progress not realize, at last, that what is here at stake is not forms of government but a new vision of the birth of man—perhaps an old, perhaps the last grand concept of the white race, probably one of the grandest realizations of the cosmic spirit itself, preluded in Goethe's hymn *To Nature?*"[34] As with many physicians in interwar Germany, Benn gravitated toward Nazi conceptions about eugenics and "racial hygiene."

To what extent was Benn an anti-Semite and a racist? In terms of the former, he appeared relatively unconcerned. Benn had Jewish friends and did not make notable anti-Semitic comments. But his racism, again true to paradoxical form, is another matter. In his essay "Breeding and the Future," Benn "again tried to establish himself as a bona fide fascist by praising the Nazi ideal of Germanic racial purity."[35] In advocating for a new "biological type," he argued that laws that limited procreation were necessary for a state. Borrowing from Oswald Spengler, he used a "language of racial and cultural doom."[36] Augustinus Dierick noted, "Benn finds in fact ample evidence in history for the existence and justification of eugenics, and even in the Bible, in the case of Moses."[37] Benn then referred to the elimination of those who were weak in order to facilitate the survival of the Israelite tribe as a whole. While he was not advocating a program to eliminate so-called sub-humans, Benn, without a doubt, was grappling with issues surrounding the biological health of a people. Already in "The New State and the Intellectuals"—the radio address that he transformed into an essay—Benn posited the triumph "of the nation-state, based on race."[38] He penned a follow-up essay called "Breeding II" (*Züchtung II*), in which he identified Nietzsche as a supporter of eugenics. He also bought into the notion of the "New Man of Nazism," writing of "the last grand conception of the white race, probably . . . one of the greatest realizations of the world spirit ever."[39] Benn's racism also found expression in a September 1933 piece he wrote for the periodical *Die Woche,* where he called for the "removal or segregation" (*ausscheidung*) of the "less valuable part of the *Volk* . . . not only for reasons to do with racial fitness, but also for macro-economic [*volkswirtschaftlichen*] reasons."[40] In short, Benn openly and forcefully articulated a racist, eugenic program. His high-brow, culture-based arguments can be seen as buttressing what would evolve into a genocidal program, although again, he himself made no call for persecution, let alone killing.

In addition to the biological component to his thinking, Benn's views dovetailed with National Socialism in other ways. He glorified the state and called for the subordination of the individual to this state. Benn rejected "the liberal demand for freedom of thought, first because he finds in history no evidence for such freedom except in the highest elite."[41] He viewed individualism as overrated, even decadent, and argued that it did not correspond to the realities of a new Germany. For someone who was a consummate outsider, an often isolated artist, the irony is palpable; but his search for community, for belonging, led him to embrace the idea of the *Volk.* He could therefore embrace the National Socialists' "call of the blood"—"the *Volk* which provided the only true relationship between the individual and community."[42] Benn's belief in the irrational and spiritual forces in life also factored in here: "Intellectual primitivism, then, was one way of escaping from the alienating economic, political and technological complications of twentieth-century society."[43] Such longings for an organic primitive community proved consonant with his anti-Marxism, anti-Americanism, and hostility to the Weimar Republic. If such views wrecked friendships, he was prepared to make the sacrifice: the new community mattered more. The concluding sentence of his "Answer to the Literary Emigrants" read, "But suddenly dangers arise, suddenly the community tightens, and everyone, the man of letters included, must stand up and choose; private hobby, or direction toward the state. I choose the latter, and I must accept it for this state if you, from your shore, bid me farewell."[44]

Despite his embrace of many racist and illiberal ideas, Benn never joined the Nazi Party. In certain respects, this is extraordinary, especially considering the administrative positions he held. In addition to heading the Poetry Section of the Prussian Academy, he became one of the vice presidents of the National Writers' Union (Union nationaller Schriftsteller), a post he assumed in January 1934. Here he served under the organization's president, Hanns Johst, an SS officer who had authored the play *Schlageter* (which was dedicated to Hitler "with unswerving loyalty").[45] This organization had formed when delegates at a congress in Ragusa (Dobrovnic) of PEN International (a worldwide organization of writers that promotes freedom of expression) had criticized the German organization. The Germans had walked out of the conference and formed their own Nazified association. That Benn could assume leadership roles in National Socialist bodies and yet not join the Party reflects the paradoxes that so intrigued him. Augustinus Dierick has noted, "The true fascination of the Nazis for Benn . . . lies in their attempt to achieve a number of syntheses which Benn until now had felt to be impossible: that of '*Geist*' and '*Macht*,' of individuality and collectivity, and of freedom and necessity."[46] Yet Benn appeared to believe that joining the Nazi Party would compromise him in some way. As he wrote in the spring of 1933, "I am not in the Party, have no contact with its leaders, and do not count on new friends. It is my purity of feeling and thought that determines my attitude."[47]

This did not prevent him from facilitating the *Gleichschaltung* of the Prussian Academy and the National Writers' Union, while simultaneously defending Expressionism. For example, on 5 November 1933, Benn published an essay titled "Apology for Expressionism" in the German weekly periodical *Deutsche Zukunft* (*German Future*). Benn wrote that Expressionism was the "last great resurgence of art in Europe," and that it had an "anti-liberal function" that had paved the way for National Socialism.[48] Benn's advocacy of certain kinds of modernism included delivering a much publicized address at the opening of the Italian *Aeropittura* exhibition in Berlin in 1934. Shortly thereafter, on 29 March 1934, he spoke at an event sponsored by the Union of German Writers. With his remarks published in the newspaper *Deutsche Allgemeine Zeitung*, he praised Marinetti and the Futurists for their boldness and efforts at spiritual renewal, as well as for their embrace of the instinctual elements in life.[49] During the early years of the Third Reich, Benn also engaged other German modernists and discussed ways that they might move forward together. Wilhelm Furtwängler, for example, sought him out in July 1933, with the conductor writing how he wished to discuss "spiritual" (*geistig*) matters; and Benn corresponded with Oskar Schlemmer about aesthetic issues in 1933 and 1934.[50] Schlemmer posed the question to Benn in an October 1933 missive, "Entirely and especially unclear is the matter of the visual arts: What then?"[51] While Benn did not have the answer sought by the painter, he showed sympathy for freedom of expression in a formalistic or stylistic sense, even as he called for restrictions on the ideas themselves.

Like many other cultural figures, Benn hoped that he would find a place in the new Reich, and there were perhaps more solid grounds for hope among writers than among almost any other branch of the arts. Peter Paret has noted, "Among non-Jewish writers a relatively large number with stronger-than-average talent were accepted by the regime—Gerhart Hauptmann, Agnes Miegel, Ernst Jünger, and Hans Carossa come to mind. Some of them had not moved far beyond the late achievements of naturalism. Others—notably Gottfried Benn—worked within the broad current of European modernism."[52] In addition to the array of talented writers with modernist inclinations, there was the fact that Hitler, although an avid reader with a massive library that eventually counted some sixteen thousand volumes, did not approach literary texts with the same passion as he did the visual arts, architecture, or even music.[53] As noted earlier, Hitler's assertiveness in the area of visual arts policy proved crucial to the resolution of the Expressionism debate.

Despite Benn's hopefulness, his romance with the regime did not last long. In June 1934, he was replaced as head of the poetry section of the Prussian Academy by Hans Friedrich Blunck, a Nazi stalwart and literary hack. To Benn's credit, his support for the National Socialists evaporated quickly. He was particularly appalled by the violence of the Night of the Long Knives in late June 1934. Toward the end of August 1934, for example, he wrote to his friend, poet Ina Seidel, "I live with completely pinched lips, inwardly and outwardly. I cannot go along anymore. Certain things recently gave the final push. Horrible tragedy!"[54] A month later, he wrote to Ina Seidel once again, expressing his disillusionment—or more specifically, his realization that certain ideals were unrealizable: "[Nietzsche's] blonde beast, its breeding chapter [*Züchtungskapitel*] still but a dream of the unity of spirit and power. That is past."[55] He recognized that the regime was unlikely to change and accept his Expressionist poetry. Theater historian William Niven, who studied the Nazi regime's suppression of the cultic "*Thing*-Plays" in 1935–36, noted how these performances contained Expressionist tendencies which threatened the regime. The *Thing*-Plays featured types, rather than individuals, an "anti-materialist thrust," and an "ecstatic asser-tiveness," and threatened to provoke social criticism and general disorder.[56] Although Hitler and his cohort glorified the irrational forces in the world and sought to exploit them for their own purposes, they also regarded them with some trepidation, fearing they could threaten the regime. In certain ways, the expressionistic *Thing*-Plays were like SA leader Ernst Röhm: while an important part of the early Nazi movement, Röhm represented turmoil and a challenge to Hitler's authority, and had to be removed.

Gottfried Benn's disaffection from the Nazi regime occurred in the wake of the Röhm purge. An early manifestation of his alienation appeared while the poet was on holiday in the Alpine town of Oberstdorf in the All-gäu in October 1934. He penned a poem titled "Am Brückenwehr" (On the Bridge), which opened with the lines

I have thought broadly,
Now I leave the things
and loosen the rings
of the new power.[57]

His disaffection from the regime had proceeded slowly, almost incremen-tally. Back in June 1934, he had written to his friend Waldemar Bonsels about having represented Hanns Johst at a meeting of the Union of Ger-man Writers, "I am not very interested in social and propagandistic things, am a 'private thinker,' and step forward unwillingly [onto the stage], but if one today is committed to work today, one must do it."[58] The spring of 1934 had also brought allegations that Benn was Jewish (he was not). Some thought his name was connected to the Hebrew *Ben* (son), which it was not. He responded to one denunciation of his racial origins by protesting that his father and grandfathers had been Protestant ministers, as was one of his brothers.[59] His art, of course, also came under attack, with certain critics objecting that his writings were "criminally indecent and immoral."[60] Although Benn did not detail all the reasons for his break from the regime, the persecution he experienced personally, when combined with the vio-lence of the Röhm Purge, lay at the heart of the matter.

Benn therefore sought a way out, and looked to his training as a physician as the means to embark on his own form of inner emigration. In November 1934, he applied for a position as a physician for the municipality in Berlin—the city where he had lived for thirty years (with the exception of World War I). However, Benn received a reply so curt as to be insulting. The response from the authorities read, "No openings. Enclosed documents returned." Benn's re-

Gottfried Benn as an army staff doctor
in 1935. Benn viewed the military as
an "aristocratic form of emigration."
(Deutsches Literaturarchiv, Marbarch)

sponse to these attacks, as he noted in a letter to Ina Seidel, was to lament, "Oh holy heart of the people, oh fatherland!"[61] The poet and physician therefore decided that joining the armed forces was the most honorable path. He enlisted in the army and, as of 1 January 1935, was appointed chief staff physician. In a later attempt to distance himself from the Nazified Wehrmacht, he claimed that he had been in the Ersatz-Offizierkorps, or replacement officer corps— most of whom were veterans where "the old Prussian principles of service prevailed." Benn maintained after 1945 that members of the regular army did not treat the Ersatz-Offizierkorps as equals and were reluctant to salute, and there is an element of truth to this account. But mythmaking factored into his thinking from the very outset as he dramatized his actions. Benn wrote to Ina Seidel about his decision to abandon writing as a profession: "One couldn't continue morally or economically; I had to release myself from all associations. It is an aristocratic form of emigration. Not an easy decision!"[62] Yet Benn, as J. M. Ritchie noted, "never publicly retracted or openly attacked the National Socialist regime."[63]

Thus began a ten-year stint as a military physician, with Benn spending the first two years stationed in Hannover. Compared to Berlin, Hannover seemed decidedly provincial and Benn missed the great Berlin library, the Staatsbibliothek, then situated on Unter den Linden. Benn wrote at the time how "I moved to an alien city, live like a student in a single room; the desk is not large; I cannot begin extensive work."[64] Benn actually resided in several single-room dwellings during his time in Hannover, but the point was that he chose to live an ascetic and private existence. A variety of invitations came from abroad—to write a piece on German Romanticism for the French periodical *Les Cahiers du Cinéma,* and to contribute to a literary magazine published in Tokyo, for example—but he largely limited himself to poetry, essays, and memoirs that he kept to himself. The year 1936 saw the publication of seventy-five selected poems from the years 1911 to 1936, so he was not completely absent from the public sphere prior to 1937. A second edition of the volume appeared shortly thereafter.

Despite his attempt to avoid conflict with the regime, Nazi radicals pursued Benn. On the occasion of his fiftieth birthday in 1936 and the appearance of the above-noted volume of selected poems, the SS paper *Das Schwarze Korps* ran a particularly vicious article labeling Benn's work as "degenerate" and "Jewish" and deriding Benn himself as a homosexual; other phrases included "obscenities contrary to nature" and "mental enfeeblement" (*Geistesverblödung*). The anonymous author also railed, "Give it up, poet Benn; the time for such obscenities has finally passed."[65] The following year, in July 1937, Wolfgang Willrich published a high-profile book titled *Die Säuberung des Kunsttempels* (*The Cleansing of the Art Temple*). This racially charged polemic came from a painter who identified with the völkisch faction of the Nazi Party and played a leading role agitating for the purge of German museums. Willrich attacked a wide range of modernists, including Ernst Barlach, Otto Dix, and George Grosz. He also included excerpts from Benn's poetry in this self-proclaimed "attack piece" (the word *Kampfschrift* figured into the book's subtitle). Willrich reproduced a stanza from Benn's volume of poetry *Twilight of Humanity* and concluded,

> It was conjointly a synthesis of consciously Bolshevist literature, created under the influence of the young generation of left-wing artists. No wonder that the imaginative brains and easily titillated temperament were often overtaxed. The debilitating awareness of a destructive literature was extended through the futuristic, dadaistic poems and prose with the purpose of unpolitical nonsense in the brains bred through a protracted carnival warble.[66]

Benn, who described Willrich as "an obscure dilettante who painted heroes and wheat-blonde women," later recalled, "I was now completely purged from this temple [and called] a cultural bolshevist, a race-defiler."[67]

A curious denouement occurred when Heinrich Himmler intervened on Benn's behalf. The Reichsführer-SS reprimanded Willrich, who was a member of the SS. In a September 1937 letter to Willrich, Himmler began by saying he "was well acquainted with the case of Benn," pointed out that Benn had behaved in an honorable manner in the years since 1933, and noted that he had "forbidden all his offices from becoming involved in matters concerning Benn."[68] Himmler had been influenced by Hanns Johst, the president of the Reich Chamber for Literature and head of the Union International Writers. Johst, who had once composed in an Expressionist style and who held the rank of SS colonel (Oberführer) and counted among Himmler's favorites (he addressed letters "Mein Reichsführer, lieber Heini Himmler!"). Johst was also a close friend of Benn's, and the latter frequently turned to him when the attacks intensified in the mid-1930s. The head of the Chamber for Literature was fanatical in other respects (harassing one writer for engaging a Jewish secretary) but nonetheless evinced sympathy for Benn. Himmler advised Willrich "that it would be more prudent for him 'to continue painting decent pictures' than to pry into people's pasts."[69]

Although Himmler had intervened on his behalf, others in the National Socialist state persisted in their attacks against Benn. Hermann Göring, who had authority over the Prussian Academy due to his position as Prussian Minister President, approached Joseph Goebbels about Benn in early 1938 and expressed his concerns about the poet. Goebbels responded by personally ordering the expulsion of Benn from the Reich Chamber for Literature, a step undertaken without the knowledge of Johst.[70] This meant, of course, that Benn was not permitted to publish or publicly engage in related professional activities. Johst, who wrote to Himmler in March 1938 protesting the Propaganda Minister's unilateral action against Benn, suspected that "an art historian, whom you had previously ordered to remain quiet," was behind the order.[71] Johst therefore assigned the blame to Wolfgang Willrich, who had emerged as a prominent figure in the effort to purge modernist art from German museums.

Despite being expelled from the Chamber for Literature, Benn kept on writing, much like proscribed artists who continued to paint. He had returned to Berlin from Hannover in July 1937—the same time that Willrich's book appeared and the *Degenerate Art Exhibition* had commenced its two-year run—and found consolation in his personal life. His first wife, Edith, had died tragically in 1922 in the wake of a gall bladder operation, and although the writer had romantic interests in the intervening years, his relationship with Herta von Wedemeyer rose to an entirely different level.

Wedemeyer was an attractive thirty-one-year-old aristocrat with refined sensibilities, and she raised Benn's spirits. The two met in 1936 and soon moved in together in an apartment in the Wilmersdorfer neighborhood. With help from other friends, he found a new medical post in the Reich capital—this time, as a physician on the Staff of the General Command of the Third Army Corps, in which he mostly carried out "routine administrative tasks." By January 1938, the couple had settled into a larger residence in Schöneberg, where he also saw patients on a private basis. They married in January, and this domestic happiness provided an environment where he could carry on writing. He now had his cherished Staatsbibliothek at his disposal and, despite the Nazi regime, could enjoy many of the cosmopolitan offerings of the capital. He maintained an active correspondence, penning letters every day. But he did more than that. Benn wrote to his friend F. W. Oelze in May 1938 that he was about to send along "my last great work, namely, *Das Weinhaus Wolf* [Wolf's Tavern]."[72]

Inspired by a Hannover locale with the same name, *Das Weinhaus Wolf* drew its inspiration from Klaus Mann's novel *Mephisto*, which had first been published in 1936 when Mann was living in exile in Amsterdam. Benn thought that Mann's veiled portrait of actor Gustaf Gründgens suffered from gross inaccuracies ("on no account is he a demonic person"), and that Mann had failed to understand the true nature of National Socialism. Benn noted in a letter to his friend, the actor Elinor Büller, "the simple-mindedness, the hate for culture, the pronounced mediocrity, the hate for all that is different. That is something that only a resident of the country, someone who remained, can see and portray."[73] Although Benn saved his harshest words about the regime for his personal correspondence—some of which remained in private papers until 2010—he painted a bleak picture of humanity in *Das Weinhaus Wolf*. Benn wrote, "Peoples who see the spirit only in historic victories and successful frontier-crossings are of low race. Peoples who allow the spirit in all its manifestations to rise to the sphere of creativeness are high-bred. So what counts is the sphere of the creative!"[74] Later in the piece, employing an aphoristic rhetorical technique, he quoted a Chinese proverb, "He who rides a tiger cannot dismount," concluding, "No one can now see history as anything but the justification of mass murder: rapine and glorification—there's the mechanism of power." In *Das Weinhaus Wolf*, Benn showed that he had not abandoned his modernist literary style. The prose is choppy, disjointed, and awkwardly self-conscious, and it contains a dream sequence, as the narrator sits in the drab tavern and beholds "a very quiet animal-keeper [leading] white-skinned human creatures around in a circle until they became discolored. Then he pried open their jaws and yelled 'spirit or life!'"[75] Of course, this book did not see the light of day during the Third Reich—it wasn't published until 1949—but it was an important element of what Benn called his *Doppelleben,* or double-life.

During the war, Benn had to conform to the restrictions imposed by life as a functionary in the military. He had noted earlier, just after rejoining the army, "Know what form is: seconds, commas, millimeters!"[76] But he was able to devote time to his poetry and essays. He had little face-to-face contact with other intellectuals, but was nonetheless able to pursue his "double life" of the mind, one at odds with his quotidian day-to-day existence. Even back in the mid-1930s, "He had tried to reestablish contact with those of his former friends who although anti-fascist were still in Germany. Understandably his advances were met with great caution and skepticism."[77] Regardless, Benn continued to engage the ideas of a wide range of contemporary thinkers. His essay "Art and the Third Reich," which he wrote in 1941, discussed figures such as Sergei Diaghilev ("the real founder of the modern stage"), Igor Stravinsky, and Anna Pavlova. In the 1943 essay "World of Expression," he wrote about American writer Thomas Wolfe and Mexican muralist Diego Rivera.[78] The international orientation of his writing stood in marked contrast to the provincialism of Nazi Germany—even of Berlin, where he remained until 1943, and certainly of Landsberg an der Warthe in Brandenburg (today Poland), to which he was evacuated when the capital became too dangerous. But wherever he resided, Benn continued to work. He noted in a letter to his friend F. W. Oelze in May 1942, "Yes, these 10 years have been of the greatest importance to me."[79]

During World War II, Benn, like many other writers, would usually phrase his formulations in a careful manner so that he would lessen the chances for persecution and arrest. For example, in one essay that he penned late in the war that he titled "Novel of the Phenotype," he wrote in the third person about a subject whom he called "the phenotype" (who was representative of his epoch or generation). That it was autobiographical was beyond question. He concluded, for example,

> The preceding consists of the phenotypes impressions, memories, and actions during the three months from 20 March to 2 June 1944—a span of time sufficient for description of his attitude. He was lodged in barracks somewhere in the East, lived on military rations, with two loaves of army bread twice a week, adequate margarine, and a bowl of soup or cabbage twice a day, so that he was well provided for, and

his room overlooked a drill ground, where the generality pursued the trend of their ideas.[80]

In this essay, which was published only in 1950, Benn still talked about "racial types," but he was clearly chastened, and appeared wholly accepting of his ascetic existence. Rather, he focused on observing what was around him in Eastern Europe: for example, "a picture of the Repin school, a wonderfully fat and beautiful woman," he noted at one point, making reference to the nineteenth-century Russian artist.[81]

Like the members of the German army who took photographs to document their involvement with historical events, Benn used his literary skills to capture the world around him. A difference, however, was that many of his contemporaries photographed atrocities—as the famous *Wehrmacht Exhibition* of the late 1990s showed—while Benn focused on more innocuous subjects, such as the onset of spring, or his immediate surroundings, describing his world in 1944 as "a table, a chair, an army cot—the world becomes small and the Alleluia begins."[82] Benn also engaged more esoteric and abstract topics, such as the spirit of history. There was an anti-war animus to his writing—he noted, for example, "that in 1948 there would be a jubilee for the fiftieth year of the machine gun's existence" and referenced the British slaughter of the Sudanese at Omdurman with the Maxim-Nordenfeldt guns, but Benn by and large took care to avoid the more dangerous topics of present-day massacres.[83]

The most critical and subversive of Benn's writings from later in the Third Reich is probably "Double Life," which he also wrote in 1944 (and published in 1950). Here, he noted that "two ranks carry the army in the fifth year of the war, the lieutenants and the field marshals—the rest is detail." He noted how the junior officers had been socialized and indoctrinated in the Hitler Youth: "They have been insulated from parents who still may be cultured, from educators trained in the old sense, from clergymen and humanist circles—in short from culture carriers of any kind—and that in peacetime; thus well-equipped, they consciously, purposefully, and deliberately set out on their Aryan mission of destroying the continent."[84] Such seditious ideas reflected considerable courage—even if he kept his notebooks secret. This essay also included the observation "Art is forbidden, the press exterminated, personal opinion answered with a bullet in the neck—to gauge the space-filling by humans and moral standards, as in civilized countries, was no longer possible on the premises of the Third Reich."[85] Strong words, to be sure, but after his statements and actions in 1933, was this too little too late?

The end of the war added more drama and tragedy to Benn's remarkable life. He and his wife, Herta, who had been allowed to follow him to Landsberg, were forced back to Berlin by the advancing Red Army. Yet the daily bombing and the impending street fighting compelled him once again to send her away from the capital—this time to the town of Neuhaus, in Lower Saxony. In July 1945, well after the end of the fighting, Herta believed that she was trapped in the Soviet zone and, rather than endure a fate at the hands of Soviet soldiers, committed suicide by way of a morphine injection. Benn, ever the survivor (he had endured house-to-house fighting and the threats of fanatical SS officers in the last days of the war), managed to rebound and by the end of 1946 had married for the third time—this time a young dentist named Ilse Kaul. Around this time, Benn reflected on the work of Rainer Maria Rilke, singling out the poet's well-known phrase "Who speaks of victory?—Survival is all!"[86]

Although Benn had attempted to distance himself from the Nazi regime after 1935, the victorious Allies viewed him as an important early supporter of Hitler and therefore put limitations on him in the early postwar years. As J. M. Ritchie noted, "He was on everybody's black-list and attacked particularly for his National Socialist affiliations by other survivors from the Expressionist years, contemporaries like J. R. Becher and Alfred Döblin, who held important positions in East and West Germany respectively."[87] The restrictions did not last long, however, and in 1951 Benn received the prestigious Georg Büchner Prize, an honor that signaled his return to the public sphere, if not his complete rehabilitation. He described the award ceremony in Darmstadt as "a glorious day, one of the most brilliant of my life, completely successful in terms of atmosphere."[88] Yet that same year he declined an invitation to speak at a poetry conference in Belgium, evidently fearing a negative response from other participants.

But the Büchner Prize and the other awards that followed, such as the Cross of Merit of 1952 mentioned at the beginning of this chapter, did a great deal to facilitate his rehabilitation. Benn enjoyed widespread acclaim in his last years and rejoined the broader community of writers. He even attended the Belgian poetry conference in 1952. J. M. Ritchie summed up his postwar career, "After 1945, Gottfried Benn, that other great survivor from the age of Expressionism, offered an exciting mixture of modernism, aestheticism, solipsism and nihilism in his esoteric poetry and dazzling essays."[89] Benn attracted a great deal of attention because he did not deny or conceal his early support for National Socialism. Unlike the literary exiles, he had remained in Germany and witnessed the horrific events of the war;

and his cool, critical perspective resonated with many postwar observers who lived in bombed-out cities with much of the weight of history upon them. J. M. Ritchie noted, "He had always been a sensationally provocative poet and essayist and there is no doubt that he enjoyed what he himself called his 'come back.' The war that raged over him was lively in the extreme, for he fascinated his new public as much by the 'unspeakable' things he said as by the manner in which he said them. In post-war Germany, he became a literary phenomenon of the first order."[90] Benn was unusual in confronting his own past so openly: in his collections of essays, he included the more problematic texts, such as "Answer to the Literary Emigrants," and in his autobiographical reflections he appeared to own up to his political naïveté. The appearance of honesty, combined with his disillusionment— and perhaps even nihilism—struck a chord that resonated with a wider German public. A "Gottfried Benn school" of poetry emerged, one marked by stylistic imitation and a similar approach to ideas; the "school" also fit in well with the increasingly popular existentialist trend in philosophy.[91]

Amid the revival of his career, Benn took time to reflect on "the tragic fate of the German Expressionist generation." In one sense, Benn counted among the victims of this generation: not only did he directly experience two world wars and endure persecution during the Third Reich, but his association with National Socialism also tarnished a great talent. Gottfried Benn, who wrote to almost the very end of his life, died from cancer of the spine on 7 July 1956. In his last poem, "No Mourning," he reaffirmed his dark, cynical worldview, and also his affinity for irony. Just as he was enjoying the fame and adulation associated with his "come-back," he wrote:

We carry in us seeds of all gods
The gene of death and gene of lust,
Who divided them: the words, the objects,
Who mixed them—the pains and the place
Where they end, wood with streams of tears,
For a few short hours, a miserable home.

There can be no mourning. Too far, too vast,
Too far removed now bed and tears,
no No, no Yes.[92]

The poem, which echoes certain ideas of Sigmund Freud—another physician turned cultural critic—places the life of an individual in a grand cosmic context. In such a perspective, all lives appear small. But tighten the focus, and Benn's experiences take on a wholly different significance. As J. M. Ritchie noted, "Benn's life was not an exceptional one, indeed some would argue that his life was more typical than exceptional, typical, that is, of certain intellectual and political developments in Germany between the wars."[93] Gottfried Benn was also sui generis, but his life is undoubtedly instructive in terms of the extremes, the mistakes, and yet the undeniable accomplishments.

7

Ernst Barlach

(1870 Wedel–1938 Rostock)

Ernst Barlach in his studio in Güstrow, Mecklenburg (1935). Behind him are figures for *The Frieze of the Listeners.* (Zentralinstitut für Kunstgeschichte, Munich)

ERNST BARLACH, A brilliant Expressionist artist and author, has been described as "one of the most powerful German sculptors since Riemenschneider"—the Renaissance master known for his elaborate wood carvings.[1] The merits of Barlach's work struck contemporaries with an immediacy that is difficult to overestimate. For example, it speaks volumes that Barlach had his first major exhibition in 1917, and was then elected to the venerable Prussian Academy just two years later in 1919. He won the prestigious Kleist Prize for literature in 1924, a vivid affirmation of his reputation as a dramatist and novelist. The artist was embraced as a modern master by a wide range of observers. More recently, historian Peter Paret stated succinctly that Barlach was "the most important German sculptor of the time."[2] Barlach was not a Nazi. He was not even sympathetic to Hitler or the dictator's cultural-political program. Barlach always identified with the downtrodden and marginalized and had no truck with an ideology of conquest and oppression. But he wanted to remain in his native country and pursue his multifaceted work. Barlach therefore sought accommodation with the Nazis. Because he drew support from a wide range of people—including the pro-modernist wing of the Nazi Party—his aspirations seemed possible, if distinctly optimistic. When Hitler came to power in 1933, the artist knew he would face difficulties, but he tried nonetheless to carve out a space in the Third Reich.

Although Ernst Barlach's rise to fame came quickly, it would be incorrect to say that he lacked training or was simply a naïve artist. He had studied art for three years at the Hamburg Arts and Crafts School (Kunstgewerbeschule) in the late 1880s, followed by four years at the Royal Academy of Fine Arts in Dresden. His development was further aided by study trips to Paris on two occasions between 1895 and 1897, where he attended the Académie Julian, and to Berlin in the years that followed. His early work had a *Jugendstil* flavor, but he also explored woodblock prints that had a more "primitive" quality to them. In 1906 Barlach experienced a transformative journey to Russia, as his work began to take on an Expressionistic quality. Even after returning to Germany, Barlach continued to depict Russian subjects—beggars and peasants, whom he viewed as "symbols of the human condition in its nakedness between heaven and earth."[3] The illustrious Berlin dealer Paul Cassirer represented Barlach after 1907. The contract he extended the artist afforded Barlach greater freedom to work where he wished, and in 1909 it facilitated his acceptance of the Villa Romana Prize in Florence. Barlach spent a year in Tuscany working and also walking the countryside, often in the company of poet Theodor Däubler. Upon his return to Germany in 1910, Barlach retreated to the town of Güstrow in Mecklenburg, where he led a simple life and devoted himself to his work. Barlach would make trips to Berlin, and in 1913 he was elected to the board of the Berlin Secession. But again, he withheld most of his work from the public and was forty-seven years old when Cassirer gave him his first retrospective exhibition in 1917.

Barlach himself expressed sophisticated, complex views that were prone to misinterpretation. For example, in 1895 while studying in Paris he had declared, "Long live the victorious German spirit!" Historian Peter Paret explains that the artist merely intended to encourage his German compatriots to develop styles of their own, and not to imitate the French: "Nothing was further from his mind than apportioning aesthetic quality according to racial or national identity."[4] In this way, he was reminiscent of Johann Gottfried von Herder, who a century earlier had sought to appreciate national distinctions, but not to value one over another. However, the phrasing of the formulation above—with the invocation of nation and victory— could later be construed in a way that would be consistent with the rhetoric of the Nazi regime. Others viewed Barlach through the prism of national identity as well. French sculptor Aristide Maillol once said to him, "Tu es Nordique—moi, je suis Mediterrané."[5] Some observers regarded Barlach as a *Niederdeutscher* (Lower German) in the tradition made popular by nineteenth-century cultural critic Julius Langbehn, who had waxed rhapsodically about Rembrandt as an artist in touch with his Nordic soul. This was similar to the view of art historian Paul Fechter, who produced a 1936 book on Barlach's drawings. Despite a racialistic argument on Barlach's behalf, Fechter's book was confiscated by the Bavarian Political Police. Throughout the Third Reich, local officials would take it upon themselves to seize editions or close exhibitions, even though similar events passed without noticeable difficulty on other occasions. Barlach attracted additional atten tion for his war memorials, which many interpreted as pacifist and hence seditious, and it did not help that he identified with the Russian people and often featured them in his work.

But, as noted above, many contemporary observers viewed him as a quintessentially German artist. Barlach had explored the art of woodblock prints while in his forties—just before World War I—and for many, woodblock prints harkened back to an earlier tradition of German old masters and to a folk culture of arts and crafts. That Barlach illustrated works of Weimar classicism, including the *Niebelungen Lied*, Goethe's *Faust*, and Schiller's *Ode to Joy*, also emphasized the Germanic quality of his art. Oftentimes he drew on everyday life in small German towns, which many observers (and many Nazis) viewed as distinctively German. Barlach himself wrote in a 1936 essay titled "When I Was Threatened with the Prohibition to Work in My Profession," that he saw himself as "an artist of German birth and roots" and added, "I know that I belong nowhere else than in the place in which I have worked until now. And because I am accused of being an alien, I want to claim a better, stronger, far deeper association with the land of my birth."[6] His file for the Reich Chamber of Culture, of which he was a member, shows him complying with the authorities by filling out, in April 1937, a questionnaire on which the artist attested that he was "Aryan." Even before this, in January 1934, when there were vague rumblings from certain agitators in the anti-modern faction that Barlach was Jewish, he submitted his "Aryan" family tree to the local Mecklenburg newspaper, which published it as proof of his "German" origins.[7]

The stylistic and thematic qualities of Barlach's work also provided grounds for hope that it would be tolerated by the Nazis. In terms of his writing, he often focused on nonpolitical subjects such as the relationship between father and son (*The Dead Day* from 1912 and *The Poor Cousin* from 1918), or on the struggle between the material world and the spiritual (*The Blue Boll* from 1926 and *The Good Time* from 1929).[8] And while his art had been represented in the Berlin Nationalgalerie starting in December 1918—that is, with the advent of the Weimar Republic—he did not conjure images of decadence, sexuality, and transgressive behavior so often associated with Weimar culture. Peter Paret noted, "It is hard to imagine an artist whose work was farther removed from the metropolis and all it represents than Barlach, and the openly erotic is absent from his sculpture."[9] The artist tended to create figures cloaked in robes and other garments as compared to those displaying the naked body. One can point to works like *The Dreamer* (from *The Frieze of the Listeners*) of 1931 or *Reading Monks* from 1932: both works

Barlach's illustration for Goethe's *Faust*. (Zentralinstitut für Kunstgeschichte, Munich)

feature Christian motifs, but the "temperature" is very low for work that was
supposedly seditious. Peter Paret added that "deformation and distortion
. . . are certainly found in many of his figures, but they cannot be said to
dominate his work as a whole."[10] Barlach's art was figurative, and in general
he avoided "radical distortion." Even critics like Alfred Rosenberg acknowledged that Barlach's work exhibited a marked technical facility.

Fritz Klimsch and Georg Kolbe, who were peers of Barlach's and fellow members of the pre–World War I Berlin Secession, enjoyed successful
careers during the Third Reich. Granted, their works were not quite as Expressionistic as Barlach's, but even Barlach has been viewed by scholars as
"near, but at the edge of Expressionism."[11] The same applied to his writing,
as he objected to being associated with any literary movement, especially
Expressionism. True, the Nazis took down certain early monuments Kolbe

had created, but this was not for stylistic reasons; rather, the interventions came about because of the subject matter, and most notably because he had portrayed Jewish subjects such as Heinrich Heine or Emil and Walther Rathenau. Kolbe had also collaborated with Mies van der Rohe on the Barcelona Pavilion in 1929, helping create the iconic modernist exhibit. Yet Kolbe not only was able to exhibit during the Third Reich, but benefited from Hitler's personal patronage: for example, the purchase of a statue of a young woman for the considerable sum of RM 18,000 ($7,200) in the mid-1930s.[12] Both Kolbe and Klimsch also received prestigious awards—the former the Goethe Medal and the latter the more exalted Eagle Plaque of the Reich—and both were listed as "irreplaceable artists" during the war (in light of their advanced age, the designation was intended as honorific).

In terms of politics, Barlach's personal history raised few problems. He was a veteran of World War I, where he had served in the army. Granted, his tenure in the infantry had lasted for only a few months. He was already forty-four in 1914 and suffered from an irregular heartbeat. But Barlach answered the call to arms—initially as a medic before being conscripted into the infantry. At this point, he was anything but a pacifist. The slaughter that ensued made him critical of the war in its later years, but he had done his patriotic duty and subsequently counted himself a veteran.[13] Barlach had never been a member of the Communist or Social Democratic Party. He had not been active in any of the left-wing artists groups that flourished in the early years of the Weimar Republic (for example, the Novembergruppe). His political views have been described by his biographer Peter Paret as "moderately liberal, with conservative tendencies"—although art historian James van Dyke has placed him further to the right and shown that Barlach had once evinced considerable sympathy for the ideas of Arthur Möller van den Bruck and his "conservative revolution."[14] Van den Bruck penned the important 1923 book *The Third Reich*, where he espoused nationalist ideas in a manner that inspired the Nazis to appropriate the phrase. Barlach belonged to the *Bildungsbürgertum,* or educated middle class, where nationalistic views were not uncommon. The artist also voted for the conservative war hero Paul von Hindenburg in the 1932 presidential elections.

Besides the support expressed by the Nazi students, there were other developments in early 1933 that gave Barlach hope that his work would find a place in the new Reich. Shortly after the seizure of power, he was awarded the Order Pour le mérite, a highly prestigious honor that was voted by the members of the Prussian Academy (albeit without purged members such as Käthe Kollwitz and Heinrich Mann). Two of his sculptures were included in an exhibition of ecclesiastical art at the Chicago World Fair in May 1933 (along with the work of Emil Nolde, among others), and he had other pieces featured in the German pavilion at the Venice Biennale of 1934. The director of the Berlin Nationalgalerie, Eberhard Hanfstaengl, along with sculptor and professor Josef Wackerle, had curated the German entry to the Venice exhibition. This was an important international event, and the German pavilion was subject to official scrutiny. Even Hitler, who visited the exhibition in June 1934, appeared to give his tacit assent to what he saw.[15] Curators at the Berlin Nationalgalerie continued to acquire his works through 1935: the sculpture *Traveler in Repose* (1910), for example, was bought by the Dresdner Bank and donated to the museum, and an anonymous patron gave six additional drawings.[16] Barlach's plays were also still performed in the early years of the Third Reich. For example, in March 1934 a theater on the outskirts of Hamburg staged twelve performances of his tragicomedy *The Blue Boll.*

Even Barlach's defeats could be viewed as having certain silver linings. In the case of the famed anti-war monument that he had executed for the Magdeburg Cathedral in 1929, a board representing the church decided to remove the sculpture from the Protestant cathedral early in the Third Reich; but it was transferred, according to the postwar restitution officer Kurt Reutti, to the Nationalgalerie.[17] Among Barlach's works, the Magdeburg Cathedral *Ehrenmal,* which depicted a coterie of soldiers and clergy standing in a cemetery, elicited the strongest criticism. Alfred Rosenberg fumed about "the small, half-idiotically staring, mixed variants of indefinable human types in Soviet helmets"—but the sculpture evidently remained in the Nationalgalerie until the 1937 purge of "degenerate art," when the artist's friend and dealer Bernhard Böhmer acquired it via the Reich Propaganda Ministry.[18] Böhmer safeguarded the work up to his death in 1945, and it was returned to the Magdeburg Cathedral after the war.

It was indeed his public monuments in the 1920s that created the greatest difficulties for Barlach. He explored the themes of suffering and death, but not in a heroic or uplifting manner. Rather, his sculptures expressed overwhelming fear or profound grief and sorrow felt by the subjects. His monuments often constituted poignant anti-war statements and were interpreted accordingly by observers. Barlach was prolific and designed many memorials during the Weimar Republic—too many to list here. Among the most famous were those in Güstrow, Kiel, Cologne, Hamburg, Lübeck, Schwerin, and of course Magdeburg—although not all were technically war memorials. His works became iconic during the Weimar Republic, and indeed, his close association with the Republic was a primary reason he came under attack from certain National Socialists. Peter Paret has observed, "Barlach may not have realized that he made political statements!—but it is not surprising that people who rejected these works did so largely on political grounds. It was not their formal attributes that offended many Germans, but their message."[19] The responses to his work were often extreme, as with the famous *Hovering Angel* from the Güstrow Cathedral, which was melted down in the later 1930s.

The Nazis indeed attacked him on many fronts, ranging from rebuking him for the pacifist messages they saw in his works to persecuting his Jewish dealers Paul Cassirer and Alfred Flechtheim. One historian noted, "His pacifist—some said defeatist—themes, which were considered an insult to the German spirit, and his frequent portrayal of 'inferior racial types' earned him inclusion in the *Entartete Kunst Exhibition.*"[20] There were also (unfounded) rumors that he was Jewish or Slavic. Barlach himself realized even prior to the Nazi seizure of power that he would likely face difficult times ahead. He had experienced right-wing opposition to his work in the 1920s, noting, for example, in 1928 as he created a bronze statue for the University Church in Kiel, "All right-wing parties join in the fight."[21] Later, in 1931, Nazi activists had mobilized to protest a war memorial he planned for Hamburg. In 1932, storm troopers broke the windows at his studio in Güstrow. Located in the conservative province of Mecklenburg-Schwerin, Güstrow had many residents who felt uncomfortable with Barlach's work: insulting notes and signs posted on his door were common fare for the artist. On 26 January 1933, he wrote his friend Hugo Sieker, "We feel we are sitting on a volcano. . . . The nationalist terror will probably outlast me . . . storm signals everywhere."[22] In short, the artist was no stranger to the attacks from the *völkisch* lobby, and part of him believed he could weather the storm. Barlach often adopted a fatalistic attitude, writing, for example, to pro-Expressionist museum director Alois Schardt in 1934, "It is important to recognize that in these cases [of attacks] that there is nothing one can do; it must remain as it is."[23] Of course, the attacks against Barlach intensified after 1933. Theater managers broke agreements to stage his plays, and plans for exhibitions of his work were scrapped. Granted, at first many of his opponents were reluctant to come forward. Barlach wrote in May 1933, "I am being robbed of my livelihood, but no one wants to have done it, no one admits responsibility. The canine cowardliness of this glorious age makes one blush to the tip of one's ears at the thought of being German."[24] Later, the regime censored his mail and put surveillance teams at his home.

Yet, as noted earlier, Barlach was not without supporters in the Nazi regime—beginning with Goebbels. Regardless of whether the Reich Propaganda Minister owned one or two of the artist's sculptures, the presence of Barlach's work in his office constituted a ringing endorsement. And if *Man in Storm* stood on or near Goebbels's desk, as was reported, this was an even bolder gesture. Goebbels also personally signed off on the inclusion of Barlach's work in the exhibition at the Chicago World Exposition of 1933 and the Venice Biennale the following year. Furthermore, Barlach received two grants from foundations that directed money to him through the Prussian Academy. Considering that the Academy, like nearly every organization in Germany, was being Nazified, these subventions conveyed a measure of official support. The artist also had four of his sculptures "prominently placed" in the *Berliner Kunst* exhibition at the Neue Pinakothek in Munich in 1935.[25] In June of that year, Barlach's friend, dealer, and assistant, Bernhard Böhmer, wrote to Goebbels, seeking the minister's support for the artist. Böhmer cited the Chicago and Venice exhibitions as evidence that Barlach fit into the new Reich. He added that Barlach was knight (Ritter) of the Order Pour le Mérite, in good standing with the Reich Chamber for the Visual Arts, and also a member of the writers' association, the Bund deutscher Schriftsteller, which had been Nazified early in the Third Reich.[26] Böhmer also approached Professor Alexander Langsdorff, a prominent art historian and "close associate of Himmler" who in 1935 promised to support Barlach.[27] Böhmer continued his dialogue with Langsdorff through at least the spring of 1936. Although the latter had influence—as a member of the Gestapo, Leader of External Relations for the Berlin State Museums, and Himmler's "very close friend"—it is unclear to what extent Langsdorff actually assisted the artist.[28] The same can be said for the Propaganda Ministry's Rolf Hetsch, who oversaw the Berlin warehouses of the purged "degenerate" art and lobbied on behalf of Barlach with considerable vigor.[29]

Because Barlach was a war veteran and had powerful supporters in the Nazi Party, his opponents had to tread more carefully than they did with many other modernist artists. In this way, he was much like Franz Marc and August Macke, who both fell on the field of battle in World War I. Even the purging committee viewed him as a "tragic case" and tried to spare his sculptures. Only two of Barlach's sculptures were actually included in the *Degenerate Art Exhibition,* which speaks to the ambivalence felt by many.

Yet the organizers of the show included his work *Christ and John the Baptist* from the Kiel Museum, and the 1926 sculpture *The Reunion,* going so far as to describe the former in the panel texts as "the portrayal of two monkeys in nightshirts."[30] They also included in a vitrine a copy of a book of his drawings. Despite the defamatory panel texts, the works did not have the desired effect on many viewers. One Swiss woman, for example, came forward and attempted to purchase the sculpture. As with Franz Marc's paintings (including his *Tower of the Blue Horses,* which found its way to Göring but disappeared at war's end), Barlach's art was removed from the exhibition once it left Munich to travel to other venues in the Reich. Barlach's works were among those sold off by the Propaganda Ministry in the wake of the purging of state collections. Seven sculptures were put up for sale at the Fischer Lucerne auction of "paintings and sculptures of modern masters from German museums."[31] The liquidation program in fact showed there was an international market for his art, and also helped support the four dealers who were charged with the sales; they received a 25 percent commission.

Peter Paret's fine study of Barlach's late years is titled *An Artist Against the Third Reich,* but it would be more appropriate to say that this was yet another instance of the Third Reich against an artist. Paret himself noted, "Because Barlach was not a Jew and had not been politically active in the Weimar Republic, the new men in power might have shrugged him off as an unimportant survivor of an earlier age."[32] Barlach sincerely believed that his art should be a part of the culture of the new, revived Germany. This belief underpinned the request that he made to his friend Friedrich Dross to compile a family tree showing that Barlach had no Jewish ancestry. Like Emil Nolde, both of his parents hailed from the borderlands between Schleswig and Denmark (but also maintained he had "pure Lower Saxon blood").[33] The family tree was put at the disposal of Alfred Hentzen, a curator at the Nationalgalerie, who used it to reassure others that the artist was not Jewish. Back in the summer of 1933, the head of the Nationalgalerie's division for modern art, Alois Schardt, had implemented a policy of providing proof of "Aryan" ancestry for the artists exhibited in the museum, Barlach among them.

The sculptor also had other patrons who helped sustain him in the difficult years after 1933. The most notable was Hermann Reemstma, who visited Barlach in Güstrow for the first time in August 1934. Reemstma, who was a member of the Hamburg-based cigarette dynasty that offered massive financial support to the Nazis (and most infamously to Göring), was enthralled with what he found in Barlach's atelier, and immediately purchased a wood sculpture from 1925 titled *The Ascetic.* A short time later, Reemstma provided financial support for *Frieze of the Listeners,* a project that engrossed the artist at the time. By the time of Barlach's death in 1938, Reemstma had purchased some twenty sculptures, as well as nearly one hundred drawings. Today, these and other works are housed at the Ernst Barlach House in Hamburg, a museum that opened after Reemstma's death in 1961.[34] Another patron, dealer Alexander Vömel, who had "Aryanized" Alfred Flechtheim's Düsseldorf gallery in 1933, exhibited Barlach's works, which were also available for purchase. Although the sales records are not extant, one exhibition in May 1937 at Vömel's gallery featured not only works by Barlach and Lehmbruck, but also a Hitler bust by Arno Breker. This was likely part of Vömel's strategy to keep the show open. The previous year, an exhibition in Hamburg, called *Painting and Sculpture in Germany 1936,* included Barlach's works, as well as those by Otto Dix, Max Beckmann, and others, although local authorities closed the show after only ten days.[35] The larger point remains that, despite considerable difficulties, Barlach was able to sell works up until his death. Munich dealer Günther Franke recalled after the war that "during the years of ostracization," he had bought "a number of bronze figures and colored plaster models" from Barlach, although, he noted, "a personal meeting with the artist never occurred."[36] Barlach appeared not to have a great deal of money during these years, but he certainly had enough to continue his work.

An empathetic and soulful human being, Ernst Barlach inspired a number of his creative cohort, and they sought to help him out in various ways. The wealthy aristocratic painter Leo von König, who rendered Barlach's portrait on two occasions in 1937, helped with financial subventions. Von König was not the only one to paint his portrait. Emil Nolde had also captured Barlach's expressive face late in his life. With regard to one of König's portraits, author Jochen Klepper noted in his diary on 14 September 1937,

> Now, following Nolde, König has painted Barlach, and by doing so, their destruction in Germany through the *'Degenerate Art' Exhibition.* These fallen ones at least give one solace that his face is preserved for his afterlife by the best painters. In the Barlach portrait resides, at the end, all the wounded anguish of the old spiritual man, before the dawning of this new time.[37]

The artist, then, emerged as a symbol for certain contemporaries—a sad, even tragic symbol who represented an earlier, better time. The fact that he wanted to work in the "new" Germany only heightened such perceptions. Previously, in 1936, his counterparts in Vienna had elected him an honorary member at both Secession and the Artists' Association of Austrian Sculptors, gestures meant to help him to continue working.

Barlach was deeply dismayed by the attacks he incurred. When Robert Scholz, the chief art critic of the Nazi Party newspaper, penned articles assailing him in 1933, Barlach responded, "The *Völkischer Beobachter* has violently vomited on me."[38] This emotional response reveals that the artist cared about the criticism—even when leveled by ardent Nazis—and that he worried about his reputation more generally. Barlach also responded by going into a kind of inner emigration. As he wrote to a sympathetic Margarete Havemann in March 1934, "The only thing I can think of doing is to isolate myself as much as possible."[39] This meant that he often declined invitations to exhibit his works, and communicated by having trusted friends deliver sensitive letters. He reportedly went so far as to burn potentially sensitive documents.

This wish to find acceptance, or at least tolerance, in Nazi Germany contributed to his decision to sign the petition of August 1934 endorsing Hitler's self-invented title of Führer. Peter Paret has described Barlach's decision to sign the petition as "the one misstep in his encounter with National Socialism."[40] Barlach evidently first refused to sign the "Declaration for Adolf Hitler!," but when an official in the Reich Propaganda Ministry telephoned him and not only expressed admiration for Barlach's work, but also listed other signatories (including Mies van der Rohe, Benn, Nolde, and Heckel), the sculptor relented. Barlach told his brother that he hoped this would stop people from labeling him a cultural Bolshevist. Because the signatories of the petition were listed alphabetically, Barlach's name came second, making it especially prominent. Goebbels's agents had apparently not wanted Barlach's name at the very top of the list and therefore approached Werner Beumelberg, "a popular author of novels glorifying war and patriotic sacrifice."[41] (Never mind that "Beumelberg" came after "Barlach" alphabetically, it was close enough to deceive most observers.) Alfred Rosenberg and others in the völkisch faction were dismayed by the inclusion of "those [against] whom we have waged a total cultural-political war for years."[42] But it also did little for the signatories and their supporters. Paret also concluded with regard to Barlach, "Although no more than a symbolic gesture given under duress, signing the appeal marred his record of detachment from National Socialism, and his rejection of it, and was a mistake even from the perspective of immediate self-interest, for it did nothing to bring the attacks on him to a halt."[43]

But again, the situation was far from clear-cut for Barlach in the mid-1930s. In 1934, the Association for Church Art elected Barlach as the Honorary President, a sign that certain admirers remained steadfast in their support. Many of Barlach's works in the mid-1930s continued to feature religious themes. He produced baptismal basins up until his death, and sculptures with biblical subjects such as *The Sinner II* and *The Believer* from 1934. As part of the Nazis' coordination measures, the Association for Church Art was absorbed into the Reich Chamber of Culture. This created a situation in which Barlach had no real power but nonetheless served as a symbol—for supporters and opponents as well. Alfred Rosenberg wrote to Goebbels in October 1934, complaining that Barlach's presidency "actually means a strengthening of the artistic direction that we are fighting and not the promotion of the National Socialist cultural viewpoint."[44] In 1936, Eberhard Hanfstaengl, the director of the Nationalgalerie, opened a new room devoted exclusively to Barlach's work (there was one for sculptor Wilhelm Lehmbruck too).[45] Barlach remained a member of the Prussian Academy until July 1937. His series the *Frieze of the Listeners,* which was being supported by Hermann Reemstma, who had commissioned another six figures to complete the ensemble, also received positive resonance.

Barlach's friend and former student Bernhard Böhmer also played a key role in the artist's later life. Böhmer had moved to Güstrow in the mid-1920s and continued to help his mentor in the studio, but in the early years of the Third Reich he became an art dealer. Böhmer developed connections to influential Party members and had written to the Reich Propaganda Ministry in the autumn of 1934, requesting official permission for Barlach to proceed with the commission from Hermann Reemtsma to continue with *Frieze of the Listeners.* Böhmer received a response from Goebbels's aides on 22 October 1934 that there were "no objections whatsoever," which gave the impression that "the ministry approved of the frieze."[46] Böhmer also later served as one of the four principal dealers of the purged "degenerate" art from state collections (along with Ferdinand Möller, Karl Buchholz, and Hildebrand Gurlitt), and during the war he worked as an agent for Goebbels, traveling to the Netherlands, France, and Switzerland to acquire art for the Reich Propaganda Minister. Böhmer's astonishing career in the Third Reich ended in Güstrow on 3 May 1945, when, upon the arrival of the Red Army, he and his wife committed suicide.[47]

Barlach and his allies continued to battle for official acceptance. In late 1935, famed Munich publisher Reinhard Piper, a longtime friend of Barlach's, published a book with fifty-six drawings by the artist, which appeared in an edition of five thousand copies. The Nazi regime immediately banned the book, although it was not entirely clear who had issued the order. Barlach felt secure enough to write Goebbels directly, which he did on 25 May 1936,

> Very honorable Reichsminister . . . I must appeal to you to rescind the confiscation order [for the book of drawings]; and so that this can happen I must first explain, clarify and resolve any misunderstandings, focusing on the points that led to the decision to confiscate. It is impossible to say that the themes portrayed in these works—reader, violinist, song of joy, dancer, two girls finishing a cloth, fisherman, Faust in Walpurgisnacht, flute-player, cold girl, man in a storm, . . . and the like, portraying purely human and timeless conditions, require an intervention to protect the public.[48]

In this May 1936 letter, he requested that the Reich Minister review the confiscation order and said that he believed "the objections were to a few drawings, not to the entire work." He then argued that because his art had recently been praised by certain distinguished museum directors, "one can hardly assume that an artist wins approval in one area of his work, and is subjected to a diametrically opposed judgment in another." He went on to say that if he was told which drawings were regarded as "unusual or even crass," then he would substitute others for them. Barlach concluded the rather obsequious letter by "assuring Goebbels that he trusts in the minister's readiness to acknowledge the reasonableness of his expectations."[49] Barlach also penned a second missive to Goebbels, which he ultimately decided not to send. Goebbels offered no reply to the first letter: he "was not in the habit of justifying his measures either to subordinates or to victims."[50]

Barlach, then, did not view his work as so hostile to the regime that it warranted repression. He communicated this to the most important official for cultural matters, and did so in a way that was not confrontational. Here was an artist trying to find a way to move forward with what he understood to be the most progressive minister in the regime. There have also been reports that Hitler tried to reconcile with Barlach in the summer of 1935. Peter Paret noted that there is no proof for this assertion, and suggested that the rumor arose due to the ongoing efforts of Otto Andreas Schreiber and others who were advancing their pro-modernist agenda.[51] It is probably fair to say that Barlach thought it best to approach Goebbels first before contemplating any further steps. Because he also held out hope that his writing would continue to be published—several books of his appeared during the Third Reich, including the *Güstrow Diaries: Excerpts, 1914–18,* and the posthumously released *Fragments from a Much Earlier Time* (1939) and *Conversations with Barlach* (1939)—he viewed a measure of official acceptance as being of the utmost importance.[52]

Not surprisingly, Barlach's complex relationship with the Nazi regime manifested itself in his work. Earlier in the Third Reich, while he did not abandon his artistic vision out of political expediency, he seemed to moderate the more distinctively Expressionist elements evident in his earlier art. His art from the mid-1930s also communicated a pronounced sense of melancholy (a quality never absent from his work).[53] The theme of resilience also appeared in several forms, such as in *Sitting Old One* from 1933, in which an elderly lady who looks like Käthe Kollwitz sits, staring with a slightly bemused expression. She seems prepared for anything but is quite calm, with her hands folded in her lap. The following year Barlach produced *Wanderer in the Wind* (1934), a wood carving from oak in which the subject keeps his head down as he holds on to his cap with his left hand and grabs his cloak with his right, pulling it closed. *The Bad Year, 1937* features a woman with a shawl, her face in a frown but largely expressionless. She stares out resolutely, with rather masculine features, but at the same time looks guarded, fatalistic, and stoic. Then there is the famous *Laughing Crone* (1937), featuring an old lady who looks delirious, even insane. She pulls back into a hearty laugh, forming a shape with elegant organic lines. Her strong hands are elongated. She has her own response to the situation. Several versions of the bronze exist, but both feature an old woman leaning back, ecstatically, or hysterically, laughing. She appears unbalanced, both figuratively and literally. Many have viewed *Laughing Crone* as an act of protest by an artist in inner-emigration. Peter Paret described it as "the outrageous fantasies of a sculptor bent on insulting the ideals of a new Germany and the aesthetic principles of its leader."[54] It is indeed far from the static, controlled, and heroic state-sponsored sculpture. That said, Barlach rendered these works in a figurative manner. They were not out-and-out subversive based on stylistic considerations. Berlin dealer Karl Buchholz was able to include *Freezing Crone*—the counterpart to *Laughing Crone*— in an exhibition titled *Ernst Barlach's New Works, Sculptures, and Drawings,* which ran from May through June 1937 in Buchholz's gallery on the Leipziger Strasse.[55]

Barlach's sculpture *Freezing Crone* from 1937. (Zentralinstitut für
Kunstgeschichte, Munich)

Although Barlach continued to have his supporters, the onslaught
against him persisted and even intensified. On 26 June 1935 the newspaper of the SS, *Das Schwarze Korps,* published an article characterizing Barlach's work as "of alien blood."[56] The artist's figures carved for the Church
of St. Catherine in Lübeck were removed in 1936; the war memorial for
the Güstrow Cathedral was dismantled in 1937 and melted down; and the
monument in Kiel was cut into three pieces in 1937–38 (these were among
the 381 works by Barlach "purged" from public collections and churches
during the Third Reich).[57] There were other insults and blows that followed:
commissioned works were rejected in Stralsund and Malchin, and the sculptor was denied permission to execute a gravestone for his friend, poet Theodor Däubler. By 1937, Barlach was clearly an artist under attack. As noted

above, some of his work was included in the *Degenerate Art Exhibition* of July 1937 and subsequent defamatory shows, such as the "anti-Bolshevism" exhibition in Nuremberg. He was expelled from the Prussian Academy in 1937 and the Reich Chamber for Literature in September 1938, the latter in principle preventing him from publishing. One also cannot underestimate the impact of the critical views toward him on the part of many locals in Güstrow. He had moved there with his son and his mother in 1910, and the hostility of certain neighbors only added to his alienation.

These broadsides against Barlach—who was a particularly sensitive individual—took a toll on him. He lost his drive to work, and his health deteriorated, with an angina causing him particular difficulty. In late October 1937 Barlach wrote to a friend, a writer who had a Jewish wife, "When day after day one has to expect the threatened deadly blow, work stops by itself. I resemble someone driven into a corner, the pack at his heels."[58] He died in his sixty-ninth year, on 24 October 1938, at the hospital in Rostock. The Nazi regime put restrictions on coverage of his death. This included no memorial plaque at the house where he was born; limitations on press coverage; and a final gratuitous insult in *Das Schwarze Korps,* in which a full page article labeled him "un-German, Slavic, unbalanced, and a lunatic."[59] However, there was an element of the "yes . . . but" in other reviews.[60] And Barlach's two-day funeral—a memorial in Güstrow on 27 October 1938, and the burial near his childhood home in Ratzeburg, Schleswig-Holstein, the following day—provided an opportunity for appreciation. His friend Käthe Kollwitz was among those in attendance. She made one final drawing of Ernst Barlach, a kind of melancholic tribute that emphasized his face and his hands, both rendered in carefully exquisite detail. One can imagine Kollwitz in Güstrow, standing by Barlach's coffin and sketching: a final act of solidarity among artists, a favor to a friend to help document an important life, and also an affirmation that art continues, no matter what.[61] Barlach would have agreed with this latter sentiment, which in itself goes far to explain his behavior during the Third Reich.

8

Emil Nolde

(1867 Nolde–1956 Seebüll)

Emil Nolde in 1937. (©Nolde Stiftung, Seebüll)

EMIL **NOLDE** was rarely what he seemed. Even his name masked reality. Born Hans Emil Hansen in the town of Nolde in Schleswig, the painter changed his name at age thirty-five when he married Danish actress Ada Vilstrup in 1902. The Expressionist painter later joined the Nazi Party in 1920, but he joined the Danish branch, which subsequently perplexed many observers, including the Nazis themselves after 1933. Well into the Third Reich, as one exchange with Nazi officials from 1938 shows, it remained unclear whether the artist was a German or a Danish citizen (the latter proved to be the case) and whether he was a Party member. Despite the complications surrounding his life history, Nolde had a sure sense of self. As he wrote to Goebbels in July 1938 with regard to the defamation that he was experiencing,

> I take this particularly hard, and especially because I was—
> before the beginning of the National Socialist movement—
> almost the only German artist in open struggle against the
> foreign infiltration of German art and fought against the un-
> clean art dealers and against machinations of the Liebermann
> and Cassirer period, a struggle against a superior power that
> brought me decades of material need and disadvantages.[1]

This passage not only communicated a deeply ingrained anti-Semitism, but reflected his long-standing sympathy for the Nazis. By using the adjective "unclean" in connection with the famed Jewish art dealer/publisher Paul Cassirer and Jewish artist Max Liebermann, who had been the Honorary President of the Prussian Academy until his ouster in 1933 (and a cousin of Walther Rathenau, a Foreign Minister during the Weimar Republic), Nolde revealed how he bought into certain Nazi conceptions.

Nolde grew up the fourth of five children in a town in the very north of Germany that belonged to the state of Prussia and hence the German Reich until 1920. His father was from Nordfriesland

and spoke the local vernacular (*Nordfriesisch*), while his mother spoke a dialect called *Südjütisch*. Nolde attended the local German school yet always spoke German with a pronounced regional accent. Ernst Ludwig Kirchner even commented that Nolde scarcely spoke the language, which was a mean-spirited exaggeration. Despite the linguistic challenges, and his subsequent Danish citizenship, Nolde believed he was German. He wrote to Ferdinand Möller in March 1937, "Having been born a German, I cannot feel myself to be anything other than a German."[2] After the 1920 plebiscite, as provided for in the Treaty of Versailles, the province of Schleswig passed to Denmark, and this brought about his Danish citizenship. Nolde later claimed during the Third Reich that he had thought it an act of German patriotism for him, an ethnic German, to remain in Denmark "in order to avoid a weakening of the Germans in North Schleswig," and he harbored irredentist feelings his entire life.[3]

From 1884 to 1888, "Nolde" enrolled in a vocational school in Flensburg, where he studied to be a woodworker and draftsman. During his time there, he even helped restore the Brüggemann Altar, the massive and elaborately carved centerpiece of the Schleswig Cathedral from 1521 that counts as one of the most important cultural artifacts in the region. Nolde continued his training at the local arts and crafts school and then relocated to Berlin, a move marred by illness when he contracted tuberculosis. After returning home to Schleswig to recover, he set out again; this time to St. Gallen in Switzerland, where he worked at the Industry and Crafts Museum teaching drawing (1892–97). Nolde was anything but a prodigy. He completed his first painting only at age twenty-nine in 1896. Without much experience, he submitted his work to the Munich Academy in 1898, but Professor Franz Stuck and the admission committee rejected him. Nolde later reflected on "how nice it could be to meet together with Kandinsky, Klee, and perhaps also Marc, who all belonged to this time."[4] Nolde nonetheless found time to travel and to educate himself in cultural centers such as Munich, Paris, Copenhagen, and Berlin. After he married Ada in 1902, the couple lived in Berlin-Grunewald for a spell, but then moved back to Friesland in the far north of Germany.

Nolde would retain ties to Berlin throughout his life. He joined Die Brücke in 1906 (for only one year) and then affiliated himself with the Berlin Secession in 1908. In the period before World War I, when Nolde became one of the greatest painters of watercolors in history and developed his expressive and powerful palette, he moved back and forth between the Reich capital and his native land. He and Ada kept a home in Berlin and cultivated an interesting circle of friends that included dancers Gret Palucca and Mary Wigman—who ostensibly influenced him, as seen in his many pictures of dancing figures. In fact, Palucca often served as a model for Nolde, and the artist painted Wigman's portrait in 1920. A path-breaking modern dancer, Palucca was of Jewish origin and was forced to give up her dance academy in 1939 (although she was able to continue to perform, appearing 99 times in 1942–43 alone).[5] That Nolde remained friends with her deserves recognition in light of his views about National Socialism. As noted earlier, Nolde was also friends with Ludwig Mies van der Rohe, whom he met before World War I. In the late-1920s, the Noldes commissioned Mies to design a home in Berlin-Zehlendorf. Although the house was never built, it engendered a correspondence between the two men—mostly with Nolde complaining about delays. Mies nonetheless managed to finish the design in 1929 and counted it as part of his oeuvre.[6]

In 1926, Nolde bought a home in Seebüll, just a few kilometers south of the Danish border. The town would become inextricably linked with the artist. Between 1927 and 1937, Nolde designed and built his home, which included an atelier. The sleek modernist structure was nonetheless quite imposing, especially with its location set in the flat northern countryside. Seebüll would become the artist's muse as he painted the landscape and flora throughout his life, and also used it as his refuge during difficult times. But that period came later. Although commencing his career as an artist at a relatively advanced age, Nolde had quickly enjoyed critical acclaim. His *Last Supper* was the first Expressionist painting purchased by a German museum: Max Sauerlandt acquired the work for the Moritzburg Museum in Halle in 1913—despite the protests of Wilhelm Bode, the General Director in Berlin. The fact that Nolde had 1,052 pictures confiscated from German museums in 1937 and 1938—the most of any artist—stands as a testament to his previous commercial and critical success.[7]

The early acclaim had brought him visibility, and in 1913 Nolde was invited to join an expedition to New Guinea sponsored by the Reich Colonial Office. The purpose of the expedition was to gain a better understanding of the reasons for the declining indigenous population. The brutal labor conditions that characterized German colonial rule clearly factored heavily in the drop. Nolde took his "responsibilities" seriously and executed numerous portraits of the locals. He focused on their racial characteristics, especially the color of their skin, which unlike in black-and-white photography could be rendered in his artworks. Nolde's worldview evolved in these years—for better and for worse. There was a decidedly racialistic quality to his thinking. For example, he came to regard Japan as the "Germany of the East" (but nevertheless thought the Japanese inferior to the Germans). While professing a racialist worldview, he also claimed to have a deep appreciation of indigenous cultures. While a member of the German New Guinea expedition of 1914, he wrote to the German Colonial Office, "condemning the rape of tribal culture by 'civilized' powers."[8] Nolde admired tribal art and thought it should be not in ethnographic museums, but in art museums. He argued, "These last traces of primal man [should be collected] while it was still possible."[9] Nolde and his wife, Ada, were on their way back from the South Seas when war broke out in 1914. Almost forty-seven years of age, he was not subject to conscription. However, he was affected almost immediately. The German ship he was on was seized by the British navy in Port Said, and his bags, including paintings he had executed during his sojourn, were confiscated. He recovered these works only in 1921. Nolde and his wife nonetheless proceeded back to Europe on a Dutch freighter, making their way back to Schleswig via Genoa, Zurich, and Berlin. Nolde proceeded to enjoy the most productive year of his career, completing eighty-eight paintings in 1915 alone. He settled on Denmark's west coast in 1916, where he continued to work at a feverish pace.

Nolde often seemed to be caught in between wildly differing circumstances, and this found expression in the organizations he joined. In 1918, for example, he enlisted in several left-wing artists' groups, including the Arbeitsrat für Kunst and subsequently, the Novembergruppe. Despite the oppositional nature of these groups, his career flourished. Already in 1920, the Berlin Nationalgalerie had a room dedicated exclusively to his work, and he was later elected to the Prussian Academy in 1931. But he also executed an about-face in 1920 and joined the North Schleswig branch of the Nazi Party. He himself later maintained that he was naïve—certainly in terms of politics. But he was acutely troubled by the German-Danish wrangles over the border and vehemently rejected the Treaty of Versailles. He wrote to his friend Professor Hans Fehr in February 1919, "The newspapers bring rather disturbing news from Schleswig. It hurts me so that the land where I was born, my *Heimat,* should be torn through the middle."[10] He concluded that the Nazi Party offered the most effective response, and in this respect he was not alone among his Schleswig compatriots. In the July 1932 elections, the province had the highest percentage of Nazi voters among the thirty-five Party districts (*Gaue*) across Germany. Schleswig had also produced the likes of Julius Langbehn, a conservative German art historian and philosopher who had considerable influence in right-wing cultural politics in the fin-de-siècle period. Nolde's political views therefore fit into a particular historic context.

While there would be much confusion over whether Nolde was technically a member of the Nazi Party, he did in fact rejoin the North Schleswig, branch in September 1934 and received a Party membership number.[11] Yet during the Third Reich, the affiliated Danish branch was not formally regarded as part of the Nazi Party. There is, for example, no Nazi membership card for him in the Federal Archives in Berlin, which houses the Party's master card register from Munich. Some Party members contemplated prosecuting him in a Hamburg Nazi Party court in early 1937—evidently for seditious art. They inquired with Nazi authorities about whether Nolde was actually a Party member, but they were told "no"—that he had not registered—so they could not proceed because he was not an official Party member.[12] Nonetheless, Nolde expressed his support for the Nazi movement in many ways, for example in September 1934 joining affiliated organizations such as the National Socialist Working Community–North (NS Arbeitsgemeinschaft–Nord). Nolde also never resigned his membership in these organizations—unlike Max Ludwig Nansen, the character based on Nolde in Siegfried Lenz's famous novel, *Deutschstunde* (*The German Lesson*).[13]

Nolde also expressed great admiration for Hitler. In one letter to his friend Hans Fehr, dated 10 November 1933, the artist wrote, "The Führer is great and noble in his aspirations and a genial man of deeds [*Tatenmensch*]."[14] In this same letter he spoke of his "beloved Germany," which captured his intense nationalism. These views changed little in the years after 1933. He wrote to Goebbels in 1938,

> After the partition of North Schleswig, it would have been easy for
> me—a celebrated artist throughout the world—to get caught up in
> political matters. This is due to my devotion to Germandom, above all
> else, which I have shown at every opportunity, both domestically and
> abroad, as I have fought for and recognized the Party and state, despite
> their defaming me. Or, perhaps, I have done this all the more because
> I am convinced of the world importance of National Socialism.[15]

In other words, Nolde saw himself as a true believer who had made great sacrifices for the German cause. Back in April 1933, he wrote that he had been "very involved in this forcefully executed and beautiful rising of the German people."[16]

As noted earlier, Nolde's racial views accorded with National Socialism, although there were certain inconsistencies in his formulations. On the one hand, as he explained in the second volume of his autobiography, which appeared in 1934, "Seen from a broader perspective, no race is worse or better than the other—before God they are all equal—but they are different, very different."[17] This respect for other races, however, ran headlong into his vulgar anti-Semitism. Nolde, for example, postulated that "Jews have great intelligence and spirituality [Geistigkeit], but little soul and little gift for creativity. . . . Jews are different people than we are."[18] The ambivalence in Nolde's thinking found expression in his having Jewish friends, like Gret Palucca, and a number of Jewish supporters. As Ernst Ludwig Kirchner wrote in December 1934, just after receiving a newly published copy of Nolde's autobiography Jahre der Kämpfe (Years of Struggle), "He, more than any other, was earlier supported by Jews—see Shapiro, etc. He has now turned himself into an anti-Semite. It is very sad that he is such an opportunist [Conjunkturjäger], but he was always that way."[19] It appears that Nolde became more openly anti-Semitic after the Nazis came to power in 1933.

One striking example of Nolde's more strident anti-Semitism occurred in the spring of 1933, when Nolde told an employee of the Reich Propaganda Ministry that his old colleague from Die Brücke, Max Pechstein, was a Jew. This was untrue, and a serious contretemps ensued.[20] Pechstein telephoned Nolde, who admitted the denunciation but refused to disclose anything more. Pechstein then sent Nolde a twenty-four-hour ultimatum, which elicited a statement that the information came from a Jewish friend of his wife. Pechstein explained that this was a "grave matter," with existential implications, and demanded that Nolde contact the Reich Propaganda Ministry with a correction, but Nolde refused. Indeed, Nolde wrote that he was "entirely disinterested in Pechstein's livelihood."[21] Pechstein decided not to take Nolde to court, and instead had the Prussian Academy investigate the matter. The Academy obtained proof of Pechstein's "Aryan" ancestry going back centuries and duly informed Nolde.[22] While one can question whether Nolde ever truly and legally joined the Nazi Party, there is no doubt that the artist was an enthusiastic supporter of Hitler and the National Socialist movement, and that he exhibited anti-Semitic views. To denounce a former colleague as a Jew, whether accurately or, in the case of Pechstein, mistakenly, showed how he tried to establish his Nazi bona fides and offers an on-the-ground example of anti-Semitism.

Granted, Nolde was far from alone among modernist cultural figures in exhibiting markedly anti-Semitic views. Ernst Ludwig Kirchner, for example, was also not immune to certain anti-Semitic views. In the mid-1920s, he commented that "the Jew, despite great intelligence, lacks a true creativity; as a German one cannot be friends with him, etc."[23] In one diary entry from 1925, he criticized Marc Chagall and called him a "halt Jude" (which might be translated as "just a Jew").[24] In July 1934, Kirchner wrote about events surrounding plans for frescoes he was preparing for the Folkwang Museum—they were never installed—expressing worry that a former employee there, Kurt-Wilhelm Kästner, would deprive him of the commission: "Kästner probably lobbies for Kandinsky or the Parisian Jew Ozefant. If this happens, then I will be finished with him forever."[25] While this formulation was not the most perniciously anti-Semitic of remarks, it appears to reveal a certain bias. He would not have been alone in this respect in the art world at this time; recent revelations have uncovered anti-Semitism in a variety of progressive and well-educated individuals, including modernist poet T. S. Eliot and Berlin museum director Wilhelm von Bode, the namesake of the current Bode Museum.[26] To be fair, unlike Nolde's, Kirchner's statements about Jews grew notably more positive during the 1930s. This came largely because he identified more with them—and, of course, in the eyes of some Nazis, he and his work became identified with Jews. Kirchner noted in his journal late in life, "As someone who will soon turn sixty, I must say it: My pictures were valued and purchased by the Jews. My best and most principled art dealer was a Jew. None were politically active in any way. None wanted me to be other than I was. They took my pictures as well as respected and explained them. It was done freely and good that way."[27] One can parse these statements, beginning with the phrase "the Jews," as well as the suggestion that by "politically active," he meant left-wing. Kirchner apparently viewed Jews as different from Christian Germans, but he lacked the hatred found among most Nazis.

Nolde persisted in his campaign for acceptance in the Third Reich. In 1934, he published the second volume of his autobiography, *Jahre der Kämpfe*, in which he explained his views about the superiority of Nordic people.[28] Scholars Bernhard Fulda and Aya Soika observed that the title seemed to echo Hitler's *Mein Kampf* (which may have been coincidental), and that "anti-Semitic and racist passages [were] now featured quite prominently."[29] In terms of his art, Nolde continued to paint "luminous colors and the flat northern landscape. He harbored a suspicion of the city and preferred as subject matter the cyclical rhythms of nature, primordial myths, and legends."[30] Nolde usually placed his luminescent canvases in simple wooden frames. These rustic affairs were akin to those found in farmers' homes. While they served to set off the bright colors of the paintings, the frames also echoed "blood and soil" notions regarding the spiritual connection between peasants and the natural landscape. Not that this made Nolde a Nazi, but it reflected his positive views toward the regime. Previously, in the early 1930s, he had tried to join the Fighting League for German Culture but had been rejected.[31] He was so incensed that he made his letter of response public, and Otto Andreas Schreiber would quote from it extensively in his speeches after the Nazi seizure of power as he battled the anti-modernist *völkisch* groups.[32] Continuing his campaign for acceptance, Nolde signed the declaration of loyalty to Hitler in August 1934 that affirmed support for Hitler's position of Führer. The artist later wrote several letters to Goebbels, including an oft-quoted missive on 2 July 1938 in which he proclaimed, "My art is German, powerful, austere, and profound."[33] There was little doubt, in the words of art historian Reinhard Müller-Mehlis, that Nolde was a "Nordic-thinking National Socialist"—even if the technicalities of his Party membership remained in doubt.[34]

While he remained frustrated in his efforts to find official acceptance, there were enough small victories to sustain his hopes. Nolde had works in the landmark NSD-Studentenbund show, *Thirty German Artists;* and while it was temporarily closed down by the authorities, he could at least point to supporters in the Nazi movement. His name came into play in the first half of 1933 as the director of the Vereinigte Staatliche Kunstschule (United State Art School) in Berlin, and Goebbels dispatched a subordinate to talk with the artist about a possible appointment.[35] Nolde also knew that Goebbels had his watercolors in his home in 1933 and most likely sensed the Reich Propaganda Minister was struggling to find a policy regarding his art, although there was no way he would have known about Goebbels's journal entry from July 1933: "Is Nolde a Bolshevik or a painter? Theme for a dissertation."[36] In November 1933, Reichsführer-SS Himmler invited Nolde and his wife, Ada, to Munich as "guests of honor" to the "Feier" (celebration) of the 1923 Beer Hall Putsch. This invitation, according to Himmler's wife, was the "personal wish" of the Reichsführer-SS.[37] As part of the commemoration Nolde joined Himmler and other high-ranking Nazis, including Ernst Röhm and Ritter von Epp, in the Löwenbräukeller, where they drank beer together. It is a striking image that Nolde described the following day in a letter to Hans Fehr. Nolde observed that he was about the only one in civilian clothing, surrounded by this panoply of high-ranking Nazis. That Himmler reached out to Nolde in the autumn of 1933 shows that the Reichsführer-SS was not always a resolute anti-modernist (writer Hanns Johst, who had worked in an Expressionist style, was also present), and that Nolde had supporters at the highest level of the Nazi regime. The artist was also friends with the Hanfstaengl family in Munich, who were close to Hitler and who had sheltered the young politician in the wake of the Beer Hall Putsch. Erna Hanfstaengl and her husband intervened on Nolde's behalf and evidently played a role in prompting Himmler to extend the invitation for the 9 November 1933 event. The painter and his wife even stayed with them on this visit to Munich.[38] Around this time Erna Hanfstaengl, who was a cousin of Eberhard Hanfstaengl (the director of the Nationalgalerie in Berlin from 1934 to 1937 and a supporter of Nolde), organized an exhibition of the artist's work at a gallery on the Karlsplatz in Munich. A number of Nazi leaders visited the show, and she arranged for her brother, Ernst ("Putzi") Hanfstaengl, who was a member of Hitler's inner circle, to put several of Nolde's watercolors in his flat, where they were seen by Hitler.[39]

Nolde's experiences in the first years of the Third Reich were decidedly mixed. He had been asked to "voluntarily" resign from the Prussian Academy in 1933 and refused to do so. This tactic seemed to work, and he retained his membership. There was even talk in the early years of the Third Reich of his becoming president of the Associated Art Schools (Vereinigten Kunstschulen). A 1934 exhibition of his watercolors sponsored by the Kestner-Gesellschaft in Hannover featured ninety-seven works, most of them for sale with prices ranging from RM 150 to RM 800 ($60 to $320). Nolde also had four works in the 1934 show on landscape painting at the Hamburg Kunsthalle. The director of the museum, Harald Busch, even purchased Nolde's painting *Hülltoft Barn* in November 1934. Busch used the funds donated by Hamburg industrialist Alfred Voss to buy the landscape, which featured red houses and a dark, threatening sky set in the area just south of Seebüll.[40] That the Hamburg Kunsthalle acquired one of his recent works— Nolde painted it in 1932—underscored the viability of the artist. Busch counted among those who believed that "modern Nordic artists" should find a place in the Third Reich, and to this end he kept modern pictures by Nolde, Kirchner, and Edvard Munch on display in the Hamburger Kunsthalle until his departure in late 1935.[41]

In January 1935, Nolde had a show at the Cologne Art Association (Kölner Kunstverein). According to a critic for the *National-Zeitung* of Essen, the exhibition had been in the works for years. The critic quoted Nolde himself, "I myself am of the opinion that, in spite of the traveling far and wide, my art is rooted deeply in the soil of the homeland [*Heimatboden*], in which I paint the land here between the two seas. Could there be a connecting link between Germany and the Nordic countries, perhaps?" The critic himself concluded the review with, "German art today is at the advent of a New Romanticism. The experience of Nolde's pictures will play a part and contribute to the recognition that the richness of the German artistic revelation is not yet exhausted by a romantic sensibility. In Nolde, and not only in him, an artistic expressiveness is evident, that, like a stream, has flowed through German art since the beginning and whose adherents include [Matthias] Grünewald."[42] Nolde also received positive press in the *Saarbrücker Zeitung.* The critic titled the review "Great Nolde-Exhibition in Cologne," called him a "German artist," and gushed that his art "is still informed by a youthful energy and undiminished ardency of an active master." He continued, "The strongest and purest [images] for the viewer are the flowers and landscapes. Nolde is a contemplative and at the same time impulsive conjurer of color."[43] According to the critic, the show was to travel from Cologne to Krefeld, Essen, Frankfurt am Main, Wiesbaden, and Hamburg. There was a hint of criticism in this piece: Nolde's works were "not easily accessible, but they were filled with a deep inner space behind the color skin of the exterior picture." But it was striking that his art received such a balanced treatment. It was also notable how visible Nolde's work was in this period: it was also featured in group exhibitions in 1935 in Chemnitz, Munich, and Bielefeld, as well as in overseas venues including Los Angeles and Belgrade.[44]

Certain museum directors tried to help Nolde with more clandestine support. In 1935, Eberhard Hanfstaengl, director of the Neue Abteilung of the Berlin Nationalgalerie, entered into a trade with Nolde. The artist received his picture *The Family* (1931) in exchange for *Young Horses* (1916). The latter was a landscape that was less provocative and had a better chance of finding a place in the museum. Hanfstaengl also reserved for purchase a portrait of Nolde by Leo von König for the Nationalgalerie. Nolde had sat for König in the winter of 1936–37, when the former Berlin Secession artist had executed two versions of the portrait.[45] Max Sauerlandt, one of the most important museum officials in Germany who directed the Museum for Arts and Crafts in Hamburg, defended Nolde's art and spoke of his "Nordic background." Sauerlandt had given a series of lectures in 1933 in which he talked about the artist's *niederdeutsche* origins and the "specifically Nordic-Protestant ancestral-element."[46] He also devoted a chapter to Nolde in his book *Kunst der letzten 30 Jahre* (*Art of the Last 30 Years*), although the book was banned in November of 1935. In the opinion of another museum official, Alois Schardt, Nolde's work expressed qualities that were both exotic and savage, and reflected the prophetic ecstasy of early medieval art.

Schardt, as noted earlier, was a key proponent of "Nordic modernism" and viewed Nolde as a striking exemplar. Even Ernst Buchner, the head of the Bavarian State Painting Collections who specialized in old German painting and who would later become complicit in the Nazis' plundering campaigns, exchanged letters with Nolde in 1935. Buchner adopted a convivial tone in one missive to the artist, where he noted that Nolde's painting *Flowers* "had an exemplary effect in the exhibition and received a lot of recognition."[47] Buchner explained that he currently had to pass on a solo exhibition, but his warm personal feelings still came through (despite the "Heil Hitler!" ending to the letter).

Perhaps the most remarkable support shown for Nolde by a Nazi came from Count Klaus Baudissin, the notorious director of the Folkwang Museum in Essen. An SS officer who once remarked that "the most beautiful object ever created was the steel helmet [*Stahlhelm*]," Baudissin would serve as a member of Adolf Ziegler's purging committee that collected the works for the *Degenerate Art Exhibition*. He also allowed Ziegler's committee to take Schlemmer's murals, the ones he promised not to harm back in 1934. Some have maintained that he ordered their destruction, but two of the panels appeared in the *Degenerate Art Exhibition*.[48] Earlier, Baudissin had organized an "exhibition of shame" (*Schandausstellung*), defaming modernist artists in Stuttgart in June 1933. Yet Baudissin was not a straightforward figure and at times expressed admiration for certain kinds of German Expressionism. He even faced charges in 1939, brought by the Gauleiters of Essen, Weimar, and Hagen, that he had "acted against the guidelines of the Party in connection with art questions."[49] Baudissin initiated negotiations with Nolde's dealer, Ferdinand Möller, in 1935 regarding a picture titled *Zinnias and Lilies*. Granted, this oil painting of flowers was among Nolde's tamer works, at least with regard to the sensibilities of most Nazis. Möller sent *Zinnias and Lilies* to Essen for Baudissin's inspection in the summer of 1936, receiving the considerable sum of RM 3,000 ($1,200) as a refundable deposit. The museum director responded to the dealer,

> The museum does not possess a single work depicting flowers by Nolde. It has helped until now that we have had a picture of sunflowers on loan, and been represented by a second loan of the work, *Peonies*. But these loans must eventually be returned, and in order to have Nolde represented in the form of a flower picture, I will try to carry out the purchase of the picture you sent here to me. I hope that I will be able to decide the matter in the next week.[50]

Baudissin and Ferdinand Möller continued their correspondence regarding the painting for well over a year until autumn 1936. Simultaneously, Baudissin deaccessioned Kandinsky's *Improvisation 28* (1912) from the museum, selling it to Ferdinand Möller. This controversial unilateral action predated the Reich Propaganda Ministry's purging program by about a year, yet it raised the funds that would have covered the Nolde painting (the Kandinsky today is in the Guggenheim Museum in New York).[51] In the end, however, the sale did not go through. Baudissin evidently could not expend the political capital that such an acquisition would entail. He, like Goebbels, apparently abandoned an earlier sympathy for Expressionism. Yet his earlier admiration for Nolde's landscapes and still lifes offered those in the modernist camp a glimmer of hope for the future.

The *Degenerate Art Exhibition* would constitute a crushing defeat for Nolde—a clear signal that official acceptance was not forthcoming. As noted earlier, Nolde had 1,052 works confiscated from state collections in 1937—more than any other artist: Erich Heckel (729) und Ernst Ludwig Kirchner (639) trailed him by a considerable margin. Nolde's important oil painting *The Life of Christ* was at the center of the first gallery of the Munich exhibition, among over three dozen works featured at that venue. The *Degenerate Art Exhibition* had come as a shock to Nolde, who had visited the show with his friend, the banker Friedrich Doehlemann: "It is so entirely unexpected," he wrote to another confidant, Wilhelm Hebestreit, on 10 November 1937. He tried to face developments with equanimity, adding stoically, "We have accepted the event as rather fateful. Very often, creators of great culture must suffer a lot."[52] But he also tried to rally support for his cause. Nolde wrote to Alfred Heuer that fall, "We have done all that is possible—but letters have not been answered." While deeply shaken by the defamatory exhibition and all it entailed, he worked hard to achieve some perspective. Nolde added in the letter to Heuer, "When I write to you in this way, it comes not from bitterness but from a sense of the grotesque, with a certain attendant humor."[53]

Nolde was so upset by vilification in the *Degenerate Art Exhibition* and corresponding measures that he cancelled the celebration he had planned for his seventieth birthday. Family and friends were to have come to Seebüll for a "simple *Gartenfest*," but he could not face them. He also worried that the celebration would be viewed as a provocation and feared the consequences.[54] In accounts of his experiences, Nolde always appeared to be "retreating" north—in 1937, 1938, 1941—and his quest for even more privacy continued during the final years of the war. He nonetheless mustered the courage to send letters to Goebbels and Rust, in which he protested the seizure of his property and affirmed his German background. In a bold if somewhat contradictory move, Nolde in 1938 sent works to the famed exhibition of twentieth-century German art at the New Burlington Galleries in London. The protest exhibition, which included Le Corbusier and Picasso on the organizing committee, had a distinctly anti-Nazi animus and was meant as a response to the *Degenerate Art Exhibition*. But the artist appeared to covet the international recognition. Nolde had eleven works in the London show.[55] In this way, he hoped to enhance the value of his artwork. The way he fought for the recovery of certain purged works that belonged to him that were housed in German state collections also sent this message. In a letter sent directly to Reich Minister Goebbels on 2 July 1938, Nolde asked for the nine-piece *The Life of Christ,* as well as *Large Sunflowers, Blonde Girl,* and *Wet Day.*[56] He proved successful in compelling the Reich Propaganda Ministry to return the seized art that he had on loan to the affected museums. These were among the 244 purged works returned by the Nazi state when it was determined that the works were owned by private parties or foreign governments.[57]

The late 1930s were nonetheless good for Nolde in certain respects. He had recovered from serious illness that had hospitalized him in 1935, and he spent considerable time in the Alps. As he recounted in his memoirs, "Every year during the winter months we would travel up to the winter world in the mountains in search of an improvement of our health. . . . However, I would also always take my watercolors with me and paint where I could—the snow covered mountains, the beauty of the clouds, the fir trees."[58] Otto Andreas Schreiber assisted them with visas and documents. It was not always easy for the Noldes to travel abroad. In 1936 they pleaded that the artist was sick and needed to travel to the Alps for his health—with Ada mentioning in one letter that her husband was a Party member and giving his number from the NSDAP-N. In the end they were permitted these trips to the Austrian and Swiss Alps. Painting in Kitzbühel and St. Moritz has not usually been part of the standard narrative of Nolde's experiences during the Third Reich (and the trips receive scant mention in his self-pitying memoirs).[59] The same can be said for the change in the Propaganda Ministry's liquidation policies in the winter of 1939–40, when Goebbels's staffers pulled back somewhat from the deaccessioning policies and returned the work of certain artists to German museums, rather than selling them abroad. This shift applied to the art of Franz Marc, Paula Modersohn-Becker, and Leo von König, among others. Nolde also saw some of his works go back to German state collections, and his painting *Young Horses,* which had been sent to the Basel Art Museum and was under consideration for purchase, was returned to Berlin, to the great disappointment of the Basel director, Georg Schmidt.[60] This change in the sales policy of the German Reich in the winter of 1939–40 also resulted in the cancellation of tentative sales agreements with the Basel Museum for works by Oskar Schlemmer, Otto Dix, and Ernst Ludwig Kirchner. While not widely publicized, the shift in the regime's sales policy raised the hopes of some insiders in the art world.

There can be no doubt that Nolde suffered ever increasing persecution in the second half of the Third Reich. On 20 March 1939, dozens of Nolde's works—mostly watercolors—were among the 1,004 paintings and sculptures and 3,825 graphic works burned at the Berlin Main Firehouse. In 1940, he was again required to submit his entire artistic production for the year to the Reich Chamber for the Visual Arts; he sent some forty-eight works, which were then seized by the police and never seen again.[61] He came under increasing scrutiny, most notably—and perhaps dangerously—in a report written by Reinhard Heydrich on 25 April 1941. The Security Services chief had just learned that "the notorious art Bolshevist and leader of degenerate art, Emil Nolde, submitted a tax declaration for 1940 for the sum of RM 80,000 ($32,000)."[62] While this report must be treated with skepticism—it is unlikely that the artist earned such an astronomical salary the previous year—the direct involvement of the head of the Reich Security Main Office signaled the decision to ratchet up the pressure on the artist. On 23 August 1941, President Ziegler informed Nolde that he had been expelled from the Chamber. Officially, he was forbidden to practice his profession or work in related professions (*nebenberufliche*). In the vast scholarly literature on Nolde and on art in the Third Reich, Nolde is almost invariably said to have experienced a *Malverbot* (prohibition on painting), but in fact that phrase was never used in any official communication to the artist—and, apparently to any other artist (Karl Schmidt Rottluff, for example, received a letter with almost the exact wording). Ziegler's 23 August 1941 letter, which Nolde produced in facsimile in his memoirs, prohibited him from any "activity in the field of the visual arts."[63] This was indeed more extreme than the ban on exhibitions (*Ausstellungsverbot*) or professional activity (*Berufsverbot*), and effectively served as a ban on painting. Nolde later told the now-famous story of how the local authorities in Seebüll were charged with preventing him from engaging in artistic activity, and how they paid several visits to his home and atelier. He claimed that they would feel and smell his brushes to see if he had been painting. Because oil paints left a distinct odor, he turned to watercolor.

In fact, the watercolors, or, as Nolde labeled them, the "unpainted pictures," began in 1938—well before Ziegler's 1941 prohibition on professional activity. In any case, during the remaining years of the Third Reich, Nolde painted over 1,300 watercolors on scraps of rice paper that he created "in a small, half-concealed room" in Seebüll. He painted a wide variety of themes, ranging from serene landscapes to "lonely people, jealous people, alienated individuals" and "anxious fantasies" from *Peer Gynt* and other dramatic works. In October 1944, Nolde wrote, "Only to you, my little pictures, do I sometimes confide my grief, my torment, my contempt."[64] These works, of course, became iconic in multiple respects. The *Ungemalte Bilder,* as art historian James van Dyke has noted, are now "enjoyed not only on their own aesthetic terms, but also as documents of persecution and resistance."[65] That he painted these pictures with odorless pigments and hid them away certainly speaks to the unease and the trepidation he felt, even if the threat from the authorities was perhaps not as great as he and others subsequently maintained. Nolde subsequently used the watercolors as the basis for more than one hundred larger oils that he executed from 1945 to 1951. In other words, the war continued to be a period of tremendous productivity for the artist. This included twelve oil paintings that he completed between 1942 and 1944—despite the oil-sniffing Nazi authorities. He later wrote, "As this painting and sales prohibition arrived [in 1941] I was in the midst of my most beautiful and productive painting. The brushes were gliding out of my hands. The nerves of an artistic person are sensitive; their ways restless and responsive. I suffered spiritually because I believed that I still had to paint my most substantial works."[66]

Nolde remained true to his artistic vision: one cannot say that his style changed dramatically during the Third Reich. He continued to paint landscapes, still lifes (especially flowers), religious themes, and portraits. Granted, there were somewhat "fewer people of color" after 1933. The catalogue raisonné of his oil paintings includes a group of pictures in 1932–33 with "non-Aryan" subjects, but he painted far fewer subsequently. Rather, his portraits featured more classically "Germanic" types, including *Red-Blonde Woman II* from 1936. A few of the wartime watercolors feature subjects with dark skin, but he also executed a series of "Viking Pictures"—including one titled *Nordic People (Nordische Menschen)*. Nolde nonetheless proved inclined to offer formulations suggestive of the Nazis' "blood and soil" philosophy. His thinking found expression in his landscapes, which, with their deep and luminous colors, seem to be spiritually infused. This theme is sometimes explicit, such as in *The Great Gardner* from 1940, which features a god-like figure tending to flowers or, more specifically, a lily. The stalks of the flowers thrust upward in a dynamic way, almost as if they are miniature trees of life. *Poppies and Red Evening Clouds,* an oil painting from 1943, features bright, optimistic colors, and the vivid sky fuses with the green marshland, with the poppies in the foreground: a pantheistic image with a reference to peace and death (the poppies). Considering contemporaneous events—he had followed the war carefully from 1939 onward and evacuated some of his paintings from Seebüll to western Germany, where he believed they would be safer—as well as the fact that he was over seventy when he created these pictures, it is not surprising that he would engage such themes.[67]

In pursuing themes that both resonated with contemporaneous events and also grew out of earlier work, Nolde's later efforts are similar to those of Ernst Ludwig Kirchner before his death in 1938. In addition to painting supercharged landscapes, Kirchner continued to depict synchronized dancers—a theme that he began exploring in the later 1920s and featured in his designs for the Folkwang Museum project, and that he continued through the late 1930s (he declared *Dancing Girls in Colorful Rays* to be unfinished in a November 1937 letter).[68] His pursuit of this theme raises questions. Even in isolation near Davos, Kirchner would have known about the Nazis' spectacles that featured athletic youth moving in a coordinated fashion. Such exercises represented nationalistic and racialized expressions of the "people's community" and were featured in newsreels, magazines, and other media.[69] The most iconic example, set at the Nuremberg Party Rally, was co-choreographed by Kirchner's friends Mary Wigman and Gret Palucca, whom he knew from Dresden. While there is no extant documentation showing that Kirchner was referencing Nazi pageants and gestures, the depiction of these coordinated figures with outstretched arms may well have been a sign that he hoped for accommodation (much like Schlemmer's murals for the Deutsches Museum, although the latter involved a proposal for a Nazi state competition). Kirchner's depictions of dancers around this time also appear to reference the recent work of Picasso and Matisse, and the images in part engaged the theme of liberation (Plates 6, 7).[70]

In a sense, the tensions raised by these images paralleled his own contemporaneous statements: he himself penned a ghostwritten essay on his art for a 1933 retrospective at the Kunsthalle in Bern, asserting that the work "created a connection between contemporary German art and international stylistic sensibilities."[71] Kirchner believed that he had discovered certain fundamental truths central to both German and European art. It is therefore understandable that he would continue with these images, even with the ambiguous resonances. His persistent engagement with these themes also indicates that Kirchner long held out hope that his work would ultimately find acceptance in the Third Reich.[72] His suicide in June 1938 suggests an eventual loss of faith in this regard, but for a number of years of Nazi rule he was not very different from his old Die Brücke friend Erich Heckel, who submitted documentation about his ancestry to the Nazi authorities in late 1936 and signed letters with a "Heil Hitler!" as he sought permission to work.[73] While Kirchner did not use that phrase in his correspondence, his response to being asked to resign from the Prussian Academy on 12 July 1937 constituted a comparable gesture.

> I never tried to get into the academy. . . . I have no personal advantage from my membership. . . . For thirty years I have fought for a strong new real German art and will continue to do so until I die. I am not a Jew, a Social Democrat, or otherwise politically active and have a clear conscience. I therefore will patiently await what the new government decides to do with the academy and put the fate of my membership faithfully into your hands.[74]

This letter was very similar to what he had written in 1933 when the Nazis' artistic policies remained in flux. But perhaps more notably, Kirchner also communicated his wish for acceptance in aesthetic terms.

Despite the increased persecution, Nolde still had allies. For example, when the Nazi regime launched the "degenerate art" action in 1937, Bernhard Sprengel, a successful chocolate manufacturer and avid art collector from Hannover, traveled to Munich to see the now notorious show. Contrary to the intentions of the exhibition's organizers, Sprengel became captivated with Nolde's works, and he took advantage of the fact that Nolde's works were still for sale in the city. Sprengel, with the support of his wife, Margrit, continued to purchase Nolde's art during the war as he amassed one of the world's most important collections of modern art, most of which is housed in the Sprengel Museum in Hannover. By 1942, the Sprengels' Nolde acquisitions included thirteen paintings, thirty-five watercolors, and an extensive collection of graphic works.[75] Nolde even had an opportunity to visit the Sprengels' collection in April 1941. In May of the following year, Nolde journeyed to Vienna to meet with Reich Governor Baldur von Schirach. The painter later suggested that the initiative came from the Nazi leader:

Nolde and Margrit Sprengel in Seebüll (July 1941). Margrit and Bernhard Sprengel were great patrons of Nolde during the latter half of the Third Reich. (Sprengel Museum Hannover)

"From Vienna came in an artistic sense a breath of fresh air . . . Gerhart Hauptmann and Richard Strauss were honored guests in Vienna. An invitation also came to me, a painter. We traveled there and were greeted with considerable understanding and warmth."[76] Despite his spending several enjoyable weeks in Vienna, Nolde did not secure an audience with Schirach. The Reich Governor, however, found time to view some the artist's recent works and was reportedly "sufficiently impressed to promise help" (Plate 5).[77] Of course, this never occurred in a meaningful way, but, like his support he received from the Sprengels, the experience provided further grounds for hope. Bernhard Fulda and Aya Soika have noted, "In 1943, [Nolde] was apparently still considering painting an SA man. And as late as 1944, Ada was writing letters to people she considered influential, pointing to Nolde's patriotism and party membership."[78]

Nolde, of course, carried on with his work, receiving support from a variety of places. In 1943, to cite another example, Otto Andreas Schreiber, who had become a division leader in the Reich Chamber for the Visual Arts, arranged for Nolde to be sent paints. Nolde responded with a letter of thanks dated 20 July 1943. In his memoirs, Nolde recalled that at some unstated point during the war, "A man from a government ministry came [to Seebüll] and saw some of my works hanging in the homes of our friends. Surprised and harmlessly he noted, 'We have some works by Nolde hanging on the walls of the ministry.'"[79] Nolde presumably was referring to Schreiber or Weidemann, but they were not alone among the cultural functionaries who continued to profess support for the artist. Others, mostly his friends in the north of Germany, helped him during the war by hiding some of his "unpainted pictures." Late in the war, Munich banker and art collector Friedrich Doehlemann, who had previously helped raise funds for the House of German Art, wrote to the president of the Reich Chamber for the Visual Arts, Wilhelm Kreis (Ziegler's successor in 1943), and pushed for Nolde's rehabilitation. For his part, Nolde kept on hoping for acceptance. He wrote Munich dealer Günther Franke on 8 October 1944, "We receive many inquiries about my watercolors and such, and even with the lasting prohibition that bans us, we answer, with the expectation that someday a change will come. But who knows what will happen next with art. [80]

Nolde's work continued to be sold throughout the Third Reich, although the commerce occurred relatively clandestinely. Reinhard Heydrich's intervention in 1941—prompted by reports of Nolde's lofty income—resulted in a closer watch on the artist. Yet a network of dealers maintained their businesses in modern art, including Nolde's work. In some cases, the customer had to have a personal relationship with the dealer—to be in an inner circle. Art historian Werner Haftmann said of the Galerie Buchholz in Berlin that "for those who were trusted, they could view the treasures as long as desired . . . it was a wonderful oasis in the abominable cultural climate of Berlin at that time."[81] This network of dealers who continued to trade in modern works until war's end included, in addition to Buchholz (who had branch galleries in Berlin, Budapest, and Lisbon), Ferdinand Möller in Berlin/East Prussia (the village of Zermützel); Ludwig Gutbier (the proprietor of the Arnold Galerie) in Munich; Günther Franke in Munich/Lake Starnberg; and Alexander Vömel in Düsseldorf. Despite the difficulties, they fared remarkably well: "im Geschäft geht es gut" (business is good) appeared as a common refrain.[82] Reich Propaganda Ministry State Secretary (and SS General) Leopold Gutterer wrote to Reinhard Heydrich in May 1941, "The reality is, the more or less strong demand in so called collectors' circles has created a market for works of decadent art, and as such, represent an extremely serious sabotage of the art policy of the Führer." To illustrate how dangerous the situation remained, Gutterer described how in his investigation he had found at the Galerie Vömel in Düsseldorf "a still life by Kokoschka and several works by Nolde."[83] The Reich authorities would cause difficulties for the dealers of modern art from time to time (Vömel had some works seized and then returned), and they monitored the art market carefully (Heydrich and the Security Service—or SD—received regular reports); but they refrained from putting a stop to this commerce.

If anything, the precarious nature of the trade in Nolde's works limited supply and inflated prices. In April 1943, dealer Ferdinand Möller wrote to fellow dealer Ludwig Gutbier that a Nolde oil painting in his possession was available for RM 6,000 ($2,400)—more than twice the average annual salary of a worker in the Third Reich. The market for Nolde's works proved so robust that the dealers could not satisfy customers. Munich dealer Günther Franke wrote to Gutbier in June 1944, "Unfortunately it is not possible for me to arrange a picture by Nolde for you. The artist has not provided any works from his atelier for two years and the owners of Nolde's works also do not part with them. I receive very many inquiries [for his work], without being able to accommodate."[84] Franke, however, did have graphic works by Nolde and was prepared to sell them. These were prewar pieces—Nolde's recent efforts were not available to these dealers—and Gutbier found this disappointing, writing to Günther Franke, "The affair with Nolde is very unfortunate. I had hoped that that you might at least offer a bit of advice."[85]

Despite notable artistic productivity, the unrelenting support of allies, and a strong demand for his works, Nolde's experiences during the war were overwhelmingly negative. In 1944, his Berlin home on the Bayernallee was flattened by Allied bombs. Nolde had taken precautions, and with the help of friends and patrons, like Bernhard Sprengel, had moved most of his art out of the heart of the Reich capital to the town of Teupitz; but forty-three of his works also perished at war's end in this depot. He later claimed they were burned along with valuable furniture by Red Army soldiers.[86] To his profound regret, the Allied bombing also destroyed much of his collection of artists whom he admired: Kokoschka, Klee, Kandinsky, Feininger, Daumier, and Gauguin, among others. Late in the war, his wife's health failed and she spent several weeks in the hospital. Ada would never recover fully.

Nolde enjoyed great success after the war and successfully rehabilitated his career. In 1946 he was appointed professor of art by the government of Schleswig-Holstein. He was awarded the Stefan-Lochner Medal of the City of Cologne in 1949; the Venice Biennale Prize for Graphic Work in 1952; the Order Pour le Mérite in 1952; and the Culture Prize of the City of Kiel in 1952. Nolde also took part in the exhibition *Documenta I* in 1955 (and posthumously in *Documenta II* in 1959 and *Documenta III* in 1964). Despite the honors and awards, Nolde remained a controversial figure.[87] His support for National Socialism was the primary reason, even though relatively little was known about his pro-Nazi views. Nolde himself adopted a conscious strategy of avoiding any discussion of the Third Reich, but allegations and rumors persisted. Nolde also raised eyebrows by the way he conducted his private life. Two years after Ada's death in 1946, the eighty-one-year-old artist married Jolanthe Erdmann (1922–2010), a much younger woman (then aged twenty-six). Attractive and vivacious, the second Frau Nolde made a striking companion to the aging artist. But he continued painting, executing not only watercolors, but also over a hundred oil paintings in the first six years after the war. Jolanthe was among his favorite subjects, and she later devoted herself to the legacy of his art. In 1951, Nolde fell and broke his left arm while working in his garden in Seebüll. The injury proved traumatic, and he never again painted in oil. But when his health permitted he continued with watercolors until shortly before his death in 1956.

Nolde was buried next to his first wife at Seebüll, and the foundation which came into existence as stipulated in his will bears both their names: "Stiftung Seebüll Ada und Emil Nolde." The foundation provided for a museum in his former home in Seebüll, which opened to great fanfare in 1957. Since then the museum has exhibited his work in ever-changing combinations and receives around a hundred thousand visitors each year. In 2007, the Nolde Stiftung in Seebüll established a *dépendance* in Berlin on the Gendarmenmarkt, where the foundation administrators mount exhibitions and promote the artist's works. The foundation also controls his *Nachlass*, or his documents and correspondence, and as a result scholars have struggled to gain unfettered access to the documents. Jolanthe Nolde's protective outlook toward her late husband seemingly played a role in limiting access to Nolde's papers, and the effects of her passing in June 2010 remain to be seen.[88] This towering figure of Expressionism, who, as we have seen, elicited admiration even from many Nazis, certainly deserves a forthright critical treatment of his life and work.

Plate 1. Advertisement for Bauhaus wallpaper made by the Firma Rasch (1938). Bauhaus-designed products continued to be sold throughout the Third Reich. (Reprinted from Winfried Nerdinger, ed., *Bauhaus-Moderne im Nationalsozialismus. Zwischen Anbietung und Verfolgung* [Munich: Prestel, 1993])

Plate 2. Poster design for the *German People–German Work exhibition*, executed by former Bauhaus Master Herbert Bayer (1934). Walter Gropius and Ludwig Mies van der Rohe were among the other former Bauhaus figures who participated in this Nazi exhibition. (Reprinted from *Deutsches Volk—Deutsche Arbeit*, exh. cat. [Berlin: n.p., 1934])

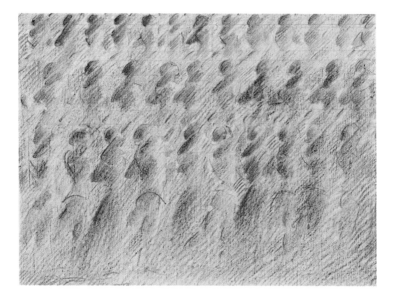

Plate 3. Sketch of a proposed mural by former Bauhaus-Master Oskar Schlemmer for the Congress Hall of the Deutsches Museum in Munich (1934). Note the outstretched hands suggestive of a Nazi salute, as well as the modernist techniques involving repetition and abstraction. (Photo Archive C. Raman Schlemmer, Oggebbio, Italy)

Plate 4. Emil Nolde, *Northern Windmill* (1932). The artist painted the north German and South Danish landscape in a way that suggested a deep spirituality—an idea that was not inconsistent with the Nazis' Blood and Soil philosophy, which posited a deep connection between the German people and the land. (©Nolde Stiftung, Seebüll; Zentralinstitut für Kunstgeschichte, Munich; and Pinakothek der Moderne, Munich)

Plate 5. Emil Nolde, *Afternoon Clouds* (1940). Chocolate manufacturer
Bernhard Sprengel and his wife, Margrit, emerged as key patrons of
the artist after 1937 and purchased this painting from Nolde in 1941.
(©Nolde Stiftung, Seebüll; and Zentralinstitut für Kunstgeschichte, Munich)

Plate 6. Ernst Ludwig
Kirchner, *Deer in the Evening* (1938), in which he
portrays peasants and their
animals in the countryside.
(Reprinted from Björn Egging and Karin Schick, eds.,
*Der Neue Stil. Ernst Ludwig
Kirchners Spätwerk* [Biele-
feld: Kerber Verlag, 2008])

Plate 7. Ernst Ludwig Kirchner, *Self-Portrait,* which he began in 1934 and completed in 1937. The figure in the lower right appears to reference the synchronized dancing figures he painted throughout the 1930s, as does the framed landscape in the background. The yellow bars that almost form a swastika seem to handcuff his wrists. Most notably, the picture reveals the psychological torment Kirchner suffered at the time. (© 2013 Ingeborg und Wolfgang Henze-Ketterer, Wichtrach/Bündner Kunstmuseum Chur)

Plate 8. Max Beckmann, *Self-Portrait with Horn* (1938), which he executed shortly after arriving in Amsterdam. The ensuing years in the Netherlands—nearly five of them under Nazi occupation—were among the most productive of his career. The horn itself is suggestive of the creative muses. (Neue Galerie New York and Private Collection; © Artists Rights Society [ARS], New York/VG Bild-Kunst, Bonn)

Plate 9. Still photo from Leni Riefenstahl's *Triumph of the Will* (1935), which featured abstraction and repetition in a way indicative of her modernist roots. (Medienarchiv LR-Produktion)

Plate 10. Synchronized dancers at Nuremberg Party Rally (1937). Choreographed by modern dancers Mary Wigman and Gert Palucca, and influenced by the conceptions of Leni Riefenstahl and Albert Speer, these events incorporated modernist aesthetics. (Getty Images)

Plate 11. Arno Breker overseeing the construction of the monumental relief *The Victim* by French laborers at his studio in Wriezen during the war. The assemblage of the piece in sections represents certain modernist strategies, including an interest in modern production methods and a mechanistic view of the human body. (© Foto Breker-Archiv, Art-Museum, Schloss Nörvenich, Germany)

Plate 12. Albert Speer, Cathedral of Light, Nuremberg. Speer used repetition, a stark angularity, and modern technology to achieve his most famous theatrical effect. (Bundesarchiv-Koblenz, Bild Nr. 183-1982-1130-502)

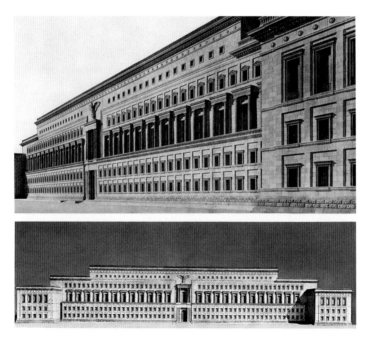

Plate 13. Albert Speer, model for the office of the Reichsmarschall. This design for Hermann Göring's headquarters featured geometric shapes and a lack of ornamentation, among other modernist techniques. (Reprinted from Léon Krier, *Albert Speer Architecture, 1932–1942* [New York: Monacelli Press, 2013 (1985)])

Part III

Accommodation Realized

ARTISTS HAD MYRIAD ways to respond to the sharper key of the National Socialists' cultural policy. Some left the country, of course, while others retreated into "inner emigration." "I have been banished to landscape painting," said painter Otto Dix in a comment that captured the avowedly nonpolitical nature of his art during the Third Reich, as well as his rural surroundings once he left Dresden for the countryside near Lake Constance.[1] But even with "inner emigration," many artists thrived. Dix, who lived in a comfortable lakeside villa in the town of Hemmenhofen after 1936, had more time to focus on painterly techniques. Despite undeniable difficulties during the Third Reich, he would travel to Dresden and other cities for "intellectual contact," and he always knew he had supporters in the Nazi hierarchy, Ribbentrop and Speer among them. Max Beckmann, to take another example, entered into one of the most productive phases of his career after being fired from his professorship in Frankfurt (Plate 8). More specifically, during his time in Amsterdam (from 1937 to 1947) Beckmann "created one-third of his entire oeuvre including five of his nine great triptychs" (granted, this figure includes five years when he did not live under Nazi rule).[2] Although Beckmann never belonged to the Netherlands' equivalent of the Reich Chamber of Culture, which was exclusively for Dutch citizens, and while he did suffer difficult moments—such as when he was identified in June 1942 as eligible for conscription (which caused so much stress that he had a mild heart attack)—he seemed to thrive artistically during the German occupation. Beckmann wrote to one of his dealers, Günther Franke, in February 1944—at a time when the Dutch faced agonizing privation and a brutal winter—"I have thrown myself into my work and am *very* well."[3]

It has become a romanticized cliché to talk about suffering artists expressing their angst via their work, but the most recent scholarship on Beckmann shows that he responded with great creativity to his challenging circumstances in wartime Amsterdam. He had extensive contacts with members of the Dutch resistance and painted these individuals on many occasions. Interestingly enough, he often used photographs and would reproduce the subjects' expressions from those images. Beckmann, according to art historians Christian Fuhrmeister and Susanne Kienlechner, also depicted the perpetrators. In their analysis of the artist's 1943 painting *Dream of Monte Carlo,* they identified two figures who represented the art plunderers Erhard Göpel and Bruno Lohse: the former, as noted earlier, worked as an agent for Hitler and Sonderauftrag Linz, and the latter served as Göring's chief representative in the art world in Paris during the war.[4] With a certain sense of black humor, and consistent with his difficult-to-decipher iconography, Beckmann portrayed the two plunderers as croupiers. These and other figures he portrayed in his wartime works embodied the larger themes—violence, despotism, and role-playing, among many others—that fascinated the artist.

Beckmann's work continued to be obscurely symbolic and allegorical. Building upon earlier pictures that explored the themes of tyranny and torture—such as *Hell of the Birds* of 1938—he incorporated specific events from his life, such as in his 1943–44 work *The Journey,* which captured the spirit of war's end in the Netherlands. With an element of wishful thinking —he began the painting well before the Germans' departure, *The Journey* features a defeated German hero, served by a bellboy wearing a cap with the word "Eden" on it—suggesting a luxury hotel and the subservience of others. A provocatively dressed woman with her legs spread, evidently representing those who had fraternized with the occupiers, bids farewell to a pair of departing men. The powerfully evocative, if not well-known, work (it remains in a private collection but was once owned by Göpel) explored the themes of collaboration, plunder, and defeat.[5] In his public statements, Beckmann proved calculatingly circumspect in what he said about the Nazis. Even in his speech in London in 1938 on the occasion of the exhibition *Twentieth Century German Art,* an exhibition organized by anti-Nazi exiles to counter the *Degenerate Art Exhibition,* he couched his words. Beckmann spoke about the dangers of "collectivism" and how it could turn "the way of living of mankind to the level of termites," but that was about the extent of his criticism of the Nazis.[6] He nevertheless found other modes of self-expression—in his pictures, diaries, and letters. As a result of the private and veiled nature of his criticisms, the Nazi officials largely left him alone after the Germans overran the Netherlands in May 1940. That the artist's son, Peter Beckmann, who was a medic stationed at a Luftwaffe hospital outside Munich, arranged for certain larger works to be transported from Amsterdam back to Germany in an ambulance, provides another fitting example of the resourceful artist finding a way to get by.[7]

Other cultural figures developed strategies that allowed them to do far more than survive. The individuals treated in this section were the most famous, and in many respects, the most representative cultural figures in the Third Reich. What is striking is how they all had previously engaged modernism in some way: either they were trained in this manner, such as Albert Speer, who studied and worked with Heinrich Tessenow, or they performed in a modernist style, such as Leni Riefenstahl, who had begun her career as an Expressionist dancer. Composer-conductor Richard Strauss rose to fame well before the Third Reich and incorporated modernist elements into his work. Although not the most modern of the figures treated in this section, and critical of many aspects of Weimar culture, Strauss figures into the broader history of modernism, stretching back into the fin-de-siècle era.

Certainly, these cultural figures showed that they were adaptable. There was perhaps no greater chameleon than actor and director Gustaf Gründgens, who moved from left-wing agitprop theater in Hamburg in the 1920s to become part of Göring's coterie in the Third Reich—living in an "Aryanized" villa as well. The figures in this chapter survived the Third Reich and adapted to their circumstances in the postwar world with remarkable success (although Strauss, who was eighty-two in 1945, lived only until 1949). There are myriad other examples: sculptors Arno Breker and Josef Thorak, both modernists in their youth, became "State Sculptors" and eagerly created works that represented the Nazi regime. Breker lived in Paris in the 1920s, studying with his acknowledged mentors Aristide Maillol and Georges Despiau—both modernists in the tradition pioneered by Rodin. This branch of modernist sculpture certainly differed from that of Constantin Brancusi, Jean Arp, and Picasso, among others who deconstructed forms in a radical way, but the Rodin-led movement was nonetheless part of the broader modernist accomplishment. And Breker did have exposure to other kinds of modernist sculpture: he recalled in a 1983 interview, for example, that he knew "Constantin Brancusi, whose atelier in Paris I often visited as a young man."[8] Josef Thorak also had worked in a modern style, exhibiting with the Berlin Secession in the 1920s. Yet during the Third Reich both Breker and Thorak were celebrated figures and cultivated friendships at the highest level of the Nazi regime. Interestingly, while both went through denazification, they continued to travel in radical right-wing networks and remained favorites of old Nazis, whose publications, such as the *Deutsche Soldaten-Zeitung,* would frequently feature their work.

Even after 1937, when Hitler had sought to settle the Expressionism debate, a considerable amount of uncertainty existed about the positive side to the Nazis' cultural program. In preparing the first *Great German Art Exhibition,* for example, the jury struggled mightily with the selection process. Adolf Ziegler, Arno Breker, and the other jurors first reduced the fifteen thousand entries to around nine hundred. Hitler and Goebbels then journeyed to Munich to view the works that had been selected. Goebbels commented, "With sculpture everything is all right, but with painting much is absolutely catastrophic. Works are being shown here that make one literally sick.... The Führer is wild with rage."[9] Hitler reportedly said, "I will not tolerate unfinished paintings."[10] The following year, in his speech to open the 1938 *Great German Art Exhibition,* Hitler admitted that he had been tempted to cancel the inaugural 1937 show. As expected, he offered platitudes about how he was confident that German artists would find a style commensurate with a great people. That said, the lack of a clear vision regarding what constituted a National Socialist aesthetic in painting afforded opportunities for many creative types. While most understood certain principles that would characterize the new official art—a racial consciousness and an appreciation of the German landscape, for instance—the actual elaboration of the idiom remained to be determined.

Moreover, certain Nazi leaders continued to embrace modernism, even if they now became more guarded in their statements. Baldur von Schirach and his wife Henriette acquired works by Pierre-Auguste Renoir, Auguste Rodin, and Vincent van Gogh for their own collection—even if some of it was plundered from Jews, such as the van Gogh *Poppies in the Field,* which came from a Nazi plundering agency in the Netherlands.[11] Their Renoir, titled *Landscape with Bathers* (1880), came from the Galerie Welz in Salzburg, whose proprietor, Friedrich Welz, was notorious for trafficking in looted works. At war's end the painting appeared on a French list of missing works, but it was never found and its disposition remains a mystery.[12] The Schirachs, however, did muster the courage to approach Hitler to discuss the art of Franz Marc. During a visit to the Berghof, Henriette von Schirach showed Hitler illustrations from the artist's early period, when Marc worked in a more realistic style with "nature-true" colors. As Hitler viewed these renderings of birds and landscapes, he begrudgingly acknowledged the quality of the artworks but also remained unappeased, commenting, "So if he could draw properly, why didn't he?" Henriette von Schirach was especially close to the dictator (she was the daughter of Hitler's photographer Heinrich Hoffmann) and, as her husband noted, "Henriette had freedoms with him that no one else could lightly undertake."[13] Attempting to induce Hitler to warm to Franz Marc was one such freedom.

While other Nazi leaders did not have the self-assuredness to defend modernist artists to Hitler, many, and perhaps even most, of the high-ranking figures engaged in activities that violated what most perceived as the official aesthetic policy. Foreign Minister Joachim von Ribbentrop, along with his wife, Annelies, collected modern French art. As indicated earlier, they had works by Claude Monet, André Derain, and others. Hermann Göring kept two landscapes by Camille Pissarro in his Berlin home—an astonishing instance of boldness, not just for stylistic reasons, but also because the Impressionist painter was Jewish. The works may have been intended as fare for barter, but Göring's collection, according to recent scholarship, certainly included works by Renoir, van Gogh, and Henri de Toulouse-Lautrec.[14] Naturally, there were other ways to push the limits of official aesthetic policy. Henriette von Schirach recalled in her memoirs how she and her friends adored Hollywood films such as *Gone with the Wind* (1939) and *Gulliver's Travels* (1939), as well as the British-made *Mrs. Miniver* (1942). She added, "The American films which reached Germany via Portugal as a sort of intellectual black-market contraband were as popular with the Nazi elite as every new issue of *Vogue* magazine."[15] Many *Bonzen* (bigwigs) subscribed to a kind of quasi-aristocratic exceptionalism. The official restrictions applied to common folk, not to those at the highest level of the regime. Nazi leaders would also sometimes signal their more liberal views about culture by professing a kind of open-mindedness. In 1937, the Gauleiter of Bavaria, Adolf Wagner, was asked whether works by Nolde and Barlach would be considered for the first *Great German Art Exhibition*. He responded, "Absolutely. Everyone who does good work must be admitted; we exclude no names, only poor work."[16] While such remarks offered scant reassurance to those supportive of modernism, they could be construed as cracks in the edifice and, as such, served to encourage those who persisted in their advocacy of a more tolerant cultural policy.

More than any other city in the Third Reich, Vienna offered opportunities for an engagement with modernism. Compared to the rest of the

Annelies Ribbentrop at her Berlin-Dahlem villa with a painting by French modernist André Derain. (Bundesarchiv-Koblenz)

"old Reich"—the pre-1938 Germany—the Austrian capital was a bastion of cultural tolerance. The famous phrase *Wien ist anders . . .* (Vienna is different . . .) had special resonance from 1938 to 1945. True, Vienna also had a history of militant anti-modernism. One need only look at the protests against Schoenberg, Schnitzler, and writer Hugo Bettauer (the latter murdered in 1925). But the Habsburg capital had given rise to such a wide range of modernist accomplishment that by the late 1930s many residents embraced a civic identity that looked with pride at Klimt, Kokoschka, Schiele, Otto Wagner, Adolf Loos, and other fin-de-siècle luminaries. When the *Degenerate Art* show came to Vienna from 7 May to 18 June 1939, huge crowds engulfed the venue—over 147,000 in the five-week run—leading some to wonder whether the Viennese were there to do something else besides ridicule and revel in Schadenfreude. Many sensed that there was genuine enthusiasm for modern art.[17]

In his postwar memoirs Baldur von Schirach, who became the Reich Governor of Vienna in August 1940, recalled that when he arrived in the city, Hitler "spoke to me of the tradition of this city and assured me of the cultural independence of the Viennese."[18] While this proved to be true in certain respects, it would be better to describe Vienna as a contested space. The reasons for this were not only the anti-modernist element, but also the rivalries among the Nazi officials who all sought influence in the city. In the cultural sphere, Goebbels came armed with not only his position as Reich Minister for Propaganda (and all his other posts), but also a huge budget for cultural activities. Schirach reported that Goebbels "must provide, on Hitler's orders, 11 million marks for art and culture in Vienna from the budget of his ministry."[19] Goebbels and von Schirach ended up fighting over the budget for cultural affairs, engaging in a veritable *Papierkrieg* (paper or bureaucratic war). The contretemps had policy implications because by 1940 Schirach was considerably more pro-modernist than Goebbels (they had held similar positions a few years earlier). Schirach later recalled, "Goebbels had already repeatedly complained to Hitler about my cultural policies in Vienna."[20]

There were a host of pro-modernists in the Nazi administration of Vienna following the *Anschluss*. Most notably, Kajetan Mühlmann, an art historian who went on to become arguably the most prolific art plunderer in history, initially held a key post responsible for art schools, museums, and monument protection in the Ostmark, as the former Austria was called after the *Anschluss*. Mühlmann admired a great deal of Austrian modernism, including the work of Anton Faistauer, a Salzburg-born painter whose work was heavily influenced by Paul Cézanne.[21] Mühlmann helped set the tone for Vienna's cultural life. While he coordinated the plundering operations aimed at the city's Jews, he also supported the exhibition of modern art and the selling of such objects at auction houses like the Dorotheum. The same can be said for the director of the Österreichische Galerie (the Austrian National Gallery) in Vienna, Bruno Grimschitz, who also held Austrian modernism in particularly high regard. Grimschitz proved a very important figure in the Nazi cultural bureaucracy: he furnished valuations of confiscated artworks, purchased seized works for the museum he directed, and yet also organized the massive Klimt retrospective in Vienna in 1943. In this exhibition Grimschitz helped "de-Jewify" (in Nazi parlance) the work of Gustav Klimt. The stand-out portrait of Adele Bloch-Bauer from 1907 (purchased by Ronald Lauder in 2006 for $135 million—then a record for a painting—and now in the Neue Galerie in New York) was simply called *Golden Portrait*. Grimschitz saw no need to mention the illustrious Viennese Jewish subject. Her widowed husband's art collection had been seized in 1938 as he fled Austria—first to his *Schloss* near Prague, then to Switzerland when the Germans invaded rump state Czechoslovakia in March 1939. Grimschitz had advised on the valuation of Ferdinand Bloch-Bauer's seized art, and then put several of the persecuted exile's Klimts on exhibition a few years later.[22] Grimschitz and Mühlmann were far from alone among those who were both pro-modernist and complicit in art plundering at the same time.

The same could be said for Baldur von Schirach, the key figure with regard to Vienna's *Kulturpolitik*. Schirach himself was a published poet who had dabbled with Expressionism, as well as an amateur painter. Beyond his sympathy for modernism, Schirach believed that cultural policy mattered. Already in April 1941, Schirach sought to use a festival called the *Wiener Kulturprogram* in order to claim "Vienna as the first city of theater in the Reich."[23] This whole idea—this "cultural initiative"—says much about Schirach. For the longtime leader of the Hitler Youth, culture was something to be organized. Yet he did an impressive job in this regard; for example, he arranged for Wilhelm Furtwängler to become Vienna's musical plenipotentiary and permanent conductor of the Vienna Philharmonic Orchestra in 1940, and then he lured Karl Böhm to the Vienna State Opera in 1943.[24]

Schirach reveled in playing the role of patron, and he used the considerable funds at his disposal as a means to influence cultural policy. To take one example, he personally allocated funds to renovate the home and atelier of Professor Fritz Klimsch, a sculptor who had worked in the modernist tradition. Schirach also engaged the Gropius-trained architect Hanns Dustmann to oversee reconstruction in Vienna and planned to include a modernist element in the reshaping of the city during and after the war. Early in 1943, his office allocated money to art plunderer and Albertina employee Bernhard Degenhart, who traveled to Italy to purchase "graphic works of important artists of the Italian modern"—an initiative whereby Degenhart bought works by Giorgio de Chirico, Gino Severino, and Mario Sironi, among others—often directly from the artists themselves.[25] These purchases involved allocations in the tens of thousands of Reichsmarks—sums that would likely have required Schirach's personal approval. The Reich Governor of Vienna relied on his cultural aide Walter Thomas, who also evinced pro-modernist views. This entailed organizing shows from the Albertina's holdings that included graphic works by Klimt, Schiele, Kollwitz, and Belgian Post-Impressionist James Ensor. Thomas also arranged a private exhibition of Nolde's watercolors in Vienna in May 1942 and helped coordinate the artist's trip to meet with Schirach.[26] The meeting, as noted earlier, resulted in Nolde's request for both a studio in Vienna, as well as official support. Although Schirach would have liked to help the artist, he knew that Hitler's strong antipathy precluded visible patronage of this kind. Nolde nevertheless had the opportunity to tour the exhibition of his watercolors and to meet with Schirach, but in the end he retreated northward to inner exile in Seebüll.

Schirach nonetheless worked to create a kind of space in Vienna where modernist artists could enjoy some measure of tolerance. One way Schirach approached his task was to argue that no true National Socialist painting style had yet to emerge. He advanced this thesis in a much-discussed article in the *Völkischer Beobachter* in November 1942. It was the published version of a talk that Schirach had given to mark the two hundred fiftieth anniversary of the Academy of Fine Arts in Vienna. In what was advertised as "a major address in which he opined on current problems in the visual arts," Schirach stated, "The crisis of painting can be explained by the absence of representatives who set a direction, as has been the case to a considerable extent with our architecture. It turns out that we not only have important architects, but also a new architecture, while at the same time, we have no painting, although we have many clever, and indeed a few important, painters."[27] Schirach, like many others, believed that the niveau of state-approved painting was dismal (the popular joke was that it was not the "Haus der Deutschen Kunst" but the "Haus der toten Kunst" [House of Dead Art]). He also discussed the great art of Rembrandt, Beethoven, and van Gogh— a comparison that was intended to be provocative. Schirach had floated many of these ideas in October 1941 when he spoke at the opening of an exhibition of Viennese art held in Düsseldorf. In this earlier address, he positioned himself as the representative of a younger generation who resisted the "academic regimentation of artistic production," but he went further in the November 1942 speech in Vienna.[28]

Although Schirach's speech on the occasion of the Viennese Academy anniversary alarmed some of the anti-modernists in the Nazi cultural bureaucracy—Alfred Rosenberg's art expert Robert Scholz among them— there were no discernible consequences for the Viennese Reich Governor. Consequently, he was emboldened to take even more radical steps, including an exhibition, *Junge Kunst im Deutschen Reich*, which opened at the Wiener Künstlerhaus on 7 February 1943. In the catalogue to the exhibition Schirach is listed as the "organizer"—and not just the "patron" (*Schirmherr*), as would be customary for a political official.[29] The Viennese governor also purchased a half-dozen works from the exhibition with RM 25,000 ($10,000) from his ministerial funds.[30] In a briefing from his cultural aide, Walter Thomas, Schirach was told that the show would feature works by younger artists who worked in an Expressionistic style. Thomas, like Schirach, also embraced modernism in the musical sphere, and "was a follower of Strauss and, to a lesser extent, Carl Orff and other Nazi tolerated modernists."[31] He had overseen the Vienna Staatstheater from 1940 to 1943, and also the Wiener Staatsoper for several months in early 1941, which afforded him platforms for his progressive views. Subsequently, in his capacity as cultural adviser to Schirach, Thomas engaged other pro-modernist staffers, such as Wilhelm Rüdiger, whom he selected to curate the *Junge Kunst* exhibition.

Rüdiger underwent a dramatic transformation in his views about modernism prior to curating the *Junge Kunst* exhibition. He had once been the art critic for the *Völkischer Beobachter*, as well as the director of the Städtische Kunstsammlung in Chemnitz, and early on had shown himself to be a staunch anti-modernist. The Chemnitz museum had a first-rank collection of works by members of Die Brücke, including Kirchner and Heckel, which Rüdiger not only defamed in the *Schandausstellungen* that he helped organize (he curated one called *Art That Did Not Come from Our Soul*), but he also deaccessioned modernist works from the Chemnitz collection.[32] Rüdiger's career as a museum director lasted for only a year, after which he focused on writing art criticism, most notably for the *Völkischer Beobachter* and the glossy periodical *Kunst im Deutschen Reich*. Although Rüdiger worked in these Rosenberg-controlled enterprises, his views about modernism shifted. For reasons that are unclear, he developed greater sympathy for Expressionism (he went on to a highly successful postwar career as an art historian).[33] In the summer of 1942, Rüdiger organized an exhibition of works by young artists for the European Youth Summit that took place in Weimar. Reports surfaced that the exhibition included "degenerate" works.[34] The Nazi Security Service (the Sicherheitsdienst, or SD) went so far as to launch an investigation, evidently prompted by a denunciation. Schirach reached out to Rüdiger in an attempt to protect the young art historian and through Walter Thomas hired him for the *Junge Kunst* show. Schirach, Thomas, and Rüdiger knew full well what they were doing, which was to

Paul Mathias Padua, *Flower-Stand.* From the catalogue of *Junge Kunst im Deutschen Reich,* a 1943 exhibition sponsored by Viennese Governor Baldur von Schirach that included many modernist works. (Reprinted from *Junge Kunst im Deutschen Reich,* ex. cat. [Vienna: Ehrlich and Schmidt, 1943])

push the limits of official cultural policy. One witness at Wilhelm Rüdiger's denazification trial in 1948 opined that *Junge Kunst* "was regarded, and had to be regarded, as an eloquent critique of all Nazi art."[35]

In preparation for the *Junge Kunst* exhibition, Rüdiger invited 175 artists to send works to Vienna. Some were established, such as Karl Albiker, Rudolf Hermann Eisenmenger, Ernst Dombrowski, Paul Mathias Padua, and Josef Wackerle—nearly all of whom had works included in the annual *Great German Art Exhibition.* But these artists also ranged beyond the officially endorsed aesthetic. In his report to Alfred Rosenberg, Robert Scholz referred to "recent painting that is still very much French-oriented"—an astute observation in that many of the young artists were influenced by the French Post-Impressionists. Scholz also acknowledged that many of the younger artists were producing even more aggressively modernist art.[36] Walter Thomas recalled in his 1947 memoir how "painters responded to the invitation to send in works from all parts of Germany—works that they had previously kept hidden out of fear of the brown dictatorship."[37] Rüdiger selected 582 works: a mixture of painting, graphic art, and sculpture. In Robert Scholz's words, they reflected "a trend directed against the *Great German Art Exhibition* in Munich."

In fact, many of the works in the *Junge Kunst* exhibition appeared quite tame—especially the sculpture, which was all figurative and mostly stiff. The catalogue contains a conventional portrait bust of Hitler by Bernhard Bleeker and another of Mussolini by Hans Wimmer. The latter is rather more daring, with Il Duce sporting a thick neck and moderately stylized features. Certain paintings stand out as bolder: for example, Gerth Biese's *Girlfriends* (vaguely resembling Oskar Schlemmer's style), or Hans Happ's work titled *Diana,* which suggests motion in a Futurist-related manner. Marianne Coenen-Bendixen's *Girl with a White Handkerchief* actually lives up to Scholz's claim of a French influence. The same can be said for Paul Mathias Padua's *Flower Stand,* which perhaps comes as no surprise because the artist was not averse to taking risks. In 1939, he had painted two versions of the notoriously sexual *Leda and the Swan* (one of which was purchased by Martin Bormann). Padua's *Flower Stand,* based on Édouard Manet's later, more Impressionistic, work, featured prominently in the *Junge Kunst* catalogue and evidently attracted the attention of Hitler, who was reportedly not pleased with it.[38]

In hindsight, many of those involved recalled the *Junge Kunst* exhibition as a triumph, as a symbol of their independence and courage. In actuality, the show might have been sub-titled "a bridge too far." Preliminary reports on the provocative exhibition made it to Hitler.[39] There was no shortage of subleaders who were prepared to rush to the dictator and present the case against the modernist show. In March 1943, Alfred Rosenberg scribbled in red crayon on Robert Scholz's memo regarding the exhibition that he hoped to go to the Führer Headquarters to give a report in person, although it is not clear if he ever did. Even Österreichsiche Galerie director Grimschitz reportedly uttered negative comments: "One must count German art as lost if this exhibition actually represented it," was one attributed to him.[40] Schirach became apprehensive and cancelled the opening, justifying the move in late January 1943 due to the "difficult battles in the East"—that is, the fighting that resulted in the German Sixth Army's defeat at Stalingrad. While most events planned for the opening did not come off, such as a performance of the concert choir of the Hitler Youth and the operetta *Wiener Blut* (*Viennese Blood*) by Johann Strauss, other related programming, including an exhibition of Gustav Klimt's paintings at the former Secession, continued as planned.[41]

Hitler reacted by sending the longtime Nazi and set designer Benno von Arent to Vienna to inspect the show. Arent worked in the Reich Propaganda Ministry as a cultural bureaucrat and specialized in the area of theater and stage design. He reported back that *Junge Kunst* was "liberal Schweinerei" (liberal troublemaking). Schirach was called to the Berghof at Obersalzberg to answer to Hitler—"a mandatory audience," the Viennese Reich Governor later called it. Schirach recounted, "Hitler did not offer me a chair and he himself remained standing. Bormann positioned himself a step behind him, quiet and ice cold." Hitler reportedly said, "I have been forced to hear downright unpleasant things."[42] He continued, "Herr von Schirach, I don't wish for such exhibitions. That is sabotage." Bormann evidently came forward with a copy of the magazine of the Hitler Youth called *Wille und Macht* (*Will and Power*), which had illustrations from works in the *Junge Kunst* exhibition. Hitler raged, "Look at this picture—a green dog! And you permitted a quarter million copies to be printed. By doing so, you mobilize all the cultural Bolsheviks and reactionaries against me. This is not a youth education; it is an education in resistance."[43] The next day, 10 March 1943, Schirach's aide Walter Thomas received the order from Berlin to close the show—a little over a month after its opening. There was also talk of suspending all financial contributions to Vienna for culture, and even of sending Schirach to the Eastern Front. Schirach testified at the Nuremberg Trials that this meeting at the Berghof "made a frightful impression" on him and constituted a conclusive break with Hitler.[44] Even though there were other strains on the relationship, it is notable that the conflict surfaced in the realm of culture.

The former Austrian capital nonetheless remained a place where modernism endured, albeit not without challenges and defeated initiatives. Perhaps the most striking case concerned Egon Schiele, whose work was never declared "degenerate" or purged from German or Austrian state collections. Arguably the most radical fin-de-siècle Expressionist, Schiele, who had died tragically along with his pregnant wife in 1918 from the influenza pandemic, avoided official condemnation. His art was exhibited publicly, including in a 1943 show at the prestigious Albertina graphic collection— a state institution.[45] The Nazi newspaper *Der Völkische Beobachter* paid a tribute to Schiele in November 1943, with a laudatory article commemorating the twenty-fifth anniversary of his death: "Egon Schiele. Zum Gedächtnis" (In Memoriam). The author, Heinrich Neumayer, offered formulations such as, "In the oeuvre of Schiele, the impression of inner truth remains. He spoke of the desolate faces that tormented him and from the holiness of a beautiful girl's face. . . . The fact that Schiele was capable, an ability for which German art can only be grateful, makes him important; his honest and deep grappling with the severity of his times is borne witness by his art- istry."[46] Schiele's works were also included in an exhibition at the Salzburg museum in 1944; and, as noted earlier, his works were sold openly within the Austrian part of the Reich during the Third Reich, including by the state-owned Dorotheum auction house in Vienna.[47]

During the war, modernism also continued in certain German-occupied territories in the West. Such was the case in Paris, for example, where the Galerie Louis Carré organized a series of exhibitions, including one in No- vember 1941 featuring Henri Matisse's drawings.[48] There were occasional demands by local German commanders to remove works because they were "degenerate" (this reportedly happened with a Picasso show at the Galerie Charpentier in Paris), but more often than not, the occupiers would tol- erate modernism in these foreign (and inferior) countries.[49] Picasso and Kandinsky kept working in France, even if works by the latter often sold in backrooms.[50] One must keep in mind that an estimated 80 percent of French dealers sold art to German buyers during the occupation.[51] Some of these works would have been modernist, and there would have been little difficulty transporting them back to the Reich. The German occupation authorities in the Netherlands also permitted modernist artists to carry on with their work, and did not prohibit the sale of modern art, which contin- ued to take place at well-established venues such as the Amsterdam auction house Mak van Waay and, until 1943, the Kunstzaal van Lier—that is, until its proprietor, Carel van Lier, was arrested and sent to Auschwitz, where he perished.[52]

The territory of the *Altreich* (old Reich) proved more of a challenge for modernists, but many endured and enjoyed some measure of success. This often entailed an alteration in the style and nature of the work, as was the case with those individuals who trained as modernists and then became celebrated figures during the Third Reich. Others, as indicated above, continued on in the shadows, or in relatively liminal spaces. Such was the case with Otto Andreas Schreiber, who persevered with his own painting. He had been forced to bring his factory exhibitions to a close in mid-1939 when Hans Schweitzer from the Reich Propaganda Ministry filed a complaint, and he had seen certain (but not all) of his works declared degenerate. His woodcut *Hay Harvest in Lithuania* was purged from the Prussian State Graphic Collection and then included in the *Degenerate Art Exhibition*.[53] Yet Schreiber continued to paint throughout the Third Reich.

In July 1944, for example, over a year after Hitler and Goebbels had pro-claimed "total war," Schreiber was writing to the Reich Chamber for the Vi-sual Arts to secure his ration of turpentine and paints.[54] His annual requests for these "painting supplies" were always approved by the Nazi bureaucrats. Schreiber could even report in 1944 that his works were still in the Prus-sian State Graphic Collection, the Kunstverein Berlin, and a museum in Königsberg.[55] He also noted that his art had been included in an exhibition in Philadelphia ("Carnegie" he scribbled on one form). Schreiber presum-ably referred to the efforts of Charlotte Weidler, an American art critic and dealer who worked for the Carnegie Foundation in the 1930s and did a great deal to support German modernist artists. Weidler, who had been ro-mantically involved with German-Jewish émigré art critic Paul Westheim and who had close ties to anti-Nazi circles, also had contacts in the Reich Propaganda Ministry, and Schreiber evidently figured into her network.[56] It is remarkable to think that Schreiber's art was exhibited in the United States during the Third Reich, but again, the stereotypes were such—then and now—that Expressionist artworks were rarely associated with National Socialism. That many of the cultural luminaries of the Third Reich had modernist roots also cuts against the grain of common understanding.

9

Richard Strauss

(1864 Munich–1949 Garmisch)

Richard Strauss, portrait by Max Liebermann from 1918.
(Bundesarchiv-Koblenz, Bild Nr. 183-S94748)

WHILE CERTAIN MODERNIST figures, such as Emil Nolde, were sympathetic to the Nazis, and others who sought to find a place in the Third Reich were more ambivalent, many who hoped for accommodation were downright critical of Hitler and his regime. The great composer Richard Strauss would fall somewhere between the latter two categories, although, as with most of the figures in this book, his views were not static, and the cordiality and optimism that prevailed at the start gave way to a distinct antipathy to Hitler's regime. Strauss signaled his initial willingness to find a modus vivendi by accepting Goebbels's offer to serve as the first president of the Reich Chamber of Music in the autumn of 1933. His reasons for this were complex. He later stated that he hoped to mitigate the regime's negative influences on music in Germany, including increased repression, deteriorated quality of instruction, and harm to the country's international reputation. He truly believed that his leadership would help other artists. This would be consistent with historian Peter Paret's take on the composer: "Richard Strauss, no admirer of Hitler, could live in any environment that did not seriously interfere with his work."[1] While true enough, this formulation misses the optimism that informed his thinking in the early years of the Third Reich.

"Optimism" is perhaps too positive a word for the crusty and difficult musical genius, who penned his first composition at age six. Strauss was patrician, arrogant, and contemptuous of the Weimar democracy—as well as much that went with it, including trade unions and a vibrant popular culture. The son of Franz Joseph Strauss, a gifted horn player for the Munich court opera and later a professor at the Bavarian Royal Music School, and Josephine Pschorr, who hailed from a beer-brewing dynasty and whose family counted among the richest in Munich, Strauss grew up in a privileged and conservative milieu. That his father was illegitimate added a sense of social insecurity, for which he overcompensated with haughtiness and rigidity. His "arch-conservative" father, who served as his first music teacher, viewed even the operas of Richard Wagner with trepidation, considering the composer too progressive. Strauss's own politics remained conservative, and the composer exhibited a marked patriotism when war broke out in 1914. That he subsequently lost millions of marks that he had invested with London banker Sir Edgar Speyer just prior to the war—funds that were seized as part of the Entente Powers' war reparations —only added to his national chauvinism.[2]

Richard Strauss proved extraordinarily complex. Although a nationalist, he counted the pacifist and left-wing writer Romain Rolland as his "best friend," and during World War I he refused to sign a famous wartime manifesto that stated the present war was about the conflict between the profound German *Kultur* and the superficial and money-driven civilization of the West. Similarly, Strauss was not an unambiguous modernist, although he certainly incorporated elements of dissonance and progressive syncopation, as well as explored new sounds and textures. Music scholars have used words like "eclectic" and "stylistic pluralism" to describe the manner in which he incorporated modernist elements into compositions—works that were often conventional in other respects.[3] In more than one sense, he straddled the nineteenth and twentieth centuries, a transitional figure between the Romantic and the modern eras. He had been declared, before the age of twenty-one, to be the successor to Brahms and Wagner (with the latter, in his day, "on the modernist edge"), and Kurt Weill acknowledged him as a major influence. Even Arnold Schoenberg "proactively sought out the master's opinion on music he had written."[4] Although Strauss has defied easy categorization, music scholars have most often identified him as a modernist.

Thematically, he explored topics favored by many modernists, including the evocation of sexual gratification (*Der Rosenkavalier*, 1910), the linkages between humans and nature (*The Alpine Symphony*, 1915), and the power of emotions and instincts. Arguably his most famous work today, *Also Sprach Zarathustra* (1896), which director Stanley Kubrick featured in *2001: A Space Odyssey*, derived its inspiration from Friedrich Nietzsche, who constructed much of the philosophical underpinning for modernism. Nietzsche's exploration of the "Dionysian" impulses—that is, the irrational, instinctive, visceral, passionate, and liberating qualities in great art—lay at the heart of the modernist project. Strauss understood this. He had studied philosophy and art history at the University of Munich in the early 1880s and evinced considerable intellectual sophistication. Later, the ideas of Arthur Schopenhauer were to exert a strong influence on the composer: the pain and suffering manifest in the world could best be overcome, albeit temporarily, by aesthetic contemplation. Schopenhauer's interest in the irrational and visceral aspects of life—expressed most purely in music—also proved important, although Strauss came to reject the metaphysics of the German philosopher in other key respects, viewing music "as nothing more than music," and not as a transcendental phenomonen.[5]

Strauss's transition away from a conservative approach to music toward modernism occurred in the later 1880s and 1890s. Influenced by composer/violinist Alexander Ritter, who had married into the Wagner family, Strauss began to explore what he and Ritter called "the music of the future" and turned to writing more artistically ambitious tone poems. His *Don Juan,* from 1889, in the words of his biographer Bryan Gilliam, "earned him international recognition as a modernist" because of "the work's provocative subject matter and musical brilliance."[6] *Don Juan* required virtuosity on the part of nearly every player in the orchestra (and for this reason is often used for auditions). Strauss's works tended to be extremely complex and difficult to play. The tone poem *Also Sprach Zarathustra* from 1896 was also part of the buildup to his most daring period, as was *Don Quixote* from 1898, which featured "torrential chromatic textures." Around the turn of the century, he moved on to opera. Strauss was, in the words of Gilliam, "a literary or pictorial composer in the sense that he required extra-musical images to charge his imagination or challenge his intellect to creativity."[7] The results included *Salome* (1905), which was based on the play by Oscar Wilde. *Salome* told the story of a woman who beheaded John the Baptist "because he refused to satisfy her lust." That he favored strong female characters provided another modernist element. The audacious opera, which featured incest, decapitation, and necrophilia, elicited strong reactions, with some members of the audience taking offense at the scandalous subject matter and others howling at the dissonance. Descriptions such as "thunder," "noise," and "orchestral cacophony" accompanied early performances of the piece.[8] Reactions were hardly less muted in the United States, and *Salome* closed at the Metropolitan Opera in New York after only one performance.

In his next opera, *Elektra* (1909), Strauss went even further with regard to atonality and dissonance. Featuring a libretto by Hugo von Hofmannsthal, the opera explored the visceral themes of passion, vengeance, and horror. The culmination of the opera is Elektra's "ecstatic dance of triumph," which counts as a dramatic expression of the Dionysian impulse.

The "*Elektra* chord," a powerful extended and bitonal chord, has also become a hallmark of the opera. Igor Stravinsky remarked about *Elektra,* "I am completely ecstatic. It is his best composition. Let them talk about the vulgarisms that are always present in Strauss. . . . Strauss's *Elektra* is a marvelous thing!"[9] Critics have compared the character of Elektra to Lulu from Frank Wedekind's dramas *Earth Spirit* (1895) and *Pandora's Box* (1904). The rebel prostitute was also at the center of Alban Berg's eponymous opera of 1935. Strauss also collaborated with modernist choreographer Sergei Diaghilev. The Russian émigré commissioned a ballet from him for the Ballets Russes in Paris, as he did from Maurice Ravel, Darius Milhaud, and other modernist composers. In short, Strauss, while a transitional figure from the nineteenth-century Romantic and Wagnerian tradition, was also part of the twentieth-century modernist movement. This is especially the case when one considers thematic factors such as his interest in the irrational and the sexual, and if one avoids defining modernism in music solely as the rejection of tonality.

Elektra marked Strauss's most adventurous foray into modernism, and his compositions subsequently became less aggressively dissonant, even as his reputation grew. He still explored chromaticism and dissonance—the jagged edges remained in his work—and he borrowed from an earlier operatic tradition in a way that anticipated post-modernist strategies. Strauss would quote and parody earlier works in a self-conscious way, thereby "forg[ing] a new relationship between composer, performer, and audience," who were expected to understand his references.[10] But he moderated the tone of his music—some would say "regressed"—so as to make it more fluid and accessible. Of course, Strauss enjoyed tremendous success. His operas *Der Rosenkavalier* (1910), *Ariadne auf Naxos* (1912), and *Die Frau ohne Schatten* (1918), among many others, became standards of the Western musical world, and he was celebrated as both a composer and a conductor. Strauss himself believed in his own greatness, declaring, "I am the last mountain of a large mountain range. After me come the flatlands."[11] His egotism would be a key factor in his decision to work with the Nazis. Strauss could imagine no other overseeing the musical life of the new Germany. Indeed, his stature was such that it was the Nazis who approached him first.

As discussed earlier, Goebbels was anxious to co-opt the nation's cultural luminaries, and Strauss was at the top of his list in the world of music. Strauss responded positively to these approaches, with smaller gestures preceding the fateful decision to become president of the Reich Chamber of Music. In April 1933, the Nazis' threats induced Jewish conductor Bruno

Walter to cancel engagements in Leipzig and Berlin, and Strauss stepped in to conduct in the capital, leading the Berlin Philharmonic (but donating his fees back to the orchestra). Arturo Toscanini quit at Bayreuth in solidarity with Walter—writing in protest to Hitler directly—and Strauss again served as a replacement.[12] Although two very complex episodes, with Strauss trying to mend fences with the Wagner family as one factor in his decision to conduct at Bayreuth, his decision to step in for both Walter and Toscanini certainly pleased Hitler (while angering others). Around the same time, in April 1933, Strauss signed a letter condemning Thomas Mann for delivering a lecture on Wagner, first at Ludwig-Maximilian-Universität in Munich in February and then in other European cities. The letter alleged that Mann was belittling Wagner and thus offending nationalist (and Nazi) sensibilities. Many observers viewed Mann's lectures as motivated by his anti-Nazi politics rather than by his views about Wagner, whose work he generally admired.[13] Strauss's signature on the letter therefore appeared to be another pro-Nazi gesture. While Strauss did not embrace many aspects of National Socialism—he did not appear a strident anti-Semite and quarreled with his son Franz Alexander over the latter's support for certain Party policies —he made an effort in 1933 to curry favor with the new regime.

Reich Minister Goebbels appointed Strauss to the post of president of Reich Chamber of Music in November 1933. While there has been considerable debate about whether the composer sought the position and lobbied for it, there is no question that, after the Nazis' initial approach, a mutual courtship ensued. Goebbels and Strauss had first met at the Bayreuth Festival in July, and the recently appointed Reich Propaganda Minister had been extremely impressed by "the great musician"; while Strauss, in turn, returned the compliment in a contemporaneous letter, writing about "the very art-inspired and sensitive Dr. Goebbels."[14] This auspicious meeting led to the appointment—one that served as an important symbol in the early years of the Third Reich. It struck people differently, but almost everyone took note. Popular author Erich Ebermayer commented: "Too bad about Strauss. The great, beloved master of *Salome, Elektra, Ariadne, Rosenkavalier,* who will be truly immortal through his music—did he really find this necessary? What can have moved him to give them his great, eternal name?" Arturo Toscanini famously quipped, "To Strauss the composer I take off my hat; to Strauss the man I put it back on again."[15]

To return to the question regarding Strauss's rationale for working with the National Socialists to the extent that he did in the first years of the regime, again his motivations proved multifaceted, and the hierarchy of reasons is somewhat different in Strauss's case than with certain other figures. Clearly, his behavior rested upon a misassessment of the Nazis. But beyond that, ego played a key role. Strauss saw no other figure of comparable standing, either as a composer or as a professional in the musical life of Germany. He believed that he should—and indeed must—set the course for the reform of German music. As historian Frederic Spotts noted, "If Furtwängler longed to be the *Führer* of musical performance, Strauss wished to be Führer of what was performed."[16] His was not a case in which he merely wanted to be left in peace to compose. If that had been his sole objective, Strauss could have retreated to his villa in Garmisch and pursued his own form of inner emigration. He accepted a political office that shaped music in the public sphere because he believed in his particular vision of German music.

Richard Strauss's self-confidence as an arbiter of music policy rested on his belief that high musical accomplishment in Germany had been jeopardized by the permissive atmosphere and cultural heterogeneity of the Weimar Republic. The influence of American popular fare was a source of particular concern. Michael Kater has noted that Strauss "had a deep distrust of 'Negroes,' constituting one seed for his unmitigated dislike of jazz."[17] Strauss also hated light entertainment music. This posed a problem because Hitler liked this genre, and Goebbels thought it useful as a kind of opiate for the masses. At several points, the composer found himself at odds with the Nazi leaders for having mocked Franz Lehár, one of the Führer's favorites. Strauss proved somewhat tone-deaf in regard to Lehár. As late as February 1941, Goebbels reprimanded him for referring to Lehár as a "street musician" and suggesting his operettas be confined to the circus. Back in 1933, Strauss undertook measures aimed at elevating the quality of music in the Reich, and this included reducing the number of venues for opera and classical music so as not to dilute the pool of talent, allowing the best musicians to perform beyond the compulsory retirement age, and improving music education of the "proper" kind. In describing Strauss's elitist impulses Michael Kater labeled him an "aesthetocrat," arguing that the musician believed Hitler's regime offered the best chances for realizing the higher standards.[18]

Considering that the Reich Chamber of Music had absorbed more than 150 professional musical associations and counted more than 170,000 members by 1939, Strauss's post as president was more than ceremonial. The Chamber had a network of local offices, with over 1,140 representatives who kept track of local musicians. They also doled out commissions, subsidies, and other forms of support. To go with these carrots, the officials also had sticks in the form of negative evaluations and recommendations to expel members from the Chamber. Yet one should not place too much weight on these efforts to censor and proscribe. More recent scholarship has emphasized the inefficiency of the control mechanisms, with music historian Pamela Potter observing, "To the extent that music censorship did exist, it was not very well organized. . . . Music censorship at most consisted of a few published and unpublished lists condemning certain Aryans as well as non-Aryans, including Alban Berg, Aaron Copland, and Serge Koussevitzky." Potter includes as one of her myths about music in the Third Reich "Myth #3: The Nazis banned all jazz and atonal music."[19] In short, she viewed Strauss and his colleagues in the Chamber as relatively laissez-faire. This is not to say that Strauss lacked influence or power. He also headed the corporatist body for composers, which was also absorbed into the Reich Chamber of Music, and then subsequently led the Permanent Council for International Cooperation among Composers, which was a Nazified agency that replaced the German chapter of the International Society for Contemporary Music.[20] This body dealt with issues such as copyrights and royalties —matters that had long concerned Strauss. He believed that a centralized organization could best represent composers, but it also afforded the Nazi state an additional measure of control. The fact remains that Strauss emerged as a powerful cultural bureaucrat.

Richard Strauss made his inaugural address to the Reich Chamber of Music in February 1934. He "expressed 'the warmest thanks' to Hitler and Goebbels on behalf of 'the entire German music world' for creating a body that would reorganize German musical life and integrate 'the German nation with its music' as closely as it had been centuries earlier."[21] Around the same time, he composed "Das Bächlein," which he dedicated to Goebbels. The piece concluded by repeating the word *Führer* three times—rendering it unambiguously propagandistic.[22] Later in 1934, before an assembly of German musicians, he delivered yet another speech praising the Nazi government. Here he proposed to limit concerts with music by foreign composers (he advocated a one-third rule). For someone as brash as Strauss, and who saw his work as central to world music in a broadly historic manner, his actions early in the Third Reich proved strikingly obsequious and parochial.

For a while Strauss and the Nazi leaders worked around their differences. Hitler, for his part, held off imposing his own views about music on the entire country. Even in 1938, in a cultural address at the Nuremberg Party Rally that constituted one of his most programmatic statements about music, Hitler not only "refrained from naming any musical styles or genres, but also stated forthrightly that music cannot and should not serve any political agenda, and that musicians should be guided by their own sense of beauty and expressiveness alone rather than by any strict rules."[23] Strauss, on the other hand, straddled his own line as a Nazi cultural bureaucrat. While he proved compliant in the ways noted above (criticizing "Negro" jazz, etc.), he could not bring himself to sign the dismissal notices related to the 7 April 1933 Law for the Protection of a Professional Civil Service. Nonetheless, he did not block other officials in the Chamber from enacting such measures. Another instance in which Strauss and Hitler sought a modus vivendi occurred in the summer of 1934, when Strauss asked Hitler to help with regard to his opera *Die Schweigsame Frau* (*The Silent Woman*), which featured a libretto written by Stefan Zweig, who was Jewish. Hitler himself examined the libretto and ruled that while the collaboration with a Jew was problematic, he had no problem with the text and the opera could be performed "on an exceptional basis."[24] Hitler even indicated that he would attend the premiere. Strauss, for his part, tried not to exacerbate the situation and avoided the most aggressively modern sounds in his compositions. Peter Paret has noted that "younger composers, like Werner Egk and Carl Orff, salvaged enough dissonance and syncopation to persuade their audiences that they were keeping up with the times."[25] Strauss, however, avoided phrasing that many Nazis would find confrontational. His efforts at supplication also included presenting Hitler with the piano score to the *Olympische Hymne* in late March 1935 (playing it personally for Hitler during an audience), and then returning on 17 April to wish the Führer a happy birthday. In his note the following day, Strauss expressed the "'warmest thanks for the precious, scintillating hour' and his hope for Hitler's prolonged health, [as well as] for the continued protection of 'German art.'"[26]

It would be a gross understatement to say that the Nazi leaders did not usually abide by compromise arrangements. Although it was no small feat for Strauss to secure special permission from Hitler and Goebbels to stage *Die Schweigsame Frau* in Dresden, the dispensation did not last. The opera, which premiered in Dresden under Karl Böhm on 24 June 1935, generated the expected criticism from Nazi stalwarts, including Alfred Rosenberg, who protested the Jewish and anti-Nazi librettist. In fact, the production closed after fewer than a half-dozen performances as a result of poor ticket sales (one show was canceled with the feigned reason that the female lead was sick). Problems also arose when Strauss demanded that Zweig's name appear on the program, which happened but not without incident. Yet it was the ancillary events that made this episode so significant. On 17 June 1935, Strauss, who was staying at the Hotel Bellevue in Dresden, attempted to send a note to Zweig, who remained abroad in Switzerland. Nazi authorities intercepted Strauss's missive, which had been hand-scribbled on hotel stationery, and passed the message up through channels to Saxon Gauleiter Martin Mutschmann, and then to Berlin.[27] The letter, however, did not reach Hitler and Goebbels until early July, well after the premiere.

In the now notorious letter to Zweig, Strauss claimed to be "aping the position of President of the Reich Chamber of Music"—a highly compromising formulation, to be sure. The composer also maintained that he took the position "to do some good and to avert a greater misfortune—simply out of an artistic sense of duty!"[28] Strauss stated that he rejected anti-Semitism and wanted to work further with Zweig, despite the objections of the Nazi leaders. Strauss's letter was prompted by the Austrian writer's decision to pull out of their partnership in February 1935, when Zweig wrote that he did not want to collaborate surreptitiously as a silent partner, which had been Strauss's preference. Zweig reaffirmed his decision in mid-June, explaining that he had qualms about working with the head of the Nazi Chamber of Music. The Austrian writer also referenced the Bruno Walter and Arturo Toscanini incidents. It was Strauss's response to this missive that was intercepted by the authorities. In hindsight, Strauss's letter shows him in a rather positive light. He added, "For me there are only two categories of people: those who have talent and those who don't. For me, the *Volk* exists at the moment when it becomes the audience. Whether this consists of Chinese, Upper Bavarians, foreigners or Berliners—for me it's all the same."[29] Yet with formulations of this kind, he sounded like anything but an official of the Nazi state.

Strauss tried to convince Zweig to undertake another collaborative project, but the composer did not want to work on one that they had discussed earlier. Strauss characterized it as a "Mexican text" and said that although it may well be good, it was not suitable for him: "I am not interested in Indians, red and white gods, and Spanish pangs of conscience!"[30] Zweig went on to write on his own, including the elegant memoir *The World of Yesterday,* which chronicled his youth in fin-de-siècle Vienna. The book was published posthumously in 1943. Zweig sent the manuscript to his publisher on 21 February 1942—the day before he and his wife, Lotte, committed suicide in Petropolis, Brazil.

When Hitler read Strauss's 17 June 1935 letter, he responded as Gauleiter Mutschmann had hoped and demanded Strauss's resignation. Goebbels carried out the order and in early July sent an aide to see the composer, who was then in Berchtesgaden. The letter had compounded Strauss's previous difficulties. For example, he had faced the issue of disorderly bookkeeping raised by fractious associates in the Reich Chamber of Music, and he had expended political capital when he defended pro-modernist composer and critic Hans Heinz Stuckenschmidt, as well as modernist composer Paul Hindemith, on whose behalf he intervened in the spring of 1935 when he tried to convince Goebbels to allow Hindemith to retain his professorship at the Berlin Hochschule für Musik. Michael Kater went so far as to argue, "Contrary to received wisdom, Strauss's difficulties with Stefan Zweig were not the solitary reason, and not even the main reason of his permanent fall from grace in the Nazi Reich."[31] The letter incident must be viewed in a broader context that includes the composer's haughty and independent behavior, and the gradual radicalization of the Nazis' policies.

Strauss complied with Goebbels's demand, but asked that "health reasons" be given as the grounds for being relieved of his duties. This was the explanation provided in the press. Strauss then wrote to Hitler on 13 July 1935. He had returned to Garmisch, aware that he faced a serious situation. He acknowledged that his resignation was warranted, but wanted to explain himself. This letter did not make for Strauss's finest hour. The core of it read,

> Mein Führer! My entire life belongs to German music and the tireless efforts to elevate German culture. I have never been active as a politician or expressed myself as such, and therefore I believe that you, as the great shaper of all of German life, will have understanding if I convey to you with deepest emotion about my dismissal as President of the Reich Chamber of Music, and where I had hoped to serve only the purest and most idealistic goals in the few years that I have left.[32]

Strauss maintained that his letter to Zweig "does not represent my worldview nor my true conviction," and then begged for an audience with Hitler so that he could further explain himself. He signed the letter, "I remain, very honorable Herr Reich Chancellor, with the expression of my deep veneration, your ever devoted subject."

Obviously, the modus vivendi between Strauss and the Nazi regime suffered major difficulties around 1935, and this was mirrored by the personal interactions between Hitler and the composer. Frederic Spotts observed, "The relationship between the two men was never more than a marriage of convenience, hopeful on Strauss's part, but bound to end in tears."[33] A key reason stemmed from the fact that Hitler was not particularly fond of Strauss's music. It had been Goebbels, after all, who had initiated Strauss's appointment to head the Reich Chamber of Music. Albert Speer recorded how Hitler expressed decidedly negative opinions regarding Richard Strauss, commenting, "Strauss is of no interest to me as a composer. Completely second rate! . . . We had to boot him out soon enough as president of the Reich Chamber of Music; Strauss had got much too involved with the Jewish riffraff."[34] Goebbels, whose views usually shifted so as to remain in alignment with Hitler's, also grew more critical of Strauss, as reflected in his diaries. By July 1936 he would write, "Furtwängler tells me about R. Strauss. . . . No one loves him. He has too little character." But Goebbels would vacillate as well, and he later made positive remarks about Strauss's work, saying of *Cäcilie* (1894), "What a wonderful song. 'In the creative breath of God.' Indescribable. An artwork. It really moves me."[35]

As with all the figures in this chapter, one must ask, why did he not emigrate? This is especially the case with someone as eminent as Richard Strauss, who could have secured appointments abroad without any difficulty. In addition to the reasons noted above about his ego and wanting to save German music, there was his Jewish daughter-in-law, Alice (née von Grab), and his two grandchildren. Strauss intervened on their behalf on numerous occasions and eventually utilized his contacts at very high levels to save their lives. Of course, Alice's presence put a strain on Strauss's relations with the Nazis, as did his Jewish publisher, his Jewish librettist, and his resistance to certain anti-Semitic measures in the Reich Chamber of Music. Yet somewhat paradoxically, despite Strauss's commitment to Jewish family members and several Jewish colleagues, he was not totally immune to the anti-Semitism so prevalent at the time. Michael Kater has argued that "Strauss, as an adolescent and a young man, was an anti-Semite in the mold of the cultured German upper bourgeoisie toward the end of the nineteenth century," and these views did not completely dissipate in the subsequent years.[36] He subscribed to certain stereotypes about greed, stubbornness, and dishonesty. He even called the light operetta genre that he despised "Jewish." Thus, Strauss remained in Germany in part to help others who were threatened, and in part because he shared a belief in certain aspects of the Nazis' worldview, among other reasons.

Strauss's resignation as president of the Reich Chamber of Music by no means brought an end to his cooperation with the Nazi regime. As Frederic Spotts noted, "Although his ardour eventually cooled, for some years he went on praising Hitler publicly and privately for his political accomplishments and his encouragement of the arts."[37] Strauss also retained several offices not related to the Reich Chamber of Music: for example, his post heading up the German branch of the international composers' union (he served as president of the entire organization). Consistent with his philosophy of exploiting cultural figures with international reputations, Goebbels realized that Strauss could be useful to the Nazi regime, especially with regard to foreign propaganda. To take one specific example, Strauss conducted at a festival in Antwerp in March 1936 at the height of the Rhineland crisis, when anti-German sentiment in Belgium was on the rise. This proved to be a propaganda coup for the Germans, and Strauss himself profited from the arrangement because his music served as the focal point of the program. He seemed to understand the mutually beneficial nature of his collaboration, writing to his wife after his return, "I would like to see another German artist do this, during this time, in those hostile foreign lands. For this feat I am actually entitled to the most golden medal of the propaganda ministry."[38] While this did not actually occur, musical historian Erik Levi noted how Strauss did indeed find a place in the Reich: "The highly dissonant language cultivated by Richard Strauss in his operas *Salome* and *Elektra* also escaped censure, and both works continued to be performed during the Third Reich."[39]

Shortly after the triumphal Belgian tour, Strauss released his Olympic hymn for the 1936 Berlin games, which he had actually completed in December 1934. Strauss had been approached by the International Olympic Committee in 1932, and accepted the assignment in early 1933. Famed author Gerhart Hauptmann had also initially agreed to write the words, but the Nazi leaders interjected themselves into the process, organizing a national competition to find suitable accompanying lyrics. The text to the hymn was actually the product of two competitions: the first, won by Wilhelm von Scholz, the president of the Reich Poets' Society, concerned Siegfried's battles and was deemed too nationalistic. The second competition, which generated over three thousand entries, yielded a poem by Robert Lubahn, an unemployed actor. It included lines such as, "The pride and the blossom of many countries came here to this celebration of struggle, all the fires that glow blaze together high and free." In short, it was a bombastic paean to martial values that invoked blood, conflict, and youthful energy. Goebbels even saw fit to tweak it lest a reference to the rule of law appear too democratic. The hymn premiered at the opening ceremonies of the Berlin Olympics on 1 August 1936. Strauss himself conducted the Berlin Philharmonic, the National Socialist Symphony Orchestra, and a chorus of one thousand. Leni Riefenstahl filmed the performance, and a segment appeared in her film *Olympia.*

It bears mentioning that Strauss was not nearly so dynamic as a conductor as Furtwängler and many other contemporaries. Of course, he was already sixty-nine years old when the Nazis came to power in 1933, but he looked even older. Strauss was rather laconic and did not exhibit much emotion when he led an orchestra. His movements were short and efficient. Some thought him disinterested—that he was looking forward to the card games that came after the performances. Yet musicians played well for Strauss, and many regarded him as a "wonderful" conductor.[40] He certainly had a presence, even a grandeur, that enhanced a performance.

It is commonly asserted that Strauss retreated from public affairs after 1936 and lived in isolation in Garmisch in the Bavarian Alps, but this is only partly correct. In fact, he was far from absent from German music life. Strauss was a perennial nominee for the prestigious German National Prize, with nods in 1938 from Alfred Rosenberg, who recognized Strauss's contacts with Jews but still regarded him as a "grosser Musikant," and from Goebbels in 1939, who posited that Strauss must "be regarded as the most representative German composer, whose life work can no longer be disassociated from German musical and cultural life."[41] Goebbels personally approached Strauss to conduct the composer's *Arabella* and *Festliches Präludium* at the Reich Music Festival in Düsseldorf in May 1938—part of a plan to implicate him in the *Degenerate Music Exhibition,* which took place at the same time.[42] Strauss accepted the invitation and basked in the publicity, even as he was exploited by the regime. His opera *Friedenstag* (*Day of Peace*), which premiered in 1938, received twenty-five different stagings and 130 performances during the Third Reich, including one for Nazi Party members in Rostock on Hitler's birthday in 1940.[43] Somewhat ironically, but reflecting the ambiguities of Strauss's career in these years, the one-act opera was set in the Thirty Years' War and featured a pacifist theme (it was also based on a sketch by Stefan Zweig, although the libretto was by the "Aryan" Joseph Gregor).[44]

Despite all his difficulties—most palpably, the forced resignation from office and the threats endured by his family as a result of the regime's racial policies—Strauss continued to curry favor with the Nazi leaders. During the latter half of the Third Reich, he dedicated pieces to Goebbels, Hans Frank (later the General Governor of occupied Poland), and Walther Funk (the Reich Economics Minister).[45] With regard to his subservient behavior, his years of experience stroking Kaiser Wilhelm II's ego and ultimately getting his way have often been cited to explain his interactions with Hit-ler: he was simply playing by the same rules he had learned over the years, even though the game itself had fundamentally changed. Strauss contin-ued to pen obsequious letters to Hitler, who sent polite responses and also attended performances of the composer's music, including *Friedenstag* in Vienna in June 1939 on the occasion of Strauss's seventy-fifth birthday. In 1942, the Reich Propaganda Ministry commissioned a film of him directing the Berlin Philharmonic. Goebbels himself had met with Strauss in Decem-ber 1941 and noted in his diary, "He has totally gotten over my earlier con-frontation with him and once again is toeing the line. . . . He is our greatest and most valuable, most representative musician."[46]

Of course, not everything went smoothly for Richard Strauss and his family. A most telling episode occurred at a meeting on 28 February 1941, at which Goebbels invited leading composers to discuss copyright payments. The Reich Minister wanted to reduce the sums received by composers of serious music and reward those who wrote more popular works, such as Franz Lehár. Goebbels had planned before the meeting to advance his agenda by way of an attack on Strauss. First, he arranged a reading of ex-cerpts of Strauss's correspondence with Stefan Zweig, in which the com-poser criticized the new government. Goebbels then yelled at Strauss, "Be quiet, and take note that you have no idea of who you are and who I am! Lehár has the masses, you don't. Stop babbling about the significance of serious music! This will not revalue your stock! Tomorrow's culture is dif-ferent from that of yesterday! You, Herr Strauss, are of yesterday!"[47] Clearly, Strauss was not regarded as an untouchable, and Goebbels had ambivalent feelings about him.

Richard Strauss's stock with Hitler and Goebbels fell even further in 1943 when he refused to open his home to evacuees who had lost their domiciles in the bombings. Strauss claimed that having them in his villa would prevent him from gaining access to his piano—with the implication being that he would be unable to carry on composing—but this answer, when combined with other factors (the letter to Zweig was scarcely forgot-ten), made him the target of threatening rumors. Hans Frank, although based in Cracow, where he served as the General Governor of what was left of Poland, managed to intervene and express support for Strauss, but in January 1944, when Strauss again resisted the measures to house refugees, Hitler ordered the annex to the Strauss estate in Garmisch to be confiscated. Goebbels wrote about the composer "who earlier could not do enough for us in terms of declarations of devotion but today says things that qualify for a people's court. . . . The Führer does not want anything done to harm Richard Strauss. He was just terribly angry because he behaved so shabbily about accepting evacuees. Nonetheless his works should be performed without hindrance."[48]

Strauss had also acquired a residence in Vienna in late 1941, largely due to his close relationship with the Nazi governor of the city, Baldur von Schirach. The two had known each other for decades, ever since Schirach's father had been the theater director in Weimar. Schirach and Strauss's son Franz had played together as children. Now, as part of his efforts to revive Vienna's cultural life, Schirach lured Strauss back, promising him artistic freedom. Schirach recalled after the war, "Richard Strauss, along with his wife, son, daughter-in-law, and grandchild moved back into his Viennese Palais."[49] He was referring to an elegant villa on the Janquingasse. In exchange for the comfortable arrangement, Strauss played along. This included receiving the first Beethoven prize awarded by the city council of Vienna in December 1942, and then in 1943 writing the *Festmusik* for the fifth anniversary of the *Anschluss*. Schirach also commissioned works from Strauss, such as the 1943 *Festmusik für den Trompeterchor der Stadt Wien*, and Strauss willingly complied. The two men got on well and socialized together from time to time—for example, at a party for dramatist Gerhart Hauptmann's eightieth birthday in November 1942, which was celebrated at the Schirachs' villa, known as the Hohe Warte.[50]

Strauss's greatest concern at this point was not his music but his Jewish daughter-in-law, Alice, and her children, who faced grave threats from the regime. Alice and Franz Strauss also resided in Garmisch, and their home had been targeted by storm troopers in November 1938 during the *Reichskristallnacht* pogrom, after which Alice had been placed under house arrest. She had fallen seriously ill, mostly likely induced by the stress. Richard Strauss had helped during this crisis—turning to Goebbels and securing limited protection. In another act that purportedly stemmed from his desire to help his family, he dedicated his symphony *Die Liebe der Danae* that he completed in 1940 to Heinz Tietjen, one of Göring's protégés and the head of the Prussian State Theater, as well as the artistic director for Bayreuth, who continued to use his influence to help the Strauss family.[51] The Nazi authorities nonetheless wanted Strauss's son to divorce Alice, which Franz refused to do. It was in this context that Strauss turned to Schirach in late 1941, and in which Strauss and his family were led to move into the villa in Vienna. Schirach, however, could offer only limited protection. In late 1943, Alice and Franz were arrested and imprisoned in a Gestapo jail for

*Reichsleiter ᵗon Schirach wohnte mit seinen Gästen Richard Strauß und Gerhart Haupt-
mann in der ~~Wiener Staats~~oper der glanzvollen Erstaufführung der Werke „Joan von
Zarissa" und „Carmina Burano" bei. Wenige Tage darauf folgte als zweites Wiener
Theaterereignis die Premiere von Hauptmanns „Iphigenie in Delphi" im Burgtheater*

Richard Strauss, Baldur von Schirach (middle), and dramatist Gerhart Hauptmann (right)
attend a performance of Carl Orff's Carmina Burana at the Viennese State Opera (February
1942). The photo was published in Goebbels's periodical, *Das Reich.*

several days. Schirach helped with an approach to the SS, and the two were
released. Alice and Franz were then permitted to move back to Garmisch,
where they remained under house arrest until Germany's surrender. Strauss
also relocated back to Garmisch for the last years of the war. More tragic
was the fate of Alice's family, including her grandmother, who was deported
to Theresienstadt. Strauss reportedly traveled to the camp outside Prague
and, arriving at the gates of the fortress-like complex, stepped out of his
limousine and proclaimed, "I am the composer Richard Strauss." The SS
guards were not impressed and turned him away. Strauss could do nothing,
and Alice's grandmother died, along with twenty-five Jewish relatives, during the Holocaust.[52]

Despite bitterness and depression, as well as physical ailments that
plagued him and his wife, Strauss kept working. Indeed, he maintained
throughout his entire career that he believed in "liberation through work,"
and the war years provided the most vivid expression of this philosophy.
Die Liebe der Danae, which as mentioned earlier was effectively completed
in 1940 and then polished in the subsequent years, elicited the phrase "mas-

terpiece" in one 2002 review that appeared in the *New Statesman* (a prestigious British periodical).[53] In other words, Strauss continued to create
high-quality work during the Third Reich—an especially remarkable feat
in light of his age (some consider the level of his work the greatest ever for
an octogenarian composer). In June 1944, on his eightieth birthday, which
in Germany customarily entailed a public celebration for major cultural
figures, Hitler and Goebbels sent congratulatory telegrams, and a new staging of *Ariadne auf Naxos* took place in Vienna, with Schirach in attendance.
While the celebration was technically "unofficial," the composer, in Frederic Spotts's words, "remained the country's most noted cultural figure."[54]
Even during the war, Strauss's operas were performed more frequently than
those of any other living composer in Germany. Granted, Strauss lost many
of the perks to which he had grown accustomed: a gardener, a chauffeur,
and foreign currency, and this perturbed him deeply. Yet he kept writing
and in April 1945 finished *Metamorphosen,* which featured an elaborate
arrangement for strings (twenty-three different solo parts). While scholars
had long believed that Strauss's composition mourned the bombing of the
Munich opera house, the Hoftheater, which he called "the greatest catastro-
phe that has ever disturbed my life," more recent research suggests that he
sought to "probe the cause of war itself, which stems from humanity's bes-
tial nature," and that he had been inspired by a poem by Goethe, "Niemand
wird sich selber kennen" (No One Can Really Recognize Himself).[55] One
critic called it "possibly the saddest piece of music ever written."[56]

The composer endured war's end and the ensuing period with remarkable ease. He was arrested by American troops at his Garmisch home in
April 1945, although he was treated with utmost respect by the commanding officer, Lieutenant Milton Weiss, who himself was a musician. When
faced with impending eviction from his villa, Strauss reportedly descended
the grand staircase and announced in heavily accented English, "My name
is Richard Strauss. I am the composer of *Der Rosenkavalier* and *Salome,*"
as he held up the pages of the scores. Lieutenant Weiss nodded with recognition, then placed an "off-limits" sign in front of the home.[57] Strauss
expressed no remorse about his actions during the Third Reich. Rather than
remain in Germany and face the consequences of his actions, he fled to
Switzerland. While Strauss sold some of his manuscripts and sketchbooks
to fund his temporary emigration—his accounts in Germany had been
frozen—he lived in relative comfort in a hotel outside Zurich. Receiving indications that he would be treated leniently if he returned to his homeland,
Strauss traveled back to what was now the American occupation zone in

early 1947 to face denazification in Garmisch and Munich. The prosecution was poorly organized and filed a series of inaccurate charges (for example, that he had been a member of the Prussian State Council, which was not true). The trial played out for seven months, with Strauss permitted periodic trips to Switzerland. On 7 June 1948, he was found "not incriminated" and cleared of all charges.

The verdict contributed to a rapid rehabilitation, and not only in Germany. Already in 1947, British conductor and impresario Sir Thomas Beecham invited the composer to London and, more specifically, to a Strauss Festival to be held at the Royal Albert Hall. Strauss himself conducted *Elektra*, for which he received a standing ovation from the entire audience. It was a remarkable gesture: a performer who was a Nazi official and currently standing trial performing in the British capital, and this two years after war's end. The entire event was broadcast on the BBC. Strauss was celebrated in the Federal Republic as well. For his eighty-fifth birthday in June 1949 he was invited back to his old orchestra, the Munich Philharmonic, which performed selections from *Der Rosenkavalier*. Strauss was greeted warmly by the members of the orchestra (presumably a number of holdovers from the Nazi era), and conducted a few passages. He was also awarded an honorary doctorate of law from the University of Munich.[58] And so he bowed out—venerated and seemingly exonerated. Strauss was even able to continue writing up until the end of his life, and he completed his *Requiem* among his last works. He did not live to see it performed. Strauss died from heart and kidney failure at his Garmisch home on 8 September 1949 at age eighty-five. When his *Requiem* premiered eight months later, the conductor of the orchestra was Wilhelm Furtwängler.

10

Gustaf Gründgens

(1899 Düsseldorf–1963 Manila)

Gustaf Gründgens as Hamlet in 1936. (Bundesarchiv-Koblenz, Bild Nr. 183-S01144)

ONE OF GERMANY'S most famous actors in the twentieth century, Gustaf Gründgens was immortalized by his one-time brother-in-law Klaus Mann in his thinly veiled novel *Mephisto*. Written in 1936, and then turned into an Academy Award–winning film in 1981, the now famous roman à clef portrayed the actor as a cynical but tortured opportunist.[1] Klaus Mann, as noted earlier (see Chapter 6), was the son of Thomas Mann and a well-known author in his own right. At the time he published *Mephisto* in the mid-1930s he claimed that his novel was about no specific individual but rather a particular type who collaborated with the Nazi regime.[2] Such protestations proved ineffectual, and nearly all observers have regarded the character of Hendrik Höfgen as a stylized version of Gründgens. A lawsuit by Gründgens's companion (and also adopted son), Peter Gründgens-Gorski, in the 1960s went all the way to the Federal Constitutional Court in Karlsruhe. The justices ruled that "Gründgens's personal freedom (Article 2 of the Basic Law) was more important than the freedom of art (Article 5)," and, as of 1968, the West German edition of the book was outlawed (the East German edition, printed by a different publisher, was not affected). A West German edition was finally published in 1980—only a year before the release of the exceptionally successful film.[3]

Regardless of one's interpretation of Klaus Mann's novel, Gründgens's high profile and successful career offer insight into the manner in which some avant-garde actors responded to the Third Reich. Although a number of famous actors emigrated and flourished in Hollywood—Marlene Dietrich, Peter Lorre, and Lotte Lenya stand out as examples—and although as many as "4,000 theater artists in all quit Germany," the majority of the Weimar theatrical talent remained in Germany after the Nazi seizure of power.[4] Actors, perhaps more than other artists, were tied to language, and mastering English proved a challenge that most Germans were unwilling to face. The spate of Hollywood films about the Nazis—

especially with the wartime propaganda efforts—meant that there was limited work for those who were prepared to be the German "heavy" (Conrad Veidt, for example, who had starred as Cesare in *The Cabinet of Dr. Caligari* in 1920, played Major Strasser in *Casablanca* in 1942, among several similar roles). Gründgens, on the other hand, acted in a breathtaking array of plays and films in Nazi Germany, and of course he continued to act after the war. A compilation of his work, which appeared in the form of a twenty compact disc set in 2004, provides a sense of his remarkably productive career.[5]

Among those associated with the theater and who stayed in Germany during the Third Reich, many had engaged in left-wing activities during Weimar. Examples include set designer Caspar Neher and director Erich Engel, both of whom had worked closely with Bertolt Brecht in the 1920s, and actors Heinrich George and Bernhard Minetti, who moved from leftist theater to the Nazi stage without serious difficulties. Gerhart Hauptmann, a pioneer of German Naturalism and an artist who had long shown sympathy toward workers and the marginalized in society (which could be construed as left-wing), continued to write and to have his plays performed during the Third Reich. Some in the theatrical world tried to adapt modernist precepts to fit into Nazi Germany, including Robert Rohde, who founded "the first Nazi experimental theatre company" in 1925. Rohde's traveling company, which endured only until the early 1930s, staged both Nazi works, like the plays of Dietrich Eckart, and also classics, such as Schiller's *The Robbers*, in which the troupe added a strong anti-Semitic element. For over two years, the Rohde company's repertoire included a relatively avant-garde production of Joseph Goebbels's *The Traveler* (*Der Wanderer*). Although the text for the play has been lost, there are a number of extant reports about its staging: the drama centered on "a character [who] made his way through Germany's 'deep night' observing phenomena such as poverty, the church, and the government."[6]

It was not just the continuity from the pre-1933 period that was so notable, but also the vitality of theater in Nazi Germany. One gains a sense by looking at the figures for the number of musicians contracted to German theaters during the Third Reich:

Season	Singers	Chorus	Orchestra
1932–33	1,859	2,955	4,889
1937–38	2,145	3,238	5,577

All categories of performers experienced increases after 1933, and the number employed in the theatrical world remained considerable up until the "total war" measures of early 1943. Germany's 197 municipal theaters, which were subsidized by the government, saw attendance increase steadily. By 1942 twice as many people went to these theaters as compared to ten years earlier.[7] These figures call to mind the observation of cultural historian Otto Friedrich, who noted, "The Germans' relationship to their theatre is quite unlike the Americans' distant view of Broadway. The German drama is not simply a series of box-office hits in a far-off metropolis but part of a nationwide tradition."[8] The fact remains that the Nazis exposed more Germans to culture than any previous regime, and this found expression at the box office.

Gründgens stands out as such a striking figure because he featured so prominently in left-wing theater during the Weimar Republic, and then subsequently received so much publicity as a representative of the "revivified" stage during the Third Reich. He was also genuinely talented, or, as Peter Watson observed in his book on "German genius," Gründgens was "the most imaginative and versatile actor/director of those times . . . [and he] could sing and dance, as well as act."[9] It is often the case that the story is more interesting when the protagonist possesses intelligence and ability, and so it was with Gründgens. The actor's story is also instructive because he brought together so many of the previously discussed factors that motivated his complicity with the Nazis, including a misassessment of the regime, a naked opportunism, an oversized ego, and a belief that his art would align well with the new Germany.

Gustaf Gründgens grew up in a bourgeois milieu in Düsseldorf. His father and other family members were industrialists, although he later characterized them as a family in decline. Gründgens demonstrated certain conservative tendencies early on. He initially trained for a career in business and, in a fit of nationalistic fervor, volunteered for the army in July 1917. However, he never saw action at the front and, after an accidental injury, was allowed to join an army theater troupe. It was a transformative experience for him, and by 1918 he had risen to become the manager of the troupe, now renamed the Bergtheater Thale. Upon demobilization in 1919, Gründgens enrolled in an acting school at the Düsseldorf Schauspielhaus and then won a scholarship to attend the highly regarded School of Dramatic Arts (Hochschule für Bühnenkunst) in Düsseldorf, led by Louise Dumont and Gustav Lindemann.[10] He showed considerable promise but also made no secret of his ambitions and soon moved into the professional ranks.

Gründgens's career began in smaller cities, such as Halberstadt in north-central Germany, where he acted in a local theater in 1920, but he gradually moved to larger venues, first in Kiel in 1921 then in Hamburg in 1923. This latter move, in which he joined the company of the Kammerspiele in Hamburg, represented a major step forward. In the five years he spent at the Kammerspiele, he experimented with a wide array of roles—seventy different characters—while also finding time to direct thirty productions between 1923 and 1928. Gründgens developed a reputation for playing villains, but his repertoire extended to "arrogant snobs, social climbers [and] morally unstable and neurotic types."[11] (Rather appropriately, he changed his name in 1925 from the conventional "Gustav" to the more unusual and affected "Gustaf.") He threw himself into his craft, often devoting sixteen hours a day to productions—and, as Klaus Mann suggested with some exaggeration, suffering a nervous collapse about once a week. But he learned a great deal from a talented cohort and became a skilled actor.

The Hamburger Kammerspiele featured agitprop theater; in line with Marxist tenets that all intellectuals should work toward the revolution, the members of the company staged plays that heightened the political consciousness of the audience. Enacting theories developed by left-wing theater pioneers such as Bertolt Brecht (for example, "epic theater," which employed technological innovations such as treadmills, strived for "the alienation effect" and aimed to have the audience "learn how to think rather than how to feel"), the Hamburg company emerged as a leading and in many ways representative exponent of Weimar culture. One critic referred to Gründgens in this period as a "flamboyant radical."[12] Gründgens rose to become a leader of the company—often directing productions himself—and his outlook was consonant with the entire company. Representative of the Kammerspiele's political orientation was a July 1926 press release that proclaimed that Gründgens was preparing a series of sketches called "Revolutionary Theater." The performances would take place on Sunday mornings, when workers were not burdened with their jobs, and invitations were extended to various workers' and youth associations. The first production was to feature Ernst Toller's *Masse-Mensch,* a classic work of left-wing agitprop theater.

The Revolutionary Theater undertaking, however, never took off. Due to financial considerations, Sunday-morning performances were abandoned, although the company did mount other left-wing productions, including Erwin Piscator's staging of Alfons Paquet's drama *Sturmflut* (*Storm Flood*). Gründgens ultimately became known more for rhetoric and cha-

Gründgens (kneeling with monocle at right) at the Hamburger Kammerspiele theater during the Weimar Republic. (Stadtmuseum Berlin)

risma than for his reform efforts. One biographer suggested that the force behind the initiatives for political theater in Hamburg was another member of the troupe, and that Gründgens was merely a kind of conjuncturist.[13] That said, the Hamburg company was both left-wing and experimental. Typical of their work was their cabaret-style staging of Shakespeare's *Hamlet* and Georg Büchner's *Danton's Death* from 1835. Gründgens also made a name for himself in Hamburg performing in plays by modernists Frank Wedekind and Carl Sternheim, both of whom incorporated Expressionist elements into their work. Gründgens directed and starred in Wedekind's *Spring Awakening* in 1926, a play that presented a critique of the sexually

217

oppressive culture of the fin-de-siècle period and was so controversial that a court order was required to clear the way in 1917 when it was first staged in English in New York (the city's Commissioner of Licenses maintained that it was pornographic).

The Hamburger Kammerspiele was also notable because the company featured Klaus and Erika Mann (two of Thomas Mann's children), and Pamela Wedekind (daughter of the above-noted dramatist). They formed a tight-knit group in more ways than one. Gründgens was married to Erika Mann from 1926 to 1929, and Erika Mann, who was bisexual, eventually became romantically involved with Pamela Wedekind (Erika Mann later married W. H. Auden in a "marriage of convenience"). The four were all glittering members of Weimar's cultural elite. Erika Mann, for example, was active in both journalism and politics. In the late 1920s, she and Gründgens had a remarkable range of friends and acquaintances who figured in the cultural life of the nation. The couple divorced in 1929, but both went on to even greater prominence. Erika, with her brother Klaus, help found the cabaret Die Pfeffermühle in Munich in January 1933, which they then reestablished in Zurich after emigrating from Germany. The cabaret emerged as a center for exile activities and helped induce the Nazi regime to withdraw the siblings' German citizenship in the mid-1930s. Erika went on to write an important tract on education in Nazi Germany, *School for Barbarians* (1939), and, along with Klaus, an account about prominent German émigrés titled *Escape to Life* (1939). Klaus himself published *Mephisto* (1936), *The Vulkan* (1939), and *The Turning Point* (1942), among other works; tragically, he suffered from acute depression and died of an overdose of sleeping pills in Cannes in May 1949.

One should not overly romanticize Gründgens's tenure with the Hamburger Kammerspiele. In addition to the theater's financial difficulties, many of its productions received negative notices. A review of the 1927 production of a comedy titled *Revue zu Vieren,* which was written by Klaus Mann and featured not only the author, but also his sister, Erika, Gründgens, and Pamela Wedekind, began, "The play and its author are a matter for a psychologist, not for theater."[14] The phrasing referred to the subject matter of the play (a doctor filling out a certificate of health), but also alluded to shortcomings of the production. Another reviewer noted, "Much is said in the dialogue about European youth. However, Klaus Mann has nothing to say to them. The leadership position of Europe's youth is not occupied."[15] That said, Gründgens stood out in this and other productions. Even in *Revue zu Vieren,* Gründgens received praise for his forceful presence. He possessed considerable talent as well as a booming voice and an ability to speak with exaggeratedly clear diction. But he refused to go on tour with the company to the provinces, fearing he would hurt his career by performing in a poorly received play in cities like Cottbus.

An element of Gründgens's modernist chic persona during the late-Weimar Republic grew out of his film work, which included edgy productions such as *M—A City Seeks a Murderer,* the Fritz Lang and Thea von Harbou film of 1931. In *M,* Gründgens played Schränker, an underworld boss who helps bring a child murderer (Peter Lorre) to justice. The gritty film, set in Depression-era Berlin with dark themes such as child murder and (implied) pedophilia, certainly pushed boundaries of popular culture. For the role, Gründgens wore a black leather trench coat and matching gloves, accompanied by a stylish bowler. His was a kind of urban gangster chic. Among the half-dozen films in which he acted in the early 1930s, only a handful could be regarded as modernist, but as with his earlier agitprop efforts in Hamburg, Gründgens did enough to earn a reputation as "fashionably radical."[16]

The actor had moved to Berlin in 1928 in order to perform on a bigger stage, and this included at Max Reinhardt's famed Deutsches Theater. His first performance there, in October 1928, was as a "sadistic homosexual" in Ferdinand Bruckner's play *The Criminals.* One biographer noted of his performance, "This slick, ice-cold, and cynical type, who in his cunningly glittering and sharply articulate way, was new for Berlin."[17] Despite making his mark on the Berlin theater world, Gründgens eventually grew dissatisfied with the roles Reinhardt gave him and looked elsewhere for work, including the film industry and the cabaret stage. During this time he met director Heinz Tietjen, the head of the Berlin Staatstheater at the Gendarmenmarkt and the artistic director in Bayreuth, among other posts. It was Tietjen who cast him in the role for which he would become most famous: Mephisto in Goethe's *Faust I.* Although Gründgens had appeared in the play earlier in his career, the timing of this production in late 1932, when so many Germans struggled with their conscience regarding political affairs, proved prescient—and too tempting for Klaus Mann to resist as a subject for a novel. The actor's Faustian bargain with the Nazis offered the perfect metaphor for many citizens of Nazi Germany. Indeed, as indicated above, Mann claimed his novel was not about his former brother-in-law, but rather a more generic treatment of collaboration in the Third Reich.

Caveats aside, Klaus Mann captured the essence of Gründgens's career in Nazi Germany, and he also referenced many true-life events. This included both Gründgens being out of the country when Hitler was appointed chancellor in January 1933 (he was in Spain filming *The Beautiful Days of Aranjuez*), and the key role played by Emmy Sonnemann (later Göring) in intervening to promote Gründgens's career. After the Nazi seizure of power, it was questionable whether the actor would even dare return to Germany. His left-wing persona left him apprehensive, and he may have had private concerns about how his homosexual proclivities would be received. Gründgens himself declared in 1950 that he returned in order to help five people for whom he felt responsible: his parents, a friend who was a dedicated Communist, a Jewish friend (Ida Liebmann), and a fifth person whom he did not identify but who lived in the United States after the war.[18]

Gründgens faced a difficult environment when he returned to Berlin. Göring had appointed dual Intendants of the Prussian State Theater: Franz Ulbrich from the Weimar Nationaltheater, and Hanns Johst, a playwright who sported an SS uniform. Johst is now best remembered for the line in his contemporaneous play *Schlageter*, "When I hear the word *culture*, I release the safety catch on my Browning" (uttered by a professor, no less).[19] The two men told Gründgens that his contract would not be renewed, and that certain roles which he had been promised—most notably Hamlet—were not consistent with the new historical circumstances. Although Johst had once shown modernist tendencies in his writing and occasionally helped modernist colleagues such as Gottfried Benn, he and Ulbrich (who had also earlier staged Expressionist productions) were Nazi stalwarts, and by 1933 that meant a very different kind of theater. With the Prussian State Theater, they thought they were reinvigorating an august institution that had turned decadent and irrelevant, when, in reality, they threatened to transform it into a provincial backwater. They showed their intentions by first attempting to fire all Jews and Communists who worked there.

Despite the new politicized leadership, Gründgens was permitted to reprise his role as Mephisto. The April 1933 performance in *Faust II* would prove fateful because Göring was in attendance. Emmy Sonnemann arranged an introduction, inviting the actor to the royal box, and this marked the beginning of an important relationship. Gründgens recalled his encounter with the Prussian Minister President that night: "Göring appeared very impressed by my portrayal of Mephisto and declared categorically that the contract between the State Theater and me remained valid—and that this must be both for the State Theater and also for me."[20] The contract in question was as an actor with the Prussian State Theater, not the position of Intendant.

Gründgens and Emmy
Sonnemann Göring, who
acted together at the
Prussian State Theater.
(Stadtmuseum Berlin)

In October 1933, Gründgens starred with Sonnemann in a staging of Hermann Bahr's comedy *The Concert*, which proved one of many popular successes. Exhibiting a free and easy charm, Gründgens delighted audiences, including the Prussian Minister President, who came to see his future wife perform. Subsequent roles at the Staatstheater for Gründgens in late 1933 and early 1934 included Frederick the Great in Hermann von Boetticher's *The King*, and Joseph Fouché in a drama about Napoleon called *The Hundred Days*, which was written by Benito Mussolini and Giovacchino Forzano (a film version followed in 1935). Gründgens showed considerable range, which contributed to a rise in his professional fortunes. His 1938 film *Dance on the Volcano*, a musical set in 1830 Paris, showcased his varied talents. Gründgens played Debureau, a minstrel who affronts King Charles X with his satirical song but who is saved from the guillotine by the masses. The costume drama-musical extended a long way from classical or avant-garde theater, although the linkages remained evident. Goebbels complained in his diary about the film, "typical Gründgens. A bit too cerebral."[21]

Gründgens also benefited from the contemporaneous rivalry between Göring and Goebbels. Hanns Johst was in Goebbels's camp—he became president of the Reich Chamber for Literature in 1935. With the Reich Propaganda Minister expanding his empire at a rapid rate—the Reich Chamber of Culture had come into existence in the autumn of 1933—Göring moved to consolidate power over the Prussian State Theater. Right after the premiere of the Mussolini-Forzano play on 26 February 1934, Göring decided to sack Johst and turn to Gründgens, offering him the leadership of the theater.[22] Gründgens had most likely been alerted by Emmy Sonnemann that the offer was coming, but he still asked for time to consider the matter. Göring pressed him, promising the utmost artistic freedom. Gründgens relented and accepted the post—albeit on a provisional (*kommissarische*) basis at first. He knew that the appointment entailed becoming one of Göring's creatures and that he was exposing himself in a politically fraught environment. Goebbels was also making a play to take over the Prussian State Theater in March 1934. But Gründgens took the leap, his appointment as Intendant becoming permanent in September 1934, thereby completing the Prussian Minister President's tactical maneuver.

Göring more or less proved good on his word and served as Gründgens's chief patron for the next eleven years. With regard to artistic freedom, the Prussian Minister President fostered an independent and more liberal *Theaterpolitik*.[23] While this did not mean that productions by Jewish authors were staged, or that the theater featured aggressively modern set design, Gründgens oversaw a wide array of productions, ranging from German classics (Goethe, Schiller, Lessing) to foreign classics (Shakespeare, Alexandre Dumas), to more contemporary drama and comedy. Gründgens was also able to employ people like Erich Ziegel, an old friend and colleague from Hamburg who had been known for promoting Expressionist drama and who was married to a Jew, Mirjam Horwitz. Ziegel remained with the Prussian State Theater until 1945. Director Jürgen Fehling continued to stage controversial works, including a rendition of *Richard III* in 1937 in which the murderers wore brown shirts and jackboots and the character Gloucester, played by Werner Krauss, hobbled about the stage with a clubfoot (a seeming reference to Goebbels).[24] Despite calls for his dismissal—apparently endorsed by Göring who had seen the play and was also offended—Gründgens defended Fehling, and the director kept his post within the Prussian state system. Other actors in the troupe also had Jewish spouses, including Wolf Trutz, Paul Bildt, Paul Henckels, and Karl Ettlinger. According to Gründgens's biographer Heinrich Goertz, the spouses were protected from the worst of the Nazi racial persecution.[25] Because it was widely known that Gründgens had Göring as a patron, many opponents avoided open criticism of the actor, and this often extended to challenging his influence in other ways.

Few people in the Third Reich were completely safe from attacks, and Gründgens himself proved no exception. In early 1936, he tackled the lead role as Shakespeare's troubled Danish prince. Several Nazi reviewers considered his performance to be too "modern"—with words like "nervous" and "aestheticized" accompanying the critiques. An article in the *Völkischer Beobachter* on 3 May 1936 noted, "Intellectualism is a typical product of Jewry . . . Gründgens is an intellectual."[26] The logic of this formulation was not lost on readers. Alfred Rosenberg and the other editors at the paper also thought Gründgens too "narcissistic rather than Nazi-istic." Although Gründgens's Hamlet was a box-office hit, and his fans continued to wait outside the theater hoping for an autograph, the attacks in the press demoralized and frightened him, prompting Gründgens to head into temporary exile in Switzerland. In fact, he left for Basel on the same day the *Völkischer Beobachter* piece appeared.[27]

Göring quickly learned that Gründgens had "immigrated" to Switzerland and telephoned the actor to request his return. The Prussian Minister President approached Gründgens with "a mixture of joviality and threat."[28] He promised him free passage back to Berlin to discuss the situation, but he also said that a failure to return might lead to consequences for Gründgens's family and friends. Göring also noted that two of the editors responsible for the negative reviews of *Hamlet* had been imprisoned. Gründgens returned almost immediately and met with Göring at the Prussian Minister President's palace on the Leipziger Platz. Göring also arranged for one of the arrested journalists to be transferred from the Gestapo cells in the Prinz-Albrecht Strasse and brought to the meeting. The latter apologized and swore that the attacks were aimed not at Gründgens, but at another actor, Alexander Moissi, who had long been associated with the pro-modernist theater producer Max Reinhardt. Gründgens therefore returned to the fold and continued to supervise the Prussian State Theater.

Göring actually oversaw all the state theaters in Prussia, including those in provincial towns like Kassel, but he cared most about "his" Prussian State Theater in Berlin. As the foremost theater in the capital—and arguably in all of Germany—its productions resonated on a national level. There was the additional factor that Göring's fiancée and future wife, Emmy Sonnemann, starred at the theater. Even though she stepped back from the stage after marrying Göring in 1935, Sonnemann remained a force with regard to the performing arts. Gerdy Schüchter, the wife of conductor Herbert von Karajan's assistant in Aachen, recalled in 1946 how von Karajan's first wife, who was a singer at the Aachen Stadttheater, "was a personal friend of Emmi [sic] Sonnemann and thereby would promote Herr von Karajan, without his volition and without his somehow being enthused about the goals and ideas of the Nazis."[29] While this is undoubtedly a very generous portrayal of von Karajan (who joined the Nazi Party twice, after all), the more striking point is the influence of Göring's wife. Gründgens would later attempt to repay her for the support she had provided him, testifying on her behalf at her July 1948 denazification trial.

Gründgens was cognizant of the Görings' tremendous power over the theater, and he played a game of supplication with skill and charm. He was rewarded handsomely for his fealty. For example, he became a Reich Cultural Senator in 1935, along with Furtwängler, Pfitzner, Clemens Krauss, and Heinz Tietjen. Although the post had little real power, it was a symbol of his position and brought some enjoyable perks—including two orchestra seats for any performance at an opera, theater, or concert. Later, on 7 May 1936, after his return from Switzerland, Göring appointed him to the Prussian State Council (Preussische Staatsrat). This was another largely honorary body, but it offered Gründgens another opportunity to interact with Göring. It also afforded him an additional measure of political protection. As Gründgens's biographer Alfred Mühr noted, "The title of privy counselor [Staatsrat] made Gründgens immune. Nothing could happen to a member of the Prussian State Council without the knowledge of Göring. He could neither be imprisoned nor displaced."[30] In December 1936, Gründgens was promoted from Intendant to General Intendant—indicative of even greater authority in the German theater world—and in July 1937 Goebbels made Gründgens a State Actor (Staatsschauspieler), an ambiguous title but meant to represent the highest honor that could be bestowed upon an actor. That same year, Goebbels appointed him to the Presidential Advisory Board of the Reich Chamber of Theater, as all the previous members had been replaced for "unspecified reasons."

Gründgens also knew well enough to cultivate Dr. Goebbels, the most powerful figure in the cultural sphere besides Hitler. Despite a certain friction in their personal and professional relationship, the actor would socialize with the Reich Propaganda Minister, as reflected in Goebbels's diaries from 13 June 1938: "Below us lies heavenly Vienna. We spend mid-day and the afternoon in the amusing company of artists. Gründgens is riotously funny. . . . And then we sit among a circle of artists in a garden in Grinzing. The moon shines above us, mild summer air; the violins weep. Hans Moser sings songs of the *Heurige* [wine gardens]. It is indescribably romantic."[31] The actor knew that his career depended on not only his work on the stage, but also his relationships with the Nazi leaders. Perceiving themselves as men of culture and enjoying the company of artists (Goebbels also worked hard to seduce many of the female persuasion), the Nazi leaders sought out figures like Gründgens, who could entertain them with witty repartee. Gründgens was also invited to meet Hitler, although he did not become a regular member of the dictator's court.

Gründgens used his connections with Göring and Goebbels to aid other actors persecuted by the regime. These interventions proved valuable after the war when he was imprisoned and denazified by the Soviets. Some of the actors whom he assisted testified on his behalf, and he was set free after nine months. Gründgens was particularly helpful to Jewish actors, such as Paul Bildt and Paul Henckels, whom he saved by approaching Goebbels. He also evidently interceded on behalf of actor Ernst Busch. Gründgens's biographer Peer Michalzik believes that the actor later exaggerated the significance of such interventions, writing they "were by a good measure not so critical and risky as Gründgens later wanted to regard them."[32] But Gründgens was not alone in this respect—in terms of both helping colleagues in peril and subsequently exaggerating the importance of his efforts.

A key question about Gründgens is whether he, during the Third Reich, attempted to utilize the modernist theater techniques that he learned earlier. The short answer would be yes, in certain ways. One need only read the reviews of his work. For example, in an early performance in the role of Mephisto around the time of the Nazi seizure of power, the Berlin critic Herbert Ihering wrote, "He is a cabaret singer and Charly's aunt, a cavalier and an ornamental lady. He flashes and sparks . . . with an amusing snobbery."[33] In other words, Gründgens's portrayal incorporated elements of cabaret, popular culture, and androgyny—and more generally featured a daring approach to the role. His style often suggested a certain decadence, and it was an open secret that he was homosexual (or bisexual). All of these characteristics were suggestive of the modernist cabaret culture of the Weimar Republic.

Gründgens's androgyny and ambiguous sexuality characterized many of his performances during the Third Reich. This was the subtext of the

Gründgens as Joseph Chamberlain in the anti-British propaganda film *Ohm Krüger* from 1941. (Stadtmuseum Berlin)

attacks on his portrayal of Hamlet in 1936, even if the journalists would couch their words in Nazi jargon—for example, that he lacked Nordic-mythic qualities. His androgynous qualities were also evident in the 1938 film *Gösta Berling,* in which he played a Hamlet-like character who pursues "the longing for freedom of the soul."[34] Even his portrayal of Joseph Chamberlain in the infamous Nazi propaganda film *Ohm Krüger* (1941) included effeminate elements. Gründgens's Joseph Chamberlain, the British Colonial Secretary and father of Prime Minister Neville Chamberlain, seemed effete and brittle, while at the same time arrogant and cruel. According to the Nazis, of course, it was the British who invented the concentration camp during the Boer War.

Göring in particular sanctioned Gründgens's sexual ambiguity. Historian Alan Steinweis noted, "The flexible approach to the purge of homosexuals is perhaps best exemplified by the case of the celebrated actor and director Gustaf Gründgens, whose homosexuality was an open secret in the Third Reich. Both Goebbels and Hitler were 'aghast' by what the former characterized as a 'swamp' of homosexuality that Gründgens had ostensibly encouraged at the Berlin State Theater. But Hermann Göring, who as Minister President of Prussia oversaw the State Theater, interceded to insulate Gründgens from the consequences of Paragraph 175" (the provision in the German criminal code that made homosexuality illegal).[35] When Reich Chamber of Culture Vice President and SS Major General Hans Hinkel tried to discipline Gründgens after reports of misconduct, Göring interceded and not only put the matter to rest but reprimanded Hinkel. Goebbels expressed frustration and resentment in a diary entry from 1937: "These 175ers are all hysterical like women. . . . The entire Gründgens shop [is] completely gay. I don't understand Göring here at all."[36]

The key point here is that Gründgens's performances in the Third Reich reflected considerable continuity with his work during the Weimar Republic. Like other cultural figures discussed in this book, Gründgens did not completely divorce himself from his modernist training. Of course, there were limits to the extent to which he could employ modernist techniques in his work. Unlike painters, who could create on their own, or composers, who could still write the music that they pleased (even if they faced difficulties performing the work in public), actors could scarcely practice their craft in private. Also, theater represents an essentially a collaborative venture and, as such, requires a kind of coordination that lends itself to control by the state.

As a star in Nazi Germany's theater and cinema establishment, Gründgens not unexpectedly found himself in productions that expressed National Socialist ideas. Goebbels, for example, recruited him to appear in *Ohm Krüger,* recognizing the actor's facility for playing villains. The ruthlessness of the British imperialist comes through in Gründgens's over-the-top performance. Gründgens initially resisted taking on the role. He wrote to the production chief of the Tobis studio, Ewald von Demandowsky, "I have granted the request made to me by Herr Reichsminister Dr. Goebbels, not as an artist, but self-evidently, as a consequence of my position within the Reich Chamber of Culture and the inner circle of the Reichsmarschall. I therefore have no particular wishes, and am waiting for your instructions."[37] He penned a similar letter to Emil Jannings, who starred in the film. Jannings had also starred in the 1930 Weimar classic *The Blue Angel* and would qualify as another cultural figure with modernist roots who found a place in the Reich. Despite the oppositional undertone of the messages, Gründgens signed both missives with "Heil Hitler!" Appearing in productions of this kind was one of the costs Gründgens paid in order to play other, more congenial roles. That same year, in 1941, he appeared in

Friedemann Bach, a historical biopic about a member of the Bach family. The film has been compared to *Amadeus,* with Gründgens in the role of the brilliant but tragic musician.

Gründgens favored historical subjects, and this was clearly reflected in the productions he organized at the Prussian State Theater. He portrayed Frederick the Great in *The Seven Years' War* in 1937 and Alexander the Great in Hans Baumann's *Alexander* in 1941. While there were ideological messages—Frederick was the duty-bound first servant of the state and Alexander sought to conquer the world—they were not explicitly political productions. Rather, Gründgens's characters typically proved more subtly supportive of the Nazi Reich. During the war, for example, Gründgens once again staged Goethe's *Faust* (he not only played the role of Mephisto, but served as director). In this wartime production, he played a blond, Nordic Mephisto. This reflected a broader trend in theater during the Third Reich, where explicitly propagandistic works were often regarded as excessively heavy-handed. As Christelle Le Faucheur noted, "With the exception of an Aryanized version of *The Merchant of Venice,* plays rarely displayed outright antisemitism, a concession to the general lack of such sentiment among audiences."[38] Not that the *Bildungsbürger* (educated bourgeoisie) weren't anti-Semitic or supportive of National Socialism, but a more subtle and *salonfähig* (socially acceptable) approach seemed more consistent with the culture of the theater world.

But relative to other theatrical enterprises, Gründgens had free rein. For example, the Staatstheater productions did not require the approval of the Reichsdramaturg, the censor that answered to Goebbels. Ironically, the main censor, Rainer Schlösser, exhibited pro-modernist tendencies.[39] But that said, no productions of stridently modernist playwrights were performed during Gründgens's tenure at the Staatstheater—no Frank Wedekind or August Strindberg, for example. In 1936, when Gründgens was promoted to General Intendant, he also became the head of a smaller Berlin theater, called the Kleine Haus in der Nürnberger Strasse, that held just over a thousand seats. Later, in 1941, he took over the Lustspielhaus, which was the former Komische Oper. This afforded Gründgens more latitude than he had in the august State Theater, and here he was able to stage works by Gerhart Hauptmann, George Bernard Shaw, and, before the outbreak of war, Oscar Wilde. He also performed the role of Louis Dubedat in Shaw's *The Doctor's Dilemma* at the Staatsoper in Berlin in October 1938.[40] That Gründgens could stage a romantic comedy by the Irish-born author and co-founder of the London School of Economics spoke to the relative latitude he enjoyed, especially in the prewar period.

Göring not only protected Gründgens, he also helped corrupt him. Of course, Gründgens became very wealthy. As of 1936, he received as salary RM 200,000 ($80,000) to serve as head of the Prussian Staatstheater (or a hundred times the wage of an average worker). Gründgens also had additional income from films, where he earned on average RM 80,000 ($32,000) per picture (and he acted in or directed twenty-eight films between 1930 and 1941 alone).[41] In 1935 Gründgens moved into an estate about an hour's drive outside Berlin that had belonged to a Jewish banker. Nazi leaders often put "Aryanized" residences at the disposal of cultural figures—there was a sense that they needed the financial assistance and that helping artists made the enterprise seem more noble—and the arrangement for Gründgens was typical in this respect.[42] The so-called Gutes Zeesen bei Königswusterhausen was an elegant *Schloss* that featured a mansard roof, a dramatic staircase, and an adjoining lake. The Jewish owner (named Goldschmidt) had died in 1934, and his son was forced to sell it to Gründgens at a extraordinarily low price—so low that questions of a forced sale emerged after the war. While these allegations were never proven, the property was ultimately restituted to the Goldschmidt family.[43] In addition to this country house, Gründgens received a more centrally located abode from Göring after the actor returned from his "emigration" to Switzerland: more specifically, the residence of the royal gardener in Schloss Bellevue. This state property came at no cost to him.

Besides appearing in Nazi propaganda films and reaping the financial benefits of stardom, Gründgens also helped provide the regime with "its beautiful veneer," to use the phrase coined by historian Peter Reichel.[44] Gründgens had married actor and movie star Marianne Hoppe in 1936, and the two frequently served as symbols of the new Reich. With her fair complexion and natural beauty, she epitomized a certain, in Goebbels's words, "Nordic attractiveness."[45] For Hoppe, Gründgens's serious theater work, especially his staging of the classics, and his more general fame as an actor, made him a suitable match. Hoppe therefore was both a movie star and a member of the ensemble of the Prussian State Theater, where she continued to perform until relatively late in the war. The couple frequently appeared in propaganda photos produced by the regime—collecting funds for the Nazi charity Winterhilfswerk or serving up helpings of *Eintopf,* the one-pot stew that symbolized the austerity program that would benefit the *Volk*. Hoppe was a favorite of Goebbels and Hitler, and the couple was invited to socialize with the Nazi elite. She later acknowledged after the war that Gründgens "was my love, but never my great love. That was [my] work."[46] And indeed, both Gründgens and Hoppe used one another to advance their careers and to ascend into Nazi Germany's "cultural aristocracy." In a sense, the public relations campaign surrounding the actors was quintessentially modern, as the popular press featured seemingly ceaseless coverage of their films and followed their private lives in mind-numbing detail. The couple divorced in 1946 but remained close friends. Hoppe, who had begun acting in the mid-1920s as a member of Max Reinhardt's Deutsches Theater, returned to modernist theater after the war—appearing in productions of plays by Jean-Paul Sartre, Heiner Müller, and Thomas Bernhard, with the latter becoming her romantic partner as well.

Despite a certain lack of ethics, Gründgens held on to certain principles. He continued to believe in the importance of theater, as reflected in his remarks to his actors and stage crew in August 1944 when the Prussian State Theater was being shuttered as part of the regime's "total war" measures. Gründgens spoke of the Staatstheater as a "temple"—the "most holy that we have."[47] He vowed not to leave the temple, which is striking in that he had also recently emerged as a high-profile volunteer for the German army. When Goebbels trumpeted the "total war" effort after the Sixth Army's defeat at Stalingrad in February 1943, Gründgens responded with a letter to Göring, pleading to be allowed to serve in the Wehrmacht. By June 1943, he was undergoing army training in the Netherlands. Gründgens, who was photographed with a rifle while stationed near Amsterdam in an air defense unit, returned to Berlin when Göring ordered his reappointment to the Staatstheater in Berlin in April 1944. But the closing of his playhouse—and all theaters in the Reich—late that summer as part of the ever-expanding "total war" measures meant that Gründgens had lost his venue. He therefore turned to a new role, that of the courageous civilian-artist, and remained in Berlin as the Soviet Red Army attacked the city. With brutal street fighting in the vicinity, Gründgens organized readings of Schiller's *The Robbers*. There appears to have been some ambiguity about Gründgens's staging of the Schiller play. While one might view it as an effort to bolster morale by turning to a German classic in a desperate time, Gründgens was also known for "cast[ing] himself as the villainous Franz Moor with a maniacal mien and a hairstyle reminiscent of Hitler's."[48] If Gründgens intended to make a subversive statement, it went unnoticed by the Nazi authorities and can scarcely be considered an act of resistance.

When the Germans capitulated, the Soviets captured Gründgens and incarcerated him for nine months. As arguably Nazi Germany's most famous actor, he held an exceptional position, and the Soviet secret police, the NKVD, kept him in a special camp in Jamlitz in rural Brandenburg. His lawyer eventually came to his rescue and found witnesses who attested to Gründgens's efforts to help others. Arssenyi Gulya, who served as a Soviet theater officer, also intervened on his behalf and argued for his release. A Soviet Military Administrative District judge agreed to release Gründgens, but on the condition that the actor/director work to promote theater in the Soviet-occupied zone of Berlin.[49] Gründgens did not remain in the East for long, although the experience made him particularly sensitive to the tribulations of former colleagues who had been compromised during the Third Reich. As noted earlier, he testified on behalf of Emmy Göring during her denazification trial in Garmisch in 1948.

Somewhat astonishingly, Gründgens returned to the Berlin stage on 9 May 1946 at the Deutsches Theater—the venue that had been the pride of Max Reinhardt (who had died in America during the war)—and began the revival of his career. Playing Christian Maske, the "snob" in the eponymous play by Carl von Sternheim, Gründgens received a raucous and prolonged ovation upon his return. With a certain poignancy, his character's first line offered the haunting formulation: "das ist grotesk."[50] The gifted actor continued his renewed ascent by serving as the General Intendant at the municipal theater in Düsseldorf from 1947 to 1955 and then returning to Hamburg, where he occupied the same position at the Deutsches Schauspielhaus from 1955 to 1963. There were occasional outcries when he performed abroad. At the Edinburgh Festival in 1949, for example, protesters produced flyers headlined, "Did You Know? Hitler's 'Senator of Culture' and Goering's Friend—in Edinburgh! Send Him Home!"[51] These critics went so far as to throw the leaflets on the stage prior to his performance, but the show went on. Gründgens reprised his role as Mephistopheles for film versions of *Faust* in 1955 and 1960. He won numerous honors in the postwar period, including the German Service Cross with Star, the highest award that can be made to civilians, which was bestowed to Gründgens "for his services to post-war German theatre."[52] He also performed in Leningrad, Moscow, New York, and Venice, among other prestigious foreign venues. In October 1963 Gustaf Gründgens died in Manila, Philippines, from an overdose of sleeping pills that he took while on a trip around the world. He was just shy of his sixty-fourth birthday. His body was cremated and an urn holding his ashes was flown to Hamburg, where it was placed in an *Ehrengrab* (honorary grave). His death made headlines around the world.

Gründgens continues to be widely regarded as one of Germany's greatest actors of all time, as reflected in the extensive literature concerning his life and career. He possessed a charisma, a power that is undeniable. Even he recognized this quality, noting in a 2 November 1946 letter, "With strength, effort and the single-mindedness of my ambition I mesmerized a lot of people many times. I ran them down, won them and lost them."[53] But he had other qualities, including a facility for self-preservation. At the entrance to an exhibition on Gründgens held at the Berlin Staatsbibliothek on the hundredth anniversary of his birth, a poster offered another quotation by the actor/director: "I want to be regarded as someone who preserved and nourished the flame in a dark period and someone who can relate how it was, how it is now, and how one could possibly rebuild."[54] Gründgens proved very adept at rebuilding, and he bridged three distinct periods in twentieth-century German history with remarkable facility.

11

Leni Riefenstahl

(1902 Berlin–2003 Pöcking am Starnberger See)

Photo from the 1920s inscribed by Leni Riefenstahl to the author (1998).

A GIFTED FILMMAKER who produced propaganda for Hitler and the Nazi regime, Leni Riefenstahl had once been a modern dancer and a serious actor known for daring projects, including mountain and adventure films. Raised in the rich cultural milieu of Berlin, and coming of age during the Weimar Republic, she utilized modernist elements in her work throughout her career, even after she entered the service of the National Socialists. Her camera angles, editing methods, and visual references all contained modernist techniques, even as she produced fascist epics. She has been called the greatest female filmmaker in history, and while this is debatable, she has certainly earned a place in the history of cinema, photography, and the visual arts. Even as late as 1974, as Susan Sontag noted, Riefenstahl was the "guest of honor at a new cinéphile-controlled film festival held in the summer in Colorado [Telluride] and the subject of a stream of respectful articles and interviews in newspapers and on TV."[1] Riefenstahl consorted with the likes of Andy Warhol, whom she met in New York; Mick and Bianca Jagger, whom she herself photographed in London and who professed admiration for her films (some of which Mick Jagger claimed to have seen "as often as fifteen times"); and she traveled to Havana, Cuba, with photographer Helmut Newton in 1987, resulting in still more publicity.[2] Riefenstahl mingled among an international cultural elite with strategic reasons in mind—just as Warhol, the Jaggers, and Newton, who made careers out of transgressive behavior, sought out Riefenstahl because of her controversial status. Regardless, considering her career during the Third Reich, Riefenstahl's acceptance into this jet-setting society showed that she had come a long way.

Riefenstahl had an ability to adapt that was not unlike that of Gustaf Gründgens or others examined in this book. During the Weimar Republic, she was a "new woman": a creative, liberated, self-confident, and ambitious artist. Riefenstahl launched her career as an expressionist dancer, staging one-person shows across central Europe, making her a virtual cliché of Weimar culture. But she was good at it and would have enjoyed a fine career as a dancer had events not taken another course. She successively transformed herself first into an actor and then, after 1932, into a "gifted filmmaker." How she negotiated these transformations had a lot to do with her personality, her ethics, and also her undeniable talent.

Riefenstahl adapted to the Third Reich, although her chameleon-like qualities did not serve as camouflage. Instead, she was one of the most visible figures in Nazi Germany. Riefenstahl was heavily promoted by the regime and, in return, reflected positively on the Third Reich—just as Goebbels had envisioned with his nationalistic cultural policy. There was also something about her relationship to Hitler that invited gossip. Some claimed that they were lovers (they were almost certainly not). But they saw one another before the war with considerable frequency—and often in private settings, including Riefenstahl's home—and clearly evinced a deeply felt mutual admiration. Because of her relationship with Hitler, Riefenstahl was the only filmmaker in the Third Reich not beholden to Goebbels, who effectively controlled the film industry. Although she never joined the Nazi Party, she was a privileged artist who enjoyed powerful political support, wide-ranging artistic freedom, and considerable wealth.

Some might dispute that Riefenstahl was truly a modernist—either in the 1920s or at any time subsequently. Yet a survey of her early work shows how Riefenstahl was originally a modernist in both spirit and style. For starters, she was raised in the modernist capital of the world in the early twentieth century (more specifically, she hailed from the working-class district of Wedding). Not that this automatically makes one a modernist, but it helped that she was raised surrounded by the culture of a *Weltstadt* (world city). Riefenstahl attended an art college—the State School of Arts and Crafts on the Prinz-Albrecht-Strasse—before studying ballet with Madame Eugenie Eduardova, "a once great ballerina from St. Petersburg," as well as modern dance at the Jutta Klamt school.[3] At age fifteen, she started taking dance lessons without her parents' knowledge at Helene Grimm-Reiter's Berlin School of Dance, a progressive academy where famed Weimar dancer Anita Berber had trained. Berber was immortalized in Otto Dix's iconic painting, although uncharacteristically she wears clothes in the portrait. Riefenstahl later studied with modern dance pioneer Mary Wigman in Dresden-Hellerau, where she trained with Gret Palucca, among others. Although this arrangement lasted only a few months—Riefenstahl found Wigman's style "too abstract, too ascetic, too severe" and had her own ideas about a more "fairy tale, dream-like" approach to dance—the fact remains that the future filmmaker received a progressive and urban education that featured extensive exposure to modernist culture.[4] In her memoirs, published in the late 1980s, she recalled her frequent visits to the modernist floors in the Nationalgalerie in the Kronprinzenpalais, where she fantasized about a collection of works by Cézanne, van Gogh, and Klee, among others. She recounted how she imagined a "personal" collection of these modernist artworks that she regarded as "mine" and how certain works (especially by van Gogh) made her "so excited that she nearly burst into tears." She also recalled that "before the start of World War II, I wrote a screenplay about Van Gogh . . . but that dream, like so many others, never came true."[5]

Riefenstahl's professional dancing would qualify as modernist because of its interpretive and expressionist elements. Dance had become part of the more general modernist movement in the early twentieth century. Its expressiveness and the effort to liberate the body proved attractive to modernists. The fin-de-siècle period also gave rise to the idea of a *Sprachkrise,* or a crisis of language: Hugo von Hofmannsthal (in his "Letter from Lord Chandos") and others realized that words were insufficient to convey the complexity of the human condition. This came at the same time as Freud's discovery of the unconscious, and at a time when the Expressionists turned to color and form as a means of communication. Dance, many believed, offered another important nonverbal means of expression. The discipline was professionalized in the early twentieth century. Or, at least schools developed and a market for star performers produced the likes of Isadora Duncan, Mary Wigman, and Gret Palucca. Along with Sergei Diaghilev, Martha Graham, and a few others, these were the pioneers of modern dance. Certain practitioners, it should be noted, espoused racist ideas and believed the discipline offered proof of their views. Dancer and choreographer Rudolf von Laban published tracts in the 1920s in which he argued "about the inherent biological inferiority of black people."[6] It is not clear whether Riefenstahl was exposed to such views and, if so, embraced them, but she certainly contributed to the integration of dance into the broader fascist culture.

Riefenstahl's debut as a dancer came on 23 October 1923 at the Tonhalle in Munich, when her boyfriend at the time, a wealthy (and Jewish) financier named Harry Sokal, paid for the event. This occurred during hyperinflation and cost him $1, for both the rental of the hall and the publicity. Leni was twenty-one and the undertaking was audacious, especially considering that she had limited training. She had taken up ballet relatively late and was still studying dance at the time back in Berlin with Jutta

Riefenstahl as modern
dancer: "study after a
gavotte." (Medienarchiv
LR-Produktion)

Klamt. But these performances were about personal expression and intense emotions, as reflected in the titles of the pieces she performed in Munich: "Three Dances of Eros," "Surrender," and "Release," among others. Riefenstahl nonetheless received rave reviews (Sokal had also arranged for critics to attend). A reporter for the *Münchener Neuesten Nachrichten* noted her "beautiful looks and obviously unorthodox temperament [that] enable her to hold the attention of her audience to the end."[7] A debut on the Berlin stage occurred a few days later, on 27 October, when she appeared at the Blüthner-Hall: "a triumph beyond my wildest dreams," she later recounted. The press reported the "prolonged applause of the house," and she returned for multiple encores, repeating several of the dances. Riefenstahl danced at Max Reinhardt's famous Deutsches Theater, as well as at the impresario's smaller venue, the Kammerspiele: to be engaged at these temples of modern theater represented a major accomplishment for the twenty-one-year-old performer. Her career took off around the time that the Berlin government brought hyperinflation under control.

Riefenstahl appeared in over seventy performances between October 1923 and May 1924 (averaging one every three days) in Frankfurt, Dresden, Innsbruck, Zurich, and Prague, among other places. Each engagement brought an honorarium of five hundred to a thousand Gold Marks, a sizable sum at that time. Yet her dreams of a career as a dancer suffered a blow in June 1924 when she tore knee ligaments and collapsed on stage during a performance in Prague. The injury probably occurred because she demanded so much of herself physically but had not developed the necessary muscles or elasticity. Riefenstahl's dancing career had thus far lasted eight months. When she was one hundred years old she lamented, "I wish with body and soul that I had stayed a dancer. Of all the things I have done in my life as an artist, it was dancing that most fascinated me and made me happy."[8] A less nostalgic perspective was offered by a critic who wrote, "She had earlier attracted attention as an expressionist dancer, a brief but addictive episode of celebrity interrupted by a knee injury."[9] Relatively little was known at the time about reconstructive knee surgery and rehabilitation, which made a full recovery rather daunting. Riefenstahl in fact returned to her first professional art form for a very short spell, and danced in a few films, but it did not offer a future in the same way that acting did. At that time it was almost unimaginable for a young woman to contemplate a career as a film director.

Riefenstahl sought the limelight, and this was reflected in many ways. For starters, she performed alone during her career as a dancer; she was not going to share the stage with others. Riefenstahl starred in all nine films in which she appeared; she exhibited no interest in supporting roles. She also entered beauty contests and made a concerted effort to cultivate the press. The young performer edited her reviews into a scrapbook, and then into a press book that she distributed to agents. She had quickly absorbed a great deal about "publicity and image building." This included carefully editing out the negative comments, as with a clipping of a review by Fred Hildenbrandt, a famous and influential critic writing for the *Berliner Tagblatt;* Riefenstahl preserved his positive remarks but omitted the critical observations. Her egotism, like her remarkable work ethic, would become defining characteristics of her long career.

The young Berliner's relatively successful tenure as a dancer led to opportunities to act in the silent films of the era. In the mid-1920s, especially after the economic stabilization ushered by Hjalmar Schacht's currency reform of 1924, Berlin rivaled Hollywood for boasting the most influential film industry. The Americans always had a commercial edge, but Berlin was the closest competitor. In terms of artistic accomplishments, the "golden age of Weimar cinema," which ranged from *The Cabinet of Dr. Caligari* in 1920 to Bertolt Brecht's *Kuhle Wampe* in 1932, proved difficult to surpass.[10] Indeed, Berlin and Hollywood held one another in high regard and cooperated on a number of projects, including *SOS Iceberg* (1933), which Riefenstahl and her co-stars filmed in two languages. The film was distributed in the United States by Universal Pictures. Riefenstahl had a strong Berlin accent, and her voice irritated many viewers; despite concerted efforts with a speech instructor, this would limit her career as a thespian. That she subsequently became closely tied to the Nazi regime also prevented her from becoming an international film star; but she was among the actors who prompted discussions of collaboration between Hollywood and Berlin, and she always retained certain ties to colleagues in America. Walt Disney invited her to Los Angeles in 1939, and she was "championed in the 1930s" by Josef von Sternberg, Douglas Fairbanks, and Charlie Chaplin, among others.[11]

Riefenstahl had undeniable audacity and physical courage when it came to her work. She was the first woman to star in *Bergfilme,* or mountain films, which in themselves were unusual, because unlike the vast majority of productions, which were shot in studios, these were filmed in outdoor settings. The filmmakers of this genre, Riefenstahl included, were the first to secure dramatic footage shot on Alpine peaks and on Icelandic ice floes. Film historian Sabine Hake observed, "The enthusiastic embrace of cinema as a technology of conquest and discovery and the preference for a camera aesthetic modeled on the pro-filmic event distinguish many mountain films as modernist works." Hake places many of "the genre's leading practitioners . . . closer to the realist aesthetics of New Objectivity, the documentary ethos of New Photography, and, of course, the non-narrative form of the cultural film." She also notes how these Bergfilme "included extensive references to mass tourism and modern technology."[12] Films were made under difficult conditions and were the province of specialists, who often spent months in extreme weather conditions. Riefenstahl had remarkable physical gifts. She learned to ski while making these films and became so adept at downhill that she qualified for the 1932 winter Olympics.[13] She also showed courage filming in remote arctic landscapes. One critic talked of her character in *The Blue Light,* Junta, who "scales the heights (literally)" as she climbs craggy peaks in the Dolomites wearing only rags.

Riefenstahl viewed these adventure films as more than technical accomplishments; she regarded them as spiritually infused artworks. Earlier, when she saw Arnold Fanck's 1924 film *Mountains of Destiny,* she recalled being captivated: "I was experiencing a world that I did not know, for I had never seen such mountains. I knew them only from postcards, on which they looked rigid and lifeless. But here, on the screen, they were alive, mysterious, and more entrancingly beautiful than I had ever dreamed mountains could be."[14] There was something modernist in this outlook, akin to Ernst Ludwig Kirchner's spiritually resonant mountain landscapes. That *The Blue Light* was based on legend, and not in the "realist" genre, also added a modernist element. Classical modernists often turned to myth in order to convey the essential or primal. Some critics have seen screenwriter Béla Balázs's influence in this regard: "a Jewish intellectual and prominent leftist," in the words of film historian Eric Rentschler, Balázs helped add an intellectual sophistication to the films on which he worked.[15] Of course, the mountain films were also anti-modernist and pre-fascist in other respects. Sabine Hake noted that "the glorification of primordial nature, the metaphysics of place and belonging, and the idealization of pre-industrial communities reveal the genre's debts to right-wing rhetoric."[16] These films offered a vehicle for anti-capitalist rhetoric and ethnic stereotyping. The Social Darwinist messages that pervaded the genre—only the "fittest" (strongest and healthiest) characters survive, and the Alpinist often appears as a "superman" —added to the pre-fascist qualities. Understandably Hitler and many other Nazis responded enthusiastically to these works, and the directors of the Bergfilme, including Arnold Fanck and his protégés Luis Trenker and Leni Riefenstahl, flourished during the Third Reich.

The Blue Light—the only film Riefenstahl directed prior to being commissioned by Hitler to record the Nuremberg Party Rally of 1933 (which became a kind of trial run for *Triumph of the Will*)—reflected her interest in modernist aesthetics. More generally, Weimar cinema from the mid-1920s onward often referenced the artistically ambitious cinema that had flourished just after World War I, even as the filmmakers attempted to make more commercial films. Fritz Lang's film *M*, for example, alluded to the work of Robert Wiene (*Caligari*) and F. W. Murnau (*Nosferatu*), even though the director abided by the conventions of mainstream cinema. The same could be said for Orson Welles, whose work was also artistically sophisticated while at the same time commercial. In *The Blue Light*, Riefenstahl showed an experimental streak, utilizing innovative lighting (including night shots with a new film created by Agfa) and different focal lengths and lenses, and at times colorizing the film with an unusual blue tint to reflect the magic crystals hidden in the Alpine cave. The blue wash of the film could be viewed as painterly. The same could be said of the shots of medieval statues in the local Alpine church: rendered in an artful manner, the figures appear almost Expressionist and call to mind the work of Ernst Barlach. The use of time-lapse photography, such as the moon rising in the Dolomites, although by no means pioneering, nevertheless placed Riefenstahl on the cutting edge of film technology. She also utilized local villagers in the Dolomites and included authentic images of their farmhouses, alpine huts, and churches in a way that later led Italian director Roberto Rossellini to acknowledge her as "the godmother of neorealism."[17] Awarded a silver medal at the 1932 Venice Biennale and a gold medal at the Paris World Exposition in 1937 after its re-release, *The Blue Light* was widely hailed as an artistically ambitious film.

Like many films of the era, *The Blue Light* functioned on multiple layers. The story itself is accessible, based on an ancient legend, and fairly simple as it concerns a strange gypsy woman played by Riefenstahl who lives in the Alps and who is the only person able to reach a strange blue light atop a mountain. A love story ensues involving Riefenstahl's character, Junta, and a young painter from Vienna, but it ends tragically with both falling off the mountain in the wake of the villagers' plundering of the crystal grotto—the source of the blue light. Of course, the film also conveyed an array of more subtle social and ideological messages. Film critic and sociologist Siegfried Kracauer famously maintained that films reveal so much about a society because they are collaborative ventures involving significant numbers of people. While this argument is debatable, Riefenstahl's first film in many ways captured the conflicted spirit of the Weimar Republic. On the more progressive side, besides the aesthetic qualities discussed above, there is the strong female heroine who comes into conflict with the ignorant misogynist villagers. This theme is perhaps not surprising considering that Riefenstahl was the only female director of note in interwar Germany. To her credit, she managed almost exclusively male crews and flourished in a male industry. But *The Blue Light* also featured the pre-fascist elements common to so many of the Bergfilme: these included the authentic peasant characters in a spiritually infused landscape, bringing to mind "blood and soil" themes and, in the words of Siegfried Kracauer, "a kind of heroic idealism," with "aspirations toward a mystic goal" that were "kindred to the Nazi spirit."[18] It remains unclear whether Riefenstahl set out to make a political statement, but as a self-aware artist she was no doubt aware of the implications of the work. The contemporaneous critical reaction, where many saw the work as harmonious with the Nazi worldview, and Riefenstahl's response to the not uncommon negative notices, which prompted emotional anti-Semitic outbursts aimed at the Jewish press, also merit consideration.[19]

Triumph of the Will (1935), of course, made Riefenstahl's career. It has frequently been recognized as one of the greatest films of all time, and along with its Communist counterpart, Sergei Eisenstein's *Battleship Potemkin* (1925), constituted an archetype for both documentaries and propaganda. She certainly pioneered right-leaning documentaries: up until then, most documentary films exhibited left-wing tendencies. Riefenstahl's treatment of the 1934 Nazi Party Rally at Nuremberg was significant not only for political reasons—Hitler's first gathering of Party leaders and followers since the Röhm Purge three months earlier, his successful plebiscite on 19 August to modify his title to Führer and Reich Chancellor, and the advent of the personal oath of loyalty to him by members of the armed forces—but also for aesthetic ones. The filmmaker utilized cutting edge technology, such as telephoto lenses, sophisticated trolley devices to move cameras, and aerial photography, to achieve visual images never before seen. The shots from above, of masses of Nazi supporters aligned in rows, referenced modernist designs of the interwar period. The use of repetition and the resulting abstraction that emerged from such images echoed, for example, Oskar Schlemmer's contemporaneous designs that showed a series of figures (sometimes with outstretched arms) appearing to move in unison (Plates 3, 9, 10). While Riefenstahl never pointed to Schlemmer as a direct influence, she certainly thought in terms informed by modernist aesthetics.[20] Riefenstahl also possessed a keen eye and was a perfectionist, both during filming and in the editing room, as she searched for particular aesthetic forms and linkages that she compared to musical compositions. Like Albert Speer and others in this book, she sometimes had difficulty bringing projects to completion.

Riefenstahl herself helped design the Nazi Party Rally of 1934. She worked closely with Albert Speer, the chief designer of the mass spectaculars staged by the regime, and they conceived both a rally and a film at the same time. For example, they consulted at length on the placement of the storm troopers and the representatives of the other branches of the National Socialist state. Speer in turn received prominent mention in the credits of *Triumph of the Will* as "the architect of the film." But Riefenstahl also had tremendous say in the organization of the Rally. Her crew of 172, which was truly extravagant by the standards of the time, provides an indication of her influence. Riefenstahl's role in the event actually provoked a backlash, as misogynist Nazi functionaries objected to submitting to her directions and intrigued against her. She later claimed in a 1965 interview with the prestigious *Cahiers du cinéma* that she merely documented what transpired in Nuremberg in 1934 ("It is *cinéma vérité*"). But these remarks clearly belied the reality. One author wrote, "Indeed, the whole spectacle looks as though choreographed," and suggested a connection to the legacy of her dancing years.[21]

A lingering debate about Riefenstahl's career has centered on the issue of "fascist aesthetics," and the filmmaker's role in shaping the uniquely National Socialist variant. Riefenstahl herself denied understanding the concept, as she stated in Ray Müller's documentary of the early 1990s.[22] Yet her remarks regarding this and many other aspects of her work during the Third Reich are scarcely credible. In 1974 Susan Sontag offered a definition of fascist aesthetics in her famous essay about Riefenstahl titled "Fascinating Fascism":

> Fascist aesthetics include but go far beyond . . . a preoccupation with situations of control, submissive behavior, extravagant effort, and the endurance of pain; they endorse two seemingly opposite states, egomania and servitude. The relations of domination and enslavement take the form of a characteristic pageantry: the massing of groups of people; the turning of people into things; the multiplication or replication of things; and the grouping of people/things around an all-powerful, hypnotic leader-figure or force. The fascist dramaturgy centers on the orgiastic transactions between mighty forces and their puppets, uniformly garbed and shown in ever swelling numbers. Its choreography alternates between ceaseless motion and a congealed, static, "virile" posing. Fascist art glorifies surrender, it exalts mindlessness, it glamorizes death.[23]

Sontag argued that Riefenstahl's career was devoted to fascist aesthetics, identifying three distinct phases—the mountain films, those of the Third Reich, and the Africa projects—that "form a triptych of fascist visuals."

Riefenstahl's postproduction work constituted a major part of her accomplishment. She threw herself into the editing process, working twenty-hour days at stretches to devise a revolutionary cinematography. She used montages and the "cross-cut method" of editing like few before her, as in the beginning of day two of the Rally when the Party faithful prepare themselves while the Nazi leaders arrive at the Luitpold Arena. Her skill interspersing reactions from the crowd (the cross-cut) and multiple camera angles (close-ups, distance shots) produced highly evocative effects and in particular captured the emotionally charged relationship between Hitler and his followers. The most iconic moment of the film—the visually impressive climax of day four, when Hitler, Himmler, and Viktor Lutze (Röhm's successor as head of the storm troopers [SA]) pass through the ranks of over 150,000 SA and SS men—resulted from Riefenstahl's filming and editing. But it was an artistically informed effort on Riefenstahl's part. She was conscious of how her work fit in with that of Walter Ruttmann (*Berlin, Symphony of a World City* from 1927) and the Soviet directors Sergei Eisenstein and Dziga Vertov. Riefenstahl went so far as to engage Ruttmann as an assistant on *Triumph of the Will*. Film scholar Eric Rentschler has noted, "The fastidiously ordered lines of these hundreds of thousands of followers take us back to the staged masses of Expressionist dramas by Ernst Toller and Georg Kaiser. They also bring to mind Siegfried Kracauer's 1927 essay on the 'mass ornament' [*Ornament der Masse*], which commented on a troupe of precision dancers, the Tiller Girls."[24] Riefenstahl's film was not purely an exercise in formalistic aesthetics. It was a political document and a political act—an effort to render the Nazis' ideas in a tangible manner and move Germany's citizens at a critical time, in the aftermath of a murderous purge that was potentially destabilizing. But the fact remains that Riefenstahl viewed herself as a kind of auteur, whose work advanced cinema as an art form (Plates 9, 10).

To the "cinematic poetry," as Riefenstahl referred to *Triumph of the Will*'s visuals, she added a rich, stirring soundtrack, drawing mostly on Wagner's music. Although Riefenstahl had some difficulty bringing around musical director Herbert Windt—a Nazi Party member since 1931 who wanted to use his own score—their collaboration proved successful. Yet they did more than appropriate Hitler's favorite composer and blend Wagner quotations with political songs, such as the Nazi anthem, the *Horst Wessel Lied.* The music "helps legitimate the Nazis by anchoring 'their' music in a familiar German musical tradition."[25] It also served, in a sense, to narrate the film, in which there was no conventional voice-over (further evidence, according to Riefenstahl, that the film was not propaganda). And the director was always attuned to the rhythm of her work, likely another legacy of her career as a dancer. In a sense, the Wagner-based motifs allowed Riefenstahl to create a new kind of *Gesamtkunstwerk,* and like Wagner she had lofty artistic aspirations. This notion of a "total work of art" is how Riefenstahl often presented her cinematic efforts, at least to highbrow audiences (for example, she visited Oxford and Cambridge in April 1934), and with Hitler, who responded with enthusiasm and offered copious financing for future productions.

To what extent was Riefenstahl a Nazi? As mentioned earlier, she never joined the Party. While this may say something about her reservations about the Nazi movement, it may have been more an outgrowth of her personality, with her fractious inclinations and self-conception as an artist. Riefenstahl clearly revered Hitler. She described seeing him speak for the first time in 1932 as a spiritual experience. She read his autobiography and political program, *Mein Kampf,* with care and "intensely engaged herself with his theories."[26] Riefenstahl also evinced considerable anti-Semitism, although she had a few Jewish friends, including a romantic interest (Harry Sokal). Riefenstahl met Hitler just after her first film, *The Blue Light,* was panned by some Jewish critics, and the two reportedly bonded while discussing the pernicious Jewish influence on the media. Riefenstahl also behaved deplorably with Hungarian Jew Béla Balázs, who had co-authored the script for *The Blue Light.* His name was removed from the credits after 1933 and Riefenstahl engaged her friend Julius Streicher, the Gauleiter of Nuremberg and a notorious anti-Semite, to help her avoid paying Balázs. In October 1933, she wrote Streicher and gave him full authority to represent her interests against her Jewish colleague. In the questionnaires and other official documents that Riefenstahl filled out in order to work in Nazi Germany, she would use freighted terms, such as describing the "racial origins" of her family as "Arisch" (Aryan)—a word she repeated over and over again on the form.[27]

Riefenstahl not only was attracted to Hitler but also fit in with the circle that surrounded the Nazi leader during the first years of the Third Reich. Goebbels recounted in his diaries evenings spent with Riefenstahl, Prince Philipp von Hessen, and actress Anny Ondra and her husband, boxer Max Schmeling, among others. In May 1933 Goebbels and Riefenstahl picnicked together as they discussed a film about the Party Rally.[28] Riefenstahl later maintained that Goebbels made sexual advances and that her rebuff transformed him into a bitter enemy. While elements of this are likely true (Goebbels's advances), Riefenstahl maintained cordial relations with all the Nazi leaders, Goebbels included. She was so close to Gauleiter Streicher of Nuremberg that they used the informal "du," and he would begin letters "liebe Leni."[29] Riefenstahl was an actress, after all. When Hitler asked her to meet with Mussolini in 1936, she took on the role. She usually performed with masterful skill. Hitler reportedly called Riefenstahl "my perfect German woman."[30] Their rapport found expression in frequent invitations to meet, and Riefenstahl visited Hitler in his private apartment at the Chancellery in Berlin, at the Obersalzberg, and at her own apartment (and later

Riefenstahl, filmmaker Luis Trenker (facing away from the camera), and Goebbels at a Nazi high society event in the 1930s. (Landesarchiv-Berlin)

Dahlem villa), among other places. At times, such as in late 1933, they dined together several times in a week.

While it is likely that their relationship was never sexual—as she maintained, although she was also known for being sexually aggressive and pursuing men she found attractive—there is no doubt that the two shared a deep mutual interest in one another. Very powerful emotions were at play. One telegram she sent to Hitler from Pera di Fassa, a town in the Italian Dolomites, on 25 August 1935 had strikingly romantic undertones: "The congratulations given to me by my Führer has made fulfillment possible and my heart has therefore led me to be thankful. Today, I hold with both arms the roses as red as the mountains all around nestled in the last of the sunlight. Thus I look up to the garden of roses, to its bright tower and walls and stroke with my hands the red flowers and I just know that I am inexpressibly happy."[31] Her use of poetry, the reference to roses that she caresses, and the passionate tone are all palpable here. In another telegram, this on 14 June 1940, when the French declared that they would not defend Paris and

Hitler visits Riefenstahl at her Berlin villa in 1937: although most observers have commented on the expressions of the two subjects, it is also worth noting the modernist painting on the wall in the background. (National Archives and Records Administration, College Park)

effectively sealed their defeat, Riefenstahl wrote Hitler the following and sent it to the Führer Headquarters in the Belgian village at Bruly-le-Pêche: "With indescribable joy, deeply moved and filled with burning gratitude, we share with you, my Führer, your and Germany's greatest victory, the entry of German troops into Paris. You exceed anything the human imagination has the power to conceive, achieving deeds without parallel in the history of mankind."[32] Riefenstahl's vanity and careerism aside, she wholeheartedly supported Hitler and the Nazi regime.

The filmmaker continued to support the Nazi state even as the regime grew more radical. For example, in April 1938, prior to the plebiscite in Austria to decide on the *Anschluss,* she made a "passionate electoral appeal in support of Hitler" in which she talked of "the greatness of the German days of destiny during which the Führer liberated his homeland, [which] was like a miracle to us all."[33] The following year, she witnessed atrocities firsthand while filming propaganda in Poland in September 1939. While Riefenstahl gradually extricated herself from the assignment and returned home, she said nothing publicly about the incident and never criticized the regime. Hitler in turn remained loyal to her; he personally, if secretly, financed her projects, including her last film during the Third Reich, *Tiefland.* Hitler's lieutenants sometimes gave her difficulties: for example, Goebbels denied her request for funds for the over-budget *Olympia* (he wrote in his journal, "Fräulein Riefenstahl becomes hysterical in front of me. There is no working with this wild woman. . . . She cries. That is the last weapon of women").[34] But she would go directly to Hitler, who assented to nearly all of her requests. Later in the war Riefenstahl also turned to Martin Bormann, Hitler's private secretary, for help. Even the threat of enlisting Bormann could be effective, as in 1944 when she wanted a cameraman named Albert Benitz to be placed at her disposal in order to complete *Tiefland.* Max Winkler, an official in the Reich film office, had other plans for Benitz, but Riefenstahl repeated her request, noting, "before I inform Herr Reichsleiter Bormann," and achieved the desired result.[35] It appears she also at times had the power to send individuals to concentration camps. In late September 1940, during the filming of *Tiefland,* Riefenstahl used Roma ("gypsies") taken from the Maxglan concentration camp; one of the extras fled the set in fear but was quickly captured. According to the extra, a young woman named Rosa Winter, Riefenstahl visited her in her cell and threatened her when she refused to beg for forgiveness, saying, "You'll go to a concentration camp!" A short time later, Winter was sent to Ravensbrück north of Berlin.[36] That Riefenstahl evidently intervened to help several threatened Jews—including the wife of *Olympia* production designer Robert Herlth, whom she reportedly saved from the Gestapo—also speaks to her influence.

Riefenstahl's power found expression is numerous ways. In March 1939 she visited with Hitler at the Obersalzberg, where they discussed the construction of her own film studio. Riefenstahl's production company was one of the last to remain independent during the Third Reich, as the major studios such as Ufa, Terra, and Tobis were nationalized. Riefenstahl secured a commitment to build a gargantuan complex that would occupy a forty-thousand-square-foot property in Berlin Dahlem. The complex would include a studio, print lab, editing facility, screening room, film archive, and gym, among other features, and was budgeted at RM 2,000,000 ($800,000)—to be financed by the Nazi regime. This undertaking would be covered by Hitler's cultural funds, which consisted of revenue generated from sales of *Mein Kampf* and from payments for his image appearing on postage stamps, among other sources (these funds were also used to pay for the purchase of artworks for the Führermuseum).[37] Riefenstahl entered into talks with Albert Speer and Martin Bormann, and although the land was purchased the project was abandoned in 1942 because of the war. Less clear was the source that paid for a newly constructed villa in Dahlem that she moved into in 1937. Abutting the Grunewald forest, it was a grand abode and featured a projection room and an indoor winter garden. While it too may have been financed by the Reich, Riefenstahl was certainly capable of paying for it with her own resources. She made millions of Reichsmarks while in the service of the Nazi regime.

Patronage was not without its costs. After *Triumph of the Will* premiered in May 1935, Hitler compelled Riefenstahl to return to Nuremberg and film the Rally for a third consecutive year. It turned out that many army generals were upset by their lack of screen time in *Triumph* and demanded redress. The last day of the 1934 Rally, which had been devoted to a military parade, had been marred by rain, and the footage did not fit with the rest of the film. Much of her own stock had also been damaged by the inclement weather, and she would have had to rely on newsreel material, which was not up to the same standards: it did not feature "beautiful pictures" and was "gray."[38] Riefenstahl insisted on retaining artistic control over *Triumph* and would not add footage of the armed forces. The film *Day of Freedom: Our Armed Forces* was the result of her return to Nuremberg in 1935. It largely reprised what she had done the year before, but with the armed forces now featured more prominently. *Day of Freedom* was used by the German military for recruitment and indoctrination—one writer has called it "a document of triumphant militarism in the initial stage of German rearmament"—but did not occupy a special place in the culture of the Third Reich.[39] There was no complete print of the film until reunification in 1989 brought together reels in the East and West. Perhaps most notable about the film was the way Riefenstahl navigated the political minefields; for example, she avoided mention of the Nuremberg Laws that had been promulgated at a special meeting of the Reichstag (the first to be held in Nuremberg since 1543). Instead of focusing on the regime's anti-Semitic measures, Riefenstahl put a more generic Hitler speech at the center of the film, along with the images of Wehrmacht leaders and marching troops. Leaving Party leaders in the background, *Day of Freedom* was more nationalistic in spirit and orientation. Of course, she incorporated Nazi symbols into the pageantry, but in a very stylized manner, such as the final image of swastika-adorned airplanes flying in a swastika formation. Even though there was little new in this film cinematically, it demonstrated political adroitness and enabled her to focus on more artistically ambitious projects.

Olympia (1938), the epic about the 1936 Berlin games, was supposed to elevate her in the eyes of the world to the level she had reached in her native land. To her credit, she produced a film that elicited international recognition, including winning the "Coppa Mussolini" for best film at the Venice International Film Festival of 1938 (beating out Walt Disney's *Snow White and the Seven Dwarfs*). Other awards followed in Greece, Sweden, Finland, Norway, and Romania, as well as from the International Olympic Committee. Most viewers believed she had accurately captured the experience of the Berlin games, Jesse Owens's victories included. *Olympia* arguably is the least offensive of her five major efforts during the Third Reich (including *Tiefland*). That said, she was unable to sell *Olympia* in the United States or the United Kingdom, even though she had one version with all the shots of Hitler deleted.[40]

Olympia, with its two sections ("Celebration of Nations" and "Celebration of Beauty") running 126 minutes and 100 minutes, respectively, stands in its own right as a monument to megalomania. With miles of raw footage (250 miles to be precise), *Olympia* required over two years of unstinting labor to edit. Even then it runs a colossal three hours and forty-six minutes. One critic observed, "As propaganda, *Olympia* is less interested in blatantly indoctrinating viewers in the principles of National Socialism than in promoting a positive, and even kind, image of Germany."[41] Showing a clean, revitalized country that was playing the role of congenial host to visitors from around the world was part of "the beautiful veneer of the Third Reich." It didn't hurt that the Germans won the most medals of any country and that an investment of RM 100 million ($40 million) to stage the games brought a return of five times that sum—accomplishments that appeared to validate the measures undertaken by the Nazi regime. That the film premiered in Berlin on Hitler's birthday, 20 April 1938, is also suggestive. Yet critics have seen even more insidious qualities in the film. Jeanne Anne Nugent, for example, wrote, "Riefenstahl's *Olympia* is surely the Third Reich's grandest artistic statement. It achieves that dubious honor . . . [by tapping] into the latent irrationalism and vitalist currents in German art and culture."[42] The cult of the perfect body, the merits of competition, and the joy of national triumph were among the themes that resonated in a particular fashion within the context of Nazi Germany. Riefenstahl may not have been making *Hetzfilme* [hate films] like *Jud Süss*, as one denazification judge noted after the war, nor was she formally recognized as a propagandist for the Third Reich, but she served the regime in her own ways. There was a reason that Riefenstahl could not sell *Olympia* on the Anglo-American market: "No one wanted to do business with a 'saleswoman for Nazi Germany.'"[43] And despite her claims that the project was financed by the German International

Olympic Committee, this was not the case: Hitler and the Reich provided the funds, including Riefenstahl's own fee of RM 400,000 ($160,000), "the highest salary in the National Socialist film industry."[44]

Leni Riefenstahl undoubtedly advanced the art of sports reportage. She filmed events in a manner never before seen. The Olympic Stadium was turned into a "film stadium," and even with all the technical resources that provided advantages—cameras on catapult-like devices, trenches that permitted low-angled shots, and Zeppelins, including the *Hindenburg,* that provided aerial shots—she and her crew of 120 intruded on the actual events. They positioned themselves so close as to distract and endanger the athletes and obstruct the officials. But Riefenstahl got her shots, including the memorable images of divers in slow motion, with the first-ever underwater cameras capturing their splashing entrances into the pool. She used her signature techniques, such as montage segments, to capture the drama and the inner experiences of the athletes. Perhaps most notably, she succeeded in this regard with the climax of the first of the two-part film, the marathon, for which she filmed the athletes up close while in training; after her careful editing, and with the addition of music, she was able, in the words of biographer Jürgen Trimborn, "to suggest the inner state of the runners, their extraordinary exertion and also their will to win."[45] Riefenstahl's filming of sport proved so successful that she formed a division within her production company that continued to turn out shorter works of this genre up until 1943. Nine of the approximately twenty that were planned were completed, and they served as short cultural films that preceded the features. While Riefenstahl was credited only as the producer, she in fact pioneered the kind of work that now dominates the television airwaves.

Riefenstahl's lofty goals also found expression in the epic *Tiefland* (Lowlands), based on the 1903 opera by Eugen d'Albert and Rudolph Lothar. The plot centers on a love triangle between a peasant gypsy girl, Marta (played by Leni Riefenstahl in her film), a wealthy landowner, Sebastiano, and a poor shepherd, Pedro. Marta ends up with Pedro, who carries her back to the mountains, but not before exclaiming, "Far up in the mountains. To sunshine and freedom and light!" Such was Riefenstahl's project for the entire war: a fantasy of being carried into the mountains by a lover.[46] The theme of the "good, unspoiled" mountains and the "evil, decadent" lowlands resonated with other works in Nazi Germany, including (at least regarding the mountains) many of the landscape paintings exhibited in the *Great German Art Exhibitions.* With connections to more modernist pictures as well—the aforementioned Alpine scenes featuring peasants rendered by Ernst Ludwig Kirchner—Riefenstahl's film exhibited her lofty artistic aspirations (one author talked of its "painterly effect"). *Tiefland,* however, was also very different from Kirchner's work. Financed by the Nazi regime on orders of Hitler, who counted the opera as among his favorites, *Tiefland* was the third most expensive film undertaken during the Third Reich (the other two being color films, *The Adventures of Baron Münchhausen* from 1943 and Veit Harlan's 1945 epic, *Kolberg*). Beginning in 1940, Riefenstahl threw herself into the film, as she did her other projects. In order to realize her vision, she decided she would need thousands of extras—extras who would be credible gypsies. As is now well documented, Riefenstahl chose to use Roma slave labor from the Maxglan camp near Salzburg. While there were no charges of mistreatment while on the set, she did make arrangements with the SS commandant of the camp and employed armed guards, and the vast majority of the extras were transported to Auschwitz after the filming wrapped up, where they were gassed and cremated.[47] Was the latter Riefenstahl's decision? No. Would this fate have befallen them if they had not been extras? It is very likely. But the fact remains that Riefenstahl used unpaid prisoners to make *Tiefland,* and she did nothing to help them once they had served her purposes. She completed the film in 1954 and then continued to offer false and misleading statements about the episode for the rest of her life.

A previous episode in Riefenstahl's career in the Third Reich also deserves closer attention. In September 1939 she had volunteered to lead a camera unit and film the German victory in Poland—her own effort at the cinéma vérité pioneered by Dziga Vertov and others. She and Albert Speer would later discuss plans to create a mammoth newsreel production company, and her expedition to Poland would be her first experience in this realm (although filming the Nuremberg Party Rally and Olympic games served her well in this respect). With the countryside still smoking from the German Blitzkrieg, Riefenstahl arrived, pistol and dagger strapped to her military uniform. While some have reported that she wore a Waffen-SS uniform, she actually designed her own outfit, which General Erich von Manstein described as "nice and jaunty—[she looked] like an elegant partisan whose costume might have been purchased on the Rue de Rivoli in Paris."[48] She and her crew ("Special Film Troop Riefenstahl") were embedded with a German army unit. Just after they entered the town of Końskie on 12 September, they witnessed the execution of a group of local Jews in retaliation for an attack on German Police General Wilhelm Roettig and four soldiers. A photographer captured Riefenstahl's response at the time of the massacre. In the image, she recoils in tears, visibly disturbed by what she has just witnessed.

When a German named Helmut Freitag approached Riefenstahl in 1951 and informed her that he had photographed her at Końskie that day in September 1939, Riefenstahl replied that she welcomed this evidence (although she later referred to him as a "blackmailer").[49] She claimed in a document submitted to a denazification court in 1952 that she had protested when the German soldiers had struck the victims who were digging their own graves, kicking them as they tried to climb out of the burial pit, and that other German soldiers had yelled that she should be "punched in the mouth"—with one going so far as to exclaim what might be loosely translated as, "Shoot the bitch!" ("Schiess das Weib nieder!").[50] The photo that surfaced in 1951, Riefenstahl said, was of her at that moment. Yet she also claimed that neither she nor her crew ever saw any actual murders, that they heard only the distant gunfire, and that she heard later that "a shot fired by a Luftwaffe officer had started a panic that in turn led to a senseless shooting spree."[51] This explanation has now been thoroughly discredited. The photos of her at the critical moment show other German soldiers standing next to her and looking in the same direction with comparably alarmed expressions—that is, they were all attuned to the same event, and no one is threatening her. Indeed, they appear sheltering and protective. Toward the end of 1999, a photo album surfaced from a German army private who was in Końskie at the time. The album contained images, taken with his own camera, showing Riefenstahl and her crew and "prove conclusively that Riefenstahl was an eyewitness to the shootings."[52] One of the photos in the album is captioned "The Jews have to dig the graves of their fallen comrades," and the next reads, "Leni Riefenstahl faints at the sight of dead Jews." As indicated above, the allegations of her presence at the massacre were made in the course of her denazification trials, but the extant evidence was such that she could deny any direct knowledge or involvement. Riefenstahl also dealt with this episode in her memoirs, a treatment that in itself is illuminating because she subtly altered facts for her own purposes. Thus, for example, she wrote that Końskie was about the deaths of "more than thirty Poles"—a formulation that omitted the fact that all the victims were Jews. She also later claimed, "I did not see one dead person in Poland, not one soldier, not one civilian."[53] Considering that she was in Poland for some three weeks after 10 September, this assertion appears highly dubious.

Riefenstahl also later claimed to have given "up my newsreel assign-

Riefenstahl, wearing a uniform, witnesses the murder of approximately
thirty Jewish civilians in the town of Końskie while making a film about the
Polish Campaign in September 1939. (Landesarchiv-Berlin)

ment that very same day [of the Końskie massacre] and left the military
zone," a statement which stretches the limits of language. For starters, she
departed Końskie and traveled to Lublinic to meet with the local commander, General Walter von Reichenau, whom she briefed concerning the
events. Although later implicated in atrocities, Reichenau took disciplinary
action against the officer who purportedly fired the first shot, stripping the
soldier of his rank and issuing a two-year prison sentence. Riefenstahl then
proceeded to fly to Danzig, where, "purely by 'accident,' Hitler arrived in the
city at the same time."[54] She then ate lunch with Hitler on 19 September at
the Hotel Kasino, where she claimed to tell him of the Końskie massacre.
He promised her the guilty individuals would be tried by a court martial
(in fact he did the opposite, and on 4 October 1939 Hitler amnestied all
Wehrmacht soldiers who participated in anti-Semitic acts, including the
officer disciplined by General von Reichenau).[55] Riefenstahl subsequently
traveled to Warsaw, where she oversaw the filming of Hitler entering the
Polish capital as the conquering hero on 5 October 1939. While she is correct in the technical sense that Warsaw was not a war zone (the Modin
Fortress just north of the city fell on 29 September), the entrance of an
invading army into a nation's capital makes for something approximating a
military zone. While she tried to portray herself as a witness or guest at the
Warsaw parade, she acknowledged standing next to three cameramen from
her team. She no doubt directed them as she stood adjacent her lieutenants.

Their footage was then featured in newsreels shown across the Reich, with Riefenstahl receiving due credit. The premier documentary filmmaker in a regime that liked to document itself had received the plum assignment of recording Hitler as he vanquished Poland. Riefenstahl had earlier been present at the Obersalzberg in late August 1939 as Hitler and his subleaders planned the invasion of Poland, and it is clear that she entertained the idea of another film glorifying Hitler. After all, she followed him from Końskie to Danzig to Warsaw. Most likely the events at Końskie, as well as the general brutality of war, clashed with her idealized image of Hitler and induced her to abandon the project.[56] Indeed, she even took steps to deny that the project ever existed.

In the wake of the Poland campaign, Riefenstahl never again did any "war filming." With Hitler directing the armed forces from the Führer Headquarters, Riefenstahl had less contact with the dictator—and with other high-ranking Nazis in general. Yet she knew that her privileges were based on her continuing support for the regime. Thus, in June 1940, just nine months after Końskie, Riefenstahl penned the aforementioned telegram to Hitler after his victory in France, gushing that he "exceed[ed] anything human imagination has the power to conceive, achieving deeds without parallel in the history of mankind" (and adding, "How can we possibly thank you?").[57] She continued to supplicate Hitler up until their last meeting, which took place on the Obersalzberg in 30 April 1944. Clearly, part of her motivation concerned her art, and sustaining her relationship was a key to the continued financing of her work. Perhaps it was her ambition that induced her to ignore the negative aspects of Hitler as a person: the most she could say, it seemed, was that the last meeting featured an hour-long trance-like monologue and that he had aged a great deal. In her postwar accounts, she blamed the Holocaust and other crimes on the subleaders, singling out Goebbels, Bormann, and Himmler.[58] Her take on history went well beyond careerism, although her self-conception as an artist and her dedication to her work motivated many of her statements.

Despite the lengthy memoirs and interviews, Leni Riefenstahl failed so abysmally in her attempts to "master" her Nazi past that it is difficult to assess certain claims about her behavior later on in the war. There were stories that she was romantically involved with Kajetan Mühlmann, the art-historian-turned-plunderer who was known as a ladies' man. Mühlmann's friend Wilhelm Höttl reported on several occasions that Riefenstahl and Mühlmann saw one another, even after the war when the Austrian art historian was a wanted man.[59] Höttl, an SS officer and intelligence agent for the

Reich Security Main Office, was a notorious liar who fed the Americans innumerable falsehoods after the war as he went about saving his neck; but he insisted that Mühlmann lived with Riefenstahl in the 1950s on the Ammersee in rural Bavaria. The art plunderer would sneak into Austria and offer (presumably looted) paintings to those whom he trusted. It is impossible to verify Höttl's story, except that Mühlmann did stash looted works with various relatives and friends at war's end. The Americans found a number of troves belonging to Mühlmann; did they account for them all? Was Riefenstahl actually involved with the Austrian plunderer, either during or after the war? We know that Mühlmann sold artworks to Riefenstahl's colleague Luis Trenker.[60] In other words, Mühlmann traveled in the same circles regarding both filmmakers and Nazi leaders. But we have no documentary evidence to verify Höttl's claim.

American and French troops arrested Riefenstahl at her home in the Austrian Alps in May 1945. She claimed not to be political or to have known anything of atrocities, even of the concentration camps. Her answers did not impress the Office of Strategic Services agents and other Allied officials who interrogated her. The concentration camps had been public knowledge in Nazi Germany going back to 1933, even if the wartime death camps were not. The American interrogators repeatedly caught her up (she had never before heard of a concentration camp and yet Goebbels threatened her with one?). Nevertheless, after her first trial, held in the American internment camp created at Dachau, she was declared "exonerated" and released on 3 June 1945. Because Riefenstahl returned to Kitzbühel, which was under French occupation, this ruling did not stand and further incarcerations and interrogations ensued. From 1948 to 1952 four different denazification courts weighed her behavior during the Third Reich: three times she was exonerated and once was declared a "fellow traveler."[61] For the latter, a 1950 trial in Freiburg, the panel noted that she was not a Party member and found that she did not make propaganda, only documentaries. The judges also dismissed the claim that she had used Roma from a concentration camp for *Tiefland* (they signed on voluntarily to work for the "artist"). Such was the nature of denazification in West Germany: justice proved frustratingly desultory. The final trial at the Special Denazification Court of the West Berlin Senate concluded on 21 April 1952 with Riefenstahl's exoneration (*nicht betroffen*), and she was therefore free to go. This verdict also resulted in the return of her Dahlem villa, which had been placed under trusteeship.[62] In a telling gesture that speaks to the importance of her art—and her tenacious personality—she sold her Berlin home in order to finance the completion of *Tiefland:* the project she had begun in 1934 was finally finished in 1954.

Riefenstahl's postwar career lasted longer than her prewar one. She distinguished herself in two key respects. First, she continued to work up to her death at age 101, with all sorts of remarkable acts of physical vitality: filming members of the Nuba tribe in Sudan (and crashing in a Russian helicopter in the process, which occurred in 2000 at age ninety-eight), as well as scuba diving (she lied about her age in 1974 in order to be certified at an Indian Ocean diving school, listing her date of birth as 1922 instead of 1902). She continued to film underwater scenes well into her nineties. She exhibited astonishing energy and physical courage throughout her life. She also showed certain intellectual abilities; for example, she learned the language of the Nuba so that she could intermingle with them and document their lives. Granted, her work was not always well received. Most critics found her film *Underwater Impressions,* which was aired on German television in 2002 when she was a hundred years old, visually stunning but dull. One called it "the world's most beautiful screensaver," while another mocked it as "Triumph of the Gill."[63] With a soundtrack by Giorgio Moroder—who won an Academy Award for the pulsing pop music in the film *Midnight Express* in 1978—*Underwater Impressions* had elements of a music video. But it was also a technically accomplished work with serious artistic aspirations. Riefenstahl herself stated late in life, "In my heart of hearts I'm always a painter, too. That's why as a photographer I always try . . . to dissolve the realism of a photograph into the painterly."[64] *Underwater Impressions* also had an environmental message, and the filmmaker became an outspoken proponent of protecting coral reefs and nature in general.

The second respect in which Riefenstahl distinguished herself was her failure to come to terms with her past. From the time the war ended, she attempted to evade responsibility for her actions during the Third Reich. Her artistic projects themselves can be viewed as attempts to escape: throwing herself into the completion of *Tiefland* and the idea of a refuge in the mountains; traveling to the remote southern Sudan in the 1960s, where virtually no other nonindigenous person was to be found; and then submersing herself underwater, where she herself admitted that she was "spared the media and journalists." Despite these efforts, Riefenstahl remained controversial. In part, this was because she never honestly engaged her past. Susan Sontag organized her famous essay on fascist aesthetics by analyzing the error-filled account of Riefenstahl's career as presented on the back cover of the filmmaker's book of photographs, *The Last of the Nuba.*[65] Sontag offered a devastating critique of the way Riefenstahl represented her earlier work, and Sontag did not know the entire story. For example, it was only some twenty years later, when Riefenstahl published her memoirs, that she revealed Albert Speer's involvement in the Nuba book. The filmmaker recalled spending five weeks with Speer and his family in Wolkenstein in the Dolomites in the late 1960s, a reunion that led to the collaboration on the Nuba book; the two "worked together, almost every day, shortening the text." Riefenstahl recalled, "Often we went strolling in the snowy forest landscape, and I asked him questions about the past." She did not divulge much of what he said—although she did interject that Speer liked her manuscript.[66] She also observed that "the Nuba cast their spell on him too," which might support Sontag's arguments about fascist aesthetics. Both Speer and Riefenstahl would share other affinities, including a problematic engagement with their respective histories during the Third Reich.

Riefenstahl's memoirs, which were published in English in 1993 (and climbed to number five on the *New York Times* best seller list), raised more questions about her career in Nazi Germany, as did the 1994 Ray Müller film *The Wonderful and Horrible Life of Leni Riefenstahl*, as it was titled in English. Müller confronted the filmmaker with facts that contradicted her own accounts; perhaps most evocatively, she maintained in highly emotional terms that she was a sworn enemy of Goebbels, even as Müller read excerpts from the Propaganda Minister's diaries in which Goebbels gushed about fabulous evenings with her.[67] "It's not so!" Riefenstahl exclaimed repeatedly, even as she had no answer for why Goebbels would invent such accounts. She appeared somewhat more poised as she maintained that she had seen the Roma extras from *Tiefland* after the war. She repeated this claim—that she had met the former extras who had not perished in Auschwitz—in several interviews, and these statements compelled state prosecutors in Frankfurt to explore filing charges for Holocaust denial. The announcement that an investigation was under way came in 2002 on the day she turned one hundred years old.[68] No charges were ever filed, but others caught out Riefenstahl in her efforts to conceal her past. This includes the trivial, such as denying that she performed topless in the 1925 film *Ways to Strength and Beauty*, to more serious allegations, such as her sequestering the outtakes and production stills from her wartime film *Tiefland*, footage that might have permitted some insight into the fate of the extras. It appears that she first culled the most incriminating images showing the subjects in a concentration camp–like environment, and then kept the material away from researchers by sequestering it in her private archive.[69]

Whenever interviewed about Hitler and National Socialism—which occurred many times over the subsequent five decades after the war—Riefenstahl maintained her innocence, stating that she was an artist committed to her artwork, and that she was not political. At most she would acknowledge that she was "inspired . . . by what was beautiful, strong, and healthy."[70] In other words, she never achieved any distance from the films she made during the Third Reich. Eric Rentschler noted that she used a "fluid position that sought to elude the grasp of anyone who wanted to take her to task for having worked with the Nazis"—either she "simply captured what was there without any ideological prejudice or political incentive" or she was a "self-conscious artist . . . guided by her formal interest and stylistic resolve."[71] Many of her critics tried to hold her more accountable. The most notable, as indicated earlier, was Susan Sontag, who wrote,

> The careers of other artists who became fascists, such as Céline and Benn and Marinetti and Pound (not to mention those, like Pabst and Pirandello and Hamsun, who embraced fascism in the decline of their powers), are not instructive in a comparable way. For Riefenstahl is the only major artist who was completely identified with the Nazi era and whose work, not only during the Third Reich but thirty years after its fall, has consistently illustrated many themes of fascist aesthetics.[72]

Riefenstahl would have liked part of this formulation—about her importance as an artist. But she would contest all charges of unethical or complicitous behavior during the Third Reich. By her own admission she brought "fifty or more" lawsuits in the postwar period; while some of these legal actions related to commercial rights for films made during the Third Reich, most concerned her historical role and reputation.[73]

At the same time that Riefenstahl battled for respectability, she remained the doyenne of the old Nazis and socialized with that crowd, especially in Bavaria, where she resided after the war. In 1978 she moved from central Munich (Schwabing) to a modern villa, secluded on the outskirts of Munich in the village of Pöcking on Lake Starnberg—an area favored by old Nazis. Her admirers, and certain scholars, would pay her visits, and she would sometimes present them with signed photographs from her days as a "movie star." The Third Reich remained the apex of her career, and like many who flourished under the Nazi regime, there remained a positive memory of what was for them in many ways "the good old days."

But there is no doubt that Riefenstahl made her mark on cinema and popular culture. The Museum of Modern Art in New York organized the first retrospective of films by and featuring her in 1966.[74] George Lucas admitted that he borrowed from *Triumph of the Will* when he made *Star Wars:* the scenes where "the film's heroes stride to martial music across a via triumphalis of granite slabs, past block formations of uniformed masses, to mount a stone tribunal and be received in the end by an ovation from the crowd."[75] Mick Jagger and David Bowie also cited her as an influence in their concert stagecraft (the latter called Hitler "history's first rock star"), while Michael Jackson used "regalia, uniforms and mass ornaments of the Nuremberg rally" and was an "uncritical poacher who [drew] on the powerful image and images of power in order to create a self-aggrandizing spectacle."[76] Eric Rentschler summed up much of her accomplishment when he observed, "Working on the cutting edge of cinematic modernism, Riefenstahl instrumentalized advanced tools of sight and sound in ways that have indelibly marked the subsequent history of mass media."[77] Trained in a modernist tradition, from which she borrowed freely for the rest of her career, this talented and ambitious artist put her work above ethics or self-awareness, and this enabled her to find a place in the Third Reich.

12

Arno Breker

(1900 Elberfeld-Wuppertal–1991 Düsseldorf)

Photo of Arno Breker from the *Berliner Illustrierte Zeitung* (November 1938).

ARNO BREKER STANDS out as a preeminent example of a modernist figure who modified his art to suit the Nazi leaders. With a "chameleon-like quality to transform himself" and also considerable technical ability, Breker adapted to the historical circumstances of his life with remarkable finesse. Two points need to be stressed in this context. First, Breker hailed from a truly modernist milieu and never entirely gave up that identity, even after 1935, as he rose to the pinnacle of the Nazi cultural establishment. Second, Breker in his own way helped to preserve certain vestiges of modernism in the Third Reich. Although consorting with an array of the most notorious Nazis—Hitler, Himmler, and Göring among them—and occasionally posturing as an opponent of "degenerate art," Breker also used his influence for more progressive purposes, and this included helping modernist artists threatened by the National Socialist regime.

The son of a stone mason, Breker grew up with a certain ambivalence about his social class. At times, he would emphasize the working-class nature of his family and take pride in the fact that he hailed from people who labored with their hands. This heritage led him to adopt more left-wing views, as he did during his years in art school at the Düsseldorf Academy. But Breker also presented himself as part of a tradition of craftsmen—an artisan who was anything but proletarian, let alone Communist. Later, after the war, Breker styled himself as an artist above politics and consorted with a wide array of individuals from very different backgrounds, ranging from radical right-wing figures such as German publisher-politician Gerhard Frey to statesmen such as Egypt's President Muhammad Anwar al-Sadat.[1] Sadat, however, as a young nationalist officer in the Egyptian army, had sympathized with the Germans during World War II.[2] While Breker became a card-carrying member of the Nazi Party in the 1930s, he exhibited left-wing, bohemian, and cosmopolitan tendencies as a young man.

Breker's early biography makes it easy to understand why he felt connections to the left-leaning working class. Educated at a vocational school and then serving as an apprentice in his father's stonecutting establishment, Breker first studied art in night courses. He showed talent and ambition at an early age, taking over his father's business in 1916 when the senior Breker was conscripted for military service. Upon his father's return from the army, the aspiring artist was freed to matriculate at the State Art Academy in Düsseldorf, where he spent five years, from 1920 to 1925. Despite his many teachers—including sculptor Hubertus Netzer and architect Wilhelm Kreis—it was the environment more generally that shaped him. The Düsseldorf Academy counted among the most important institutions for those with modernist inclinations. Otto Dix, who arrived in 1922, held radical left-wing political views and at that time produced some of his most provocative art, including his incendiary *Lustmord* pictures that featured graphic portrayals of sexual violence.[3] Breker sculpted a portrait bust of Otto Dix in 1926, which speaks to a degree of familiarity. But the atmosphere was also contentious. Wilhelm Kreis, for example, although a proponent of the progressive German arts and crafts movement and an early supporter of his student Max Pechstein and other Expressionists, was more politically and stylistically conservative. Kreis would become an important early patron of Breker, arranging for the young sculptor to exhibit at the high-profile 1926 show in Düsseldorf called *The Great Exhibition for Health Care, Social Welfare, and Physical Exercise* (known by the German acronym GESOLEI).[4] The exhibition drew over seven million visitors, making it one of the most significant cultural events of the Weimar Republic. During his tenure at the Düsseldorf Academy, Breker learned a great deal about cultural politics. He came to appreciate the strong emotions provoked by the debates, the nature of patronage and alliances, and the wisdom of avoiding enemies.

Although Breker imagined that he could reconcile classicism and modernism, his early work in many ways followed the tradition of Auguste Rodin and the French naturalists—Aristide Maillol and Charles Despiau, among them. Rodin, according to art historian Peter Chametzky, had "exploited studio accidents and mistakes to create powerful metaphors and heighten awareness of the intrinsic qualities of specific materials."[5] These rough, textured, and often seemingly incomplete figures both engaged and "rephrased" the classical precursors. The "modernist synecdoche [allowed] the part to speak for the whole"—visual references to an inherited tradition.[6] Breker evidently encountered Rodin's *The Age of Brass* at the Düsseldorf Museum around 1915, and then read Rainer Maria Rilke's 1919 study of the French artist—both of which shaped his thinking. Yet Breker's early sculpture, such as his *Sitting Woman* from 1921, also resembled the work of Pablo Picasso and Edwin Scharff, and later efforts suggested the influence of Barlach and even Alberto Giacometti. For example, his sculptures *Torso of Saint Matthew* (1927) and *Small Dancer* (1929) have elements of abstraction, rough-hewn features, and sinewy, elongated arms.[7] During this period, he was exposed to a wide array of modernist art. He made a pilgrimage to Weimar, for example, in order to visit the Bauhaus and see the work of the *Bauhäusler,* but he left virtually no record of what he did there. Yet Breker certainly gained a sense of the contested cultural politics that plagued the art school and that shortly thereafter induced Gropius to move it to Dessau. Breker's experiences in the 1920s clearly shaped his aesthetic sensibility. Later, when he became a wealthy and powerful figure in the Nazi cultural establishment, he collected modern art.

Breker traveled to Paris in 1926 and developed an affinity for the city that would last his entire life. His initial stay lasted seven months, and he returned the following year for what became a four-year sojourn in the French capital. Having developed a facility with the language, he was embraced by Maillol and other French artists, including Fauve painter Maurice de Vlaminck. Breker also met his future wife, Demetra Messala, in Paris. A Greek model (Breker was a Philhelline), she had posed for Picasso and Maillol, among others. Living in Montmartre, the couple soon became prominent fixtures in the local art scene. The young German sculptor exhibited works at the Salon des Tuileries and the Salon d'Automne, among other venues. Breker's career advanced at an impressive pace, and did so on a distinctly modernist track. A contemporary of Breker, Dominique Egret, recalled, "Whenever we mention these three names [Rodin, Despiau, and Maillol], however, a fourth must also be added, one which is representative of that Parisian school for which human vitality was the focal point of artistic creation: Arno Breker. Breker, who was two years younger than I, stood out because of his all-encompassing vision, his tolerance and his open-mindedness."[8] Egret also noted that Breker at one point shared a studio in Paris with Alexander Calder. The American had begun his famous *Cirque Calder* series in the autumn of 1926. The juxtaposition of Calder's whimsical creations from wire, cloth, and other found objects and Breker's naturalist but increasingly monumental works is among the more interesting pairings in art history. Breker later remarked with a certain sadness, "Calder, whom I lost contact with later—just as others from our young Paris years—through political developments."[9]

Arno Breker, *Torso of Saint Matthew* (1927), a work showing Breker's modernist roots. (© Foto Breker-Archiv, Art-Museum, Schloss Nörvenich, Germany)

Another unlikely pairing developed when famed modernist dealer Alfred Flechtheim began "to promote Breker's work" in 1929.[10] Flechtheim, a German Jew from Westphalia, had a network of galleries, with those in Berlin and Düsseldorf standing out as the flagship establishments. Flechtheim was arguably the most important dealer of modernist art in the

Weimar Republic, representing Picasso, George Grosz, Paul Klee, and Max Beckmann, among others. Breker's work was less daring than that of these other artists—as was often the case for sculptors at the time—but he still incorporated elements of abstraction. Breker's early efforts were sufficiently modernist to warrant removal from German collections a few years later in the "degenerate art" action. His sculpture *Crouching Model,* which featured a kneeling female figure, was removed from the municipal art collection in Duisberg and given the inventory number 15106.[11] Breker also received a positive review in the journal *Die Kunst für Alle* by "Jewish ex-Dadaist" Luise Straus-Ernst in 1929, who praised him as "the very model of the virtuous artist, conscious of the limits and aware of the potential of his medium, and attentive to both tradition and contemporary innovations."[12] Luise Straus-Ernst, of course, had no way of knowing about future developments, including her own murder at Auschwitz in 1944.

Breker's career flourished in the latter years of the Weimar Republic. Many in the art world regarded him an up-and-coming sculptor. This high regard found expression in a prestigious fellowship jointly awarded in late 1932 by the Prussian Education Minister and the Prussian Academy of the Arts, and it enabled him to spend six months in Rome at the prestigious Villa Massimo. Breker traveled to the capital of Fascist Italy and worked on a re-creation of a lost sculpture by Michelangelo called the *Rondanini Pietà.* This project also followed the path of Rodin, who had explored lost and unfinished fragments of earlier masters. Another *Stipendiat* that year was Felix Nussbaum, a German-Jewish painter who often worked in a Surrealist idiom. Nussbaum would be captured in Belgium during the war—after being denounced by an acquaintance—and then murdered in Auschwitz in 1944.[13] But in April 1933, some eleven years earlier, when Nussbaum and Breker were holders of the prestigious fellowship and residents of the elegant Villa Massimo, the newly appointed Reich Propaganda Minister Joseph Goebbels graced them with a visit. According to Breker, Goebbels encouraged "the artists to return to Germany where a great future was awaiting them."[14] There is no record of whether Nussbaum made himself available to Goebbels, but Breker seems to have been profoundly moved by the minister's exhortations.

Goebbels was not the only one to encourage Breker to return to Germany. Similar advice came from the sculptor's friend Max Liebermann, the honorary president of the Prussian Academy and a chief proponent of the Berlin Secession school, which was modernist but in a more conservative vein. A prominent Jewish figure in Germany, Liebermann detested the Nazis but hoped that more tolerant and humane types like Breker would moderate the behavior of the new leaders. Breker himself later presented similar reasons for his return to Germany. He claimed that he sought "to save what could be saved," and also pointed to the anti-German sentiment in Paris after Hitler's rise to power, which made him uncomfortable there. But these explanations come up short and are outweighed by the strong element of career advancement that entered into his thinking. Even before his return, he had commissions for a number of portrait busts—from Bertha Siemens, a member of the famed industrialist family, among others—and he was offered the use of a Berlin studio belonging to Professor August Gaul. Breker correctly adduced the great opportunities available to him in the Reich capital.

Although reluctant to admit it after the war, Breker knew that he would need to alter the style of his work to reap the maximum rewards offered by the Nazi leaders. The time he had spent in Italy exposed him to monumental Fascist sculpture. Moreover, his fellowship coincided with the rise of the new "empire style" in the early 1930s, when Mussolini and his cohort encouraged gigantic figures and themes relating to the reestablishment of the Roman Empire in the Mediterranean. Breker also witnessed how Italian artists had state support to acquire the expensive materials required for such sculptures, and he came to appreciate how these works could overwhelm the viewer. Breker's art, therefore, changed before his political views did. His senior colleague, Georg Kolbe, noted about Breker's return to Germany in 1934, "From then on, a change in his artistic views became visible; the earlier one which stood close to the French view sank under the strongest Nazi influence."[15] Yet this transformation did not occur overnight. In 1935, for example, Breker exhibited at the Galerie Vömel in Düsseldorf, the same gallery that showed Nolde and other modernists. That same year, Breker also helped organize an important show in Munich featuring the works of Berlin artists, many who worked in a modernist vein. In the words of Breker's defender Dominique Egret, "As members of the judges' panel, Breker, Arthur Kampf, Georg Kolbe and Leo von König express their support for tolerance in art, so that artists considered controversial by the Nazi regime are also given the chance to participate. Breker is particularly supportive of Käthe Kollwitz, whom he knows and whose work he admires. In the end Gauleiter Wagner . . . imposes his own choice. Breker protests in vain. In spite of this, Breker begins campaigning against the policy of 'Entartete Kunst' [degenerate art], which leads to tension with Adolf Hitler on this issue. Nevertheless, Breker receives commissions."[16]

It was only in 1936, with Breker's work for the Berlin Olympics, that he emerged as an official artist representing the Nazi regime.[17] In the arts competition that coincided with the games, the jury singled out his *Decathlete,* awarding him a silver medal. Alfred Rosenberg also began lauding him as a promising talent. Breker's sculptures were showcased in the inaugural *Great German Art Exhibition* in 1937. All told, forty-two of Breker's works would appear in the annual Munich exhibitions. Hitler, Goebbels, and others expressed relief that there was finally an artist who could credibly represent their regime. Breker took center stage in the Nazis' propaganda, and he made the necessary adjustments. He joined the Nazi Party in January 1937, just prior to being appointed a professor by Hitler. Breker held a professorship at the University of Berlin until war's end. Later in 1937, he was named a member of the Prussian Academy, along with Josef Thorak and architects Hermann Giesler and Ernst Sagebiel—all of them "the Führer's creatures."[18] Breker would receive many other honors and awards during the Third Reich, including the Golden Badge of the Nazi Party, bestowed by Hitler personally on Breker's fortieth birthday in 1940.

Arno Breker gradually emerged as the most publicized artist in Nazi Germany. In early 1939, Speer's New Reich Chancellery building was unveiled to immense fanfare, with newsreels, special edition books, and widespread coverage in an array of media. Breker's twin sculptures, known as *The Party* and *The Army,* stood guard over a key entrance to the building. Images of Breker's sculpture and Speer's architecture would become iconic for the culture of the Third Reich. Before long, Speer had commissioned the artist to make two additional sculptures—forty-five-foot-tall figures of Atlas and Tellus—for the entrance to the Great Hall. *Grosse Halle* was Speer's venue for the masses so that they could worship Hitler, and although it was never constructed, the publicity surrounding the project, featuring large-scale models and images of Breker's works, brought even more attention to the sculptor. Arno Breker was also clearly the referent in the feature film *Venus on Trial* from 1941. The "hero is a young sculptor in the Classical tradition" and is named Peter Brake, which in German would make the last name sound very similar to Breker.[19] In 1944 Goebbels's propaganda machine also produced a "culture film," titled *Arno Breker: Hard Times, Strong Art,* that mythologized the artist's life and work. Notably, one of the filmmakers, Arnold Fanck, had been a pioneer of the mountain film genre and an early mentor of Leni Riefenstahl, whose production company oversaw the documentary. Hitler explicitly identified Breker as his favorite sculptor, and this induced other Nazi leaders to praise him and articulate the ideological messages implicit in his work. Alfred Rosenberg, for example, announced that Breker's "monumental figures [were] a representation of the force and willpower of the age."[20]

Breker in turn became well practiced at churning out sculptures for the Nazi state, and these pieces could easily be read as symbols of National Socialism. With a monumentality that dominates the viewer, and the violent themes, which are common (but not present in every piece), Breker's art from 1935 to 1945 seemingly shouted out Nazi tenets: the racially superior *Übermenschen,* for example, struggling—or fighting—heroically. Scholar Jost Hermand noted that Breker's works were "a beautification of militarism and racial soundness based on the struggle against and even liquidation of all things not beautiful."[21] The artworks and architectural designs of the Third Reich were not mere window dressing to a brutal regime, but fundamental to the Nazi leaders' worldviews. For example, Breker's early Nazi sculpture *Prometheus* (1935), which was placed in front of the Reich Propaganda Ministry building on the Wilhelm Strasse, developed a theme that Hitler had elaborated in *Mein Kampf.* Hitler represented Prometheus as an "Aryan," and then argued, "All the human culture, all the results of art, science, and technology that we see before us today, are almost exclusively the creative product of the Aryan."[22] Breker's selection of Prometheus as a subject was not accidental. He returned to the theme in 1942, and in doing so offered a kind of visual quotation of Hitler in these works. More generally, as Albert Speer acknowledged about the monumental building projects he designed with Hitler, "These monuments were an assertion of his claim to world dominion long before he dared to voice any such intentions even to his associates."[23] Breker, who counted among Speer's closest friends and colleagues, helped give artistic expression to the dictator's program of conquest and genocide.

One can also point to Breker's idealizing portraits of Hitler, which supported the idea of a Hitler cult. In 1945 a monuments officer named Kurt Reutti, who was working in the eastern region of Germany, inspected Breker's Berlin-Grünewald atelier, where he found "a mass production of Hitler busts out of ceramics. They were 'stored' by the hundred in the pond that adjoined the property."[24] In a certain sense, one could see an element of modernism in the mass production of these busts. Breker would help bring "art" into homes and offices in a manner somewhat akin to the ideas conceived by the Bauhäusler, turning to the modern means of reproduction in a way not entirely dissimilar from what Walter Benjamin imagined in his 1936 essay "The Work of Art in the Age of Mechanical Reproduction"— although Benjamin did not believe that such means were useful "for the purposes of fascism."[25] Art historian Peter Chametzky has also discerned another modernist aspect to Breker's production method. Breker would create certain works, such as his reliefs, in segments. The focus on the process, in which the "sculptural object reaches back to incorporate the duration of its creation into its physical appearance," constituted part of the modernist project.[26] The dismemberment or disaggregation of the human body also stands out as a characteristic of modernism (think Picasso, perhaps the prime example). While Breker gave the impression that his sculptures offered a whole and complete human form, recently discovered photographs documenting his creative process show these works being constructed in a piecemeal, modernist manner. His relief *The Victim,* with the head and arms still missing, offers a striking example (Plate 11). It marked a departure from pre-modern sculptors like Michelangelo, who imagined the release of an organic form from within a block of stone. Breker's deconstructivist approach with certain (but not all) works realized what George Steiner described as "an assembly-line and piecework model of human relations. . . . A brilliantly exact *figura* of the division of labor on the factory floor."[27] The production of Führer busts at Breker's Jäckelsbruch factory represented an extension of such principles.

The key point is that Breker did not completely abandon his modernist roots as he ascended to the acme of the Nazi artistic establishment. A contemporary, Victor Dirksen of the Städtisches Museum in Wuppertal-Elberfeld, noted, "That his artistic style went through a change after 1933 is not to be disputed. . . . He became a state sculptor . . . From his freestanding works and portrait busts of the time one can see that he never entirely gave up his earlier style. Otherwise, I occasionally had the impression that Breker deep down was unhappy about the development which he had experienced."[28] Breker's connection to modernism is one of the reasons that so many French artists attended the opening of the exhibition of his sculpture at the Musée de l'Orangerie in Paris in July 1942. Granted, Vichy officials put pressure on Aristide Maillol, Jean Cocteau, and others to attend the event, but the French artists went further than simply participating. Both Maillol and Cocteau offered fulsome words of praise for their old friend, with the latter penning a fawning front-page homage in the journal *Comoedia.* French sculptor Charles Despiau authored, or was credited with authoring, a biography of Breker that the Germans publicized with considerable fanfare (and then translated into seventeen languages). The French artists, to be sure, expressed some disapproval among themselves. With regard to Breker's statues assembled in l'Orangerie, Sacha Guitry quipped to

The famed French modernist writer and impresario Jean Cocteau with Arno Breker at the latter's exhibition in Paris (1942). Cocteau also evinced sympathy for fascism. (© Foto Breker-Archiv, Art-Museum, Schloss Nörvenich, Germany)

Cocteau, "If they all have erections, we won't be able to move around."[29] But of course such mocking and irreverent remarks were meant only for private consumption; the newsreels and press coverage gave a very different impression. Breker, for his part, made sure that some of his more modernist pieces were included in l'Orangerie exhibition. It made sense in terms of German-French cultural diplomacy—reaching out to the more pro-modernist French audience—but the selection also reflected Breker's own self-conception as a figure who transcended the pro- and anti-modernist divide.

The course of Breker's career during the Third Reich shows an artist in the gray zone in numerous respects. First, Breker's transformation from independent modernist to Nazi monumentalist brought him enormous riches. Individual works sold for high sums: for example, RM 100,000 ($40,000) for the relief *Comradeship* in 1938. The state commissions, such as those issued by Speer, brought him millions more.[30] Hitler also gave him tax-free case awards (*Dotationen*)—RM 250,000 ($100,000) in 1942, for example—as well as a castle in Wriezen that once belonged to Frederick the Great. Breker's *Staatsatelier* in Berlin Grunewald itself cost more than RM 1 million ($400,000), and in November 1939 he and his wife were given use of Walter Rathenau's former villa located nearby on the Königsallee (and this is by no means a comprehensive list of the properties and resources at his disposal).[31] With his vast wealth, Breker was able to amass a large art collection—much of it acquired in occupied France, where Germans had a tremendous advantage as a result of the exploitative exchange rates. Among the works in his collection were those by modern artists, including paintings by Cubists Pablo Picasso, Georges Braque, and Jacques Villon, as well as Fauves André Derain, Fernand Léger, and Maurice de Vlaminck.[32] Breker also played a role in organizing the visit of French artists to Germany in 1941. Those participating in this officially sanctioned propaganda spectacle included modernists Derain and Vlaminck, as well as Charles Despiau and Kees van Dongen.[33]

Breker was a powerful figure in occupied France, living both at the Ritz Hotel and in the "Aryanized" apartment of Helena Rubinstein on the Île Saint-Louis (Quai de Béthune 24).[34] The artist was one of the luminaries of occupied Paris, with the French side offering collaborationists Maurice Chevalier, Edith Piaf, and Coco Chanel among those who interacted with the Germans. According to a recent estimate, approximately twenty-five thousand French collaborated with German occupiers. The Franco-German elite often enjoyed extravagant luxury. Ernst Jünger, for example, recounted seeing Breker at a soirée at the Hotel Ritz in 1942, where occupation high society was in full swing.[35] The sculptor also frequently mixed into political matters: for example, engaging in discussions with the Vichy Commissioner General of Social Policy for French Working in Germany because he had French workers at his Wriezen production facility and spoke fluent French. He accompanied Hitler on his "art trip" around Paris on 23 June 1940. The evening before, while dining outside the capital in the town of Givet, Hitler had exclaimed, "Now the door is open. I am going to this metropolis of the arts with my art advisers, so that we can test, by the standards of the French capital, our own plans for civic reconstruction." During the Paris excursion he said to Breker, "I would have studied art in Paris, as you did, if destiny had not thrust me into politics."[36] Breker's longtime friend Jean Cocteau commented that Hitler viewed the sculptor as his adopted son and "loved him."[37]

Despite climbing to the pinnacle of the cultural establishment of the Third Reich, Breker was not without ambiguity. This extended not only to the modernist elements in his own art, but also to helping individuals victimized by the Nazi regime. Breker continued his friendship with Jewish painter Max Liebermann, and when the eighty-seven-year-old artist died in 1935 Breker, upon the request of Liebermann's widow, crafted the death mask. The sculptor also helped mitigate the persecution suffered by various friends and colleagues in Nazi-controlled Europe. The threats at times came close to home: his "companion," Demetra Messala, "a Greek woman, [was] suspected to be Jewish."[38] While this accusation was never proven during the Third Reich, other friends found themselves in even more serious trouble. Publisher Peter Suhrkamp, for example, whose authors included modernists Bertolt Brecht and Samuel Beckett, had been sent to the Sachsenhausen concentration camp in 1944, and Breker went to Speer, Himmler, and Reich Security Main Office chief Ernst Kaltenbrunner in a successful effort to free the publisher, who had become gravely ill with a lung ailment.[39]

The artist was arguably most effective helping friends in German-occupied France. Breker used his influence to prevent the deportation of Maillol's Russian-born and Jewish model, Dina Vierny, intervening with the head of the Gestapo, Heinrich Müller. Vierny had already been sent to the camp at Fresnes and was in imminent danger of being transported to her death in the East. But after six months of incarceration, she was set free. While Breker was completing his portrait bust of Maillol in 1943, visiting the French sculptor at Banyuls-sur-Mer, he provided updates about Vierny as he worked.[40] In the same year, Breker came to the aid of Picasso, who was trying to live quietly in Paris. Apparently, the Gestapo had discovered that the artist was trying to smuggle currency to both Spain and the Soviet Union and placed him under closer surveillance. According to Dominique Egret, "At Cocteau's request, Breker becomes involved in what comes to be known after the war as Operation 'White Dove' which saves Picasso from arrest by the German Gestapo and deportation to a disciplinary camp."[41] Picasso had received a letter on 16 September 1943 from German authorities, requiring him to appear on 20 September for a physical in anticipation of his deportation to Essen, where he would participate in a forced labor program. Breker evidently helped Picasso evade the summons. Breker also later claimed he went to Heinrich Müller in Berlin in 1943 and told him that he couldn't arrest Picasso (without specifying the reason why, but suggesting it would be bad public relations).[42] There is no extant archival documentation proving that Breker intervened with the Gestapo chief Müller, but other postwar testimony, Picasso's and Cocteau's included, affirmed Breker's account. Art historian Gertje Utley has also suggested that Breker may have been "Picasso's mysterious source of bronze for the casting of his sculptures."[43] Even as the French were melting down bronze public monuments (but not their church bells, which were spared), and sending most of the raw material to Germany for use in the war effort, Picasso managed to have his sculptures cast in bronze. Breker's own source of bronze for his Paris 1942 exhibition turned out to be his friend Albert Speer, who paid the Rudier Foundry to cast the sculptures. Of course, this bronze could very well have come from smelted French statues.

But lest one conclude that Breker was a humanitarian who simply happened to make Nazi art, it is important to remember that he was an opportunist. Breker first and foremost looked out for his own interests. How else can one interpret Robert Scholz's assertion that Breker backed him in opposing the Vienna exhibition *Junge Kunst im Deutschen Reich*, sponsored by the city's governor, Baldur von Schirach, in March 1943?[44] Scholz also claimed that Breker was opposed to Schirach providing Emil Nolde with a studio. If Scholz's report is true, which it likely is, then Breker appears to have been protecting his political interests. He was then a vice president of the Reich Chamber for the Visual Arts—having been appointed in April 1941—and did not want to expend the political capital on a cause that would anger and potentially alienate Hitler.[45] Breker may have been one of those artists "graced by God"—or, in Nazi parlance, an "irreplaceable artist"—but he was not invulnerable.

Breker assisted others when it did not diminish his own political capital. Helping or saving threatened individuals enabled him to exercise his own considerable power. By aiding persecutees, he demonstrated his power and thereby increased it. Albert Speer had understood that power needed outward expression—and even though Breker's interventions would have been known only to a relative few consisting of artists and political leaders, they were the ones that mattered to him. "The other Breker," as one scholar called him in light of his efforts to help certain persecutees, could not be divorced from the opportunistic, self-promoting, and greedy figure who wielded such power in the Third Reich.[46] Breker was also guilty of breathtaking hubris. A telling episode occurred in 1939, when, in Dominique Egret's words, "Aviation pioneer Charles Lindbergh visit[ed] Breker in his studio while the latter [was] working on his 'Flight of Icarus' relief. Lindbergh [said] to Breker, 'you have forgotten to include Icarus's fall in your portrayal.' Breker conclude[d] their discussion of his Icarus relief with a smile, saying, 'my Icarus does not fall.'"[47] This episode in itself was not important, but it nonetheless represented a larger and deeper personality trait in the artist.

In the postwar period, Breker's arrogance found expression in his failure to master his own past. He had come through denazification with a minor fine of 100 deutsche marks (about $24) and a judgment that labeled him a "fellow-traveler." This helped Breker rehabilitate his career, as he became, in the words of one East German critic, "Hofkünstler des deutschen Wirtschaftswunder" (the court artist of the German economic miracle).[48] In a project for the Gerling insurance concern in Cologne, Breker designed not only the sculptures and reliefs, but the entire building. Other projects in the 1950s followed for buildings in Düsseldorf, Munich, Essen, and Siegen. Chancellor Konrad Adenauer admired Breker so much that he sat for a portrait bust and supported him publicly with statements like, "Since Breker remains true to the quintessential in his artistic creations, he knows to be hopeful in the future; for without hope, there is no future for humanity."[49] Beyond inspiring the founding chancellor of the Federal Republic to metaphysical reflection, Breker became the doyen of the radical right in the Federal Republic, consorting with the likes of Robert Scholz, Gerhard Frey, and others whose views about the Third Reich stood well outside the mainstream. In a 1980 interview Breker denied that French Jews had been dispossessed of their property—a viewpoint approaching Holocaust denial. That same year he admitted that his friendship with the considerably more apologetic Albert Speer had come to an end, stating, "I haven't had any contact with him for four years. . . . I don't like his view of the past. . . . I can't condemn my work. . . . I have nothing to regret, nothing to repent for, nothing to add."[50]

Breker became a more visible artist in the 1980s, although he remained a highly polarizing figure. In 1981, vocal protests ensued when his work was included in an exhibition at the Centre Pompidou. Many on the Left and in the art world (often overlapping populations) regarded Breker as toxic. As art historian Ursel Berger noted, "In 1983, a 'non-artist' such as Breker, for example, was not allowed to be represented by originals in the Berliner Akademie."[51] Instead, here as in a number of exhibitions, Breker's work was represented via photographs. Berger added, "At the time, though, that was not regarded as a shortcoming, but rather as a matter of principle."[52] This kind of treatment prompted responses, perhaps most notably by chocolate manufacturer and art patron Peter Ludwig, who defended Breker's art throughout the decade, thereby stoking the debate about whether to include "Nazi art" in museums. Typical of those in the Ludwig camp, art historian John Zavrel maintained in a 1983 interview that Breker counted as "the greatest living sculptor in the classical tradition of this century."[53]

Unsurprisingly, such views formed the basis of the Museum Arno Breker, which opened in 1985 in *Schloss* Nörvenich, an imposing castle located between Aachen and Cologne. Founded by his postwar art dealers, Joe and Marco Bodenstein, the Breker Museum has catered to the artist's various supporters (the museum was renamed The Museum of European Art in the 1990s and expanded to include the art of Salvador Dalí and "Viennese Fantastic Realist painter and anti-modern art agitator" Ernst Fuchs). The Bodensteins propagate what Peter Chametzky has described as "self-defeating tactics when they aggrandize him as a genius on the order of Michelangelo."[54] The museum's website, to offer one example, includes the claim that "Breker is the most important sculptor of the classical tradition in the twentieth century."[55] The museum has attracted its share of political leaders and celebrities, and one can even join the Arno Breker Society. In 1991, German Foreign Minister Hans-Dietrich Genscher attended the opening of the Salvador Dalí exhibition in Schloss Nörvenich—the Surrealist's works surrounded by Breker's sculptures. Despite the temptation to label the spectacle "surreal," the larger point speaks to Breker's gradual rehabilitation.

Even with the widespread historical amnesia, a number of observers have offered cogent insights into the problematic artist. On Breker's ninetieth birthday in 1990, Eduard Beaucamp wrote in the *Frankfurter Allgemeine Zeitung,* "He is the classic example of a seduced, deluded, and also overbearing talent. Breker's case teaches that the modern artist may not give into blind creative illusions, that one needs 'self-awareness.' Breker's all too conspicuous, all too unreflective natural gift became his fate. He put his talent at the disposal of his patrons and identified with their will."[56] As he came out of the shadows in the 1980s, after having lived a guarded and fairly private life since the war, Breker not only received accolades, but also suffered increased scrutiny by historians and journalists. He did not endure probing questions to the same extent as his onetime friend Albert Speer, who faced allegations about his knowledge of the Holocaust back in the early 1970s (and who then became the subject of a series of critical biographies), but Breker had to answer a number of queries about his experiences in the Third Reich. He mostly feigned ignorance—for example, not knowing the source of the bronze for his l'Orangerie sculptures at a time when the French were melting down thousands of statues across the country. He also attempted to play the role of victim. But above all, he saw himself as an artistic genius, and this came with a corresponding ego of truly epic proportions. In a sense he saw himself as a Greek god, someone who was flawed but nonetheless endowed with special gifts.[57] Breker died in his sleep at his longtime home in Düsseldorf in February 1991, still believing that he was an artist of world historical importance and that he had reconciled modernism with classicism.

The conflicted nature of Breker's career and worldview is perhaps best evident in the subjects of his portrait busts. Among them were the following:

Otto Dix (1926)
Isamu Noguchi (1927)
Albert Giacometti (1929)
Max Liebermann (1934 and 1935)
Gottfried Bermann-Fischer (1935)
Joseph Goebbels (1937)
Gerda Bormann (1940)
Edda Göring (1941)
Greta Speer (1941)
Bernhard Rust (1941)
Albert Speer (1941)
Gerhart Hauptmann (1942)
Hans Schweitzer ("Mjölnir") (1942)
Aristide Maillol (1942–43)
Maurice de Vlaminck (1943)
Wilhelm Kreis (1943)
Jean Cocteau (1963)
Ezra Pound (1967)
Louis-Ferdinand Céline (1970)
Salvador Dalí (1974–75)
Winifred Wagner (1977)
Cosima Wagner (1978)
Ernst Jünger (1981–82)
Peter Ludwig (1985)

Some of the individuals may not be familiar names, such as the Nazi illustrator Hans Schweitzer, who published images of steel-jawed storm troopers and went by the Norse mythological name "Mjölnir." Yet more generally the group represents a mixture of modernist and fascist figures (and in some cases both). It also includes several Jewish subjects (Liebermann, Bermann-Fischer). One of the most striking messages conveyed by the list, however, concerns Breker's familiarity with the Nazi leaders and their families (three spouses or daughters). Despite his pro-modernist roots and inclinations, Arno Breker navigated a course that made him one of the most powerful cultural figures in Nazi Germany. He, like Albert Speer, looked to reconcile modernism and classicism and to use this "third way" as a means to find a place in the Reich.[58]

13

Albert Speer

(1905 Mannheim–1981 London)

Albert Speer (left) and Arno Breker admire a bust of Richard Wagner. (Bundesarchiv-Koblenz)

IN AN INTERVIEW with critic Robert Hughes in the 1970s, not long removed from a twenty-year stint in an Allied jail cell, and by that time a best-selling author, Albert Speer ruminated on present-day architects whom he admired. The first name he uttered was Philip Johnson—one of the titans of modernism.[1] Johnson himself had been sympathetic to Fascism in the 1930s. He had been dazzled by the Nuremberg Party Rally of 1938 and had been invited by the Reich Propaganda Ministry to witness the German invasion of Poland in 1939, where he commented that the Wehrmacht soldiers in their "green uniforms made the place look gay and happy."[2] Yet this was not the reason for Speer's admiration for his American peer. The Nazi architect asked Hughes "to send the compliments of the Masterbuilder to the Formgiver," and he inscribed a book on his architecture to Johnson; he added that he thought that Johnson's recent AT&T building "was more in the spirit of his own work than anything he had seen by an American architect since 1945."[3] On other occasions, Speer also praised Ludwig Mies van der Rohe, whose work he admired because Mies "used noble materials" and was a "classicist." Philip Johnson also saw similarities between the two architects, noting in 1947, "In fact, the somewhat abstracted classicism of Speer's early work, for example, the *Zeppelin-Feld* in Nuremberg, was not so far from that of Mies's project for the Neue Wache."[4] The fact remains that "Hitler's architect" was a modernist at heart. By suppressing certain, but not all, modernist inclinations he gained the opportunity to play a leading role—arguably *the* leading role—in what promised to be a historic building program.

Speer was a modernist, one might say, both by nature and by nurture. Regarding the former, he was a highly rational individual who attempted to organize his world in logical and efficient ways. It is telling that his first love was mathematics, and he would have taken that path if not for the influence of his overbearing father, who was himself a successful architect (as was Speer's paternal grandfather). The design of the younger Speer reflected a passion for order: symmetry, mathematically determined proportions, and an appreciation for the mechanistically linked specific as it related to the larger whole. It comes as no surprise that years later, when imprisoned in Spandau, Speer studied atlases and made the calculations to transform his perambulations in the prison courtyard into an imaginary walking trip around the world (he ended up short, somewhere just south of Guadalajara in Mexico). While most architects show an affinity for math (Michelangelo, Schinkel, etc.), and this in itself does not make one a modernist, a belief that applied math can solve the problems of social life in the industrial world provides a foundation or starting point for a modernist outlook. In many ways Speer thought like Walter Gropius. His rational worldview also extended to a belief in architecture as a means of social engineering.

In terms of "nurture," or the influence of his surroundings, the critical figure for Albert Speer was Heinrich Tessenow, a professor of architecture at the prestigious Technische Universität in Berlin. Tessenow was both an architect and an urban planner. He is best known for his pre–World War I contribution to the Hellerau "Garden City" (*Gartenstadt*) outside of Dresden, where he and his colleagues attempted to integrate modernist architecture into a green environment. It was the first time that the precepts underpinning the English garden city movement had been applied in Germany. In 1925, Tessenow joined the modernist art society Novembergruppe, and he later became a member of the Ring, where he and others (including Gropius and Mies van der Rohe) focused on reforming apartment-building design. A functionalist who influenced other important modernists—including architect Bruno Taut and urban planner Ernst May—Tessenow advocated simplicity and was perhaps best known for his saying, "The simplest form is not always best, but the best form is always simple."[5] Like Adolf Loos and most other modernist architects, he was particularly critical of historicist ornamentation and instead advocated a streamlined architectural and design aesthetic—even if he preferred stone façades to glass and metal. Tessenow himself oversaw the 1930–31 refurbishment of the Neue Wache guardhouse in Berlin on Unter den Linden. In reconfiguring Schinkel's structure into a memorial for those who fell in the Great War, Tessenow stripped the site to its bare essentials, which highlighted the sweeping lines of the original design.

Speer revered his professor, under whom he studied beginning in 1925. After he graduated as a *Diplom-Ingenieur* in February 1928, his mentor selected him to serve as his *Assistent* (a kind of assistant professorship). To serve as an Assistent was considered a high honor, and the two had a close relationship. Speer was only twenty-three at the time, and Tessenow's support meant more to him than the modest salary—although Speer later recalled that the job permitted him to marry. Speer had previously been rejected by another modernist architecture professor, Hans Poelzig, at the Technische Universität Berlin because of poor drawing technique. One should note, however, that other important architects have struggled with drawing (Walter Gropius among them). Speer's relationship with Tessenow proved significant in many ways. He later noted about Tessenow, "He must have felt an affinity for me; it can't have been for my talent: all I did was copy him."[6] In other words, Speer began his career imitating his modernist mentor. As this quote indicates, there was also a strong emotional component to the relationship. Even after Speer had moved on and become Nazi Germany's most famous architect, he remained loyal to Tessenow. Speer continued to consult him about design issues and used his considerable influence in an attempt to protect Tessenow's academic position—even though the mentor was often critical of Speer's work. Tessenow was never enthusiastic about National Socialism, and there was some talk that he had Jewish ancestry. Linked in many regards to the Weimar Republic, he temporarily lost his teaching post in 1934 and remained suspect throughout the Third Reich. Yet Tessenow continued to submit proposals for official projects and, according to architect Léon Krier, "sympathized with some of the Führer's ideas."[7] In 1936, for example, Tessenow completed a design for the Strength Through Joy facility on the island of Rügen (his submission featured swastikas), and for an exhibition hall planned in conjunction with the Berlin Olympics (his design featured the Reich Eagle over the Olympic Rings). He also worked on a monument to President Hindenburg in Magdeburg until 1939. A complex and independent figure, Tessenow also undertook a design for Ernst Barlach's grave in Ratzeburg in the far north of Germany, although his actual memorial to the sculptor remained uncompleted.[8]

Speer's training also included encounters with the more traditional architects German Bestelmeyer and Hermann Billing. Bestelmeyer was a traditionalist, perhaps best known in the United States for Adolphus Busch Hall of the Busch-Reisinger Museum at Harvard University; the structure is a charming if totally artificial assemblage of European design motifs that included plaster casts of German architectural wonders, such as a Romanesque arch copied from the cathedral in Freiberg, Saxony. Adolphus Busch Hall was completed in the early 1920s, and Bestelmeyer remained a staunch critic of modernism. His work—like the pastiche of Gothic, Renaissance, and Romantic styles in the Harvard museum—reflected a commitment to historicism. Billing, another important teacher, was best known as an exponent of *Jugendstil* design, although many of his buildings featured a simplified neoclassicism, such as the Kunsthalle that Billing completed in Baden-Baden in 1909. Billing increasingly turned toward an austere neoclassicism in the 1920s. Speer was therefore exposed to a range of aesthetic philosophies, including more traditional views. He would incorporate such ideas into his work, although not always in a straightforward manner. After the war, Speer suggested that he had espoused certain pre-modern ideas during the Third Reich: his "ruin value" theory, for example, in which he eschewed rebar and other iron supports because they would later become unsightly as his buildings decayed. More recent research has shown, however, that his notion of "ruin value" was entirely a postwar construct, a fiction first articulated in his 1969 memoirs.[9] Speer therefore took a hybrid approach to design, yet the modernist element was paramount.

Speer had joined the Nazi Party in March 1931 with the belief that he could continue to exhibit pro-modernist sympathies. He joined, he later said, for a variety of reasons: the Nazis were anti-communist, membership offered a means to subvert the hated Treaty of Versailles, and, most important, he was fascinated with Hitler. One can surmise that he also hoped Party membership would lead to architectural and design commissions (which it eventually did). Speer entered the storm troopers at the same time, an act frequently overlooked by postwar observers. This presumably reflected his enthusiasm for the Nazi cause, but it also likely represented a certain opportunism. The paramilitary organization offered more contacts and possibilities for commissions. These steps, however, did not yield immediate benefits. In biographer Joachim Fest's words, "There followed nearly eighteen months of idleness, emptiness, and a sense of wasted time. Now and then Speer took part in competitions, but he never did better than a third prize. . . . In early 1932, as the Depression approached its nadir, academic salaries were cut to the point where they were no longer viable, Speer gave up his post with Tessenow."[10] The budget cuts of Chancellor Heinrich Brüning's government hit him directly (even though his parents had set up a trust fund in Vaduz, Liechtenstein, in 1930 to help support him).[11] This financial distress and his failed attempts to secure commissions shaped Speer and helped make him the pliant architect whom Hitler would manipulate.

After leaving the Technische Universität and Berlin, Speer returned to Mannheim and managed his parents' properties. He was far from alone among the cultural figures during the Weimar Republic who felt a profound sense of economic vulnerability. This undoubtedly made many of them more open to Hitler. Speer recalled in his memoirs, "Even well-established architects in Mannheim were not getting any commissions in those times."[12] He eventually moved back to Berlin but was still underemployed. With his abundance of free time, Speer volunteered to assist the local Nazis. He owned a car—itself an indication of his pro-technology outlook at this time, if also an outgrowth of his concerns about status—and he put it at the disposal of the Party, becoming the sole member of the National Socialist Automobile Corps (NSKK) in Wannsee, the Berlin suburb where he and his wife, Margarete, lived. The car turned out to be his way of meeting and impressing a key future patron, Karl Hanke, the local district leader, who went on to work in Goebbels's ministry and then as a Gauleiter in Silesia.

Hanke liked Speer, but he also sought to exploit him. He first granted the young architect a commission to refurbish his "official residence," a villa in Grünewald near Lake Wannsee, but he did so on a nonpaying basis. Speer, who enjoyed a curious relationship with Hanke, later recalled, "The young district leader chose Bauhaus wallpapers at my suggestion, although I had hinted that these were 'Communistic' wallpapers. He waved that warning aside, with a grand gesture: 'We will take the best of everything, even from the Communists'" (Plate 1). [13] Both Hanke and Speer were brash and arrogant, and these traits found expression in their views about modernist design. They would take what they liked and disregard any attacks from more conservative Party rivals. Such was the spirit exhibited by many who congregated in and around Goebbels's Ministry, including Schreiber and Weidemann.

Karl Hanke had recommended Speer to Goebbels, who became the next important patron in the progression toward Hitler. Their first collaboration involved the renovation of a section of the Nazi Party's Berlin Headquarters on the Voss Strasse in 1932. Speer gave up a vacation with his wife in East Prussia and completed the assignment in a timely manner. Subsequently, in the spring of 1933, Hanke arranged for Speer to oversee the renovations of Goebbels's new quarters in the Wilhelmstrasse. The recently minted Propaganda Minister had taken over the ministerial residence in the government quarter from the previous Reich Minister of Nutrition, Alfred Hugenberg. Speer placed several paintings by Emil Nolde on the wall. Speer recalled how he "borrowed a few watercolors by Nolde from Eberhard Hanfstaengl, the director of the Berlin Nationalgalerie. Goebbels and his wife were delighted with the paintings." Speer also recounted how he worked with Hans Weidemann, "an old party member from Essen who wore the gold party badge," and who represented Reich Minister Goebbels. Weidemann had "assembled an exhibition of pictures more or less of the Nolde-Munch school and recommended them to the minister as samples of revolutionary nationalist art."[14] By this time, however, Goebbels had grown more cautious about modernist art and ordered the paintings removed.

Speer first rose to fame not as an architect or interior designer, but as the creator of elaborate political festivals. The story goes that he saw plans for a May Day rally in 1933 in the hands of his friend Karl Hanke—now Goebbels's personal aide—and that Speer suggested he could do better. An extravaganza of flags at the Tempelhof airfield ensued, followed by an even greater opportunity as the principal designer of the September 1933 Nazi Party Rally at Nuremberg. These events depended on modernist principles in many respects. They involved geometric formations, with symmetry, repetition, and mechanization. Biographer Dan van der Vat observed, "The key element was hugeness, the impression of infinite space, which dwarfed the [onlooker]"; he added, "Here all the world was indeed a stage, and all the men and women merely players, their many imperfections concealed by the darkness of the rally field, made all the darker by the surrounding columns of light. It was a stunning effect."[15] His dramatic, liturgical pageants affected viewers on a visceral level, tapping into the irrational impulses so admired by both modernists and Nazi leaders. Another modern, if not modernist, aspect of Speer's work came about through the bureaucratization of his work. That is, Hitler had him appointed to a Nazi Party post, giving him the title "Commissioner for the Artistic and Technical Presentation of the Party Rallies and Demonstrations."

The death of architect Paul Ludwig Troost on 21 January 1934 repositioned Albert Speer onto center stage. Previously, Speer had served as a liaison between Troost and Hitler as the dictator embarked on his ambitious building program, which included Troost's House of German Art in Munich. Speer now took a position on Rudolf Hess's staff as head of the Office for Construction. His first assignment in this post, issued to him personally by Hitler in early 1934, was the stadium and parade grounds in Nuremberg on the Zeppelin-Feld (so-named after Count Ferdinand Zeppelin landed one of his dirigibles there in 1909). This was a radical expansion of a project Troost had begun—now five times as large, totaling twenty-eight square kilometers. The monumental complex would hold 340,000 people. Speer claimed the tribune was influenced by the Pergamon Altar— the Hellenic temple sitting in Berlin as a symbol of colonial power. Yet the complex was also streamlined and modernist—especially when put to its intended use. With columns of marching uniforms and rows of flags characterized by bold primary colors, it took on a more recognizably modernist form. The 130 anti-aircraft searchlights that created the "cathedral of light" (*Lichtdom*) were iconic from their inception in 1936 (Plate 12). Speer later described them as his "most beautiful architectural concept, but after its fashion, the only one that has survived the passage of time."[16] Speer has been called a "master of light," and his Nuremberg designs were modernist not only in a technological sense, but also in a Russian Constructivist kind of way, or in a manner reminiscent of Hungarian-French artist Victor Vasarely, with his intricate and repetitive patterns. Lest one view Speer's Nuremberg structures in purely aesthetic terms, it is important to keep in mind that most of the stone for later projects, like the German Stadium, was quarried by prisoners in concentration camps.[17]

Speer's portfolio of duties in the early years of the Third Reich included consulting on special projects identified by Hitler, and this came to involve "fixing" the problem of Werner March's Olympic Stadium, which Hitler deemed too modern. As Joachim Fest described,

> The architect, Werner March, had envisaged a steel and concrete structure with extensive use of glass and enamel, but when he inspected the shell Hitler was beside himself with fury and threatened to cancel the Games. He would not dream of entering a "glass box" of this kind, and would not therefore open the Games. Speer thereupon hurriedly removed all the glass, faced the concrete with natural stone and added cornices everywhere until eventually both March and Hitler approved the changes.[18]

Speer therefore intervened and, by adding a stone exterior, found a compromise that proved acceptable to all. Werner March continued to design in Berlin, including a modernist-influenced Yugoslav Embassy built between 1938 and 1940. The larger point is that Speer could give the impression that he rejected modernist design, when he was actually adroit at incorporating modernist elements or making alterations that permitted accommodation.

Beyond his efforts as an architect and designer, Speer held a succession of government posts throughout the Third Reich in which he often advanced modernist principles. Beginning in 1934, for example, Speer served as head of the Office for the Beauty of Labor (Schönheit der Arbeit) within the Strength Through Joy organization. In this capacity, he utilized modern design to combat unsightly or dangerous environments in largely industrial workplaces. Speer later recalled about the agency, "We undertook the standardization of simple, well-formed tableware and practically designed furniture, which were mass-produced in large quantities."[19] This effort to simplify and to standardize, as well as his more general belief that design could effect social change, reflected the modernist impulses in his thinking. He even turned to employees of the Deutscher Werkbund as colleagues—that is, a modernist organization that the Nazi regime disbanded in 1938. Design historian Sabine Weissler noted, "The Office for the Beauty of Labor took notice of the Werkbund's call for quality work and for 'form without ornament' and modeled itself on the German Werkbund."[20] Speer would later be in charge of street design and management (*Strassenwesen*) and would conceive modernist-inspired street lamps for the Reich capital. A double row of lampposts on the Strasse des 17. Juni (then the East-West Axis) in the Tiergarten remain in place today, part of a limited array of Speer's works that have survived.

Speer's most important appointment as an architect, of course, was as Inspector General of Building for the Reich Capital, Berlin. This appointment did not come until January 1937, and the preceding two years were marked by intense competition between the Reich's leading architects as they jockeyed for position. Speer had lobbied Hitler to become a kind of "architectural czar of Germany," but Hitler was not yet prepared to invest the young man with such authority. Elaine Hochman also observed,

> Had Troost been alive, he would have been his first choice, Hitler told
> [Berlin Lord Mayor Julius] Lippert. Schultze-Naumburg was out of
> the question; and he needed someone more malleable than either German Bestelmeyer or Paul Schmitthenner, two architects whose severe
> and sternly monumental public style was in keeping with the national
> socialist image. Speer was young and unproven; and Hitler was unsure
> if he had the experience and ability to handle so vast a project. Before
> considering Speer, he wanted to see how he handled the design of the
> party's buildings in Nuremberg, a commission that Hitler had assigned to him in 1934. By June 1936, his mind was still not made up;
> at this time he showed Speer his plans for the city with no mention of
> giving him the commission.[21]

Among others in consideration for the position as the Reich's leading architect were Hermann Giesler, whose brother Paul was a high ranking Party leader (and later the Gauleiter in Munich); Ernst Sagebiel, who had made a bold statement with the Berlin Reich Air Ministry in 1935; Wilhelm Kreis, an architect known for designing grand monuments; Roderich Fick, who would undertake major buildings in Linz and Obersalzberg; and Leonhard

Gall, who had worked for Paul Ludwig Troost and who helped see the Haus der Deutschen Kunst through to completion.

The matter was therefore to be decided by a test, and this test would come at the Paris World Exposition in 1937. With the position of "Führer's architect" hanging in the balance, Speer would have to impress both Hitler and the world. The Germans had been given a prime location at the Paris fair, just below the Palais de Chaillot and across from the Soviet Union's pavilion. Speer recalled later,

> The French directors of the fair had deliberately arranged this con-
> frontation. While looking over the site in Paris, I by chance stumbled
> into a room containing the secret sketch of the Soviet pavilion. A
> sculptured pair of figures thirty-three feet tall, on a high platform,
> were striding triumphantly toward the German pavilion. I therefore
> designed a cubic mass, also elevated on stout pillars, which seemed
> to be checking this onslaught, while from the cornice of my tower
> an eagle with the swastika in its claws looked down on the Russian
> sculptures.[22]

This was the time of the anti-Comintern Pact, as Germany grew closer to Italy and Japan in opposition to Stalin's state. Speer understood that his design had political ramifications, and he treated the matter as a competi-tion (which, in fact, it was—the architects and designers received medals to reward their successes). The most notorious manifestation of this competi-tive drive came in the form of a mission to spy on the model of the Soviet pavilion after it had been submitted to the French authorities. Speer later maintained that he "by chance stumbled into a room containing the secret sketch of the Soviet pavilion" while inspecting the site in Paris, but this ac-count, like the fiction of his theory of ruin value, should be treated with skepticism. Art historian Karen Fiss noted, "Speer's account fails to explain how he actually came to possess French copies of the Soviet sketches, but it seems plausible that he obtained the secret plans from a French official in-volved in the planning of the fairground."[23] Fiss suspects that Jacques Greber, the chief architect for the Exposition, a "great admirer of Nazi architecture," and an acquaintance of Speer, was the culprit. Indeed, she found in Speer's papers housed in Munich "a copy of the plan for the side elevation and princi-pal façade of the Soviet building, marked with annotations in French."[24] The ruthlessly ambitious architect and self-mythologizing memoirist undoubt-edly posed challenges for both contemporary rivals and later historians.

Speer and his team succeeded in trumping the Soviets—and did so with

Albert Speer, German Pavilion at Paris World Exposition (1937). Josef Thorak's muscular statues at the base serve to emphasize the clean, soaring lines of Speer's structures. (National Archives and Records Administration, College Park)

some fine drama as the Nazi Eagle squared off with Vera Mukhina's Social-ist Realist sculpture *Worker and Kolkhoz Woman*, the seventy-nine-foot-tall centerpiece of the Soviet pavilion. The Germans, to be sure, integrated their own human forms into the design by way of Josef Thorak's three muscle-bound figures in bronze standing to the front-left of the building. Speer had overall control of the pavilion, and therefore Thorak's works were his own choice (made in consultation with Hitler and others). But they proved a viable solution for the young architect: they kept his own structure free of ornamentation (save the over-the-top Reich Eagle, which sat atop a swastika, as per the design of Kurt Schmid-Ehmen). With a flat roof and a simplified cornice, not to mention a steel infrastructure, the pavilion incorporated modernist elements. Speer's streamlined neoclassicism strived to be imposing and, at the same time, graceful. The building certainly soared, and its exaggeratedly narrow width, when combined with fluted columns, achieved a powerful effect.

The architect consciously aspired to work in the tradition of predecessors such as Étienne Boullée, a visionary neoclassical architect known for his grandiose and geometrical structures. Boullée exhibited a fascination with lighting, symbolism, and funerary monuments. One critic noted, "Boullée's designs have been interpreted both as prototypes of modernist architecture (pure geometrical forms) and of Nazi architecture (monumental scale and abstracted classical ornamentation)."[25] The German pavilion in Paris, which some viewed as suggesting "an immense, windowless sarcophagus," and which played into the Nazis' "architectural death cult," invoked certain funerary motifs.[26] Speer, of course, also studied the work of Karl Friedrich Schinkel, whose magisterial columns and neoclassicism did so much to define "the Prussian style." Speer was known to say, "My dreams were concerned purely with building. I did not want power, but to become a second Schinkel."[27] The German pavilion, which was in part inspired by the Prussian master, would be Speer's means of achieving this goal, with the Frenchman Boullée, who was just then being rediscovered by architects and scholars, also serving as a source of inspiration.

Speer won a gold medal at the 1937 Paris World Exposition for his design of the German pavilion (the Soviet architect also won gold). But the building, pardon the pun, cemented his reputation. It did not hurt that Speer was also recognized with a *Grand Prix* for his model of the Nuremberg complex, an award that surprised both him and Hitler. The plan was to combine the two, relocating the German pavilion after the Paris exposition to Nuremberg, but the war intervened and this never took place. In 1937, Speer was also invited by the French ambassador to Berlin, André François-Poncet, to display his work in Paris—this, in exchange for an exhibition of "modern French painting" in Berlin.[28] While Hitler effectively vetoed this proposal, much to Speer's disappointment, the fact remains that Speer won widespread international recognition for his designs, especially before the onset of war. It is also striking that so many observers viewed his work as a way to advance the modernist cause, both internationally and within

Germany. Speer himself basked in attention that came from abroad and, indeed, cultivated it. He facilitated exhibitions of his work in neutral countries during the war, and he would often attend the openings, permitting at least brief exchanges with his foreign contemporaries.

The young architect always saw himself as part of an international movement that expressed the spirit of the times—that is, that had an essentially modernist component. He wrote after seeing the Palais de Chaillot and other new buildings in France, "It surprised me that France also favored neo-classicism for her public buildings. It has often been asserted that this style is characteristic of the architecture of totalitarian states. That is not at all true. Rather it was characteristic of the era and left its impression upon Washington, London, and Paris, as well as Rome, Moscow, and our plans for Berlin."[29] Although this comment came as part of Speer's postwar efforts to shape his image in history, he and his work were part of an international movement. It was a movement informed by Art Deco, with "its sharp lines and blunt massing of material," to use Susan Sontag's description of the international movement that reached its apogee in the 1930s.[30] It is probably not coincidental that one of the most important museums in the world exhibiting Fascist design, the Wolfsonian-FIU, is in Miami, a center for Art Deco architecture. While Speer's efforts to relativize his architectural and design program are easy to understand, it is also apparent that he thought in such international terms during the Third Reich itself.

Despite feeling part of an international movement, Speer emerged as a unique figure as a result of his appointment as Inspector General of Building for Berlin (GBI) in January 1937, and of the expansion of his authority that came in decrees issued on 5 November 1937 and 20 January 1938. These decrees, which reflected his success at the Paris World Exposition, extended his influence to cover other cities beyond Berlin and made him the most powerful architect in Germany. While "only" a state secretary in terms of government rank, Speer had extraordinary power, especially in Berlin. He was also made a professor, although he rarely used the title and thought less of it because people like photographer Heinrich Hoffmann also received the honor. Speer felt greater pride after being appointed to the Prussian Academy of the Arts, even though he took the place of a recently expelled non-Nazi member (the Jewish ones being long gone).[31] Among Speer's other titles before becoming a Reich Minister in 1942, he was a delegate in the Reichstag, a member of the Presidential Commission of the Reich Chamber for the Visual Arts, and a Reich Cultural Senator. Even if he later portrayed himself and his architectural work in a decidedly self-effacing manner, Speer was an astonishingly powerful arbiter of culture in Nazi Germany.

Most important, of course, Speer had Hitler, and this enabled him to "aspire to control design in the Reich as a whole."[32] The working relationship that emerged between the two men remains somewhat unclear, although both clearly fed off one another. Elaine Hochman has provided a vivid description of Hitler visiting the models of "Germania" (as the capital would be renamed) in Speer's GBI office in the Arnim Palace on the Pariser Platz (the Prussian Academy having been evicted). After dinner, Hitler would invite a few favored guests to accompany him:

> With flashlights beaming and keys jangling, Hitler—like some proud and mischievous Pied Piper—would lead his guests through the special doors and corridors he had ordered installed to link his office with those of Speer in the Arnim Palace. There, Hitler's guests were astonished to see their usually stiff and formal Führer drop to his knees, his eyes sparkling, his manner vivacious, before the vast model of the grand boulevard, which stretched one hundred feet down the darkened hall, where spotlights illuminated models of the "new Berlin."[33]

Speer and Hitler could appear like children as they played with the elaborate models that helped actualize their ideas. Speer recalled later that "the only times with Hitler where I experienced real liveliness, joy, and spontaneity was when we together were engrossed in architectural plans or inspecting his beloved massive-form models of the future Berlin."[34]

Speer had tremendous opportunities to realize his creative vision within the GBI agency itself, what with his political power and vast financial resources. By the early years of the war, the GBI counted about a thousand employees (including the freelance personnel and others who helped implement the GBI projects). Speer realized that he could not design all the buildings and limited himself to a few high-profile projects. But he was able to direct work to other architects in the Reich, some of whom were senior to him in age and experience: Paul Bonatz, Wilhelm Kreis, and German Bestelmeyer. Speer directed one important assignment to Peter Behrens, the aforementioned teacher of Gropius and Mies, who received the commission for a new administrative building for AEG on, in Speer's words, "the grand boulevard in Berlin" (presumably the three-mile-long *Prachtallee*). Others of the modernist persuasion who worked for the GBI included Caesar Pinnau, Friedrich Tamms, and Werner March.[35] Several of Gropius's former associates, including Hanns Dustmann, Ernst Neufert, and Herbert Rimpl, also worked on GBI projects. Biographer Joachim Fest has noted,

> Speer confidently ignored "schools" and "camps," using his position with Hitler to silence any opposition from adherents of the national spirit or from Alfred Rosenberg, who was responsible for ideological surveillance. More and more commissions and jobs went to "New Style" architects and close collaborators of the Bauhaus, although the movement still elicited disapproval. Those who took on assignments, like Hanns Dustmann and Ernst Neufert, realized the unique opportunities the regime's building passion offered them. . . . Only Tessenow was courageous enough to continue to stand aloof and refuse to cooperate, despite repeated invitations to do so.[36]

Tessenow was forced to relinquish his teaching post at the Academy of Fine Arts in 1934, but Speer, who "stood steadfastly by him," intervened on his behalf, and his mentor was reinstated.[37] The two men continued to meet until the end of the Third Reich.

Speer was responsible not only for overseeing the design of the buildings for Berlin (and elsewhere), but also for decorating them. He and his colleagues bought paintings by the hundreds, sometimes taking them from the storerooms of the Haus der Deutschen Kunst, but also purchasing them from dealers on a lavish scale. Extant records show Speer buying art in Munich, Berlin, Vienna, Salzburg, and Paris, although this list is certainly not exhaustive. Some of the GBI purchases reflected a pro-modernist sensibility, such as the watercolor of flowers by Viennese Secessionist Josef Dobrowsky that Speer picked up at the Galerie Welz in Salzburg in 1944.[38] Both the artist and the gallery were known for modernist associations. Speer also purchased from the Neue Galerie in Vienna, which was founded by Otto Kallir-Nirenstein and then transferred in 1938 to his non-Jewish secretary, Victoria ("Vita") Künstler, just before the *Anschluss.* Known as one of the premier galleries of Austrian modernism, the Neue Galerie now sold a mixture of traditional and modernist works, including those by Egon Schiele. The ten paintings Speer purchased in 1944 seemed to be more in the traditional vein, but other works in the GBI's collection appear more pro-modernist: six watercolors and two oil paintings by Otto Dix stand out in this regard (the oil paintings were titled *Winter* and *Landscape*).[39] There was also a "Klee" drawing, described as a landscape, but it is not clear whether it is by Paul Klee or another artist. Works by Auguste Rodin and

Gustav Klimt also stand out in the Speer agency's collection. The lists of paintings acquired by the GBI also show the presence of more progressive "Nazi" artists, such as Austrian Albert Janesch (best known for his rowers), although there were no works by Schreiber, Nolde, or certain other "controversial" artists.

Privately, the architect-minister was an avid collector who filled his various homes with magnificent objects. He earned a considerable fortune for his work during the Third Reich, contrary to his claim in *Inside the Third Reich,* where he wrote, "My income remained low. For in an idealistic spirit which seemed to accord with the temper of the time, I had renounced any architect's fees for all my official buildings."[40] Speer, like Arno Breker and a few other cultural figures in Nazi Germany, commanded huge fees for his efforts. Because many of his projects remained uncompleted, he did not receive the tens of millions of Reichsmarks he was due; yet historians Heinrich Breloer and Rainer Zimmer calculated that he received RM 4.8 million ($1.92 million) by war's end.[41] This included a RM 250,000 ($100,000) "gift" from Göring that came in the form of a 247-acre land grant near the Oder River where Speer planned to build his estate. Like Gründgens, Breker, and a number of other cultural luminaries, Speer also derived financial advantages from "Aryanized" residences. He acquired real estate in Berlin-Schwanenwerder at an advantageous price from Marie-Anne Goldschmidt-Rothschild. Speer had begun negotiations with her in October 1938 as she tried to raise funds to finance her emigration, including payment of the Reich Flight Tax. He did not actually live on this property but envisioned it as a future site of one of his estates. Instead, he rented a nearby "Aryanized" villa from film star Gustav Fröhlich, who had purchased the residence from a persecuted Jew. Speer had rented out his own house in the Schlachtensee neighborhood of Berlin—a more modest dwelling which he had designed in 1935—and moved to the more fashionable Nazi enclave on the Schwanenwerder, where he counted Joseph Goebbels among his neighbors. In 1943, he received a lavish "official residence" adjacent the Tiergarten that cost RM 1.8 million ($720,000), but that was bombed out shortly thereafter, severely limiting his enjoyment of the dwelling.[42] Speer also had use of a house on the Obersalzberg, a comfortable abode near Hitler's Berghof and the last of the Nazi leaders' residences on the mountainside that remains standing today.

Albert Speer's art collection befitted a man who enjoyed a luxurious lifestyle. He collected mostly German Romantics, with Jacob Phillip Hackert, Karl Friedrich Schinkel, and Arnold Böcklin among his favorites. He claimed at war's end that most of the works of his sizable collection were destroyed. One GBI report pointed to losses at the Berlin Zoo Flakturm—a massive concrete tower for anti-aircraft guns that also served as a storage facility—that was burned and its contents subsequently plundered by the Soviet Red Army.[43] In fact, Speer had entrusted most of his collection to a friend, Robert Frank, who took the artworks to Mexico and refused to part with them for the rest of his life. Speer subsequently came to terms with Frank's heirs and was then found selling them through Lempertz auction house in Cologne in the late 1970s.[44] Speer also claimed in his memoirs that he kept an etching called *La Carmagnole,* by Käthe Kollwitz, in his collection. It is a strange picture for him to have had in that it featured, in Speer's words, "a yowling mob dancing with hate-contorted faces around a guillotine," with a weeping woman on the ground off to the side.[45] Speer proved inconsistent when it came to modern art. He liked some of it and could support a more progressive agenda, but he avoided expending political capital on the modernists. Indeed, he gave indications on several occasions that he was anti-modernist: convincing Goebbels that he stood behind the "degenerate art" measures in 1937 (which induced the minister to rejoice in his diaries), and writing to Himmler in 1944 in defense of a painter, Julius Bretz, who had a Jewish wife, noting that he "actively and always worked against the appearance of decadence in art, also before the seizure of power."[46] These formulations can be seen more as acts of expediency on Speer's part. Deep down, his sympathies lay with the pro-modernist camp. As he himself noted, "Goebbels had simply groveled before Hitler [in abandoning modern art]. We were all in the same boat. I too, though altogether at home in modern art, tacitly accepted Hitler's pronouncement."[47]

Albert Speer, then, grew out of the modernist tradition and felt comfortable among modernist cultural figures. His understanding of himself is conveyed in an episode of his memoir, *Inside the Third Reich,* where he recalled, "At the beginning of the war, I had formed a theory which I explained at a dinner in Maxim's in Paris to a group of German and French artists. Cocteau and Despiau were among the latter. The French Revolution, I said, had developed a new sense of style which was destined to replace the late rococo."[48] What is so striking here is not what Speer said, but the company and the setting. Speer stood out as a kind of artist-prince, even after he became Reich Armaments Minister and took over the other responsibilities from the deceased engineer-builder Fritz Todt in 1942. Speer saw himself as a friend to all creative types and was a conciliator by nature. He went so far as to boast, both during and after the war, that even Stalin had wanted to consult with him in the late 1930s: "Hitler, half amused and half irritated, vetoed it. Stalin would put Speer in a rat-hole, Hitler suggested, and not let him out again until the new Moscow had arisen."[49] That Speer could imagine building for the Soviet dictator speaks to his self-confidence and his adaptability, among other qualities.

The reality, of course, was that Speer could also be ruthless and even brutal when so inclined. He was complicit in a number of Nazi art plundering operations. For example, Speer liaised with the SD (Security Service) in Vienna on the removal of decorative items from the Rothschild Palace in 1938. He and his colleagues participated in the meetings led by Goebbels starting in August 1939 about the return (*Rückführung*) of Germanic cultural property from neighboring countries.[50] Speer did Hitler's bidding with regard to the removal of cultural property from Poland in 1939 and 1940. The treasures of the cathedral of Pelpin would be a prime example, whereby Speer interacted with Gauleiters Arthur Greiser and Albert Forster to negotiate who would keep the objects. The chief administrator of the Reich Chancellery, Hans Lammers, initially argued that the quality paintings would go to German museums, but the Gauleiters prevailed. Speer communicated Hitler's orders that the cathedral treasures should remain intact in Pelpin as a monument of the "time of the knights" (*Ordensritterzeit*), albeit in German hands.[51] Speer also handled a number of matters relating to Sonderauftrag Linz, coordinating with Führermuseum director Hans Posse, Martin Bormann, and Prince Philipp von Hessen, among others.[52] And he himself had no compunction about purchasing Jewish property for his own collection. He bought at least two works from the Hans W. Lange auction house in Berlin in December 1940 that came from the Goudstikker collection in the Netherlands, relinquished by the widow of the recently deceased Jewish dealer who had been forced by Göring and his agents to sell the great collection. The displacement of tens of thousands of Berlin's Jews, who were deported to the East (most to their deaths), the exploitation of slave labor at armaments facilities (despite Speer's orders to improve conditions at Mittelbau Dora), and the GBI construction operations carried out at Auschwitz, which entailed the expenditure of millions of Reichsmarks, all implicate Speer in more serious crimes.[53]

Speer appeared unconcerned about most moral issues, but he could be a particularly ruthless adversary when he felt blocked or threatened by others. This proved to be the case with the Lord Mayor of Berlin, Julius Lippert, who lost both his struggle with Speer and his post in 1940, whereupon he went off to serve in the Wehrmacht. Speer's relationship with his chief architectural rival, Hermann Giesler, also proved illuminating. Giesler received major commissions that included the rebuilding of Munich (and Hitler's residence) in 1938, and significant parts of the cultural Mecca planned for Linz, as well as the *Ordensburg* Sonthofen, a Nazi academy constructed largely out of stone in the hills of the Allgäu in southwest Germany, a project that was actually completed in 1938. The Speer-Giesler rivalry overshadowed any other among the elite architects during the Third Reich. Few appreciated the intensity of the feelings, or the importance of Giesler, until the 1980s. Speer had something to do with this. As Frederic Spotts has noted, "in his memoirs Speer seldom mentioned his rival's name and, when he did, he always misspelled it" (as "Giessler").[54] Giesler in turn said that Speer was "obsessed with power," that he "lacked historical consciousness," and that he had "been brainwashed by twenty years of prison," among other charges.[55]

One question that arises is whether the Speer-Giesler rivalry had its basis in aesthetic issues. Giesler's designs were undoubtedly more backward looking and historicist, as he built structures with clear Gothic and Romantic undertones. Giesler had trained at the Technische Hochschule in Munich under Richard Riemerschmid, who stood out as a famous proponent of the Jugendstil/Arts and Crafts movement. While this represented a different branch of modernism as compared to Tessenow's efforts to reconcile Classicism and Modernism, Giesler was at least exposed to alternatives to the stodgy historicism of the fin-de-siècle period. Giesler's work therefore sometimes included modernist touches, including clean lines, little ornamentation, and a penchant for symmetry. Such qualities were apparent in the Gauforum (or complex for Nazi Party events) that Giesler designed in Weimar, which featured horizontal lines and rectilinear windows. A modernist element was also evident in his paintings, which showed the influence of New Objectivity.[56] Speer's buildings may have been larger than his chief rival's—Giesler leveled the common charge that Speer suffered from "gigantomania"—but for both, the scale depended on the project. The cultural center at Linz overseen by Giesler would have been massive. In assessing the careers of both architects, however, it appears that overriding factors in the rivalry were ambition and self-advancement. Both men sought Hitler's approbation and wanted to build with the almost unlimited resources provided by the dictator.

As indicated above, there were also political differences between the two architects. Even though Speer had joined the Party in 1931 and was anything but apolitical—in contrast to the image he tried to cultivate after the war—Giesler was the more convinced National Socialist. Speer's rival was an ultra-Nazi who conspired with Bormann and other Party radicals. Gitta Sereny has noted, "Giesler and Bormann had already developed a very special relationship based on their unquestioning devotion to the party and to Hitler, and perhaps, too, on their mutual distrust and envy of Speer."[57] In the postwar period, Giesler was part of the network of old Nazis and published his memoirs with a radical right-wing house. His closest friends included Arno Breker, Hitler's adjutant Otto Günsche, Hitler's former secretary Gerda Christian, and Franz Alfred Six (the former dean of the economics faculty at the University of Berlin who became a Security Services agent and an officer in Einsatzgruppe B, which murdered tens of thousands in the Soviet Union). Giesler also cooperated extensively with Holocaust denier David Irving and took efforts to relativize the crimes of the Third Reich. For example, Giesler raised the question in one 1980 essay of the Soviets' murder of Polish army officers at Katyn and Stalin's postwar treatment of the soldiers who had fought with General Wlassov's pro-Axis forces. Speer, it should be noted, also supported Irving's work. Despite different views about architecture and politics, the larger point remains that the Speer-Giesler rivalry was ultimately about self-advancement.

Speer has also been charged with distorting the architectural record "to exaggerate his role and to diminish Hitler's."[58] Indeed, this is a central argument of Frederic Spotts, who maintained that Hitler was far more active in their collaborative designing of buildings; the architect merely helped the dictator carry out his ideas. Speer had a formidable public relations machine in operation during the Third Reich and then did a masterful job manipulating his image once released from Spandau in 1966. Throughout he presented himself as a shy artist who spoke in public with great reluctance. While this may have been true, he was clearly a gifted self-promoter. Speer had staff at the Inspector General of Building keep careful tabs on the press and publicity, and he did what he could to raise his own profile. Consequently, one must always be suspicious of the motives behind his statements. When he wrote Hitler on 29 March 1945, "I am an artist [*ich bin Künstler*] and as such, completely alien and difficult tasks have been given to me," it suggested that he knew of the crimes committed by a regime in which he was a leading figure and that he sought to distance himself from what had transpired. But with typical vanity he could not help but add, "I have accomplished much for Germany. Without my work the war would perhaps have been lost in 1942/43."[59]

With all these caveats—that Speer was not the sole architect in the

Reich, that his collaboration with Hitler leaves a degree of uncertainty about the contribution of each, and that Speer crafted his own myth—the fact remains that he designed a number of important buildings in the late 1930s and early 1940s, and even built a few of them. Joachim Fest is not alone among scholars who consider the New Reich Chancellery to be Speer's most important building: "The proportions were more modest and the blustering manner of the regime was less in evidence than in any other work of his design."[60] Amid much fanfare, Speer completed the New Reich Chancellery ahead of schedule. He had been approached by Hitler in January 1938 and given a deadline of 10 January 1939—the date of the annual New Year's reception for diplomats. Speer devised an ambitious production plan and made full use of the many resources and privileges afforded him, including paying for multiple shifts. Regardless, Speer completed the project on time, which only added to the impression that the massive, lavishly appointed chancellery was a technical marvel. Hitler called him "a brilliant shaper and master builder." Tessenow was more critical of "the nine-month wonder," commenting acerbically, "I would rather you had devoted nine years to the project."[61]

Speer's designs in 1938 and 1939 were notable for not only the scale but also the modernist elements. For example, Speer's Marble Hall in the New Reich Chancellery, which featured a striking red marble containing interwoven threads of white and black, stretched 160 yards, almost twice the length of the Hall of Mirrors at Versailles. The Mosaic Chamber, with the painstaking work of Hermann Kaspar, was also stunningly grand (and instantaneously iconic). The entire edifice was meant to intimidate, to communicate the power of the person inhabiting the space. This message notwithstanding, there were clear modernist elements at play in the New Reich Chancellery. The building featured symmetry, clean lines, and thematic repetition. The stone appeared almost industrial. At times, as with the Mosaic Chamber, it has a minimalist quality. Even in ruins, the New Reich Chancellery had modernist qualities: its geometric qualities became more pronounced, and the bomb-blackened stone cladding lent it an urban, postindustrial quality. For many observers the ruins possessed a strange beauty. Another design of that period, the South Railway Station of 1939 (never built), had an even more industrial quality to it. Built largely of steel and glass, it featured repetitious geometric patterns—which soared to a 180-foot-high ceiling that achieved the desired sense of monumentality —that corresponded to its function. And with cinemas, a shopping gallery, and hotels, it was not a structure that looked back in time. When function dictated it, such as with the electrical substation and water tower for the Nuremberg Rally grounds, Speer turned to more austere modernist designs. The substation, although clad in limestone (that is, a material with historicist associations), featured rectilinear lines, a cube-like functional shape, and a lack of ornamentation (save for a Reich Eagle). And certain observers have characterized Speer's ideas about urban planning as "modernist"—especially in terms of mass transportation and urban functionality.[62]

So what does one make of Albert Speer? Of course, if Speer, like Hitler, had stopped in the late 1930s, the record would look very different. That he oversaw armaments production at a key time in the war, that his system depended on slave labor, and that he held high office in a regime that undertook a genocidal program cannot be ignored in any assessment of his career during the Third Reich. Speer would maintain that he was always first and foremost an architect/designer, and that he never completely gave up work on either the Berlin or the Nuremberg projects even after becoming Reich Armaments Minister in early 1942. Indeed, he continued to pursue construction projects during the war. He had set up his own transportation network (*Transportflotte Speer*) that provided him with a means of circumventing wartime restrictions on vital goods and services, and he protected workers from conscription into the Wehrmacht. While Speer helped design other, more practical buildings for the Luftwaffe and the other branches of the armed forces, he also made progress on the German Stadium at Nuremberg and on various representational Berlin projects. Speer's workers continued to build at these sites after 1940 with the stone obtained with forced and slave labor. Concentration camp labor, especially at Flossenbürg, Gross-Rosen, and Natzweiler, quarried the stone for Speer's projects.[63] The pace of the building slowed appreciably after the defeat at Stalingrad in 1943, and as a result much of Speer's work from the Third Reich was never completed. Most of his designs were left in unfinished form or in plans and models. These models were remarkably elaborate and detailed. Monumental models, one could say.

The models for structures in "Germania" are in themselves disturbing, and offer evidence that one cannot separate his artistic work from his political career. There was something criminal in these grandiose plans. The Great Hall that he designed at one end of the three-mile-long North-South Axis would have featured a ceiling of almost seven hundred feet (210 meters), and would have had its own microclimate—one that included periodic rain. The scale of the structure so dwarfed and alienated the observer that it sometimes elicited humorous comments: one critic described the Great

Hall as an "elephantine Valkyrian breast."[64] A triumphal arch farther down the axis (known as the Prachtstrasse) would rise some four hundred feet (120 meters), such that the Parisian counterpart would fit inside it. Speer later reflected on his thinking during the summer of 1940: "Even if [Hitler] had not carried out his war in the Soviet Union, completing all of the building plans then on the drawing boards within the ten years he had set as a limit would have been impossible. The projects together amounted to the biggest construction programme in history."[65] Speer's building projects would have exacerbated the already dire labor shortage in the Third Reich and would have required the enslavement of millions more to realize the 1950 target date (three million workers by one calculation). His driving, frenetic pace of work had earlier precipitated labor unrest in Nuremberg when workers were pressed to complete the *Zeppelinwiese.* Conquest allowed the Nazis to secure certain raw materials in short supply: for example, granite and marble in the Soviet Union. When Speer's father saw the model of Berlin, he responded to his son, "You've all gone completely insane." There is some evidence "that Speer, driven by ambition, designed projects that actually surpassed Hitler's mammoth dreams."[66] Speer pushed the limits of the possible: there were even questions whether the marshy soil of Berlin could accommodate certain buildings, lest they sink into the ground.

Yet, in all of this "gigantomania," there was something modern and even modernist, as Joachim Fest has noted:

> Overstepping all the established boundaries of scale had less to do with Hitler or Speer than with the spirit of the age and its ambition to go to the extreme, or beyond, not only intellectually but also technologically. Bruno Taut's glass visions, Mies van der Rohe's design for a high-rise building on Berlin's Friedrichstrasse, Le Corbusier's residential towns, and Boris M. Iofan's Lenin Palace and his plans for Moscow all sprang from the same hubris, as did the competing skyscrapers of New York and Chicago, except that these were not linked to a boundless zeal for world conquest.[67]

It is important to preserve these distinctions, while affirming certain modernist affinities (Plate 13).

Albert Speer proved a consummate survivor and conjuncturist. It is therefore not surprising that during his career as an architect his work dovetailed with the widespread international movement in the architecture of the 1930s. His designs resonated, according to Barbara Miller Lane, with that of "Marcello Piacentini, Paul Cret, Charles Holden, Leon Azéma, Giuseppe

Vago, Alexei Shchusev, and B. M. Iofan, to mention only a few, [who] shared in an effort to create dignified, formal, yet accessible-looking official buildings in the 1930s and early 1940s."[68] Granted, many of these architects were inspired by Beaux Arts or classicist traditions and do not represent the most modernist wings of the respective nations, and internationalism should not be collapsed with modernism. Arguing that Speer was part of an international movement has also been a way to advocate for his architectural designs—a tactic that he himself utilized starting with the publication of *Inside the Third Reich.* But the fact remains that Speer not only began his career as a modernist, but also retained certain connections to modernist contemporaries. The clean lines, the Art Deco touches, and the notion of integrating architecture and design offer points of comparison. The Royal Society in London continues to occupy a Speer-designed space (7–9 Carlton House Terrace having been the German Embassy when Speer undertook the remodel in 1936–37). Stripped of the Nazi fixtures, the townhouse does not stand out and suggests that Speer would have been a capable if relatively unremarkable architect if he had worked in Great Britain.

Speer's skill at surviving served him well in other respects. He avoided being declared a traitor by Hitler at war's end, like so many others in similar positions (Göring, Himmler, etc.). He was also very fortunate to escape with his life at the International Military Tribunal at Nuremberg. As chief British prosecutor Baron Hartley Shawcross reflected several decades later, Speer was "quite lucky to have avoided a death sentence. . . . My own view was one of great surprise that Speer was so leniently dealt with, and I still think it quite wrong that his subordinate, Sauckel, who worked under his instructions, was sentenced to death while Speer escaped."[69] Three of the eight justices (two Soviet and one American) had initially voted for a death sentence for Speer, and only difficult negotiations saved his life. In avoiding responsibility for the Nazis' use of slave labor, concealing the murderous implications of his displacement of Jewish residents in Berlin, and denying specific knowledge of the Holocaust (he told historian Joachim Fest in 1969 that he had never heard the name "Auschwitz"), but at the same time, appearing to share in the collective responsibility for the Nazi regime, Speer trod a now famously fine line.[70]

Speer told lies at Nuremberg to save his life, and he subsequently misrepresented his career to save his image as an artist-technocrat. Throughout, he convinced most observers that he was devoid of personal ambition and ideological conviction. Harvard lecturer Erich Goldhagen was the first to put a dent in Speer's armor, with his October 1971 article in *Midstream,* in which Goldhagen alleged that Speer was present in Posen on 6 October 1943 when Himmler delivered a speech informing high-ranking Nazi officials of the "Final Solution." While Speer organized a spirited defense— asserting that he left the gathering before Himmler's speech and was on his way to see Hitler at Rastenburg—and while Goldhagen was later shown to have fabricated evidence, the truth eventually won out.[71] According to the most recent research by Heinrich Breloer and Rainer Zimmer, Speer apparently was in the audience during Himmler's Posen address. Moreover, he was not at the Rastenburg Führer Headquarters later that evening as he maintained, which significantly undermines his alibi.[72] An earlier but important biographer, Gitta Sereny, who had interviewed Speer at length, remained agnostic about the controversy surrounding his presence during the address of the Reichsführer-SS, but concluded, "I believe that after Posen—whether he actually attended Himmler's speech or not—he knew about the long-planned and almost complete genocide of the Jews, including women and children."[73]

Despite his efforts to deceive historians and to misrepresent his career, Albert Speer and his work stand out as poignant embodiments of the Third Reich. The monumentality of most of his structures, combined with the building procedures that often relied on exploitative practices, capture something essential about the Nazi regime. Then there is Speer's close collaboration with Hitler, which set him apart from his cohort in Nazi Germany. It is safe to say that this close working relationship with the dictator is among the myriad reasons why "Speer's" designs, then as now, have such symbolic import. Even in rubble, Speer's New Reich Chancellery overflowed with meaning—a metaphor for German traditions gone awry, the consequences of hubris, and the grim reality of "the downfall," as artist Anselm Kiefer and others have observed.[74] These resonances no doubt factored into the decisions by the Allies and the successor regimes in postwar Germany to destroy so much of Speer's work, including the war-damaged New Reich Chancellery (with the marble going to create the Soviet Cenotaph in Treptower Park and the Mohrenstrasse U-Bahn station in central Berlin), the 328-yard-long colonnade at Nuremberg that was razed in 1967, and the Runder Platz structure in the Tiergarten quarter that was leveled to make way for Mies van der Rohe's New National Gallery.[75] In exploring Speer's "synthesis" that connected his Nazi work to the modernist tradition, it is important to preserve distinctions. Speer was not Mies or Gropius, but a very different kind of modernist.

Conclusion

FORMER CHANCELLOR HELMUT Kohl's favorite writer, Ernst Jünger, "who clearly flew too close to the fascist sun," was, in historian Hans-Ulrich Wehler's opinion, one of "the greatest criminals of modern German cultural history."[1] Wehler's judgment deserves closer examination. How was it that this proponent of literary modernism was such a "criminal"? The answer, it would seem, lies in his glorification and aestheticization of war, and how this helped shape the sensibility of a generation. Jünger regarded World War I as "the school of modernity," and the formative experience for him and his generation. Jünger was also a kind of chameleon—a militant nationalist, a reclusive artist, and a privileged soldier in occupied France during World War II, among his many personae.[2] He was indeed unique, but the way in which this modernist gravitated toward fascism in the interwar period proved representative to a greater extent than most realize.

Wehler's judgment of Jünger appears overly harsh, especially compared to the figures in the last section of this book who successfully found a place in the Third Reich. Although perhaps less alienated than those who failed in their efforts to find accommodation with the Nazi regime, Jünger retreated to a private sphere—his own version of inner emigration. His novel *Auf den Marmorklippen* (*On the Marble Cliffs*) even represented a critique of the oppressive Nazi state, albeit a veiled, allegorical one. Yet in many regards, Jünger played the role of conjuncturist in a manner similar to the other figures discussed in this book, and also with a sizable portion of the German population. As historian Charles Maier noted,

> In the 1930s the authoritarian party and regime seemed the wave of the future. Disciplined collective man was apparently

on the march. Liberalism appeared the effete indulgence of a beleaguered Anglo-American elite or some aging West European philosophers. . . . In the 1930s the spokesmen for democracy were divided and apparently demoralized. The League of Nations seemed powerless before aggression.[3]

The fascist leaders in 1930s Europe could point to seemingly effective foreign policies and relatively robust economies, among other accomplishments. Many modernist figures therefore pursued accommodation with self-interest in mind, and tried to benefit from the myriad opportunities that came with Nazi cultural initiatives and building projects.

One can also see why the Nazi leaders would seek to cultivate these artists—or, at a minimum, retrain them. As Goebbels proclaimed in 1936, expressing some frustration with the younger generation, "One cannot manufacture artists."[4] His Nazi peer Göring observed, "It is always easier over time to make a decent National Socialist out of an artist than to make a great artist out of a minor Party member. Why was Hitler-the-artist not the first to recognize this?"[5] The regime force-fed the population a diet of culture—far more than they had ever had before. The Nazis needed "cultural workers" of all kinds to realize their ambitions of indoctrination and the creation of a glamorous façade for the Third Reich. Or, in the words of David Schoenbaum, the Nazis shaped a "subjective social reality" that differed from its "objective" (or statistically measurable) counterpart.[6] Germans perceived shifts in society—class divisions, income distribution, and gender roles, among others—that did not correspond to actual events. The state-directed culture and propaganda convinced many of the illusory transformations.

The regime made sure that the public was not only exposed to this culture, but participated in it as much as possible. To take the example of music, the Nazis commissioned thousands of political hymns, fighting songs, and choral works, among other genres, which were then taught to members of an array of Nazi organizations, ranging from the Hitler Youth to the storm troopers to the Strength Through Joy cadres. Popular choral societies like the Deutsche Sängerbund (with over eight hundred thousand members) were Nazified too: "Thousands of choral works with patriotic texts were submitted to the many party and state sponsored competitions, festivals, and traditional performance halls."[7] There were more concerts, public performances, competitions, and parades in the Third Reich than ever before. The Nazis also used the radio, with millions listening on their inexpensive People's Receiver, to provide a soundtrack to events.[8] With considerable psychological acuity, Goebbels and his staffers used music to bolster spirits and forge social solidarity (for example, through the *Wunsch-konzerte,* or "Wish Concerts," that we today might recognize as having a reality show element). There was so much musical activity in the Third Reich that, as historian Michael Kater has noted, "it was too decentralized to be effectively controlled over an extended period of time."[9] This is not to say that the performance of atonal symphonies was a regular occurrence in wartime Germany, but there were spaces—someone's country house with eighty people in attendance, or a living room that held a dozen—where modernism lived on. One might well call it "the secret life of modernism in the Third Reich."

It depended on the individual as to whether he or she could find those spaces and remain content with them. A central theme of this book concerns the elusiveness of clear categories—or, at least, the broad width of a gray zone—with regard to the cultural life of the Third Reich. While the historian's job is to preserve distinctions and to reject uncritical relativization, recent scholarship has also shown that facile or uncomplicated judgments do not hold up under scrutiny. The rich but often tortured cultural life of the Third Reich featured a wide array of figures who had roots in the modernist tradition. Considering how modernism had thrived as an avant-garde movement before World War I, and then had become more mainstream during the Weimar Republic, this was only natural. The Nazi leaders who made cultural policy adapted existing styles and idioms across the various arts and utilized them to their own ends.[10] While many modernists tried but ultimately failed to find accommodation with the Nazi regime, countless others altered the style of their work—and engaged in other forms of accommodation—in the interest of finding a modus vivendi with the Nazis. With regard to the latter, the rich array of figures tempts one to compile a cultural "hall of shame" of complicity. Indeed, along the lines of the Reich Chambers of Culture, one could have multiple discipline-specific categories. Irony aside, a "hall of shame" might include the following figures.

In music, there was an extra measure of opportunity because the Nazi authorities "had no precise philosophy about what constituted acceptable contemporary, newly created music."[11] Among the composers who had connections to modernism and then flourished in the Third Reich—besides the already discussed Strauss—Carl Orff stands out. His *Carmina Burana* was well received on its premiere by the Frankfurt Opera in June 1937, and then grew in popularity. Whether Orff's *Carmina Burana* was infused with

Nazi qualities has been a subject of debate among scholars, with George Steiner and other critics making a compelling case that it reflected the spirit of the times. Steiner argued that it is "terrifying when the singers spit out their Latin fricatives like jack-booted automatons."[12] The *Carmina Burana* certainly poses a challenge to the claim of musicologist Rudolf Stephan that National Socialism "played no role in those masterpieces that did arise" between 1933 and 1945 (he added, "It created nothing positive, it only destroyed").[13] Regardless, Orff affirmed the Nazi musical establishment in other ways. For example, he wrote incidental music for Shakespeare's *A Midsummer Night's Dream,* providing "one of forty-four efforts during the Third Reich to produce a substitute for the classic by the Jew Mendelssohn."[14] In this instance, Orff received a commission of RM 5,000 ($2,000) from the city of Frankfurt in order to compose the piece. Orff finished it in August 1939, with a premiere in Frankfurt in October, much to the pleasure of the Lord Mayor of the city, Fritz Krebs, who was also the head of the local Fighting League for German Culture. Orff has often been viewed as a modernist, albeit of a type appreciated by many Nazis. Musicologist Gerald Abraham noted, "The only kind of modernism acceptable in the Third Reich was the rhythmically hypnotic, totally diatonic neo-primitivism of Orff's scenic cantatas."[15]

Hitler and Wilhelm Furtwängler met in the summer of 1932. The Nazi leader had tried unsuccessfully to mediate a conflict between Furtwängler and Winifred Wagner about artistic control of the Bayreuth Festival—a dispute over artistic autonomy, which would be an issue in their relationship throughout the Third Reich. Yet Furtwängler's career flourished after 1933, and he remained the principal conductor of the Berlin Philharmonic until 1945 (with a short intermission)—a position he resumed from 1952 to 1954. Although Furtwängler lost the dispute with Winifred Wagner in 1932, he emerged as "the Führer's favourite."[16] He conducted performances of Wagner's *Die Meistersinger* to commemorate "Potsdam Day"—when the Third Reich was "festively inaugurated" on 21 March 1933, and then again to open the Nazi Party Rallies in Nuremberg in September 1933 and 1935. He subsequently performed at two gala concerts in Vienna to celebrate the *Anschluss* in 1938 (with Hitler and Goebbels seated in the state box), at a birthday concert for Hitler in April 1942, and at a famous 12 January 1945 concert at the Berlin State Opera House—the Philharmonic having been destroyed in a November 1943 bombing. During the war, Furtwängler took the Berlin Philharmonic on foreign tours. He later claimed that he went on these trips as a private individual and that he never conducted in a

German-occupied land. Neither of these assertions was true. These concert tours were organized by Goebbels's Ministry and were widely recognized in the neutral countries as propaganda efforts. Furtwängler's commitment to the German cause actually grew stronger as the war advanced. In February 1942, Goebbels noted that Furtwängler returned from a concert abroad "practically bursting with nationalistic enthusiasm [and] most willing to place himself at my disposal for any of my activities."[17] His concerts were often broadcast across Europe, and he was meant to symbolize the cultured German, so important to the nation's self-image and psyche. Very telling is Joseph Goebbels's journal entry for 13 January 1944: "To my pleasure I find that with Furtwängler the worse things go for us, the more he supports our regime."[18]

The conductor in fact displayed a certain independence from the Nazi leaders, which was no small feat considering he dealt directly with Goebbels (the Berlin Philharmonic), Göring (the State Opera in Berlin), and Hitler (Bayreuth and beyond). On a symbolic level, he generally managed to avoid giving the Hitler greeting by keeping his baton in his right hand at all times. More significantly, he intervened on behalf of Jewish musicians and helped certain half-Jewish members of the Berlin Philharmonic retain their positions.[19] While Furtwängler's true passion was the music of Beethoven, Wagner, Bruckner, and Mahler, he also made efforts to include modern music in his programs. His advocacy for modernism was arguably motivated by his desire to protect the relative autonomy of the artistic realm, yet among the performances of the Berlin Philharmonic initiated and conducted by Furtwängler one counts the music of Paul Hindemith (the symphony *Mathis der Maler* in March 1934) and Béla Bartók (January 1938), as well as Maurice Ravel and Igor Stravinsky (both on 11–13 December 1938).[20] Playing music by these composers represented a bold gesture. Bartók, for example, was linked to Central European Jewish circles, and the Russian-born Stravinsky, who lived in France during the interwar period, stood as the personification of cosmopolitanism. Furtwängler therefore did not renounce modernist music during the Third Reich, although such programs became increasingly rare during the war years and he made clear his preference for tonality.

Why did Furtwängler remain in Nazi Germany (he had ample opportunity to emigrate) and become a state artist? Certainly his ego played a role. He grew up in a privileged milieu—his father earned renown as an archeologist and a professor at the University of Munich—and Furtwängler never lacked self-assuredness. As Plenipotentiary for the Entire Musical Life of

Vienna after the Anschluss, he was jokingly referred to as the "Music Pope of Vienna." He also genuinely believed that his art corresponded to the spirit of the times. After a hiatus of over twenty years, when his own compositions were rarely played, he exhibited a renewed confidence in his work and permitted performances starting in 1937.[21] Money was also a factor: Furtwängler, for example, signed a five-year contract with Göring's Berlin State Opera in January 1934 for the extravagant sum of RM 36,000 ($14,400) per year. The conductor would revisit this contract almost every year and make demands for more money and improved arrangements—an occurrence that left the Reichsmarschall "exasperated."[22] And this was but one of his myriad positions. Competition with his contemporaries also loomed large: Furtwängler's rivals included Heinz Tietjen and, above all, the Salzburg-born and -trained Herbert von Karajan.[23] Tietjen, who held many posts including Intendant of the Prussian State Theater and artistic director of the Bayreuth Festival from 1931 to 1944, was described by one writer as "one of the most mysterious and yet phenomenally influential individuals in the history of opera performance in Germany in this century."[24] It was Tietjen who "discovered" von Karajan and brought him to Aachen in 1938. The charismatic maestro was soon dubbed the "young magician." Later that year, after his debut conducting at the Berliner Staatsoper, Karajan received a glowing review from the music critic at the *Berliner Zeitung am Mittag* (the review was later referred to in musical circles as the "Wunder-Kritik" due to its headline, "Das Wunder Karajan"). In short, Karajan was viewed by many as the future of classical music in Germany. The critic, Edwin von der Nüll, also charged that Furtwängler "belonged to the previous generation, who undoubtedly rendered a great service, but in whose blank eyes one is more or less forced to see that his time has passed, and it is now the turn of men like von Karajan."[25] Furtwängler was not prepared to step aside or, so to speak, pass the baton. At his denazification trial, allegations surfaced that Furtwängler had arranged in 1940 for Edwin von der Nüll to be sacked from his newspaper because of negative pieces about the conductor, as well as his praise for Karajan. The music critic was drafted in 1940 (along with others born in his year), but there was no evidence that this was a punitive measure or that Furtwängler played a role.

After the war, at the second of his two denazification trials, Furtwängler maintained that he had stayed in Germany to forestall "acts of terror of the Nazi Party." He also maintained that his "position regarding National Socialism was clear from the beginning." He portrayed himself as selfless, as a true patriot: "As a German, I did not want and could not forsake my people [*Volk*], my public, my orchestra, [and] my music, especially when I considered [the true nature] of National Socialism."[26] There is something to this. One biographer claims to have documented eighty instances in which Furtwängler intervened with Nazi authorities on behalf of another person; although historian Michael Kater, on closer inspection, has also pointed out that many of these beneficiaries were pro-Nazi.[27] Ronald Harwood's 1995 play, *Taking Sides*, which was made into a film by István Szabó in 2001, dramatized some of the key issues surrounding Furtwängler's behavior during the Third Reich. The plot concerned an imagined interrogation prior to his 1946 denazification trial, with Furtwängler and the American prosecuting officer facing off over issues of personal responsibility and art. Harwood made it clear that Furtwängler was not a Nazi, but he dwelt on the moral ambiguity of the maestro, who had tried to find and preserve his place in the Reich. On the scholarly side, Michael Kater opined, "Furtwängler's self-defense for staying in the Third Reich was that one could do so as an apolitical artist, especially if one tried to intercede on behalf of Jews."[28] But there are still lingering images that raise doubts: Furtwängler, for example, conducting in the Spanish Hall of the Prague Castle on 16 March 1944, with those in attendance including Reich Minister Frick, Gauleiters Eigruber and Henlein of the Upper Danube and Sudetenland, respectively, and a host of Nazi functionaries.[29] A concert in this seat of evil—the Hradčany had been Heydrich's office until his assassination in mid-1942—was filmed by newsreels so as to be grist for the Nazi propaganda mill.

Another fascinating and talented figure who flourished during the Third Reich was soprano Elisabeth Schwarzkopf, who sang her way through the dictatorship. Schwarzkopf joined at least three different Nazi organizations and served as a "leader" in a Nazi student group at the Berlin Hochschule für Musik. She also later joined the Nazi Party. Perhaps more important, she triumphed as a star at the Goebbels-led Deutsche Oper (albeit the second opera in Berlin after Göring's Staatsoper), where she spent four years on the stage (1938–42). Her complicity may have gone even further, as she developed a close personal relationship with Goebbels.[30] Other problematic parts of her biography have been documented, including her performance before SS troops in German-occupied Posen in September 1942, when she participated in the Posen Music Week. While Schwarzkopf hailed from Cottbus on the Polish border, and could naturally be expected to want to return home, it stirs the imagination to think of her in this SS milieu at a time when Himmler's legions were at their most murderous. Due to the influence and patronage of Baldur von Schirach, she was able to move to

Vienna in 1944, where she appeared at the State Opera with Karl Böhm (she had tried to make this move earlier, but had been blocked by Goebbels, who sought to keep her in Berlin). At war's end, Schwarzkopf shared a house on the Attersee in the Austrian Salzkammergut with Hilde Mühlmann, the wife of art plunderer SS-Colonel Kajetan Mühlmann. Reports also surfaced that Schwarzkopf had an SS officer for a lover (according to one source this was Hugo Jury, the Gauleiter of lower Austria and an SS general).[31] Even if she left many unanswered questions, Schwarzkopf enjoyed a spectacular career, one that stretched into the postwar period. She suffered some difficulties after 1945 and was not invited to perform at the Metropolitan Opera in New York until 1964, but she eventually counted among the world's greatest divas, performing regularly at La Scala in Milan and gaining renown as a singer of *Lieder*. Whether Elisabeth Schwarzkopf qualifies as a modernist is debatable (even doubtful), but she certainly provides another example of a talented artist finding accommodation with the Nazi regime, and then later rehabilitating her career in the postwar period. In 1953 she married British impresario Walter Legge, thereby becoming a British citizen. Interestingly, Legge was Jewish. Queen Elizabeth II later awarded Schwarzkopf the title Dame Commander, and she received an honorary doctorate from Cambridge University in 1976.

In the film industry, director Veit Harlan and actors Werner Krauss and Emil Jannings stand out. Harlan was only in training as a director during the Weimar Republic, but he learned his craft at the hands of Max Reinhardt and worked on the Berlin stage in the 1920s. Harlan went on to make several anti-Semitic films, including the notorious *Jud Süss* in 1940. The widely circulated film might count as the second most significant propaganda film of the Third Reich, after *Triumph of the Will* (some have talked of it "preparing the German populace for the 'final solution'").[32] Harlan's *Jud Süss,* however, would scarcely count as a modernist work. One scholar described it as "baroque fascist."[33] It tells the story of eighteenth-century court Jews in a conventional fashion, even if the plot, which involves the Jewish villain compelling a "German" woman to have sex with him in order to secure the release of her husband, is unconventional. It is notable that in making the film Harlan traveled to the Lublin ghetto and brought back 120 Jews for various roles in the film.[34] This element of cinéma vérité might be considered a modernist technique, although the Nazi censors prohibited any mention of these Jewish actors in the press. Harlan's first wife, cabaret singer Dora Gerson (1899–1943), whom he divorced in 1924, was Jewish, and she and her family ended up victims of Auschwitz after they were captured trying to flee the Netherlands for Switzerland in late 1942. Harlan's second wife, Kristina Söderbaum, was a star actor in Nazi Germany, and he directed her in a number of films, including *Jud Süss*.[35] The other key anti-Semitic film of the Third Reich, Fritz Hippler's *The Eternal Jew*, as noted earlier, utilized certain modernist elements, including photomontage, dissolves, and artful camera work. Eric Rentschler has noted, "Modernism persisted in Nazi cinema, to be sure, not in features, but rather in short subjects and nonfiction films (for instance, in the documentaries of Leni Riefenstahl, Willy Zielke, and Walter Ruttmann)."[36]

It is difficult to fathom that Werner Krauss, who starred in *Jud Süss*, earlier played the lead in *The Cabinet of Dr. Caligari,* providing one of the iconic images of Weimar Germany. The expressionist thriller of 1920 made the case, arguably for the first time, for the creative potential of film and helped usher in a golden era in German cinema. Krauss went on to make *The Joyless Street* (1925) with G. W. Pabst, a classic in the *Neue Sachlichkeit* genre, as well as films with Jean Renoir and F. W. Murnau, among others. Despite his importance to the history of Weimar culture, Krauss was, in the words of director Willi Forst, "the last great chameleon," and he became a Nazi.[37] Goebbels appointed him a State Actor, and Krauss appeared in a wide range of roles in the Third Reich, including Napoleon in *Hundred Days* (1935), co-starring with Gründgens (who played Fouché). Krauss also played Dr. Rudolf Virchow in *Robert Koch: The Adversary of Death* (1939), and Paracelsus in the eponymous 1943 film directed by G. W. Pabst. Krauss specialized in playing nefarious Jews, as seen in both the film *Jud Süss* (1940), in which he appeared as two distinct characters (Rabbi Loew and Secretary Levy), and a notorious production of *The Merchant of Venice* at the Burgtheater in Vienna in 1943, in which he played Shylock. From his roots in Weimar theater and film to his role as Nazi propagandist, Krauss conformed to a pattern seen frequently in this book. He also proved emblematic in that he avoided serious penalties in the postwar period. Werner Krauss acted in several films in the 1950s and lived quietly in Vienna until his death at the end of the decade.

Emil Jannings, a Swiss-born actor, starred in films in both Hollywood and Berlin. The first recipient of the Academy Award for best actor in 1927 for his performance in *The Way of All Flesh*—and one of the biggest film stars of the interwar period—Jannings had also worked with Max Reinhardt at the Berlin theater, and with F. W. Murnau, with whom he made three films in the first half of the decade. The highlight of Jannings's career came in 1929, when he starred with Marlene Dietrich in *The Blue Angel*.

Playing Heinrich Mann's Professor Immanuel Rath, Jannings delivered a timeless performance, with his humiliation at the end suggesting an early kind of method acting. His creative and even daring work during Weimar eventually gave way to Nazi propaganda, and Jannings appeared in numerous iconic films, including *The Youth of Frederick the Great* (1935), *The Ruler* (1937), and *Ohm Krüger* (1941). Each had its own Nazi themes, with the latter concerning the Boers' heroic fight against the British imperialists (Jannings played Uncle Krüger). Goebbels proclaimed Jannings to be a "state artist" in 1941, thereby protecting him from military service.[38] Jannings did not work in the postwar period, but he had precious little time, succumbing to liver cancer in 1950 while living in Strobl, a mountain town near Salzburg.

In the realm of the visual arts, the list of those with modernist roots who found accommodation with the regime would include not only the figures mentioned earlier (Otto Andreas Schreiber, Arno Breker, and Josef Thorak, among others), but also Fritz Klimsch, who had been a co-founder of the Berlin Secession in 1898. Klimsch benefited enormously from Nazi patronage, for example receiving RM 300,000 ($120,000) from Goebbels's Reich Propaganda Ministry for the monument to Mozart in Salzburg. Klimsch signed the June 1938 letter confirming the commission, "Mit deutschen Gruss und heil Hitler!"[39] He had twenty-one works exhibited in the *Great German Art Exhibitions,* and modeled busts of Interior Minister Wilhelm Frick and Adolf Hitler, among various Nazi clients. He also created sculptures for the gardens of Goebbels and Ribbentrop at the Reich Propaganda Ministry and Foreign Ministry, respectively. Klimsch had modernist roots but adapted his work to suit the new regime. He received the highly prestigious Eagle Plaque of the Reich award in 1940 and was declared an "irreplaceable artist" during the war.[40] Many sculptors with modernist roots conformed to the Nazi aesthetic, including Georg Kolbe, Richard Scheibe, Karl Albiker, and Josef Wackerle.[41] Of course, it was not exclusively sculptors who found accommodation, but also painters, including Fritz Erler, who did post-Impressionist-like paintings prior to World War I and then later became known for his iconic Hitler portraits.[42] Paul Mathias Padua, who worked in a variety of styles, including Neue Sachlichkeit and an Albin-Egger-Lienz–kind of modernist realism, executed explicitly propagandistic works like *The Führer Speaks,* a commission of the Reich Radio Office. Yet he also explored abstraction during the Third Reich, perhaps most notably with regard to his submissions for the *Junge Kunst im Deutschen Reich* exhibition in Vienna during the war. Padua went on to work in an avowedly Expressionist style after 1945.[43] Even some of the German combat artists engaged by the Reich Propaganda Ministry during the war included modernist elements in their depictions of battle scenes and other wartime experiences.[44]

For architecture, one could include not only Speer and the Bauhaus architects discussed earlier who found meaningful work in Nazi Germany, but also Wilhelm Kreis, who once advocated a sleek, modernist-informed style and became a designer of Nazi burial memorials (*Totenhalle* and *Totenburgen*). Kreis was a modernist in many respects, having taught Max Pechstein and other future Expressionists in Dresden; but he was also a Nazi, serving as the last president of the Reich Chamber for the Visual Arts beginning in September 1943.[45] Kreis represented a progressive tendency in Nazi architecture—even if he was also known as the "architect of death" because of his penchant for designing memorials (Hitler appointed him General Architect for War Cemeteries in 1941). Many of his designs during the Third Reich incorporated modernist elements, including the museum complex he planned for Albert Speer's GBI in Berlin and the stark yet eerie Soldiers' Hall designed for the army (neither was ever built). Paul Bonatz, who designed Nazi military academies (*Ordensburgen*) and the Munich Central Railway Station—with even grander plans for the Bavarian capital on the drawing board—also had a very successful career after 1933. The railway station that Bonatz designed for Hitler would feature the largest dome in the world (six times the size of Saint Peter's) and would be built of steel and glass. Bonatz has been described as a "Modernist of a functionalist stamp."[46] He tried to work with Hitler as he developed a contemporary monumental style, but the task proved daunting. Late in the design process of the Munich *Hauptbahnhof,* for example, Hitler introduced the idea of broad-gauge rail, which required the diameter of the dome to increase from 918 to 1148 feet to accommodate the wider tracks. Bonatz at first welcomed the challenge, but he then came to view it as "utterly mad." Bonatz ended up leaving Nazi Germany, taking a position in Ankara in 1943 to "flee from this insanity."[47] It bears reiteration that modernist architects more generally were never entirely phased out. Especially with regard to industrial buildings, they continued to work using flat roofs, glass, metal, and other modernist elements.

There were modernists of other kinds too, beyond the aforementioned genres. Or rather there were figures that engaged and advanced modernity in various ways. The pathbreaking philosopher Martin Heidegger, while Rector of Freiburg University, told the assembled students on 3 November 1933, "Theses and 'ideas' are not supposed to be the rules of your existence;

the Führer himself and alone is the present and future German reality and your law."[48] Heidegger served as rector for only one year, until April 1934, and arguably belongs in Chapter 2 with the figures who sought accommodation with the Nazis but became alienated. Regardless, Heidegger's academic work as a philosopher from 1933 to 1945 appears to have been profoundly influenced by National Socialism. One could also turn to the area of popular culture to find the persistence of modernist culture. Jazz, for example, continued to find supporters from a diverse array of individuals—from oppositional "swing kids" and "Edelweiss Pirates" to relatively sophisticated officers in the Luftwaffe.[49] Most jazz in the Third Reich tended toward tamer fare—swing- and jazz-inflected popular tunes—but this music still represented a linkage to the more daring popular music of the Weimar Republic. The realm of popular culture included the expansion of mass market sports. Boxer Max Schmeling, who was on-again, off-again world champion in the 1930s, fighting a series of famous bouts against Joe Louis that captivated the public's imagination, and race car driver Rudolf Caracciola, who competed for Mercedes Benz during the company's dominant "Silver Arrows" period, were important figures in the emergence of modern media, whose exploits were conveyed to the masses in an unprecedentedly immediate manner.[50] While not modernists per se, these figures engaged the concept of modernity more generally and certainly contributed to the culture in which the modernists lived and worked.

Across the disciplines, those who found a place in the Reich usually possessed character traits that included ambition, talent, and fortitude, as well as a certain amount of selfishness and opportunism. It is therefore not surprising that most knew one another and established networks during the Third Reich. One can point, for example, to the relationships between Speer, Riefenstahl, and Breker, or to the linkages between Gründgens, Heinz Tietjen, and Werner Krauss, with the latter cohort all in Göring's stable. It also comes as no surprise that most of them also adapted to the post-1945 order. The continuities between the Weimar Republic and Third Reich proved stronger than those between the Third Reich and the post-1945 era in all three German successor states, but *Stunde Null* was by no means a complete caesura. Just as there were strategies for survival after 1933, including altering the style of one's work, modifying one's political views, and finding a patron, the compromised figures in the post-1945 world found ways to continue their work and rebuild their careers. Key among them was the use of myths and the obfuscation of history. The misrepresentations of the French Resistance have been exposed and now usually bring a knowing smile to most well-informed observers who recognize that it was ludicrous to think that everyone could have participated in the anti-German underground. Some find it almost comical that the French would even try to maintain such an idea, even though the fights over the issue (and definition) of collaboration have often been fierce. The myths about modernists, however, have proved more enduring.

AFTER 1945, MANY observers believed that modern art was de facto anti-Nazi, and it is chiefly for this reason that Expressionism was embraced by so many in the fledgling Federal Republic of Germany. It was common for government offices, embassies, and other representational spaces to be decorated with modern art. One example would be the office of Christian Democratic Union Party chair Rainer Barzel, who in 1966 adorned his work space in the Bonn Federal Parliament building with three large abstract paintings by his friend Otto Andreas Schreiber.[51] All fine and good, except that Schreiber, as discussed earlier, had been an ardent Nazi, a member of the storm troopers, and an early leader of the Berlin National Socialist German Students' League. Schreiber had led a brutal attack on art school professors in February 1933, at which time he and his fellow storm troopers beat up faculty they considered "Jewish and Marxist," and he subsequently became a close associate of Reich Propaganda Minister Goebbels. Yet because his paintings were in an Expressionist style, Barzel believed he could exhibit them without arousing suspicions or provoking controversy. As art historian Christian Saehrendt noted, Expressionism had "once more become the cultural advertisement of democratic Germany" (the first time being during the Weimar Republic).[52]

Many myths about artists during the war took hold in the early postwar years, especially when the issue of collaboration with the Nazis was at stake. A telling example is provided by Pablo Picasso, the great Spanish artist who lived his adult life in France. Many Americans embraced him, especially after the Armory Show of 1913—the first international exhibition of modern art in the United States—and an entire mythmaking machine emerged in the following decades. Picasso was promoted by, among others, Alfred Barr Jr., the founding director of the Museum of Modern Art in New York. An example of the artist benefiting from an apocryphal story about his anti-fascist views was already evident in August 1943, when the museum reinstalled Picasso's *Guernica,* which had been stranded in America when the war broke out in Europe. The museum's wartime press release included a report from an anonymous source: "There is a story that after the fall of

Paris, Otto Abetz, Hitler's agent in the city, visited Picasso's studio, where the artist was still living. He saw a study sketch of the mural on Picasso's wall and asked the artist, 'Did you do that?' 'No,' Picasso replied, 'you did.'"[53] This account was then repeated over and over again and became part of the Picasso myth. After 1944, Americans would make pilgrimages to his studio in Paris. Most visitors coveted a souvenir photo with him, such as the one in September 1944 that features the artist with American photographer Lee Miller.[54] The photos seemed to complement the myths, which continued to multiply. In January 1945, Alfred Barr maintained that Picasso "was not allowed to exhibit publicly and he made no overt gestures but his very existence in Paris encouraged the Resistance artists, poets and intellectuals, who gathered in his studio or about his café table." Barr also cited an American living in Paris by the name of Gladys Demas, who gushed, "Picasso's presence here during the occupation became of tremendous occult importance. . . . [H]is work has become sort of a banner of the Resistance Movement."[55] Picasso as hero of the Resistance would sum up the myth.

The reality, of course, was very different. Art historian Christian Zervos, who actually was in the Resistance, observed, "The participation of Picasso in the Resistance is false. Picasso simply kept his dignity during the Occupation the way millions of people did here. But he never got involved in the Resistance. Realize that his work itself is the greatest form of Resistance."[56] In fact, even this formulation is exceedingly generous to the artist and grew out of an admiration for Picasso's art. It also came about because Picasso was a political artist both before the war—executing works such as *Composition with Minotaur* (1936), *Dream and Lie of Franco* (1937), and *Guernica* (1937)—and after the Liberation, when he joined the French Communist Party in October 1944. The latter, a very theatrical gesture, was made for complicated reasons but certainly entailed an effort to shape perceptions of his wartime experiences.[57]

Picasso's behavior during the war is analogous to one of his Cubist paintings: a static image proves elusive, and one is bombarded simultaneously with multiple perspectives. One image involves the German authorities leaving Picasso alone during the war. Although he had opportunities to leave Paris, he did so only once during the occupation. He clearly had supporters who weighed in on his behalf, including Arno Breker. As noted earlier, certain contemporaries, such as Jean Cocteau, later talked about "Operation White Dove," an effort to assist Picasso in the latter part of the war when he was suspected of having violated the strict currency statutes during the German occupation. There is considerably more truth to James Lord's

Photographer Lee Miller with Pablo Picasso in his studio in the rue des Grands-Augustins in late August or early September 1944. (Lee Miller Archives, Chiddingly, U.K.)

comments just after the Liberation: "All [Picasso] wanted in life was to be free to keep on working. By an irony, he [Picasso] added, the war years had been the most peaceful of his career. Denounced as degenerate and subversive, forbidden to exhibit, he had been left in peace to work as he pleased."[58] Like many other cultural figures in France, Picasso continued with his art and is credited with producing 1,473 works between the outbreak of war and the Liberation. He rendered many of them in black and white or shades of gray—an acknowledgment of the tragic circumstances that surrounded him—but he experienced one of the most productive periods of his long career.[59] This is akin to the 220 feature films that were produced in wartime France, of which all but 35 were made in the German-occupied zone. Across France, more than four hundred plays were performed. Culture continued to be produced during the war, and much of it was modernist in inspiration and orientation: Henri Matisse, Louis-Ferdinand Céline, Jean Cocteau, and Le Corbusier were among those who remained and continued their work. Le Corbusier, to elaborate briefly on one figure, held a position on a Vichy planning committee and developed designs for Algiers and other cities. Historian Julian Jackson has observed that "the post-war reputations of those [artists and intellectuals] who stayed in France have often been based more on rumour and innuendo than a balanced assessment of their conduct during the Occupation."[60]

Another image of Picasso during the war emerges from his friendship and business relationship with Martin Fabiani, a notorious dealer of looted artworks. Fabiani had taken over the stock of famed gallerist and publisher Ambroise Vollard after his death in 1939. Vollard counted Cézanne, Renoir, and Picasso among the artists he represented and stands as one of the most important dealers in the history of modern art. Vollard's death in July 1939 remains a subject of considerable controversy—officially, a "monumental" sculpture by Maillol fell on him when his car, a Talbot convertible, knocked it off its moorings—but rumors persisted that Fabiani himself was responsible for the dealer's death.[61] Regardless, Picasso was friends with Fabiani. In 1942 the "Corsican adventurer" had published an edition of Comte de Buffon's *Histoire naturelle* with illustrations by Picasso, and their relationship flourished during the war. Picasso sketched Fabiani on 28 July 1943—about the same time Fabiani sold off works from the Paul Rosenberg collection, which had been looted by the Nazis in Paris. Rosenberg was another of Picasso's dealers, now cut off from him after fleeing to the United States. Picasso reportedly purchased a looted painting from Fabiani: a work by "Le Douanier" Rousseau taken from the Wertheimer family. Although there is some uncertainty about the matter, Picasso reportedly returned it to Germaine Wertheimer after the war and has been quoted as saying, "Okay, I'll give it back to you and I'll ask Fabiani for the money."[62] For Picasso to consort with such a dubious character raises many questions. Fabiani, for his part, published self-serving memoirs after the war—claiming, for example, never to have sold any stolen objects—and he boasted about his relationship with the artist, titling one chapter "Picasso le Magnifique."[63]

Picasso proceeded very carefully when it came to his wartime experiences. In official interrogations, he would answer truthfully if exceedingly artfully. When art historian James Plaut of the Office Strategic Services' Art Looting Investigation Unit put some questions to Picasso about what he did during the war, there was a sense that Picasso had told the truth (he said "no" to the question of whether Resistance forces had met in his studio).

Yet Plaut also bemoaned that the artist's answers had been, "in some degree, evasive and unsatisfactory."[64] Picasso indicated that he did not exhibit his art under German auspices—a claim repeated in the *New York Times Magazine* in October 1944.[65] While this might have been true with regard to the contemporaneous works he produced during the war, his earlier creations were displayed in both the occupied zone and in Vichy France on numerous occasions. For example, his works were in the collection of Paul Jamot, which was donated to the French state museums and shown at the Musée de l'Orangerie in June 1941. Picasso's works were also sold at auction, including at Paris's famous Hôtel Drouot. In fact, he had stashed enough money in Switzerland before the war such that he did not need the income. The postwar reports also overlooked the fact that German officers during the war frequently visited Picasso's studio on the rue des Grand-Augustins. It was only later that historians learned that Picasso often received them with considerable warmth and hospitality. Ernst Jünger, who called on the artist in July 1942, noted in his diary that Picasso declared, "The two of us, just as we're sitting here, we could negotiate peace this afternoon. This evening men could smile."[66]

This raises the important question about how myths evolved. Clearly, they began early, gaining momentum with the denazification trials—and the equivalent measures for collaborators in the occupied countries, such as the French *épuration légale*. After the end of the war, most courts looking into cultural figures' complicity did not reach judgments that had long-lasting effects; the verdicts meted out before May 1945 were often much harsher, such as the death sentence received by French writer Robert Brasillach, who was convicted of "intellectual crimes" (treason) and executed by firing squad in February 1945.[67] Yet the bureaucratization of the judicial process in the postwar period generally moderated the penalties. And how could one sentence a writer when members of the Nazis' mobile killing squads were often not arrested or prosecuted? That the Americans transferred jurisdiction for the denazification proceedings to the Germans in 1946 added to the challenges. There were sporadic expressions of outrage at the verdicts of cultural figures as the tribunals let them off. Arno Breker's fine of DM 100 ($24) was ridiculed in certain newspapers in 1947 (with mocking titles about "Hitler's Michelangelo"), even if the journalists did not appreciate the full measure of his earlier recompense, which included the millions of Reichsmarks that he had been paid by the Nazi state.[68]

The most common response to the lenient treatment of cultural figures during denazification proceedings was indifference or apathy. When art

Der „Michelangelo Hitlers"

Der Bildhauer Arno Breker als „Mitläufer" eingestuft / 100 Mark Sühne

Donauwörth (Eig. Ber.)

Die Spruchkammer Donauwörth stufte den Bildhauer Arno Breker, geb. 1900 in Elberfeld, als Mitläufer ein, nachdem der Oeffentliche Kläger seine Einreihung in die Gruppe II (Aktivisten) gefordert hatte. Der Kreis der „Mitläufer" wurde damit um ein weiteres, angesehenes Mitglied erweitert.

*

Die Spruchkammer Donauwörth ist im Erdgeschoß des Landbauamtes untergebracht. Der Sitzungssaal, an seinem vorderen Ende in einen durch einen Mauerbogen gebildeten Alkoven auslaufend, wirkt düster und die drückende Kälte des Raumes wird durch ein großes Kruzifix über der Türe nicht gemildert. Das einzig Freundliche an diesem Saal sind einige Sonnenstrahlen, die sich durch die mit wildem Weingeranke verwachsenen Fenster stehlen.

*

Links vor dem Richtertisch, an dem eine Frau den Vorsitz führt, steht ein Mann und erzählt aus seinem Leben. Es ist Arno Breker, der große Bildhauer, der einmal der „Michelangelo des Dritten Reiches" genannt wurde. Als Sohn eines Bildhauers geboren, besuchte er die Kunstakademie in Düsseldorf, schnitt bei mehreren künstlerischen Wettbewerben nicht schlecht ab, ging 1926 nach Paris und eroberte sich durch seine starke Begabung bald einen Namen. Gelegentlich eines Besuches in Rom traf er 1934 die Nichte

Unser Bild zeigt Arno Breker (Mitte) während der Spruchkammerverhandlung in Donauwörth. Links von ihm sein Verteidiger Dr. Windhaus und rechts der ehemalige Verteidiger von Reichsminister Speer in Nürnberg, Dr. Flesner.

Photo: Fosch/Weiz

Max Liebermanns und ließ sich von ihr überreden, nach Deutschland zurückzukehren.

*

Zwei Jahre lang kämpfte er nach seiner Schilderung mit wirtschaftlichen Sorgen, bis er, der schon bei den Olympischen Spielen 1928 in Amsterdam im Wettbewerb der freien Künste mit der Bronzemedaille ausgezeichnet worden war, bei

den Olympischen Spielen 1936 in Berlin im selben Wettbewerb eine Silbermedaille erhielt. Das hatte zur Folge, daß sich Dr. Goebbels an Arno Breker wandte und eine Büste bei ihm bestellte, die ihm bei der Ablieferung allerdings nicht mehr gefiel, so daß er sie zurückschickte und vergaß, seinen Auftrag zu honorieren. Aber zwei Jahre später trat Reichsmini-

(Fortsetzung auf Seite 2, Spalte 2)

Newspaper coverage of Breker's denazification trial in Donauwörth, October 1948. The headline reads: "Hitler's Michelangelo: The Sculptor Arno Breker Is Classified as a 'Fellow Traveler' and Fined 100 Marks." (*Abendzeitung*, Munich)

historian Franz Roh learned that Adolf Ziegler had been let off as a "blosser Mitläufer" (simple fellow-traveler) in a Hannover denazification trial, he wrote the then head of the Nationalgalerie in Berlin, Paul Ortwin Rave, and asked if Rave would sign his rather fiery letter, in which he wrote of the grave harm done to German culture by Ziegler and his purging commission. Rave, however, demurred, saying that he had no desire to make life any more difficult for Ziegler, and that the former president of the Reich Chamber for the Visual Arts had "to live in his own skin."[69] Rave added that Ziegler should "go by grace of God," and that is what effectively happened. If there was dissatisfaction with the sentences of cultural figures, it was scarcely noticeable in the public sphere. The same applied to Robert Scholz, Alfred Rosenberg's art expert and the leader of Rosenberg's Special Staff for the Visual Arts, who went through denazification in an Augsburg internment camp in late 1947 and early 1948. Although prosecutors initially argued that he should be categorized as a "main offender," the three-judge panel placed Scholz in a far lesser category—"exonerated"—and allowed him to return to private life. The French sought to bring him to justice, but the West German authorities did not extradite him and he was tried in absentia in Paris in 1950. Although convicted and sentenced to ten years, he never served a day in jail. Living in Fürstenfeldbruck, a town near Munich, Robert Scholz actually continued to work as an art critic, writing for marginal yet important publications of the old Nazis and the radical right, such as Gerhard Frey's *National-Zeitung,* the *Deutsche Soldaten-Zeitung,* and the *Deutsche Klüter Blätter.*[70] Despite his prominence in this right-wing subculture, he avoided both further legal entanglements and any critical assessment by historians prior to his death in 1981.

Most of the cultural collaborators accepted their lenient sentences, retreated from public life for a spell, and then reemerged, sometimes on the margins, sometimes as stars. Otto Andreas Schreiber represented an example of the former. He lived quietly near the Dutch border and then moved in 1954 to the town of Dormagen on the west bank of the Rhine, where he kept a network of friends—like politician Rainer Barzel, mentioned above. Schreiber would correspond with scholars writing about the Third Reich, such as Paul Ortwin Rave, whom he wrote in 1949 in response to Rave's book *Kunstdiktatur im Dritten Reich.* Rave was also the director of the Berlin Nationalgalerie at this time, and he responded graciously to Schreiber's letter, thanking him in particular for information on the factory exhibitions of the 1930s (which, Rave noted, merited much more extensive treatment). Rave also evinced genuine interest in Schreiber's painting, writing the artist, "I would be delighted to have the occasion to get to know you and your work better."[71] Rave and others in leadership positions in the West German art world were seeking a new art that would reflect the newly reformed nation, and Schreiber's neo-Expressionist work seemed to merit consideration. But nothing appears to have come from the artist's overture, at least as indicated in the archives, and Schreiber lived the rest of his life as an unremarkable provincial painter. He exhibited at the Cologne Kunstverein in the 1960s, and his paintings still appear at auction today.[72] But it was a quiet career for someone who had started with such audacious tactics. Schreiber died in Dormagen, Westphalia, in 1978.

Others complicit in the Nazis' cultural initiatives revived their careers as stars, as was the case with both Herbert von Karajan and Elisabeth Schwarzkopf. In the words of Michael Kater, "Both [were] denazified in Austria by concealing their Nazi pasts . . . and joined Furtwängler in the concert rounds."[73] More specifically, von Karajan, who in 1942 had divorced his first wife and married a wealthy textile heiress—who had a Jewish grandparent and would therefore be considered a *Mischling* second degree according to the Nuremberg Laws—maintained after the war that this marriage caused him to answer to a Nazi Party court, whereby he resigned his Party membership. Michael Kater, however, has demonstrated that this was a complete lie: "His party papers in the archives are intact, and there is no record of any resignation." Kater added, "The denazification authorities believed him, however, and once again this opportunistic ploy helped to revive Karajan's spectacular career after World War II."[74] Elisabeth Schwarzkopf denied having joined the Nazi Party—as late as 1983 she repeatedly made this claim to journalists from the *New York Times*. She also refused to answer Michael Kater's questions in the early 1990s, first by referring the historian to her lawyer and then by providing no response.[75] She was not alone in avoiding her past. The high degree of complicity and accommodation among artists in the Third Reich meant that there were many who concealed parts of their personal history in order to work in the postwar period.

There was often public support for the rapid rehabilitation of the compromised artistic figures. Wilhelm Furtwängler, for example, was "denazified" at the end of April 1947 when he was placed in the "fellow traveler" category. This classification enabled him to move freely between all the occupied zones, and three weeks later, on 22 May 1947, he returned to lead the Berlin Philharmonic for the first time since the war. It was Whitsunday, and the performance took place at the Titaniapalast in Berlin-Steglitz. Furtwängler planned an all-Beethoven program: the Egmont Overture followed by the "idyllic" Sixth Symphony and the "heroic" Fifth as a finale. Some people queued for fourteen hours in hopes of obtaining tickets, which became so expensive that purchasing one on the black market would equal "the coal needed by an entire middle class family for the entirety of the next winter." But also among the audience could be found the uniforms of the occupation armies. The concert ended with a thundering applause that lasted fifteen minutes. Actor/writer Erika Mann, who had returned from emigration and was present at the concert, found herself "deeply disturbed" and even "suspected the return of the Nazis," although she had the temerity to publish her views in the *Herald Tribune*.[76] The Americans, it must be stressed, played a role in celebrating Furtwängler and hence rehabilitating him. Furtwängler himself knew that he was viewed as a representative of German music and took advantage of the Americans' pride in the reestablishment of his renowned orchestra in the western zone of Berlin.

Artists themselves also fabricated myths. Otto Dix included in his résumé in 1950, "During the entire Nazi period the Gestapo often made house searches and I was forbidden to exhibit or sell my pictures."[77] He also portrayed himself in a 1948 painting as Christ behind barbed wire in a concentration camp, exploring the theme of *Ecce Homo* (behold the man). Dix, as noted earlier, was famous for his formulation that he had been "banished to landscape painting." Yet art historian Lutz Tittel has noted with considerable reserve, "The facts of the matter speak another language."[78] A review of Dix's oeuvre from the Third Reich, and even from the war, shows that he produced work with many different subjects, including portraits. And not only did he evidently paint the children of Reich Foreign Minister Joachim von Ribbentrop, but he also received financial support from Ribbentrop's parents-in-law, the Schniewinds. That Dix received commissions to execute works for a Nazi *Ordensburg* (an ideological school set in a castle-like structure) and an army building office in Magdeburg, and that his paintings were purchased by Albert Speer's office for the rebuilding of Berlin, also speak to the complexity of his experiences during the Third Reich.[79] Yet none of this came out in his postwar statements. Artist Max Pechstein devoted fewer than three pages in his memoir to the years 1933–45.[80] Art historian, dealer, and plunderer Eduard Plietzsch, who had a remarkable career that ranged from friendships with George Grosz, Max Pechstein, and poet Else Lasker-Schüler to a wartime stint stealing art from Jews in the Netherlands with Kajetan Mühlmann, published his memoir in 1955 while living in Cologne. They dealt only with the period up to 1933—this after he burned his and many of the Mühlmann Agency's papers in 1945 and blamed it on the Soviets. Plietzsch also concealed the fact that he lived with Max Pechstein in the artist's Berlin apartment at war's end (his own Berlin apartment, which had rooms designed by Henry van de Velde and Walter Gropius, had been destroyed by bombs).[81] To this day, several bronze busts of Plietzsch that were executed by Pechstein are in the collections of German museums, with few observers aware that Plietzsch counts as one of the most notorious art looters of all time. Until his death in 1961, Plietzsch continued to publish books on Dutch painting and provide expert reports for well-known collectors like Heinz Kisters and Günter Henle.[82]

Emil Nolde was arguably the master of concealment and myth. His memoir featured eleven pages treating the period, and this includes transcriptions of letters from Nazi authorities denying him the right to pursue his profession. Clearly, one cannot call these eleven pages a forthright engagement with this history. Nolde filled his account with questionable assertions, stating, for example, that Moscow radio in the years after 1937 defended the art of "Barlach and Nolde." This would seem doubtful in that Stalin had banned abstract art. Nolde also claimed that there was a "secret decree" (*Geheimerlass*) that prevented the mention of certain artists in the press, including himself and Alfred Kubin; however, both in fact were mentioned frequently in articles up until 1945.[83] Nolde also stated that the president of the Reich Chamber for the Visual Arts forbade the sale of his works—a claim, as we have seen, that was patently false. The thrust of Nolde's account is that he was a victim who suffered deeply, and that he and others had not known what was transpiring. He wrote, "We artists, often trusting and somewhat unworldly, really didn't know what was happening."[84] There was little in the way of nuance, let alone remorse, for his positive views about Hitler and National Socialism.

Scholars often contributed to these myths about virtuous and noble modernists. Many historians, art historians, and experts in other fields have had a tendency to view the culture of the first half of the twentieth century in black-and-white terms. For some scholars, the integrity of the creator was bound with the quality of the work. When added to the natural propensity to become invested in the person whom one studies, objectivity could prove elusive. The director of the Hindemith Institute in Frankfurt, according to Pamela Potter, "dismissed any past 'incriminating' findings about the composer and scrutinized the reception history of *Mathis der Maler* in an effort to demonstrate the work's inherently 'antifascist' nature"; and the Carl Orff Center in Munich "apparently refused to publish the proceedings of a [1999] conference . . . that revealed Orff's compromising behavior in the 1930s and 1940s."[85]

The cult surrounding the Bauhaus, which was fostered by Gropius, Mies, and others, offers another prime example.[86] On the hundredth anniversary of Gropius's birth, the Bauhaus-Archive in Berlin celebrated him as a "declared enemy of Fascism."[87] There is no shortage of sanitized biographies, such as Siegfried Giedion's 1992 study of Gropius, in which the words "National Socialist," "Nazi," and "Hitler" do not appear in the index, and Gropius's experiences during the Third Reich are not engaged in a meaningful way.[88] Mies van der Rohe's six-volume set of drawings, which documents most of his archive housed in the Museum of Modern Art (MoMA), has noticeable omissions. The drawings of his plans for the Brussels Pavilion of 1934–35, for example, include only one with a swastika—and even then, one with a less prominent *Hakenkreuz*.[89] His original plans included considerably more drawings with the Nazi symbol, some of which have surfaced in other places. The Ludwig Mies van der Rohe Archive was created in 1968, shortly before his death, and contains some eighteen thousand drawings and prints. MoMA acquired the Mies archive in 1970–71, with the transfer overseen by his grandson, Dirk Lohan. The current supervisor of the Study Center for Architecture and Design at MoMA, Paul Galloway, explained that "many drawings were kept in Chicago; some because certain projects were still on-going, and some were kept by Dirk for (presumably) personal reasons."[90] In other words, MoMA officials may not have been responsible for omitting the drawings with swastikas, but rather the decision may have come from Mies or his grandson. Galloway added, "Only Dirk knows why certain early German drawings remained with him, but he kept a large range of materials."[91] Did Mies and Lohan withhold the drawings in an attempt to protect the architect's reputation? Galloway and others do not believe so, but the exclusion of such problematic images from the archive that went to MoMA raises questions. It was not until nearly two decades later—with Richard Pommer's pathbreaking essay of 1989—that Mies's relationship with the Nazi regime received anything approaching a critical treatment.[92]

The reasons for withholding compromising materials varied from case to case, and it is usually difficult to know the precise thinking behind the omissions. But omissions there were. Oskar Schlemmer's sketches and pastel renditions of figures with outstretched arms, works that he executed in preparation for his submission for the 1934 competition to decorate the Congress Hall of the German Museum, for example, rarely saw the light of day until the late 1970s. Art historian Karin V. Mauer's 1979 catalogue raisonné of the artist's work includes reproductions of many images from the Congress Hall project, and the notation "unpublished" appears in most cases (and when not, the only public showing seems to have been in Stuttgart in 1977).[93] In certain instances, scholars seemed to give the impression that the figure in question did not even live during the period of Nazi rule. This was the case with Ernst Ludwig Kirchner, as many early compendia of his letters and notebooks scarcely extended beyond 1933.[94] Granted, these sanitized treatments tended to be more common in the first three decades after the war, when myths about modernists largely still prevailed. But many remain protective about the legacies of the artists—first and foremost, family members. The daughter of painter Franz Radziwill, for example, required American art historian James van Dyke to translate his manuscript into German so that she could review what he wrote before she would grant permission for him to quote from the artist's private papers.

Many documents were destroyed, sometimes during the war and sometimes after 1945. The latter often occurred, it must be assumed, to conceal events that transpired during the Third Reich. Paul Ortwin Rave, who effectively directed the Berlin Nationalgalerie from 1937 to 1950, and who wrote the pioneering study on art in the Third Reich, left his papers to the Central Archive of the Berlin State Museums, but the finding aid for them includes a note that states, "Some of the volumes are missing, destroyed by P. O. Rave before he died."[95] Which diaries did Rave destroy, and why? Rolf Rave, the son of the museum director, maintains that the journals concerned Rave's postwar difficulties with Count Klaus von Baudissin, who had sued the city of Essen in 1949–50 for wrongful termination during the Third Reich. Baudissin won the case and received a lifetime pension from the city (he died in 1961). Rave's son asserts that a part of his father's diaries were seized and destroyed by the court, which had subpoenaed them as part of the proceedings.[96] The destruction of personal documents by a court would seem an unusual occurrence, but regardless they are not in the Rave *Nachlass*. Similar questions about the sanitizing of papers arise with the Nachlass of Nazi art dealer Karl Haberstock in Augsburg, although here there is no doubt that his widow, Magdalena Haberstock, culled his papers after his death in 1956—so much so that the Munich City Archive refused to accept them on the grounds that they were a corrupted source. They did not wish to dignify them with official status, and so Haberstock's papers went to Augsburg, where they were off-limits to scholars until 2000. Despite his widow's efforts, important documents remain, and more papers relating to Haberstock have turned up in recent years (in Gauting, for example, where materials from one of his lawyers turned up).[97] But one can only dream of what the unexpurgated archive would have yielded.

Some dealer archives remain but a dream, ostensibly destroyed by bombing during the war. Such was the case with the files of Alexander Vömel, who "Aryanized" Alfred Flechtheim's gallery in Düsseldorf in 1933 and had a very active career during the Third Reich, and with the Adolf Weinmüller auction house in Munich (that was taken over by Rudolf Neumeister in 1958), which laundered vast quantities of plundered Jewish art. Both Vömel and Weinmüller/Neumeister claimed that their records were destroyed by Allied bombs. An annotated business ledger for the years 1936 to 1945 did turn up in the basement of the Neumeister house in 2013—the important document, which lists many consigners and buyers, had been locked away in an old cupboard since the war—a development that also offers hope for future discoveries.[98] But the fact remains that many records simply disappeared with no explanation, as with Bernhard Böhmer's papers in Güstrow: "He left behind numerous paintings, but no business papers," remarked his biographer.[99] Of the four main dealers of "degenerate art"— of which Böhmer was one—only the files of Karl Buchholz are anywhere near extensive, and even then, significant gaps remain.[100]

Therefore, the corollary to the main argument of this book—that modernist artists continued to work during the years of the Third Reich—is that many artists and their accomplices wittingly or unwittingly misrepresented and concealed what actually transpired. They did this in various ways, of course. Albert Speer just out-and-out lied, starting with his declaration at Nuremberg that he had not known about Auschwitz and the Holocaust. He also provided the German Federal Archives a censored version of a journal that documented the activities of his GBI during the war—the so-called *Speerchronik*—although a complete version that detailed events such as the deportation of Berlin's Jews eventually surfaced and helped reveal Speer's efforts at obfuscation.[101] Others, like Leni Riefenstahl and Gustaf Gründgens, used the courts to quash negative information. But the public, as indicated above, played into their strategies. For many reasons, it was easier to embrace the notion of virtuous anti-Nazi modern cultural figures. The Germans wanted to move on in pursuit of the "Economic Miracle," the Americans had the Cold War as their foremost concern, and the Soviets were not known for a careful or objective historical understanding. For all involved, to use Charles Maier's phrase, the myths provided a "usable past."[102]

Most of the responsibility for the myths about modernists lies with those in the West. Developing myths about the "good" modernists fit in with the broader phenomenon of concealing the problematic pasts of those who could be useful during the Cold War: rocket scientists, intelligence assets, ministers in West German Chancellor Adenauer's cabinet, and so on.[103] There were numerous ways to foster and buttress these myths: creating the Fritz Höger Prize for outstanding brick architecture, an award that comes with €10,000, brought attention to the great achievements of the architect and promoted building with brick (the prize is sponsored by a brick-industry organization). Höger's Nazi Party membership and pro-Hitler views receive scant attention on the official website for the prize—although there is mention of Höger's "sympathy" for National Socialism and his unfulfilled desire to become a *Staatsarchitekt*. [104] In Munich, naming streets, squares, and parks after Richard Strauss and his operas (Richard-Strauss-Strasse, Rosenkavalierplatz, and the Arabella Park, for example) have brought positive associations with the composer. It is doubtful that many know about his tenure as the president of the Reich Chamber of Music. Even today, the European Union has named its top prize in architecture after Mies van der Rohe—an honor that seemingly has produced no discussion, let alone controversy.

Such myopia was most acute during the Cold War, when U.S. leaders used modernism as a weapon in the ideological fight against the Soviets and their allies. A few politicians—mostly conservative types—railed against modern art as "Communistic" and subversive. Congressman George Dondero, a Republican from Missouri, proclaimed "modernism to be, quite simply part of a worldwide conspiracy to weaken American resolve," and rumors even circulated that certain abstract works were encoded maps to U.S. missile fields and military installations. Most observers, however, took a very different view of modernism. As historian Frances Stonor Saunders has noted, "America's cultural mandarins detected a contrary virtue: for them, [modernism] spoke to a specifically anti-Communist ideology, the ideology of freedom, of free enterprise."[105] Abstraction was the opposite of Soviet Socialist Realism, and of Nazi art as well. Saunders's 1999 study documented how the CIA promoted modernism in the postwar period, organizing exhibitions, arranging purchases for American museums, and financing artists. More benign was John F. Kennedy inviting Walter Gropius to his presidential inauguration, sending the Bauhaus founder a Western Union telegram that read, "During our forthcoming administration we hope to seek a productive relationship with our writers, artists, composers, philosophers, scientists and head of cultural institutions. As a beginning, in recognition of their importance, may we extend you our most cordial invitation to attend the inaugural ceremonies in Washington, DC on January 19 and 20."[106] Efforts such as this, well intentioned and well informed or not, contributed to the myth that all modernists had fought "the good fight."

Financial considerations also played a role in the efforts to foster positive reputations among modernist cultural figures. In short, damaging the reputations of modernist cultural figures could prove costly to dealers, collectors, and others in the art world. To return to the phrase of historian Peter Gay, it was a case of the "outsider as insider." The formerly marginalized avant-garde figures had become members of a powerful establishment in the 1950s, perhaps even more than during the Weimar Republic, the period Gay had in mind when he coined the phrase. Many modernists and their supporters enjoyed great financial success after the war when the art market truly took off. Emil Nolde, for example, saw a tremendous rise in the price of his paintings and became in the words of art historian Christian Saehrendt, "Emil Nolde Superstar."[107] The market for Expressionist works steadily increased in the postwar decades. It was a long road to Kirchner's *Berlin Street Scene* realizing a price of $38.1 million, or Klimt's *Portrait of Adele Bloch-Bauer* selling for $135 million (both in 2006).[108] But for many years, modernist artworks were more quietly profitable, and there was no desire to rock the boat on the part of dealers, museum officials, and many others. When the prices of modernist art moved into the stratosphere, the marketing of modernism became more pronounced. In 2007, the town of Güstrow officially added the phrase "Barlachstadt" to its name—a symbol of the residents' pride in the artist, of course, but the honor also had financial ramifications. The name would bring tourists to the local Barlach museum and to visit the Barlach-related sights (for example, his "angel" in the cathedral) in what is a very charming and well-preserved historic town. In short, it has proved easier and more lucrative to celebrate the modernists.

Generational change has certainly been an important factor in the critical assessment of the modernist cultural figures. This became evident at different moments, such as the 1968ers questioning authority, and asking their elders what they did during the war. The answers they received were not always satisfactory. When Sibyl Moholy-Nagy talked about Mies van der Rohe's "desperate attempts to play up to National Socialism" at a 1964 symposium on modern architecture at Columbia University, questions soon found their way to the modernist hero. But Mies refused to engage the subject. He is quoted as saying, "It is not possible to move forward and look backwards"; and "he who lives in the past cannot advance."[109] Despite the desire to know more about what actually took place during the Third Reich, the inquiries of the '68ers were often deflected. Ernst Holzinger, who continued on as director of the Frankfurt Städel until his death in 1972—despite his complicity in expropriating Jewish property during the war—simply blocked all access to the museum's archives, as did his successor, Herbert Beck, who as late as 1998 refused to release the key files.[110] We are still learning about cultural figures who had a different relationship to National Socialism than had been initially assumed. A recent biography of Joseph Beuys, the great mythmaker who told of being saved in the Soviet Union during the war by Tatar tribesmen who covered him with animal fat and felt cloth, portrays the pathbreaking artist as "fairly reactionary and dangerous" and recounts how, after the war, he surrounded himself with "former and long-time Nazis."[111]

Considerable progress was made in this sphere in the 1980s and 1990s. Oftentimes, apparent defeats led to a more critical engagement with the Nazi past. For example, the controversy surrounding Kurt Waldheim's activities during the Third Reich provoked a more honest exploration of Austrians' behavior after the Anschluss. While the Austrian people twice elected Waldheim to the presidency, the resulting debate induced many to challenge the myth of the Moscow Declaration of 1943—in short, that Austrians were the first victims of Nazi aggression—and to examine their role in the persecution of European Jews (many of the "Eichmann-men" were Austrians). A more critical engagement with the Nazi past also emerged in other countries: for example, the French confronted the myth of the ubiquitous Resistance. It helped that scholars gradually gained access to archives. In part, this was a function of time. Data protection laws in Germany, for example, had long prevented scholars from shedding light on second-rank figures. The laws basically said that for individuals not of world historical importance the files should remain closed until thirty years after the person's death. Most cultural figures were not considered to be of "world historical importance"—as compared to a Hitler or a Himmler. Gaining access to the documents has been key to reassessing the cultural history of the Third Reich.

As mentioned at the outset, the purpose of this book has not been to sully the reputations of modernist cultural figures; rather, the goal has been to achieve a more nuanced understanding of these people who lived through very trying circumstances. It is indeed the "gray zone" of behavior that is so fascinating and so human. Joachim Fest noted, for example, about British historian Hugh Trevor-Roper, "At the end, Trevor-Roper said he had been toying with the idea of writing a biography of Speer, or perhaps a long biographical essay like the one on [Soviet spy Kim] Philby. For Speer, precisely because of his contradictions, is the key figure for what happened in 1933 and the following period. The Streichers or Sauckels pose no questions. The 'social criminal' or 'political desperado' types, as he called them, can be found in every society, including in Britain. It does not take long to get on top of them."[112] This book does not, and cannot, answer every question about those modernist figures who tried to find a place in Nazi Germany; but it hopefully contributes to our understanding of culture during the Third Reich, showing that modernists and modernism continued on, despite the often hostile environment.

NOTES

Because of the abundance of sources associated with the cultural history of Nazi Germany, the bibliography has been placed online and can be accessed at: http://www.claremontmckenna.edu/hist/Artists-Under-Hitler/bibliography.php.

The following abbreviations are used in the notes.

ALIU	Art Looting Investigation Unit
BAB	Bundesarchiv Berlin-Lichterfelde (German Federal Archives, Berlin)
BAK	Bundesarchiv Koblenz (German Federal Archives, Koblenz)
Bd.	Band (volume)
BDC	Berlin Document Center
BG	Berlinische Galerie
BSGS	Bayerische Staatsgemäldesammlungen (Bavarian State Painting Collections)
CDJC	Centre Documentation Juive Contemporaine, Paris (Documentation Center for Contemporary Jewry)
DBFU	Der Beauftragte des Führers für die Überwaching der gesamten geistigen und weltanschaulichen Schulung und Erziehung der Partei und gleichgeschalteten Verbände (The Representative of the Führer for the Supervision of the Entire Spiritual and Ideological Schooling of the Party and Affiliated Organizations)
DKA	Deutsches Kunstarchiv, Germanisches Nationalmuseum, Nuremberg (German Art Archive, German National Museum)
ERR	Einsatzstab Reichsleiter Rosenberg (Special Task Force of Reichsleiter Rosenberg)
GBI	Inspector General of Building, Berlin
GFM	Galerie Ferdinand Möller, Berlin
GRI	Getty Research Institute, Los Angeles
GSAPK	Geheimes Staatsarchiv Preussischer Kulturbesitz, Berlin (Secret State Archives of the Prussian Cultural Foundation)
LAB	Landesarchiv Berlin (Provincial Archive, Berlin)
NARA	National Archives and Records Administration, College Park
NL	Nachlass (papers)
NS	Nationalsozialistische (National Socialist)
NSDAP	Nationalsozialistische Deutsche Arbeiter Partei (National Socialist German Worker's Party)
RKK	Reichskulturkammer
SC	Special Collections
SMB-ZA	Staatlichen Museen Berlin—Zentralarchiv (Central Archives of the Berlin State Museums)

The exchange rate used throughout corresponds to the existing rate in 1939: RM 2.50 = $1.

PREFACE

1. See, among other works, Roger Griffin, *Modernism and Fascism: The Sense of Beginning Under Mussolini and Hitler* (Houndsmills: Palgrave Macmillan, 2007); Peter Gay,

Modernism: The Lure of Heresy from Baudelaire to Beckett and Beyond (New York: Norton, 2008); Michael Levenson, *The Cambridge Companion to Literary Modernism* (Cambridge: Cambridge University Press, 1999); Peter Nichols, *Modernism: A Literary Guide,* 2d ed. (London: Palgrave Macmillan, 2009); Christopher Wik, ed., *Modernism: Designing a New World, 1914–1939* (London: V and A Publishing, 2006); Frank Kermode, *The Sense of an Ending: Studies in the Theory of Fiction* (New York: Oxford University Press, 2000 [1967]); and Raymond Williams, *The Politics of Modernism: Against the New Conformists* (London: Verso, 1989). See also The Modernism Lab at Yale University at http://modernism.research .yale.edu/wiki/index.php/Main_Page (accessed 1 June 2010).

INTRODUCTION

1. DKA, NL Arnold/Gutbier, I, B-740, Möller to Gutbier (26 February 1945); and Gutbier to Möller (9 March 1945).

2. Reginald Isaacs, *Walter Gropius. Der Mensch und sein Werk II* (Berlin: Gebr. Mann, 1984), 637.

3. Golo Mann, "Der Pädagoge als Politiker: Kurt Hahn," in *Zwölf Versuche* (Frankfurt: S. Fischer, 1973), 61–104.

4. Herbert Bayer, *The Bulletin of the Museum of Modern Art: Bauhaus Exhibition 6/5* (1938), 2–23; Nicholas Fox Weber, *Patron Saints: Five Rebels Who Opened America to a New Art, 1928–1943* (New York: Alfred Knopf, 1992), 118–20; and Karen Koehler, "The Bauhaus, 1919–1928: Gropius in Exile and the Museum of Modern Art, N.Y., 1938," in *Art, Culture, and Media Under the Third Reich,* ed. Richard Etlin (Chicago: University of Chicago Press, 2002), 287–315.

5. Elaine Hochman, *Architects of Fortune: Mies van der Rohe and the Third Reich* (New York: Weidenfeld and Nicolson, 1989), 56.

6. Ibid., 53. Philip Johnson, quoted in Charles Jenks, *Modern Movements in Architecture* (Garden City: Doubleday, 1973), 40. To take another example, Ernst Ludwig Kirchner's first biographer, Will Grohmann, called him "an idealist as well as egocentric," with "dictatorial fantasies about artistic and human problems" Will Grohmann, *E. L. Kirchner* (New York: Arts Inc., 1961), 7.

7. Peter Gay, *Weimar Culture: The Outsider as Insider* (New York: Harper and Row, 1968).

8. Bernhard Fulda and Aya Soika, "Emil Nolde and the National Socialist Dictatorship," in *Degenerate Art: The Attack on Modern Art in Nazi Germany 1937,* ed. Olaf Peters (Munich: Prestel, 2014), 189.

9. Albert Speer, *Erinnerungen* (Berlin: Ullstein 1969), 40; and Ernst Klee, *Das Kulturlexikon zum Dritten Reich. Wer war was vor und nach 1945* (Frankfurt: S. Fischer, 2007), 437.

10. For Weidemann helping acquire *Begging Woman (Die Bettlerin),* see Getty Research Institute (GRI), Special Collections (SC), Alois Schardt Papers, box 1, file 7, Weidemann to Schardt (14 March 1949); Peter Paret, *An Artist Against the Third Reich: Ernst Barlach, 1933–1938* (Cambridge: Cambridge University Press, 2003), 172; Heinrich Hoffmann, *Hitler wie ich ihn sah* (Munich: Herbig, 1974), 146; and the entry for 29 August 1924 in Joseph Goebbels, *Die Tagebücher von Joseph Goebbels. Sämtliche Fragmente,* ed. Elke Fröhlich (Munich: K. G. Sauer, 1987), I, I, 78.

11. For the purge of Freiherr von König's *Good Samaritan (Barmherziger Samariter),* see Franz Roh, *"Entartete" Kunst. Kunstbarbarei im Dritten Reich* (Hannover: Fackelträger, 1962), 133; and BAB, R55/20748, Hofmann to Biebrach (8 August 1935), and Krape to Biebrach (13 September 1935). See also Alexandra Bechter, *Leo von König, 1871–1944* (Darmstadt: WP, 2001).

12. For the Ribbentrops and Dix, see Arno Breker, *Im Strahlungsfeld der Ereignisse. Leben und Wirken eines Künstlers* (Preußisch Oldendorf: K. W. Schütz, 1972), 134; H. W. Koch, *In the Name of the Volk: Political Justice in Hitler's Germany* (London: Tauris, 1997), 66; Brigitte Hamann, *Winifred Wagner: A Life at the Heart of Hitler's Bayreuth* (Orlando: Harcourt, 2006), 270; Jonathan Petropoulos, *Art as Politics in the Third Reich* (Chapel Hill: University of North Carolina Press, 1996), 201–12; and Jost Hermand, *Kultur in finsteren Zeiten. Nazifaschismus, Innere Emigration, Exil* (Cologne: Böhlau, 2010), 195.

13. Ulrich Gerster, "Der Schützling des Stellvertreters. Georg Schrimpf und sein Gemälde 'Mädchen vor dem Spiegel,'" in *Das Verfemte Meisterwerk. Schicksalswege Moderner Kunst im "Dritten Reich"* ed. Uwe Fleckner (Berlin: Akademie Verlag, 2009), 348; and more generally, Olaf Peters, *Neue Sachlichkeit und Nationalsozialismus. Affirmation und Kritik 1931–1947* (Berlin: Reimer, 1998).

14. Marla Stone, "The State as Patron: Making Official Culture in Fascist Italy," in *Fascist Visions: Art and Ideology in France and Italy,* ed. Matthew Affron and Mark Antliff (Princeton: Princeton University Press, 1997), 208, 212–13. See also Pierre Bourdieu, *Distinction: A Social Critique of the Judgement of Taste* (Cambridge: Harvard University Press, 1984).

15. Emilio Gentile, "The Myth of National Regeneration," in *Fascist Visions: Art and Ideology in France and Italy,* ed. Matthew Affron and Mark Antliff (Princeton: Princeton University Press, 1997), 27, 31.

16. Dr. v. L., "Streit um 'moderne Kunst,' in Italien. Gegen jüdische Einflüsse. Marinetti verteidigt den Futurismus," *Niedersächsische Tageszeitung* (8 December 1938), among other similar articles, in BAB, NS 15/140; and Maike Steinkamp, *Unerwünschte Erbe. Die Rezeption 'entarteter' Kunst in Kunstkritik, Ausstellungen und Museen der SBZ und Frühen DDR* (Berlin: Akademie Verlag, 2008), 56.

17. Ruth Ben-Ghiat, *Fascist Modernities: Italy, 1922–1945* (Berkeley: University of California Press, 2001), 104.

18. George Steiner, *In Bluebeard's Castle. Some Notes Towards the Redefinition of Culture* (New Haven: Yale University Press, 1971), 30.

19. Harold Rosenberg, "The Art Galleries: The Politics of Art," *New Yorker* (25 May 1963); and J. P. Stern, *Hitler: The Führer and the People* (Berkeley: University of California Press, 1988 [1975]), 66–97.

20. Richard Wolin, *The Seduction of Unreason: The Intellectual Romance with Fascism from Nietzsche to Postmodernism* (Princeton: Princeton University Press, 2004).

21. For the argument that Expressionism helped "prepare the way" to National Socialism, see Paul Fechter, "Der Zusammenbruch des Kunstbetriebes," *Deutsche Rundschau* (February 1933), 11. For more expansive discussions of modernism and fascism, see Peter Gay, *Modernism: The Lure of Heresy from Baudelaire to Beckett and Beyond* (New York: Norton, 2008); Mark Antliff, "Fascism, Modernism, and Modernity," *Art Bulletin* 84/1 (March 2002), 148–69; and Roger Griffin, *Modernism and Fascism: The Sense of Beginning Under Mussolini and Hitler* (Houndsmills: Palgrave Macmillan, 2007).

22. Fritz Lang, "Autobiography," in *Fritz Lang,* ed. Lotte Eisner (London: Secker and Warburg, 1976), 14; Larissa Schütze, *Fritz Lang im Exil: Filmkunst im Schatten der Politik* (Munich: Meidenbauer, 2006), 21–23; and Willi Winkler, "Ein Schlafwandler bei Goebbels," *Der Spiegel* 48 (26 November 1990), 236–43.

23. Nigel Hamilton, *The Brothers Mann* (New Haven: Yale University Press, 1979), 268. Thomas Mann's wife, Katia Mann (born Pringsheim), however, hailed from a secular Jewish family.

24. Peukert, quoted in Michael Kater, "The Impact of American Popular Culture on German Youth," in *The Arts in Nazi Germany: Continuity, Conformity, Change,* ed. Jonathan

Huener and Francis Nicosia (New York: Berghahn, 2006), 33. See also Jeffrey Herf, *Reactionary Modernism: Technology, Culture and Politics in the Weimar Republic and the Third Reich* (Cambridge: Harvard University Press, 1984); Mark Roseman, *Hitler and the Modernization of German Society* (London: Hodder Arnold, 2007); and Zygmunt Bauman, *Modernity and the Holocaust* (Cambridge: Polity Press, 1989).

25. Jeremy Aynsley, *Graphic Design in Germany, 1890–1945* (Berkeley: University of California Press, 2000); and John Heskett, "Modernism and Archaism in Design in the Third Reich," in *The Nazification of Art: Art, Design, Music, Architecture & Film in the Third Reich,* ed. Brandon Taylor and Wilfried van der Will (Winchester: Winchester Press, 1990), 110–27.

26. Patrick Rössler, *Die neue Linie, 1929–1943. Das Bauhaus am Kiosk* (Bielefeld: Kerber, 2007).

27. Nicholas Fox Weber, "Deadly Style: Bauhaus's Nazi Connection," *New York Times* (23 December 2009), Arts, 23–24.

28. Ibid.; and Debórah Dwork and Robert Jan van Pelt, *Auschwitz* (New York: Norton, 1996), 263.

29. Hildegard Brenner, *Ende einer bürgerlichen Kunst-Institution: die politische Formierung der Preussischen Akademie der Künste ab 1933* (Stuttgart: DVA, 1972), 124. Kirchner wrote a similar letter when being forced out of the Preussische Akademie in July 1937. See Kirchner to Dr. Schumann (12 July 1937), in Joseph Wulf, *Die Bildenden Künste im Dritten Reich* (Gütersloh: Sigbert Mohn, 1963), 309.

30. Regarding Belling, see Max Pechstein to George Grosz (28 March 1933), quoted in Bernhard Fulda and Aya Soika, *Max Pechstein. The Rise and Fall of Expressionism* (Berlin: DeGruyter, 2012), 305.

31. Bruno Paul to the President of the Preussische Akademie (11 July 1937), in Brenner, *Ende einer bürgerlichen Kunst-Institution,* 144–45.

32. Max Pechstein, *Erinnerungen* (Wiesbaden: Limes, 1960), 116–17; and Andreas Hüneke, ed., *Oskar Schlemmer. Idealist der Form. Briefe, Tagebücher, Schriften, 1912–1943* (Leipzig: Reclam-Verlag, 1990), 321.

33. Fox Weber, "Deadly Style," 23.

PART I. "THE SUMMER OF ART" AND BEYOND

1. Hildegard Brenner, "Art in the Political Power Struggle of 1933 and 1934," in *Republic to Reich: The Making of the Nazi Revolution,* ed. Hajo Holborn (New York: Vintage Books, 1972), 402.

2. Peter Paret, *Artist Against the Third Reich: Ernst Barlach, 1933–1938* (Cambridge: Cambridge University Press, 2003), 66.

3. Ibid., 64.

4. Brenner, "Art in the Political Power Struggle," 403, 429; and Elaine Hochman, *Architects of Fortune: Mies van der Rohe and the Third Reich* (New York: Weidenfeld and Nicolson, 1989), 166.

5. Paul Ortwin Rave, *Kunstdiktatur im Dritten Reich* (Berlin: Gebr. Mann, 1949), 42; and Brenner, "Art in the Political Power Struggle," 404.

CHAPTER 1. THE FIGHT OVER MODERNISM

1. SMB-ZA, Paul Ortwin Rave NL, Nr. 95, Ernst Holzinger to Eberhard Hanfstaengl (25 July 1937).

2. Johnson reportedly agreed to a sum of RM 30,000 ($12,000), but paid Schlem-

mer only RM 3,000 ($1,200). Karin V. Maur, *Oskar Schlemmer* (New York: Spencer Samuels, 1969), 31; and Karin V. Maur, *Oskar Schlemmer. Oeuvrekatalog der Gemälde, Aquarelle, Pastelle, und Plastiken* (Munich: Prestel, 1979), 58. Andreas Huyssen, "Oskar Schlemmer Bauhaus Stairway. 1932," in *Bauhaus 1919–1933*, ed. Barry Bergdoll and Leah Dickerman (New York: Museum of Modern Art, 2009), 318–21; Karoline Hille, "Beispiel Thüringen: Die Machtergreifung auf der Probebühne, 1930," in *1933—Wege zur Diktatur*, ed. Staatliche Kunsthalle Berlin (Berlin: Staatliche Kunsthalle Berlin, 1985), 207; Wulf Herzogenrath, "Fanal einer neuen Zeit. Die Zerstörung von Oskar Schlemmers 'Bauhaus-Fresken' im Jahr 1930," in *Das Verfemte Meisterwerk. Schicksalswege Moderner Kunst im "Dritten Reich,"* ed. Uwe Fleckner (Berlin: Akademie Verlag, 2009), 245–58.

3. Hildegard Brenner, *Die Kunstpolitik des Nationalsozialismus* (Reinbek: Rowholt, 1963), 169; and Christoph Zuschlag, *"Entartete Kunst": Ausstellungsstrategien im Nazi-Deutschland* (Worms: Wernersche Verlagsgesellschaft, 1995), 35.

4. Elaine Hochman, *Architects of Fortune: Mies van der Rohe and the Third Reich* (New York: Weidenfeld and Nicolson, 1989), 78. See also GRI, SC, Wilhelm Arntz Papers, box 28, file 86, Karl Haberstock lecture, "Der Bildersturm 1937" (n.d.).

5. Berthold Hinz, *Art in the Third Reich* (New York: Random House, 1979), 45.

6. Maike Steinkamp, *Unerwünschte Erbe: Die Rezeption 'entarteter' Kunst in Kunstkritik, Ausstellungen und Museen der SBZ und Frühen DDR* (Berlin: Akademie Verlag, 2008), 53; and Hinz, *Art in the Third Reich*, 26.

7. Hildegard Brenner, "Art in the Political Power Struggle of 1933 and 1934," in *Republic to Reich: The Making of the Nazi Revolution*, ed. Hajo Holborn (New York: Vintage Books, 1972), 396.

8. Joan Clinefelter, *Artists for the Reich. Culture and Race from Weimar to Nazi Germany* (Oxford: Berg, 2005), 7–24; Jürgen Gimmel, *Die politische Organisation kulturellen Ressentiments: Der Kampfbund für deutsche Kultur und das bildungsbürgerliche Unbehagen an der Moderne* (Münster: LIT, 2001), 40–43; and Bettina Feistel-Rohmeder, *Im Terror des Kunstbolschewismus. Urkundensammlung des 'Deutschen Kunstberichtes' aus den Jahren 1927–33* (Karlsruhe: C. F. Müller, 1938).

9. DBFU stands for Der Beauftragte des Führers für die Überwaching der gesamten geistigen und weltanschaulichen Schulung und Erziehung der Partei und gleichgeschalteten Verbände, or The Representative of the Führer for the Supervision of the Entire Spiritual and Ideological Schooling of the Party and Affiliated Organizations.

10. Brenner, "Art in the Political Power Struggle," 398.

11. Erik Levi, *Music in the Third Reich* (New York: St. Martin's Press, 1994), 175.

12. Michael Meyer, "A Musical Façade for the Third Reich," in *"Degenerate Art": The Fate of the Avant-Garde in Nazi Germany*, ed. Stephanie Barron (Los Angeles: Los Angeles County Museum of Art, 1991), 173. More generally, see Hildegard Brenner, *Ende einer bürgerlichen Kunst-Institution: die politische Formierung der Preussischen Akademie der Künste ab 1933* (Stuttgart: DVA, 1972); Charles Rosen, *Arnold Schoenberg* (Chicago: University of Chicago Press, 1996); and Joseph Auner and Jennifer Shaw, eds., *The Cambridge Companion to Schoenberg* (Cambridge: Cambridge University Press, 2010).

13. See Otto Dix's Reich Chamber of Culture card at http://forschung.gnm.de/down load/GNM_DKA.pdf. Gropius's identity card is reproduced in Walter Scheiffele, "Das neue Bauen unter dem Faschismus," in *Kunst Hochschule Faschismus*, ed. Hochschule der Künste Berlin (Berlin: Elefanten Press, 1984), 229.

14. Alan Steinweis, *Art, Ideology, and Economics in Nazi Germany: The Reich Chambers of Music, Theater and the Visual Arts* (Chapel Hill: University of North Carolina Press, 1993), 108–14.

15. The Jüdischer Kulturbund counted nearly forty thousand members in Berlin

alone, with forty to fifty events per week. Meyer, "Musical Façade," 178. More generally, Henryk Broder and Eike Geisel, *Premiere und Pogrom. Der jüdische Kulturbund 1933–1941* (Berlin: Siedler, 1992); and Rebecca Rovit, "Jewish Theatre: Repertory and Censorship in the Jüdischer Kulturbund, Berlin," in *Theatre Under the Nazis,* ed. John London (Manchester: Manchester University Press, 2000), 187–221.

16. Hermann Simon, ed., *Was vom Leben übrig bleibt, sind Bilder und Geschichten. Max Liebermann zum 150. Geburtstag. Rekonstruktion der Gedächtnisausstellung des Berliner jüdischen Museums von 1936* (Berlin: Heenemann, 1997).

17. Furtwängler to Goebbels (dated 12 April 1933), reproduced in Jonathan Huener and Francis Nicosia, eds., *The Arts in Nazi Germany: Continuity, Conformity, Change* (New York: Berghahn, 2006), 165–66; and Hochman, *Architects of Fortune,* 105.

18. Frank Schulze, *Mies van der Rohe: Critical Essays* (Cambridge: MIT Press, 1989), 186. Hochman, *Architects of Fortune,* 120–24. See also Raner Haubrich, "Wie das Bauhaus wirklich endete," *Die Welt* (2 October 2009).

19. Hochman, *Architects of Fortune,* 122.

CHAPTER 2. OTTO ANDREAS SCHREIBER AND THE PRO-EXPRESSIONIST STUDENTS

1. Michael Kater, "Der NS-Studentendbund von 1926 bis 1928: Randgruppe zwischen Hitler und Strasser," *Vierteljahreshefte für Zeitgeschichte* 22 (1974), 148–90; and Geoffrey Giles, *Students and National Socialism in Germany* (Princeton: Princeton University Press, 1985), 28.

2. Elaine Hochman, *Architects of Fortune: Mies van der Rohe and the Third Reich* (New York: Weidenfeld and Nicolson, 1989), 81. See also, for example, the charge that Hans Weidemann was "extraordinarily presumptuous and arrogant," in BAB, VBS 1/1130014796, Ried and Schieder, "Besuchs-Vermerk" (24 December 1937).

3. Fritz Hippler, *Die Verstrickung* (Düsseldorf: Mehr Wissen, 1981).

4. Hildegard Brenner, "Art in the Political Power Struggle of 1933 and 1934," in *Republic to Reich: The Making of the Nazi Revolution,* ed. Hajo Holborn (New York: Vintage Books, 1972), 401, 429.

5. David Childs, "Fritz Hippler: Nazi Filmmaker Under Joseph Goebbels," *The Independent* (18 October 2002), at http://www.independent.co.uk/news/obituaries/fritz-hippler-614326.html (accessed 28 July 2011).

6. Eric Rentschler, *The Ministry of Illusion: Nazi Cinema and Its Afterlife* (Cambridge: Harvard University Press, 1996), 149.

7. Ibid., 159–60, 266.

8. David Culbert, "The Impact of Anti-Semitic Film Propaganda on German Audiences," in *Art, Culture, and Media Under the Third Reich,* ed. Richard Etlin (Chicago: University of Chicago Press, 2002), 156.

9. Dieter Scholz, "Otto Andreas Schreiber, die *Kunst der Nation* und die Fabrikausstellungen," in *Überbrückt: Ästhetische Moderne und Nationalsozialismus. Kunsthistoriker und Künstler, 1925–1937,* ed. Eugen Blume and Dieter Scholz (Cologne: Walther König, 1999), 93. See also Schreiber's file for the Reich Chamber for the Visual Arts in BAB, R 55/24831.

10. Peter Paret, *An Artist Against the Third Reich: Ernst Barlach, 1933–1938* (Cambridge: Cambridge University Press, 2003), 63; Brenner, "Art in the Political Power Struggle," 400–401; and SMB-ZA, Rave NL, Nr. 97, Schreiber to Otto Pankok (10 March 1933). See also Andreas Hüneke, "Der Versuch der Ehrenrettung des Expressionismus als 'deutsche Kunst' 1933," in *Zwischen Anpassung und Widerstand. Kunst in Deutschland, 1933–1945,* ed. Akademie der Künste, Berlin (East) (Berlin: Akademie der Künste, 1978).

11. SMB-ZA, Rave NL, Nr. 97, Schreiber to Otto Pankok (10 March 1933); and SMB-ZA, Rave NL, Nr. 97, Pankok to Rave (12 November 1949).

12. "Weidemann—derart belastet," *Der Spiegel* 51 (14 December 1970), 88–89; and BAB, VBS 1/1130014796 (former-BDC file of Hans Weidemann), Weidemann to NSDAP Reichsleitung (21 September 1931). For more on Weidemann, see James van Dyke, "Walter Kaesbach und der Pyrrhussieg des Expressionismus," in *Wounded Time. Avantgarde zwischen Euphorie und Depression,* ed. Veit Stoers (Mönchengladbach: Städtisches Museum, 2000), 39–52; BAB, VBS 286, 6400048615, Weidemann, "Lebenslauf," (n.d. [1933]).

13. Brenner, "Art in the Political Power Struggle," 404; and Barbara Miller Lane, *Architecture and Politics in Germany, 1918–1945* (Cambridge: Harvard University Press, 1985 [1968]), 176–77.

14. GRI, SC, Schardt Papers, box 1, file 7, Weidemann to Schardt (14 March 1949).

15. Frederic Spotts, *Hitler and the Power of Aesthetics* (Woodstock: Overlook, 2003 [2002]), 153; and Christian Fuhrmeister, "Adolf Ziegler (1892–1959), nationalsozialistischer Künstler und Funktionär," in *200 Jahre Akademie der Künste München,* ed. Nikolaus Gerhart, Walter Grasskamp, and Florian Matzner (Munich: Hirmer, 2008), 88–95.

16. Weidemann also sought a post in the SD (Sicherheitsdienst, or Security Service), but that did not come about. BAB, VBS 286, 6400048615 (former-BDC file of Hans Weidemann), Weidemann to SS-Gruppenführer Zech (3 February 1938).

17. BAB, VBS 286, 6400048615 (former-BDC file of Hans Weidemann), Gunter d'Alquen to SS-Führungshauptamt (19 February 1943). See also Volker Dahm, "Künstler als Funktionäre. Das Propaganda-Ministerium und die Reichskulturkammer," in *Hitlers Künstler. Die Kultur im Dienst des Nationalsozialismus,* ed. Hans Sarkowicz (Frankfurt: Insel, 2004), 101.

18. BAB, VBS 286, 6400048615 (former-BDC file of Hans Weidemann), Gunter d'Alquen to SS-Führungshauptamt (19 February 1943); GRI, SC, Schardt Papers, box 1, file 7, Weidemann to Schardt (14 March 1949) and Schardt to Weidemann (10 June 1949); and Ernst Klee, *Das Kulturlexikon zum Dritten Reich. Wer war was vor und nach 1945* (Frankfurt: S. Fischer, 2007), 586.

19. Paret, *Artist Against the Third Reich,* 63–65; James van Dyke, *Franz Radziwill and the Contradictions of German Art History, 1919–45* (Ann Arbor: University of Michigan Press, 2010), 46, 56; and Eric Michaud, *The Cult of Art in Nazi Germany* (Stanford: Stanford University Press, 2004 [1996]).

20. Paret, *Artist Against the Third Reich,* 66.

21. BG, GFM C, II 1, 185–1, 209, 0235, Möller to Baudissin (25 August 1936).

22. Ibid.

23. BG, GFM-F I, 1–61: Mappe 66 Film 5317, 0787, Möller to Annelies Ribbentrop (9 November 1938).

24. Alfred Rosenberg, "Revolution in der bildenden Kunst [Teil I]," *Völkischer Beobachter* 187 (6 July 1933), and Alfred Rosenberg, "Revolutionäre an sich!" *Völkischer Beobachter* 195 (14 July 1933).

25. Alfred Rosenberg, "Revolution in der bildenden Kunst [Teil II]," *Völkischer Beobachter* 188 (7 July 1933). See also Ernst Piper, *Alfred Rosenberg. Hitlers Chefideologe* (Munich: Blessing, 2005), 372; and Miller Lane, *Architecture and Politics,* 152.

26. Brenner, "Art in the Political Power Struggle," 406; Hochman, *Architects of Fortune,* 167; and van Dyke, *Franz Radziwill,* 122–27, 139–46.

27. Brenner, "Art in the Political Power Struggle," 406; and more generally, Kirsten Baumann, *Wortgefechte: völkische und nationalsozialistische Kunstkritik, 1927–1939* (Weimar: VDG, 2002).

28. Miller Lane, *Architecture and Politics,* 178; and Brenner, "Art in the Political Power Struggle," 406.

29. Brenner, "Art in the Political Power Struggle," 406.

30. Otto Friedrich, *Before the Deluge: A Portrait of Berlin in the 1920s* (New York: HarperPerennial, 1995 [1972]), 3.

31. Hochman, *Architects of Fortune,* 168; Hildegard Brenner, *Die Kunstpolitik des Nationalsozialismus* (Reinbek: Rowholt, 1963), 71.

32. Brenner, "Art in the Political Power Struggle," 411.

33. Richard Grunberger, *The Twelve-Year Reich: A Social History of Nazi Germany, 1933–1945* (New York: Holt, Rinehart, and Winston, 1971), 423; Alfred Hentzen, exhibition review, "Das Bildnis in der Plastik" *Kunst der Nation* 2/23 (1 December 1934); Stefan Germer, "Kunst der Nation. Zu einem Versuch, die Avantgarde zu nationalisieren," in *Kunst auf Befehl? Dreiunddreissig bis Fünfundvierzig,* ed. Bazon Brock and Achim Preiss (Munich: Klinkhardt and Biermann, 1990), 21–58; Baumann, *Wortgefechte,* 152–79, 281–87; and Joan Clinefelter, *Artists for the Reich: Culture and Race from Weimar to Nazi Germany* (Oxford: Berg, 2005), 72.

34. Brenner, "Art in the Political Power Struggle," 410.

35. W. von Schramm, "Van Gogh als niederdeutsches Problem," *Kunst der Nation* 2/5 (March 1934), 3, cited in Germer, "Kunst der Nation," 21.

36. BG, GFM, MF, C, II-1, 551-1, 555 (Mappe 10), 0475, Schreiber to Jansen (29 January 1934) and BAB, NS 8/171, doc. 140, Rosenberg to Goebbels (9 March 1936), and docs. 163–64, Rosenberg to Goebbels (19 February 1936). See also Scholz, "Schreiber," 92–94; Eberhard Roters, *Galerie Ferdinand Möller. Die Geschichte einer Galerie für moderne Kunst in Deutschland, 1917–1956* (Berlin: Gebr. Mann, 1984); and Ferdinand-Möller Stiftung, *Ferdinand-Möller Stiftung. 15 Jahre* (Berlin: Ferdinand-Möller Stiftung, 2010).

37. Otto Andreas Schreiber, "Haben wir jungen Maler eine neues Kunstideal?," *Kunst der Nation* 1 (1 November 1933), 6, quoted in Scholz, "Schreiber," 94–95.

38. Otto Andreas Schreiber, "Maler, Artisten, Dilettanten. Nach der Eröffnung der Reichskulturkammer," *Kunst der Nation* 1 (1 December 1933), 3, quoted in Scholz, "Schreiber," 95.

39. Otto Andreas Schreiber, "Worin zeigt sich das deutsche Wesen in der deutschen Kunst?" *Der Betrieb* 4 (15 January 1934), quoted in Scholz, "Schreiber," 97. David Dennis, *Inhumanities: Nazi Interpretations of Western Culture* (Cambridge: Cambridge University Press, 2012), 230.

40. Paret, *Artist Against the Third Reich,* 65–66; and Otto Andreas Schreiber, "Fortsetzung des Expressionismus," *Kunst der Nation* 2/7 (1 April 1934), 1.

41. More generally, see James van Dyke, "Über die Beziehungen zwischen Kunst, Propaganda und Kitsch in Deutschland 1933 bis 1945," in *Kunst und Propaganda im Streit der Nationen 1930–1945,* ed. Hans-Jörg Czech and Nikola Doll (Dresden: Sandstein, 2007), 250–57.

42. Brenner, "Art in the Political Power Struggle," 411; Scholz, "Schreiber," 92; and Otto Andreas Schreiber, *Der Arbeiter und die bildenden Kunst. System und Aufgabe der Kunstausstellungen in den Betrieben (Werkausstellungen, Fabrikausstellungen)* (Berlin: NS-Gemeinschaft "Kraft durch Freude," 1938).

43. Berliner Staatlichen Museen-Zentralarchiv (hereafter BSM-ZA), Rave NL, Nr. 97, Schreiber to Rave (20 September 1949).

44. Scholz, "Schreiber," 101–4; Ekkehard Böhm, ed., *Kulturtagebuch. 1900 bis heute* (Braunschweig: G. Westermann, 1984), 349; Hochman, *Architects of Fortune,* 173. Brenner, "Art in the Political Power Struggle," 410–11.

45. Otto Andreas Schreiber, "Die Fabrikausstellungen der dreissiger Jahre," in *Die dreissiger Jahre: Schauplatz Deutschland* (Munich: Haus der Kunst, 1977), 96; and BSM-ZA, Rave NL, Nr. 97, Schreiber to Rave (20 September 1949).

46. BG, GFM, MF 5316, 0227, Möller to Ada Nolde (10 February 1936); and BSM-ZA, Rave NL, Nr. 97, Schreiber to Rave (20 September 1949).

47. BSM-ZA, Rave NL, Nr. 97, Schreiber to Rave (20 September 1949).

48. Ibid.

49. Peter Adam, *Art of the Third Reich* (New York: Harry Abrams, 1992), 57; and Baumann, *Wortgefechte,* 178.

50. The exhibition was opened at the Hamburger Kunstverein on 24 February 1934 under the title *Luft- und Flugmalerei;* and at the Neue Galerie in Vienna in February–March 1935 with the title *Italienische Futuristische Luft-und Flugmalerei.* Ruggero Vasari, *Flugmalerei. Moderne Kunst und Reaktion* (Leipzig: Max Möhring, 1935); and more generally, Franco Passoni, *Aeropittura Futurista* (Milan: Maggio-Giugno, 1970), and Stefano De Rosa, *Aeropittura 1930–1944. Settanta opere da collezioni private* (Florence: Maschietto and Musolino, 1996).

51. Brenner, "Art in the Political Power Struggle," 414. See the *Frankfurter Zeitung* (7 April 1934).

52. Brenner, "Art in the Political Power Struggle," 414. See *Die Weltkunst* (8 April 1934).

53. Brenner, "Art in the Political Power Struggle," 414; and G. H. Theunissen, *Kunst der Nation* (15 April 1934).

54. Brenner, "Art in the Political Power Struggle," 415. Otto Andreas Schreiber, "Fortsetzung des Expressionismus," *Kunst der Nation* 2/7 (1 April 1934), 1.

55. Robert Scholz, "Für und gegen den Futurismus," *Völkischer Beobachter* 87 (28 March 1934). See also his follow-up article, "Futuristische Flugmalerei," *Völkischer Beobachter* 94 (4 April 1934).

56. Robert Scholz, "Zwei Ausstellungen," *Steglitzer Anzeiger* 20 (24 January 1933); and "Neuordnung im Kronprinzenpalais," *Steglitzer Anzeiger* 40 (15 February 1933). See Alois Schardt's description of Scholz as pro-modernist in GRI, SC, Schardt Papers, box 8, file 1, Schardt, "Art Under the Nazis," and more generally, SMB-ZA, Neue Abteilung der Nationalgalerie, V/059: clipping files for Robert Scholz, with most articles appearing in the *Völkischer Beobachter* from 1934 to 1937; Amtsgericht Munich, denazification file of Robert Scholz, Fritz Höger, "Eidesstattliche Erklärung" (22 July 1947); and Andreas Hüneke, "On the Trail of Missing Masterpieces," in *"Degenerate Art": The Fate of the Avant-Garde in Nazi Germany,* ed. Stephanie Barron (Los Angeles: Los Angeles County Museum of Art, 1991), 128.

57. James Plaut, "Detailed Interrogation Report No. 3: Robert Scholz" (Washington, D.C.: OSS, ALIU, 15 August 1945); Jonathan Petropoulos, *The Faustian Bargain: The Art World in Nazi Germany* (New York: Oxford University Press, 2000), 113–53; Andreas Hüneke, *Der Fall Robert Scholz: Kunstberichte unterm Hakenkreuz* (Cologne: AICA, 2001); and Armin Zweite, "Franz Hofmann und die Städtische Galerie, 1937," in *Die "Kunststadt" München 1937. Nationalsozialismus und "Entartete Kunst,"* ed. Peter-Klaus Schuster (Munich: Prestel, 1987), 282–85.

58. Brenner, "Art in the Political Power Struggle," 417. See CDJC, CXLII, Rosenberg to Goebbels (30 August 1934).

59. Dennis, *Inhumanities,* 245–48; and GRI, SC, Schardt Papers, box 1, file 7, Weidemann to Schardt (14 March 1949); note that Weidemann said he drafted the telegram for Munch's sixtieth birthday, but he meant seventieth in December 1933. Dan van der Vat, *The Good Nazi: The Life and Lies of Albert Speer* (Boston: Houghton Mifflin, 1997), 50.

60. Joseph Goebbels, *Die Tagebücher von Joseph Goebbels. Sämtliche Fragmente,* ed. Elke Fröhlich (Munich: K. G. Sauer, 1987), I, 2/III, 369 (8 February 1934); Hochman, *Architects of Fortune,* 204.

61. Hochman, *Architects of Fortune,* 205.

62. BAB, NS 8/171, docs. 209–14, Goebbels to Rosenberg (25 September 1934).

63. Albert Speer, *Erinnerungen* (Berlin: Ullstein, 1969), 41.

CHAPTER 3. THE CONTINUATION OF MODERNISM IN NAZI GERMANY

1. Hildegard Brenner, "Art in the Political Power Struggle of 1933 and 1934," in *Republic to Reich: The Making of the Nazi Revolution*, ed. Hajo Holborn (New York: Vintage Books, 1972), 419. See Goebbels's "Rede vor den Theaterleitern" (8 May 1933), in *Dokumente der Deutschen Politik* I (Berlin: Deutsche Hochschule für Politik, 1939), 321.

2. For Goebbels's acquiring Franz von Stuck, *Portrait of Mary*, see BAB, R 55/21013, doc. 163, bill from Bayerische Hofkunsthandlung Georg Stuffler (19 May 1938).

3. For Goebbels patronizing Fritz Klimsch, which involved placing a sculpture by the artist in the garden of the Reich Propaganda Ministry in 1939, see BAB, R 55/21013, doc. 97, Biebrach to Goebbels (17 May 1939); and ibid., doc. 177, Klimsch to Goebbels (15 June 1938).

4. BG, GFM, MF 5316, 0234, Möller to Nolde (11 June 1936); and Brenner, "Art in the Political Power Struggle," 404.

5. Massimo Magistrati, *L'Italia a Berlino, 1937–1939* (Milan: Mondadori, 1956), 87.

6. Adolf Hitler, *Mein Kampf* (Boston: Houghton Mifflin, 1971), 262. See Otto Karl Werckmeister, "Hitler the Artist," *Critical Inquiry* 23 (Winter 1997), 270–97; Peter Paret, *Artist Against the Third Reich: Ernst Barlach, 1933–1938* (Cambridge: Cambridge University Press, 2003), 109–30; Peter Adam, *Art of the Third Reich* (New York: Harry Abrams, 1992), 57; and more generally, Thomas Mathieu, *Kunstauffassungen und Kulturpolitik im Nationalsozialismus* (Saarbrücken: Pfau, 1997).

7. Elaine Hochman, *Architects of Fortune: Mies van der Rohe and the Third Reich* (New York: Weidenfeld and Nicolson, 1989), 80, 169; Schlemmer to Baumeister (9 October 1933), in Andreas Hüneke, ed., *Oskar Schlemmer. Idealist der Form. Briefe, Tagebücher, Schriften, 1912–1943* (Leipzig: Reclam-Verlag, 1990), 280; and LAB, Reichskulturkammer/PV 676, doc. 998, Lederer to Hönig (8 March 1936).

8. James van Dyke, *Franz Radziwill and the Contradictions of German Art History, 1919–45* (Ann Arbor: University of Michigan Press, 2010), 1–2; and Hitler speech at Nuremberg (5 September 1934), quoted by Brenner, "Art in the Political Power Struggle," 422.

9. Hochman, *Architects of Fortune*, 171.

10. Ibid., 79.

11. Jörn Grabowski and Annegret Janda, *Kunst in Deutschland 1905–1937. Die Verlorene Sammlung der Nationalgalerie im ehemaligen Kronprinzenpalais* (Berlin: Gebr. Mann, 1992); and Jonathan Petropoulos, *The Faustian Bargain: The Art World in Nazi Germany* (New York: Oxford University Press, 2000), 25, 68.

12. Anja Heuss, "Die Sammlung Littmann und die Aktion 'Entartete Kunst,'" in *Raubkunst und Restitution. Kulturgut aus jüdischem Besitz 1933 bis Heute*, ed. Inka Bertz and Michael Dorrmann (Göttingen: Wallstein, 2008), 69; and Timothy Ryback, "'An Even Bigger Scandal,'" *ARTnews* 98 (December 1999), 153.

13. Karl Buchholz to Eberhard Hanfstaengl (28 April 1937), reproduced in Godula Buchholz, *Karl Buchholz. Buch- und Kunsthändler im 20. Jahrhundert* (Cologne: DuMont, 2005), 73. See also Esther Tisa Francini, "Ein künstlerisches Vermächtnis. Verfemung und Rettung von Lovis Corinths 'Ecce Homo,'" in *Das Verfemte Meisterwerk. Schicksalswege Moderner Kunst im "Dritten Reich*," ed. Uwe Fleckner (Berlin: Akademie Verlag, 2009), 197–226. The exchange rate used throughout corresponds to the existing rate in 1939: RM 2.50 = \$1.

14. Dieter Scholz, "Otto Andreas Schreiber, die *Kunst der Nation* und die Fabrikausstellungen," in *Überbrückt: Ästhetische Moderne und Nationalsozialismus. Kunsthistoriker und Künstler, 1925–1937*, ed. Eugen Blume and Dieter Scholz (Cologne: Walther König, 1999), 102–3.

15. Amtsgericht Munich, denazification file of Robert Scholz, Fritz Höger, "Eidesstatt-liche Erklärung" (22 July 1947); and more generally, Piergiacomo Bucciarelli, *Fritz Höger. Hanseatische Baumeister, 1877–1949* (Berlin: Vice Versa, 1992).

16. Amtsgericht Munich, denazification file of Robert Scholz, Fritz Höger, "Eidesstatt-liche Erklärung" (22 July 1947); and Hans Hesse, "Die Norddeutsche Kunsthochschule für bildenden Kunst," *Arbeiterbewegung und Sozialgeschichte* 23/24 (2009), 85–104.

17. LAB, Max Peichstein Reichskulturkammer file, F 0122, Hans Hinkel to Walter Stang, 22 May 1936, and A. von Livonius to Hans Hinkel, 16 May 1936.

18. LAB, Max Peichstein Reichskulturkammer file, F 0122, Dr. Griebert to Reichskam-mer der bildenden Künste, Landesleiter Pommern (29 July 1936); and Bernhard Fulda and Aya Soika, *Max Pechstein. The Rise and Fall of Expressionism* (Berlin: DeGruyter, 2012), 313.

19. Annegret Janda, ed., *Schicksal einer Sammlung. Aufbau und Zerstörung der Neuen Abteilung der Nationalgalerie im ehemaligen Kronprinzen-Palais Unter den Linden 1918–1945* (Berlin: Staatliche Museen zu Berlin, 1988), 68; and Max Pechstein, *Erinnerungen* (Wiesbaden: Limes, 1960), 119.

20. Pechstein to Preussische Akademie (12 July 1937), in Hildegard Brenner, *Ende einer bürgerlichen Kunst-Institution: die politische Formierung der Preussischen Akademie der Kün-ste ab 1933* (Stuttgart: DVA, 1972), 147.

21. Pechstein to Kampf (22 July 1937), in Brenner, *Ende einer bürgerlichen Kunst-Insti-tution,* 149; and LAB, Max Peichstein Reichskulturkammer file, F 0122.

22. Frederic Spotts, *Hitler and the Power of Aesthetics* (Woodstock: Overlook, 2003 [2002]), 319.

23. Ibid., 318.

24. Albert Speer, *Spandau: The Secret Diaries* (New York: Pocket Books, 1977), 192; Adam, *Art of the Third Reich,* 211–15; and C. A. Bembé in Munich (1936) in Ralph Johannes and Gerhard Wölki, *Die Autobahnen und Ihre Rastanlagen* (Petersberg: Michael Imhof, 2005), 18.

25. Spotts, *Hitler and the Power of Aesthetics,* 321.

26. Barbara Miller Lane, *Architecture and Politics in Germany, 1918–1945* (Cambridge: Harvard University Press, 1985 [1968]), 152. Note that criticisms of the Bauhaus also ap-peared in the *Völkischer Beobachter.* See David Dennis, *Inhumanities: Nazi Interpretations of Western Culture* (Cambridge: Cambridge University Press, 2012), 347.

27. Winfried Nerdinger, ed., *Bauhaus-Moderne im Nationalsozialismus. Zwischen An-bietung und Verfolgung* (Munich: Prestel, 1993), 20. See also Ruth Heftrig, "Neues Bauen als Deutscher 'Nationalstil'? Modernerezeption im 'Dritten Reich' am Beispiel des Prozesses gegen Hans Weigert," in *Kunstgeschichte im Nationalsozialismus. Beiträge zur Geschichte einer Wissenschaft zwischen 1930 und 1950,* ed. Nikola Doll, Christian Fuhrmeister, Michael Sprenger (Weimar: VDG, 2005), 119–38.

28. Jeffrey Herf, *Reactionary Modernism: Technology, Culture and Politics in the Weimar Republic and the Third Reich* (Cambridge: Harvard University Press, 1984). See also Volker Böhnigk and Joachim Stamp, eds., *Die Moderne im Nationalsozialismus* (Bonn: University Press, 2006); and Neil Gregor, *How to Read Hitler* (New York: Norton, 2005), 79.

29. NARA, M 1941, roll 18, Hellmut Lehmann-Haupt to Richard Howard (15 Novem-ber 1947).

PART II. THE PURSUIT OF ACCOMMODATION

1. Richard Pommer, "Mies van der Rohe and the Political Ideology of the Modern Movement in Architecture," in *Mies van der Rohe: Critical Essays,* ed. Frank Schulze (Cam-bridge: MIT Press, 1989), 97.

2. John London, "Introduction," in *Theatre Under the Nazis,* ed. John London (Manchester: Manchester University Press, 2000), 2; and Hugh Ridley, "Irrationalism, Art and Violence: Ernst Jünger and Gottfried Benn," in *Weimar Germany: Writers and Politics,* ed. Alan Bance (Edinburgh: Scottisch Academic Press, 1982), 26–37.

3. Will Grohmann, *E. L. Kirchner* (New York: Arts Inc., 1961), 79; Donald Gordon, *Ernst Ludwig Kirchner* (Cambridge: Harvard University Press, 1968), 141, 412.

4. Elaine Hochman, *Architects of Fortune: Mies van der Rohe and the Third Reich* (New York: Weidenfeld and Nicolson, 1989), xv.

5. Albert Speer, *Inside the Third Reich* (New York: Avon Books, 1970), 116.

6. Ruth Negendanck, *Die Galerie Ernst Arnold (1893–1951): Kunsthandel und Zeitgeschichte* (Weimar: Verlag für und Datenbank für Geisteswissenschaften, 1998), 199; and Maike Steinkamp, *Unerwünschte Erbe. Die Rezeption 'entarteter' Kunst in Kunstkritik, Ausstellungen und Museen der SBZ und Frühen DDR* (Berlin: Akademie Verlag, 2008), 62.

7. Gesa Jeuthe, *Kunstwerte im Wandel. Die Preisentwicklung der Deutschen Moderne im National und Internationalen Kunstmarkt 1925 bis 1955* (Berlin: Akademie Verlag, 2011); Meike Hopp, *Kunsthandel im Nationalsozialismus. Adolf Weinmüller in München und Wien* (Cologne: Böhlau, 2012); Angelika Enderlein, *Der Berliner Kunsthandel in Weimarer Republik und im NS-Staat. Zum Schicksal der Sammlung Graetz* (Berlin: Akademie Verlag, 2006): Christine Fischer-Defoy and Kaspar Nürnberg, eds., *Gute Geschäft. Kunsthandel in Berlin 1933–1945* (Berlin: Aktives Museum Faschismus und Widerstand in Berlin, 2011); Ute Haug and Meike Steinkamp, eds., *Werke und Werte: über das Handeln und Sammeln von Kunst im Nationalsozialismus* (Berlin: Akademie Verlag, 2010); and Hanns Christian Löhr, *Das Braune Haus der Kunst. Hitler und der "Sonderauftrag Linz"* (Berlin: Akademie Verlag, 2005).

8. Michael Meyer, "A Musical Façade for the Third Reich," in *"Degenerate Art": The Fate of the Avant-Garde in Nazi Germany,* ed. Stephanie Barron (Los Angeles: Los Angeles County Museum of Art, 1991), 175.

9. Götz Aly, *Hitler's Beneficiaries: Plunder, Racial War, and the Nazi Welfare State* (New York: Metropolitan Books, 2005); Frank Bajohr, *Parvenüs und Profiteure. Korruption in der NS-Zeit* (Frankfurt: S. Fischer, 2001); and Gerd Ueberschär and Winfried Vogel, *Dienen und Verdienen: Hitlers Geschenke an seine Eliten* (Frankfurt: S. Fischer, 2000).

10. Frederic Spotts, *Hitler and the Power of Aesthetics* (Woodstock: Overlook, 2003 [2002]), 177.

11. Max Beckmann, quoted by Axel Rüger, "Foreword," in *Max Beckmann in Amsterdam, 1937–1947,* ed. Beatrice von Bormann (Amsterdam: Van Gogh Museum, 2006), 7.

CHAPTER 4. WALTER GROPIUS

1. Peter Gay, *Weimar Culture: The Outsider as Insider* (New York: Harper and Row, 1968), 97–102.

2. Walter Gropius, *The New Architecture and the Bauhaus* (Cambridge: MIT Press, 1965).

3. J. D. Shand, "The *Reichsautobahn:* Symbol for the Third Reich," *Journal of Contemporary History* 19/2 (1984), 189–95.

4. Barbara Miller Lane, *Architecture and Politics in Germany, 1918–1945* (Cambridge: Harvard University Press, 1985 [1968]),152.

5. See Gropius's discussion of planned communities (Siedlungen) with Nazi architect Paul Schmitthenner, in Bauhaus-Archiv, Berlin, Gropius Papers, Mappe 103/4, Gropius to Schmitthenner (10 June 1934).

6. Gropius's 1922 Monument to the Kapp Putsch Victims in the Weimar Cemetery

was subsequently destroyed. See Philip Johnson, *Mies van der Rohe* (New York: Museum of Modern Art, 1947), 109; and Elaine Hochman, *Architects of Fortune: Mies van der Rohe and the Third Reich* (New York: Weidenfeld and Nicolson, 1989), 87.

7. Hochman, *Architects of Fortune*, 86; and Frank Whitford, *Bauhaus* (London: Thames and Hudson, 1984), 44.

8. Winfried Nerdinger, "Bauhaus-Architekten im 'Dritten Reich,'" in *Bauhaus-Moderne im Nationalsozialismus. Zwischen Anbietung und Verfolgung*, ed. Winfried Nerdinger (Munich: Prestel, 1993), 158; and Kathleen James-Chakraborty, ed., *Bauhaus Culture. From Weimar to the Cold War* (Minneapolis: University of Minnesota Press, 2006).

9. Hochman, *Architects of Fortune*, 41.

10. Reginald Isaacs, *Gropius. An Illustrated Biography of the Creator of the Bauhaus* (Boston: Bulfinch Press, 1991), 175; and Alan Steinweis, *Art, Ideology, and Economics in Nazi Germany: The Reich Chambers of Music, Theater and the Visual Arts* (Chapel Hill: University of North Carolina Press, 1993), 107–20.

11. Bauhaus-Archiv, Berlin, Gropius Papers, Mappe 103/1, Gropius to Hönig (18 January 1934).

12. Bernhard Fulda and Aya Soika, *Max Pechstein. The Rise and Fall of Expressionism* (Berlin: DeGruyter, 2012), 311. Hönig often clashed with the conservative Rosenberg, such as with the latter's exhibition *Kunst am Wege* in 1935. For the exchange of letters, see BAB, NS 8/253, docs. 122–55. For more on Hönig, see the newspaper clippings in SMB-ZA, V/057; and Ernst Klee, *Kulturlexikon zum Dritten Reich. Wer war was vor und nach 1945* (Frankfurt: S. Fischer, 2007), 256.

13. Hochman, *Architects of Fortune*, 220; and Walter Scheiffele, "Das neue Bauen unter dem Faschismus," in *Kunst Hochschule Faschismus*, ed. Hochschule der Künste Berlin (Berlin: Elefanten Press, 1984), 233. See also the Gropius-Hönig correspondence in Bauhaus-Archiv, Berlin, Gropius Papers, Mappe 103/1.

14. Nerdinger, "Bauhaus-Architekten im 'Dritten Reich,'" 157. The letter is in the Bauhaus-Archiv, Berlin, GN 5/92.

15. Bauhaus-Archiv Berlin, Gropius Papers, Mappe 388, Gropius to Hesse (1 September 1936).

16. Bauhaus-Archiv, Berlin, Gropius Papers, Mappe 103/3/GN 13/77–80, Gropius to Hönig (27 March 1934). See also Reginald Isaacs, *Walter Gropius. Der Mensch und sein Werk II* (Berlin: Gebr. Mann, 1984), 180; and Nerdinger, "Bauhaus-Architekten im 'Dritten Reich,'" 157.

17. Nerdinger, "Bauhaus-Architekten im 'Dritten Reich,'" 158.

18. Hochman, *Architects of Fortune*, 229. She cites Gropius to Hönig (27 March 1934), quoted in Miller Lane, *Architecture and Politics*, 181. See also Frank Schulze, *Mies van der Rohe: Critical Essays* (Cambridge: MIT Press, 1989), 200, where Gropius tried to reconcile the New Architecture and the German spirit: "I myself see a valid union of the two great spiritual heritages of the classical and the Gothic traditions."

19. Bauhaus-Archiv, Berlin, Gropius Papers, Mappe 103/1/GN 13/3, Gropius to Hönig (18 Januay 1934); Mappe 103/4, Gropius to Schmitthenner (10 June 1934).

20. Richard Pommer, "Mies van der Rohe and the Political Ideology of the Modern Movement in Architecture," in *Mies van der Rohe: Critical Essays*, ed. Frank Schulze (Cambridge, Mass: MIT Press, 1989), 97, where he cites Joan Campbell, *The German Werkbund: The Politics of Reform in the Applied Arts* (Princeton: Princeton University Press, 1978). See also Frederic Schwartz, *The Werkbund: Design Theory and Mass Culture before the First World War* (New Haven: Yale University Press, 1996); and Sabine Weissler, ed., *Design in Deutschland 1933–1945. Ästhetik und Organisation des Deutschen Werkbundes im "Dritten Reich"* (Giessen: Anabas, 1990).

21. Dan van der Vat, *The Good Nazi: The Life and Lies of Albert Speer* (Boston: Houghton Mifflin, 1997), 54.

22. Winfried Nerdinger, "Modernisierung, Bauhaus, Nationalsozialismus," in *Bauhaus-Moderne im Nationalsozialismus. Zwischen Anbietung und Verfolgung,* ed. Winfried Nerdinger (Munich: Prestel, 1993), 18–19.

23. Bauhaus-Archiv, Berlin, Gropius Papers, Mappe 106, Gropius, "Theaterbau" lecture (October 1934). See also ibid., Mappe 103/4, Gropius to Hönig (10 September 1934); Scheiffele, "Das neue Bauen unter dem Faschismus," 233; and more generally, Ruth Ben-Ghiat, *Fascist Modernities: Italy, 1922–1945* (Berkeley: University of California Press, 2001), 24, 35.

24. Isaacs, *Walter Gropius. Der Mensch und sein Werk II,* 663.

25. Nerdinger, "Bauhaus-Architekten im 'Dritten Reich,'" 18–19, 162; Isaacs, *Gropius,* 177; and Walter Prigge, ed., *Ernst Neufert. Normierte Baukultur im 20. Jahrhundert* (Frankfurt: Campus, 1999).

26. Nerdinger, "Modernisierung," 20; and Nerdinger, "Bauhaus-Architekten im 'Dritten Reich,'" 172.

27. Beate Marks-Hanssen, *Inner Emigration? "Verfemte" Künstlerinnen und Künstler in der Zeit des Nationalsozialismus* (Berlin: dissertation.de, 2006), 162.

28. Schlemmer to Gunta Stölzl on 16 June 1933, quoted in Nerdinger, "Modernisierung," 20.

29. Magdalena Droste, "Bauhaus-Maler im Nationalsozialismus," in *Bauhaus-Moderne im Nationalsozialismus. Zwischen Anbietung und Verfolgung,* ed. Winfried Nerdinger (Munich: Prestel, 1993), 131; Andreas Hüneke, ed., *Oskar Schlemmer: Idealist der Form. Briefe, Tagebücher, Schriften, 1912–1943* (Leipzig: Reclam-Verlag, 1990), 275; and Karin V. Maur, *Oskar Schlemmer. Oeuvrekatalog der Gemälde, Aquarelle, Pastelle, und Plastiken* (Munich: Prestel, 1979), 360–64.

30. Droste, "Bauhaus-Maler im Nationalsozialismus," 131.

31. Uwe Schneede, ed., *"The Most Beautiful Museum in the World: The Folkwang Museum until 1933* (Essen: Folkwang Museum, 2010).

32. GRI, SC, Arntz Papers, box 28, files 10–15, Baudissin to Schlemmer (4 May 1934); and Anna Jolly, "Biographien," in *Junge Deutsche Kunst. Der Folkwang-Wettbewerb 1934,* ed. Mario-Andreas Lüttichau (Essen: Museum Folkwang Essen, 1993), 106.

33. Eberhard Roters, *Galerie Ferdinand Möller. Die Geschichte einer Galerie für moderne Kunst in Deutschland, 1917–1956* (Berlin: Gebr. Mann, 1984), 138; and Olaf Peters, "On the Problem of Continuity of New Objectivity Painting during the Consolidation of the Third Reich: The Case of Rudolf Schlichter," *History of European Ideas* 24/2 (1998), 93–112. For more on Schlemmer having supporters in Nazi circles, see Verband Bildender Künstler Württemberg, *Künstlerschicksale im Dritten Reich in Würrttemberg und Baden* (Stuttgart: Verband Bildender Künstler Württemberg, 1987), 26. For Grohmann, see Monika Wucher, "Dr. Grohmanns Empfehlungen. Leitmotive moderner Kunstpublizistik im Nationalsozialismus," in *Überbrückt: Ästhetische Moderne und Nationalsozialismus. Kunsthistoriker und Künstler, 1925–1937,* ed. Eugen Blume and Dieter Scholz, eds. (Cologne: Walther König, 1999), 109–23.

34. Droste, "Bauhaus-Maler im Nationalsozialismus," 132; and more generally, v. Maur, *Oskar Schlemmer.*

35. For Gropius's materials for the Reichsbank, see Bauhaus-Archiv, Berlin, Gropius Papers, GS 20, Mappe 95; and Winfried Nerdinger, *Der Architekt Walter Gropius* (Berlin: Gebr. Mann, 1996 [1985]), 180, 262.

36. Bauhaus-Archiv, Berlin, Gropius Papers, GS 20, Mappe 95, "Wettbewerb Reichsbankneubau, Berlin 1933" (3 May 1933).

37. Johnson, *Mies van der Rohe,* 123; and Isaacs, *Gropius,* 178.

38. Hochman, *Architects of Fortune,* 155; Schulze, *Mies van der Rohe,* 195; and Arthur Drexler, ed., *An Illustrated Catalogue of the Mies van der Rohe Drawings in the Museum of Modern Art,* 4 vols. (New York: Garland, 1986), III:432–505.

39. Hochman, *Architects of Fortune,* 155. See also Wolf Tegethoff, "Catching the Spirit: Mies's Early Work and the Impact of the Prussian Style," in *Mies in Berlin,* ed. Terence Riley and Barry Bergdoll (New York: Harry Abrams, 2001), 134–52. Note that Moeller van den Bruck in many respects advanced arguments that prefigured the Nazis. See Fritz Stern, *The Politics of Cultural Despair: A Study in the Rise of the Germanic Ideology* (Berkeley: University of California Press, 1961).

40. Hochman, *Architects of Fortune,* 171–72; and Peter Paret, *An Artist Against the Third Reich: Ernst Barlach, 1933–1938* (Cambridge: Cambridge University Press, 2003), 60.

41. Detlev Lücke and Jens Rötzsch, "Das Haus der Tausend Fenster," *Zeitmagazin* 180/10 (2000), 68–71; Pommer, "Mies and Political Ideology," 119; Frederic Spotts, *Hitler and the Power of Aesthetics* (Woodstock: Overlook, 2003 [2002]), 341; Matthias Donath, *Architecture in Berlin, 1933–1945. A Guide Through Nazi Berlin* (Berlin: Lukas, 2006), 24–25; and Thomas Friedrich, *Hitler's Berlin: Abused City* (New Haven: Yale University Press, 2012), 343–44.

42. Bauhaus-Archiv, Berlin, Gropius Papers, GS 20, Mappe 95, includes an array of press clippings. See, for example, J. Tiedemann, "Wie wird die neue Reichshauptbank aussehen? Das Ergebnis des engeren Wettbewerbs," *Völkischer Beobachter* 188 (7 July 1933).

43. "Unterhaltung mit Walter Gropius" *Laporta* (24 April 1933).

44. Bauhaus-Archiv Berlin, Gropius Papers, Mappe 103/1/GN 13/2, Weidemann to Gropius (18 January 1934).

45. Hochman, *Architects of Fortune,* 210.

46. *Deutsches Volk—Deutsche Arbeit* (Berlin: n.p., 1934); and Nerdinger, *Der Architekt Walter Gropius,* 184–87.

47. Sabine Weissler, "Bauhaus-Gestaltung in NS-Propaganda-Ausstellungen," in *Bauhaus-Moderne im Nationalsozialismus. Zwischen Anbietung und Verfolgung,* ed. Winfried Nerdinger (Munich: Prestel, 1993), 48.

48. Hochman, *Architects of Fortune,* 287. See also the illustrations in Elke Dittrich, *Ernst Sagebiel. Leben und Werk, 1892–1970* (Berlin: Lukas, 2005), 217–18; Weissler, "Bauhaus-Gestaltung in NS-Propaganda-Ausstellungen," 60–61; as well as in the contemporaneous publication *Monatshefte für Baukunst und Städtebau* 21 (1937).

49. Scheiffele, "Das neue Bauen unter dem Faschismus," 239; and Wolfgang Christian Schneider, "Die Stadt als nationalsozialistischer Raum," in *Figurative Politik: zur Performenz der Macht in der modernen Gesellschaft,* ed. Hans-Georg Soeffner and Dirk Tänzler (Opladen: Leske and Budrich, 2002), 155–63.

50. Isaacs, *Walter Gropius. Der Mensch und sein Werk II,* 636–37.

51. Bauhaus-Archiv, Berlin, Gropius Papers, Mappe 103/1, Gropius to Hönig (18 January 1934).

52. Nerdinger, "Bauhaus-Architekten im 'Dritten Reich,'" 155.

53. Lane, *Architecture and Politics in Germany,* 184; and Isaacs, *Walter Gropius. Der Mensch und sein Werk II,* 638–40.

54. Petra Leser, *Der Kölner Architekt Clemens Klotz (1886–1969)* (Cologne: Universität Köln, 1991); and Jürgen Rostock and Franz Zadni ek, *Paradiesruinen. Das KdF-Seebad der Zwanzigtausend auf Rügen* (Berlin: Christoph Links, 2008 [1992]).

55. Schulze, *Mies van der Rohe,* 199; Johnson, *Mies van der Rohe,* 125; Pommer, "Mies and Political Ideology," 125; and Drexler, *Catalogue of the Mies van der Rohe Drawings,* IV:84–110.

56. Hochman, *Architects of Fortune,* 226; and Pommer, "Mies and Political Ideology," 125–29.

57. Hochman, *Architects of Fortune,* 228.

58. Ruegenberg, quoted in ibid., 228.

59. Bauhaus-Archiv Berlin, Gropius Papers, Mappe 103/12/GN 13/42, Gropius to Weidemann (2 February 1934); and Isaacs, *Gropius,* 179.

60. Isaacs, *Gropius,* 179; and Malgorzata Omilanowska, "Das Frühwerk von Walter Gropius in Hinterpommern," in *Landgüter in den Regionen des gemeinsamen Kulturerbes von Deutschen und Polen,* ed. Birte Pusback and Jan Skuratowicz (Warsaw: Instytut Polskiej Akademii Nauk, 2007), 133–49.

61. Scheiffele, "Das neue Bauen unter dem Faschismus" 238–39; Nerdinger, "Bauhaus-Architekten im 'Dritten Reich,'" 157; and Isaacs, *Gropius,* 177.

62. Kathleen James, "Changing the Agenda: From German Bauhaus Modernism to U.S. Internationalism. Ludwig Mies van der Rohe, Walter Gropius, Marcel Breuer," in *Exiles and Émigrés: The Flight of European Artists from Hitler,* ed. Stephanie Barron and Sabine Eckmann (Los Angeles: Los Angeles County Museum of Art, 1997), 242.

63. Scheiffele, "Das neue Bauen unter dem Faschismus" 241.

64. Isaacs, *Gropius,* 204.

65. Ibid., 203, 231, 244; and Isaacs, *Walter Gropius. Der Mensch und sein Werk II,* 915–16; and Nerdinger, "Bauhaus-Architekten im 'Dritten Reich,'" 157.

66. See the 1937 correspondence about Gropius between the president of the Reich Chamber for the Visual Arts (Ziegler) and the NSDAP Auslandsorganisation referenced in BAB, RK 60025, doc. 936, Gropius file card (n.d.); and Isaacs, *Walter Gropius. Der Mensch und sein Werk II,* 817–19.

67. Gropius to Hönig (31 December 1936), quoted in Scheiffele, "Das neue Bauen unter dem Faschismus," 241.

68. Isaacs, *Gropius,* 219; and Axel Drecoll, *Der Fiskus als Verfolger. Die steuerliche Diskriminierung der Juden in Bayern, 1933–1941/42* (Munich: Oldenbourg, 2009), 133.

69. Isaacs, *Walter Gropius. Der Mensch und sein Werk II,* 821.

70. Drecoll, *Der Fiskus als Verfolger,* 129, 140–41.

71. Isaacs, *Walter Gropius. Der Mensch und sein Werk II,* 821.

72. Karen Koehler, "The Bauhaus, 1919–1928: Gropius in Exile and the Museum of Modern Art, N.Y., 1938," in *Art, Culture, and Media Under the Third Reich,* ed. Richard Etlin (Chicago: University of Chicago Press, 2002), 287; and Anthony Heilbut, *Exiled in Paradise: German Refugee Artists and Intellectuals in America from the 1930s to the Present* (Boston: Beacon Press, 1983), 28.

73. James, "Changing the Agenda," 243; Isaacs, *Gropius,* 239; and Isaacs, *Walter Gropius. Der Mensch und sein Werk II,* 888, 892–95, 897–99. Gropius also arranged for Josef Albers to come to Harvard in 1938, but the former Bauhäusler decided to remain at Black Mountain College in North Carolina before ultimately moving to Yale University in 1950.

74. Gropius to Fray (7 June 1937), quoted in Isaacs, *Walter Gropius. Der Mensch und sein Werk II,* 854; Jonathan Petropoulos, "Saving Culture from the Nazis," *Harvard Magazine* 92/4 (March 1990), 34–42; and Reginald Isaacs, *Gropius at/in Harvard* (Berlin: Bauhaus-Archiv, 1983).

75. Isaacs, *Gropius. An Illustrated Biography,* 264–67.

76. Nerdinger, "Bauhaus-Architekten im 'Dritten Reich,'" 160; and James, "Changing the Agenda," 235–52.

77. Peter Gay, *Art and Act: On Causes in History—Manet, Gropius, Mondrian* (New York: Harper and Row, 1976).

78. Barry Bergdoll and Leah Dickerman, eds., *Bauhaus 1919–1933* (New York: Museum of Modern Art, 2009).

CHAPTER 5. PAUL HINDEMITH

1. There is an extensive historical and musicological literature on Hindemith. A useful starting point is Stephen Luttmann, *Paul Hindemith: A Research and Information Guide* (New York: Routledge, 2009 [2004]).

2. Michael Kater, *Composers of the Nazi Era: Eight Portraits* (New York: Oxford University Press, 2000), 31; and more generally, Ian Kemp, *Hindemith* (New York: Oxford University Press, 1970), 7–10, 21–22.

3. Kemp, *Hindemith,* 10–11.

4. Ibid., 24.

5. Smith, quoted in Kater, *Composers of the Nazi Era,* 33; and more generally, David Neumeyer, *The Music of Paul Hindemith* (New Haven: Yale University Press, 1986), 187–238.

6. Paulding, quoted in Kater, *Composers of the Nazi Era,* 33.

7. Walter Salmen, "'Alte Töne' und Volksmusik in Kompositionen von Paul Hindemith," *Yearbook of the International Folk Music Council* 1 (1969), 89–122; and Douglas Bomberger, "European Perceptions of Ragtime: Hindemith and Stravinsky," in *Jazz and the Germans: Essays on the Influence of "Hot" American Idioms on 20th Century German Music,* ed. Michael Budds (Hillsdale: Pendragon, 2002), 83–97.

8. Andres Briner, Dieter Rexroth, and Giselher Schubert, *Paul Hindemith. Leben und Werk im Bild und Text* (Mainz: Schott, 1988), 21.

9. Luther Noss, *Paul Hindemith in the United States* (Urbana: University of Illinois Press, 1989), 4.

10. Hindemith letter from 23 September 1914 to Dr. Weber, quoted in Briner, Rexroth, and Schubert, *Paul Hindemith,* 34; and Ian Kemp, "Paul Hindemith," in *The New Grove Modern Masters* (London: Macmillan, 1984), 230.

11. Kater, *Composers of the Nazi Era,* 49.

12. Noss, *Paul Hindemith in the United States,* 7–8.

13. Ibid., 9.

14. Hindemith to the Strecker brothers (5 September 1933), quoted in Kater, *Composers of the Nazi Era,* 36.

15. Pamela Potter, "Dismantling a Dystopia: On the Historiography of Music in the Third Reich," *Central European History* 40 (2007), 635; and more generally Michael Meyer, *The Politics of Music in the Third Reich* (New York: Peter Lang, 1993).

16. Potter, "Dismantling a Dystopia," 635, and Alan Steinweis, *Art, Ideology, and Economics in Nazi Germany: The Reich Chambers of Music, Theater and the Visual Arts* (Chapel Hill: University of North Carolina Press, 1993), 138–42.

17. Potter, "Dismantling a Dystopia," 635; and Michael Walter, *Hitler in der Oper. Deutsches Musikleben 1919–1945* (Stuttgart: Metzler, 1995), 175–213.

18. Celia Appelgate, "The Past and Present of *Hausmusik* in the Third Reich," in *Music and Nazism: Art Under Tyranny,* ed. Michael Kater and Albrecht Riethmüller (Laaber: Laaber Verlag, 2003), 136–49.

19. Potter, "Dismantling a Dystopia," 636; and Michael Kater, *Twisted Muse: Musicians and Their Music in the Third Reich* (New York: Oxford University Press), 178–79.

20. Potter, "Dismantling a Dystopia," 631.

21. Fred Prieberg, *Trial of Strength. Wilhelm Furtwängler and the Third Reich* (London:

Quartet Books, 1991), 46–47; and Erik Levi, *Music in the Third Reich* (New York: St. Martin's Press, 1994), 18–19.

22. Levi, *Music in the Third Reich,* 108.

23. Geoffrey Skelton, ed., *Selected Letters of Paul Hindemith* (New Haven: Yale University Press, 1995), 76.

24. Potter, "Dismantling a Dystopia," 647. For Gerigk as a plunderer, see Willem de Vries, *Sonderstab Musik. Organisierte Plünderungen in Westeuropa 1940–45* (Cologne: Dittrich, 1998), 16.

25. Herbert Gerigk, "Eine Lanze für Schoenberg," *Die Musik* (November 1934), quoted in Levi, *Music in the Third Reich,* 103. More generally, Claudia Mauer Zenck, "Zwischen Boycott und Anpassung an der Charakter der Zeit," in *Hindemith Jahrbuch* IX (1980), 65–129.

26. Walter Berten, quoted in Levi, *Music in the Third Reich,* 108.

27. Hindemith to Strecker (15 April 1933), quoted in Skelton, *Selected Letters of Paul Hindemith,* 69.

28. Luttmann, *Paul Hindemith,* 76.

29. Hindemith to Strecker (5 February 1934), quoted in Skelton, ed., *Selected Letters of Paul Hindemith,* 76.

30. Potter, "Dismantling a Dystopia," 631.

31. Ibid., 631.

32. Levi, *Music in the Third Reich,* 114; and Geoffrey Skelton, *Paul Hindemith: The Man Behind the Music—A Biography* (London: Victor Gallancz, 1977), 127.

33. Kater, *Composers of the Nazi Era,* 32, 53.

34. Potter, "Dismantling a Dystopia," 631; and more generally, Siglind Bruhn, *The Temptation of Paul Hindemith: Mathis der Maler as a Spiritual Testimony* (Stuyvesant: Pendragon Press, 1998).

35. Gieselher Schubert, "The Aesthetic Premises of a Nazi Conception of Music," in *Music and Nazism: Art Under Tyranny, 1933–1945,* ed. Michael Kater and Albrecht Riethmüller (Laaber: Laaber, 2003), 64–73.

36. Kater, *Composers of the Nazi Era,* 34.

37. Kemp, *Hindemith,* 30.

38. Paulding, quoted in Kater, *Composers of the Nazi Era,* 33.

39. Kater, *Composers of the Nazi Era,* 33.

40. Kemp, *Hindemith,* 31.

41. Briner, Rexroth, and Schubert, *Paul Hindemith,* 139.

42. Maurer Zenck, "Zwischen Boycott und Anpassung," 119.

43. Hindemith to Strecker (5 February 1934), quoted in Skelton, *Selected Letters of Paul Hindemith,* 76.

44. Neumann, quoted in Kater, *Composers of the Nazi Era,* 35.

45. Kater, *Composers of the Nazi Era,* 37.

46. Hindemith to Strecker (9 February 1934), quoted in Skelton, *Selected Letters of Paul Hindemith,* 77; Prieberg, *Trial of Strength,* 119–20; and Levi, *Music in the Third Reich,* 109.

47. Potter, "Dismantling a Dystopia," 649; Levi, *Music in the Third Reich,* 84; and Fred Prieberg, *Musik im NS-Staat* (Frankfurt: Fischer Taschenbuch, 1982), 61–70.

48. Preussner, quoted in Kater, *Composers of the Nazi Era,* 37; and Levi, *Music in the Third Reich,* 112.

49. Hindemith to Strecker (15 November 1934), quoted in Skelton, *Selected Letters of Paul Hindemith,* 84; and the account of his secretary, Berta Geissmar, *Musik im Schatten der Politik* (Zurich: Atlantis, 1945).

50. Kater, *Composers of the Nazi Era,* 37.

51. Prieberg, *Trial of Strength*, 122, 349; and Kater, *Composers of the Nazi Era*, 37.

52. Wilhem Furtwängler, "Der Fall Hindemith," *Deutsche Allgemeine Zeitung* (25 November 1934); Prieberg, *Trial of Strength*, 84–85, 138, 152; Kater, *Twisted Muse*, 181, 196–99; Sam Shirakawa, *The Devil's Music Master: The Controversial Life and Career of Wilhelm Furtwängler* (New York: 1992), 183.

53. Furtwängler, quoted in Levi, *Music in the Third Reich*, 113.

54. Ibid., 113.

55. Shirakawa, *Devil's Music Master*, 184; and Prieberg, *Trial of Strength*, 141.

56. Prieberg, *Musik im NS-Staat*, 47–48; and Levi, *Music in the Third Reich*, 48.

57. Joseph Wulf, *Musik im Dritten Reich. Eine Dokumentation* (Berlin: Ullstein, 1983 [1963]), 86–87; Shirakawa, *Devil's Music Master*, 151–52; and Michael Meyer, "Wilhelm Furtwängler: Collaboration and a Struggle of Authority," in *The Politics of Music in the Third Reich*, ed. Michael Meyer (New York: Peter Lang, 1990).

58. BAB, R56I /140, docs. 13–16, Furtwängler to Bernhard Rust (4 June 1933); Prieberg, *Trial of Strength*, 190; and Shirakawa, *Devil's Music Master*, 151.

59. BAB, R56I/140, Georg Gerullis to Hans Hinkel (20 July 1933); BAB, R56I/140, doc. 2, W. Ralf-Rex "Meldung" (16 June 1933); and more generally, Prieberg, *Trial of Strength*, 94.

60. Erich Roeder, "Warum Vorschusslorbeeren für Konjunktur-Musiker Hindemith," *Der Angriff* (28 November 1934), 1. A facsimilie of the article is reproduced in Briner, Rexroth, and Schubert, *Paul Hindemith*, 147.

61. Goebbels, quoted in Levi, *Music in the Third Reich*, 114; and Goebbels, "Reichsminister Dr. Goebbels: Aus der Kulturkammerrede vom 6. Dezember 1934," *Die Musik* 27/4 (January 1935), 246–47.

62. Prieberg, *Trial of Strength*, 140.

63. For facsimilies of Furtwängler's letters of resignation in December 1934, see ibid., 142–44.

64. Ibid., 150.

65. Kater, *Composers of the Nazi Era*, 39; and Kemp, *Hindemith*, 28.

66. Prieberg, *Trial of Strength*, 219.

67. Hindemith to Schüler (November/December 1934), quoted in Skelton, *Selected Letters of Paul Hindemith*, 86.

68. Maurer Zenck, "Zwischen Boycott und Anpassung," 110–20; and Kater, *Composers of the Nazi Era*, 39. For Hindemith as a passive figure, see Briner, Rexroth, and Schubert, *Paul Hindemith*, 138.

69. Hindemith to Strecker (13 February 1935), quoted in Kater, *Composers of the Nazi Era*, 39–40. See Arnold Reisman, *Turkey's Modernization: Refugees from Nazism and Atatürk's Vision* (Washington, D.C.: New Academia, 2006).

70. Kater, *Composers of the Nazi Era*, 40.

71. Hindemith report (18 June 1935), quoted in ibid., 40.

72. Ibid., 40.

73. Hindemith to Strecker (15 June 1935), quoted in Skelton, *Selected Letters of Paul Hindemith*, 89.

74. Kater, *Composers of the Nazi Era*, 40.

75. Goebbels, *Tagebücher* 3/I (5 July 1935), 257.

76. Kater, *Composers of the Nazi Era*, 41.

77. Ibid., 42, 51.

78. Levi, *Music in the Third Reich*, 114.

79. Hindemith to Strecker (23 January 1936), quoted in Skelton, *Selected Letters of Paul Hindemith*, 91.

80. Hindemith to Strecker (23 January 1936), quoted in ibid., 91.

81. For the article in *Deutsche Zukunft* (9 February 1936), see Levi, *Music in the Third Reich*, 115.

82. Hindemith to Strecker (29 June and 8 July 1936), quoted in Skelton, *Selected Letters of Paul Hindemith*, 92–94; and Kemp, "Paul Hindemith," 236.

83. Noss, *Paul Hindemith in the United States*, 10–30.

84. Furtwängler, quoted in Kater, *Composers of the Nazi Era*, 42.

85. Albrecht Dümmling, and Peter Firth, eds., *Entartete Musik. Zur Düsseldorfer Ausstellung von 1938. Eine kommentierte Rekonstruktion* (Düsseldorf: Kleinherne, 1988).

86. Kater, *Composers of the Nazi Era*, 43.

87. Ibid., 44.

88. Ibid., 45.

89. Luttmann, *Paul Hindemith*, 74. For a particularly critical view of Hindemith and his views regarding Jewish colleagues, see Berndt Heller and Frieder Reininghaus, "Hindemiths heikle Jahre: eine Dokumentation," *Neue Zeitschrift für Musik* 145/5 (May 1984), 4–10.

90. Kemp, "Paul Hindemith," 235.

91. Paul to Gertrud Hindemith (14 February 1940), quoted in Kater, *Composers of the Nazi Era*, 46.

92. Ibid., 32.

93. Shirakawa, *Devil's Music Master*, 46, 51; and Kater, *Twisted Muse*, 198.

94. Levi, *Music in the Third Reich*, 108.

95. Ibid., 102.

96. Ibid., 116–17.

97. Potter, "Dismantling a Dystopia," 641.

98. Levi, *Music in the Third Reich*, 168.

99. Ibid., 49.

100. Friedrich Welter, quoted in Levi, *Music in the Third Reich*, 111.

101. Kater, *Composers of the Nazi Era*, 46. More generally, see Noss, *Paul Hindemith in the United States*.

102. Kater, *Composers of the Nazi Era*, 47.

103. Hindemith to Gertrud Hindemith (15 July 1940), quoted in Noss, *Hindemith in the United States*, 74–75; and Kemp, "Paul Hindemith," 237.

104. Hindemith to Strecker (30 May 1941), quoted in Kater, *Composers of the Nazi Era*, 48.

105. Ibid., 34.

106. Kemp, *Hindemith*, 28.

107. Prieberg, *Trial of Strength*, 148–49.

108. Kater, *Composers of the Nazi Era*, 48; and Noss, *Hindemith in the United States*, 91–92.

109. Paul Hindemith to Gertrud Hindemith (3 April 1937), quoted in Skelton, *Selected Letters of Paul Hindemith*, 98.

110. Skelton, *Hindemith*, 241.

111. Kater, *Composers of the Nazi Era*, 48–49.

112. Kemp, *Hindemith*, 28.

113. Noss, *Hindemith in the United States*, 29.

114. Ibid., 24.

115. Hindemith to Gertrud Hindemith (2 March 1939), quoted in ibid., 47.

116. Hindemith to Gertrud Hindemith (27 March 1939), quoted in ibid., 52.

117. Hindemith to Gertrud Hindemith (12 April 1940), quoted in ibid., 75.

118. Hindemith's journal (17 April 1937), quoted in ibid., 4.

119. Potter, "Dismantling a Dystopia," 624.

120. Ibid., 624.

121. Ibid., 629.

122. Prieberg, *Trial of Strength,* 216.

123. Kemp, *Hindemith,* 36.

124. Levi, *Music in the Third Reich,* 142, 159–62.

125. Kater, *Composers of the Nazi Era,* 49–50; and Maurer Zenck, "Boycott," 109–10.

126. Otto Schumann, quoted in Levi, *Music in the Third Reich,* 116.

CHAPTER 6. GOTTFRIED BENN

1. Elaine Hochman, *Architects of Fortune: Mies van der Rohe and the Third Reich* (New York: Weidenfeld and Nicolson, 1989), 135.

2. John Collins, "Gottfried Benn," in *Twentieth-Century Culture: A Biographical Companion,* ed. Alan Bullock and R. B. Woodings (New York: Harper and Row, 1983), 61; and J. M. Ritchie, *Gottfried Benn: The Unreconstructed Expressionist* (London: Oswald Wolff, 1972), 58.

3. Collins, "Gottfried Benn," 61.

4. Edgar Lohner, quoted by Ritchie, *Gottfried Benn,* 24.

5. See, among other volumes, Holger Hof, ed. *Briefwechsel 1949–1956. Gottfried Benn/ Ernst Jünger* (Stuttgart: Klett-Cotta, 2006); and Ann Fehn, ed., *Briefe. Band III: Briefwechsel mit Paul Hindemith* (Stuttgart: Klett-Cotta, 1993).

6. Holger Hof, *Benn. Sein Leben in Bildern und Texten* (Stuttgart: Klett Cotta, 2007), 20.

7. Benn, "Der deutsch Mensch. Erbmasse und Führertum" (August 1933), quoted in ibid., 25.

8. Ibid., 26.

9. J. M. Ritchie, *German Literature Under National Socialism* (London: Croom Helm, 1983), 52.

10. Ritchie, *Gottfried Benn,* 14–15.

11. Hof, *Benn,* 53.

12. Benn, "Mann und Frau gehn durch die Krebsbaracke," quoted in facsimilie in ibid., 60; and Benn to Leo Königsmann (2 May 1912), quoted in ibid., 62.

13. Collins, "Gottfried Benn," 61. See also Walter Sokal, *The Writer in Extremis: Expressionism in Twentieth-Century German Literature* (Stanford: Stanford University Press, 1968 [1959]).

14. See the facsimilie advertisements for Cassirer's "Kunstsalon" and Benn's poem "Alaska" in *Die Aktion* (25 June 1913), in Hof, *Benn,* 64, 68; Ritchie, *Gottfried Benn,* 56; and Frederick Levine, *The Apocalyptic Vision: The Art of Franz Marc as German Expressionism* (New York: Harper and Row, 1979).

15. Benn, "Lebenslauf" (19 August 1921), quoted in Hof, *Benn,* 80, 84.

16. Benn, "In Memoriam Höhe 317," in ibid., 83.

17. Ritchie, *German Literature Under National Socialism,* 52; and Benn to Antonia Vallentin (12 August 1918), in Hof, *Benn,* 92.

18. Hof, *Benn,* 94–95; Alfred Richard Meyer, "Alfred Lichtenstein and Gottfried Benn," in *The Era of German Expressionism,* ed. Paul Raabe (Woodstock: Overlook, 1974), 49–52; and Egbert Krispyn, *Anti-Nazi Writers in Exile* (Athens: University of Georgia Press, 1978), 25.

19. Gottfried Benn, "Alexanderzüge Mittels Wallungen," *Der Querschnitt* 4/4 (1924); his essay "Das Unaufhörlich" in Flechtheim's modernist periodical *Omnibus* in 1932; and Hermann Kasack's radio address in 1927 on Benn, Kafka, and "the modern self" (*Das moderne Ich*). See Hof, *Benn,* 122, 127, 132–33, 138–39.

20. Augustinus Dierick, *Gottfried Benn and His Critics: Major Interpretations 1912–1992* (Rochester: Camden House, 1992), 97.

21. Ritchie, *Gottfried Benn,* 48, 96–105; Ritchie, *German Literature Under National Socialism,* 53.

22. Brenner, *Ende einer bürgerlichen Kunst-Institution,* 29–43, 75; and Gerhard Loose, *Die Ästhetik Gottfried Benns* (Frankfurt: Vittorio Klostermann, 1961), 111.

23. Ritchie, *German Literature Under National Socialism,* 48; and Christine Fischer-Defoy, "Artists and Art Institutions in Germany 1933–1945," *Oxford Art Journal* 9/2 (1986), 17.

24. Hochman, *Architects of Fortune,* 137.

25. Hans Sarkowicz, "'Bis Alles in Scherben Fällt . . .' Schriftsteller im Dienst der NS-Diktatur," in *Hitlers Künstler. Die Kultur im Dienst des Nationalsozialismus,* ed. Hans Sarkowicz (Frankfurt: Insel, 2004), 176; Brenner, *Ende einer bürgerlichen Kunst-Institution,* 58–60; and Ernst Klee, *Das Kulturlexikon zum Dritten Reich. Wer war was vor und nach 1945* (Frankfurt: S. Fischer, 2007), 222–23.

26. Volker Probst, "Arno Breker: Biography," in John Zavrel, *Arno Breker: The Divine Beauty in Art* (Clarence, N.Y.: Est-Art, 1986), 95.

27. Brenner, *Ende einer bürgerlichen Kunst-Institution,* 60–71; Fischer-Defoy, "Artists and Art Institutions," 17; and Sarkowicz, "Schriftsteller im Dienst der NS-Diktatur," 177.

28. Jünger to Werner Beumelburg (18 November 1933), in Brenner, *Ende einer bürgerlichen Kunst-Institution,* 88; and Sarkowicz, "Schriftsteller im Dienst der NS-Diktatur," 178.

29. Krispyn, *Anti-Nazi Writers in Exile,* 25.

30. Benn address at the Berlin Friedhof Heerstrasse (26 April 1933), quoted in Hof, *Benn,* 154.

31. Krispyn, *Anti-Nazi Writers in Exile,* 26; Ritchie, *German Literature Under National Socialism,* 49–50.

32. Gottfried Benn, "Answer to the Literary Emigrants," in Gottfried Benn, *Primal Vision: Selected Writings of Gottfried Benn,* ed. E.B. Ashton (The Hague: New Directions, 1969), 50.

33. Ibid., 47; and Dierick, *Gottfried Benn and His Critics,* 97; Krispyn, *Anti-Nazi Writers in Exile,* 11; Ritchie, *German Literature Under National Socialism,* 50.

34. Benn, "Answer to the Literary Emigrants," 48–49.

35. Krispyn, *Anti-Nazi Writers in Exile,* 27; and Ritchie, *Gottfried Benn,* 30.

36. Ritchie, *Gottfried Benn,* 63.

37. Dierick, *Gottfried Benn and His Critics,* 98.

38. Ibid., 97; and Ritchie, *Gottfried Benn,* 30.

39. Gottfried Benn, "Der neue Staat und die Intellektuellen," in *Essays und Reden. Gesammelte Werke in vier Bänden,* ed. Bruno Hillebrand (Frankfurt: 1989), 464.

40. Gottfried Benn, "Geist und Seele künftiger Geschlechter," in *Essays und Reden. Gesammelte Werke in vier Bänden,* ed. Bruno Hillebrand (Frankfurt: 1989), 255.

41. Dierick, *Gottfried Benn and His Critics,* 97; and Sarkowicz, "Schriftsteller im Dienst der NS-Diktatur," 179.

42. Ritchie, *Gottfried Benn,* 31.

43. Ibid., 31.

44. Benn, "Answer to the Literary Emigrants," 52–53.

45. Volker Dahm, "Künstler als Funktionäre. Das Propaganda-Ministerium und die Reichskulturkammer," in *Hitlers Künstler. Die Kultur im Dienst des Nationalsozialismus,* ed. Hans Sarkowicz (Frankfurt: Insel, 2004), 91–93. Hanns Johst, *Schlageter,* trans. Ford Parkes-Perret (Stuttgart: Akademischer Verlag Hanns-Dieter Heinz, 1984).

46. Dierick, *Gottfried Benn and His Critics,* 99. He references Ernst Nef, *Das Werk Gottfried Benns* (Zurich: Arche, 1964).

47. Benn, "Answer to the Literary Emigrants," 52.

48. Brenner, "Art in the Political Power Struggle," 411.

49. Gottfried Benn, "Gruss an Marinetti," *Deutsche Allgemeine Zeitung* (30 March 1934), reproduced in Hof, *Benn,* 163.

50. Wilhelm Furtwängler to Benn (30 July 1933) reproduced in Hof, *Benn,* 157.

51. Schlemmer to Benn (22 October 1933), in Andreas Hüneke, ed., *Oskar Schlemmer, Idealist der Form. Briefe, Tagebücher, Schriften, 1912–1943* (Leipzig: Reclam-Verlag, 1990), 280–82.

52. Peter Paret, *An Artist Against the Third Reich: Ernst Barlach, 1933–1938* (Cambridge: Cambridge University Press, 2003), 73.

53. Timothy Ryback, *Hitler's Private Library: The Books That Shaped His Life* (New York: Alfred Knopf, 2009), xi.

54. Benn to Ina Seidel, 27 August 1934, in Gottfried Benn, *Briefe an Ernst Jünger, E. R. Curtius, Max Rychner U. A.* (Zurich: Arche, 1960), 26; and Loose, *Die Ästhetik Gottfried Benns,* 139.

55. Benn, quoted in Loose, *Die Ästhetik Gottfried Benns,* 139.

56. William Niven, "The Birth of Nazi Drama? *Thing* Plays," in *Theatre Under the Nazis,* ed. John London (Manchester: Manchester University Press, 2000), 84.

57. Gottfried Benn, "Am Brückenwehr," in Ludwig Greve, *Gottfried Benn 1886–1956* (Marbach: Deutsche Schillergesellschaft, 1986), 230.

58. Benn to Waldemar Bonsels (21 June 1934), quoted in Hof, *Benn,* 163.

59. Ritchie, *Gottfried Benn,* 12; and Benn to F. W. Oelze (25 April 1934), in Gottfried Benn (Harald Steinhagen and Jürgen Schröder), *Gottfried Benn, Briefe an F. W. Oelze, 1932–1945* (Wiesbaden: Limes, 1977), 33; Hof, *Benn,* 164; and Greve, *Gottfried Benn,* 232.

60. Krispyn, *Anti-Nazi Writers in Exile,* 27.

61. Benn to Ina Seidel (12 December 1934), in Gottfried Benn, *Briefe an Ernst Jünger, E. R. Curtius, Max Rychner U. A.,* 30.

62. Benn to Ina Seidel (18 November 1934), in ibid., 30; and Gottfried Benn, *Doppelleben* (Wiesbaden: Limes, 1950), 112.

63. Ritchie, *Gottfried Benn,* 20.

64. Benn, quoted in Hof, *Benn,* 170; and Rolf Becker, "Liebes Morchen, kleiner Mor," *Der Spiegel* (6 February 2011).

65. "Der Selbsterreger!" *Das Schwarze Korps* (7 May 1936), reproduced in Hof, *Benn,* 175.

66. Wolfgang Willrich, *Die Säuberung des Kunsttempels. Eine kunstpolitische Kampfschrift zur Gesundung Deutscher Kunst im Geiste nordischer Art* (Munich: J. F. Lehmanns, 1937), 23–24.

67. Benn, *Doppelleben,* 116.

68. Himmler to Willrich (22 September 1937), in Greve, *Gottfried Benn,* 241–42.

69. Annegret Janda, "The Fight for Modern Art: The Berlin Nationalgalerie After 1933," in *"Degenerate Art": The Fate of the Avant-Garde in Nazi Germany,* ed. Stephanie Barron (Los Angeles: Los Angeles County Museum of Art, 1991), 112; Jay Baird, *Hitler's War Poets: Literature and Politics in the Third Reich* (Cambridge: Cambridge University Press, 2008), 61; Sarkowicz, "Schriftsteller im Dienst der NS-Diktatur," 181; and Griffin, *Modernism and Fascism,* 288.

70. Göring's role is reported by Hanns Johst in his letter to Himmler (29 March 1938), in Greve, *Gottfried Benn,* 244; and Sarkowicz, "Schriftsteller im Dienst der NS-Diktatur," 182.

71. Johst to Himmler (29 March 1938), in Greve, *Gottfried Benn,* 244.

72. Benn to F. W. Oelze (17 May 1938), in Benn, *Gottfried Benn, Briefe an F. W. Oelze,* 192; Ritchie, *Gottfried Benn,* 21; Benn, *Doppelleben,* 111; and Becker, "Liebes Morchen."

73. Becker, "Liebes Morchen."

74. Gottfried Benn, "Wolf's Tavern," in Gottfried Benn, *Primal Vision: Selected Writings,* ed. E. B. Ashton (The Hague: New Directions, 1969), 67; Becker, "Liebes Morchen"; and more generally, Gottfried Benn, *Gottfried Benn, Briefe an Elinor Büller 1930–1937,* ed. Marguerite Valerie Schlüter (Stuttgart: Klett Cotta, 2010).

75. Benn, "Wolf's Tavern," 71, 78.

76. Benn to F. W. Oelze (23 October 1935), in Benn, *Gottfried Benn, Briefe an F. W. Oelze,* 83.

77. Krispyn, *Anti-Nazi Writers in Exile,* 27; Ritchie, *Gottfried Benn,* 20; and Becker, "Liebes Morchen."

78. Benn, "Art and the Third Reich" and "Excerpts from World of Expression," in Gottfried Benn, *Primal Vision: Selected Writings of Gottfried Benn,* ed E. B. Ashton (The Hague: New Directions, 1969), 91–92, 109–12.

79. Benn to F. W. Oelze (2 May 1942), in Benn, *Gottfried Benn, Briefe an F. W. Oelze,* 314.

80. Benn, "Excerpts from Novel of the Phenotype," in Gottfried Benn, *Primal Vision: Selected Writings of Gottfried Benn,* ed. E. B. Ashton (The Hague: New Directions, 1969), 131–32.

81. Ibid., 122.

82. Benn to F. W. Oelze (15 October 1944), in Benn, *Gottfried Benn, Briefe an F. W. Oelze,* 372–73; and Hannes Heer and Klaus Naumann, eds., *Vernichtungskrieg. Verbrechen der Wehrmacht, 1941 bis 1944* (Hamburg: Hamburg Edition, 1995).

83. Benn, "Excerpts from Novel of the Phenotype," 133.

84. Benn, "Excerpt from Double Life," in Gottfried Benn, *Primal Vision: Selected Writings of Gottfried Benn,* ed. E. B. Ashton (The Hague: New Directions, 1969), 139.

85. Ibid., 140.

86. Ritchie, *Gottfried Benn,* 21.

87. Ibid., 22.

88. Hof, *Benn,* 243; and Henry Grosshans, *German Dreams and German Dreamers: Gottfried Benn's German Universe* (Wyndham Hall, 1987).

89. Ritchie, *German Literature Under National Socialism,* 256.

90. Ritchie, *Gottfried Benn,* 38–40.

91. Ibid., 40; and Benn, *Doppelleben.*

92. Hof, *Benn,* 261. From the poem, "Kann keine Trauer sein." See also Perry Anderson, "A New Germany," *New Left Review* 57 (May–June 2009), at http://www.newleftreview.org/II/57/perry-anderson-a-new-germany (accessed 5 June 2012).

93. Ritchie, *Gottfried Benn,* 23.

CHAPTER 7. ERNST BARLACH

1. Frederic Spotts, *Hitler and the Power of Aesthetics* (Woodstock: Overlook, 2003 [2002]), 180.

2. Peter Paret, *An Artist Against the Third Reich: Ernst Barlach, 1933–1938* (Cambridge: Cambridge University Press, 2003), 1.

3. Ibid., 32; Friedrich Schult, *Ernst Barlach. Werkverzeichnis, Band II. Das graphische Werk* (Hamburg: Hauswedell, 1958); and Jürgen Doppelstein and Heike Stockhaus, *Barlach und Russland: Ernst Barlachs Russlandreise im Sommer 1906* (Bonn: Verein August-Macke-Haus, 2002).

4. Paret, *Artist Against the Third Reich,* 21.

5. Ibid., 144.

6. Ibid., 144–45. He cites Barlach's "Als ich von dem Verbot der Berufsausübung bedroht war," in Friedrich Dross, ed., *Die Prosa* (Munich: R. Piper, 1959), 2, 428. See also Figura Starr, ed., *German Expressionism: The Graphic Impulse* (New York: MoMA, 2011).

7. BAB, RK 10017, docs. 256–59, Ernst Barlach, "Fragebogen" (1 April 1937); and Beate Marks-Hanssen, *Inner Emigration? "Verfemte" Künstlerinnen und Künstler in der Zeit des Nationalsozialismus* (Berlin: dissertation.de, 2006), 84; she cites the *Mecklenburgische Monatshefte* from January 1934.

8. See Barlach's works: *Der tote Tag* (1912); *Der arme Vetter* (1918); *Der blaue Boll* (1926); *Die gute Zeit* (1929); and, more generally, Henry and Mary Garland, eds., *The Oxford Companion to German Literature* (New York: Oxford University Press, 1997), 59.

9. Paret, *Artist Against the Third Reich*, 27, 146–47.

10. Ibid., 27, 28, 31.

11. Ibid., 25; Paret cites the catalogue of the Centre Pompidou–organized exhibition *Paris-Berlin.*

12. Ibid., 35; Josephine Gabler, "Georg Kolbe in der NS-Zeit," in *Georg Kolbe, 1877–1947,* ed. Ursel Berger (Munich: Prestel, 1997), 87–94; and Josephine Gabler, "Conformity in Dissent: Sculptors in the Third Reich," in *Taking Positions: Figurative Sculpture and the Third Reich,* ed. Penelope Curtis (Leeds: Henry Moore Institute, 2002), 42–59.

13. Peter Paret, "Field Marshal and Beggar: Ernst Barlach in the First World War," in *German Encounters with Modernism* (Cambridge: Cambridge University Press, 2001), 144–84. See also Ernst Barlach, *Ein selbst-erzähltes Leben* (Berlin: Cassirer, 1928). His diary from World War I, titled "Güstrower Tagebuch," is included in Friedrich Dross, ed., *Die Prosa* (Munich: R. Piper, 1959).

14. Paret, *Artist Against the Third Reich,* 36; James van Dyke, "Ernst Barlach and the Conservative Revolution," *German Studies Review* 36 (2013), 281–305.

15. James van Dyke, *Franz Radziwill and the Contradictions of German Art History, 1919–45* (Ann Arbor: University of Michigan Press, 2010), 1–2; and Gian Luigi Rondi, *La Biennale di Venezia. Le Esposizioni Internazionali d'Arte 1895–1995* (Venice: Electa, 1997), 89.

16. Annegret Janda, "Die Beziehungen zwischen Ernst Barlach und der Nationalgalerie," in *Staatliche Museen zu Berlin. Forschungen und Berichte,* vol. 25 (Berlin: Akademie Verlag, 1985), 62.

17. GRI, SC, Arntz Papers, box 30, file 1, Kurt Reutti to the Generaldirektor der Nationalgalerie (26 February 1950).

18. Ibid., and Paret, *Artist Against the Third Reich,* 46.

19. Paret, *Artist Against the Third Reich,* 48.

20. Stephanie Barron, ed., *"Degenerate Art": The Fate of the Avant-Garde in Nazi Germany* (Los Angeles: Los Angeles County Museum of Art, 1991), 197.

21. Paret, *Artist Against the Third Reich,* 42–43.

22. Ibid., 5, 24.

23. GRI, SC, Schardt Papers, box 1, file 8, Barlach to Schardt (25 December 1934). See also GRI, SC, Ernst Barlach letters, 1892–1936: letters (25 January 1936, 3 March 1936, and 25 May 1936).

24. Paret, *Artist Against the Third Reich,* 25; Barron, "Degenerate Art," 197.

25. Karsten Müller, "'Violent Vomiting Over Me': Ernst Barlach and National Socialist Cultural Policy," in *Degenerate Art: The Attack on Modern Art in Nazi Germany 1937,* ed. Olaf Peters (Munich: Prestel, 2014), 181.

26. BAB, former BDC file for Ernst Barlach, Bernhard Böhmer to Goebbels (12 June 1935), Hans Hinkel to Böhmer (5 August 1935).

27. James van Dyke, "Something New on Nolde, National Socialism, and the SS," *Kunstchronik* 65/5 (May 2012), 270.

28. Böhmer to Reinhard Piper (27 April 1936), in Ernst Piper, ed., *Ernst Barlach und die Nationalsozialistische Kunstpolitik* (Munich: R. Piper, 1983), 142–43.

29. Christian Fuhrmeister, "Dr. Phil. Rolf Hetsch, 'Einziger Zünftiger Kunsthistoriker' im Reichsministerium für Volksaufklärung und Propaganda," in *"Führerauftrag Monumentalmalerei." Eine Fotokampagne 1943–1945*, ed. Christian Fuhrmeister, Stephan Klingen, and Iris Lauterbach (Cologne: Böhlau, 2006), 107–26.

30. Paret, *Artist Against the Third Reich*, 130–31; and Barron, *"Degenerate Art,"* 197.

31. Note that only five of the seven sculptures by Barlach sold and that prices were below the estimates, but the results showed there was still a market for his art. Gesa Jeuthe, "Die Moderne unter dem Hammer," "Zur 'Verwertung' der 'entarteten' Kunst durch die Luzerner Galerie Fischer 1939," in *Angriff auf die Avantgarde: Kunst und Kunstpolitik im Nationalsozialismus*, ed. Uwe Fleckner (Berlin: Akademie Verlag, 2007), 189–306.

32. Paret, *Artist Against the Third Reich*, 6.

33. Müller, "'Violent Vomiting Over Me,'" 178.

34. Sebastian Giesen, ed., *Der Bildhauer Ernst Barlach. Skulpturen und Plastiken im Ernst Barlach Haus* (Hamburg: Barlach Haus, 2007); Eva Caspars, *Ernst Barlach Haus Hamburg* (Munich: Prestel, 2000); Curd Ochwadt, *Ernst Barlach, Hugo Körtzinger und Hermann Reemstma* (Hannover: Hejo-Verlag, 1988); and Erik Lindner, *Die Reemstmas. Geschichte einer deutschen Unternehmerfamilie* (Hamburg: Hoffmann und Campe, 2007).

35. Heinrich Stegemann, ed., *Malerei und Plastik in Deutschland 1936* (Hamburg: Hamburger Kunstverein, 1936); Ralph Jentsch, *Alfred Flechtheim–George Grosz, Zwei deutsche Schicksale* (Bonn: Weidle, 2008), 47; Roswitha Neu-Kock, "Alexander Vömel, Alfred Flechtheim, und die Verhältnisse in Düsseldorf, 1930 bis 1934," in *Kunst sammeln, Kunst handeln. Beiträge des internationalen Symposiums in Wien*, ed. Eva Blimlinger (Vienna: Böhlau, 2012), 155–66; and Roman Norman Ketterer, *Dialogue. Bildende Kunst. Kunsthandel* (Stuttgart: Belser, 1988), 390–99.

36. Günther Franke, "Günther Franke über sich Selbst," in *Briefe an Günther Franke. Porträt eines deutschen Kunsthändlers*, ed. Doris Schmidt (Cologne: DuMont, 1970), 32.

37. Piper, *Barlach und die nationalsozialistische Kunstpolitik*, 21–22.

38. Müller, "'Violent Vomiting Over Me,'" 176–85. Paret, *Artist Against the Third Reich*, 83.

39. Ibid., 87.

40. Ibid.

41. Ibid., 88.

42. Ibid., 89. See also BAB, NS 8/171, doc. 208, Rosenberg to Goebbels (30 August 1934); and the draft letter from Rosenberg to Goebbels (20 October 1934), in Reinhard Piper, *Nationalsozialistische Kunstpolitik* (Munich: R. Piper, 1987), 116–17.

43. Paret, *Artist Against the Third Reich*, 89.

44. BAB, NS 8/171, doc. 203, Rosenberg to Goebbels (20 October 1934).

45. Maike Steinkamp, *Das Unerwünschte Erbe: Die Rezeption 'entarteter' Kunst in Kunstkritik, Ausstellungen und Museen der SBZ und Frühen DDR* (Berlin: Akademie Verlag, 2008), 76.

46. Paret, *Artist Against the Third Reich*, 94; Steinkamp, *Unerwünschte Erbe*, 142.

47. Böhmer has fascinated scholars and given rise to a rich historiography. See, for example, Meike Hopp, "Bernhard A. Böhmer. Ein unbekannter Bildhauer brilliert im NS-Kunsthandel," in *Kunst sammeln, Kunst handeln. Beiträge des internationalen Symposiums in Wien*, ed. Eva Blimlinger (Vienna: Böhlau, 2012), 197–208; and Meike Hoffmann, ed., *Ein Händler "entarteter" Kunst: Bernhard A. Böhmer und sein Nachlass* (Berlin: Akademie Verlag, 2010).

48. Barlach to Goebbels (25 May 1936), in Anita Beloubek-Hammer, *Ernst Barlach, Zeichnerische und graphische Meisterwerke* (Berlin: E. A. Seemann, 1997), 136.

49. Barlach to Goebbels (25 May 1936), in Ernst Barlach, *Die Briefe, 1888–1938,* ed. Friedrich Dross (Munich: R. Piper, 1968), 636–38; and Paret, *Artist Against the Third Reich,* 101–2.

50. Paret, *Artist Against the Third Reich,* 102. See also Piper, *Barlach und die national-sozialistische Kunstpolitik,* 177–78.

51. Brenner, "Art in the Political Power Struggle," 403, 429; and Paret, *Artist Against the Third Reich,* 175.

52. Ernst Barlach, *Güstrower Tagebuch im Auszug: 1914–18* (S.I.: S.N., 1938); Ernst Barlach, *Fragmente aus sehr früher Zeit* (Berlin: Reimerschmidt, 1939); and Ernst Barlach and Friedrich Schult, *Barlach im Gespräch* (Güstrow: Opitz, 1939). Note that a range of books concerning Barlach's work in the visual arts were also published during the Third Reich.

53. Annie Bardon, "Ernst Barlach und die Melancholie," in *Ernst Barlach: Artist of the North,* ed. Jürgen Doppelstein, Volker Probst, and Heike Stockhaus (St. Ottillien: EOS, 2000), 304–9.

54. Paret, *Artist Against the Third Reich,* 136; and Friedrich Hewicker and Wolf Stubbe, *Ernst Barlach, Plastik* (Munich: R. Piper, 1959), 86, 91, 98, 99.

55. Godula Buchholz, *Karl Buchholz. Buch- und Kunsthändler im 20. Jahrhundert* (Cologne: DuMont, 2005), 73; and Paret, *Artist Against the Third Reich,* 135–36.

56. Paret, *Artist Against the Third Reich,* 95.

57. Barron, *"Degenerate Art,"* 197.

58. Paret, *Artist Against the Third Reich,* 134. Barlach to Heinz Priebatsch (23 October 1938), in Barlach, *Briefe,* 2, 735.

59. Barron, *"Degenerate Art,"* 198. "War Barlach ein Kulturbolschewist?" *Das Schwarze Korps* (3 November 1938). See also the analysis of this article in Paret, *Artist Against the Third Reich,* 140–44.

60. Paret, *Artist Against the Third Reich,* 139.

61. Martin Fritsch, ed., *Ernst Barlach–Käthe Kollwitz im Zwiegespräch* (Berlin: E. A. Seamann, 2006), 6.

CHAPTER 8. EMIL NOLDE

1. BAB, R 55/21014, doc. 64, Nolde to Goebbels (2 July 1938). For a thoughtful consideration of Nolde's anti-Semitism, see Peter Vergo, "Emil Nolde: Myth and Reality," in *Emil Nolde,* ed. Peter Vergo and Felicity Lunn (London: Whitechapel Art Gallery, 1996), 56. See also Russell Berman, "German Primitivism/Primitive Germany," in *Cultural Studies of Modern Germany. History, Representation, and Nationhood,* ed. Russell Berman (Madison: University of Wisconsin Press, 1993), 112–22; and Peter Selz, *Emil Nolde* (New York: Museum of Modern Art, 1963), 28.

2. Eberhard Roters, *Galerie Ferdinand Möller. Die Geschichte einer Galerie für moderne Kunst in Deutschland, 1917–1956* (Berlin: Gebr. Mann, 1984), 275; and Vergo, "Nolde: Myth and Reality," 59.

3. BG, GFM, MF 5316, 0245–46, Nolde to Möller (2 March 1937).

4. Martin Urban, *Werkverzeichnis der Gemälde. Band I, 1895–1914* (Munich: C. H. Beck, 1987), 14, 52; and Stephanie Barron, ed., *"Degenerate Art,": The Fate of the Avant-Garde in Nazi Germany* (Los Angeles: Los Angeles County Museum of Art, 1991), 315.

5. Susanne Beyer, *Palucca. Die Biografie* (Berlin: Aviva, 2009), 65, 81, 197–98; Peter Jelavich, "Dance of Life, Dance of Death," in *German Expressionism: The Graphic Impulse,*

ed. Starr Figura (New York: Museum of Modern Art, 2011), 36–53; and Manfred Reuther, ed., *Nolde in Berlin: Tanz, Theater, Cabaret* (Seebüll: Nolde Stiftung, 2007).

6. Arthur Drexler, ed., *An Illustrated Catalogue of the Mies van der Rohe Drawings in the Museum of Modern Art*, 4 vols. (New York: Garland, 1986), II: 520–39; and Wolf Tegethoff, *Mies van der Rohe: The Villas and the Country Houses* (Cambridge: MIT Press, 1985), 99–104.

7. James van Dyke, "Something New on Nolde, National Socialism, and the SS," *Kunstchronik* 65/5 (May 2012), 266; and Urban, *Werkverzeichnis der Gemälde I*, 19.

8. Andrew Zimmerman, "From Natural Science to Primitive Art: German New Guinea and Emil Nolde," in *Die Schau des Fremden: Ausstellungskonzepte zwischen Kunst, Kommerz und Wissenschaft*, ed. Cordula Grewe (Stuttgart: Franz Steiner, 2006), 279–300; Peter Vergo, "The South Seas," in *Emil Nolde*, ed. Peter Vergo and Felicity Lunn (London: Whitechapel, 1996), 140; and Manfred Reuther, ed., *Emil Nolde. Die Südseereise 1913–1914* (Cologne: DuMont, 2008).

9. Barron, *"Degenerate Art,"* 315. See also Nolde, "Urvölkerkunst, 1912" in Emil Nolde, *Mein Leben* (Cologne: DuMont, 1979 [1976]), 201.

10. GRI, SC, 2004.M34, folder 4, Nolde to Hans Fehr (6 February 1919); Barron, *"Degenerate Art,"* 315; Vergo, "Nolde: Myth and Reality," 38, 49; Urban, *Werkverzeichnis der Gemälde I,* 22; Martin Urban, *Die Stiftung Seebüll Ada und Emil Nolde* (Seebüll, Stiftung Seebüll, 1991), 10; Peter Selz, *German Expressionist Painting* (Berkeley: University of California Press, 1974 [1957]), 313; Elaine Hochman, *Architects of Fortune: Mies van der Rohe and the Third Reich* (New York: Weidenfeld and Nicolson, 1989), 322.

11. See, for example, Joseph Wulf, *Bildenden Künste im Dritten Reich* (Gütersloh: Sigbert Mohn, 1963), 44; Diether Schmidt, *In letzter Stunde, 1933–1945. Schriften Deutscher Künstler des 20. Jahrhunderts. Teil II* (Dresden: Verlag der Kunst, 1964), 271–72; Ian Dunlop, *The Shock of the New. Seven Historic Exhibitions of Modern Art* (London: Weidenfeld and Nicolson, 1972), 235; Reinhard Müller-Mehlis, *Die Kunst im Dritten Reich* (Munich: Heyne, 1976), 150–51; and Franz Roh, *Streit um die moderne Kunst* (Munich: List, 1962), 24.

12. BAB, OPG, D 108, doc. 236, Sauerteig to Gaugericht Hamburg der NSDAP (18 March 1937); BAB, R 55/409, doc. 68, Dr. Richter to Pressebeirat Frielitz in the German Embassy in Copenhagen (7 April 1941). See also Monika Hecker, "Ein Leben an der Grenze. Emil Nolde und die NSDAP," *Nord Friesland* 110 (June 1995), 10; and Vergo, "Nolde: Myth and Reality," 49.

13. Siegfried Lenz, *The German Lesson* (New York: Hill and Wang, 1972); and Hecker, "Ein Leben an der Grenze," 9.

14. Van Dyke, "Something New on Nolde," 269. Van Dyke cites GRI, SC, 2004.M34, folder 5, Nolde to Hans Fehr (10 November 1933).

15. BAB, R 55/21014, doc. 64, Nolde to Goebbels (2 July 1938).

16. Bernhard Fulda and Aya Soika, "Emil Nolde and the National Socialist Dictatorship," in *Degenerate Art: The Attack on Modern Art in Nazi Germany 1937*, ed. Olaf Peters (Munich: Prestel, 2014), 186.

17. Stefan Koldehoff, *Die Bilder sind unter uns. Das Geschäft mit der NS-Raubkunst* (Frankfurt: Eichborn, 2009), 166; quoting Emil Nolde, *Jahre der Kämpfe* (Berlin: Rembrandt, 1934), 122.

18. Koldehoff, *Die Bilder sind unter uns,* 166, quoting Nolde, *Jahre der Kämpfe,* 101, 124.

19. Kirchner to Schiefler (20 December 1934), in Ernst Ludwig Kirchner, *Briefwechsel 1910–1935/1938* (Stuttgart: Belser, 1990), 706.

20. Bernhard Fulda and Aya Soika, *Max Pechstein. The Rise and Fall of Expressionism* (Berlin: DeGruyter, 2012), 303. They quote a letter from Pechstein to Kraus (7 October 1933) in the Preussische Akademie der Künste Archive (1104, f. 120).

21. Ibid., 302–3.

22. Ibid.

23. Lothar Grisebach, *E. L. Kirchners Davoser Tagebuch. Erste Veröffentlichung der wichtigsten Schriften E. L. Kirchners* (Cologne: DuMont, 1968), 94, 288.

24. Kirchner entry (19 September 1925), in Grisebach, *Kirchner,* 94–95. For another expression of anti-Semitism by Kirchner, see his letter to Hansgeorg Knoblauch (29 December 1930), in Eberhard Kornfeld, ed., *Ernst Ludwig Kirchner. Briefwechsel mit einem jungen Ehepaar, 1927–1937. Elfriede Dümmler und Hansgeorg Knoblauch* (Bern: Verlag Kornfeld, 1989), 122–23.

25. Kirchner, quoted in 6 July 1934 letter in Hubertus Froning, *E. L. Kirchner und die Wandmalerei. Entwürfe zur Wandmalerei im Museum Folkwang* (Recklinghausen: Verlag Aurel Bongers, 1991), 94.

26. Anthony Julius, *T. S. Eliot, Anti-Semitism and Literary Form* (London: Thames and Hudson, 2003); and Rita Pokorny, "Archives Cast a Shadow over Revered State Museum Director," *Art Newspaper* 220 (January 2011).

27. Grisebach, *Kirchner,* 288.

28. The first volume of Nolde's autobiography was titled *Das eigene Leben. Die Zeit der Jugend, 1867–1902* (1931). The second volume, *Jahre der Kämpfe 1902–1914* (1934), was followed by the third, *Welt und Heimat. Die Südseereise 1913–1918* (Cologne: DuMont, 1965), and finally by *Reisen–Achtung–Befreiung, 1919–1946* (Cologne: DuMont, 1967). They have been combined in Emil Nolde, *Mein Leben.*

29. Fulda and Soika, "Emil Nolde and the National Socialist Dictatorship," 191.

30. Barron, *"Degenerate Art,"* 315.

31. Brenner, *Kunstpolitik des Nationalsozialismus,* 67; and Vergo, "Nolde: Myth and Reality," 64.

32. Hildegard Brenner, "Art in the Political Power Struggle of 1933 and 1934," in *Republic to Reich: The Making of the Nazi Revolution,* ed. Hajo Holborn (New York: Vintage Books, 1972), 402.

33. BAB, R 55/21014, doc. 64, Nolde to Goebbels (2 July 1938). See also, Thomas Knubben, "'Mein Leid, meine Qual, meine Verachtung.' Emil Nolde im Dritten Reich," in *Emil Nolde. Ungemalte Bilder. Aquarelle 1938 bis 1945 aus der Sammlung der Nolde-Stiftung Seebüll,* ed. Tilman Osterwold and Thomas Knubben (Ostfildern-Ruit: Hatje Cantz, 1999), 143.

34. Müller-Mehlis, *Kunst im Dritten Reich,* 150–51.

35. Fulda and Soika, "Emil Nolde and the National Socialist Dictatorship," 187.

36. Peter Paret, *Artist Against the Third Reich: Ernst Barlach, 1933–1938* (Cambridge: Cambridge University Press, 2003), 18. See the diary entry for 2 July 1933 in Joseph Goebbels, *Die Tagebücher von Joseph Goebbels. Sämtliche Fragmente,* ed. Elke Fröhlich (Munich: K. G. Sauer, 1987), I:2, III:219.

37. Van Dyke, "Something New on Nolde," 268–70.

38. Nolde to Hans Fehr (10 November 1933), quoted by van Dyke in ibid., 268–70.

39. Fulda and Soika, "Emil Nolde and the National Socialist Dictatorship," 190.

40. Urban, *Werkverzeichnis der Gemälde I,* 25; and Kestner-Gesellschaft, ed., *Emil Nolde Aquarelle* (Hannover: Kestner-Gesellschaft, 1934). For Nolde's works in the exhibition, *Das Bild der Landschaft,* see Urban, *Werkverzeichnis der Gemälde I,* 590. Nolde's *Hülltoft Hof* was sold off via Karl Buchholz, but the painting was reacquired at auction by the Voss family and given to the Hamburg Kunsthalle for a second time in 2002. See http://www.hamburger-kunsthalle.de/archiv/seiten/nolde1.html (accessed 2 August 2011).

41. Koldehoff, *Die Bilder sind unter uns,* 167–68. See also BAB (former BDC-file), OPG, Personalakte Harald Busch, RKK 2100.

42. Dr. C. P., "Emil Nolde in Kölner Kunstverein," *National-Zeitung* (Essen) (13 January 1935).

43. K. H. B., "Grosse Nolde-Ausstellung in Köln," *Saarbrücker Zeitung* (12 January 1935).

44. Urban, *Werkverzeichnis der Gemälde I*, 590.

45. GRI, SC, 2004.M35, Nolde to Alfred Heuer (21 October 1937); and Maike Steinkamp, *Das Unerwünschte Erbe. Die Rezeption 'entarteter' Kunst in Kunstkritik, Ausstellungen und Museen der SBZ und Frühen DDR* (Berlin: Akademie Verlag, 2008), 75.

46. Hecker, "Ein Leben an der Grenze," 15; Barron, *"Degenerate Art,"* 319. See more generally, Max Sauerlandt, *Die Kunst der letzten 30 Jahre: Eine Vorlesung aus dem Jahre 1933* (Hamburg: Laatzen, 1948); and Max Sauerlandt, ed., *Emil Nolde. Briefe aus den Jahren 1894–1926* (Berlin: Furche-Kunstverlag, 1927).

47. BSGS, Nr. 1755, Ernst Buchner to Nolde (9 May 1935); Barron, *"Degenerate Art,"* 315; and Nolde, *Mein Leben,* 391.

48. Pamela Kort, "Oskar Schlemmer," in *"Degenerate Art": The Fate of the Avant-Garde in Nazi Germany,* ed. Stephanie Barron (Los Angeles: Los Angeles County Museum of Art, 1991), 336; and Laura Lauzemis, "Die nationalsozialistische Ideologie und der 'neue Mensch.' Oskar Schlemmers Folkwang-Zyklus und sein Briefwechsel mit Graf Klaus von Baudissin aus dem Jahr 1934," in *Angriff auf die Avant-Garde. Kunst und Kunstpolitik im Nationalsozialismus,* ed. Uwe Fleckner (Berlin: Akademie Verlag, 2007), 5–88.

49. Anna Jolly, "Biographien," in *Junge Deutsche Kunst. Der Folkwang-Wettbewerb 1934,* ed. Mario-Andreas Lüttichau (Essen: Museum Folkwang Essen, 1993), 106.

50. BG, GFM, C, II 1, 185-1, 209, 0236, Möller to Baudissin (21 August 1936); and Baudissin to Möller (9 September 1936).

51. Andreas Hüneke, "Immer wieder Ferdinand Möller," and Ute Haug, "'Private Schlupfwinkel' in der Öffentlichkeit. Die Provenienz des Gemäldes 'Improvisation Nr. 10' von Wassily Kandinsky," in *Das Verfemte Meisterwerk. Schicksalswege Moderner Kunst im "Dritten Reich,"* ed. Uwe Fleckner (Berlin: Akademie Verlag, 2009), 489–508 and 509–42.

52. GRI, SC, 890235, Emil Nolde Correspondence, 1932–1937, Nolde to Wilhelm Hebestreit (10 November 1937).

53. GRI, SC, 2004.M35, Nolde to Alfred Heuer (21 October 1937).

54. See the invitation to the Heuers in GRI, SC, 2004.M35, Ada Nolde to Frau Heuer (9 April 1937); and Nolde, *Mein Leben,* 394–95.

55. Urban, *Werkverzeichnis der Gemälde I,* 27. For more on the *Exhibition of Twentieth Century Germany Art* (July 1938), see Keith Holz, *Modern German Art for Thirties Paris, Prague, and London. Resistance and Acquiescence in a Democratic Public Sphere* (Ann Arbor: University of Michigan Press, 2004), 127–29, 194–222; and Eberhard Roters and Bernhard Schulz, eds., *Stationen der Moderne* (Berlin: Berlinische Galerie, 1989), 314–36.

56. BAB, R 55/21014, doc. 64, Nolde to Goebbels (2 July 1938).

57. See http://www.geschkult.fu-berlin.de/e/db_entart_kunst/geschichte/beschlagnahme/index.html (accessed 16 June 2013).

58. Nolde, *Mein Leben,* 380; and BG, GFM, MF 5316 (Nolde), 0227, Ferdinand Möller to Ada Nolde (10 February 1936).

59. BG, GFM, MF 5316 (Nolde), 0228, Ada Nolde to Eugen Hönig (n.d. [January 1936]); and Vergo, "Nolde: Myth and Reality," 38–40.

60. Georg Kreis, "'Entartete Kunst' in Basel: Eine Chronik ausserordentlicher Ankäufe im Jahre 1939," *Baseler Zeitschrift für Geschichte und Altertumskunde* 78 (1978), 186–97.

61. Urban, *Werkverzeichnis der Gemälde I,* 27; Franz Roh, *"Entartete" Kunst. Kunstbarbarei im Dritten Reich* (Hannover: Fackelträger, 1962), 139–40; and SMB-ZA, Rave NL, Nr. 95, Rave notes (n.d.).

62. Paul Ortwin Rave, *Kunstdiktatur im Dritten Reich* (Berlin: Gebr. Mann, 1949), 73; and Alexander Vömel, "40 Jahre Kunsthandel in Düsseldorf," in *Alex Vömel, Daniel-Henry Kahnweiler, Fritz Nathan. Freuden und Leiden eines Kunsthändler,* ed. Karl-Heinz Hering (Düsseldorf: Arbeitsgemeinschaft kultureller Organisationen Düsseldorf, 1964), 17.

63. Ziegler to Nolde (23 August 1941), reproduced in Urban, *Werkverzeichnis der Gemälde* I, 29; Nolde, *Reisen—Achtung—Befreiung,* 124, and Marlborough Fine Arts, *Nolde: Forbidden Pictures* (London: Marlborough Fine Arts, 1970), 5. For Ziegler's letter to Schmidt-Rottluff (3 April 1941), see Rave, *Kunstdiktatur im Dritten Reich,* 94.

64. Barron, *"Degenerate Art,"* 319; Selz, *Emil Nolde,* 71; and Nolde, *Mein Leben,* 394. See also Tilman Osterwold and Thomas Knubben, eds., *Emil Nolde. Ungemalte Bilder. Aquarelle 1938 bis 1945 aus der Sammlung der Nolde-Stiftung Seebüll* (Ostfildern-Ruit: Hatje Cantz, 1999).

65. Van Dyke, "Something New on Nolde," 266.

66. Nolde, *Mein Leben,* 394; Barron, *"Degenerate Art,"* 319; and Urban, *Werkverzeichnis der Gemälde I,* 29.

67. GRI, SC, 2004.M35, Nolde to Alfred Heuer (18 September 1939). Martin Urban, *Werkverzeichnis der Gemälde. Band II, 1915–1951* (Munich: C. H. Beck, 1990), 440–42, 456, 513–14.

68. Hyun Ae Lee, "Tanz der Farben im Spätwerk Kirchners," in *Der Neue Stil. Ernst Ludwig Kirchners Spätwerk,* ed. Björn Egging and Karin Schick (Bielefeld: Kerber, 2008), 123.

69. John London, "Introduction," in *Theatre Under the Nazis,* ed. John London (Manchester: Manchester University Press, 2000), 19; Lilian Karina and Marion Kant, *Hitler's Dancers: German Modern Dancers in the Third Reich* (New York: Berghahn, 2003); Susan Laikin Funkenstein, "There's Something About Mary Wigman: The Woman Dancer as Subject in German Expressionist Art," *Gender & History* 17/3 (November 2005), 826–59; and Björn Egging, "'Der Stil ist neu': Anmerkungen zum Stilwandel in Kirchners Spätwerk," in *Der Neue Stil. Ernst Ludwig Kirchners Spätwerk,* ed. Björn Egging and Karin Schick (Bielefeld: Kerber, 2008), 20.

70. Hyuan Ae Lee, "Tanz der Farben im Spätwerk Kirchners," 123.

71. Egging, "'Der Stil ist neu,'" 17, 20. See also Louis de Marsalle (= E. L. Kirchner), "Über Ernst Ludwig Kirchner," in *Ernst Ludwig Kirchner. Spontan und doch Vollendet,* ed. Andrea Wandschneider (Paderborn: Städtische Galerie, 2008), 31–35.

72. Froning, *Kirchner und die Wandmalerei,* 88, 96 (the latter references a letter from Kirchner discussing his work on the fresco design from 29 April 1937); and the work titled *Allegory* (Nr. 1004) from 1937, in Donald Gordon, *Ernst Ludwig Kirchner* (Cambridge: Harvard University Press, 1968), 412.

73. BAB (former BDC-file of Erich Heckel), RKK files, Heckel to Landesleiter der Reichskammer der bildenden Künste (3 October 1936 and 21 November 1942).

74. Kirchner to Dr. Schumann, 12 July 1937, in Wulf, *Bildenden Künste im Dritten Reich,* 309; Brenner, *Ende einer bürgerlichen Kunst-Institution,* 146–48; and Grisebach, *Kirchner,* 198.

75. Vanessa-Maria Voigt, *Kunsthändler und Sammler der Moderne im Nationalsozialismus. Die Sammlung Sprengel 1934 bis 1945* (Berlin: Reimer, 2007), 33–59, 65; Markus Heinzelmann and Ulrich Krempel, eds., *Emil Nolde und die Sammlung Sprengel 1937 bis 1956: Geschichte einer Freundschaft* (Hannover: Sprengel Museum, 1999); and Mirka Knauf, "Bernhard Sprengel Zeigt und Schenkt—Der Sammler und Die Sammlung Sprengel," in *Die 1960er Jahre in Hannover. Künstler, Galerien und Strassenkunst,* ed. Stephen Lohr and Ludwig Zerull (Hannover: Sprengel Museum Hannover, 2007), 143–51.

76. Nolde, *Mein Leben,* 395; and Selz, *Emil Nolde,* 71.

77. Fulda and Soika, "Emil Nolde and the National Socialist Dictatorship," 193.

78. Ibid.

79. Nolde, *Mein Leben*, 393, 403; Dieter Scholz, "Otto Andreas Schreiber, die *Kunst der Nation* und die Fabrikausstellungen," in *Überbrückt: Ästhetische Moderne und Nationalsozialismus. Kunsthistoriker und Künstler, 1925–1937*, ed. Eugen Blume and Dieter Scholz (Cologne: Walther König, 1999), 104, 108. See "Jetzt schreite ich aber ein," *Der Spiegel* 42 (2 March 1992), 238–43.

80. Nolde to Franke (8 October 1944), in Doris Schmidt, ed., *Briefe an Günther Franke. Porträt eines deutschen Kunsthändlers* (Cologne: DuMont, 1970), 197–98; and Hans-Joachim Hecker, "Missbrauchtes Mäzentum?," in *Die "Kunststadt" München 1937. Nationalsozialismus und "Entartete Kunst,"* ed. Peter-Klaus Schuster (Munich: Prestel, 1987), 59.

81. Werner Haftmann, "Ein Deutscher Kunsthändler in Amerika," *Jahresring* 58/59 (1958), 179; and Magdalena Droste, "Bauhaus-Maler im Nationalsozialismus," in *Bauhaus-Moderne im Nationalsozialismus. Zwischen Anbietung und Verfolgung*, ed. Winfried Nerdinger (Munich: Prestel, 1993), 138–40.

82. SMB-ZA, Buchholz NL, Karton 9, Erika Berndt to Marie Louise Buchholz (23 March 1943); and an unidentified employee of the Buchholz Gallery to Marie Louise Buchholz (13 October 1943).

83. BAB, R 55/21018, Leopold Gutterer to Reinhard Heydrich (6 May 1941).

84. DKA, NL Arnold/Gutbier, I, B-740, Möller to Gutbier (10 April 1943); and DKA, NL Arnold/Gutbier, I, B-674, Franke to Gutbier (6 June 1944).

85. DKA, NL Arnold/Gutbier, I, B-674, Gutbier to Franke (10 June 1944).

86. Urban, *Werkverzeichnis der Gemälde I,* 29. Nolde, *Mein Leben,* 401. Voigt, *Kunsthändler und Sammler der Moderne im Nationalsozialismus,* 65.

87. Selz, *Emil Nolde,* 77; Barron, *"Degenerate Art,"* 320; and Werner Haftmann, *Emil Nolde* (Cologne: DuMont, 1958).

88. Manfred Reuther, "Jolanthe Nolde. Emil Noldes späte Liebe," *Schleswig-Holstein Zeitungsverlag* (19 June 2010), at http://www.shz.de/nachrichten/schleswig-holstein/kultur/artikeldetail/article//emil-noldes-spaete-liebe-1.html (accessed 26 August 2011).

PART III. ACCOMMODATION REALIZED

1. Beatrice von Bormann, ed., *Max Beckmann in Amsterdam, 1937–1947* (Amsterdam: Van Gogh Museum, 2006) 14; and Lutz Tittel, "Dix–neu gesehen," in *Otto Dix. Die Friedrichshafener Sammlung Bestandskatalog*, ed. Lutz Tittel (Friedrichshafen: Moser, 1992), 58, 95.

2. Bormann, *Max Beckmann in Amsterdam,* 11.

3. Beckmann to Franke (22 February 1944), in Doris Schmidt, ed., *Briefe an Günther Franke. Porträt eines deutschen Kunsthändlers* (Cologne: DuMont, 1970), 84.

4. Christian Fuhrmeister and Susanne Kienlechner, "Max Beckmann und der Widerstand in den Nederlanden," in *Max Beckmann von Angesicht zu Angesicht*, ed. Susanne Petri and Hans-Werner Schmidt (Ostfildern-Ruit: Hatje Cantz, 2011), 42–43, 352. See also Olaf Peters, *Vom Schwarzen Seiltänzer. Max Beckmann zwischen Weimarer Republik und Exil* (Berlin: Reimer, 2005), 336–39; Christian Lenz, ed., *Hefte des Max Beckmann Archivs, 11/12. Erwerbungen 2008–2010* (Munich: Max Beckmann Gesellschaft, 2012), 49.

5. Erhard Göpel and Barbara Göpel, eds., *Max Beckmann. Katalog der Gemälde* (Bern: Kornfeld and Cie, 1976), 396 (and vol. II, Tafel 242). The provenance for the painting, which is in a private collection, lists Erhard Göpel as the owner in 1944. See also Carla Schulz-Hoffmann, ed., *Frauen* (Munich: Pinakothek der Moderne; and Ostfildern: Hatje Cantz, 2012), 290–91.

6. Bormann, *Max Beckmann in Amsterdam*, 17.

7. Beckmann to Franke (22 February 1944), in Schmidt, *Briefe an Günther Franke*, 29, 84; and Reinhard Müller-Mehlis, "Zum Tode von Günther Franke," *Weltkunst* 21 (1 November 1976), 2120.

8. Breker, quoted in a 22 September 1983 interview in John Zavrel, *Arno Breker: The Divine Beauty in Art* (Clarence, N.Y.: Est-Art, 1986), 32.

9. Peter Paret, *An Artist Against the Third Reich: Ernst Barlach, 1933–1938* (Cambridge: Cambridge University Press, 2003), 127. See Goebbels's entry for 6 June 1937, in Joseph Goebbels, *Die Tagebücher von Joseph Goebbels. Sämtliche Fragmente*, ed. Elke Fröhlich (Munich: K. G. Sauer, 1987), I, 4, 170.

10. Paret, *Artist Against the Third Reich*, 127–29.

11. For a list of some two dozen paintings purchased by Schirach from or through Mühlmann, see Jean Vlug, *Report on Objects Removed to Germany from Holland, Belgium, and France During the German Occupation in the Countries* (Hague: Stichting Nederlands Kunstbesit, 1945), 96.

12. Fritz Koller, *Das Inventarbuch der Landesgalerie Salzburg, 1942–1944* (Salzburg: Salzburger Landesarchiv, 2000), 142. For more on the Schirachs' art collection, see Jonathan Petropoulos, *Art as Politics in the Third Reich* (Chapel Hill: University of North Carolina Press, 1996), 220–26; and Gert Kerschbaumer, *Meister des Verwirrens. Die Geschäfte des Kunsthändlers Friedrich Welz* (Vienna: Czernin, 2000), 156–57.

13. Henriette von Schirach, *The Price of Glory* (London: Frederick Muller, 1960), 32; Baldur von Schirach, *Ich glaubte an Hitler* (Hamburg: Mosaik, 1967), 289; and Isgard Kracht, "Verehrt und verfemt. Franz Marc im Nationalsozialismus," in *Angriff auf die Avant-Garde. Kunst und Kunstpolitik im Nationalsozialismus*, ed. Uwe Fleckner (Berlin: Akademie Verlag, 2007), 307–59.

14. Doreen Carvajal, "Prominent French Families Battle over a Missing Monet," *New York Times* (19 March 2012), 1; and Nancy Yeide, *Beyond Dreams of Avarice: The Hermann Goering Collection* (Dallas: Laurel, 2009), 166, 167, 211, 452.

15. Von Schirach, *Price of Glory*, 196. Note that many Hollywood films were accessible to the German public, at least in large cities, until 1940. See Jost Hermand, *Kultur in finsteren Zeiten. Nazifaschismus, Innere Emigration, Exil* (Cologne: Böhlau, 2010), 162.

16. Paret, *Artist Against the Third Reich*, 127. See also Mario-Andreas von Lüttichau, "'Deutsche' Kunst und 'Entartete Kunst': Die Münchner Ausstellung 1937," in *Die "Kunststadt" München 1937. Nationalsozialismus und "Entartete Kunst,"* ed. Peter-Klaus Schuster (Munich: Prestel, 1987), 90.

17. Oliver Rathkolb, "Nationalzoialistische (Un-) Kulturpolitik in Wien, 1938–1945," in *Im Reich der Kunst. Die Wiener Akademie der bildenden Künste und die faschistische Kunstpolitik*, ed. Hans Seiger, Michael Lunardi and Peter Josef Populorum (Vienna: Verlag für Gesellschaftskritik, 1990), 250; and Jan Tabor, "Die Gaben der Ostmark. Österreichische Kunst und Künstler in der NS-Zeit," in *Im Reich der Kunst. Die Wiener Akademie der bildenden Künste und die faschistische Kunstpolitik*, ed. Hans Seiger, Michael Lunardi and Peter Josef Populorum (Vienna: Verlag für Gesellschaftskritik, 1990), 291.

18. Schirach, *Ich glaubte an Hitler*, 285.

19. Ibid.

20. Ibid.

21. Mühlmann led art plundering operations in Vienna, Poland, and the Netherlands. See Jonathan Petropoulos, *The Faustian Bargain: The Art World in Nazi Germany* (New York: Oxford University Press, 2000), 170–204; Rathkolb, "(Un-) Kulturpolitik in Wien," 264; and Gert Kershbaumer, *Faszination Drittes Reich. Kunst und Alltag der Kunstmetropole Salzburg* (Salzburg: Otto Müller, 1988).

22. Alexandra Caruso, "Raub in geordneten Verhältnissen," in *NS-Kunstraub in Öster-reich und die Folgen,* ed. Gabriele Anderl and Alexandra Caruso (Vienna: Studien Verlag, 2005), 98; Hubertus Czernin, *Die Fälschung. Der Fall Bloch Bauer und das Werk Gustav Klimts* (Vienna: Czernin, 2006); and Anne-Marie O'Connor, *The Lady in Gold: The Extraordinary Tale of Gustav Klimt's Masterpiece, Portrait of Adele Bloch-Bauer* (New York: Alfred Knopf, 2011).

23. Rathkolb, "(Un-) Kulturpolitik in Wien," 268.

24. David Monod, *Settling Scores: German Music, Denazification, and the Americans, 1945–1953* (Chapel Hill: University of North Carolina Press, 2005), 85; Oliver Rathkolb, *Führertreu und Gottbegnadet. Künstlerelite im Dritten Reich* (Vienna: Österreichischer Bundesverlag, 1991), 99–105; and Erik Levi, "Opera in the Nazi Period," in *Theatre Under the Nazis,* ed. John London (Manchester: Manchester University Press, 2000), 136–86.

25. Christian Fuhrmeister and Susanne Kienlechner, "Tatort Nizza: Kunstgeschichte zwischen Kunsthandel, Kunstraub und Verfolgung," in *Kunstgeschichte im "Dritten Reich": Theorien, Methoden, Praktiken,* ed. Ruth Heftrig, Olaf Peters, and Barbara Schellewald (Berlin: Akademie Verlag, 2008), 426. Degenhart, an expert on Renaissance art, worked for the Dienststelle Mühlmann in the Netherlands and later directed the Staatlichen Graphischen Sammlung in Munich from 1965 to 1970. See "Dictionary of Art Historians," at http://www.dictionaryofarthistorians.org/degenhartb.htm (accessed 30 June 2011).

26. Thomas Weyr, *The Setting of the Pearl: Vienna Under Hitler* (New York: Oxford University Press, 2005), 211. See also W. Th. Anderman (pseudonym for Walter Thomas), *Bis der Vorhang fiel. Berichtet nach Aufzeichnungen aus den Jahren 1940 bis 1945* (Dortmund: Karl Schwalvenberg, 1947).

27. Baldur von Schirach, "Der Grosse Auftrag," *Völkischer Beobachter* 305 (1 November 1942).

28. BAB, NS 8/170, docs. 96–97, Scholz to Rosenberg (16 November 1942).

29. Wilhelm Rüdiger, *Junge Kunst im Deutschen Reich, Wien 1943. Veranstaltet vom Reichsstatthalter in Wien Reichsleiter Baldur von Schirach* (Vienna: Ehrlich and Schmidt, 1943).

30. Schirach consulted Professor Bruno Grimschitz and purchased works by Karl Albiker, Theo Champion, Franz Gebhardt, and Hans Wimmer, among others. Österreichisches Staatsarchiv, Archiv der Republik, Bundesministerium für Unterricht und Kultus, 1780–1943, No. U-71, Walter Thomas, memoranda (19 February 1943 and 8 March 1943).

31. Michael Kater, *Composers of the Nazi Era: Eight Portraits* (New York: Oxford University Press, 2000), 169.

32. Stefan Koldehoff, *Bilder sind unter uns. Das Geschäft mit der NS-Raubkunst* (Frankfurt: Eichborn, 2009), 159–64; and Christoph Zuschlag, *"Entartete Kunst": Ausstellungsstrategien im Nazi-Deutschland* (Worms: Wernersche Verlagsgesellschaft, 1995), 93; and David Dennis, *Inhumanities: Nazi Interpretations of Western Culture* (Cambridge: Cambridge University Press, 2012), 40–46.

33. See, among other works, Wilhelm Rüdiger, *Die Welt der Renaissance* (Munich: K. Desch, 1970).

34. Koldehoff, *Bilder sind unter uns,* 169–71.

35. BAB, NS 8/170, docs. 96–97, Scholz to Rosenberg (16 November 1942); and Emil Preetorious, quoted by Koldehoff, *Bilder sind unter uns,* 171.

36. BAB, NS 8/170, docs. 110–113, Robert Scholz, "Bericht für den Reichsleiter, Besichtigung der Ausstellung 'Junge Kunst im Deutschen Reich' in Wien" (24 March 1943).

37. Tabor, "Die Gaben der Ostmark," 294. Anderman [Thomas], *Bis der Vorhang Fiel,* 216.

38. Volker Probst, *Paul Mathias Padua. Maler zwischen Tradition und Moderne* (Neuss: Silesia Hanke, 1988), 9, 56.

39. BAB, NS 8/170, docs. 110–113, Robert Scholz, "Bericht für den Reichsleiter, Besichtigung der Ausstellung 'Junge Kunst im Deutschen Reich' in Wien" (24 March 1943).

40. Ibid.

41. DKA, NL Arnold/Gutbier, I, B-540, Rüdiger to Gutbier (24 January 1943); DKA, NL Arnold/Gutbier, I, B, 292, program and materials related to *Junge Kunst* exhibition.

42. Tabor, "Die Gaben der Ostmark," 294.

43. Schirach, *Ich glaubte an Hitler,* 288.

44. International Military Tribunal, *Trial of the Major War Criminals* (Nuremberg: International Military Tribunal, 1947), vol. XIV, 428.

45. Schiele's works were included in the exhibition at the Albertina, "Deutsche Zeichnungen nach der Jahrhundertwende," February–April 1943. For Schiele being tolerated, see Weyr, *Setting of the Pearl,* 210–11.

46. Heinrich Neumayer, "Egon Schiele. Zum Gedächtnis," *Völkischer Beobachter* 307 (3 November 1943), 4.

47. Well over a dozen pictures by Egon Schiele were sold at the Dorotheum auction house in Vienna during the war, including: *Häuser* (1914) and *Weiblicher Akt* (n.d.) at auction 458 in 1940; and *Torso* (n.d.) in auction 479 of 3–6 November 1942. Thanks to Andreas Hüneke for this information.

48. Michael Fitzgerald, "Reports from the Home Fronts: Some Skirmishes over Picasso's Reputation," in *Picasso and the War Years: 1937–1945,* ed. Steven Nash and Robert Rosenblum (New York: Thames and Hudson, 1999), 117.

49. Steven Nash, "Chronology," in *Picasso and the War Years,* ed. Steven Nash and Robert Rosenblum (New York: Thames and Hudson, 1999), 221.

50. Lynn Nicholas, *The Rape of Europa: The Fate of Europe's Treasures in the Third Reich and the Second World War* (New York: Alfred Knopf, 1994), 180.

51. Elizabeth Campbell Karlsgodt, *Defending National Treasures: French Art and Heritage Under Vichy* (Stanford: Stanford University Press, 2011), 227.

52. Adriaan Venema, *Kunst-Handel in Nederland 1940–1945* (Amsterdam: Uitgeverij De Arbeiderpers, 1986), 67–71; and Gerard Aalders, *Nazi Looting: The Plunder of Dutch Jewry During the Second World War* (Oxford: Berg, 2004), 185–88, 194, 274.

53. SMB-ZA, Rave NL, Nr. 97, Schreiber to Rave (20 September 1949); Paret, *Artist Against the Third Reich,* 72.

54. LAB, A Rep. 243–04, F 0156, Schreiber to President of the RkdbK [Reich Chamber for the Visual Arts] (12 July 1944).

55. LAB, A Rep. 243–04, F 0156, Schreiber questionnaire (6 July 1944).

56. Ralph Jentsch, *Alfred Flechtheim–George Grosz, Zwei deutsche Schicksale* (Bonn: Weidle, 2008), 112–22; Koldehoff, *Bilder sind unter uns,* 41–54; and Ines Rotermund-Reynard, "Erinnerung an eine Sammlung. Zu Geschichte und Verbleib der Kunstsammlung Paul Westheims," in *Exilforschung. Ein internationales Jahrbuch* (28/2010), ed. Claus-Dieter Krohn and Lutz Winckler (Munich: Richard Booberg, 2010), 151–93.

CHAPTER 9. RICHARD STRAUSS

1. Peter Paret, *An Artist Against the Third Reich: Ernst Barlach, 1933–1938* (Cambridge: Cambridge University Press, 2003), 74. See more generally, Gerhard Splitt, *Richard Strauss 1933–1935. Ästhetik und Musikpolitik zu Beginn der nationalsozialistischen Herrschaft* (Praffenweiler: Centauraus, 1987).

2. Michael Kater, *Composers of the Nazi Era: Eight Portraits* (New York: Oxford University Press, 2000), 213–15; Oliver Rathkolb, *Führertreu und Gottbegnadet. Künstlerelite im Dritten Reich* (Vienna: Österreichischer Bundesverlag, 1991), 182; and Bryan Gilliam,

"Richard Strauss," in *The New Grove Dictionary of Music and Musicians*, vol. 24, ed. Stanley Sadie (London: Macmillan, 2001), 497.

3. Gilliam, "Richard Strauss," 497; and Peter Watson, *The German Genius: Europe's Third Renaissance, the Scientific Revolution, and the Twentieth Century* (New York: Harper-Collins, 2010), 643.

4. Kater, *Composers of the Nazi Era*, 211–12, 217; and Gilliam, "Richard Strauss," 506.

5. Gilliam, "Richard Strauss," 505, 507; and Steve Smith, "Strauss's Take on the Life of Strauss," *New York Times* (1 November 2010).

6. Gilliam, "Richard Strauss," 499.

7. Ibid., 505; and more generally, Mark-Daniel Schmid, *The Richard Strauss Companion* (Westport: Praeger, 2003).

8. Joachim Herz, "Salome—Tragödie in der Zeitenwende oder Perversionen am Küchentisch?" in *Richard Strauss. Essays zu Leben und Werk*, ed. Michael Heinemann, Matthias Hermann and Stefan Weiss (Laaber: Laaber, 2002), 135–46; Gilliam, "Richard Strauss," 511; Modris Eksteins, *Rites of Spring: The Great War and the Birth of the Modern Age* (Boston: Houghton Mifflin, 1989), 83; and Petra Dierkes-Thrun, "'The Brutal Music and the Delicate Text'? The Aesthetic Relationship Between Wilde's and Strauss's *Salome* Reconsidered," *Modern Languages Quarterly* 69/3 (2008), 376.

9. Michael Heinemann, "Elektras Erwartung," in *Richard Strauss. Essays zu Leben und Werk*, ed. Michael Heinemann, Matthias Hermann, and Stefan Weiss (Laaber: Laaber, 2002), 147–58; and Eksteins, *Rites of Spring*, 85–86.

10. Gilliam, "Richard Strauss," 513.

11. Kater, *Composers of the Nazi Era*, 217. He quotes Anderman [Thomas], *Bis der Vorhang Fiel*, 241.

12. Toscanini to Hitler (29 April 1933), reproduced in Hans Mayer, *Richard Wagner in Bayreuth, 1876–1976* (Stuttgart: Belser, 1976), 211. See also Kater, *Twisted Muse*, 79–80; Kater, *Composers of the Nazi Era*, 220–25; and Frederic Spotts, *Hitler and the Power of Aesthetics* (Woodstock: Overlook, 2003 [2002]), 299.

13. Matthias Herrmann, "'Mir geht nichts über mich!' Richard Strauss im 'Dritten Reich,'" in *Richard Strauss. Essays zu Leben und Werk*, ed. Michael Heinemann, Matthias Hermann, and Stefan Weiss (Laaber: Laaber, 2002), 218; Kater, *Composers of the Nazi Era*, 223–25; and Hans Vaget, "Thomas Mann und Richard Strauss: Zeitgenossenschaft ohne Brüderlichkeit," *Thomas Mann Jahrbuch* 3 (1990), 59–64.

14. Kater, *Composers of the Nazi Era*, 219, 228; and Alan Steinweis, *Art, Ideology and Economics in Nazi Germany: The Reich Chambers of Music, Theater and the Visual Arts* (Chapel Hill: University of North Carolina Press, 1993), 47.

15. Michael Kennedy, review of "A Confidential Matter: The Letters of Richard Strauss and Stefan Zweig, 1931–1935," *Music and Letters* 59/4 (4 October 1978), 472–75; and Spotts, *Hitler and the Power of Aesthetics*, 299.

16. Spotts, *Hitler and the Power of Aesthetics*, 300.

17. Kater, *Composers of the Nazi Era*, 215.

18. Ibid., 218, 230, 231.

19. Pamela Potter, "Music in the Third Reich: The Complex Task of 'Germanization,'" in *The Arts in Nazi Germany: Continuity, Conformity, Change*, ed. Jonathan Huener and Francis Nicosia (New York: Berghahn, 2006), 89; and Michael Meyer, "A Musical Façade for the Third Reich," in *"Degenerate Art": The Fate of the Avant-Garde in Nazi Germany*, ed. Stephanie Barron (Los Angeles: Los Angeles County Museum of Art, 1991), 175.

20. Kater, *Composers of the Nazi Era*, 229–30; Meyer, "Musical Façade," 177; and Fred Prieberg, *Musik im NS-Staat* (Frankfurt: Fischer Taschenbuch, 1982), 208.

21. Spotts, *Hitler and the Power of Aesthetics*, 299.

22. Ibid., 299–300.

23. Potter, "Music in the Third Reich," 87; and Meyer, "Musical Façade," 176.

24. Spotts, *Hitler and the Power of Aesthetics,* 301; Pamela Potter, "Strauss and the National Socialists: The Debate and Its Relevance," in *Richard Strauss: New Perspectives on the Composer and His Work,* ed. Bryan Gilliam (Durham: Duke University Press, 2007), 95; and Albrecht Riethmüller, "Stefan Zweig and the Fall of the Reich Music Chamber President Richard Strauss," in *Music and Nazism: Art Under Tyranny,* ed. Michael Kater and Albrecht Riethmüller (Laaber: Laaber Verlag, 2003), 269–91.

25. Paret, *Artist Against the Third Reich,* 74.

26. Strauss to Hitler (18 April 1935), quoted in Kater, *Composers of the Nazi Era,* 239.

27. For more on the Strauss-Zweig relationship, see Hermann, "Mir geht nichts," 221–25; and Erik Levi, *Music in the Third Reich* (New York: St. Martin's Press, 1994), 29–30. See also BAB, NS 10/111, doc. 141, Martin Mutschmann to Adolf Hitler (1 July 1935). The file includes a photostat of Strauss's 17 June 1935 letter, as well as a typed transcription.

28. BAB, NS 10/111, docs. 142–45, Richard Strauss to Stefan Zweig (17 June 1935); Kater, *Composers of the Nazi Era,* 242; Levi, *Music in the Third Reich,* 30; and Sam Shirakawa, *The Devil's Music Master: The Controversial Life and Career of Wilhelm Furtwängler* (New York: 1992), 187.

29. BAB, NS 10/111, docs. 142–45, Richard Strauss to Stefan Zweig (17 June 1935).

30. Ibid.

31. Kater, *Composers of the Nazi Era,* 32–33, 233–40; and Steinweis, *Art, Ideology and Economics,* 59.

32. BAB, NS 10/111, docs. 146–47, Strauss to Hitler (13 July 1935). George Marek, in his biography of Strauss, called the letter, "the nadir of Strauss's morality." See George Marek, *Richard Strauss: The Life of a Non-Hero* (New York: Simon and Schuster, 1967), 283; and Kater, *Composers of the Nazi Era,* 24, 243.

33. Spotts, *Hitler and the Power of Aesthetics,* 301.

34. Joachim Fest, *Albert Speer. Conversations with Hitler's Architect* (Cambridge: Polity Press, 2005), 45–46.

35. See the entries for 20 June 1936, 22 July 1936, and 8 August 1936, in Joseph Goebbels, *Die Tagebücher von Joseph Goebbels. Sämtliche Fragmente,* ed. Elke Fröhlich (Munich: K. G. Sauer, 1987), I, 3/II, 112, 137, 153.

36. Kater, *Composers of the Nazi Era,* 242–47.

37. Spotts, *Hitler and the Power of Aesthetics,* 299.

38. Richard Strauss to Pauline Strauss (25 March 1936), quoted in Kater, *Composers of the Nazi Era,* 248–49.

39. Levi, *Music in the Third Reich,* 42, 103.

40. *The Art of Conducting. Great Conductors of the Past: Richard Strauss,* 1994, at http://www.youtube.com/watch?v=doJVlS7nn_g&feature=related (accessed 19 June 2010).

41. BAB, NS 8/179, docs. 3–6, Rosenberg to Bormann, 19 July 1938. BAB, R 55/1017, doc. 10, Biebrach to Goebbels (20 April 1939).

42. Kater, *Composers of the Nazi Era,* 249; and Albrecht Dümmling, "Rassenreinheit statt Kulturaustausch. 'Entartete Musik' im Nationalsozialismus," in *Die Moderne im Nationalsozialismus,* ed. Volker Böhnigk and Joachim Stamp (Bonn: University Press, 2006), 55–84.

43. Hanns-Werner Heister, "Maskierung und Mobilisierung. Zur Rolle von Musik und Musiker im Nazismus," in *Hitlers Künstler. Die Kultur im Dienst des Nationalsozialismus,* ed. Hans Sarkowicz (Frankfurt: Insel Verlag, 2004), 316. See also Pamela Potter, "Strauss's *Friedenstag:* A Pacificst Attempt at Political Resistance," *Musical Quarterly* 69 (1983), 409.

44. Potter, "Strauss and the National Socialists," 96.

45. Spotts, *Hitler and the Power of Aesthetics*, 303; and Rathkolb, *Führertreu und Gott-begnadet*, 187.

46. Kater, *Composers of the Nazi Era*, 250. See the entry for 5 December 1941 in Goeb-bels, *Tagebücher* II/2, 436.

47. Richard Evans, *The Third Reich at War: How the Nazis Led Germany from Conquest to Disaster* (London: Allen Lane, 2008), 583. See also Fred Prieberg, *Musik im NS-Staat*, 222–23; and Kater, *Composers of the Nazi Era*, 252.

48. Spotts, *Hitler and the Power of Aesthetics*, 303; and Shirakawa, *Devil's Music Master*, 286.

49. Baldur von Schirach, *Ich glaubte an Hitler* (Hamburg: Mosaik, 1967), 286; and Thomas Weyr, *The Setting of the Pearl: Vienna Under Hitler* (New York: Oxford University Press, 2005), 211.

50. Schirach, *Ich glaubte an Hitler*, 288; Hans Sarkowicz, "'Bis Alles in Scherben Fällt . . .' Schriftsteller im Dienst der NS-Diktatur," in *Hitlers Künstler. Die Kultur im Dienst des Nationalsozialismus*, ed. Hans Sarkowicz (Frankfurt: Insel, 2004), 184; Heister, "Maskierung und Mobilisierung," 320; and Rathkolb, *Führertreu und Gottbegnadet*, 176.

51. Kater, *Composers of the Nazi Era*, 253–54; and Fred Prieberg, *Musik und Macht* (Frankfurt: Fischer Taschenbuch, 1991), 224.

52. Kater, *Composers of the Nazi Era*, 254–57; Evans, *Third Reich at War*, 582; and Her-mann, "Mir geht nichts," 226.

53. Peter Conrad, "The Golden Touch," *New Statesman* (16 September 2002).

54. Spotts, *Hitler and the Power of Aesthetics*, 304; Gilliam, "Richard Strauss," 504; and Kater, *Composers of the Nazi Era*, 258.

55. Gilliam, "Richard Strauss," 509–10; and Melvin Jules Bukiet, "A Synagogue Is No Place to Perform Richard Strauss," *Forward* (26 June 2008).

56. Alan Jefferson, quoted in Gilliam, "Richard Strauss," 510.

57. Kater, *Composers of the Nazi Era*, 259; Walter Panofsky, *Richard Strauss. Partitur eines Lebens* (Munich: R. Piper, 1965), 331; and Gilliam, "Richard Strauss," 504.

58. Panofsky, *Strauss*, 344.

CHAPTER 10. GUSTAF GRÜNDGENS

1. Klaus Mann, *Mephisto* (New York: Random House, 1977).

2. Klaus Mann, "Selbstanzeige: Mephisto" (1936), in *Heute und Morgen. Schriften zur Zeit* (Munich: Nymphenburger Verlagshandlung, 1969), 53.

3. John London, "Introduction," in *Theatre Under the Nazis*, ed. John London (Man-chester: Manchester University Press, 2000), 1.

4. Ibid. Stefan Steinberg, "The Rehabilitation of Gustav Gründgens: *Gustav Gründgens —A German Career*: An Exhibition at the Berlin Staatsbibliothek" (29 December 1999), at http://www.wsws.org/articles/1999/dec1999/gust-d29.shtml (accessed 15 January 2010). See the chapter "In Hollywood We Speak German" in Joseph Horowitz, *Artists in Exile: How Refugees from Twentieth-Century War and Revolution Transformed the American Performing Arts* (New York: HarperCollins, 2008), 217–309.

5. *Gustaf Gründgens—Theaterstücke, Hörspiele, Monologe, Reden, Chansons.* twenty audio-CD set (Los Angeles: Universal Music: 2004).

6. London, "Introduction," 2, 7.

7. Erik Levi, *Music in the Third Reich* (New York: St. Martin's Press, 1994), 181; Peter Watson, *The German Genius: Europe's Third Renaissance, the Scientific Revolution, and the Twentieth Century* (New York: HarperCollins, 2010), 644; Richard Grunberger, *The Twelve-Year Reich: A Social History of Nazi Germany, 1933–1945* (New York: Holt, Rinehart, and Winston, 1971), 363; John Willett, *The Theatre of the Weimar Republic* (New York: Holmes

and Meier, 1988), 184; Boguslaw Drewniak, *Das Theater im NS-Staat. Szenarium Deutscher Zeitgeschichte 1933–1945* (Düsseldorf: Droste, 1983); and Bruce Zortman, *Hitler's Theater: Ideological Drama in Nazi Germany* (El Paso: Firestein Books, 1984).

8. Otto Friedrich, *Before the Deluge: A Portrait of Berlin in the 1920s* (New York: HarperPerennial, 1995 [1972]), 248.

9. Watson, *German Genius,* 648.

10. Hennig Rischbieter, "'Schlageter'—Der 'Erste Soldat des Dritten Reichs.' Theater in der Nazizeit," in *Hitlers Künstler. Die Kultur im Dienst des Nationalsozialismus,* ed. Hans Sarkowicz (Frankfurt: Insel Verlag, 2004), 228; Dagmar Walach, *Aber ich habe nicht mein Gesicht. Gustaf Gründgens. Eine deutsche Karriere* (Berlin: Henschel, 1999), 21–24; Heinrich Goertz, *Gustaf Gründgens* (Reinbek: Rowohlt, 1982), 14.

11. Steinberg, "Rehabilitation of Gustav Gründgens," 1; Walach, *Aber ich habe nicht mein Gesicht,* 221; and Goertz, *Gründgens,* 22.

12. Steinberg, "Rehabilitation of Gustav Gründgens." For more on experimental theater, see, among others, John Willett, ed., *Brecht on Theatre: The Development of an Aesthetic* (London: Methuen, 1964).

13. Goertz, *Gründgens,* 23.

14. R. W., "Revue zu Vieren," *Hamburger Zeitung* (26 April 1927), in *Gustaf-Gründgens-Ausstellung anlässlich seines achtzigsten Geburtstages am 22. Dezember 1979,* ed. Heinrich Riemenschneider (Düsseldorf: Dumont-Lindemann-Archiv, 1980), 40.

15. Arthur Kürschner, "Revue zu Vieren," *Das Theater* 10 (1927), in *Gustaf-Gründgens-Ausstellung anlässlich seines achtzigsten Geburtstages am 22. Dezember 1979,* ed. Heinrich Riemenschneider (Düsseldorf: Dumont-Lindemann-Archiv, 1980), 41. See also Klaus Mann, *Der Wendepunkt. Ein Lebensbericht* (Reinbek: Rowohlt, 2006).

16. Herbert Holba, Günter Knorr, and Peter Spiegel, *Gustaf Gründgens Filme* (Vienna: Action, 1978).

17. Goertz, *Gründgens,* 26; and John Willett, *The Theatre of the Weimar Republic* (New York: Holmes and Meier, 1988), 111, 164.

18. Goertz, *Gründgens,* 36.

19. Hanns Johst, *Schlageter,* trans. Ford Parkes-Perret (Stuttgart: Akademischer Verlag Hanns-Dieter Heinz, 1984), 87; London, "Introduction," 7; and Gustaf Gründgens, *Briefe, Aufsätze, Reden,* ed. Rolf Badenhausen and Peter Gründgens-Gorski (Hamburg: Hoffmann und Campe, 1967), 16.

20. See the statement written by Gründgens in early 1946 in connection with his denazification trial in Walach, *Aber ich habe nicht mein Gesicht,* 87.

21. Goebbels's entry for 18 November 1938, quoted in Mary Elizabeth O'Brien, *Nazi Cinema as Enchantment: The Politics of Entertainment in the Third Reich* (Rochester: Camden House, 2006), 19, and more generally, 18–30.

22. Göring also prohibited productions of Johst's drama about Martin Luther, titled *Prophets.* See Goertz, *Gründgens,* 38–40; and Carola Stern, *Auf den Wassern des Lebens. Gustaf Gründgens und Marianne Hoppe* (Reinbeck: Rowohlt, 2005), 114.

23. Jan-Pieter Barbian, "Die Beherrschung der Musen. Kulturpolitik im 'Dritten Reich,'" in *Hitlers Künstler. Die Kultur im Dienst des Nationalsozialismus,* ed. Hans Sarkowicz (Frankfurt: Insel Verlag, 2004), 53; and Sam Shirakawa, *The Devil's Music Master: The Controversial Life and Career of Wilhelm Furtwängler* (New York: 1992), 146.

24. Peter Watson, *The German Genius: Europe's Third Renaissance, the Scientific Revolution, and the Twentieth Century* (New York: HarperCollins, 2010), 648.

25. Goertz, *Gründgens,* 40–41; Oliver Rathkolb, *Führertreu und Gottbegnadet. Künstlerelite im Dritten Reich* (Vienna: Österreichischer Bundesverlag, 1991), 142; and O'Brien, *Nazi Cinema as Enchantment,* 20.

26. Alfred Mühr, *Mephisto ohne Maske. Gustaf Gründgens. Legende und Wahrheit* (Munich: Langen Müller, 1981), 60.

27. Stern, *Auf den Wassern des Lebens,* 372.

28. Mühr, *Mephisto ohne Maske,* 61.

29. LAB, A Rep. 243-01, Nr. 301–302, Gerdy Schüchter to Redaktion der "Telegraf" (15 December 1946). Karajan joined the Nazi Party in Salzburg in March 1933, and then did so again in Ulm in 1935. David Monod, *Settling Scores: German Music, Denazification, and the Americans, 1945–1953* (Chapel Hill: University of North Carolina Press, 2005), 91; Heister, "Maskierung und Mobilisierung," 319; and Rathkolb, *Führertreu und Gottbegnadet,* 211.

30. Mühr, *Mephisto ohne Maske,* 63, 164; and Volker Dahm, "Künstler als Funktionäre. Das Propaganda-Ministerium und die Reichskulturkammer," in *Hitlers Künstler. Die Kultur im Dienst des Nationalsozialismus,* ed. Hans Sarkowicz (Frankfurt: Insel, 2004), 101.

31. Goebbels, quoted in Felix Moeller, "'Ich bin Künstler und sonst nichts.' Filmstars im Propagandaeinsatz," in *Hitlers Künstler. Die Kultur im Dienst des Nationalsozialismus,* ed. Hans Sarkowicz (Frankfurt: Insel, 2004), 138; and Rischbieter, "'Schlageter,'" 230.

32. Peter Michalzik, *Gustaf Gründgens. Der Schauspieler und die Macht* (Berlin: 1999), 114.

33. Rischbieter, "'Schlageter,'" 227.

34. Walach, *Aber ich habe nicht mein Gesicht,* 58; and Rischbieter, "'Schlageter,'" 231.

35. Alan Steinweis, *Art, Ideology and Economics in Nazi Germany: The Reich Chambers of Music, Theater and the Visual Arts* (Chapel Hill: University of North Carolina Press, 1993), 130. In a 28 December 1934 letter to Heinz Tietjen, correspondence that was also meant for Göring, Gründgens offered to resign and identified his sexual proclivities as a reason (although he talked of mastering his homosexual urges). Göring rejected his offer to resign. Rischbieter, "'Schlageter,'" 228–30.

36. Stern, *Auf den Wassern des Lebens,* 170; and the entry for 29 July 1937, in Joseph Goebbels, *Die Tagebücher von Joseph Goebbels. Sämtliche Fragmente,* ed. Elke Fröhlich (Munich: K. G. Sauer, 1987), I, 4, 238.

37. Walach, *Aber ich habe nicht mein Gesicht,* 62; and Rischbieter, "'Schlageter,'" 231.

38. Christelle Le Faucheur, review of Gerwin Strobl, *The Swastika and the Stage* (May 2009), at http://www.h-net.org/reviews/showrev.php?id=24743 (accessed 25 July 2013).

39. Boris von Haken, *Der "Reichsdramaturg": Rainer Schlösser und die Musiktheater-Politik in der NS-Zeit* (Hamburg: Von Bockel, 2007); and Rischbieter, "'Schlageter,'" 232.

40. See the list of roles in Mühr, *Mephisto ohne Maske,* 339–42; Walach, *Aber ich habe nicht mein Gesicht,* 232; and Stern, *Auf den Wassern des Lebens,* 125–27.

41. Steinberg, "Rehabilitation of Gustav Gründgens," 3; Stern, *Auf den Wassern des Lebens,* 171; and, more generally, for the salaries of film stars, Eric Rentschler, *The Ministry of Illusion: Nazi Cinema and Its Afterlife* (Cambridge: Harvard University Press, 1996), 136.

42. For an even more striking case of a cultural figure being given an "Aryanized" residence, see the file for marine painter Adolf Bock, which includes letters from Eichmann, Bormann, and Heydrich in 1941 in BAB, R43II/1250a.

43. Stern, *Auf den Wassern des Lebens,* 158; and Walach, *Aber ich habe nicht mein Gesicht,* 231.

44. Peter Reichel, *Der Schöne Schein des Dritten Reiches. Faszination und Gewalt des Faschismus* (Munich: Hanser, 1991).

45. Stern, *Auf den Wassern des Lebens,* 109.

46. Ibid., 107; O'Brien, *Nazi Cinema as Enchantment,* 20; Jana Bruns, *Nazi Cinema's New Women* (Cambridge: Cambridge University Press, 2009), 27; and the obituary of Marianne Hoppe, *Independent* (29 October 2002).

47. Rischbieter, "'Schlageter,'" 234.

48. Walach, *Aber ich habe nicht mein Gesicht,* 110; Steinberg, "Rehabilitation of Gustav Gründgens," 1–3; and Grunberger, *Twelve-Year Reich,* 370.

49. Steinberg, "Rehabilitation of Gustav Gründgens," 3.

50. Rischbieter, "'Schlageter,'" 234.

51. Walach, *Aber ich habe nicht mein Gesicht,* 134.

52. Steinberg, "Rehabilitation of Gustav Gründgens," 1.

53. Walach, *Aber ich habe nicht mein Gesicht,* 138.

54. Steinberg, "Rehabilitation of Gustav Gründgens," 1.

CHAPTER 11. LENI RIEFENSTAHL

1. Susan Sontag, "Fascinating Fascism," in Susan Sontag, *Under the Sign of Saturn* (New York: Vintage, 1981), 84.

2. Leni Riefenstahl, *A Memoir* (New York: St. Martin's Press, 1993 [1987]), 595–96, 601–2; Bianca Jagger, "Leni's Back and Bianca's Got Her," *Interview* 5 (January 1975), 35–37; Stephen Schiff, "Leni's Olympia," *Vanity Fair* (September 1992), 252–61, 291–96; Angelika Taschen, ed., *Leni Riefenstahl, Africa* (Cologne: Taschen, 2010), 384; and Eric Rentschler, *The Ministry of Illusion: Nazi Cinema and Its Afterlife* (Cambridge: Harvard University Press, 1996), 27–28.

3. Steven Bach, *Leni: The Life and Work of Leni Riefenstahl* (New York: Vintage Books, 2007), 24; and Jürgen Trimborn, *Leni Riefenstahl: A Life* (New York: Faber and Faber, 2007), 10–15. See also LAB, B Rep. 031-02-01, Nr. 2654, Bd. 5, Riefenstahl "Lebenslauf" (1 November 1948).

4. Trimborn, *Riefenstahl,* 16.

5. Riefenstahl, *A Memoir,* 35.

6. John London, "Introduction," in *Theatre Under the Nazis,* ed. John London (Manchester: Manchester University Press, 2000), 4.

7. Bach, *Leni,* 28; and Trimborn, *Riefenstahl,* 21–22.

8. Bach, *Leni,* 29–30; and Trimborn, *Riefenstahl,* 20–22.

9. Bach, *Leni,* 4, 31; and Sontag, "Fascinating Fascism," 75–76.

10. See, for example, Laurence Kardish, ed., *Weimar Cinema, 1919–1933. Daydreams and Nightmares,* exh. cat. (New York: Museum of Modern Art, 2010).

11. Sontag, "Fascinating Fascism," 80; Trimborn, *Riefenstahl,* 33; and Rentschler, *Ministry of Illusion,* 28.

12. Sabine Hake, *German National Cinema* (New York: Routledge, 2008), 45.

13. Susan Tegel, *Nazis and the Cinema* (London: Hambledon Continuum, 2007), 79–80; Kardish, ed., *Weimar Cinema,* 195.

14. Bach, *Leni,* 36.

15. Rentschler, *Ministry of Illusion,* 29, 42; and Tegel, *Nazis and the Cinema,* 80.

16. Hake, *German National Cinema,* 45; and Trimborn, *Riefenstahl,* 34–35.

17. Trimborn, *Riefenstahl,* 43; Eric Rentschler, "The Situation Is Hopeless but Not Desperate: UFA's Early Sound-Film Musicals," in *Weimar Cinema, 1919–1933. Daydreams and Nightmares,* ed. Laurence Kardish (New York: Museum of Modern Art, 2010), 48; and Eric Rentschler, "The Elemental, the Ornamental, the Instrumental: *The Blue Light* and Nazi Film Aesthetics," in *The Other Perspective in Gender and Culture: Rewriting Women and the Symbolic,* ed. Juliet Flower MacCannell (New York: Columbia University Press, 1990), 161–88.

18. Siegfried Kracauer, *From Caligari to Hitler: A Psychological History of the German Film* (Princeton: Princeton University Press, 1947), 110–11, 258–59; Bach, *Leni,* 36; and Tegel, *Nazis and the Cinema,* 78.

19. Trimborn, *Riefenstahl,* 49, 55–56.

20. Hake, *German National Cinema,* 74; and Richard Meran Barsam, *Filmguide to Triumph of the Will* (Bloomington: Indiana University Press, 1975).

21. M. Delahaye, "Leni et le Loup," *Cahiers du cinema* 170 (September 1965), 48, cited in Tegel, *Nazis and the Cinema,* 76. See also Tegel, *Nazis and the Cinema,* 84; Sontag, "Fascinating Fascism," 71–105; and Bach, *Leni,* 288.

22. Ray Müller's film *The Wonderful, Horrible Life of Leni Riefenstahl* (*Die Macht der Bilder: Leni Riefenstahl*) (1993). See also Ray Müller and Linda Schulte-Sasse, "Leni Riefenstahl Feature Films and the Question of a Fascist Aesthetic," *Cultural Critique* 18 (Spring 1991), 142.

23. Sontag, "Fascinating Fascism," 86, 91.

24. Eric Rentschler, "The Legacy of Nazi Cinema: *Triumph of the Will* and *Jew Süss* Revisited," in *The Arts in Nazi Germany: Continuity, Conformity, Change,* ed. Jonathan Huener and Frank Nicosia (New York: Berghahn, 2006), 67; and Trimborn, *Riefenstahl,* 116.

25. Riefenstahl, interviewed by Ray Müller, *The Wonderful Horrible Life of Leni Riefenstahl;* Rentschler, "Legacy of Nazi Cinema," 68; and Tegel, *Nazis and the Cinema,* 50, 86.

26. Trimborn, *Riefenstahl,* 57; Tegel, *Nazis and the Cinema,* 78; and Ernst Klee, *Kulturlexikon zum Dritten Reich. Wer war was vor und nach 1945* (Frankfurt: S. Fischer, 2007), 485.

27. BAB, RK Fachschaft Film, Z39, doc. 706, Leni Riefenstahl, "Fragebogen" (2 October 1933); BAB, RK Fachschaft Film, Z39, doc. 756, Riefenstahl to Streicher (11 October 1933); Tegel, *Nazis and the Cinema,* 78–79; and Rentschler, *Ministry of Illusion,* 31, 46.

28. Entry for 17 May 1933, Joseph Goebbels, *Die Tagebücher von Joseph Goebbels. Sämtliche Fragmente,* ed. Elke Fröhlich (Munich: K. G. Sauer, 1987), I/2/III, 188. Note that Goebbels mentioned Riefenstahl in his diaries on well over a dozen occasions in 1933.

29. BAB, RK Fachschaft Film, Z39, doc. 824, Streicher to Riefenstahl (27 July 1937).

30. Sontag, "Fascinating Fascism," 86; Riefenstahl, *A Memoir,* 181–84; and Trimborn, *Riefenstahl,* 63–64.

31. LAB, B Rep 031-02-01, Nr. 2654 (Riefenstahl denazification files), vol. III: Riefenstahl to Hitler (25 August 1935); and Trimborn, *Riefenstahl,* 62–70.

32. LAB, B Rep 031-02-01, Nr. 2654 (Riefenstahl denazification files), vol. III: Riefenstahl to Hitler (June 1940). See also Kay Sokolowsky, "Die neue Rechte," *Konkret* 3 (1999): 12–17.

33. Trimborn, *Riefenstahl,* 147.

34. LAB, B Rep 031-02-01, Nr. 2654 (Riefenstahl denazification files), vol. III: Riefenstahl to Karl Hanke (19 October 1936). Entry for 6 November 1936 in Goebbels, *Tagebücher,* I, 3/II, 240. See also Timothy Ryback, *Hitler's Private Library: The Books That Shaped His Life* (New York: Alfred Knopf, 2009), 99.

35. Bach, *Leni,* 207.

36. Trimborn, *Riefenstahl,* 207–17; Bach, *Leni,* 198; BAB, RK Fachschaft Film, Z39, docs. 922–24, Riefenstahl to Max Winkler (18 June 1944); and ibid., Muller-Goerne to Riefenstahl (3 July 1944).

37. Trimborn, *Riefenstahl,* 155, 157–58, 195; and more generally, Wulf Schwarzwäller, *Hitlers Geld. Bilanz einer persönlichen Bereicherung* (Rastatt: Moewig, 1986). See also Tegel, *Nazis and the Cinema,* 80; and BAB, R4606/4526, Speer to Pilli Körner (13 July 1939).

38. Riefenstahl, *A Memoir,* 162.

39. Trimborn, *Riefenstahl,* 130; and Tegel, *Nazis and the Cinema,* 94, 97.

40. Tegel, *Nazis and the Cinema,* 98.

41. Robert Schneider and William Stier, "Leni Riefenstahl's '*Olympia*': Brilliant Cinematography or Nazi Propaganda" (2001), at http://www.thesportjournal.org/article/leni

-riefenstahls-olympia-brilliant-cinematography-or-nazi-propaganda (accessed 15 October 2008).

42. Jeanne Anne Nugent, "Germany's Classical Turn from the Great Disorder to a Kingdom of the Dead," in *Chaos and Classicism. Art in France, Italy, and Germany, 1918–1936,* ed. Kenneth Silver (New York: Guggenheim Museum, 2010), 164.

43. Tegel, *Nazis and the Cinema,* 98; and LAB, B Rep. 031-02-01, Nr. 2654, Bd. 5, Badisches Staatskommissariat für politische Säuberung, "Entscheidung" for Leni Riefenstahl-Jacob (10 January 1950).

44. Trimborn, *Riefenstahl,* 133.

45. Ibid., 137, 145.

46. Roger Russi, "Escaping Home: Leni Riefenstahl's Visual Poetry in *Tiefland,*" in *Cultural History Through a National Socialist Lens. Essays on the Cinema of the Third Reich,* ed. Robert Reimer (Rochester: Camden House, 2000), 155–75; and Trimborn, *Riefenstahl,* 182.

47. Bach, *Leni,* 282–83; Trimborn, *Riefenstahl,* 184–92, 208; Tegel, *Nazis and the Cinema,* 81; and Russi, "Escaping Home," 162–64.

48. Trimborn, *Riefenstahl,* 164. For the Waffen-SS uniform, see the entry for Riefenstahl at http://www.newworldencyclopedia.org/entry/Leni_Riefenstahl (accessed 11 August 2010). See also Sontag, "Fascinating Fascism," 95–96; and BAB, R3 Anhang/33, Willi Nerlich report (25 September 1945).

49. LAB, B Rep. 031-02-01, Nr. 2654, Bd. 5, Riefenstahl to Helmut Freitag (April 1951).

50. Bach, *Leni,* 188.

51. Riefenstahl, *A Memoir,* 384–88; and Bach, *Leni,* 189.

52. Trimborn, *Riefenstahl,* 166.

53. Ibid., 167; Riefenstahl, *A Memoir,* 259; and Bach, *Leni,* 189.

54. Trimborn, *Leni Riefenstahl,* 167.

55. Ibid.

56. Riefenstahl, *A Memoir,* 261; and Trimborn, *Riefenstahl,* 167–77.

57. Bach, *Leni,* 192.

58. Riefenstahl, *A Memoir,* 293–95; and Trimborn, *Riefenstahl,* 201, 225.

59. Jonathan Petropoulos, *The Faustian Bargain: The Art World in Nazi Germany* (New York: Oxford University Press, 2000), 202–3.

60. "Report on Objects Removed to Germany from Holland, Belgium, and France During the German Occupation in the Countries" (Hague: Stichting Nederlands Kunstbesit, 1945), 121.

61. For a 1950 verdict as Riefenstahl as "Mitläufer," see BAB, RK, Fachschaft Film, Z 39, docs. 1258–64, Spruchkammer Freiburg, "Entscheidung" (13 January 1950); and Trimborn, *Riefenstahl,* 233.

62. LAB, B Rep. 031-02-01, Nr. 2654, Bd. 5, "Leni Riefenstahl lief 'nur' mit," *Der Berliner Anzeiger* (22 April 1952).

63. Bach, *Leni,* 293.

64. Trimborn, *Riefenstahl,* 265.

65. Sontag, "Fascinating Fascism," 73–81; and Trimborn, *Riefenstahl,* 246, 263.

66. Riefenstahl concluded a letter to Speer (8 June 1976), "Perhaps—and I very much hope so—we can meet again—without talking about the past." Riefenstahl, *A Memoir,* 575–76, 626–28.

67. Tegel, *Nazis and the Cinema,* 78; Riefenstahl, *A Memoir;* and Trimborn, *Riefenstahl,* 277.

68. The Frankfurt prosecutors responded to a complaint of the Cologne Association of Roma. See "Jubilare. Riefenstahl. Der Staatsanwalt ermittelt," *Frankfurter Allgemeine Zeitung* (22 August 2002).

69. Steven Bach claims that Riefenstahl donated the controversial materials from *Tiefland* to the German Federal Archives and placed restrictions on accessing them, but it appears that she retained them in her own private archive in her Pöcking home, which has not been open to researchers. Bach, *Leni*, 3, 284, 356; and Trimborn, *Riefenstahl*, 287.

70. Trimborn, *Riefenstahl*, 257, 261.

71. Rentschler, "Legacy of Nazi Cinema," 68-69.

72. Sontag, "Fascinating Fascism," 90.

73. While Riefenstahl was not always successful in the lawsuits regarding the Reich and Nazi Party–financed films, she still managed to secure some income from them. Bach, *Leni*, 283; and Trimborn, *Riefenstahl*, 240-42.

74. Trimborn, *Riefenstahl*, 274.

75. Ibid., 276.

76. Ibid., 276; and Rentschler, "Legacy of Nazi Cinema," 69-70. With regard to the latter, Rentschler refers to the "teaser" for the compilation film *Michael Jackson: History 2* (1997).

77. Rentschler, "Legacy of Nazi Cinema," 70.

CHAPTER 12. ARNO BREKER

1. John Zavrel, *Arno Breker: The Divine Beauty in Art* (Clarence, N.Y.: Est-Art, 1986), 81.

2. Jeffrey Herf, *Nazi Propaganda for the Arab World* (New Haven: Yale University Press, 2009), 230.

3. Ida Katherine Rigby, *An alle Künstler! War, Revolution, Weimar* (San Diego: University Gallery, San Diego State University, 1983), 64; and Maria Tatar, *Lustmord: Sexual Murder in Weimar Germany* (Princeton: Princeton University Press, 1997).

4. GESOLEI stands for Gesundheitspflege, soziale Fürsorge, und Leibesübungen. See Jürgen Wiener, ed., *Die GeSoLei und die Düsseldorfer Architektur der 20er Jahre* (Cologne: Bachem, 2001).

5. Peter Chametzky, *Objects as History in Twentieth-Century German Art: Beckmann to Beuys* (Berkeley: University of California Press, 2010), 138.

6. Ibid., 138-39; and Claudia Schönfeld, "Breker und Frankreich," in *Zur Diskussion gestellt: der Bildhauer Arno Breker*, ed. Rudolf Conrades (Schwerin: Verlagsgruppe Schwerin, 2006), 102-45.

7. Iris Kalden-Rosenfeld, "Künstler und Chamälon. Herleitung und Formanalyse der Bildwerke Arno Brekers," in *Zur Diskussion gestellt: der Bildhauer Arno Breker*, ed. Rudolf Conrades (Schwerin: Verlagsgruppe Schwerin, 2006), 65; Schönfeld, "Breker und Frankreich," 107, 114.

8. Dominique Egret, *Arno Breker. Ein Leben für das Schöne* (Tübingen: Edition Grabert, 1996), 13; Zavrel, *Arno Breker*, 25; and William Hamscher, *Albert Speer: Victim of Nuremberg?* (London: Leslie Frewin, 1970), 104.

9. Zavrel, *Arno Breker*, 33.

10. Egret, *Arno Breker*, 56; Hans Albert Peters, ed., *Alfred Flechtheim—Sammler, Kunsthändler, Verleger* (Düsseldorf: Kunstmuseum Düsseldorf, 1987); and Ottfried Dascher, *"Es ist was wahnsinniges mit der Kunst": Alfred Flechtheim. Sammler, Kunsthändler, Verleger* (Wädenswil: Nimbus, 2011), 291-412.

11. See the database (Datenbank zum Beschlagnahmeinventar der Aktion 'entartete Kunst') of the Forschungsstelle "Entartete Kunst," Freie Universität Berlin, at http://emuseum .campus.fu-berlin.de/eMuseumPlus?service=RedirectService&sp=Scollection&sp=SfieldV alue&sp=0&sp=0&sp=3&sp=SdetailList&sp=0&sp=Sdetail&sp=0&sp=F (accessed 5 July 2010).

12. Chametzky, *Objects as History,* 139, citing Luise Straus-Ernst, "Der Bildhauer Arno Breker," *Die Kunst für Alle* 44 (1928–29), 370–75.

13. Peter Junk and Wendelin Zimmer, *Felix Nussbaum. Leben und Werk* (Cologne: Du-Mont, 1982), 90–95, 148–98; Chametzky, *Objects as History,* 138; and Rosalind Krauss, *Passages in Modern Sculpture* (Cambridge: MIT Press, 1977), 29–30.

14. Dietmar Schenk and Gero Seelig, "Die Deutsche Akademie in Rom: Felix Nussbaum und Arno Breker in der Villa Massimo, 1932/1933," in *"Die Kunst hat nie ein Mensch allein besessen": Die Akademie der Künste: Dreihundert Jahre Hochschule der Künste,* ed. Monika Hingst et al. (Berlin: Henschel, 1996), 433.

15. Amtsgericht Munich, Breker file, Georg Kolbe to Spruchkammer, Donauwörth (16 July 1947).

16. Egret, *Arno Breker,* 19, 57; and Arno Breker, *Im Strahlungsfeld der Ereignisse. Leben und Wirken eines Künstlers* (Preußisch Oldendorf: K. W. Schütz, 1972), 132.

17. Breker received a commission from the Reich Finance Ministry in 1935, but this work attracted little attention. See Chametzky, *Objects as History,* 141.

18. Note that Breker was on the original jury for the 1937 *Great German Art Exhibition.* Frederic Spotts, *Hitler and the Power of Aesthetics* (Woodstock: Overlook, 2003 [2002]), 342; Jonathan Petropoulos, *The Faustian Bargain: The Art World in Nazi Germany* (New York: Oxford University Press, 2000), 225; and Christoph Zuschlag, *"Entartete Kunst": Ausstellungsstrategien im Nazi-Deutschland* (Worms: Wernersche Verlagsgesellschaft, 1995), 187.

19. Chametzky, *Objects as History,* 145–51, 158; and Spotts, *Hitler and the Power of Aesthetics,* 360.

20. Rosenberg, quoted in Christian Zentner and Friedemann Bedürftig, eds., *The Encyclopedia of the Third Reich* (New York: Macmillan, 1991), 12.

21. Jost Hermand, *Old Dreams of a New Reich: Volkisch Utopias and National Socialism* (Bloomington: Indiana University Press, 1992), 233.

22. Adolf Hitler, *Mein Kampf* (Boston: Houghton Mifflin, 1971), 290.

23. Albert Speer, *Inside the Third Reich* (New York: Avon Books, 1970), 110.

24. GSAPK, I HA Rep. 92, Kurt Reutti *Nachlass,* NL 1, Kurt Reutti, "Erinnerungen," 193.

25. Walter Benjamin, "The Work of Art in the Age of Mechanical Reproduction," in Walter Benjamin, *Illuminations* (New York: Schocken, 1969), 217–52.

26. Chametzky, *Objects as History,* 138–39; and Rudolf Conrades, "Warum Breker?," in *Zur Diskussion gestellt: der Bildhauer Arno Breker,* ed. Rudolf Conrades (Schwerin: Verlagsgruppe Schwerin, 2006), 18.

27. George Steiner, *In Bluebeard's Castle. Some Notes Towards the Redefinition of Culture* (New Haven: Yale University Press, 1971), 49–50.

28. Amtsgericht Munich, Breker file, Dirksen to Spruchkammer Donauwörth (12 July 1947).

29. Alan Riding, *And the Show Went On: Cultural Life in Nazi-Occupied Paris* (New York: Alfred Knopf, 2010), 177; Elizabeth Campbell Karlsgodt, *Defending National Treasures: French Art and Heritage Under Vichy* (Stanford: Stanford University Press, 2011), 46–47; Egret, *Arno Breker,* 60; Jean Cocteau, "Salut à Breker," *Comoedia* 48 (29 May 1942), 1; Charles Despiau, *Arno Breker* (Paris: Flammarion, 1942); and BAB, R58/190, Reichssicherheits Hauptamt, "Meldungen" (1 November 1943), 9.

30. Petropoulos, *Faustian Bargain,* 230; and Richard Grunberger, *The Twelve-Year Reich: A Social History of Nazi Germany, 1933–1945* (New York: Holt, Rinehart, and Winston, 1971), 431. For Breker's declared income, see BAB, R 43II/986, doc. 52: income chart (April 1942). He reports a rise from RM 2,300 ($920) in 1934 to RM 919,885 ($368,000) in 1941. Breker received payments totaling RM 27,396,000 ($10,958,400) prior to 1945, but

this includes funds to cover fabrication costs. See BAB, R/4606/4738, "Vermerk" (21 March 1945).

31. BAB, R 43II/986, doc. 51, Bormann "Vermerk" (21 April 1942); BAB, R3 Anhang/208, doc. 4, Willi Nerlich, "Akten-Notiz" (25 September 1945); and Trimborn, Breker, 219–21, 327.

32. Amtsgericht, Munich, Breker file, Friedrich Tamms to Spruchkammer Donauwörth (27 August 1947); and ibid., Werner Windhaus to Spruchkammer Donauwörth (2 August 1948). See also Breker, Im Strahlungsfeld der Ereignisse, 134–35.

33. Michèle Cone, Artists Under Vichy: A Case of Prejudice and Persecution (Princeton: Princeton University Press, 1992), 156; and Laurence Bertrand Dorléac, L'art de la défaite, 1940–1944 (Paris: Seuil, 1998), 104–6.

34. CDJC, LXXI-98, Karl Theodor Zeitschel to Gesandter Rahn (3 June 1942); Petropoulos, Faustian Bargain, 233, 243; and Trimborn, Breker, 325–28.

35. Allan Mitchell, The Devil's Captain: Ernst Jünger in Nazi Paris, 1941–1944 (Cambridge: Cambridge University Press, 2011), 25; Christopher Lloyd, Collaboration and Resistance in Occupied France: Representing Treason and Sacrifice (New York: Palgrave Macmillan, 2003), 27; Hal Vaughan, Sleeping with the Enemy: Coco Chanel's Secret War (New York: Alfred Knopf, 2011); and Riding, And the Show Went On.

36. Hamscher, Albert Speer, 105, 108; and Petropoulos, Faustian Bargain, 233–38.

37. Schönfeld, "Breker und Frankreich," 129.

38. Egret, Arno Breker, 19, 57.

39. See Rainer Hackel, "Der andere Breker. Engagement für politisch Verfolgte," in Zur Diskussion gestellt: der Bildhauer Arno Breker, ed. Rudolf Conrades (Schwerin: Verlagsgruppe Schwerin, 2006), 146–59.

40. Volker Probst, "Arno Breker: Biography," in John Zavrel, Arno Breker: The Divine Beauty in Art (Clarence, N.Y.: Est-Art, 1986), 96; and Cone, Artists Under Vichy, 161.

41. Egret, Arno Breker, 62. See also Gertje Utley, Picasso: The Communist Years (New Haven: Yale University Press, 2000), 31.

42. A. P., "Picasso: oder die Kunst zu erben. Die Schwierigkeiten mit dem Nachlass. Arno Brekers Erklärung," Frankfurter Allgemeine Zeitung 92 (18 April 1973), 28; and Steven Nash, "Chronology," in Picasso and the War Years, ed. Steven Nash and Robert Rosenblum (New York: Thames and Hudson, 1999), 222.

43. Utley, Picasso, 31; BAB, R3 Anhang/41, doc. 10, GBI "Auszahlungsordnung" (23 January 1942); "Picasso entlastet Arno Breker," Die Neue Zeitung 83 (2 October 1949); Egret, Arno Breker, 14–15; and Kirrily Freeman, Bronzes to Bullets. Vichy and the Destruction of French Public Statuary, 1941–1944 (Stanford: Stanford University Press, 2009), 1–3, 48.

44. BAB, NS 8/243, doc. 110, Scholz "Bericht für den Reichsleiter" (24 March 1943).

45. "Arno Breker und Leonhard Gall—Vize-Präsidenten der Reichskammer der bildenden Künste ernannt," Münchener Neueste Nachrichten 97 (7 April 1941); and Reinhard Merker, Die bildenden Künste im Nationalsozialismus (Cologne: DuMont, 1983), 167.

46. Hackel, "Der andere Breker," 146–59; and Albert Speer, Spandau: The Secret Diaries (New York: Pocket Books, 1977), 126.

47. Egret, Arno Breker, 60; Zavrel, Arno Breker, 34–35.

48. GSAPK, I HA Rep. 92, Kurt Reutti Nachlass, NL 1, Kurt Reutti, "Erinnerungen," 197; and Probst, "Arno Breker," 96–97.

49. Stefan Koldehoff, Die Bilder sind unter uns. Das Geschäft mit der NS-Raubkunst (Frankfurt: Eichborn, 2009), 203, who cites Norbert Seitz, Die Kanzler und die Künste. Die Geschichte einer schwierigen Beziehung (Munich: Siedler, 2005), 23.

50. Ben Witter, "Arno Brekers Kunstschaffen geht weiter," Die Zeit 26 (20 June 1980), 23; and Petropoulos, Faustian Bargain, 246–50.

51. Ursel Berger, "'Modern Sculpture' versus 'The Decoration of Power.' On the Perception of German Sculpture of the Twenties and Thirties After 1945," in *Taking Positions: Figurative Sculpture and the Third Reich,* ed. Penelope Curtis (Leeds: Henry Moore Institute, 2001), 69.

52. Ibid., 69.

53. Zavrel, *Arno Breker,* 32; Andreas Bluhm, "Ludwigs Lücken," *Kunstchronik* 48/9 (September 1993), 513–22; and more generally Klaus Staeck, ed., *NS-Kunst ins Museum?* (Göttingen: Steidl, 1988).

54. Chametzky, *Objects as History,* 153, 156; Trimborn, *Breker,* 502–28; and Egret, *Arno Breker,* 73.

55. See http://www.museum-arno-breker.org/deutsch/d-museum-0.html (accessed 20 January 2011).

56. Beaucamp, "Dienstbarer Athletiker: Arno Breker, der Bildhauer wird neunzig," *Frankfurter Allgemeine Zeitung* 165 (19 July 1990).

57. Zavrel, *Arno Breker,* 41–46.

58. For more on "a modernist classicism" in Nazi Germany, see Roger Griffin, *Modernism and Fascism: The Sense of Beginning Under Mussolini and Hitler* (Houndsmills: Palgrave Macmillan, 2007), 291–94; Alexander Scobie, *Hitler's State Architecture: The Impact of Classical Antiquity* (University Park, Pa.: Pennsylvania State University Press, 1990), and more generally, Kenneth Silver, ed., *Chaos and Classicism: Art in France, Italy, and Germany, 1918–1936* (New York: Guggenheim Museum, 2010).

CHAPTER 13. ALBERT SPEER

1. Robert Hughes, "Master Builders," *New York Review of Books* 54/14 (27 September 2007).

2. Hilton Kramer, "Philip Johnson's Brilliant Career," *Commentary* (September 1995). See also Benjamin Forgey, "An Architect on Many Levels: Philip Johnson, Blueprinter of Change," *Washington Post* (27 January 2005), C01; and Kazys Varnelis, ed., *The Philip Johnson Tapes. Interviews by Robert A. M. Stern* (New York: Moacelli Press, 2008), 33, 72–75.

3. Varnelis, *Philip Johnson Tapes,* 186–87.

4. Philip Johnson, *Mies van der Rohe* (New York: Museum of Modern Art, 1947), 123.

5. Gerda Wangerin and Gerhard Weiss, *Heinrich Tessenow. Ein Baumeister* (Essen: Richard Bacht, 1976), 54; and Marco De Michelis, *Heinrich Tessenow, 1876–1950* (Stuttgart: Deutsche-Verlags-Anstalt, 1991), 303–9.

6. Gitta Sereny, *The Healing Wound: Experiences and Reflections, Germany, 1938–2001* (New York: Norton, 2001), 276; Albert Speer, *Inside the Third Reich* (New York: Avon Books, 1970), 40; and Dan Van der Vat, *The Good Nazi: The Life and Lies of Albert Speer* (Boston: Houghton Mifflin, 1997), 35.

7. Léon Krier, *Albert Speer Architecture, 1932–1942* (New York: Monacelli Press, 2013 [1985]), xiv; Martin Ebert, *Heinrich Tessenow. Architekt zwischen Tradition und Moderne* (Weimar: edition m, 2006), 132. See also Wangerin and Weiss, *Tessenow,* 67; and Joachim Fest, *Albert Speer. Conversations with Hitler's Architect* (Cambridge: Polity Press, 2005), 26.

8. De Michelis, *Tessenow,* 319–26. Wangerin and Weiss, *Tessenow,* 248–50; and Krier, *Albert Speer Architecture,* XIV.

9. Christian Fuhrmeister and Hans-Ernst Mittig, "Albert Speer und die 'Theorie vom Ruinenwert' (1969)—der lange Schatten einer Legende," in Inge Marszolek and Marc Buggeln, eds., *Bunker. Kriegsort, Zuflucht, Erinnerungsraum* (Frankfurt: Campus, 2008), 225–44.

10. Fest, *Speer,* 29. See also Speer, *Inside the Third Reich,* 52–53.

11. Heinrich Breloer and Rainer Zimmer, *Die Akte Speer. Spuren eines Kriegsverbrechers* (Berlin: Propyläen, 2006), 428.

12. Speer, *Inside the Third Reich,* 52; and Fest, *Speer,* 29.

13. Speer, *Inside the Third Reich,* 51.

14. Ibid. 58.

15. Van der Vat, *Good Nazi,* 49.

16. Speer, *Inside the Third Reich,* 96–97.

17. Paul Jaskot, *The Architecture of Oppression: The SS, Forced Labor and the Nazi Monumental Building Economy* (New York: Routledge, 1999), 56–68.

18. Fest, *Speer,* 56.

19. Speer, quoted in Heiner Boehncke, "Von 'Stillen' und 'Lauten' Formen. Design im Nationalsozialismus," in *Hitlers Künstler. Die Kultur im Dienst des Nationalsozialismus,* ed. Hans Sarkowicz (Frankfurt: Insel, 2004), 301. See also Anson Rabinbach, "Beauty of Labour: The Aesthetics of Production in the Third Reich," *Journal of Contemporary History* 11 (1976), 43–74; and Mathias Schmidt, *Albert Speer. The End of a Myth* (New York: Collier Books, 1982), 45.

20. Weissler, quoted by Boehncke, "Von 'Stillen' und 'Lauten' Formen," 301. See more generally, Sabine Weissler, ed., *Design in Deutschland 1933–1945. Ästhetik und Organisation des Deutschen Werkbundes im "Dritten Reich"* (Giessen: Anabas, 1990); and Winfried Nerdinger, "Bauhaus Architecture in the Third Reich," in *Bauhaus Culture. From Weimar to the Cold War,* ed. Kathleen James-Chakraborty (Minneapolis: University of Minnesota Press, 2006), 148.

21. Elaine Hochman, *Architects of Fortune: Mies van der Rohe and the Third Reich* (New York: Weidenfeld and Nicolson, 1989), 268; Breloer and Zimmer, *Akte Speer,* 49; and Frederic Spotts, *Hitler and the Power of Aesthetics* (Woodstock: Overlook, 2003 [2002]), 345.

22. Speer, *Inside the Third Reich,* 124.

23. Karen Fiss, *Grand Illusion: The Third Reich, the Paris Exposition, and the Cultural Seduction of France* (Chicago: University of Chicago Press, 2009), 60; and Speer, *Inside the Third Reich,* 81.

24. Karen Fiss, "In Hitler's Salon: The German Pavilion at the 1937 Paris Exposition Internationale," in *Art, Culture, and Media Under the Third Reich,* ed. Richard Etlin (Chicago: University of Chicago Press, 2002), 322.

25. Christopher John Murry, ed. *Encyclopedia of the Romantic Era, 1760–1850* (New York: Fitzroy Dearborn, 2004), 107; and Speer, *Inside the Third Reich,* 213. See also Helen Rosenau, *Boullée and Visionary Architecture* (London: Academy Editions, 1976); and Richard Etlin, *The Architecture of Death: The Transformation of the Cemetery in Eighteenth Century Paris* (Cambridge: MIT Press, 1984).

26. Fiss, "In Hitler's Salon," 319.

27. Speer, quoted in Alexander Scobie, *Hitler's State Architecture: The Impact of Classical Antiquity* (University Park, Pa.: Pennsylvania State University Press, 1990), 18; and G. F. Koch, "Speer, Schinkel und der Preussischen Stil," in *Architektur. Arbeiten, 1933–1942,* ed. Albert Speer (Berlin: Propyläen, 1978), 136–50.

28. Speer, *Inside the Third Reich,* 124; and Fest, *Speer,* 61.

29. Speer, *Inside the Third Reich,* 124–25.

30. Susan Sontag, "Fascinating Fascism," in Susan Sontag, *Under the Sign of Saturn* (New York: Vintage, 1981), 94.

31. BAB, R55/1017, Albert Speer Lebenslauf (1939); Otto Thomae, *Die Propaganda-Maschinerie. Bildende Kunst und Öffentlichkeitsarbeit im Dritten Reich* (Berlin: Gebr. Mann, 1978), 197; Speer, *Inside the Third Reich,* 118–19; Schmidt, *Albert Speer. End of a Myth,* 218; and Robert Scholz, "Speer gegen Speer. Verrat an seiner eigenen Architektur," *Die Klüter-Blätter* 30/4 (April 1979), 12–15.

32. Barbara Miller Lane, "Architects in Power: Politics and Ideology in the Work of

Ernst May and Albert Speer," in *Art and History. Images and Their Meaning*, ed. Robert Rotberg and Theodore Rabb (Cambridge: Cambridge University Press, 1986), 285.

33. Hochman, *Architects of Fortune*, 292.

34. Speer, quoted in 1971 *Playboy* interview in Breloer and Zimmer, *Akte Speer*, 117.

35. Speer, *Inside the Third Reich*, 145; and Lars Olof Larsson, *Die Neugestaltung der Reichshauptstadt. Albert Speers Generalbebauungsplan für Berlin* (Stockholm: Almquvist and Wiskell, 1978).

36. Fest, *Speer*, 81; and BAB, R3/1736, "Speerchronik," 33 (20 April 1942).

37. Fest, *Speer*, 81.

38. BAB, R/4606/4520, doc. 167, Hofmann to Hauptamt Verwaltung und Wirtschaft (7 September 1944). For purchases in Paris, see BAB, R120/2883, Finanzabteilung to Amtskasse (9 October 1943).

39. BAB, R3/175, "Aufstellung der dem früheren Reichsministerium Speer gehörenden Gemälde und Plastiken," (n.d.); and BAB, R/4606/4520, doc. 173, Hofmann to Hauptamt Verwaltung und Wirtschaft (8 September 1944).

40. Speer, *Inside the Third Reich*, 63.

41. Breloer and Zimmer, *Akte Speer*, 74–81.

42. Ibid., 77.

43. BAB, R3 Anhang/175, doc. 2, Abteilung Kultur, *Vermerk* (n.d.); Speer, *Inside the Third Reich*, 43; and Horst Kessler, ed. *Karl Haberstock. Umstrittener Kunsthändler und Mäzen* (Munich: Deutscher Kunstverlag, 2008), 281–91.

44. Stefan Koldehoff, "Nazi Gemälderaub. Kunst und Kriegsverbrecher," *Spiegel Online* (3 September 2007), at http://www.spiegel.de/kultur/gesellschaft/0,1518,503001,00.html (accessed 6 July 2010); and Breloer and Zimmer, *Akte Speer*, 415–23.

45. Speer, *Inside the Third Reich*, 422.

46. BAB, R3/1583, doc. 126, Speer to Himmler (14 November 1944).

47. Speer, *Inside the Third Reich*, 27.

48. Ibid., 220.

49. Fest, *Speer*, 78–79.

50. BAB, R55/1476, Goebbels to Lammers (30 August 1940); BAB, R43II/1269g, docs. 8–30, (April–August 1940); and Jonathan Petropoulos, *Art as Politics in the Third Reich* (Chapel Hill: University of North Carolina Press, 1996), 168.

51. BAB, R3/1588, doc. 7, Speer to Lammers (16 November 1940); BAB, R3/1578, doc. 82, Speer to Forster (19 November 1940); BAB, R43II/1269f, doc. 48, Speer to Greiser (21 October 1940); and R43II/1269g.

52. For Speer buying from Haberstock for Hitler, see BAB, NS10/339 (June 1938); and BAB, R 3/1594, doc. 144, Speer to Posse (29 May 1941).

53. Breloer and Zimmer, *Akte Speer*, 74–75, 83–241; Susanne Willems, *Der entsiedelte Jude. Albert Speers Wohnungsmarktpolitik für den Berliner Hauptstadtbau* (Berlin: Edition Hentrich, 2000), 90–116; Hans Reichhardt and Wolfgang Schäche, *Von Berlin nach Germania* (Berlin: Transit, 1998), 159–79; and Paul Jaskot, "Anti-Semitic Policy in Albert Speer's Plans for the Rebuilding of Berlin," *Art Bulletin* 78/4 (December 1996), 622–32.

54. Spotts, *Hitler and the Power of Aesthetics*, 346; Schmidt, *Albert Speer. End of a Myth*, 52, 220; Michael Früchtel, *Der Architekt Hermann Giesler. Leben und Werk (1898–1987)* (Munich: Edition Altavilla, 2008); Hermann Giesler, *Ein anderer Hitler. Bericht seines Architekten Hermann Giesler* (Leoni: Drüffel, 1977); and Franz Albert Heinen, *NS-Ordensburgen: Vogelsang, Sonthofen, Krössinsee* (Berlin: Christoph Links, 2011).

55. Hermann Giesler, *Nachtrag. Aus unveröffentlichten Schriften* (Essen: Heitz and Höffkes, 1988), 80, 87; and Giesler, *Ein Anderer Hitler*, 318–60.

56. See, for example, Giesler's self-portrait from 1949 in Giesler, *Nachtrag*, 5.

57. Gitta Sereny, *Albert Speer: His Battle with Truth* (New York: Alfred Knopf, 1995), 236; Giesler, *Nachtrag*, 165–70; and Früchtel, *Architekt Hermann Giesler*, 354, 369.

58. Spotts, *Hitler and the Power of Aesthetics*, 347.

59. BAB, R3/1538, doc. 25–30, Speer to Hitler (29 March 1945); and Breloer and Zimmer, *Akte Speer*, 304.

60. Fest, *Speer*, 106; Krier, *Albert Speer Architecture*, 125–61.

61. Schmidt, *Albert Speer: End of a Myth*, 49.

62. Krier, *Albert Speer Architecture*, 47, 116–18, 173.

63. Jaskot, *Architecture of Oppression*, 63–68, 98. See also the website of Susanne Willems at http://www.susannewillems.de/archiv.php?page=Speers_Geschaefte_mit_der_SS (accessed 17 July 2013).

64. Michael Sorkin, "Hitler's Classical Architect," *Nation* (10 June 2013).

65. Spotts, *Hitler and the Power of Aesthetics*, 382; Speer, *Inside the Third Reich*, 212–13; and Sereny, *Speer*, 217; Krier, *Albert Speer Architecture*, 72–79.

66. Schmidt, *Albert Speer: End of a Myth*, 44; Jaskot, *Architecture of Oppression*, 56–79; Sereny, *Speer*, 158; and Spotts, *Hitler and the Power of Aesthetics*, 384.

67. Fest, *Speer*, 77.

68. Sereny, *Speer*, 30. See also "Speer's Hidden Hand at Auschwitz," *Der Spiegel* (5 October 2005), at http://www.spiegel.de/international/0,1518,355376,00.html (accessed 22 March 2009). This report discusses documents found by historian Susanne Willems showing that Speer knew of the "Final Solution" by May 1943 at the latest. More generally, see Willems, *Der entsiedelte Jude*.

69. Breloer and Zimmer, *Akte Speer*, 180; and Heinrich Breloer, *Unterwegs zur Familie Speer. Begegnungen, Gespräche, Interviews* (Berlin: Proplyäen, 2005).

70. Erich Goldhagen, "Albert Speer, Himmler, and the Secrecy of the Final Solution," *Midstream* 17/8 (October 1971), 43–50; and Albert Speer, "Antwort an Erich Goldhagen," in *Albert Speer. Kontroversen um ein deutschen Phänomen*, ed. Adelbert Reif, ed (Munich: Bernard and Graefe, 1978), 395–403.

71. The documents show Speer arriving at Hitler's headquarters the following day. Breloer and Zimmer, *Akte Speer*, 224–26, and more generally, 180–226, 388–414.

72. Sereny, *Speer*, 703–7.

73. Miller Lane, "Architects in Power," 301, 305. For more on comparisons of this kind, see Sandro Scarrocchia, *Albert Speer e Marcello Piacentini. L'architettura del totalitarismo negli anni trenta* (Milan: Skira, 1999).

74. Lisa Saltzman, *Anselm Kiefer and Art After Auschwitz* (Cambridge: Cambridge University Press, 1999).

75. Krier, *Albert Speer Architecture*, XII.

CONCLUSION

1. Helmuth Kiesel, *Ernst Jünger: Die Biographie* (Berlin: Siedler, 2007), 16, 260. See also Eliah Bures's review of Kiesel's biography of Jünger on H-German, H-Net Reviews (May 2009), http://www.h-net.org/reviews/showrev.php?id=23751 (accessed 25 May 2009).

2. Allan Mitchell, *The Devil's Captain: Ernst Jünger in Nazi Paris, 1941–1944* (Cambridge: Cambridge University Press, 2011).

3. Charles Maier, *Dissolution. The Crisis of Communism and the End of East Germany* (Princeton: Princeton University Press, 1997), 57.

4. See the entry for 16 June 1936 in Joseph Goebbels, *Die Tagebücher von Joseph Goebbels. Sämtliche Fragmente*, ed. Elke Fröhlich (Munich: K. G. Sauer, 1987), I, 3/II, 108.

5. Frederic Spotts, *Hitler and the Power of Aesthetics* (Woodstock: Overlook, 2003 [2002]), 174–75.

6. David Schoenbaum, *Hitler's Social Revolution: Class and Status in Nazi Germany, 1933–1939* (New York: Norton, 1997 [1966]), 285.

7. Michael Meyer, "A Musical Façade for the Third Reich," in *"Degenerate Art": The Fate of the Avant-Garde in Nazi Germany,* ed. Stephanie Barron (Los Angeles: Los Angeles County Museum of Art, 1991), 174–75; Vernon Lidtke, "Songs and Nazis: Political Music and Social Change in Twentieth-Century Germany," in *Essays on Culture and Society in Modern Germany,* ed. Gary Stark and Bede Karl Lackner (Arlington: University of Texas Press, 1982), 167–200; and Pamela Potter, "Dismantling a Dystopia: On the Historiography of Music in the Third Reich," *Central European History* 40 (2007), 85–110.

8. Richard Grunberger, *The Twelve-Year Reich: A Social History of Nazi Germany, 1933–1945* (New York: Holt, Rinehart, and Winston, 1971), 390–406; and Horst Bergmeier and Rainer Lotz, *Hitler's Airwaves: The Inside Story of Nazi Radio Broadcasting and Propaganda Swing* (New Haven: Yale University Press, 1997).

9. Michael Kater, *Twisted Muse: Musicians and Their Music in the Third Reich* (New York: Oxford University Press), 189.

10. Jürgen Trimborn, *Leni Riefenstahl: A Life* (New York: Faber and Faber, 2007), 260.

11. Sam Shirakawa, *The Devil's Music Master: The Controversial Life and Career of Wilhelm Furtwängler* (New York: 1992), 171.

12. George Steiner and Elissa Poole are quoted by Michael Kater, *Composers of the Nazi Era: Eight Portraits* (New York: Oxford University Press, 2000), 113–14.

13. Rudolf Stephan, quoted in Potter, "Dismantling a Dystopia," 623.

14. Meyer, "Musical Façade," 178. See also Alex Ross, "In Music, Though, There Were No Victories," *New York Times* (20 August 1995).

15. Kater, *Composers of the Nazi Era,* 113–14, 126–28.

16. Spotts, *Hitler and the Power of Aesthetics,* 289; Susan Tegel, *Nazis and the Cinema* (London: Hambledon Continuum, 2007), 85–86; and Meyer, "Musical Façade," 171.

17. See the entry for 28 February 1942 in Goebbels, *Tagebücher,* II, 3, 387; and Kater, *Twisted Muse,* 202.

18. See the entry for 13 January 1944 in Goebbels, *Tagebücher,* II, 11, 82.

19. Fred Prieberg, *Trial of Strength. Wilhelm Furtwängler and the Third Reich* (London: Quartet Books, 1991), 356–57.

20. Ibid., 58; and Mark Swed, "'Wilhelm Furtwängler: The Legacy' Is 107 CDs of Musical Hypnotism," in *Los Angeles Times* (1 July 2012).

21. Shirakawa, *Devil's Music Master,* 16, 417.

22. Prieberg, *Trial of Strength,* 117; Spotts, *Hitler and the Power of Aesthetics,* 294; and Erik Levi, *Music in the Third Reich* (New York: St. Martin's Press, 1994), 173–75, 267.

23. Kater, *Twisted Muse,* 55–65, 186.

24. Shirakawa, *Devil's Music Master,* 102; and Spotts, *Hitler and the Power of Aesthetics,* 298.

25. LAB, A Rep. 243-01, Nr. 301–302, Annalise Theiler statement (17 December 1946); LAB, A Rep. 243-01, Nr. 301–302, Wolfgang Schmidt, memorandum (30 April 1947); David Monod, *Settling Scores: German Music, Denazification, and the Americans, 1945–1953* (Chapel Hill: University of North Carolina Press, 2005), 88, 91; and Oliver Rathkolb, *Führertreu und Gottbegnadet. Künstlerelite im Dritten Reich* (Vienna: Österreichischer Bundesverlag, 1991), 194–220.

26. LAB, A Rep. 243-01, Nr. 305, "Protokoll der zweiten Hauptverhandlung in Sachen des Dirigenten Dr. Wilhelm Furtwängler" (17 December 1946).

27. Kater, *Twisted Muse,* 196.

28. Ibid., 196.

29. Prieberg, *Trial of Strength,* 306.

30. Michael Kater, "Triumph of the Wilful," *Guardian* (24 August 2006); Kater, *Composers of the Nazi Era,* 30, 163–64, 170; and Kater, *Twisted Muse,* 55–65.

31. Kater, "Triumph of the Wilful."

32. Eric Rentschler, *Ministry of Illusion: Nazi Cinema and Its Afterlife* (Cambridge: Harvard University Press, 1996), 149; Frank Noack, *Veit Harlan: "des Teufels Regisseur"* (Munich: Belleville, 2000); Linda Marie Schulte-Sasse, *The Jew as Other Under National Socialism: Veit Harlan's Jud Süss* (American Association of Teachers of German, 1988); Rathkolb, *Führertreu und Gottbegnadet,* 220–24; and Mary Elizabeth O'Brien, *Nazi Cinema as Enchantment: The Politics of Entertainment in the Third Reich* (Rochester: Camden House, 2006), 168–70. Tegel, *Nazis and the Cinema,* 129–48.

33. Rentschler, *Ministry of Illusion,* 167. See also Linda Schulte-Sasse, *Entertaining the Third Reich: Illusions of Wholeness in Nazi Cinema* (Durham: Duke University Press, 1996); and Grunberger, *Twelve-Year Reich,* 381.

34. David Welch, *Propaganda and the German Cinema, 1933–1945* (London: Oxford University Press, 1985), 285; and Erwin Leiser, *Nazi Cinema* (London: Macmillan, 1974), 81.

35. Jana Bruns, *Nazi Cinema's New Women* (Cambridge: Cambridge University Press, 2009), 171–224.

36. Rentschler, *Ministry of Illusion,* 160, 216; Christian Hardinghaus, *Filmpropaganda für den Holocaust?: eine Studie anhand der Hetzfilme "Der Ewige Jude" und "Jud Süss"* (Marburg: Tectum, 2008).

37. Rentschler, *Ministry of Illusion,* 157–58; and Rathkolb, *Führertreu und Gottbegnadet,* 251–58.

38. Rathkolb, *Führertreu und Gottbegnadet,* 245–51; Emil Jannings, *Theater, Film und Ich,* ed. C.C. Bergius (Berchtesgaden: Zimmer and Herzog, 1951); Erich Ebermayer, *Eh' ich's vergesse—. Erinnerungen an Gerhart Hauptmann, Thomas Mann, Klaus Mann, Gustaf Gründgens, Emil Jannings, und Stefan Zweig* (Munich: Langen-Müller, 2005); and Thomas Saunders, *Hollywood in Berlin: American Cinema and Weimar Germany* (Berkeley: University of California Press, 1994), 208–19.

39. BAB, R55/21013, doc. 177, Klimsch to Goebbels (15 June 1938).

40. Entry for 6 February 1940, Goebbels, *Tagebücher,* I, 7, 298. Hermann Braun, *Fritz Klimsch. Eine Dokumentation* (Cologne: Kunsthaus am Museum Carola van Ham, 1991); and Otto Thomae, *Die Propaganda-Maschinerie. Bildende Kunst und Öffentlichkeitsarbeit im Dritten Reich* (Berlin: Gebr. Mann, 1978), 282–83.

41. Josephine Gabler, "Georg Kolbe in der NS-Zeit" in *Georg Kolbe, 1877–1947,* ed. Ursel Berger (Munich: Prestel, 1997); and more generally, Penelope Curtis, ed., *Taking Positions: Figurative Sculpture and the Third Reich* (Leeds: Henry Moore Institute, 2001).

42. Christina Schroeter, *Fritz Erler. Leben und Werk* (Hamburg: Christians, 1992).

43. Volker Probst, *Paul Mathias Padua. Maler zwischen Tradition und Moderne* (Neuss: Silesia Hanke, 1988), 9, 47.

44. Gregory Maertz, "The Invisible Museum: Unearthing the Lost Modernist Art of the Third Reich," *Modernism/Modernity* 15/1 (January 2008), 79; Gregory Maertz, *The Invisible Museum: The Secret Postwar History of Nazi Art* (New Haven: Yale University Press, 2010); and Barbara McCloskey, *Artists of World War II* (Westport, Conn.: Greenwood, 2005), 41–67.

45. BAB, (former BDC file for Wilhelm Kreis), RKK files, Hans Hinkel to Kreis (24 September 1943). See also Karl Arndt, "Problematischer Ruhm—die Grossaufträge in Berlin, 1937–1943," in *Wilhelm Kreis. Architekt zwischen Kaiserreich und Demokratie, 1873–*

1955, ed. Winfried Nerdinger (Munich: Klinkhardt and Biermann, 1994); Hans Stephan, *Wilhelm Kreis* (Oldenburg: Gerhard Stalling, 1944); Wilhelm Kreis, *Wilhelm Kreis* (Berlin: Gebr. Mann, 1997); and Spotts, *Hitler and the Power of Aesthetics*, 350.

46. Ibid., 370; Paul Bonatz, *Leben und Bauen* (Stuttgart: A. Spemann, 1950); Wilhelm Bader, ed., *Paul Bonatz zum Gedenken* (Stuttgart: Technische Hochschule Stuttgart, 1957); Ralf Rummel, ed., *Paul Bonatz (1877–1956). Bauten und Projekte im Norden* (Delmenhorst: Aschenbeck and Holstein, 2005); and Hartmut Frank, "Bridges: Paul Bonatz's Search for a Contemporary Monumental Style," in *The Nazification of Art: Art, Design, Music, Architecture and Film in the Third Reich*, ed. Brandon Taylor and Wilfried van der Will (Winchester: Winchester Press, 1990), 144–57.

47. Spotts, *Hitler and the Power of Aesthetics*, 370–71.

48. Hildegard Brenner, *Die Kunstpolitik des Nationalsozialismus* (Reinbek: Rowholt, 1963), 189. See more generally, Emmanuel Faye, *Heidegger: The Introduction of Nazism into Philosophy in Light of the Unpublished Seminars of 1933–1935* (New Haven: Yale University Press, 2009); Victor Farias, *Heidegger and Nazism* (Philadelphia: Temple University Press, 1989); and George Steiner, *Martin Heidegger* (Chicago: University of Chicago Press, 1991). Other figures in the Third Reich with modernist connections who do not always fit neatly in arts-specific rubrics can be found in Wolfgang Bialas and Anson Rabinbach, eds., *Nazi Germany and the Humanities* (Oxford: Oneworld, 2007).

49. Michael Kater, *Different Drummers: Jazz in the Culture of Nazi Germany* (New York: Oxford University Press, 1992); Michael Kater, "Forbidden Fruit? Jazz in the Third Reich" *American Historical Review* 94 (1989), 11–43; Otto Bender, ed., *Swing Unterm Hakenkreuz in Hamburg 1933–1944* (Hamburg: Christians, 1993); Franz Ritter, ed., *Heinrich Himmler und die Liebe zum Swing. Erinnerungen und Dokumenten* (Leipzig: Reclam, 1994); and Bernd Polster, ed., *"Swing Heil." Jazz im Nationalsozialismus* (Berlin: Transit, 1989).

50. Max Schmeling, *Max Schmeling: An Autobiography* (Chicago: Bonus Books, 1998); and David Margolick, *Beyond Glory: Joe Louis vs. Max Schmeling and a World on the Brink* (New York: Vintage Books, 2006). For Caracciola, see Eberhard Reuss, *Hitler's Motor Racing Battles: The Silver Arrows Under the Swastika* (New York: Simon and Schuster, 2002), 188; and Peter Stevenson, *Driving Forces: The Grand Prix Racing World Caught in the Maelstrom of the Third Reich* (Cambridge: Bentley Publishers, 2002), 84–85, 134–36. See also Neil Gregor, *Daimler-Benz in the Third Reich* (New Haven: Yale University Press, 1998).

51. Hermann Schreiber, "Der Junge Mann und das Mehr," *Der Spiegel* 13 (21 March 1966); Dieter Scholz, "Otto Andreas Schreiber, die *Kunst der Nation* und die Fabrikausstellungen," in *Überbrückt: Ästhetische Moderne und Nationalsozialismus. Kunsthistoriker und Künstler, 1925–1937*, ed. Eugen Blume and Dieter Scholz (Cologne: Walther König, 1999), 104; Joseph Wulf, *Die Bildenden Künste im Dritten Reich* (Gütersloh: Sigbert Mohn, 1963), 17–22; and more generally, Wolfgang Ullrich, *Macht Zeigen. Kunst als Herrschaftsstrategie* (Berlin: Deutsches Historisches Museum, 2010).

52. Christian Saehrendt, *"Die Brücke" zwischen Staatskunst und Verfemung. Expressionistische Kunst als Politikum in der Weimarer Republik, im "Dritten Reich" und im Kalten Krieg* (Stuttgart: Franz Steiner, 2005), 82.

53. Michael Fitzgerald, "Reports from the Home Fronts: Some Skirmishes over Picasso's Reputation," in *Picasso and the War Years: 1937–1945*, ed. Steven Nash and Robert Rosenblum (New York: Thames and Hudson, 1999), 115.

54. David Scherman and Antony Penrose, *Lee Miller's War: Photographer and Correspondent with the Allies in Europe, 1944–1945* (Boston: Bulfinch Press, 1992), 73–74; Gertje Utley, *Picasso: The Communist Years* (New Haven: Yale University Press, 2000), 41; and Michèle Cone, *Artists Under Vichy: A Case of Prejudice and Persecution* (Princeton: Princeton University Press, 1992), 131–53.

55. Alfred Barr Jr., "Picasso 1940–1944: A Digest with Notes," *Museum of Modern Art Bulletin* (January 1945), quoted in Fitzgerald, "Reports from the Home Fronts," 118.

56. Fitzgerald, "Reports from the Home Fronts," 119.

57. Gertje Utley, "From *Guernica* to *The Charnel House:* The Political Radicalization of the Artist," in *Picasso and the War Years: 1937–1945,* ed. Steven Nash and Robert Rosenblum (New York: Thames and Hudson, 1999), 77.

58. Fitzgerald, "Reports from the Home Fronts," 118; Alan Riding, *And the Show Went On: Cultural Life in Nazi-Occupied Paris* (New York: Alfred Knopf, 2010), 181. See also Michael Carlo Klepsch, *Picasso und der Nationalsozialismus* (Düsseldorf: Patmos, 2007), 13–50.

59. Herschel Chipp and Alan Wofsy, eds., *The Picasso Project. Picasso's Paintings, Watercolors, Drawings and Sculpture. A Comprehensive Illustrated Catalogue. Nazi Occupation, 1940–1944,* vol. 8 (San Francisco: Alan Wofsy Fine Arts, 1999).

60. Julian Jackson, *France: The Dark Years 1940–44* (Oxford: Oxford University Press, 2001), 301; Riding, *And the Show Went On,* 187; Frederic Spotts, *The Shameful Peace: How French Artists and Intellectuals Survived the Nazi Occupation* (New Haven: Yale University Press, 2008), 15–24; and Jean-Louis Cohen, *Architecture in Uniform: Designing and Building for the Second World War* (Paris: Editions Hazan, 2011), 12, 253, 365.

61. Michael Fitzgerald, *Making Modernism: Picasso and the Creation of the Market for Twentieth Century Art* (New York: Farrar, Straus and Giroux, 1995), 262; Ben Hoyle, "Was Ambroise Vollard Murdered? As Vollard's Lost Hoard of Masterpieces Resurfaces, the Death of the 20th Century's Greatest Art Dealer Still Intrigues," *Times* (London) (12 June 2010); David D'Arcy, "The Mysterious Mr. Slomovic," *Art & Auction* (September 2006); and Rudolf Koella and Rudolf Velhagen, eds., *Renoir, Cézanne, Picasso and ihr Galerist Ambroise Vollard* (Heidelberg: Edition Braus, 2006).

62. Riding, *And the Show Went On,* 171; and Fitzgerald, "Reports from the Home Fronts," 117, 121.

63. Martin Fabiani, *Quand j'étais marchand de tableaux* (Paris: Julliard, 1976), 124–31. Note that the copy of the book in the GRI was owned by art historian/dealer/collector Douglas Cooper and contains extensive marginalia with words like "nonsense" and "rubbish."

64. James Plaut, quoted in Fitzgerald, "Reports from the Home Fronts," 119.

65. G. H. Archambault, "Picasso," *New York Times Magazine* (29 October 1944); and Fitzgerald, "Reports from the Home Fronts," 118–19.

66. Riding, *And the Show Went On,* 171, 182; Fitzgerald, *Making Modernism,* 264; Fitzgerald, "Reports from the Home Fronts," 118; and Steven Nash, "Chronology," in *Picasso and the War Years,* ed. Steven Nash and Robert Rosenblum (New York: Thames and Hudson, 1999), 216.

67. Irith Dublon-Knebel, "A Dual Life—The Fate of Nazi Painters and Sculptors, 1945–1990," in *Tel Aviver Jahrbuch für deutsche Geschichte,* vol. XXXIV, ed. Moshe Zuckermann (2006), 205–31; and Beate Marks-Hanssen, *Inner Emigration? "Verfemte" Künstlerinnen und Künstler in der Zeit des Nationalsozialismus* (Berlin: dissertation.de, 2006), 17–31. Alice Kaplan, *The Collaborator: The Trial and Execution of Robert Brasillach* (Chicago: University of Chicago Press, 2000).

68. See, for example, the newspaper article "Der 'Michelangelo Hitlers,'" *Die Abendzeitung* (Munich) (2 October 1948), reproduced in Jonathan Petropoulos, *The Faustian Bargain: The Art World in Nazi Germany* (New York: Oxford University Press, 2000), 242.

69. SMB-ZA, Rave NL, Nr. 97, Rave to Roh (15 July 1949).

70. Amtsgericht, Munich, Robert Scholz file, "Klageschrift" (15 December 1947), and Spruch (8 April 1948); and Petropoulos, *Faustian Bargain,* 144–53.

71. SMB-ZA, Rave NL, Nr. 97, Rave to Schreiber (27 September 1949).

72. Otto Andreas Schreiber, *Gouachen, 1959–1963* (Cologne: Kölner Kunstverein, 1963); and Kunsthandlung Goyert, *Otto Andreas Schreiber: Gemälde und Gouachen* (Cologne: Kunsthandlung Goyert, 1987).

73. Kater, *Composers of the Nazi Era*, 276.

74. Kater, *Twisted Muse*, 60–61.

75. Ibid., 61.

76. Eleonore Büning, "Schluss mit Rumpeln, Raspeln, Rauschen," *Frankfurter Allgemeine Zeitung* 184 (11 August 2009), 28.

77. Tittel, "Dix–neu gesehen," 58.

78. Ibid., 58; and Fritz Löffler, *Otto Dix. Leben und Werk* (Dresden: VEB Verlag der Kunst, 1977).

79. Lutz Tittel, "Dix–neu gesehen," in *Otto Dix. Die Friedrichshafener Sammlung Bestandskatalog*, ed. Lutz Tittel (Friedrichshafen: Moser, 1992), 58, 172, 173; and Franz Larese, quoted in a 1991 interview in Lutz Tittel, ed., *Otto Dix. Die Friedrichshafener Sammlung Bestandskatalog* (Friedrichshafen: Moser, 1992), 95; and BAB, R3/175, "Aufstellung der dem früheren Reichsministerium Speer gehörenden Gemälde und Plastiken," (n.d.).

80. Max Pechstein, *Erinnerungen* (Wiesbaden: Limes, 1960), 114–16.

81. Eduard Plietzsch, ". . . Heiter ist die Kunst." *Erlebnisse mit Künstlern und Kennern* (Gütersloh: Bertelsmann, 1955); Laura Meier-Ewert, "Eduard Plietzsch. Dem Zeitgeist Stets zu Diensten," in *Gute Geschäft. Kunsthandel in Berlin 1933–1945*, ed. Christine Fischer-Defoy and Kaspar Nürnberg (Berlin: Aktives Museum Faschismus und Widerstand in Berlin, 2011), 87 92; Jean Vlug, *Report on Objects Removed to Germany from Holland, Belgium, and France During the German Occupation in the Countries* (Hague: Stichting Nederlands Kunstbesit, 1945), 8, 13; and Bernhard Fulda and Aya Soika, *Max Pechstein. The Rise and Fall of Expressionism* (Berlin: DeGruyter, 2012), 364, 399. Jan Köhler, Jan Maruhn, and Nina Senger, eds., *Berliner Lebenswelten der zwanziger Jahre: Bilder einer untergegangenen Kultur photographiert von Martha Huth* (Frankfurt: Eichborn, 1996), 112–13.

82. Stefan Koldehoff, *Die Bilder sind unter uns. Das Geschäft mit der NS-Raubkunst* (Frankfurt: Eichborn, 2009), 215.

83. Emil Nolde, *Mein Leben* (Cologne: DuMont, 1979 [1976]), 390–91. With regard to the war, he also referred to an adage, "Artists and children don't know anything." See ibid., 396.

84. Emil Nolde, *Reisen—Achtung—Befreiung, 1919–1946* (Cologne: DuMont, 1967), 115. See also Brandon Taylor, "Post-Modernism in the Third Reich," in *The Nazification of Art, Design, Music, Architecture and Film in the Third Reich*, ed. Brandon Taylor and Wilfried van der Will (Winchester: Winchester Press, 1990), 130.

85. Potter, "Dismantling a Dystopia," 631.

86. See, for example, Gropius's and Mies's self-mythologizing statements in Richard Pommer, "Mies van der Rohe and the Political Ideology of the Modern Movement in Architecture," in *Mies van der Rohe: Critical Essays*, ed. Frank Schulze (Cambridge: MIT Press, 1989), 108, 118. For example, Mies said that he urged the Bauhaus faculty to vote to close the school in the spring of 1933 because it "enabled him to have the closing celebrated with champagne," implying that he wished to make a show of spurning the Nazis' offer."

87. Walter Scheiffele, "Das neue Bauen unter dem Faschismus," in *Kunst Hochschule Faschismus*, ed. Hochschule der Künste Berlin (Berlin: Elefanten Press, 1984), 241.

88. Siegfried Giedion, *Walter Gropius* (New York: Dover, 1992).

89. For the Brussels Pavilion drawings, see Arthur Drexler, ed., *An Illustrated Catalogue of the Mies van der Rohe Drawings in the Museum of Modern Art* (New York: Garland, 1986), IV:84–110. The drawing with an abstracted swastika is on page 108. The text does

note, however, that the design "was, if anything, quite remarkable for the way in which the architect united an unmistakably Nazified program with a design manner he had made his own." Ibid., 84.

90. Paul Galloway to author (24 February 2011); and Terence Riley, "Making History: Mies van der Rohe and the Museum of Modern Art," in *Mies in Berlin,* ed. Terence Riley and Barry Bergdoll (New York: Harry Abrams, 2001), 10–23.

91. Paul Galloway to author (24 February 2011).

92. Pommer, "Mies van der Rohe and the Political Ideology," 99. See also Winfried Nerdinger, "Bauhaus-Architekten im 'Dritten Reich,'" in *Bauhaus-Moderne im National-sozialismus. Zwischen Anbietung und Verfolgung,* ed. Winfried Nerdinger (Munich: Prestel, 1993), 157, 216. A drawing of the Brussels Pavilion with the swastika flags appears in the Museum of Modern Art exhibition catalogue from 2001, with the lender identified as "private collection, courtesy Max Protetch Gallery." See Terence Riley and Barry Bergdoll, eds., *Mies in Berlin* (New York: Harry Abrams, 2001), 286.

93. Karin V. Maur, *Oskar Schlemmer Oeuvrekatalog der Gemälde, Aquarelle, Pastelle, und Plastiken* (Munich: Prestel, 1979), 362–64. She also notes that many of the images were not reproduced in the previous reference works on Schlemmer by Hans Hildebrandt (1952) and Wulf Herzogenrath (1973). The latter, a study of Schlemmer's wall decorations for new architecture, has two pages devoted to the Deutsches Museum project and does not include the most incendiary images. See Wulf Herzogenrath, *Oskar Schlemmer. Die Wandgestaltung der neuen Architektur* (Munich: Prestel, 1973), 229–30.

94. See, for example, Lothar Grisebach, ed., *E. L. Kirchners Davoser Tagebuch. Erste Veröffentlichung der wichtigsten Schriften E. L. Kirchners* (Cologne: DuMont, 1968); and more generally, "A Blank Space in Historical Accounts," in Cohen, *Architecture in Uniform,* 12–13.

95. SMB-ZA, Rave NL, Findbuch, 1.

96. Rolf Rave to author (3 August 2011). Rolf Rave also noted with regard to his father, "The Nazi period did not come to an end with the culmination of the war." See also Laura Lauzemis, "Die nationalsozialistische Ideologie und der 'neue Mensch.' Oskar Schlemmers Folkwang-Zyklus und sein Briefwechsel mit Graf Klaus von Baudissin aus dem Jahr 1934," in *Angriff auf die Avant-Garde. Kunst und Kunstpolitik im Nationalsozialismus,* ed. Uwe Fleckner (Berlin: Akademie Verlag, 2007), 67.

97. For the "Gautinger Fund" of Haberstock documents, see Horst Kessler, "Der Kunst-händler als Opportunist: Karl Haberstock im 'Dritten Reich,'" in *Werke und Werte: über das Handeln und Sammeln von Kunst im Nationalsozialismus,* ed. Maike Steinkamp and Ute Haug (Berlin: Akademie Verlag, 2010), 23–40; Horst Kessler, ed., *Karl Haberstock. Umstrit-tener Kunsthändler und Mäzen* (Munich: Deutscher Kunstverlag, 2008), and the review of this volume by Nikola Doll and Christian Fuhrmeister in *Kunstchronik* 63/12 (December 2010), 620–23; Horst Kessler and Christof Trepisch's response in *Kunstchronik* 64/4 (April 2011), 215–17; and Doll and Fuhrmeister, "Zur Zuschrift von Kessler/Trepesch," *Kunst-chronik,* 64/5 (May 2011), 273–74.

98. Meike Hopp, *Kunsthandel im Nationalsozialismus. Adolf Weinmüller in München und Wien* (Cologne: Böhlau, 2102), http://www.zikg.eu/projekte/projekte-zi/weinmueller (accessed 17 April 2014).

99. Meike Hoffmann, "Bernhard A. Böhmer. Januskopf im NS-Kunsthandel," in *Gute Geschäft. Kunsthandel in Berlin 1933–1945,* ed. Christine Fischer-Defoy and Kaspar Nürn-berg (Berlin: Aktives Museum Faschismus und Widerstand in Berlin, 2011), 23; and Maike Steinkamp, *Unerwünschte Erbe. Die Rezeption 'entarteter' Kunst in Kunstkritik, Ausstellungen und Museen der SBZ und Frühen DDR* (Berlin: Akademie Verlag, 2008), 225–30. Note that

East German monuments officer Kurt Reutti played a key role in attending to Böhmer's estate.

100. Besides Böhmer, there are is virtually nothing extant for Hildebrand Gurlitt; and only a *Teilnachlass,* or partial set of papers, for Ferdinand Möller located at the Berlinische Galerie. Karl Buchholz's records are housed in the Bundesarchiv in Berlin (see R55/2017) and in the Zentralarchiv of the Berlin State Museums.

101. Joachim Fest, *Albert Speer. Conversations with Hitler's Architect* (Cambridge: Polity Press, 2005), 122–24. The full version of the *Speerchronik* went to the Federal Archives (Bundesarchiv) in Koblenz in 1983.

102. Charles Maier, *The Unmasterable Past: History, Holocaust, and German National Identity* (Cambridge: Harvard University Press, 1997 [1988]), 121–59.

103. See, among other works, Norbert Frei and Johannes Schmitz, *Journalismus im Dritten Reich* (Munich: C. H. Beck, 1989); Christopher Simpson, *Blowback: The First Full Account of America's Recruitment of Nazis and Its Disastrous Effect on Our Domestic and Foreign Policy* (New York: Weidenfeld and Nicolson, 1988); Hartmut Lehmann and James Van Horn Melton, eds., *Paths of Continuity: Central European Historiography from the 1930s to the 1950s* (Cambridge: Cambridge University Press, 1994); and Michael Neufeld, *Von Braun: Dreamer of Space, Engineer of War* (New York: Alfred Knopf, 2007).

104. See http://www.backstein.com/3.0/kk_templates/show.php?sel_rubrik=20&sel_subrubrik=66&sel_artikel=393 (accessed 18 July 2011).

105. Frances Stonor Saunders, *The Cultural Cold War: The CIA and the World of Arts and Letters* (New York: The New Press, 1999), 253–54; and Hugh Wilford, *The Mighty Wurlitzer: How the CIA Played America* (Cambridge: Harvard University Press, 2008), 101–2.

106. Bauhaus-Archiv Berlin, Gropius Papers, *Korrespondenz-Nachlass,* 1937–1969, 1167/1, President John F. Kennedy to Gropius (12 January 1961).

107. James van Dyke, "Something New on Nolde, National Socialism, and the SS," *Kunstchronik* 65/5 (May 2012), 266. See also Christian Saehrendt, "Emil Nolde Heute," in *Emil Nolde,* ed. Manfred Reuther (Cologne: DuMont, 2010), 9; and more generally Fitzgerald, *Making Modernism.*

108. Peter Schjeldahl, "Golden Girl: The Neue Galerie's New Klimt," *New Yorker* (24 July 2006).

109. Hochman, *Architects of Fortune,* xiv; Pommer, "Mies van der Rohe and the Political Ideology," 117.

110. Koldehoff, *Bilder sind unter uns,* 121. The Städel reversed course in 2008 and granted access to a research group led by Uwe Fleckner and Max Hollein; their results were published in Uwe Fleckner and Max Hollein, eds., *Museum im Widerspruch. Das Städel und der Nationalsozialismus* (Berlin: Akademie Verlag, 2011).

111. Ulrike Knöfel, "Beuys Biography: Book Accuses Artist of Close Ties to Nazis," *Der Spiegel* (17 May 2013); and Hans Peter Riegel, *Beuys. Die Biographie* (Berlin: Aufbau, 2013).

112. Fest, *Speer,* 121. Julius Streicher was the Gauleiter of Nuremberg, and Fritz Sauckel the Reich Minister for Labor. Neither was known for being particularly intelligent.

ACKNOWLEDGMENTS

THIS BOOK HAS had a lengthy gestation period, and throughout it three great friends have provided unwavering and invaluable support. I owe a special debt of gratitude to Dennis Mulhaupt, Christopher Walker, and David Hetz. For an even longer time, I have been honored to hold a chair in European history endowed by Jack and Kingsley Croul. They have continued to support me and my research and I view every book I write as implicitly dedicated to them. Their interest in history, their commitment to education and a range of good causes, and their warm friendship have been nothing short of inspirational. My literary agent, Michael Carlisle, and his colleague Lauren Smythe of InkWell Management have also exhibited great faith in this project over the years. I thank them for both their guidance and sage advice. My editor at Yale University Press, Steve Wasserman, and his colleague Erica Hanson helped make this a better and more readable book. I look forward to future collaborations with them.

Other individuals have assisted me in myriad ways—most often with help in the archives or by reading drafts of the manuscript. I thank Florian Beierl, Hubert Berkhout (Netherlands State Institute for War Documentation), Inka Bertz (Jüdisches Museum in Berlin), Ulf Bischof, Ralf Burmeister (Berlinische Galerie), Peter Cheremushkin, Christopher Clark, Scott Denham, Marion Deshmukh, Raymond Dowd, Philip Eliasoph, Tanja Fengler-Veit (Deutsches Literaturarachiv, Marbach), Christian Fuhrmeister (Zentalinstitut für Kunstgeschichte in Munich), Karen Furey, Paul Galloway (MoMA), Christian Goeschel, Kristen Hartisch (Bundesarchiv-Berlin), Richard Heffern, Patricia Hertlinge, Meike Hopp (Zentalinstitut für Kunstgeschichte in Munich), Christian Huemer (Getty Research Institute), Andreas Hüneke, Richard Hunt, Paul Jaskot, Birgit Joos (Deutsches Kunstarchiv, Nuremberg), Irene Kacandes, Michelle Lynn Kahn, Michael Kater, Herr Klein (Bundesarchiv-Berlin), Stephan Klingen (Zentalinstitut für Kunstgeschichte in Munich), Roger Labrie, Iris Lauterbach (Zentalinstitut für Kunstgeschichte in Munich), Sigrid and Stephan Lindner, Wendy Lower, Annegret Neupert (Bundesarchiv-Koblenz), Carolin Pilgermann

(Zentralarchiv der Berliner Staatlichen Museen), Pamela Potter, David Roland, Celina Rosas, Adam Rosenkranz (Honnold-Mudd Library at the Claremont Colleges), Charles Rossow (Special Collections of the Getty Research Institute), David Rowland, Benjamin Royas, Marie-Louise and Timothy Ryback, Wolfgang Schöddert (Berlinische Galerie), Susanna Schraftstetter, Sylvester Segura, Alan Steinweis, Bridgette Stokes, Anja Tiedemann, Clemens Toussaint, James van Dyke, Louise Volwahsen, Christine Wilkes, Andreas Wirsching (Institut für Zeitgeschichte, Munich), and Torsten Zarwel (Bundesarchiv-Berlin). I offer a special word of thanks to Jeffrey Schier for his careful and thoughtful efforts as the copy editor.

Finally, I would thank my family. My father, George Petropoulos, raised me such that I developed a strong interest in European history, and my mother, Maureen Petropoulos, exhibited a confidence in her only son that has proven invaluable. My wife, Kimberly Petropoulos, and our daughters Isabel and Astrid, have provided additional support. They tolerate, and indeed encourage, my research trips, and even enjoy coming along when possible. My family and friends have helped me in innumerable ways as I have pursued this project, and it is to them more generally that this book is dedicated.

INDEX

Page number in *italics* refer to illustrations.